America's Founding Food

AMERICA'S
founding
FOOD

The Story of New England Cooking

KEITH STAVELY & KATHLEEN FITZGERALD

The University of North Carolina Press   Chapel Hill & London

© 2004
The University of North Carolina Press
All rights reserved
Set in Adobe Caslon and Emigre Mrs Eaves types
by Tseng Information Systems, Inc.
Manufactured in the United States of America
The paper in this book meets the guidelines for
permanence and durability of the Committee on
Production Guidelines for Book Longevity of the
Council on Library Resources.
Library of Congress Cataloging-in-Publication Data
Stavely, Keith W. F., 1942–
America's founding food: the story of New England
cooking / Keith Stavely and Kathleen Fitzgerald.
p. cm.
Includes bibliographical references and index.
ISBN 0-8078-2894-7 (cloth)
1. Cookery, American—New England style—History.
I. Fitzgerald, Kathleen, 1952– II. Title.
TX715.S.N48S743 2004
741.5974—dc22 2004007412

08 07 06 05 04 5 4 3 2 1

To the memory of my mother, Edith E. Fitzgerald

K. F.

To my mother, Elizabeth W. Stavely

K. S.

Contents

Illustrations

Preface

We have spent a number of years (we shudder to recall how many!) thinking about the taste of New England's past. This book is the result. It represents the convergence of our interests in both culinary and New England history. But aspects of our personal histories have also been involved.

One of us was raised in New England, but as an Irish Catholic apart from the Yankee culture that still dominated the region during her childhood in the 1950s. The other grew up in the 1940s outside New England but most distinctly as New England–descended. These two different, at times opposed, worlds were in some small measure joined when we married in Boston in 1978.

Given our experiences as, on the one hand, a cultural outsider living in the Yankee world and, on the other, a geographic outsider to his own Yankee heritage, each of us has had moments of feeling both bound up with and detached from the New England fold. Being thus in various ways possessed of and dispossessed by the culture we have chosen to study informs and, we hope, humanizes our work. Such a dual perspective helps to attune us to the muted voices of history, while avoiding unfruitful exercises in blame.

A further benefit of occupying the unstable position of simultaneous insider and outsider is that it gives us entrée into one of the defining dynamics of New England culture. If this is a slippery foothold in New England's psychosocial terrain, it is not a unique one — the likes of Roger Williams and Anne Hutchinson had similar, if far more personally extreme and historically important, experiences. The Calvinism that dominated New England for so long defined itself as much by exclusion as by inclusion. This powerful dynamic can be seen in culinary history as clearly as it has been seen in religious and political history, and, with our own lives attuning us to it, we hope we have been successful in bringing it to light here.

It is a pleasure to acknowledge those who have helped us. First, we are grateful to the libraries that efficiently and graciously provided us with materials. It is no exaggeration to say that without the unfettered access to its culinary collection provided by the Schlesinger Library, Radcliffe Institute, Harvard University, this book would not exist. The Schlesinger's distinct virtues as a research library are evident both in its generous access policies and also in its staff, the expertise and welcoming spirit of which were for us exemplified by reference librarian Sarah Hutcheon.

HELIN, a consortium of Rhode Island academic libraries, and especially the University of Rhode Island Library, have also been generous with both materials and assistance, as have the Fall River Public Library, the Cambridge Public Library, the Newport Public Library, and the other member libraries in the SAILS, Minuteman, and CLAN networks. We thank the American Antiquarian Society, Worcester, Massachusetts, for permission to quote from unpublished manuscript portions of the diary of Ebenezer Parkman.

We are also grateful to Jean Williams, Mark Hirsch, Emily Sollie, Andrew F. Smith, and Joseph M. Carlin, who provided both suggestions that helped shape our inquiries and support at crucial junctures. At a later stage, Jeffrey R. Dykes lent luster to the book with his photographic expertise. In Elaine Maisner this project found its ideal editor. Indeed, the entire staff of the University of North Carolina Press, and especially our project coordinator, Pamela Upton, and our copyeditor, Bethany Johnson, have gone the extra mile to make this the best book it can be. Finally, we thank our families, Fitzgeralds and Stavelys, and especially Jonathan, for the many intangible ways in which they have lent this project support by giving us their love.

A brief word on some of the procedures we have chosen to follow. Quotations from primary sources are spelled exactly as they appear in the editions in which we found them. In footnoting, we have attempted to strike a balance between readability and immediate identification of sources. Citations are grouped at the ends of paragraphs, or in a few cases after two or more paragraphs, in the order in which the cited material appears in the text.

One issue that has proven to be unexpectedly knotty has been that of verb tense. We were both trained in the conventions of literary criticism, according to which documents are discussed in the present tense. With so many of our sources, including cookbooks, being "literary" in the broad sense, the use of this convention threatened to obscure the sense of pastness that is essential to any historical narrative. We have therefore opted to use the past tense throughout, even when talking about such sources as the novels of Harriet Beecher Stowe.

America's Founding Food

L ike the dusty spinning wheel or the unfired hearth in one of New England's many colonial house museums, the historic foods of the region by and large enter our consciousness as worthy of remembrance and reverence, but not as something we would expect to see in our own homes today. For some, especially those with ancestral connections to the region and its Puritan founders or Yankee farmers, the thought of baked beans, served "in the pot, as the Pilgrims did," carries with it warm familial associations that override mere considerations of how the food tastes. For others with fewer direct connections to the New England past, patriotic sentiment nevertheless flavors the beans. But for many, understanding the impulse to glorify our American roots simply does not translate into understanding the gustatory appeal of the plain dishes that typify New England cooking. One historian colorfully exemplifies this point of view: "For three centuries, New England families gave thanks to their Calvinist God for cold baked beans and stale brown bread, while lobsters abounded in the waters of Massachusetts Bay and succulent gamebirds orbited slowly overhead."[1]

Our great annual American feast, Thanksgiving, perhaps provides the best example of the dual approaches to that part of our national cuisine based on historic New England cooking. On the one hand, the nation still celebrates the day at the family table with roasted turkey, cranberry sauce, and pumpkin pie, all foods long associated with the region. On the other hand, not many of us serve these foods on other days of the year, although their cost is well within most family budgets.

But this distance between the tastes of our day and the historic cuisine of New England not only provides an opportunity to partake of a culinary form of patriotism once a year. It also allows us to think dispassionately about the origins and meaning of foods that have become museum pieces but that once dominated American tastes. Throughout this book, we ask such questions as: Why these particular dishes? Why baked beans, pumpkins, Johnny cakes, and boiled cod? What did they taste like when they first came from the colonial bake oven or fireplace? Did ways of making them change over time, given changes in available foodstuffs and cooking equipment? But along with these questions, we also ask: What did these foods mean to those who cooked them, wrote about them, and elevated such culinary wallflowers to virtually canonical status?

The answers to these questions involve practical considerations, such as what grew well and what didn't in New England soil, what sold well in the expanding markets of Europe and the Caribbean, and what was best suited to the kitchen conditions of the colonial and nineteenth-century home. But to paint a full picture of the region's culinary contribution also requires a close look at the society in which the foods were prepared and consumed. What, for instance, most appealed to Anglo-American appetites, and why? What did the colonists think about eating what were in essence the same foods as those consumed by their "savage" neighbors? And in connection with a later period, why have some of the simplest and plainest dishes in the New England culinary repertoire come to be considered definitive of it? This question has particularly intrigued us, in that the period in which this definition of New England cooking was emerging—the later nineteenth century—was also the period in which economic development and increasing wealth made a greater variety of foods more widely available. Just when edible luxuries were brought within more people's reach, the foods long associated with necessity began to be celebrated. How come?

Because questions about New England's cooking legacy range from the practical to the philosophical, coming up with answers requires considering a diversity of material. Therefore, although we treat them at length and with respect, we do not limit ourselves to what might be considered the conventional material of culinary history—cookbooks and domestic guides. In the following pages the reader will find evidence about foods and their meanings drawn from sources somewhat removed from the kitchen, such as economic and environmental histories, but also novels, memoirs, essays, and poems. Gathered together with faithfulness to the material but also with imagination, these disparate elements of the historical record provide a more complete portrait than we have until now had of an important part of America's culinary and cultural heritage.

Since we are telling a story about cooking, we have organized the narrative in a way that highlights different types of foodstuffs and the things that cooks created with them. The broader social trends and issues that influenced New England cooking, and the cultural myths and meanings that accrued to it, are treated recurrently as they become pertinent in diverse foodstuff contexts. Thus, for example, Thanksgiving is considered in relation to pumpkin pie, then in relation to turkey, and finally in relation to pies of all types.

Our approach to the material is infused with both appreciation and skepticism. As far as the latter is concerned, the result of our irreverence concerning the more hagiographic understandings of New England food traditions is not the type of unrelieved debunking that has generated a backlash against "political correctness." We insist that the people of New England were not saints not in order to see them instead as sinners, but rather the better to see them as humans. Like those of all people, their motives and actions were mixed and imperfect.

Actually, we have found that our skepticism has made possible our appreciation. The culture of New England, once taken off its pedestal and placed where it belongs on a level with the cultures of other peoples, becomes a great deal more interesting and entertaining. One of the primary benefits of an iconoclastic approach is that it thereby becomes possible to retell the many particular stories that New Englanders have told about their foods without the self-satisfaction and sentimentality that have too often accompanied them.

It is our hope, then, to have set a plentiful table on the theme of New England's foods and cooking styles, not one groaning under a burden of self-congratulatory lore and sanctimoniously lauded dishes, but rather one full of more varied, and ultimately more tasty, historical fare.

CHAPTER I

This Beautifull Noble Eare

Corn

*W*hen the small band of separatists from the Church of England whom we call the Pilgrims arrived at Cape Cod in November 1620, they entered an abundant land. But they faced some major obstacles to enjoying the foods around them. While there was much talk in Europe at the time about the wondrous plants and animals of the New World, few Europeans could distinguish fact from fancy among claims about new discoveries. The fish and game looked similar to Old World species, but much of the plant life seemed unfamiliar. There are few places in North America where the vegetation more resembles that of the British Isles, but the Pilgrims, like many wayfarers, were more struck by differences than similarities. In their ignorance, they saw their new home as, in the words of William Bradford, "a hideous and desolate wilderness, full of wild beasts and wild men."[1]

However, for the thousands of native people who called the region home, the land was most certainly not "a hideous and desolate wilderness." For these people, members of different tribes and language groups, whom Europeans soon lumped together under the generic and inaccurate term "Indian," the region provided rich hunting and fishing grounds. It was also, in its southern portions, an excellent place to grow corn, beans, pumpkins, and other squashes. And it abounded with many types of edible wild plants, berries, and nuts. As the English eventually came to see and the native peoples already knew, New England was a fruitful place.[2]

Why Begin with Corn?

It was sadly prophetic of the relations that would eventually develop between the colonists and the Indians that the colonists' first taste of indigenous food was an illicit one. Edward Winslow and William Bradford described the incident in one of the earliest accounts of the settlement of Plymouth Colony. Shortly after the *Mayflower* dropped anchor off the outer end of Cape Cod, a party was sent inland to explore the area. Before long, the men came across a harvested field and an adjacent mound of sand. Buried in the sand was "a fine great new basket, full of very fair corn of this year . . . some yellow, and some red, and others mixed with blue, which was a very goodly sight; the basket . . . held about three or four bushels, which was as much as two of us could lift up from the ground, and was very handsomely and cunningly made." The explorers took the basket with them, and its contents were added to the available provisions aboard the ship.[3]

This small theft (Bradford and Winslow took pains to say that the Indians from whom the corn was stolen were later compensated) began the Pilgrims' indebtedness to the native peoples. One month after finding the cache of corn, unable to travel farther south because of the approach of winter, the newcomers decided to settle across Cape Cod Bay from the place where they had first dropped anchor. The site they chose for their settlement was an abandoned Algonquian village. It had been decimated a few years earlier by an epidemic imported from Europe. The settlers considered this "a place . . . fit for situation," as Bradford said, because of its nearby brooks and open fields, which had been cleared by the Algonquians for growing corn.[4]

The Pilgrims were unfit for the life of settlers for reasons other than their unfamiliarity with American flora and fauna. Before crossing the Atlantic, they had lived for over a decade in the Dutch town of Leiden, supporting themselves as artisans and laborers. Even in England, most of them had been townspeople, although many were but a generation removed from an agricultural background. During their first winter in America, half their number died of scurvy and other diseases. They had few tools, making the work of building houses long and arduous.[5]

Even if the Pilgrims had been better equipped, they could not have avoided the suffering and struggle that comes with adjustment to a new environment. They soon discovered that New England weather fluctuated dramatically through the year, from winters that were "sharp and violent, and subject to cruel and fierce storms," to summers that could be extremely hot and humid. One problem they did not have to confront as yet was the need to clear forested land for English-style tillage and livestock pasturage. The Pilgrims established their settlement on a site that the native inhabitants of the region had cleared before an epidemic had killed most of them. But the "light, sandy, and gravelly soil" of this and other conveniently cleared spots nearby proved inhospitable to the English grains that the settlers preferred to grow. Such soil should have been "ideal for rye" at least, though not for wheat, but for some reason, as one writer would state in 1637, even "our rye likes it not." The implications of this difficulty will be explored throughout this chapter.[6]

The most immediate obstacle, of course, was that it was winter when the Pilgrims established their settlement, making planting impossible for many months. Fortunately, the time they finally could plant, March 1621, was also the time that the straggling band of settlers made contact with the two representatives of the neighboring group of Wampanoag Indians who more than anyone else would make it possible for them to survive. One of these was the sachem Massasoit. As was noted in *Mourt's Relation*, Massasoit was eager to conclude a peace treaty with the newcomers, "especially because hee hath a potent Adversary the *Narowhiganseis* [Narragansetts], that are at warre with him, against whom hee thinks wee may be some strength to him, for our peeces [guns] are terrible unto them."[7]

The treaty was duly concluded and was soon turned into a practical reality by the actions of the other Indian whose acquaintance the settlers made that spring — Squanto. We all know about Squanto from our elementary school lessons. He had been taken by European traders years earlier to be a slave in Spain, but he had escaped to England. In 1617 he returned to the New England coast by way of Newfoundland, after learning that an epidemic had killed most of his tribe. It was the same epidemic that had caused the abandonment of the village that subsequently became Plymouth Plantation.

After the successful termination of the treaty negotiations and Massasoit's return to his home place, "Squanto continued with them and was their interpreter and was a special instrument sent of God for their good beyond their expectation. He directed them how to set their corn, where to take fish, and to procure other commodities." The following spring, he showed them some crucial points of corn agriculture, including the use of fish as fertilizer (a technique he may actually have learned during his sojourn in England and Newfoundland): "Squanto stood them in great stead, showing them both the manner how to set it, and after how to dress and tend it. Also he told them, except they got fish and set with it in these old grounds it would come to nothing."[8]

But Corn Can't Stand Alone

When Europeans arrived in the Americas, nutrition-deficiency diseases were unheard of among the natives of the hemisphere. This fact becomes even more surprising when we consider that such diseases were common in Europe at the time. It appears that the Indians had come to understand the hazards of a diet consisting exclusively of corn. Such at least is a reasonable inference from the fact that they either supplemented corn with other foods, or cooked it in ways that released all its nutrients, or both.

These supplementary foods were most often beans or pumpkins and other squashes, but they also included fish, game, and occasionally maple syrup. As far as nutritious methods of cooking corn itself were concerned, the principal one was the addition of ash. Whether the ash was specially made from burnt hickory or roasted, crushed shells, or whether it was simply swept up from the fire, throughout the vast geographic area of corn's predominance, native peoples pinched a little of it into their corn mixtures.[9]

We now know that these practices had a sound nutritional basis. Without supplementation or special treatment, corn provides neither niacin, a member of the vitamin B family, nor tryptophan, an amino acid from which, as Betty Fussell explains, "the human body can synthesize niacin." The primary supplement to corn was beans, which are rich in niacin and tryptophan. If the corn is not supplemented by other foods in the eating, then adding an alkali such as ash in the cooking both increases the availability of tryptophan and also assists in converting tryptophan to niacin, thereby releasing the vitamin "for the body's use."[10]

These procedures exemplify the substantial, if intuitive, wisdom that underlay many premodern traditions. By following them, the Indians were spared the horrors of pellagra, a vitamin-deficiency disease that afflicted the peasantry of those parts of Europe that had adopted corn as a dietary staple after its introduction from the Americas in the sixteenth century.[11]

All Indian tribes who relied on corn knew how to extract the maximum nutritional value from their most important crop. But how did corn become the quintessential Indian crop in the first place?

She Who Sustains Us

Corn is a species of grass, albeit an unusually large one. A giant, in fact. Originating in Mexico or Central America approximately 8,000 years ago, it spread throughout the hemisphere. Columbus's men found it growing in

Cuba in 1492. The original English word for the grain, "maize," comes from the Tainos, the Arawak people of Cuba, the Greater Antilles, and the Bahamas, whom the Spanish expedition encountered. The Tainos called their grain "mahiz," from which were derived the Spanish "maíz" and the English "maize."[12]

As corn was passed along from one group to another, people developed the strains that best suited their soils, climates, growing conditions, and tastes. By preserving seeds from plants of the type they wished to grow and discarding the rest, native farmers practiced sophisticated agriculture. In finding that cache of corn during their very first explorations, the *Mayflower* voyagers stumbled upon something that gave the lie to their idea that they had come to tame a wilderness.[13]

They also encountered one of the plant's most useful properties. Thoroughly dried, and kept free from moisture, corn can be stored indefinitely. During a dig in Mexico, an archaeologist discovered one of the expedition's pack mules "contentedly munching on . . . Aztec maize that was perhaps a thousand years old." A. Hyatt Verrill recounts the story of a farmer in Northfield, Massachusetts, in the 1930s who discovered pots filled with corn buried in his field. It had been over 150 years since Indians had lived in the area, but these earthen pots were nevertheless of Indian manufacture. To the farmer's astonishment, the eighteenth-century grain was still in perfect condition. The Indians had covered the openings with rawhide, then smeared pitch over it to make the containers watertight.[14]

The names given to this grain by the hemisphere's original inhabitants say a great deal about its importance in their lives. What we call corn translates in various native languages as "Our Mother," "Our Life," and "She Who Sustains Us." It is unfortunate that one of the greatest agricultural gifts of Indian America to the world is now primarily known by its most pedestrian name.[15]

Some Grains Are More Equal Than Others

Very little of what we now know about corn was known to the first settlers. Realizing that it would be essential to survival in their new environment, they began cultivating it immediately, and with great success, as indicated by this 1630 testimony of Francis Higginson: "the aboundant encrease of [Indian] Corne proves this Countrey to bee a wonderment. Thirtie, fortie, fiftie, sixtie are ordinarie here: yea *Josephs* encrease in *Ægypt* is out-stript here with us. Our planters hope to have more then a hundred fould this yere." When

Edward Johnson looked back two decades later on the first years of settlement, he echoed Higginson's appreciation of how well corn had thrived in the soil of New England and how important this had been to the initial success of the colonial venture: "and assuredly when the Lord created [Indian] Corne, hee had a speciall eye to supply these his peoples wants with it, for ordinarily five or six graines doth produce six hundred."[16]

Despite the gratifying productivity of their cornfields, the settlers' attitude toward their new staff of life was, to say the least, ambiguous. When the niece of John Winthrop Jr. wrote to her uncle from her home in Stamford, Connecticut, in 1649 about her many troubles, one of the ways she chose to summarize and praise her husband's willingness to place her needs before his own was to note that he "eats Indian [corn] that I might eat whet [wheat]." Likewise, Edward Johnson recalled that "the want of English graine, Wheate, Barly, and Rie proved a sore affliction to some stomacks, who could not live upon Indian Bread and water, yet were they compelled to it till Cattell increased, and the Plows could but goe."[17]

As one scholar has recently stated, the primary tendency in these early accounts was less to complain openly about Indian corn, these various comments notwithstanding, than to say as little about it as possible, thereby minimizing its importance in the colonists' diet. When Johnson turned to brag about the prosperity that he claimed had been achieved in New England by the 1650s, he mentioned corn only in order to draw a contrast between the past and present penury of the natives, forced to live on "parch't Indian corn incht out with Chestnuts and bitter Acorns," and the current well-being of the English, among whom "now good white and wheaten bread is no dainty." The foods of the good life, in Johnson's representation, were wheat bread, meat from domesticated livestock, poultry, wine, sugar, and such fruits as apples and pears.[18]

The corn that had served "to the great refreshing of the poore servants of Christ, in their low beginnings" in the 1630s was treated in the 1650s as though it no longer played any part whatsoever in the settlers' increasingly comfortable way of life. But we know that this was not true: corn remained a crucial component of the diet of the New World English throughout the colonial period and well into the nineteenth century. What accounts for the reluctance of Edward Johnson and others to acknowledge the importance of a foodstuff that was making it possible for the new colonies not just to survive but to flourish?[19]

Part of the answer is simply that the colonists were homesick for the familiar foods they had left behind in England. However, considerably more than nostalgia was involved. The nature of the grain that one consumed had been a matter laden with social significance since ancient times. Beginning with what William G. Panschar calls the "momentous discovery [of] the art of leavening" in Egypt in about 3,000 B.C.E., bread made from wheat had tended to be reserved for the upper classes, initially because wheat was much more expensive than barley, the other major grain of the Mediterranean basin.[20]

There was also a long-established hierarchy regarding the degree of processing to which the wheat had been subjected: the more the processing and the whiter the resulting bread, the greater the prestige. Darkness in bread could be the result either of limited bolting (bran removal) in the processing of the wheat or of the use of less highly regarded grains such as barley or rye (or the mixing together of such inferior ingredients). But whatever the method of preparation, black or dark bread had been associated with low social status at least since the time of the Roman dramatist Plautus, who had a man in one of his comedies ridicule a woman with whom he is quarreling as having lived "on black bread in rags and poverty" prior to his acquaintance with her.[21]

If such evaluations of white versus dark breads had not already existed in Britain, they were certainly brought there by the Romans, whereupon they probably became "even more pronounced," since the British climate was less conducive than the Mediterranean to growing wheat: "more rye or barley must have been added to the cheaper grades of bread, as well as a greater proportion of bran." Throughout the Middle Ages, the darker blends that were necessarily produced in large numbers were almost universally disparaged, and the rarer light and white loaves were correspondingly esteemed. This attitude could be seen in the seventh century, when pagan Saxon princes viewed with "greedy interest" the "shining white" wheaten Communion wafers dispensed by a Christian bishop. And it could be seen again in the fourteenth century, when Geoffrey Chaucer described in his *Canterbury Tales* on the one hand a poor widow who had to content herself with "brown breed," and on the other hand a prioress, a high-ranking nun, who could easily afford to lavish "wastelbreed," white bread, on her "smale houndes," her lap dogs.[22]

At the time of the colonization of New England, this grain and bread hierarchy remained entrenched. According to William Harrison, writing in 1577, "the gentility commonly provide themselves sufficiently of wheat for their own tables, whilst their household and poor neighbors in some shires are enforced to content themselves with rye or barley, yea, and in time of dearth, many with bread made either of beans, peason [peas], or oats, or of all together and some acorns among." Meanwhile, the unleavened hearth-baked oat cakes that were daily fare in the north and west of England as well as in Wales and Scotland were "frowned upon" by the inhabitants of the southern lowland regions of England, from which the majority of the colonists originated.[23]

Since the bread and social hierarchies coincided, Fernand Braudel's estimate that no more than 4 percent of the European population of the fifteenth, sixteenth, and seventeenth centuries ate white bread is plausible. At the same time, in England and no doubt elsewhere, the *desire* to eat such bread was far more widespread. In the late fourteenth century the poet William Langland referred unsympathetically in *Piers Plowman* to beggars who demanded bread of "clean wheat." Although the "movement in favor of white wheaten bread" was to gain full momentum only in the eighteenth century, when improved agricultural methods made possible a wider cultivation of wheat, it had developed by the early seventeenth century to the point that, according to the Grocers' Company of London, the lower orders would purchase barley or rye only as part of a mixture, four-fifths of which was wheat. This question of preferences among and prestige accorded to different grains and grain blends is explored in greater detail in chapter 7.[24]

The reluctance on the part of the earliest English inhabitants of New England to talk about their reliance on Indian corn for survival is becoming more comprehensible. Although not necessarily the primary motivation, a desire to escape from the adverse economic circumstances that were prevalent in late-sixteenth- and early-seventeenth-century England certainly played a part in the decisions of many of the emigrants to leave their native country. Yet upon arrival in their new homeland, they were immediately confronted with a sharp downturn in their fortunes, especially as far as diet was concerned. For a variety of reasons, attempts to grow wheat, the staple of choice in the Western world for millennia, proved unsuccessful. Moreover, Indian corn, the one grain that would grow and thrive, almost without effort on the English settlers' part (as it seemed), was not even on the charts in the terms of the venerable traditions of grain desirability.[25]

The situation was then further and sharply exacerbated by the fact that the staple food the English settlers were driven to cultivate and consume was also, as indicated by the name they bestowed upon it, the staple food of the natives. According to the justification of the colonizing enterprise propounded by its principal leader, John Winthrop, it was legitimate for the English to dispossess the natives of the territories comprising New England because "[the natives] inclose noe Land, neither have they any setled habytation, nor any tame Cattle to improve the Land by, & soe have noe other but a Naturall Right to those Countries. Soe as if we leave them sufficient for their use, we may lawfully take the rest, there being more then enough for them & us." In other words, lacking settled residence and methods of "improving" the land, the natives were savages, with no grounds for objecting to being displaced (if it should come to that) by the civilized English.[26]

But if that were the case, if the advent of the English was designed to move the New World from barbarism to civilization, then the fact that the civilizers were subsisting on the savages' food was, at a minimum, highly embarrassing. In this basic respect, the currents of influence appeared to be running in the wrong direction. Instead of the natives becoming civilized, the civilizers were "going native." The lack of discussion of Indian corn in early accounts of New England strongly suggests psychological denial of an emerging gap between high-minded, self-serving rationales and more complex realities that had the potential to call such rationales into serious question.[27]

Boiled Bag Puddings

We will return to the question of bread later in this chapter, when we consider the specific breads or breadlike foods cooked and eaten in colonial New England. For the moment, suffice it to say that edible results in the use of Indian corn as English food were difficult to achieve with the breadmaking techniques to which the settlers were accustomed, since corn lacks the gluten that makes it possible for wheat and, to a lesser degree, rye to produce an elastic bread dough. Successful adaptations were developed more readily not with bread but rather with a type of dish that had only evolved into its contemporary form quite recently—pudding.[28]

In its earlier forms, pudding was one of the methods of utilizing all the parts of a slaughtered animal—specifically, the blood. Blood or black pudding has a venerable history in Britain going back to Roman times. In the course of the Middle Ages, it came to be supplemented by "white" pudding, in which the offal of livestock was lightened up with such ingredients as breadcrumbs, cream, and eggs. The requirement to abstain from meat during Lent promoted the development of wholly meatless versions of white pudding. Like black ones, such puddings were boiled in containers of animal guts, which had the disadvantages both of being "awkward to clean and inconvenient to fill" and of being unavailable except at the time of year that livestock were slaughtered.[29]

After a period of experimentation with hollowed-out carrots, turnips, and cucumbers as pudding containers, the major breakthrough in English pudding technology occurred in the early seventeenth century when the pudding cloth came into general use. One early recorded instance of a pudding cooked in a pudding cloth was a recipe for Cambridge pudding (served to Cambridge University students in their dining halls) from 1617, just before the English settlement of New England. Given the high proportion of emigrants to New England with direct or indirect ties to Cambridge, it is not surprising that pudding cloth or boiled bag puddings became mainstays of the New England diet.[30]

Corn was easily adapted to pudding recipes. It functioned as well as any grain in making this hearty staple. To the Indians' basic corn and water mixture (of which more anon), the colonists began to add what they had on hand to sweeten the batter—whortleberries (the English word for what we now call huckleberries), currants, and other fruits and berries. They took the mixture and boiled it in a bag placed in a pot filled with water.[31]

Boiled bag corn puddings were one of the most successful adaptations of a New World food to English tastes. They were ideally suited to the cooking methods of the time. In early New England the kitchen hearth might be large enough for an adult to stand up in. There was space for pots to be suspended over the fire at varying heights, and there were areas for roasting joints of meat, perhaps even whole carcasses, on spits. Increasingly, there was also a built-in bake oven.

The fire in the colonial hearth was rarely allowed to go out, as it was far simpler to revive a smoldering fire than to start a fresh one. In fact, an unfired hearth was generally viewed with disapproval—only an inattentive housewife would allow her fire to burn out completely. We can hardly imagine the labor required to maintain these fires.

Besides vigilantly maintaining the fire, the housewife had to understand it well enough to know which foods to cook over (or in) which type of blaze. A young roaring fire called for roasts. A long-burning, slower fire was perfect for stews. With the need to keep their fires perpetually burning, frugal housewives made sure they had something cooking all the time. Roasting required considerable attention to avoid burning the food or, even worse, starting a house fire. But boiled foods, such as pottages, stews, and boiled bag puddings, could be left unattended for long periods, provided there was sufficient liquid in the pot to prevent scalding. These types of dishes, therefore, became the favorites of housewives whose many daily chores left them limited time to watch over what they were preparing.[32]

Boiled bag puddings held another advantage for the early American housewife — they could be prepared in reusable pieces of cloth and hung inside a pot or cauldron that was being used to cook other foods at the same time. Even the poorest household had an extra piece of old cloth for the purpose. Iron cooking pots were expensive, but most families owned at least one. With a minimal supply of pots, the housewife had to accommodate as many foods as possible in one pot at one time. Fortunately, the dense, compact boiled bag puddings also did not take up much room.

The name notwithstanding, the bags used to make boiled bag puddings were not bags at all. They were really just "large flat strips of stout cloth with no sewing to give them shape." When being readied for use, the cloth was first soaked in boiling water and wrung out. Then it was spread over a deep bowl and sprinkled with meal. The pudding batter was poured into the center, and the loose ends were gathered together and tied with a string. Finally, the bag was set on a trivet inside the stew pot or kettle and left there to simmer for three or four hours. The pudding could now cook unattended. No harm would come if the fire burned a little hotter or cooler than expected, or if the pudding was left to cook a little longer than usual.[33]

In addition to berries and other fruit, these puddings were enriched with molasses, maple syrup, eggs, butter, and spices. They could be served hot or sliced cold; the texture when chilled was that of a dense cake. Boiled bag puddings remained a staple of New England cooking for almost three hundred years, continuing to be called for in standard cookbooks into the twentieth century.[34]

Even though it had been sweetened (not to mention distanced from its origins in the slaughter of animals), pudding was not regarded as a dessert during the colonial era. Through the early years of American independence, for instance at John Adams's home, boiled bag puddings made of corn and sweetened with molasses were still brought to the table during the earlier stages of the meal. Ella Shannon Bowles and Dorothy S. Towle note that well into the nineteenth century "the invitation, 'Come at pudding time,' was a way of saying, 'Come in time for dinner.'"[35]

Nevertheless, by the late eighteenth century Americans were developing different ideas about when their puddings should be eaten. The debate even took on political significance. In Salem, Massachusetts, the Federalists, following the example of their leader John Adams, ate their puddings first, while the Jeffersonians began eating them at the end of the meal. The family of Caroline Howard King, who grew up in Salem in the 1820s and 1830s, had presumably been Federalists, for King had "heard my father say that in my grandfather's house the pudding was served first." The Jeffersonian practice won out, and puddings have become almost exclusively a dessert dish.[36]

Indian Pudding

With one exception to be discussed below, bags or metal containers are no longer used in the preparation of puddings. Nevertheless, several enduring New England dishes are descended from puddings that were prepared that way. The most significant of these is Indian pudding. The name refers not to native peoples but rather to the main ingredient, Indian meal or "Indian."

The first cookbook by an American author was Amelia Simmons's *American Cookery*, published in 1796. Adapting British and Continental sources, such as Susannah Carter's *The Frugal Housewife*, a British cookbook reprinted in Boston in 1772, to ingredients available on this side of the Atlantic, *American Cookery* was an enormous success. It filled the need of American housewives for a cookbook specifically designed for them, containing several distinctively American recipes along with the European adaptations.

Among the American recipes were no fewer than three Indian puddings, two of them to be baked, one to be boiled in a bag or a metal or stoneware container:

A Nice Indian Pudding

No. 1. 3 pints scalded milk, 7 spoons fine Indian meal, stir well together while hot, let stand till cooled; add 7 eggs, half pound raisins, 4 ounces butter, spice and sugar, bake one and half hour.

No. 2. 3 pints scalded milk to one pint meal salted; cool, add 2 eggs, 4 ounces butter, sugar or molasses and spice . . . it will require two and half hours baking.

No. 3. Salt a pint meal, wet with one quart milk, sweeten and put into a strong cloth, brass or bell metal vessel, stone or earthen pot, secure from wet and boil 12 hours.[37]

As he recalled them in 1879, the baked Indian puddings of Thomas Robinson Hazard's early-nineteenth-century childhood in Narragansett, Rhode Island, were in accordance with Simmons's recipes, consisting of cornmeal (which Hazard called "ambrosia"), milk, eggs, and sugar or molasses. Instead of Simmons's raisins, Hazard remembered huckleberries and blackberries in

AMERICAN COOKERY,

OR THE ART OF DRESSING

VIANDS, FISH, POULTRY and VEGETABLES,

AND THE BEST MODES OF MAKING

PASTES, PUFFS, PIES, TARTS, PUDDINGS, CUSTARDS AND PRESERVES,

AND ALL KINDS OF

C A K E S,

FROM THE IMPERIAL PLUMB TO PLAIN CAKE.

ADAPTED TO THIS COUNTRY,

AND ALL GRADES OF LIFE.

By Amelia Simmons,

AN AMERICAN ORPHAN.

PUBLISHED ACCORDING TO ACT OF CONGRESS.

HARTFORD

PRINTED BY HUDSON & GOODWIN.

FOR THE AUTHOR.

1796

Title page from American Cookery, *Hartford edition, 1796.*
(Courtesy American Antiquarian Society)

both baked and boiled bag Indian puddings. Best of all had been "green fox-grape boiled pudding, none of your tasteless catawba or Isabella insipids." Accompanying all varieties had been "luscious brown sugar sauce."[38]

The next highly successful Yankee cookbook was *The American Frugal Housewife*, by Lydia Maria Child. Child's recipes for Indian pudding, both baked and boiled, varied from those of Simmons primarily in the direction indicated by her title. Molasses as the only recommended sweetener, water as a possible substitute for milk, and the omission of eggs from the baked version all bespoke frugality. She noted that some people stirred "thin slices of sweet apple" into boiled Indian pudding.[39]

Other puddings from the first half of the nineteenth century also exhibited only minor variation. Mrs. N. K. M. Lee copied Child's recipe for boiled Indian pudding almost verbatim, though she restored the eggs and the (brown) sugar option to baked Indian pudding, which she said required a mere half hour (versus Child's three or four hours) in a Dutch oven. Sarah Josepha Hale added whortleberries and cranberries to the list of fruits that might be added.[40]

Two writers of the 1840s, perhaps following the Philadelphia authority Eliza Leslie rather than Child, mentioned lemon juice or grated peel for flavoring. One of these writers proposed eating her "Rich Boiled Indian Pudding . . . with sauce made of drawn butter, wine and nutmeg." Such indulgence was certainly far removed from a Child-like frugality. This same writer, Mrs. A. L. Webster, did provide some measure of economy with her suggestion that leftover boiled Indian pudding could be "cut in slices and fried, when cold."[41]

During the eighteenth and early nineteenth centuries, Indian pudding in its baked form was usually cooked on Saturday night in the brick oven, as part of the weekly preparations for the Sabbath, alongside baked beans, pies, and loaves of bread. (We will discuss this custom further in the next chapter.) Although the episode did not take place on the Sabbath, Harriet Beecher Stowe, in her 1859 novel *The Minister's Wooing*, which was set in Newport, Rhode Island, in the 1790s, showed baked Indian pudding, "its gelatinous softness, matured by long and patient brooding in the motherly old oven," forming a meal in company with baked beans and brown bread.[42]

Later in the same novel, Stowe indicated that density and firmness were among the properties of the boiled bag form of Indian pudding that were the most highly prized. A young female character, who was being teased about her matrimonial prospects, stated, "I've been practising on my pudding now these six years, and I shouldn't be afraid to throw one up chimney with any girl." Stowe proceeded to explain: "This speech was founded on a tradition, current in those times, that no young lady was fit to be married till she could construct a boiled Indian-pudding of such consistency that it could be thrown up chimney and come down on the ground, outside, without breaking."[43]

As the nineteenth century progressed, baked Indian pudding became by far the predominant form. One author writing in 1864 clarified the somewhat enigmatic instructions Lydia Maria Child had given regarding what to do "if you want whey": "When you place it [the pudding] in the oven, turn a half pint of milk on the top of the pudding without stirring it, and let it bake three or four hours, moderate fire. It should be taken from the oven two hours before it is used, that the whey may cool, which makes a most delicious jelly." Some recipes from this era called for wheat flour along with cornmeal, at most half as much wheat as cornmeal.[44]

In the twentieth century a popular Indian pudding recipe was that of Durgin Park, the restaurant in Boston's Faneuil Hall market. The renowned eatery was described thus in 1954: "At Durgin-Park's, in the heart of the market district, the crockery is thick and durable as gravestones, and the tablecloths are red-checkered. Strangers sit side by side. White-frocked butchers in straw hats bump elbows with State Street brokers and Harvard professors. And almost everybody orders Indian pudding."[45]

Although Indian pudding remains a *specialité de la maison* at Durgin Park, it is doubtful that many twenty-first-century diners continue to partake of it in the spirit implicitly recommended by this mid-twentieth-century author—as a reaffirmation of the rock-solid, serious, and well-ordered yet democratic New England tradition. Now located in the trendsetting Quincy Market historic district and tourist mall, Durgin Park, and the tradition it embodies, has become merely one attraction among the many the area offers to postmodern passersby, competing, thus far successfully, with a wide variety of non-Yankee venues.

As presented in a 1939 cookbook, the most noteworthy feature of the Indian pudding that "almost everybody" ordered at Durgin Park was its topping of whipped cream or vanilla ice cream. Elsewhere in this cookbook, the author wrote that Nelson Eddy, "radio and movie star," was wont to be served Indian pudding with whipped cream for dessert, after a main course of New England boiled dinner, when he would visit his mother in Pawtucket, Rhode Island. Mrs. Eddy's Indian pudding "varies from the Durgin-Park recipe in that she uses a variety of Rhode Island corn meal that is made from a strain of the original Indian maize that has been grown continuously on the Carr Homestead, Quononoquott Farm, Jamestown, Rhode Island, since Governor Carr's time. It is slowly ground between fine grained stones of Rhode Island granite." This passage swept "original Indian maize" into extravagant claims, similar to those made in the 1950s account of Durgin Park, for the virtues of the New England tradition—its long continuities, its measured patience, its solid foundations.[46]

Hasty Pudding

Acquiring its name from the speed with which it supposedly could be prepared, hasty pudding was also called stirabout pudding. In Britain, hasty pudding had been made from such things as grated bread and oatmeal, although as time went on, the oatmeal version tended to be confined to the north and west. Recipes utilizing a wheat flour base were common in eighteenth-century cookbooks. In New England, of course, cornmeal rapidly became the key ingredient.[47]

Simple as it was, hasty pudding still admitted of a degree of variation in methods of preparation. In the earliest Yankee cookbook recipe, in Child's *American Frugal Housewife*, spoonfuls of sifted cornmeal were dissolved in a bowl of water, and then the solution was poured into boiling water, the amount varying "according to the size of your family." Salt and handfuls of additional meal were thrown into the kettle, while the mixture was being constantly stirred. "When it is so thick that you stir it with great difficulty, it is about right." According to Child, that would have been after half an hour, which was perhaps just in time to prevent the name from becoming a misnomer. The dish was to be eaten with milk or molasses. Rye meal was preferable to corn "if the system is in a restricted state."[48]

Regarding the requisite cooking time, Catharine Beecher had a quite different idea, abandoning all pretense of connection between name and thing, by stating that two or three hours was needed. Beecher was perhaps attempting to salvage her credibility by adding another name, calling her recipe "Mush, or Hasty Pudding." She recommended that it only be eaten after it had been chilled, sliced, and fried. Hasty pudding as fried mush remained prominent in most subsequent recipes, with many authors calling for an admixture of wheat flour to facilitate slicing.[49]

Possibly the plainest preparation in a culinary repertoire that was nothing if not plain, hasty pudding nevertheless provided the inspiration for one of the earliest instances of the use of Yankee food for cultural mythmaking about New England. We refer to "The Hasty Pudding," a poem written by

"The Hasty Pudding," Harper's New Monthly Magazine, *July 1856.*
(Courtesy Fall River Public Library)

the Revolutionary-era "Connecticut wit" Joel Barlow while he was living in France in 1793.

With the Indians now reduced to a wholly subordinate status, Barlow felt free to imagine that hasty pudding was derived from Indian cuisine. It must have been some "lovely squaw" who "in days of yore, / (Ere great Columbus sought thy native shore) / First gave thee to the world." This conjecture was valid only in the broad sense that the Indians did indeed add cornmeal to boiling water, but usually, along with "additives of many kinds," as part of succotash, described later in this chapter.[50]

The poem actually provided the first New England recipe for hasty pudding, depicting a housewife who "strews" the cornmeal into a kettle of boiling water until it "thickens all the flood." Barlow did not shrink from noting that, again in spite of the name of the dish and his poem, "Long o'er the simmering fire she lets it stand." It was extremely important that a high degree of thickness be achieved, he went on; such a thickness indeed that "To stir it well demands a stronger hand; / The husband takes his turn."[51]

In Barlow's view, the knowledge required for eating hasty pudding in the proper fashion was more complex and hard-won than that for cooking it: "For rules there are, tho' ne'er unfolded yet, / Nice rules and wise, how pudding should be ate." He grudgingly allowed that hasty pudding eaten with molasses was "A wholesome dish, and well-deserving praise," but he insisted that the true aficionado chose milk instead. Only with milk was hasty pudding truly itself:

> First in your bowl the milk abundant take,
> Then drop with care along the silver lake
> Your flakes of pudding; these at first will hide
> Their little bulk beneath the swelling tide;
> But when their growing mass no more can sink,
> When the soft island looms above the brink,
> Then check your hand: you've got the portion's due,
> So taught our sires, and what they taught is true.

The poem continued with prescriptions about the type of spoon and bowl that would most conduce to an authentic experience of hasty pudding, concluding with an admonition to "Fear not to slaver; 'tis no deadly sin."[52]

While doubtless included partly for comic effect, these detailed instructions regarding tableware, utensils, eating, and manners were appropriate to the period in which the poem was composed. It was in the later eighteenth century that the array of dishes, implements, and modes of dining that have since come to be considered proper first began to take hold among large segments of the population.[53]

Those familiar with the Italian dish polenta, or as Barlow calls it "*Palanta*," may not realize that it is essentially hasty pudding under the name given to it by "the soft nations round the warm Levant." Barlow noted another, more objectionable instance of linguistic and cultural diversity in connection with the dish when he exclaimed, "how I blush / To hear the Pennsylvanians call thee *mush*." Under its true name, "a sound to every Yankey dear," hasty pudding was dense with significance:

> My father lov'd thee through his length of days:
> For thee his fields were shaded o'er with maize;

From thee what health, what vigour he possesst,
Ten sturdy freemen sprung from him attest;
Thy constellation rul'd my natal morn,
And all my bones were made of Indian corn.

The soil, the agriculture and cookery, and the sturdy political spirit of Barlow's native Connecticut were offered as constituting the firmest possible foundation for the new nation. As later in the mid-twentieth century, here at the dawning of New England's self-presentation to the larger American world, Indian corn, and with it Indians, were reborn as Yankee food, Yankee culture, and Yankees.[54]

Samp and Hominy

Roger Williams, maverick Puritan and founder of Rhode Island, was an open-minded and acute observer of the native way of life, and he provided a good deal of the information upon which later students of the indigenous peoples of New England have relied. In his account of the Narragansett group with which he was most familiar, written in the 1640s, Williams referred to a corn preparation called "Nasàump" and went on to describe both native and English methods of cooking it: "A kind of meal pottage, unparched. From this the English call their samp, which is the Indian corn, beaten and boiled, and eaten hot or cold with milk or butter, which are mercies beyond the natives' plain water, and which is a dish exceeding wholesome for the English bodies." Williams's friend John Winthrop Jr. felt that "Sampe" was "the best sort of Food which the English make of [Indian] Corne."[55]

Williams's comparison of a boiled native food to pottage was echoed by many other seventeenth-century European observers and will be considered later on in the chapter in connection with succotash. "Nasàump" was also called rockahominie, tackhummin, and sagamite by the Indians, just as samp was also called hominy, great hominy, whole hominy, pearl hominy, lye hominy, hominy grits, and grits by the English. One of the founders of Dorchester, Massachusetts, Roger Clap, illustrated the imprecision that was customary in speaking of these preparations when he recalled of those earliest years of settlement that "it was not accounted a strange thing in those Days to Drink water, and to eat *Samp* or *Homine* without Butter or Milk."[56]

These differences in names corresponded, but with far from perfect consistency, to differences in methods of removing the hulls from the corn kernels and breaking up (or not) the kernels thus hulled. According to Betty Fussell, "Indians distinguished between two kinds of hulled corn: one was made of kernels broken into coarse pieces in a mortar, then cleared of skins by winnowing; the other was cleared of skins by boiling the kernels in lye."[57]

If John Winthrop Jr. is to be believed, the seventeenth-century English colonists made their samp by combining aspects of these two methods:

> They first Water the Corne, if with Colde Water a little longer, if with Water a little warmed a shorter time about halfe an hower more or less, as they find it needfull, according to the driness of the Corne, then they either beate it in a Mortar . . . to be about the Biggness of Rice, . . . or Grind it gross as neere as they can about the bigness of Rice in handmills or other Mills, out of which they sift the Flower, or Meale very cleane . . . then they winnow it in the wind, and so separate the hulls from the rest[.] this is to be boyled or Stued with a gentle Fire, till it be tender, of a fitt consistence, as of Rice so boyled, into which if Milke, or butter be put either with Sugar or without, it is a food very pleasant and wholesome.

In this case, Winthrop did not acknowledge the native origins of these procedures, although in his presentation of other areas of corn culture and cookery he did.[58]

After providing instruction in the boiling-in-lye method noted by Fussell, two early-twentieth-century authors noted that "few care to take this trouble, since the corn already hulled can be purchased in most large towns." They then offered two recipes, one for hominy itself (soaking the hulled corn overnight in cold water, boiling it for ten minutes, and steaming it for "several hours"), and one for "Hominy Cakes" (beating egg and butter into cold hominy and frying "like griddle cakes").[59]

William Cobbett recommended hominy, which he called samp, to his English readers, claiming not only that it was far more healthful and nutritious than corresponding preparations made from beans, peas, and other pulses, but also that it was an aphrodisiac.[60]

Ryaninjun and Brown Bread

As we have seen, the English settlers arrived in New England in the early seventeenth century possessed of an ancient set of attitudes about which kinds of bread were more and less desirable. Their longing for breads made exclusively with wheat could only begin to be satisfied in the second quarter of the nineteenth century, after the opening of the Erie Canal made wheat shipped in from areas to the west affordable. In Plymouth in the first few decades after settlement, wheat ranked well behind corn in acreage planted and amounts yielded. According to the calculations of Darrett B. Rutman for the 1640s and 1650s, more than twice as many acres tended to be planted in corn as in wheat, and each acre of corn yielded more than double what each acre of wheat yielded. A typical farm might produce one hundred bushels of corn for every eighteen bushels of wheat.[61]

Thereafter, throughout New England even this level of success with wheat became more difficult to achieve, due to a variety of impediments, most especially those arising from a wheat fungus known as the blast. The region therefore became an importer of wheat in the eighteenth century, bringing supplies in from Pennsylvania and other Middle Colonies. This trade, however, was never carried on in sufficient volume to make wheat bread a dietary staple for all levels of society.[62]

As wheat declined, rye tended to take its place. In Middlesex County, Massachusetts, probate inventories in the third quarter of the seventeenth century, the proportion containing wheat declined from over 50 percent to around 20 percent, while those containing rye rose from 33 percent to almost 40 percent. By the first quarter of the eighteenth century, rye "had become the chief bread grain of English origin." Other European grains, such as field peas, barley, and oats, "were distinctly minor crops throughout the [seventeenth] century" in Plymouth and elsewhere. Barley was grown in great part as the basis of beer, but even the limited allocation of resources for this purpose tended to be reduced as beer was steadily displaced by cider as the staple beverage. Oats served mostly as fodder, in accordance with the regional prejudice most memorably expressed in Samuel Johnson's definition of oats as "a grain which is generally given to horses but in Scotland supports the people."[63]

As a result, the colonists' predicament was that they had abundant supplies of a grain that at best was unfamiliar and at worst was tainted with savagery, along with limited supplies of other grains that they had never particularly liked back home, but that they had, except for the few of them that were of gentry stock, always reluctantly incorporated into their bread. From these unpromising ingredients they fashioned what became the principal bread of colonial and early national New England—Rye and Indian. The full name was soon elided in common parlance, becoming Ryaninjun.

John Winthrop Jr., writing in 1662 before the difficulties of growing wheat in New England had become fully apparent, provided one of the earliest descriptions of Ryaninjun: "There is . . . very good Bread made of [Indian corn], by mixing half, or a third parte, more or less of Ry, or Wheate-Meale, or Flower amongst it, and then they make it up into Loaves, adding Leaven or yeast to it to make it Rise."[64]

In chapter 7 we will discuss at length the rise (and fall) of yeast in relation to the leavening of cakes, but in the meantime let us not imagine that obtaining good quality yeast in the seventeenth century was as simple as Winthrop made it sound. Elizabeth David has written of the ancient pedigree of both ale or beer barm and the "spontaneous leaven and sourdough systems"—the latter being the growing of wild yeasts in solutions or worts of "fermented grain, potatoes, flour," or the like. Such yeasts had been known in Britain at least since the Iron Age, but they were "temperamental . . . their strength was uncertain, so were their keeping qualities." Temperamental or not, they were what was most available to the seventeenth-century English and colonial bread baker, especially the ale or beer barm, which came to be known as "emptins" from its origin at the bottoms of beer barrels.[65]

By all accounts, Ryaninjun quickly ascended to the status of "the standard bread for brick-oven cookery." In the earliest colonial period, when pans and other cooking utensils were expensive to import and forges for making local wares were few, this food's advantage was its convenience. The dome-shaped loaves could be baked without pans, directly on the oven floor or atop a bed of oak or cabbage leaves spread across the bottom of the oven. The leaves were said to impart a distinctive flavor to the bread.[66]

One method of depositing the loaves atop the oak or cabbage leaves involved the use of a hoe or bread peel, which was a long-handled paddle for placing the bread deep into the oven. As Alice Morse Earle described the process, "the peel was sprinkled with meal, great heaps of dough were placed thereon, and by a dextrous twist they were thrown on the cabbage or oak leaves." Ella Shannon Bowles and Dorothy S. Towle state that "Rhode Island housewives" placed both the leaves and the dough on the bread peel, thrust the peel into the oven, "and with a quick turn of the handle deposited both leaves and bread on the bottom." However the placement of the bread in the oven to bake over the leaves was accomplished, considerable skill was evidently required. The children of the family also participated in the process of making Ryaninjun. In autumn they would "go leafing" for large, unblemished oak leaves, gathering the best ones and stringing them on sticks "to keep them in order."[67]

According to Thomas Robinson Hazard, two methods of baking "Rhineinjun bread" were commonly utilized in his grandfather's early-nineteenth-century southern Rhode Island household. In one, "late in the evening, when the logs . . . were well burned down," two iron basins filled with kneaded dough were placed in the midst of the open hearth fire, "the one on top of the other, so as to inclose their contents and press them into one loaf. The whole was then carefully covered with hot ashes with coals on top, and left until morning." The other method was to place the loaves in "a long-heated and well-tempered brick oven . . . into which a cup of water was also placed to make the crust soft."[68]

In the earliest published recipes, starting in 1829, the names "Rye and Indian" and "brown bread" were used interchangeably. "Some like to have it half Indian meal and half rye meal; others prefer it one third Indian, and two thirds rye," wrote Lydia Maria Child, confirming John Winthrop Jr.'s statement above regarding the varying proportions of the grains. Sarah Josepha Hale added the option of two-thirds cornmeal and one-third rye. Since these cookbooks appeared after the opening of the Erie Canal had made wheat more generally available, they also sometimes mentioned yet another option—one-third cornmeal, one-third rye, and one-third wheat.[69]

Hale used the two-to-one cornmeal-to-rye formula in her own 1839 recipe:

Take *four quarts* of sifted indian meal; put it into a glazed earthen pan, sprinkle over it a table-spoonful of fine salt; pour over it about two quarts of boiling water, stir and work it till every part of the meal is thoroughly wet; indian meal absorbs a greater quantity of water. When it is about milk-warm, work in *two quarts of rye meal, half a pint* of lively yeast, mixed with a pint of warm water; add more warm water if needed. Work the mixture well with your hands: it should be stiff, but not firm as flour dough. Have ready a large, deep, well buttered pan; put in the dough, and smooth the top by putting your hand in warm water, and then patting down the loaf. Set this to rise in a warm place in the winter; in the summer it should not be put by the fire. When it begins to crack on the top, which will usually be in about an hour or an hour and a half, put it into a well-heated oven, and bake it three or four hours. It is better to let it stand in the oven all night, unless the weather is warm. Indian meal requires to be well cooked. The loaf will weigh between seven and eight pounds. Pan bread keeps best in large loaves.

With her eight-pound loaf, Hale certainly followed her own advice about producing Ryaninjun in substantial quantities. Her use of the phrase "lively yeast," which echoed the exact language found in Child's earlier instructions for this same bread, raised the specter of yeast that was not lively and thus indicates that yeast remained a problem in the second quarter of the nineteenth century. All the cookbooks of this era included information on various ways of utilizing what Elizabeth David called the venerable "spontaneous leaven and sourdough systems." They explained how to make yeast from "the settlings" of beer and also from hops, wheat or rye bran, milk, and potatoes.[70]

Catharine Beecher called for saleratus, sodium bicarbonate, instead of yeast in her recipe for what she called "Eastern Brown Bread." Another cookbook published the year before, in 1845, gave a reason for this choice: "Bread made so will not sour so quick as when yeast is put into it." Both this author and Beecher also recommended including molasses, which was to become standard procedure.[71]

A British traveler of the 1820s opined that the breads made of "Indian-corn" that one was apt to be served at the "better class" of New England inns were "very good." Thomas Robinson Hazard, intent upon demonstrating the superiority of all things southern Rhode Island and early nineteenth century, claimed that when the door of his grandfather's brick oven was opened in the morning after a night of baking Ryaninjun, "it was customary to raise one or two windows in the kitchen, the fragrance from the bread being so enrapturing as sometimes to affect persons whose nerves were not very strong."[72]

Nevertheless, the leavened cornmeal breads of New England had, predictably, their detractors. Josiah Quincy recalled the tedium of a steady diet of Rye and Indian at the parsonage where he had boarded during his student days at Phillips Academy in Andover, Massachusetts, in the 1780s: "As to bread, there being little or no intercourse with the South, rye and Indian bread was our only supply, and that not always thoroughly baked. The minister alone was indulged in white bread, as brown gave him the heart-burn, and he could not preach upon it." The American Revolution had not, at least as yet, disturbed the grain hierarchy. Such limited supplies of wheat bread as were available went to the minister, who occupied the pinnacle of village society.[73]

In *Oldtown Folks*, another of Harriet Beecher Stowe's novels set in late colonial/early national New England, the narrator began his paean to Ryaninjun with an apology for the bread's darkness and ended it by invoking the peculiarly rugged circumstances of a New England winter as the requisite context for celebration of this particular type of bread: "Our bread, to be sure, was the black compound of rye and Indian which the economy of Massachusetts then made the common form, because it was the result of what could be most easily raised on her hard and stony soil; but I can inform all whom it may concern that rye and Indian bread smoking hot, on a cold winter morning, together with savory sausages, pork and beans, formed a breakfast fit for a king, if the king had earned it by getting up in a cold room, washing in ice-water, tumbling through snow-drifts, and foddering cattle." The mechanisms by which a virtue was fashioned from a necessity were rather obvious in this instance.[74]

Until the mid-nineteenth century, brown bread was simply another name for Ryaninjun. Around that time, however, as wheat bread became more widely available, nostalgia began to ennoble "the old brown bread" that had previously been mostly tolerated. The long-established mixture of cornmeal and rye was placed in a tin (as opposed to bag) pudding container and thus was born steamed Boston Brown Bread.[75]

A related development was the health food movement of the 1830s spearheaded by Sylvester Graham, "the prophet of bran bread and pumpkins," as Ralph Waldo Emerson called him. As early as 1839, Graham's spirited efforts to overturn the ancient bias in favor of bolted wheat flour had met with success sufficient to lead Sarah Josepha Hale to acknowledge that her recipe for "brown or dyspepsia bread" might better have been called "Graham bread." However, Hale's brown bread was not steamed Boston Brown Bread but rather a version of "bran bread," in our terms, oven-baked whole wheat bread. Catharine Beecher contributed to the confusion of terminology by giving the name brown bread both to her Ryaninjun bread ("Eastern Brown Bread") and to her graham or bran bread ("Walnut Hill's Brown Bread"). Neither one was steamed.[76]

A typical recipe for steamed brown bread from the second half of the nineteenth century, "Mrs. Reed's Brown Bread," consisted of sour milk, baking soda, salt, two level cups of "Indian meal," three heaping cups of "flour or Graham meal," and a cup of molasses. The mixture was to be steamed for four hours and then browned lightly in an oven. In allowing for either graham meal or bolted wheat flour, this recipe reflected the fact that throughout this period some cookbooks called for one of these, some for the other, in varying ratios to corn and rye. (The recipe is somewhat atypical in its omission of rye.) The rye and graham components could be called either meal or flour, while the wheat was invariably flour and the corn invariably meal. The proportion of sweetener in "Mrs. Reed's Brown Bread," one cup to five-plus of meal and flour, was much higher than in that of contemporaneous baked brown or Ryaninjun recipes, which remained at the level of approximately half a cup of sweetener to three or four quarts of flour or meal.

The modern preference for (some might say addiction to) sweetness seems to have emerged early on in connection with this dish, not only as compared with its baked bread cousin but also, as we shall see in the next chapter, as compared with baked beans.[77]

In the mid-twentieth century Bowles and Towle gave us brown bread in jingle form: "Three cups of corn meal, / One of rye flour; / Three cups of sweet milk, / One cup of sour." And so on. Boston Brown Bread thus became the stuff of twentieth-century nostalgia. But to Thomas Robinson Hazard, it represented the most arrant degeneration from the true "Rhineinjun bread" that he had known as a child and that continued to be properly made in the household he headed as an adult. "Even before" this alleged triumph of Boston culinary art had been rendered "utterly worthless by the introduction of Western [i.e., Midwestern] corn meal, made often of damaged corn, and tasteless Western rye to match," Hazard had brought home "after a visit to that city, a loaf of the famous material, that my children might compare its quality with our family bread." But the children were unwilling to partake of more than one mouthful of "the famous luxury they had heard so much of."[78]

They were not the only dissatisfied diners: "After breakfast I took the loaf and placed it in the trough for an old Berkshire sow to eat, that I knew was very fond of our Rhineinjun bread, a piece of which I used almost daily to treat her with. The old creature—which had not been fed that morning—dove her nose greedily into it; but at the first taste she dropped the morsel, and regarding me askance, with a suspicious and sinister expression in her eye, she hastened to a stagnant, muddy pool in the corner of the yard, and rinsed her mouth."[79]

Johnny Cake: Where It Came From

In recent times, owing in part to the efforts of mid-twentieth-century Yankee cookbook writers of a self-consciously traditionalist cast, the most popular of all colonial corn breads has been Johnny cake. Thoroughfares called "Johnnycake Lane" are currently found in at least two New England communities—Portsmouth, Rhode Island, and Chelsea, Vermont. Johnny cake might not have an Indian name, but (unlike Ryaninjun) it was derived from a bread eaten by native peoples. The time has come to examine in somewhat greater detail the place of corn in native cooking.[80]

In his 1634 pamphlet *New Englands Prospect*, written for the purpose of encouraging emigration, William Wood stated that the natives "seldome or never make bread of their Indian corne." Other seventeenth-century European observers disputed this, however. Samuel de Champlain testified that the natives "reduce [corn] to flour, of which they then make cakes like the Indians of Peru." Roger Williams saw the Narragansetts taking their cornmeal and mixing it with powdered strawberries to make what he called "Strawberry bread," or with dried and powdered currants to make "a delicate dish which they call *Sautáuthig*; which is as sweet to them as plum or spice cake to the *English*." Williams also referred to a practice of using boiled clam juice to make native bread "seasonable and savory, instead of Salt." The natives known to Daniel Gookin, a colleague of John Eliot, early New England's chief Christian missionary, "sometimes . . . beat their maize into meal and sift it through a basket made for that purpose. With this meal they make bread, baking it in the ashes, covering the dough with leaves."[81]

In her comprehensive study of the native people living in the New England area during the time of contact with Europeans, Kathleen J. Bragdon concludes from this testimony and other evidence that cornmeal was used by the natives to make "cakes, and other baked or fried breads sounding remarkably like tamales or tortillas." In other words, the breads that were among the core constituents of the native diet resembled the unleavened, hearth-baked oat cakes of Scotland, Wales, and northern and western England at which the migrants to New England from the southern and lowland portions of England had been in the habit of turning up their noses. In the words of a recent writer, tortillas, "eastern Amerindian pone breads," and British oat cakes were all "conceptually the same product."[82]

We must now take another look at the discrepancy between the founding New Englanders' self-image and the realities of their situation. They perceived a stark contrast between themselves as civilized human beings and the natives as savages. Nevertheless, they were forced to use native grain to make breads, such as Ryaninjun and brown bread, that resembled the coarser leavened breads of England's lowlands that they had never considered particularly satisfactory, even without this alien ingredient. But an even wider gap between perception and reality resulted from the fact that the settlers found themselves using native grain to make a bread similar to the one that the "savages" had always made. Back home, their abstention from breads of this sort had distinguished them, or so they thought, from the semisavage Scots, Welsh, and northern English. Now this distinction had collapsed in practice, which probably made clinging to it in theory all the more vital.[83]

To understand how Johnny cake is derived from Indian "bread," we must consider the origin of the name "Johnny cake." William Wood provided a description of a form of native corn cookery in which corn was turned into meal not before it was cooked, as in the Gookin account above, but rather after it was cooked: "the best of their victuals for their journey is Nocake, (as they call it) which is nothing but Indian Corne parched in the hot ashes; the ashes being sifted from it, it is afterward beaten to powder, and put into a long leatherne bag, trussed at their backe like a knapsack; out of which they take thrice three spoonefulls a day, dividing it into three meales." Roger Williams recast Wood's "Nocake" as "Nókehick," making the orthography more closely resemble Algonquian speech patterns, and he was perhaps the first Englishman to give this dish a favorable review: "With a *spoonfull* of this *meale* and a *spoonfull* of water from the *Brooke*, have I made many a good dinner and supper."[84]

It is worth mentioning that the parallel between "eastern Amerindian pone breads" and Scottish oat breads extended to this use as provision for travel. In the fourteenth century the chronicler Sir John Froissart noted that Scottish soldiers, on their raids into England, came equipped with flat stones and bags of oatmeal. They would mix the oatmeal with water, form it into small cakes, and cook the cakes on the stones in the embers of their campfires. "It is therefore no wonder that they perform a longer day's march than other soldiers," Froissart remarked, just as William Wood was later impressed that the New England natives, sustained by their "strange viaticum" of parched cornmeal and water, "will travell foure or five daies together, with loads fitter for Elephants than men."[85]

To return to the name: Wood's "Nocake" doubtless reflected more accurately than did Williams's scholarly "Nókehick" how the Algonquian terminology sounded to English ears. What we wish to stress, however, is that Wood, the same observer who asserted that the natives "seldome or never make bread of their Indian corne," was also the one who linguistically transformed this native traveling food into cake. It is likely that the connection, noted by Wood and other early English observers, between Indian journeying and Nocake ("their victuals for their journey is Nocake") was elided in common parlance to "journey cake."

But what about the further mutation from journey cake into Johnny cake? Thomas Robinson Hazard, that devoted nineteenth-century student of Rhode Island corn cookery in general and of "jonny-cake" in particular (the spelling variation will be discussed shortly), claimed:

This name journey-cake was retained until the close of the War of Independence, about which time, in compliance with the prayers of memorials from the women of Connecticut and Rhode Island to the respective Legislatures of these commonwealths—the term journey, as applied to the favorite food of the gods and of the Yankee nation, was abrogated by sovereign authority, and that of jonny substituted in its place, in honor of Gov. Jonathan Trumbull, the honored and trusted friend of General Washington, who always addressed the sterling patriot with the affectionate pet name of Brother Jonathan. It was for this latter reason that the whole Yankee nation, and especially New England, became finally sobriqueted, characterized, and identified in the person of Brother Jonathan Trumbull, a plain, unassuming, honest, common-sense man, who resided in Lebanon, which is situated in the south-eastern part of Connecticut, over which colony he presided as Governor throughout the War of Independence.[86]

A check of the official records of Connecticut and Rhode Island from the beginning of American independence to the end of the eighteenth century confirms the whimsicality of Hazard's allegation that the change from journey cake to Johnny cake was the result of legislative action. But otherwise his account of how "Jonathan" came in the early years of the new nation to be "a generic name for the people of the United States, and also for a representative United States citizen" is substantially in agreement with the *Oxford English Dictionary*. That there may be a link between this development and the emergence around the same time of a similar name for a representative United States food preparation is far from implausible.[87]

Certainly there is no doubt that the earliest uses in print of the name Johnny cake date from this same period, as in the first cookbook by an American author, Amelia Simmons's *American Cookery* of 1796:

Johny Cake, or Hoe Cake
Scald 1 pint of milk and put to 3 pints of indian meal, and half pint of flower [flour]—bake before the fire. Or scald with milk two thirds of the indian meal, or wet two thirds with boiling water, add salt, molasses and shortening, work up with cold water pretty stiff, and bake as above.

In calling for either milk or water as the liquid agent, for an admixture of wheat flour to the cornmeal in a ratio of one to six, and for salt, molasses, and shortening, Simmons's recipes reflected some of the developments in the colonial New England food economy that had occurred since the initial English encounter with native Nocake/journey cake.[88]

Primarily however, these two varieties of "Johny Cake," baked "before the fire," were similar to and descended from the "bread," as Daniel Gookin had called it, that the Indians had made, "baking it in the ashes, covering the dough with leaves." Behind Simmons's recipes stood a conflation (which had doubtless been effected several generations before) of one thing, the Indians' bread (in which the corn was turned into meal, then cooked in the fire), with the name(s) of another thing, Nókehick/Nocake/journey cake (in which the corn was first parched in the fire, then turned into meal).[89]

Thomas Robinson Hazard's explanation implied a patriotic motivation for the change in name from journey cake to Johnny cake. Simmons's use of "Johny Cake," evoking the typical New Englander and American, for one of her most distinctively American dishes was fully consistent with such a motivation. As Mary Tolford Wilson states, *American Cookery*, with its Indian puddings, "pumpkin" pies, and "Johny" cakes, was "in its minor sphere, another declaration of American independence."[90]

However, the most interesting aspect of this alteration in the name of the dish has to do with the relation of "Johny" as generic New Englander or American to the native associations of "journey." According to James Axtell and most other recent scholars, one of the principal ways in which the polarity between savage natives and civilized Englishmen played itself out from the seventeenth century onward was in a perceived contrast between native mobility and wandering and English stability and rootedness. The natives were not "securely anchored to one plot of ground." In the terms of our discussion, they were constantly going on journeys and eating their journey cakes.[91]

But, as far back as anyone could remember, the English, unlike the natives, had been securely anchored to single plots of ground, and they reestablished themselves in this respect as quickly as they could once they had made it across the Atlantic. They speedily set up their stationary yeoman households, partly by means of house plans based on chimneys and open hearth cookery and partly by means of the early importation of cattle. As their temporary status as journeying emigrants began to evolve into their eventual identity as settled Jonathan/Johnny New Englanders, so they put milk from their cows into the journey cakes they got from the natives, baked the cakes in the massive homestead fireplaces that sharply distinguished them from the natives, and turned native journey cakes into New England and American Johnny cakes.[92]

Other names for essentially this same dish included Shawnee cake, Indian cake (used by Lydia Maria Child), hoe cake (Simmons put this alongside "Johny Cake" at the head of her recipe), corn cake, and corn bread (although some cooks maintain that Johnny cake and corn bread are completely different). Another common name was spoon bread, possibly from "suppawn," a native term for porridge, and/or from the fact that soft forms of corn bread could be eaten with a spoon. Finally there was spider cake, named for the pan in which the bread was baked.[93]

In the seventeenth and eighteenth centuries the use of the word "cake" did not mean that the food was a dessert. Cakes resembled our modern sweetened batters, but they were also any small bread, baked or pan-fried, such as pancakes or, as we have seen, Scottish oat cakes. The ambiguities seen in the alternative names corn cake and corn bread went back to the Middle Ages, when "the line between enriched breads and cake was not . . . very easily drawn." An example would be gingerbread, which is now primarily a cake but which developed in medieval times with "compacted breadcrumbs" as its basis. This subject, including a section on gingerbread, is considered in detail in chapter 7.[94]

One of the names listed above, Shawnee cake, has been implausibly proposed as the source of the principal name, Johnny cake. Another, hoe cake, probably derived from the fact that the cakes were often baked on flat, hoe-like paddles. Possibly there was also a link to William Wood's Nocake. Like Simmons, Joel Barlow gave hoe cake and Johnny cake as two different names for the same thing, stating that under the "Hoe-cake" name the dish was "fair Virginia's pride." Barlow's use of the term "Johnny-cake" preceded by a few years that of Simmons. If he is to be given credence as a source of information regarding culinary practices, then "in dear New-England" Johnny cake "receive[d] a dash of pumpkin in the paste, / To give it sweetness and improve the taste." Johnny cake and hoe cake appeared in Barlow's poem as part of a list of dishes which "please [him] well" but which were nevertheless inferior to hasty pudding.[95]

Johnny Cake: How It Was Made

Many of the variations that later became familiar in Johnny cake cookery were initially suggested by Lydia Maria Child, who, as already noted, called the dish "Indian Cake." She immediately introduced yet another possible name, "bannock," reminding us again with this Scottish term of the close similarity between native journey cake, New England Johnny cake, and Scottish oat cake. After giving Simmons's second formula of cornmeal, "scalding water," molasses, salt, and shortening, mixed together and baked "before a quick fire," Child validated Barlow's claims about traditional New England practice by stating that "a little stewed pumpkin, scalded with the meal, improves the cake." She also proposed "a richer Indian cake" that included not only the milk Simmons had used in her first version but also egg and ginger or cinnamon. This enriched mixture could be baked in a spider (described below) or Dutch oven. In spite of its being more readily available than in Simmons's day, Child omitted the wheat that Simmons had included.[96]

As late as the 1850s, the method of baking Johnny cake "on a board before the fire" was still being recommended, although by that time it had become necessary to give "on a tin in a stove" as an alternative. The transition from open hearths to wood-fueled cookstoves will be considered in the next chapter. But already in the previous decade, Catharine Beecher had told her readers simply to pour her "Indian Bannock" batter "into square buttered tins an inch thick, and bake fifteen minutes." Thus was Johnny cake to be cooked directly in the oven, either the traditional colonial brick oven or one built into a new cookstove. For Beecher, the use of an open fire to cook a simple cake of any type had become a self-consciously historical gesture. She also gave a recipe for "Pilgrim Cake," consisting of either wheat flour or cornmeal, butter, and water, to be placed in the fire and covered with hot ashes and coals: "This method was used by our pilgrim and pioneer forefathers."[97]

Regarding the issue of the use of wheat in Johnny cake, Beecher's Indian bannock was more in line with what we might expect, now that it had been fully twenty years since supplies of wheat had become more plentiful in New England. Beecher drastically increased the proportion of wheat to cornmeal from what Simmons had recommended, so that it reached the level of one to one.[98]

In another cookbook of the 1840s, the name of the dish was given as "Journey or Johnny Cakes." Possibly the massive westward movements in the years since the American Revolution were now being acknowledged with this reversion to colonial terminology. In any case, this recipe is worth reproducing in its entirety:

Journey or Johnny Cakes

Sift and scald a quart of Indian meal with water enough to make a very thick batter; add two or three teaspoonfuls of salt, and mould it into small cakes with the hands. In moulding up, the hands will need a good deal of flouring to prevent their sticking. Fry them in nearly sufficient fat to cover them. When brown on the under side, turn them. Cook them about twenty minutes. When done, split and butter them.

Another way which is nice. Put to a quart of scalded Indian meal a teaspoonful of salt, the same of saleratus dissolved in milk, adding two or three spoonfuls of wheat flour. Drop the batter by spoonfuls into the frying pan. The batter should be very thick, and there should be just fat sufficient to prevent the cakes sticking to the frying pan.[99]

Rhode Islanders have long claimed that "Jonny cakes" originated in their state. They maintain that the "h" should be left out when spelling Johnny cake, so that the name becomes Jonny cake (and occasionally, to compound the possibilities for confusion, Jonne cake). This was necessary, wrote Thomas Robinson Hazard, so as not to place "Johnny Bull's Christian name before a genuine Rhode Island Jonny-cake, and thereby immortalize the name of America's former perfidious foe, instead of the honored name of Jonathan Trumbull, the sterling American patriot."[100]

According to Sandra L. Oliver, in the 1870s Rhode Island "Jonnycakes without an 'h'" remained "a distinct food item." By that time, they were no longer being baked "before the fire" in the traditional colonial manner retained by Simmons and Child and recalled in loving detail by Hazard, but rather were usually fried on a griddle. In Oliver's view, "Jonnycakes without an 'h'" are to be sharply distinguished from "Johnnycake with an 'h,'" which had become by the mid-nineteenth century "a quick bread very similar to our modern day cornbread."[101]

The recipe above suggests that this account should be modified somewhat. Appearing in a mid-nineteenth-century cookbook with no particular associations with Rhode Island, the recipe recommended the frying of "Johnnycake with an 'h,'" in a manner entirely consistent with later Rhode Island practice. Mrs. A. L. Webster, the author of the quoted recipe, gave versions with and without milk, and the person Oliver interviews as an authority on Rhode Island Jonny cake stated that the use of milk was a matter of individual discretion. One of Webster's versions used so much grease as to amount virtually to deep-fat frying; the other used as little as possible, just enough to prevent sticking. Oliver's interviewee recommended "plenty of grease," while other Rhode Island, or allegedly Rhode Island, sources specified a "slightly greased skillet" or simply a "greased griddle." In this last recipe, the dish was called "Johnny Cakes," with an "h."[102]

So people in Rhode Island were not the only ones to fry their "Jonny cakes." And there were apparently some in Rhode Island who did not insist on that particular orthography. Nevertheless, the "Jonny cake" tradition did certainly exist in the state, and the spelling fetish was a major part of it. In the 1890s the Rhode Island legislature mandated that the term be spelled without the "h." During the same decade, a debate between two Rhode Island counties, Newport and South, concerning the proper way to make Jonny cake, almost caused legislators to come to blows. Betty Fussell relates that the spokesman for Newport County in this debate considered South County Jonny cake unfit even for pigs; South County's champion retorted that over in Newport, they were wasting their time in the preparation of "hick feed." As is often the way with old political disputes, the distinction, in retrospect, appears to be almost without a difference: in Newport County, Jonny cakes were usually made with cornmeal, salt, and cold milk, in South County, with cornmeal, salt, and boiling water. As we have seen, there was precedent for both methods in early New England cookbooks.[103]

The distinction between fried Rhode Island Jonny cake and the oven-baked Johnny cake more characteristic of the rest of New England is also without a difference, at least insofar as either one is supposed to be more "authentic" than the other. As methods of cooking simple cornmeal doughs, both represented departures from the colonial and Indian practice of unmediated contact between the dough and the heat of an open fire. Both arose at about the same time, around the middle of the nineteenth century. Moreover, the inclusion of eggs and sweetener predated the emergence of this distinction, going back to Child and, in the case of sweetener, Simmons. Basically, "Jonny cake" took Simmons's austere first version of liquid and meal, poured it into a skillet, and fried it. "Johnny cake" took the second version, in which enriching and seasoning components were added to the liquid and meal, poured it in a pan, and stuck it in the oven.

Although these two categories are in general valid, a quick survey of recipes from the second half of the nineteenth century and into the twentieth indicates that cooks were quite capable of producing variations that blurred them. For example, of the two Johnny cakes in an 1864 cookbook, an "Old Times Johnny Cake" of mere liquid and meal was baked, while a straightforward "Johnny Cake" of buttermilk or sour milk, cornmeal and wheat flour in a ratio of one to one, and molasses was apparently to be fried (no cooking method was specified, but the recipes given before and after it were both designed for frying). A fried Johnny cake (with an "h") from a non–Rhode Island 1910 cookbook included sugar.[104]

As mentioned previously, Johnny cake was sometimes called spider cake after the frying pan or "spider" in which it was often baked. Lydia Maria Child, for example, allowed that her enriched form of Indian cake or bannock might be baked in a spider. One mid-twentieth-century New England cook extolled spider cake thus: "In our house we used a seasoned spider (Yankee for frying pan), black as your shoe. We broke the Johnnycake into wedge-shaped pieces (hot bread, we were told, should never be cut), and slathered it with butter."[105]

We have noted some of the instances from the early nineteenth century in which Johnny cake was called Indian bannock or simply bannock. Some cookbooks of that day did make a distinction between Johnny cake and bannock, however. Sarah Josepha Hale's Johnny cake was essentially the simpler of Simmons's two versions, while her bannock was essentially Child's enriched Indian cake or bannock, with eggs, sugar, butter, and cinnamon or ginger.[106]

According to one tradition, people on Nantucket drew a similar distinction between bannock and Johnny cake. An elderly Nantucket miller interviewed in 1915 fondly recalled his mother's "johnnycake" and "corn cakes" as two different things. Similarly, it was said of a much earlier Nantucket miller that his family ate a cornmeal bread they called bannock for breakfast and one they called Johnny cake for dinner.[107]

As noted above, when prepared so as to remain soft, Johnny cake has been called spoon bread, a name that some believe is derived from the word, "suppawn" or "saupawn," that was used by the Massachusetts natives to denote cornmeal softened by water. If such a derivation has any validity, then the fact that spoon bread has become associated primarily with southern rather than Yankee cooking is somewhat curious. Recipes for softened forms of Johnny cake, not called spoon bread, did appear in a few New England cookbooks of the early and mid-twentieth century.[108]

Many varieties of Johnny cake were thus appreciated throughout New England. We have mentioned Roger Williams's testimony regarding the Indians' addition of strawberries to their corn pone. They also enriched it with raspberries, blackberries, blueberries, elderberries, and cherries. "Above all other edibles, in the estimation of the olden-time children of Narragansett," wrote Thomas Robinson Hazard regarding his childhood in the early nineteenth century, "loomed up the huckleberry jonny-cake, which, to be first-

rate, must be made half and half of meal and fresh gathered ripe berries. . . .
It used to be held in Narragansett," he continued, "that the faces of little
boys and girls that were fed during the whole berry season on half and half
huckleberry jonny-cake grew into the shape of a smile that remained until
berries came again the next summer."[109]

It is fitting to conclude this discussion with one of Hazard's reveries. In
the 1830s the determinedly gourmandizing Mrs. N. K. M. Lee, perhaps in a
reprise of the colonial denial of Indian contributions to the American diet,
had included in her (purported) "Complete Culinary Encyclopedia" not one
single form or name of Johnny cake or corn bread. Half a century later, the
determinedly mythologizing Hazard placed this plebeian dish at the heart
of traditional New England life, while at the same time only minimally acknowledging any indebtedness to Indian cuisine and culture. After another
half century, the presence in at least three cookbooks of recipes for corn rolls
associated with the Parker House Hotel indicated that Johnny cake cookery,
its ties to its Indian origins now totally severed and those to Yankee agrari-
anism thoroughly attenuated, had ascended to the very pinnacle of Boston
society.[110]

Succotash

"Their food is generally boiled maize, or Indian corn, mixed with kidney
beans, or sometimes without," wrote Daniel Gookin in 1674 of the native
diet, testimony corroborated by John Josselyn in the same year. "Also they
frequently boil . . . fish and flesh of all sorts" in this corn or corn-and-bean
mixture, Gookin added. Gookin thus provided the fullest early description
of succotash. A scholar who fifty years ago surveyed the available evidence
regarding southern New England native foods in the seventeenth century
concluded that succotash "was in fact the central feature of Indian cookery
and the most common meal."[111]

Gookin explicitly called this fundamental native dish "pottage," thus
linking it to a preparation of corresponding centrality in the diet of British
peasants and yeomen. According to a mid-sixteenth-century observer, "pottage is not so much used in all Christendom as it is used in England." Oatmeal was not subjected to the same degree of disparagement in the pottage context as in the bread, and in fact it was used throughout Britain as
one of pottage's principal bases. William Wood referred to this fact in his
caustic account of native boiled food, which he characterized as "their un-
oat-meal'd broth, made thicke with Fishes, Fowles, and Beasts boyled all

Eastern woodland Indians cooking succotash, engraving by Theodor de Bry, from Grands Voyages, *2d ed., 1624, MSS 115. (Courtesy Mashantucket Pequot Museum and Research Center, Archives and Special Collections)*

together; some remaining raw, the rest converted by over-much seething to a loathed mash, not halfe so good as Irish Boniclapper." Distancing himself, as an Englishman, as far as possible from this hideous hodgepodge of the raw and the cooked, Wood deemed succotash inferior to the cookery even of Ireland.[112]

Pottage in Britain usually consisted of a grain base (often but not necessarily oatmeal), to which might be added such meats as cut-up boiled beef or mutton, along with herbs and such vegetables as peas, beans, cabbages, carrots, turnips, and onions. In Gervase Markham's *The English Housewife* (1615), a widely read cookbook that would have been familiar to many of the first New Englanders, there appeared instructions for "the best ordinary Pottage" (consisting of mutton or beef, oatmeal, and herbs) and "pottage of the best and daintiest kind" (with the same basic ingredients but a greater variety of herbs and seasonings).[113]

In New England and the other colonies, English and native pottage traditions came to form a seamless whole. Throughout the seventeenth century and, though to a lessened extent, into the eighteenth, the diet of colonial New England was essentially "daily 'pottage' fare, and many families ate 'one continued round' of meat and legume or vegetable stews morning, noon, and night." More specifically, "the most widely distributed . . . dish of the potage type" in the American colonies, especially New England, was succotash. And it was essentially the same succotash that had been "the central feature of Indian cookery and the most common meal."[114]

Here the problems posed for the English ideology of colonization by the realities of subsistence took a slightly different form. In this instance, it was not that the English were turning into savages, but rather that the alleged savages were not that different from the English after all. The one-pot meals that the English had always eaten were in essence the same one-pot meals that the natives had always eaten. But although the form of the problem was different, the problem itself remained the same—that the justification for taking possession of another people's homeland was being eroded. And naturally, as long as the situation of the colonists seemed in any way precarious, the response to the problem—namely, silence and denial—remained the same as well.

The name "succotash" has become predominant among the many transliterations from Indian languages. Others include "sukquttahash" or "sauquaquatash" and "msakwitash" or "m'sick-quotash." Perhaps because its native origins are only thinly disguised (or perhaps simply because in its modern form it is exceedingly insipid), succotash has not attained as high a position in New England cultural mythology as have other dishes. It made a promising start, however, with its inclusion in one of the earliest exercises in romanticized New England history, as part of the menu for the first celebration of Forefathers' Day in Plymouth in 1769.[115]

In 1793 Joel Barlow placed succotash at the beginning of his compilation of dishes that were, though perfectly worthy, inferior to hasty pudding:

> Let the green Succatash with thee contend,
> Let beans and corn their sweetest juices blend,
> Let butter drench them in its yellow tide,
> And a long slice of bacon grace their side;
> Not all the plate, how fam'd soe'er it be,
> Can please my palate like a bowl of thee.

Thomas Robinson Hazard made no invidious comparisons among corn delicacies, but he did state that his grandmother "used to always caution me about eating too much [succotash], as she had once known a naughty boy who burst asunder in the middle from having eaten too heartily of the tempting dish."[116]

A few years before Hazard's memoir, Harriet Beecher Stowe, in *Oldtown Folks*, gave succotash back to the natives: "By and by, the old [Indian] woman poured the contents of the pot into a wooden trough, and disclosed a smoking mess of the Indian dish denominated succotash,—to wit, a soup of corn and beans, with a generous allowance of salt pork."[117]

Although both Barlow and Stowe, whose novel was set at the time Barlow's poem was written, mentioned a meat component—salt pork or bacon—in their accounts of succotash, meat was by no means a constant in nineteenth-century succotash recipes. Stowe's own sister, Catharine Beecher, omitted it:

If you wish to make succotash, boil the beans from half to three quarters of an hour, in water a little salt, meantime cutting off the corn and throwing the cobs to boil with the beans. Take care not to cut too close to the cob, as it imparts a bad taste. When the beans have boiled the time above mentioned, take out the cobs, and add the corn, and let the whole boil from fifteen to twenty minutes, for young corn, and longer for older corn. Make the proportions two-thirds corn and one-third beans. Where you have a mess amounting to two quarts of corn and one quart of beans, take two tablespoonfuls of flour, wet it into a thin paste, and stir it into the succotash, and let it boil up for five minutes. Then lay some butter in a dish, take it up into it, and add more salt if need be.[118]

The aspect of Beecher's recipe that was a constant in other succotash recipes of the day was the boiling of the corncobs. Some specified lima beans, some added milk or cream, and some did indeed call for salt pork or simply pork. But all stated that the cobs should be boiled during the cooking process. This would, in the words of one of the recipes, "improve the flavor, as there is great sweetness in the cob." Perhaps the reduced presence of the flesh element in nineteenth-century as opposed to colonial succotash indicates a further evolution away from the native succotash the English settlers had originally encountered.[119]

According to Ella Shannon Bowles and Dorothy S. Towle, in the nineteenth century there was an attempt to assimilate succotash to New England boiled dinner, with a recipe purporting to be based on the succotash served at the 1769 Forefathers' Day banquet. Corned beef, chicken, potatoes, and a turnip supplemented the corn, beans, and salt pork mentioned by Stowe and included in other nineteenth-century recipes. The meat and poultry were to be boiled together, but separately from the corn, beans, and other vegetables. The faunal components were also to be served separately from the floral. Similar procedures were recommended in "Original Plymouth Succotash" from the twentieth century.[120]

While appearing to restore to succotash its original pottage-like hospitality to meat and vegetable combinations, these recipes, by their insistence on segregation in cooking and serving, did not really do so. They were more boiled dinner than succotash, instances of "the ideal American meal of meat, potato, and vegetable" that, as James Deetz argues, had by the end of the eighteenth century supplanted the "mixed dishes" that were "typical of English" (and native) "cookery at the time of the colonization of America." Boiled dinner is discussed further in chapter 5.[121]

Husking and Bussing

In spite of their ambivalence about corn, the English adopted many aspects of Indian corn culture. For example, at colonial husking bees, if a man found a red ear of corn, he could demand a kiss from the girl of his choice. According to Joel Barlow, a woman who found such an ear had a corresponding right to "cull one favor'd beau," and if she found a "smut ear," she might "smut [strike] the luckless swains."[122]

On occasion, the red ear ritual led to considerable excitement. In 1661 on Long Island, "where the customs were very like those of New England, one James Chichester found a red ear, and said that he must kiss 'Bette' Scudder. That lively and turbulent damsel replied that she 'would whip his brick;' these endearments ended in a scuffle, whereupon Goody Scudder interfered. The result was a summons before the 'Town Court,' an examination of witnesses, and a fine of 12s. with costs for James." Betty Scudder was apparently utilizing the female prerogative of smiting in cases of smut ear discovery as a defensive tactic in a case of red ear discovery.[123]

In Indian practice, more than a kiss would be claimed when a red ear was discovered, as appears indeed to have been the situation between this Long Island pair. The custom could even verge on the orgiastic among some not-so-staid colonial New England farmers. Jacob Bailey, while serving as a schoolmaster in a New Hampshire village in the eighteenth century, recorded in verse his impressions of a husking bee. Right from the start, "kisses and drams set the virgins on flame." As supper was being served, "The girls in a huddle stand snickering by / Till Jenny and Kate have fingered the pie." All this was but titillating prelude, however, to the scene after supper when a great number of the males present "lay tussling the girls in wide heaps on the floor."[124]

Bailey's quaint diction only barely disguised the importance of the sexual transactions that took place within the safe, ritualized context of the social

"Gathering Roasting Ears," Harper's New Monthly Magazine, *July 1856.*
(Courtesy Fall River Public Library)

gathering known as the husking bee. A food that had been central to, and centrally ritualized and mythologized by, the Indians was now playing an equally important role in the social life of the white settler community. No one in that community, of course, would openly acknowledge the extent to which a quintessentially native foodstuff, and native attitudes and customs surrounding it, had come to fit the settler situation.[125]

Corn did indeed become ubiquitous in the colonial home, serving not only as food for humans and their cattle, but also as the raw material with which to make innumerable household implements, from corncob pipes to bottle stoppers and scrubbing brushes. Mattresses were stuffed with corn husks; colonial children played with corn husk dolls and other corn toys, and sharpened their wits playing with checkerboard pieces made of corn, often while sitting on corn husk chair seats. Even in the outhouse, corn husks played a useful role, or perhaps we should say roll.[126]

Corn was used as fodder for hogs, but it was also on its way to becoming the primary fodder for Americans themselves, in another form, that is. As Henry Adams pointed out, by the turn of the nineteenth century, "Indian corn was the national crop, and Indian corn was eaten three times a day in another form as salt pork."[127]

Given the importance of corn to the New England way of life, it certainly comes as no surprise that social rituals such as husking bees were constructed around this food. Sadly, neither is it a surprise that the sexual potency within the husk could as easily be transformed into a weapon of war. It is with one such tale of war that we conclude this chapter.

If Their Corn Were Cut Down

Although William Bradford described the first few months of settlement at Plymouth as a "general calamity," it was in fact the Indians for whom English settlement turned out to be cataclysmic. Despite the hope for co-existence expressed by the Wampanoags' early treaty with the English, by 1675 the tensions inherent in massive English immigration had come to a head. There were vast differences between the two societies in agricultural practice, and a combination of treaty violations, sharp business dealings on both sides, and competition for natural resources had reduced the Indians' hold on their land and way of life. The result was war.[128]

The story of King Philip's War has been told many times. Our concern here is not the overall narrative of the conflict but rather the ways in which food was used as a weapon. Both Indians and English destroyed crops and stores of grain, killed cattle and horses, and set fire to woodlands and homes. Corn, essential to both groups, often became a pawn in their struggles.

In 1682 a narrative was published describing the experiences of a colonial woman held captive by the Indians during the war. Commonly known as Mary Rowlandson's captivity narrative, the book was intended as propaganda against the Indians. However, it is also an invaluable source of information about their response to crisis.

In guiding us through her own emotional terrain, Rowlandson set the scene of a landscape of war: "After a restless and hungry night there we had a wearisome time of it the next day. The swamp by which we lay was, as it were, a deep dungeon and an exceeding high and steep hill before it. Before I got to the top of the hill, I thought my heart and legs and all would have broken and failed me. What through faintness and soreness of body it was a grievous day of travel to me." While we have only their silent presence within her narrative, the Indians too, we realize, were traveling through this dismal countryside. They were not only the cause of Rowlandson's finding herself in a swamp of misery. To the extent that their own country had been alienated from them by war, they were, like Rowlandson, inhabitants of this bleak night-filled world. The landscape had become saturated with weariness for all. Such was the vortex of war.[129]

Rowlandson's narrative is as valuable for identifying the issues at stake in King Philip's War as it is for recreating the experience of being caught up in the war itself: "As we went along, I saw a place where English cattle had been. That was comfort to me, such as it was. Quickly after that we came to an English path which so took with me that I thought I could have freely laid down and died."[130] Here was an inevitable confrontation between the Indians' small-scale farming, foraging, and hunting society and the Europeans' large-scale farming and mercantile one. The type of agriculture introduced by the English was bound to alter the ecology of New England. On land where the Indians had hunted, fished, and foraged only for their own needs, planted small crops, and traveled in small groups, the English now began to clear tracts of woodlands for broadcast planting and pasture, to graze large herds, to harvest timber for ships, carts, and roads, to cut broad thoroughfares ("English paths") for easier cart and horse travel and cattle transport, and to establish densely populated permanent settlements.[131]

Rowlandson intended her descriptions of her captors' methods of obtaining food and of the kinds of foods they ate as confirmation of her view of them as savages. But at this historical distance, her account has a different effect. While some of the Indians' foraging methods were undoubtedly arduous, and some of the things they ate unappetizing to modern palates, we cannot fail to understand that these warriors were simply utilizing the one advantage they had over the English—their knowledge of the land and its natural resources. Of course, that was not Rowlandson's perspective: "That day, a little after noon, we came to Squakeag where the Indians quickly spread themselves over the deserted English fields, gleaning what they could find; some picked up ears of wheat that were crickled [broken] down; some found ears of Indian corn; some found groundnuts, and others sheaves of wheat that were frozen together in the shock, and went to threshing them out. . . . That night we had a mess of wheat for our supper."[132]

At another point, Rowlandson recounted that the Indians, in preparing for a day of battle "fell to boiling of groundnuts and parching of corn (as many as had it) for their provision." As we might expect, on a forced march the natives sustained themselves with parched corn, the basis of their "journey cake." They also made succotash when they could: "I went into another wigwam where they were boiling corn and beans, which was a lovely sight to see."[133]

Without seeming to comprehend the brutality of the English behavior she described, or the evidence that her narrative provided of the resilience of the Indians' response, Rowlandson told this tale of warfare upon an entire population: "It was thought if their corn were cut down they would starve and die with hunger, and all their corn that could be found was destroyed, and they driven from that little they had in store into the woods in the midst of winter. And yet how to admiration did the Lord preserve them for His holy ends and the destruction of many still amongst the English! Strangely did the Lord provide for them that I did not see (all the time I was among them) one man, woman, or child die with hunger."[134]

While she was critical of the Indians for doing so, Rowlandson nevertheless conceded that they could rely on knowledge of wild foods and on their remarkable capacity to endure pain and deprivation as their primary weapons against a technologically superior enemy:

> Though many times they would eat that that a hog or dog would hardly touch, yet by that God strengthened them to be a scourge to His people. . . .
>
> They would pick up old bones and cut them to pieces at the joints, and if they were full of worms and maggots, they would scald them over the fire to make the vermin come out and then boil them and drink up the liquor and then beat the great ends of them in a mortar and so eat them. They would eat horses' guts and ears, and all sorts of wild birds which they could catch; also bear, venison, beaver, tortoise, frogs, squirrels, dogs, skunks, rattlesnakes yea, the very bark of trees. . . . Many times in a morning the generality of them would eat up all they had and yet have some further supply against they wanted.[135]

King Philip's War was fought scarcely two generations after corn was first offered to the English settlers by the Indians. But corn was a gift that the settlers had always regarded with ambivalence, and this made it all the easier—indeed, made it appropriate—for them to utilize its destruction as a key element in their struggle to eliminate the native way of life as a serious threat to their own. Psychological denial of the extent of their dependence on native foodstuffs and foodways could be more comfortably sustained, and in the future it would be more comfortably sustained, if native corn culture were removed from the scene along with the native cultivators. It would not be until a century later, the natives thought to have "dwindled to a few scattered families, living an uncertain and wandering life on the outskirts of the thrift and civilization of the whites," that denial would relax its grip and allow the native agricultural and culinary contribution to the Yankee way of life to surface—bathed in condescension—in Yankee consciousness.

The words just quoted were those of Harriet Beecher Stowe, who like many New Englanders of her generation expressed pity for the Indians, seeing them as victims of "the doom which seems to foreordain that [the native] races shall dry up and pass away with their native forests." But such sentiments demonstrate that if denial had relaxed its grip in the nineteenth century and later, it certainly had not let go altogether. Pity for the natives was characteristically conjoined with displacement of responsibility for what had happened to them from Stowe's ancestors to a comfortably abstracted doom or fate.[136]

But the purpose of an honest understanding of the American heritage is best served by neither aspect of this lingering form of denial. Just as the conquest of North America was carried out not by some mysterious metaphysical force but rather by identifiable European and English people, so the Indians who stood in their way should not be reduced to mere victims. The people who had given the gift of corn demonstrated in the pages of Mary Rowlandson's narrative that they also knew how to live without it. The resilience they displayed when their essential crop was destroyed was no less remarkable for the fact that, as we know in retrospect, they were waging a losing battle for their way of life.

Hominy, corn breads and cakes, succotash—versions of these dishes were eaten by the peoples of southern New England for many centuries before the Pilgrims arrived on Cape Cod. The most telling indication of how thoroughgoing was the English conquest is the fact that for three centuries these gifts of "she who sustains us" have been considered Yankee fare.

CHAPTER 2

Baked & in a Pie

Beans & Pumpkins

O ne of the earliest observations of the native practice of horticulture was made by the French explorer Samuel de Champlain, while traveling through what is now southern Maine. The area was among the northernmost in which climatic conditions permitted a partially horticultural, as opposed to a primarily hunting and gathering, way of life:

> Sieur de Monts and I landed to observe their tillage on the bank of the [Saco] River. We saw their Indian corn, which they raise in gardens. Planting three or four kernels in one place, they then heap up about it a quantity of earth with shells. . . . Then three feet distant they planted as much more, and thus in succession. With this corn they put in each hill three or four Brazilian beans, which are of different colors. When they grow up, they interlace with the corn, which reaches to the height of from five to six feet; and they keep the ground very free from weeds. We saw there many squashes and pumpkins . . . which they likewise cultivate.[1]

We have been looking at the role of corn in the survival and flourishing of the English settlers. We turn now to the part played by beans and pumpkins.

Corn was unknown to the first English settlers until the Indians taught them how to grow and prepare it. But beans were a different story. Peas and beans had long been central components of the British diet. In the Middle Ages, three kinds of pea—green, white, and gray—were commonly cultivated, along with beans of the broad bean family (*Vicia faba*). Chickpeas (which are actually beans rather than peas) and lentils "were raised in a few places."[2]

Legumes (the overarching name for peas, beans, and lentils) were hardly prestige foods. One medieval authority recommended that church dignitaries avoid the consumption of beans, since "by oft use thereof the wits are dulled." Similarly, William Harrison stated in the late sixteenth century that even among the poor, legumes were utilized in breadmaking only with great reluctance, in times of scarcity. Two centuries earlier, in William Langland's allegorical poem *Piers Plowman*, "two loaves of beans and bran" symbolized the extreme penury to which countryfolk had been reduced. And much later on, in the nineteenth century, William Cobbett went so far, in his advocacy of corn as a replacement for traditional British staple foodstuffs, to allege that "all the pulse kind, if eaten, by man or beast, to anything approaching to excess, are always dangerous, and frequently kill."[3]

Nevertheless, for centuries before the English came to North America, legumes had been grown by yeoman farmers "in due rotation" with cereal grains and harvested and stored along with them as well. They remained "in constant demand for pottage," the other dish besides bread on which peasants and yeomen principally subsisted.[4]

Cultivation of "a vast range of beans" of the *Phaseolus* type first took place in the Americas, probably in the Peruvian Andes, about 8,000 years ago. Within this broad category are such familiar varieties as the lima bean, the turtle or black bean, the kidney bean, the pinto bean, the red bean, and the various strains of "round white beans ranging from the large marrow bean to the small pea or navy bean." During the same exploratory tour of Cuba on which he and his men first saw corn, Christopher Columbus also recorded the first European encounter with New World beans, "very different from ours."[5]

As also proved to be the case with pumpkins, between the time of Columbus's voyages and the English colonization of North America, American beans were taken to Europe and cultivated there. Jay Allan Anderson states that broad beans and kidney beans formed part of the annual growth and harvesting cycle of early-seventeenth-century English yeomen, many of whom emigrated to New England. In the realm of beans, therefore, the colonists hardly needed to adapt to their new environment at all. Before long, they came to prefer the little white pea bean above all others. According to Amelia Simmons, this type was "best for winter use, and excellent." Pea beans were the ones most often chosen for making pots of baked beans.[6]

Although succotash, the native corn and bean one-pot dish, was recognized early on as a form of pottage and came to be widely consumed throughout New England and the other British colonies, it was baked beans that eventually, among all the colonial pottage fare, gained the highest status as a cultural icon. Not only did baked beans come to be associated—as Boston

Baked Beans—with the region's primary urban center, the region's primary urban center also came to be associated with the humble "pulse kind" whenever it went by the nickname Beantown.[7]

Where Baked Beans Came From

According to one recent writer, "baked beans and succotash may be the closest to signature dishes for [New England]—one based on Old World traditions and the other on those of the New World." In an immediate sense, this statement is correct. We have already explored the New World origins of succotash. As for the Old World origins of baked beans, peas or beans and bacon have been claimed to be among the oldest of English dishes. Despite the generally low position of beans in English food-status hierarchies, one version of beans and bacon is said to have been enjoyed by the medieval gentry. The specifically baked form of bean pottage was prevalent among Staffordshire yeomen, who soaked their dried beans overnight, then baked them along with honey-and-mustard-cured ham and onions or leeks in a narrow-necked earthenware pot especially reserved for the purpose. This "dark, sweet cassoulet" has been identified as the immediate progenitor of New England baked beans.[8]

There is a tradition that, like succotash, baked beans was of native origin. "Beans were abundant, and were baked by the Indians in earthen pots just as we bake them today," wrote Alice Morse Earle in 1898. Three-quarters of a century later, Sally Smith Booth was not the first to include the use of underground beanholes among the native methods of baking beans: "Indians probably originated this dish, for many tribes baked bean stews in earthen pots placed into pits and covered with hot ashes." However, as Howard S. Russell has acknowledged, there is no direct evidence of natives' baking beans, either in earthenware pots or in beanholes in the ground.[9]

On the other hand, baked beans "prepared by the bean-hole method were by far the most important single food" in late-nineteenth-century Maine lumbering camps. A vogue for outdoor and wilderness experience, including culinary experience, that was supposed to approximate the lifeways of the North American Indians, had emerged at this time and gave encouragement to the idea that another form of popular underground New England cookery, the clambake, had originated with the Indians. Similar notions about the native sources of beanhole baked beans may also have germinated in this cultural soil, so to speak.[10]

Skepticism regarding romanticized conceptions of native and settler culinary practices should not, however, lead us to dismiss altogether the possibility of a relationship between the bean cookery of the two groups. In her recent study of the way of life of the Indians of New England from 1500 to 1650, Kathleen J. Bragdon states that baking was one of the methods of cooking beans the Indians utilized. Another scholar notes that baking was characteristically accomplished either "on hot ashes, the food sometimes wrapped in leaves" or "on a hot flat stone under an inverted kettle covered with coals," adding that while there are no eyewitness accounts of cooking in pits, "the lack of mention probably does not preclude use" of this method. Possibly the "bean cakes" mentioned by Daniel Gookin were baked by one of these procedures.[11] According to archaeologists, cooking in pits, or "earth ovens," was a technique known to at least "some tribes" in what became the northeastern United States, such as the Abenaki of the Maine and the Iroquois of the New York regions. Thousand-year-old excavated sites on Long Island and coastal Connecticut reveal both "shallow pits that were used as baking ovens for shellfish and deeper pits that were used for either cooking or storage."[12]

So although the English clearly brought with them a well-established tradition of bean-and-bacon pottage that, in at least one of its variants, was baked in a beanpot in an oven, it is also possible that the natives they encountered upon arrival had a similar tradition of preparing legume pottage by baking. Moreover, the immigrants did not scruple to integrate New World beans into their Old World pottage, just as they incorporated New World grain into their bread.

The indebtedness of the English to the Indians was not as significant in the case of beans as it was in that of corn. Nevertheless, here was another instance in which the general contrast between savage Indians and civilized English was belied by a particular mirroring in the realm of food customs. While it is proper to distinguish the New World origins of succotash from the Old World origins of baked beans, it should also be emphasized that, in the case of both dishes, culinary encounter pointed to the need to reconsider the rationale for and the nature of the colonial enterprise. Needless to say, baked beans availed no more than did succotash or Johnny cake in promoting such a reconsideration.

There Is No Such Home–Splendor Now

We have noted in the previous chapter that baked beans was usually cooked in "the brick oven at the side of the fireplace," alongside "the baked Indian puddings . . . the chicken pies . . . [other] pies, loaves of bread, dowdies, and cakes." As is perhaps indicated by the existence of a "brick oven" brand of canned baked beans, the mystique of the beanpot is closely bound up with the mystique of the kitchen hearths of colonial and post-Revolutionary New England. We have already considered some aspects of the practical functioning of the open fireplace kitchen in our discussion of boiled bag puddings. Before proceeding further with our discussion of beans, we offer some thoughts on its cultural significance.[13]

In her memoir, *A New England Girlhood*, Lucy Larcom provided a description of the New England open hearth kitchen as it was on the eve of its displacement. The depredations of modernity were implicit in her opening depiction of her birthplace, Beverly, Massachusetts, as already wearing "a half-rustic air of antiquity" at the time she had been born, when the nineteenth century was "just rounding the first quarter of her hundred years." When Larcom was a girl, "primitive ways of doing things had not wholly ceased."[14]

Specifically, "we . . . sat by open fireplaces." Actually, as the fireplace was deep as well as open, the children sat not merely by it but within it: "there was a 'settle' in the chimney corner, where three of us youngest girls could sit together and toast our toes on the andirons (two Continental soldiers in full uniform, marching one after the other), while we looked up the chimney into a square of blue sky, and sometimes caught a snow-flake on our foreheads; or sometimes smirched our clean aprons (high-necked and long-sleeved ones, known as 'tiers') against the swinging crane with its sooty pot-hooks and trammels." Never have the sentimental, even spiritual, advantages of "primitive" inconvenience been better expressed.[15]

Larcom went on to evoke the various components of open hearth cookery: the coffeepot resting "on a three-legged bit of iron called a 'trivet'"; the potatoes "roasted in the ashes"; the "great bakings" occurring in the "brick ovens in the chimney corner"; and the "'Dutch oven,' in which delicious bread could be baked over the coals at short notice." One item in Larcom's Massachusetts household was made the same way Johnny cake had been made several decades before in Thomas Robinson Hazard's grandfather's Rhode Island household: "there never was anything that tasted better than my mother's 'fire-cake,'—a short-cake spread on a smooth piece of board, and set up with a flat-iron before the blaze, browned on one side, and then turned over to be browned on the other. (It required some sleight of hand to do that.)" And of course there was "the Thanksgiving turkey in a 'tin-kitchen.'"[16]

Larcom eventually identified the development that was turning open hearth cookery into a thing of the past: "Cooking-stoves were coming into fashion." Jack Larkin explains that as a result of "improvements in the technology of cast iron, [the cookstove] marked the most significant change in the technology of cooking since the widespread adoption of the fireplace and hearth. By the 1830s cookstoves were coming into use among middling city families and in Northern commercial villages. . . . With their stove-top heating surfaces at waist height, their somewhat lighter-weight 'boilers' and kettles of various sizes, cookstoves, as the editor of the *New England Farmer* noted in 1837, saved 'much female strength, which over a fireplace has to be exerted over heavy pots and kettles.'"[17]

But in the Larcom household, as the drift of Larcom's recollection clearly indicated, cookstoves were regarded as "clumsy affairs, and our elders thought that no cooking could be quite so nice as that which was done by an open fire." Moreover, Larcom also emphasized that these plain-spoken elders took care to perpetuate their traditional way of life by encouraging the active participation of the rising generation: "What magic it seemed to me, when I was first allowed to strike that wonderful spark, and light the kitchen fire! . . . the business of turning the spit [on which the Thanksgiving turkey was impaled] being usually delegated to some of us small folk, who were only too willing to burn our faces in honor of the annual festival. . . . If I could only be allowed to blow the bellows—the very old people called them 'belluses'—when the fire began to get low, I was a happy girl."[18]

As we know, the hearthside tradition was not perpetuated in fact. Larcom was among those who were particularly alert to the march of technological and social change, having been a pioneer participant in the American Industrial Revolution. She worked in the 1840s in the new textile mills in Lowell, Massachusetts, and wrote about the experience in the magazine the young female operatives produced. But precisely because of these experiences, Larcom was also particularly sensitive to the cost of such change: "When supper was finished, and the tea-kettle was pushed back on the crane, and the backlog had been reduced to a heap of fiery embers, then was the time for listening to sailor yarns and ghost and witch legends. . . . We younger ones reveled in the warm, beautiful glow, that we look back to as to a remembered sunset. There is no such home-splendor now."[19]

The elders were not successful in keeping the open hearth way of life alive in society and history. But they succeeded brilliantly in keeping it alive in culture and literature. The nostalgia of their fireside "sailor yarns and ghost and witch legends" eventually became Larcom's masterly memoir of a paradise lost.[20]

Cooking Baked Beans

In England the installation of bake ovens into the chimneys of nongentry households had begun to take place only in the decades immediately preceding the migration to North America. The standard design had a rectangular base, approximately twenty-four by eighteen inches, with sloping sides ascending to a domed roof. In the colonies the domed roof was retained, but the rectangular base became circular, with a diameter of about thirty inches. This was the classic "beehive" arrangement. Baking was done most often on Saturday. Some households had a second weekly baking day, usually Wednesday, while those who were particularly well off would heat the oven every day.[21]

The fire was usually constructed of dry pine or birch wood. Catharine Beecher recommended that the pieces be "of equal size and length" and that the fire be laid toward the back of the oven. It was allowed to burn until the blackness had disappeared from the dome and the inside of the oven had become uniformly light in color. Coals and ashes were then removed by shoveling and sweeping, the items to be baked were placed within, in pans or on tin sheets or leaves, and the oven door was shut and sealed with clay to prevent heat loss.[22]

Lydia Maria Child offered more detailed instructions for gauging whether an oven had been properly heated: "A smart fire for an hour and a half is a general rule for common sized family ovens, provided brown bread and beans are to be baked." "Flour bread," an occasional option even for Child's frugal readers after the opening of the Erie Canal, required only an hour's preheating, as did most pies. "Pumpkin pies will bear [require] more," however. A test for overheating was to throw in some flour. If it blackened after a minute or so, the oven was too hot; "if it merely browns, it is right. Some people wet an old broom two or three times, and turn it round near the top of the oven till it dries; this prevents pies and cakes from scorching on the top."[23]

Catharine Beecher's recommendation of uniform dimensions for wood was intended as an aid to ascertaining oven heat: "Find, by trial, how many [sticks] are required to heat the oven, and then require that just that number be used, and no more." Along with Child's tests, Beecher added these two:

"If you cannot hold your hand in longer than to count twenty moderately, it is hot enough. If you can count thirty moderately, it is not hot enough for bread." However, "these last are not very accurate tests, as the power to bear heat is so diverse in different persons."[24]

Since in most households the oven was not heated every day, many items were baked at the same time. Young people thus received an indelible impression of cornucopia. Here is Lucy Larcom again:

> The Saturday's baking was a great event, the brick oven being heated to receive the flour bread, the flour-and-Indian, and the rye-and-Indian bread, the traditional pot of beans, the Indian pudding, and the pies; for no further cooking was to be done until Monday. We smaller girls thought it a great privilege to be allowed to watch the oven till the roof of it should be "white-hot," so that the coals could be shoveled out.

"Oh what things came out of that oven," exclaimed a woman who had grown up in a household with twice-a-week baking.[25]

Not every household had a bake oven as part of its kitchen arrangements. In late-eighteenth-century Maine Martha Ballard's neighbors brought their breads and cakes to her house for baking, since they themselves had no ovens. In England prior to the widespread installation of bake ovens in yeoman households, baking had been carried out, for a fee, at either the manor house or a public cookshop, and cookshop baking continued into Victorian times. Likewise, in colonial New England "the large cooking ovens of taverns and inns served as communal-baking facilities for the entire community. Once a week, usually on Saturday, bean pots filled with raw ingredients would be carried to the inn from houses throughout the town." Beginning in 1747, Wright's Tavern in Concord, Massachusetts, was one such venue of weekly communal bean baking.[26]

Lucy Larcom recalled that in Beverly, communal baking developed later, as the hearthside bake oven went into decline in individual households:

> In those early days, towns used to give each other nicknames, like schoolboys. Ours was called "Bean-town"; not because it was especially devoted to the cultivation of this leguminous edible, but probably because it adhered a long time to the Puritanic custom of saving Sunday-work by baking beans on Saturday evening, leaving them in the oven over night. After a while, as families left off heating their ovens, the bean-pots were taken by the village baker on Saturday afternoon, who returned them to each house early on Sunday morning, with the pan of brown bread that

went with them. The jingling of the baker's bells made the matter a public one.

The towns through which our stage-coach passed sometimes called it the "bean-pot." The Jehu who drove it was something of a wag. Once, coming through Charlestown, while waiting in the street for a resident passenger, he was hailed by another resident who thought him obstructing the passage, with the shout—

"Halloo there! Get your old bean-pot out of the way!"

"I will, when I have got my pork in," was the ready reply.

If Larcom is to be believed, the penumbra of nickname and anecdote that contribute to the creation of a cultural mystique had begun to form around baked beans during the years of her childhood. We will return to this subject later in the chapter.[27]

Though she commended the white pea bean, Amelia Simmons did not include a recipe for baked beans. Lydia Maria Child took a no-nonsense approach, calling baked beans "a very simple dish." Despite its simplicity, few people cooked it properly, she felt, so her instructions were quite detailed:

[The beans] should be put in cold water, and hung over the fire, the night before they are baked. In the morning, they should be put in a colander, and rinsed two or three times; then again placed in a kettle, with the pork you intend to bake, covered with water, and kept scalding hot, an hour or more. A pound of pork is quite enough for a quart of beans, and that is a large dinner for a common family. The rind of the pork should be slashed. Pieces of pork alternately fat and lean are the most suitable; the cheeks are the best. A little pepper sprinkled among the beans, when they are placed in the bean-pot, will render them less unhealthy. They should be just covered with water, when put into the oven; and the pork should be sunk a little below the surface of the beans. Bake three or four hours.[28]

From a modern perspective, the most striking feature of Child's recipe is that the pepper "to render them less unhealthy" was the only seasoning. There was no sweetener whatsoever. A sweetening element has come to be considered the sine qua non of baked beans, and we have seen that honey went into the baked bean and ham pottage that was a Staffordshire specialty at the time of the settling of New England. Nevertheless, Child did not sweeten her baked beans, and according to Sandra L. Oliver, sweeteners, usually molasses, did not begin to be added to the dish until the last quarter of the nineteenth century.[29]

Oliver states that when molasses began to appear as an ingredient in baked beans, the amounts were relatively small—no more than a tablespoonful per quart of beans. Such was the case in an 1881 recipe for "New England Baked Beans." A couple of years later, in "Yankee Pork and Beans," a doubling or tripling of the molasses was recommended. By the turn of the twentieth century and into its early decades, this amount had become standard. With *The Home Science Cookbook* by Mary J. Lincoln and Anna Barrows, the molasses began to be measured by the cup. Around this time sugar became an additional sweetening option in baked beans.[30]

Another trend in baked bean cookery after 1875 or so was a reduction in the proportion of pork, reflecting (as we shall see in chapter 5) the steadily deteriorating reputation of this particular meat in the later nineteenth century. In "Yankee Pork and Beans," the author went so far as to suggest the substitution of "a fresh spare-rib" if "salt pork is too robust for the appetites to be served." Lincoln and Barrows indulged in extremes of precision regarding the presence of salt pork: "Wash one-quarter to one-half of a pound of salt pork, part fat and part lean, scrape the rind until white, and cut it one inch deep in half-inch strips." After all that, they allowed that vegetarians were wont to omit the pork altogether, while others replaced it with "fat corned beef."[31]

There appears to have been considerable room for disagreement on the issue of where the pork should reside vis-à-vis the beans in the pot. Whereas Child wanted it "a little below" the beans, our 1881 author of "New England Baked Beans" wanted it "a little above." Catharine Beecher placed the top of the pork "even" with the beans, which seems in accordance with Sarah Josepha Hale's command to "put the pork down in the beans, till the rind only appears." Down to the mid-twentieth century, there persisted such varying prescriptions as "crowd well down into the beans," "leaving ¼ inch above the beans," "leaving only the rind in sight," and "press it down so that it will lie more than half its thickness in the water."[32]

We conclude our survey of Yankee baked bean cookery by noting a recipe from the mid-twentieth century that went by what had become the definitive name for the dish—Boston Baked Beans. Besides exhibiting the characteristics we have been chronicling, such as directions to "force" the salt pork "down among the beans until it just shows at the top of the pot" and the inclusion of almost a cup, all told, of brown sugar and molasses, this recipe is of interest for its use of onion and dry mustard. It thus amounted to a re-creation, of sorts, of the Staffordshire "dark, sweet cassoulet," made with honey, mustard, and onion or leek, that some of the emigrating yeomen may indeed have brought over to these shores.[33]

Consuming Baked Beans

In the previous chapter, we noted that pottage constituted the basis of the colonial diet. People ate it, in one form or another, every day, especially in the seventeenth century. A historian of Weare, New Hampshire, stated that "the most common dish of those times was bean porridge. It was made by boiling the beans very soft, thickening the liquor with a little meal and adding a piece of pork to season it. A handful of corn was often put in." Perhaps we can see in this description an evolution from succotash toward baked beans, as a "native" pottage of corn, beans, and flesh turned into a more "English" quotidian fare in which the beans had achieved predominance over the corn.[34]

In Beverly, Massachusetts, in the first half of the nineteenth century, beans were eaten once a week rather than every day. In Lucy Larcom's account, the beans were baked on Saturday night and eaten on Sunday. Other sources indicate that they were baked during the day on Saturday and eaten both Saturday night and Sunday. No doubt the pattern varied somewhat.[35]

But the more interesting question has to do not with weekly bean consumption patterns, but rather with how a weekly, as opposed to a daily, consumption pattern came into existence in the first place. How did New England get from "daily 'pottage' fare," beans endlessly stewing, to baked beans served up weekly on the Sabbath?

Sarah F. McMahon, from whom we have quoted the phrase "daily 'pottage' fare," argues that techniques of food production, storage, and preservation gradually improved during the colonial period. As a result, by the second half of the eighteenth century an "increase in the variety of staple foods provided new possibilities for varying the daily fare and enhancing the enjoyment of family meals." So here was the first prerequisite for the transition from daily to weekly consumption patterns, the capability of providing enough different kinds of foodstuffs so that different things could be eaten on different days. By 1750, New Englanders were able to shift from monotony to routinized variety in their diet.[36]

But what about the emergence of baked as opposed to stewed legume pottage? Although there was an established English tradition of baking beans, bake ovens were certainly not widely available from the beginning of settlement. "The first fireplaces had no ovens, all cooking being done in and over the fire," and as late as the 1790s, in at least one frontier district, many families still lacked ovens, sharing the one bake oven in the neighborhood. Even those who had them could not necessarily afford to heat their ovens up every day, leading to the pattern of weekly or semiweekly baking already described.[37]

Nevertheless, the creation of a situation in which bake ovens were more or less readily available, either in one's own home, in that of a neighbor, or at the village tavern, probably coincided with the creation of conditions for a more varied diet. After 1750, different meals could be had on different days of the week, and once or twice a week parts of the meal would be baked. The relative infrequency of baking made baked goods relatively scarce, therefore relatively special; and hence the beginnings of the transformation of beans from their lowly status as the dregs of the English breadmaking process, that "by oft use" of which "the wits are dulled," into a more esteemed cultural position.

Lucy Larcom explained that eating beans on Saturday and Sunday, as opposed to other days, was due to "the Puritanic custom of saving Sunday-work." Although the date by which this custom became widespread remains uncertain, Larcom's idea is plausible, in that a particular reverence for the Sabbath was indeed one of the features of English and American Puritanism that distinguished it from Continental Protestantism. A further dimension of New England Sabbath dining is suggested by the report of a traveler from Maryland, visiting Boston in 1744, that "salt cod fish" was "a common Saturday's dinner" there.[38]

No meat on Saturday at midday and a semimeatless meal on Saturday night and Sunday: it begins to appear that Sabbath eve and Sabbath day baked bean eating was part of an adaptation of the fast day and Lenten traditions of medieval Catholicism that New England Protestants developed. According to Christopher Hill, a major reason that English Puritans came to emphasize the Sabbath was to replace sporadic traditional Catholic saints' days and festival observances. Abstinence from work routines would thereby be made more regular and predictable. A New England weekly Sabbath interval of meat abstinence, replacing Lent and other fast and "fish" days scattered throughout the year, would thus fit this pattern.[39]

The hallowing of baked beans, however, was far from fully established in 1750. What else happened to turn it into one of the definitive New England dishes? We have referred in the previous chapter to the first celebration of Forefathers' Day in Plymouth in 1769. This festival was initiated by an organization called the Old Colony Club, founded in that same year to pay respect to "the first landing of our worthy ancestors in this place."[40]

The Old Colony Club and Forefathers' Day did not constitute the genesis of New Englanders' fond and reverential commemoration of their own history and culture. There had been a centennial observance in Plymouth in 1720; before that there had been Cotton Mather's monumental retrospective in book form, *Magnalia Christi Americana*, published in 1702; and before that, dating roughly from the 1660s, there had been a more diffuse but nevertheless distinct pattern of "jeremiad" sermonizing, in which each generation of New Englanders compared itself unfavorably to the first settlers.[41]

But if the establishment of Forefathers' Day as an annual observance should not be seen as the starting point of New England's construction of a myth about itself, it is fair to describe it as a sign of the emergence of such mythmaking into consolidated, institutionalized form. The sole purpose of the Old Colony Club was to perpetuate the memory of "our worthy ancestors." It is probably not coincidental that such activity was becoming more visible at the same time that there had developed sufficient resources for the creation of agricultural surpluses and the building of bake ovens. A society can devote itself to cultural elaboration, from a varied diet to the remembrance of things past, only when it has surplus wealth at its disposal.

At any rate, it is certain that from this point on, the recalling of New England history and the creation of fit symbols of New England tradition became increasingly prominent features of New England life. Lawrence Buell argues that from the American Revolution to the Civil War, New Englanders energetically propagated, in Forefathers' Day orations among other ways, the idea that the key ideals of the new nation had originated in their region. In Daniel Webster's summary phrasing of this theme in an 1820 oration, the "free nature of our institutions" had "come down to us from the Rock of Plymouth."[42]

New England foods played an important part in this highly successful propaganda campaign. As we have seen, Joel Barlow was already in the 1790s hailing hasty pudding as the prime sustenance of a race of "sturdy freemen." By 1842, baked beans was included in the array of dishes invested with symbolic glamour. In a "sketch of New England" written by a descendant of one of "those stern old Puritans who chartered the Mayflower," baked beans was placed in the midst of determined celebration of the special virtues of the New England way of life:

On Saturday evening, whatever may be the season of the year, no festivities can take place. The work and the play of the farmer's boy have then ceased, and young and old all prepare for the approach of holy time. . . . The house has been thoroughly cleansed and "put to rights," from the disorder which the week's movements have occasioned; the long rows of shining pewter upon the dresser have been newly scoured; the proceeds of the last churning have been thoroughly worked and neatly put away; the new-made cheese is placed under the press; the beer has been brewed; and the batch of Indian bread—with its Sunday-noon concomitants, baked pork and beans—is safely deposited in the oven.

As evening comes on, the children are called into the house to undergo the weekly ablution, and then, one after another, are called to learn the Bible questions for Sunday school. The men drop in, as each one finishes his duties; the boy has collected and put by all the farming utensils for the next week; the rich store of milk is brought in from the barnyard; and sunset finds the whole family partaking of the evening meal. All loud talk or boisterous merriment is, as if by common consent, suspended.

In this purportedly typical scene of Sabbatarian reverence, discipline, and order, the evening meal was represented as virtually a partaking of the sacrament. Meanwhile, the next sacramental occasion, the Sunday noon repast, was already in preparation. It would consist of Ryaninjun and baked beans.[43]

Harriet Beecher Stowe's depiction of a baked bean meal also radiated a sacramental aura:

[Aaron] Burr accepted the invitation [to dinner at the Scudders] with a frank and almost boyish abandon, declaring that he had not seen anything, for years, that so reminded him of old times. He praised everything at table,—the smoking brown-bread, the baked beans steaming from the oven, where they had been quietly simmering during the morning walk, and the Indian pudding, with its gelatinous softness, matured by long and patient brooding in the motherly old oven. He declared that there was no style of living to be compared with the simple, dignified order of a true New England home, where servants were excluded, and everything came direct from the polished and cultured hand of a lady. It realized the dreams of Arcadian romance.

In this passage from Stowe's *The Minister's Wooing*, first published in 1859, there was a complex interplay of judgment and celebration. Aaron Burr, grandson of New England's most influential religious thinker, Jonathan Ed-

Bean and pudding dish, nineteenth century.
(Courtesy Peabody Historical Society; photograph by Jeffrey R. Dykes)

wards, was depicted in the course of the novel as he had been in the 1790s, a rising politician already immersed in the sort of devious scheming that would eventually lead him to be branded a traitor. Worse, from the New England point of view, he was an infidel, an abysmal apostate from his grandfather's heroic theology. He was also an inveterate womanizer.[44]

Burr's praise of baked beans, brown bread, and the simple, dignified order of a true New England home thus represented the false nostalgia of worldly sophistication and was moreover spoken primarily for effect, in order to impress the mother of the novel's beautiful heroine, Mary Scudder. Yet alongside all this, Stowe was in fact looking back on the 1790s from the vantage point of 1859 and celebrating baked beans, brown bread, and Indian pudding as truly appropriate symbols of what was indeed, to her, truly valuable—the simple, dignified order of a true New England home.

This scene in Stowe's novel took place on a Wednesday. Perhaps the Scudder household was one of those in which the baking was undertaken twice rather than once a week. In any case, we may construe this transfer of the sacramental meal to a weekday as a sign that the symbolizing capacity of baked beans was being secularized; it would no longer necessarily be attached to

New England religion but could henceforth be used to invoke the entire spectrum of uniquely valuable New England virtues and ways.

The exaltation of baked beans entered into maturity in the twentieth century. Recipes began insisting that "the beans be baked in a pot small at the top, and bulging in the middle—the New England bean pot. They are not nice baked in any other dish." In the latter-day Staffordshire baked pottage recipe described above, the reader is urged to serve these Boston Baked Beans "in the pot, as the Pilgrims did." Thus were mid-twentieth-century American suppers turned into patriotic sacraments.[45]

The fullest evocation of baked beans was probably one published in 1945 that confined the dish, insofar as it was to be considered authentic, to rural Maine: "They say it's hard to find a decent bean today in Boston, but that isn't so, because we sell a lot of beans down there." Genuine baked beans required a genuine beanpot, not merely small at the top and bulging in the middle, but one whose "pores" had taken on "a mellowing that comes from weekly bakings. It takes barrels of beans, gallons of molasses, whole saltings of pork, bushels of onions, and months of blue moons to fire the quintessence of a good bean pot." Furthermore, "it takes the loving care of a mother to pick and choose only the right beans, and the right kind of beans. . . . But even the beans aren't all-important. It takes hot hardwood fires over a long period of time, and none but the old and established families really get the best baked beans."[46]

No new steel beanpots and electric ovens from the store in town were allowed. The excellence conferred by nostalgia had now been passed on, along with a well-seasoned crockery pot, from the brick oven to the wood range that replaced it: "They find their sparkling electric range has a number of advantages our wood range can't boast, but it seems to us a fine stove in the kitchen is a poor substitute for good beans in the dining room. . . . If a steel bean pot bakes better beans than a stone one, all I can say is I don't want any better beans than come out of our traditional vessels." Even the threshing of the crop of beans was best done by hand: "if we had a power threshing machine we'd finish up the beans in no time and then have nothing to do in bad weather."[47]

In this author's representation, time, lovingly protracted, was of the essence: "Anyway, really enjoyable beans are not a simple thing to prepare. They start in the spring with the planting, and follow along through the months. And the cooking itself is nothing you do quickly, at the last minute before eating time." The author's great-grandmother would work on her baked beans from Friday night all through Saturday, stoking the fire, keeping

them now properly moist, now "a little dry, which browned them up good. After she thought they were dry enough, she would pour water on again, and the pot would sizzle, a cloud of steam would pour out in the room, and each and every bean would assume its rightful share of essence and power."[48]

The entire traditional way of life of rural New England—as still exemplified by old and established families, traditional cooking vessels and methods, and even by farming procedures that remain unchanged from those of the yeomen of premigration England—all of this went into the production and consumption of the best baked beans. And what it all produced, here at the close of New England mythmaking as it did at its dawning in Joel Barlow's hymn to hasty pudding, was sturdy New England individualism: each bean, each person, assuming "its rightful share" of the essence and power of the entire pot of beans, the entire community.[49]

Pumpkins

At the beginning of the seventeenth century, Samuel de Champlain saw the natives of the Saco River region cultivating squashes and pumpkins, along with beans and corn. First domesticated, like corn, in Central America, pumpkins had eventually been brought to North America, where they came to form a part of the diet of the New England Indians. After Columbus's voyages, pumpkins were brought to Europe, and at some point in the sixteenth century they were introduced into England from France. According to William Harrison, writing in 1577, the cultivation of "pompions" was part of a general resumption, after a few centuries' hiatus, of vegetable growing in sixteenth-century England, "not only . . . among the poor commons," but also among "delicate merchants, gentlemen, and the nobility." The last three groups, Harrison continued, "made their provision yearly for new seeds out of strange countries, from whence they have them abundantly." Pumpkins would certainly have qualified at that time as a new seed out of a strange country.[50]

Early English observers of native culinary practices had relatively little to say about squashes and pumpkins. According to William Wood, Indians relied on "Isquoutersquashes [squashes] . . . a fruite like a young Pumpion" for sustenance in the summertime, "when their corne is spent." Roger Williams praised "Askutasquash" (squash) as being "sweet, light[,] wholesome[,] refreshing." As for specific cooking methods, Daniel Gookin mentioned "pumpions and squashes" among the items sometimes added to succotash.[51]

Otherwise, direct testimony regarding pumpkin and squash cookery of the natives of New England is lacking. Algonquian groups elsewhere on the east coast were reported to have boiled them whole and stewed them "in their own steam in pots covered with large pumpkin leaves." According to another source, pumpkin was roasted in strips over the fire. "For winter use all eastern tribes dried squash and pumpkins in great quantities and later ground or soaked the flesh" prior to its utilization in cooking, writes Howard S. Russell.[52]

Despite the cultivation and consumption of pumpkins in sixteenth-century England, Edward Johnson, one of the major chroniclers and celebrants of early New England, found it necessary in 1654 to apologize for the early colonists' dependence on them, just after acknowledging a similar dependence on corn: "let no man make a jest at Pumpkins, for with this fruit the Lord was pleased to feed his people to their good content, till Corne [i.e., grain] and Cattell were increased." A bit later on, Johnson implied that pumpkins were a poor substitute for familiar English fruits, just as corn was a poor substitute for familiar English grain: "instead of Apples and Peares, they had Pomkins and Squashes of divers kinds." Johnson was doubtless writing with an eye to the fact that pumpkins and squashes, like corn, were a staple among the Indians.[53]

If, as Johnson said, the people of New England had been fed to their good content with pumpkin before "cattell were increased," after dairy cattle were increased they continued to be so fed, for one method of cooking pumpkins in colonial times was to empty them of fiber and seeds, place them, either empty or filled with milk, in a tin baker or brick oven, and bake them for several hours. Sometimes the shell was wrapped in cabbage or pumpkin leaves during the baking. When removed from the oven, the meaty vegetable was filled or refilled with milk or cream, and a savory pumpkin custard in its own container was ready to be served. This dish probably derived from the practice of the common people of sixteenth-century England of emptying pumpkins of their "seeds and pith" and baking them stuffed with apples.[54]

Pumpkin was also boiled, or boiled and mashed, by the New England colonists. The "pumpkin sauce" served to Sarah Knight in 1704 at a Connecticut inn, on her way back to Boston from New York, was probably prepared by the latter method. In the mid-nineteenth century, Catharine Beecher proposed utilizing the former method in a recipe for pumpkin preserves. Strips of pumpkin fruit were to be soaked overnight in sugar and lemon juice. The next day, lemon peel was added to the mixture, after which

it was boiled and cooled. The syrup was then strained and poured back on: "If there is too much lemon peel, it will be bitter."[55]

Pumpkin pulp produced by boiling and mashing was also added to various forms of bread or cake "to flavor and sweeten" them. Joel Barlow's testimony from the 1790s that "a dash of pumpkin" was what distinguished New England Johnny cake from Virginia hoe cake has been noted in the preceding chapter, as has Lydia Maria Child's inclusion three decades later of "a little stewed pumpkin" in her "Indian cake, or bannock." An early-twentieth-century recipe for Boston Brown Bread, probably copied from an earlier source, stated that "such bread is improved by the addition of a gill of boiled pumpkin or winter squash."[56]

Back in 1846 Catharine Beecher had offered a variation on Ryaninjun relying almost entirely on pumpkin: "Stew and strain some pumpkin, stiffen it with Indian meal, add salt and yeast, and it makes a most excellent kind of bread." Beecher was thus at odds with Sarah Knight, who had found during her 1704 travels "such an aspect" to the "Pumpkin and Indian-mixed bread" she was served at another Connecticut stopping point that she refused to eat it.[57]

Like the Indians, the colonists preserved pumpkins for use in winter by drying them; one use of dried pumpkin was as a sweetener in flip, a popular alcoholic drink described more fully in chapter 8. Pumpkin and/or apple parings were used to make a beer of sorts, immortalized in the following rhyme: "Oh we can make liquor to sweeten our lips / Of pumpkins, of parsnips, of walnut-tree chips." The Indians made mats out of dried pumpkin strips, and the colonists found nonculinary uses for dried pumpkin as well—for example, as containers for seeds, grain, yarn, and cloth. Nowadays, of course, the main use of pumpkins is to brighten and frighten during Halloween.[58]

Pumpkin Pie

In chapter 6 we will talk about the major importance of pie in general, first in English and then in Yankee cookery. As for pumpkin pie in particular, in sixteenth- and seventeenth-century England "people of substance" were familiar with a form of pumpkin pie that both followed the medieval tradition of "rich pies of mixed ingredients" and also bore resemblance to the consumption of apple-stuffed pumpkins typically engaged in by people of lesser substance: "The pumpkin was first sliced and fried with sweet herbs and spices, sugar and beaten eggs. Then it was put into a pastry shell with alternate layers of apples and currants."[59]

Pumpkin pie went out of fashion in Britain during the eighteenth century. Perhaps Edward Johnson reflected this emerging attitude in the 1650s when he offered as a sign of New England's progress toward prosperity the fact that in most households people were eating "apples, pears, and quince tarts instead of their former Pumpkin Pies." Pumpkin had been superseded by the more civilized fruits (free of association with the natives), of which the settlers had been at first deprived.[60]

Such an anticipation that pumpkin pie was on the way out was premature, as far as developments on this side of the Atlantic were concerned. In the 1760s, just before the American Revolution, an upper-class Boston family, the Gardiners, carried on the English tradition sketched above with a pie of layered pumpkin and apple slices. Given that the Gardiners, like most of the colonial elite at this time, "mingled with British officials and patterned their behavior on the upper-class English model," this is not surprising. The Gardiners opposed the Revolution and spent the war years in England, presumably taking their ancien régime pie with them.[61]

A couple of decades later, after the Revolution, Amelia Simmons's two pumpkin pie recipes became another case in point that her cookbook "was, in its minor sphere, another declaration of American independence":

> No. 1. One quart [pumpkin] stewed and strained, 3 pints cream, 9 beaten eggs, sugar, mace, nutmeg and ginger, laid into paste No. 7 or 3, and with a dough spur, cross and chequer, and baked in dishes three quarters of an hour.
>
> No. 2. One quart of milk, 1 pint pumpkin, 4 eggs, molasses, allspice and ginger in a crust, bake 1 hour.

The "paste" in the first recipe was pie crust, a topic which will receive due consideration in chapter 6. The main point here is that Simmons's pumpkin pie was recognizably different from traditional English pumpkin pie and recognizably similar to the pumpkin pie we know today: a pie crust filled with spiced pumpkin custard. Simmons did retain the traditional top crust. The contrast between Simmons's Americanized custard-pumpkin pie and English or Anglophile apple-pumpkin pie can perhaps be traced to the similar contrast between the colonial baking of whole pumpkins filled with milk or cream and the premigration English baking of whole pumpkins stuffed with apples.[62]

Given that most of us today would gladly sit down to a piece of Simmons's pumpkin pie, it is not surprising that later recipes mostly offered minor variations on her themes. Lydia Maria Child said nothing at all on the question of the crust. Her recipe was intended for either pumpkin or squash, and she mentioned that "the part nearest the seed is the sweetest part of the squash." While calling for salt and cinnamon along with ginger, she stated that "ginger will answer very well alone for spice, if you use enough of it." "The outside of a lemon grated in is nice," she went on, concluding that "the more eggs, the better the pie."[63]

Ten years later, in 1839, Sarah Josepha Hale's recipe implied that the identity of pumpkin pie as one with a bottom crust only had become fully established: "Roll the paste rather thicker than for fruit pies, as there is only one crust." Like Child, Hale referred to ginger as the crucial spicing element, and like Simmons, she offered versions with either cream or milk. Of Catharine Beecher's two pumpkin pie recipes, one specified baking "with a bottom crust and rim."[64]

The subsequent history of pumpkin pie cookery in New England need not be followed in detail. During the 1880s and 1890s, *Godey's Lady's Book and Magazine*, that arbiter of nineteenth-century domesticity (Sarah Josepha Hale had just completed her long run as editor a few years before), offered five pumpkin pie recipes.[65]

One of the *Godey's* recipes stipulated that a "Yankee pumpkin" be used, and this brings us onto the terrain of pumpkin pie as yet another icon from the kitchen, evocative of New England traditions and values. An 1831 cookbook stated that a liking for pumpkin pie was one of the defining characteristics of "the universal Yankee nation." Hale called pumpkin pie in her 1839 recipe "this real yankee pie," which was "prepared in perfection" only in rural districts. In 1876 "Punkin Pies" were part of the menu, along with baked beans, "Boiled Vittles" (probably boiled dinner), and doughnuts, for a "Centennial Tea Party or Supper of ye Antient Times," held at the Mystic, Connecticut, Methodist Church. Part of Thomas Robinson Hazard's 1879 repertoire of nostalgia was "the famous old-time pumpkin pies."[66]

The *Godey's* recipes appeared in fall or winter, after the harvest. Three of them were timed with Thanksgiving dinner specifically in mind. In Lydia Maria Child's classic poem, "The New England Boy's Song about Thanksgiving Day," first published in 1845 and now far better known from its first line, "Over the River and through the Wood," the final line was "Hurra for the pumpkin pie!" Sarah Josepha Hale, who would later lead the campaign for the establishment of Thanksgiving as a national holiday, had already stated in a fictional description of Thanksgiving dinner that "custards and pies of every name and description ever known in Yankee land" were to be found on the holiday table, "yet the pumpkin pie occupied the most distinguished niche."[67]

Pumpkins, corn, and beans, the triumvirate of native horticulture and cookery, were central ingredients in many foods that are now identified as distinctively belonging to New England. Like corn and beans, pumpkins eventually bore symbolic as well as dietary weight in the formation of Yankee culture. They persisted from their not always appetizing contribution to colonial breadmaking to their apotheosis as a symbol of the Anglo-American heritage on the Thanksgiving dinner tables of today. The earliest culinary efforts of the English settlers in regard to this native fruit were aimed at perpetuating its absorption into medieval haute cuisine that had been effected just prior to their immigration to New England. But even as this brief tradition was dying out, Yankee housewives came up with a truly worthy invention: pumpkin pie, as it has been known and loved ever since the birth of American independence.

CHAPTER 3

A Knowen & Staple Commoditie

Fish & Shellfish

*A*s a commercial product, fish was the foundation on which New England's economic life was built. From the fishing industry came the shipbuilding and carrying trades and, eventually, the American Industrial Revolution, in which New England led the way. Yet despite fishing's centrality to the history of the region, the actual activity of catching fish was generally held in low regard among the English settlers and their Yankee descendants. When young, men might go to sea and fish, but their purpose in doing so was to make enough money to establish themselves as farmers. It was from farming, not fishing, that New Englanders crafted their self-image.[1]

This unfavorable view of catching fish had its roots in Puritan culture. An unfavorable view of eating fish had more venerable sources in English and European tradition. Yet, with England being "an island surrounded by fish," English attitudes toward such an abundant food resource could not be entirely negative. This proved to be the case for the colonists as well. Living near the sea, New Englanders ate what the sea provided, with diminishing distaste as time went on, ultimately with relish. We shall explore these various cultural ambivalences about fish and fishing more fully later on. First we take a look at the beginnings of the cod fisheries.[2]

Excellent Fishing for Cod

Although our school lessons begin the story of New England with the Pilgrim settlement, for the English who first became interested in the region, the story began somewhat earlier, and the plot revolved around fishing rather than farming. In 1602 Bartholomew Gosnold, on a trading and sassafras-gathering journey to the region, returned to England with glowing reports of his "ship's deck covered" with his crew's catch. It appeared to him that the

New England coastal waters would prove superior to those off Newfoundland, heretofore England's premier fishing grounds.[3]

The Bristol merchants who had long underwritten fishing expeditions from the English West Country next sent Martin Pring to investigate. He too found "excellent fishing for cod which are better than those of Newfound-land and withall we saw good and rockie ground fit to drie them upon." A decade later, Captain John Smith continued to promote New England waters for commercial fishing: "let not the meanness of the word *fish* distaste you, for [fishing] will afford as good gold as the mines of Guiana or Potosi, with less hazard and charge." Note Smith's anticipation of prejudice against fish among his readers.[4]

Expectations of lucrative fishing played a part in the settlement of both the Plymouth and Massachusetts Bay colonies. Just prior to his departure for North America, John Winthrop spoke of fish as "a knowen and staple Commoditie" that Massachusetts Bay ought to exploit. John White likewise told the planters that fishing would be "the first means that will bring any income into your lande."[5]

But the anticipated ascendancy of New England's fishing grounds over Newfoundland's did not immediately materialize. Scholars have offered various explanations for this: political maneuvering over fishing licenses; the inexperience of small entrepreneurs; the problems of residential fisheries as opposed to encampments and trading posts; and the "lack of capital, small numbers, the distances between settlements, and the uncertain returns" of these smaller ventures.[6]

In time, however, the pattern of small but efficient fisheries was successful. As established settlements grew, they in turn set up fisheries farther afield, all along the coasts of what were to become Massachusetts and Maine. The success of Salem, Massachusetts, after 1628 is both the earliest and foremost example.[7]

At first, the primary market for the embryonic New England fishing industry was the fiercely competitive one of Catholic Europe. While this trade, primarily with the Iberian peninsula, was to remain significant, the most profitable outlet for the fish, mainly cod, caught by New Englanders proved to lie elsewhere, in the Caribbean.[8]

By the late 1640s, the West Indian sugarcane industry had developed sufficiently to provide a market for the so-called refuse cod that New England merchants had hitherto found left on their hands. Such fish, which could amount to half of each catch, had been poorly split or cured and were therefore not saleable in Europe or the Portuguese Atlantic islands. But they were considered adequate as food for the slave labor force of the sugar industry. Refuse cod was sold to Caribbean plantation owners for two-thirds of the price of top-grade goods. This factor—a reliable outlet for the sale of an inferior product—was more important than any other to New England's commercial success. We shall discuss the West Indian sugarcane industry in its role as a seller to New England, rather than as a buyer from it, in chapters 6 and 8.[9]

The fact that sugar plantation slavery was fed on New England codfish would not come to the fore as a moral concern among New Englanders until the late eighteenth century, after the fisheries had been superseded by maritime trade in other goods as the region's primary wealth-creating enterprise. The moral and religious objections to the fishing industry that the Puritans of early New England did express came from a different direction: they disapproved of the behavior and religious beliefs of most fishermen.

We can begin to understand the issues at stake by noting the distinction between the "core" of a society and its "periphery" that Daniel Vickers has outlined. "In a less mobile age than our own," Vickers writes, "people who moved out to earn their livings on the . . . fringes of society" were apt to be considered marginal not only geographically but also morally. In the eyes of those who lived closer to the center of settlement, "the independent husbandmen and craftsmen who worked together with their families on the property they owned," the people out on the periphery seemed to be "persons of casual habits, often without families, brushing shoulders daily with others they scarcely knew." Such transients might be capable of anything.[10]

Several features of the colonial New England fishing industry sharpened this polarity between core and periphery. First, the economic relationship between fishermen and those who financed their voyages was profoundly unequal, like that of a servant to a master. The first inhabitants of the coastal fishing communities, dependent upon merchants for vessels, tools, supplies, provisions, and the sale of their catch, were entangled in a system of credit, often for their entire working lives. What this situation also resembled, therefore, was our modern economy, in which most people are employed by the few with capital resources. The fishermen and their families out on the social periphery were caught in exactly the trap of wage labor, and associated loss of independence, that (as we shall see in the next chapter) the great majority of the farmers inhabiting the social core had come to New England to avoid.[11]

Such demeaning conditions of employment would already have been sufficient to attract into the fishing industry mostly people whose style of living was the opposite of Puritan restraint. But even if there had been any fishermen imbued with Puritan precepts, they would have found it difficult to remain on the straight and narrow path. To the Puritan, work was the cornerstone of Christian life. But work "was pleasing to God only when performed in a regular and disciplined manner." In the fishing industry, it was impossible to live up to this standard. Part of the year, men exerted themselves furiously, but by venturing beyond even the periphery into the wild. They either pursued a wild species across the treacherous ocean, or, while the catch was being dried and salted, they languished on "an isolated stretch of shoreline." Throughout the fishing season, they were separated from the restraining and softening influences of family and community life.[12]

Other parts of the year, between fishing seasons, the men were back home but were forced into inactivity. They were therefore, according to the Puritan authorities in the Massachusetts General Court (legislature), all too likely to lapse into "idling, gameing, or spending their time unproffitably." This "alternation of frantic activity and idleness . . . was a necessary feature of [the] seasonal and market-oriented calling" of fishing, but its necessity was invisible to the Puritans. They damned the fishermen when they did, and worked, and likewise when they didn't, and rested.[13]

Viewed as dangerous aliens by respectable folk, the people inhabiting and setting forth from Salem, Marblehead, and other fishing locales responded by creating an alternative culture. Not only did they engage disproportionately in Sabbath-breaking and blasphemy (one Marblehead fisherman declared in 1649 that he wished his dog to be christened); and not only did they commit themselves to clergymen with High Church views, anathema to the Puritans, to the point of paying their salaries; fishermen also subscribed to "forms of spirituality—the invocation of Saints' names . . . or the use of certain lucky charms and ceremonies" that the Puritans abhorred but that were meaningful to the fishermen themselves. Daniel Vickers argues that such a religious outlook made sense to men who constantly faced "economic uncertainty and physical danger."[14]

Moreover, "maritime culture further distinguished itself by the importance it placed upon organized social drinking." Fishing boats sailed forth with a quart's worth of beverage—beer, cider, and brandy—per crew member per day. On shore, there was an equally ample supply of taverns, and "Marblehead generated close to three times the number of liquor-related offenses that one would have expected from a town of its size."[15]

The problem was not only that the patterns of organization and activity of the fishing industry made it virtually impossible for a fisherman to be-

Massachusetts fisherman, Harper's New Monthly Magazine, *June 1875.*
(Courtesy Fall River Public Library)

come or remain a Puritan. It was also that for those few "family heads with orthodox religious beliefs" who did engage in fishing, "land was too easy . . . to acquire, and the order and security of life on shore too difficult to resist."[16]

The Puritan core of early New England despised its anti-Puritan periphery. But it was unable to get along without it. Basically, "the surpluses generated by independent producers in New England's rocky soil were . . . inadequate." Such surpluses were essential to acquire English manufactured items, such as cooking pots and farm implements, that the colonists desperately needed. So the fisheries were a necessary evil, tolerated as a means to generate a spendable surplus in a predominantly barter economy.[17]

It took many years for fishing to become wholly a New England enterprise. Indeed throughout the seventeenth century it was not. Crucial parts of the process remained under the control of English rather than New English capitalists. By the eighteenth century, however, the merchants of Boston and other domestic seaports had amassed sufficient resources to manage and manipulate all phases and aspects of the transactions.[18]

Fysshe Dayes

While the Puritans had their own special reasons to dislike the fisheries, they also shared in more widespread English trepidations about the sea and its products. The English attitude about "the meanness of . . . fish," to borrow Captain Smith's phrase, was, it seems, embedded in their language. As Sandra L. Oliver points out, evidence of long-standing misgivings about fish linger in the historical repository of idiomatic English expressions: "Consider the implications of the word 'fishy' compared to the word 'beefy.' When we want to improve something we 'beef it up,' when we feel suspicious we think a thing is 'fishy.'"[19]

There were a variety of reasons for this low opinion. To some extent, the sheer abundance of fish bred what familiarity usually does. According to one fourteenth-century description of England, the "grete plente of small fysshe of samen [salmon] and of eeles" available at that time meant that "the people in some place[s] fedeth thyr swyne with fysshe." In New England as well, shellfish served not only as cheap nourishment for indentured servants and slaves, but also on occasion as fodder for swine. Regarding clams, William Wood noted that "these fishes be in great plenty in most places of the countrey, which is a great commoditie for the feeding of Swine."[20]

The early modern diner disparaged fish primarily because fish-eating represented the dietary deprivation of the meatless fast days so prevalent in the medieval religious calendar. Such meatless days did not disappear with the end of medieval religiosity. The linkage between fish and impoverishment of diet was actually strengthened in post-Reformation England. During the reign of Queen Elizabeth, laws requiring the observance of "fysshe dayes" remained in force, not for "religions sake" but rather on distinctly worldly grounds:"for the preservation of the navie, and maintenance of convenient numbers of sea faring men" and "to the end our numbers of cattell may be the better increased." In other words (at least as far as the second reason was concerned), people had to continue to eat fish because there was not enough meat.[21]

With frequent periods of food scarcity in the early years of New England, the association of fish-eating with bad times was only strengthened. William Bradford summarized a period of shortage in Plymouth in 1623 by recalling that the "best dish" anyone had been able to offer to a neighbor or guest had been "a lobster or a piece of fish without bread or anything else but a cup of fair spring water." Edward Johnson depicted the women of Massachusetts Bay gathering mussels and clams in 1631 during another interval of severe grain shortage. While engaged in this activity, they found it necessary to prop each other up with holy sentiments, "encouraging one another in Christ's careful providing for them." Whereupon, "they lift up their eyes and saw two Ships comming in," laden with "Victualls," which they clearly anticipated would be greatly superior to that afforded by their shellfish harvest. Describing a period of dearth in 1643 in the Massachusetts Bay colony, Governor John Winthrop lamented that "many families in most towns . . . were forced to live off clams, muscles [mussels] . . . dry fish."[22]

The "dry fish" Winthrop referred to was dried cod. Since the early fifteenth century, before they began commercial fishing on a large scale, the English had imported cod in quantity from Iceland; it had become "the most plentiful and least loved of Lenten delicacies." That "dry fish" was consumed with so little relish becomes immediately clear from such cooking instructions as: "it behoves to beat it with a wooden hammer for a full hour, and then set it to soak in warm water for a full two hours or more, then cook and scour it very well like beef."[23]

Fish and Fishing among the Indians

The Indians of New England considered fish a bounty unencumbered by negative connotations. As Daniel Gookin observed, fish was as likely as meat to be added to the Indians' "standing dish," succotash. Roger Williams similarly noted fish's parity with meat in the Indian cuisine: "*Sometimes* God *gives them* Fish or Flesh."[24]

Although they were skilled fishing folk, New England Indians did not venture far from shore in their birch bark and dugout canoes. M. K. Bennett tells us that "along the coast and in lakes and streams the Indians used hook (of bone until the colonists brought iron) and line, as well as nets made of some kind of indigenous hemp. They built weirs on streams. They shot fish with arrows and speared them, perhaps especially from canoes, by torchlight at night."[25] In appreciative tones, William Wood vividly described one such scene: "lightning a blazing torch . . . they weave it too and againe by their Cannow side, which the Sturgeon much delighted with, comes to them tumbling and playing, turning up his white belly, into which they thrust their launce, his backe being impenetrable; which done they haile to the shore their strugling prize." Wood and John Josselyn also reported that the Indians ice-fished in winter.[26]

More than eighty kinds of fish and shellfish were known, and most eaten, by southern New England Indians in the seventeenth century. According to one estimate, fish and shellfish comprised 9 percent of their diet. In the north, where agriculture was rare, fish was probably eaten in even greater proportions. Of course, different species dominated in different locations, but common types were lobsters, clams, crabs, scallops, oysters, mackerel, herring, salmon, shad, sturgeon, bass, pickerel, trout, and eels. In general, women were responsible for gathering shellfish, men for fishing. Inland, "even tribes hostile to each other" gathered at key spots during the spring runs of shad and herring to capture their shares of the bounty. But the New England coastline offered the most striking evidence of the importance of fish in the Algonquian diet, in the form of the great middens of shells, mostly clams, found there by the early English settlers.[27]

As we mentioned in chapter 1, Roger Williams reported that the natives used clams "and the naturall liquor of it" both for broth and as an ingredient in bread, "making it seasonable and savory, instead of Salt." Archaeological evidence indicates that clams and oysters were roasted or baked, sometimes in shallow round pits. According to John Josselyn, lobsters were also "rosted or dryed in the smoak." Other fish were broiled over coals on flat stones or placed directly on the coals. Some natives were known to cook salmon (or shad) by fastening it to a piece of driftwood, sealing in its juices by holding it over a high flame, then letting the wood burn to embers, thereby smoking it. This method is still used to produce expensive planked salmon.[28]

Despite their inherited ambivalence about fish, the colonists found much

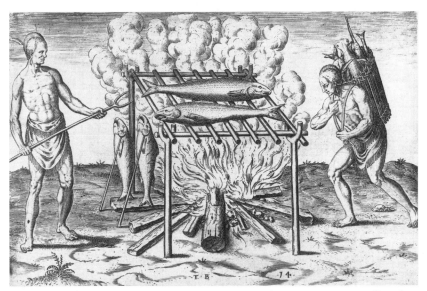

Eastern woodland Indians cooking fish, engraving by Theodor de Bry, from Grands Voyages, *2d ed., 1624, MSS 115. (Courtesy Mashantucket Pequot Museum and Research Center, Archives and Special Collections)*

in the Indians' fish repertoire to like, as indicated in these verses by William Wood: "The luscious lobster with the crabfish raw, / The brinish oyster, mussel, periwig, / And tortoise sought for by the Indian squaw, / Which to the flats dance many a winter's jig, / To dive for cockles and to dig for clams."[29] (Wood's boosterism aside, shellfish gathering was no occasion for dancing, as we shall see below.) Wood also spoke of "Clamms as big as a pennie white loafe," so good that they were "great dainties amongst the natives, and would bee in good esteeme amongst the English were it not for better fish." Farther from shore, the rich fishing grounds off Plymouth were remarked upon with approval by Edward Winslow as a reason for the fitness of the site for English habitation: "Skote, Cod, Turbot, and Herring wee have tasted of; abundance of Musles the greatest & best that ever we saw; Crabs and Lobsters, in their time infinite." The English, it seemed, were losing their distaste for fish in the presence of the astounding bounty enjoyed by the Indians of New England.[30]

England Is Best Served of Fysshe

Even in England, however, some degree of legitimacy had long been conferred on at least some types of fish or fish preparations. With the exception of clams, the species of shellfish listed by Wood had been eaten in Britain since prehistoric times. During the Middle Ages, mollusks were the most affordable, and "a farthings worth of mussels or a farthings worth of cockles was a feast for [the average English person] on a Friday," according to William Langland's *Piers Plowman*.[31]

Oysters had always been the most popular type of shellfish. A late-sixteenth-century traveler, who noticed that they were "cried in every street," thought English oysters superior to those he had seen in Italy. Oysters— stewed, fried, pickled, baked in a pie—dominated the first two courses of a banquet menu in the 1630s. The English also had, like the native inhabitants of southern New England, a long tradition of roasting oysters.[32]

As with shellfish, so with all fish. The same or similar species that were eaten by New England Indians had formed part of the English diet from very early days. In the sixteenth century Andrew Boorde opined that "of all nacyons and countres, England is best served of Fysshe, not onely of al maner of see-fysshe, but also of fresshe-water fysshe, and of all maner of sortes of salte-fysshe." On the eve of the English colonization of America, fish were thus "a near staple" component of the yeoman diet, although most English people of the middling classes, wherever they lived, purchased their fish in the town marketplace.[33]

Drawing on recollections of these happier aspects of English fish cookery, experiencing the gustatory delights of New England's aquatic reserves, and anticipating the financial dividends those reserves would yield, the Puritans mostly overcame their many reservations about catching and eating fish. In time, their Yankee descendants would fully exploit—in both myths and menus, for both trade and sustenance—the resources of New England's watery kingdom.

Eels

Although eel is the vernacular name of any fish, both marine and freshwater, of the order *Anguilliformes*, the common freshwater eels found in Great Britain and the similar species found in rivers along the Atlantic coast of North America were the food fish commonly referred to in British and American cookbooks. These creatures spawn and die at sea but enter rivers to develop from tiny elvers to adults. The males spend their lives at the mouths of rivers; the females travel upstream, spending from five to twenty years in freshwater. Their flesh is oily, and their skin is so scaly it was once used as leather.[34]

We begin our survey with eels because it is likely that the colonists would have done so. Edward Winslow boasted to a friend back home regarding the new settlement at Plymouth that "in September we can take a Hogshead [about 150 gallons] of Eeles in a night, with small labour, & can dig them out of their beds, all the Winter." The English were not alone in their liking. The Indians also avidly consumed eels, broiling and stewing them, and sometimes preserving them with smoke for later eating. Squanto was said to have instructed the Pilgrims in such practical fishing methods as "treading out eels from the brook with his feet and catching them with his hands."[35]

In early modern England, too, eels were often what was for dinner. In 1577 they were among the one hundred kinds of fish that William Harrison recorded as being consumed in Britain. By that time, the English taste for eels was already centuries, possibly millennia, old. Eel fisheries were mentioned by the eighth-century monk, the Venerable Bede. These "wickerwork traps" caught the fish as they congregated in the streams that fed Britain's many watermills. Eels were listed in the *Treatyse of Fysshynge with an Angle*, a fifteenth-century disquisition by Dame Juliana Berners, Abbess of Sopwith. Eel pies were long bartered for rent in East Anglia, where eels bred in the swampy fens. Many of the Puritans came from this region. In spite of the indigenous supplies in Britain, eels were also imported from the Netherlands.[36]

Like all fish consumption during the Middle Ages, eel-eating revolved around observance of fast days. But why eels above other varieties of fish? Mostly because they were cheap, which also made them "probably the only fresh variety, other than shellfish, bought by poor people." By the sixteenth century, however, English demand exceeded fresh supplies, and eels were often purchased dried; the boxes in which they arrived at the fish vendor were a common sight on market day.[37]

Given their long familiarity with eels, the colonists considered their availability in New England a boon. Serpentine, scaly, and oily to us, to them eels were easily caught, cleaned, and cooked—a familiar food, tasting of Old England while confirming their expectations that their new home was a place of natural abundance.[38]

Price, availability, and sentiment, however, do not fully explain the preference for eels over other fish. Even after the years when dietary choices were limited, the colonists continued to place eels high on their list of favorite fish. Reporting to the Royal Society in the 1670s on two voyages he had made to New England, John Josselyn communicated the colonial enthusiasm: "I never eat better *Eals* in no part of the world that I have been in, than are here. . . . There is several wayes of cooking them, some love them roasted, others baked, and many will have them fryed; but they please my palate best when they are boiled." Having succumbed to the allure of colonial eels, Josselyn dispensed with any pretense of disinterested reporting and sent along a succulent-sounding recipe: "a common way it is to boil them in half water, half wine with the bottom of a manchet, a fagot of Parsley, and a little winter savory, when they are boiled they take them out and break the bread in the broth, and put to it three or four spoonfuls of yeast, and a piece of sweet butter, this they pour to their *Eals* laid upon sippets and so serve it up."[39]

Putting fish or meat stew over pieces of bread was an ancient English practice that derived from the use of trencher-bread as an edible container for sauced foods. As C. Anne Wilson explains, "during the sixteenth and seventeenth centuries fish were still served upon sops." Several other elements mark Josselyn's recipe as a typical seventeenth-century English dish. The manchet, a small roll made of the finest quality wheat flour, the bottom of which was here used to flavor and thicken the wine and water broth, also stood on its own as a valued food in the mother country. The addition of this costly ingredient to the broth signaled that, although found in the colonies, these eels would be fit for consumption by genteel English persons.[40]

The emphasis on butter in the recipe—the "piece of sweet butter" in the broth as well as the sippets, which are pieces of bread fried in butter—reflected a new trend in English cuisine. Butter is ubiquitous in modern cooking, of course, but in Josselyn's time it was a novel flavoring. All in all then, Josselyn's colonial eel recipe had a thoroughly English pedigree. Its presence in New England amounted to evidence that while the colony might be an exotic place in many respects, it had already made considerable progress toward full concurrence with English norms.[41]

Eel recipes continued to find a prominent place in eighteenth-century English cookbooks, such as those of E. Smith, Hannah Glasse, and Susannah Carter. These English best-sellers attracted many readers in the American colonies.

Smith gave recipes for collared eels and roasted fresh eels. The recipe for collared eels, part of a section on preserved foods, was placed after a number of savory pies and before a recipe for potted lobster. The eels thus stood between dishes that could have graced a medieval banquet table and a dish that employed the newly stylish butter-preservation method. But in seasoning, the collared eels were more medieval than modern. They were to be sprinkled with sage, black pepper, nutmeg, and salt, then simmered in a broth of water, salt and pepper, cloves, mace, and bay leaf. After cooking, the eels were kept in a cold broth composed of yet more spices and their own bones. This was a common method of short-term preservation. The roasted fresh eels were coated with egg yolk, stuffed, and seasoned rather more lightly than the collared eels.[42]

Hannah Glasse included recipes for eel soup (soup was becoming popular as a distinct course) and, in the medieval savory pie tradition, eel pie, as well as traditional stewed eel, the newly popular potted eel, and "To pitchcock Eels," all within a section designated "For a Fast-Dinner, a Number of good Dishes, which you may make use of for a Table at any other Time." The almost three hundred recipes in this section bespoke a meatless fasting day tradition that was still very much alive and well, and the nine eel recipes indicated that eels remained a standard fast day choice.[43]

Susannah Carter's book was printed in Boston in 1772, with illustrations by Paul Revere. Her broiled eels were essentially Glasse's "pitchcocked" eels: seasoned with those medieval spices that remained in widespread use during the early modern period—mace, nutmeg, salt, and pepper; coated with breadcrumbs and butter; broiled; and served in a sauce of butter and anchovy, accompanied by a piece of lemon (lemon was also included in the seasoning). The butter in the sauce distinguished this recipe as an eighteenth-century creation, but the anchovies added a piquant flavor that would have pleased any early modern, or even ancient Roman, diner.[44]

As noted in the previous chapter, Anne Gibbons Gardiner's family manuscript recipe book was an example of the particularly marked imitation of English ways among wealthy colonial merchants and gentry. Ninety of Gardiner's 225 recipes have been attributed to Hannah Glasse, fifty to another well-known English author, Elizabeth Raffald. Gail Weesner states that "nowhere in these pages does one find even the slightest hint of an emerging national American cookery."[45]

Weesner allows that in the section on fish and fish sauces, which comprised close to one-third of the manuscript, there was a higher quotient of original recipes. This serves as "a reminder that Massachusetts was a seafaring colony and that the fruits of the sea were an important part of the regional diet." The fruits of the muddy rivers and marshes were apparently also important, for Mrs. Gardiner included a number of eel dishes.[46]

In one stewed eel recipe, the directions simply to "add a little Spice," then finish "with some small Herbs and Chives [and] Butter rolled in Flour" indicated a typically mild, eighteenth-century dish. But another version of stewed eel reflected the older, more strongly seasoned style: "put in a small Onion stuck with Cloves," and tied in a muslin rag, "a little bundle of sweet herbs, a blade of Mace, and some whole Pepper." Gardiner's eel pie called for cut up eels, pepper, salt, "a little beaten Mace," and water. It was to be baked in "a good Crust," which by this time meant an edible paste, as opposed to the medieval hard shell (sometimes called a "coffin") that had served primarily as a preservative container.[47]

With directions for "how to choose the best in market," Amelia Simmons seemed to expect most readers to purchase rather than to fish for the eels they would consume. Nevertheless, she still wanted them to know how to catch the best eels, should they choose to do so. For most fresh fish, such as those "noble pan fish" the perch and roach, she advised that "the deeper the water from whence taken, the finer are their flavors." For eels, however, she declared that those captured in the shallows, "from muddy bottoms," were the ones that were "best to jump in the pan." The glossary to a modern edition of Simmons's cookbook explains "jump in the pan" as "a characteristic action of eels while in the process of cooking."[48]

Such vigorous activity was also characteristic of live eels. The "Boston Housekeeper," Mrs. Lee, asserted that the best live eels were "quite fresh, full of life, and 'as brisk as an eel.'" (She seems to have had no qualms about figurative redundancy.)[49]

The first edition of Amelia Simmons's cookbook had included no recipes for eels, and next to none for other fish as well. In Lee's pages, three decades later, American eel cookery remained derivative of English practice. We find the standard English methodology of baking, boiling, collaring, frying, potting, stewing, spitchcocking, and placing in a pie crust. Lee apparently learned about spitchcocking from French rather than English sources: "this the French cooks call the English way of dressing eels." The process she described was indisputably English, with the eels set high on a gridiron over a "clear fire" until they were "of a fine crisp brown." Mrs. Lee, as we shall see, often applied a patina of additional refinement, in this case by frenchification, to a recipe.[50]

In the middle of the nineteenth century, luminaries of American domestic economy such as Catharine Beecher and Sarah Josepha Hale, as well as lesser known authors, continued to include eel recipes in their cookbooks. Mrs. A. L. Webster, in *The Improved Housewife*, offered boiled, broiled, and baked eels, although these recipes constituted the tail of her fish section. They still won a place before shellfish, however. It would be almost the next century before the tables were turned and shellfish took precedence over fish.

Mrs. Webster's eel dishes were almost devoid of spices. The strong, spicy, salty flavors of the Middle Ages, which lingered in early modern mixtures of mace, nutmeg, pepper, and anchovies, had just about disappeared. In "To

Boil Eels," she recommended cooking in salted water and serving with a simple parsley and drawn butter sauce. Her broiled eels were a close cousin to the classic spitchcock, utilizing egg yolk and breadcrumbs. Although the fish in this recipe were not grilled on a gridiron, a dripping pan produced virtually identical results. The term broiling, once interchangeable with grilling, was now used exclusively. Perhaps it sounded more refined to nineteenth-century ears. The colorful if slightly vulgar term spitchcock had also disappeared. Along with the traditional breading, the eels were dressed only with "pepper, salt, and sage" (no amounts were given, although the offhand instruction might imply light seasoning), and they were served with the same simple parsley-butter sauce as above. The overall impression was of a modern fish dish.[51]

Contemporaneous with Webster but still adhering to the older style of eel cookery, with its distinct spicing and a classic repertoire of recipes, was Ann H. Allen. Noting that "eels are fine fried," she also offered recipes for them in a pie, spitchcocked (which she gave as "spilchrock"), and collared. The recipe for cold collared eels, with its liberal use of herbs and spices and its unsqueamish retention of the eel skin, follows:

> Bone a large eel, but do not skin it; mix pepper, salt, mace, pimento, and a clove or two, in the finest powder, and rub over the whole inside; roll it tight, and bind it with a tape. Boil it in salt and water till done; then add vinegar, and, when cold, keep the collar in pickle. Serve whole, or in slices, garnished with parsley. Chopped sage, parsley, thyme, knotted marjoram, and summer savory, mixed with the spices, greatly improve the taste.[52]

Catharine Beecher devoted little space to eels, with only one dish, "To Cook Eels," placed at the end of the fish section, after oysters and lobsters, although still before the lowly scallops and clams. Her brief recipe bespoke inattention: "Dress them, lay them open flat, rub them with salt and pepper, cut them in short pieces, and broil them. Small ones are best skinned and fried." The long Anglo-American history of favoring eels was winding down.[53]

Before the end, however, Sarah Josepha Hale entered the discussion with a thoroughly modern concern for the eels themselves: "Eels should be alive and brisk in movement when they are purchased, but the 'horrid barbarity,' as it is truly designated, of skinning and dividing them while they are so, is without excuse." She proposed an alternative: "they are easily destroyed 'by piercing the spinal marrow close to the back part of the skull with a sharp pointed knife or skewer. If this be done in the right place all motion will instantly cease.' We quote Dr. Kitchener's assertion on this subject . . . boiling water also will immediately cause vitality to cease, and is perhaps the most humane and ready method of destroying the fish."[54]

Hale's call for humane slaughtering echoed the overall moral tone of her book. For example, in explaining why she included "a greater variety of receipts for preparing *Fish, Vegetables, and Soups*," she cited "the large and increasing class of persons in our country who abstain from flesh meats during Lent." Of course, the recipes would also be useful "to all families during the hot season." Continuing in this open-minded vein, she proclaimed: "As our Republic is made up from the people of all lands, so we have gathered the best receipts from the Domestic Economy of the different nations of the Old World; emigrants from each country will, in this 'New Book of Cookery,' find the method of preparing their favorite dishes."[55]

Regarding edible matter from the oceans, Hale lived up to her claim. Her fish chapter, which spanned twenty pages and was followed by a five-page shellfish chapter, included a full page on eels. She also gave some shopping tips: "when in high condition [eels] have a bright, glossy appearance on the back, and brilliant white on the belly. Unless eels weigh at least half a pound in weight [*sic*], they are hardly worth purchasing." After cleaning, gutting, and skinning, the head and tail were to be removed and the remaining meaty portion cut "into short pieces of 3 to 4 inches in length, and left for an hour or two in salt water."[56]

In Hale's four eel recipes — boiled, fried, broiled, and stewed "the French way" — only the last involved the high spicing once common to eel dishes. Even here, the "few peppercorns, cloves, and a little salt" and the "cream flavored with a grate of nutmeg" were hardly up to the level of those robust medieval preparations. Eels had themselves become a seasoning: "a gravy should be got ready, to be made in the following manner: — Take out all the bones, cut off the heads and tails [of the fish], and, if this should not be sufficient, add an eel, or any small common fish."[57]

The popularity of eels waned as other inexpensive sources of protein, including canned fish, became available. But they remained quotidian fare well into the nineteenth century. On Cape Cod in 1849, Henry David Thoreau was served "eels, buttermilk cake, cold bread, green beans, doughnuts, and tea" for breakfast by the wife of a Wellfleet oysterman. After careful observation of the way in which the oysterman had ejected "his tobacco-juice right and left into the fire . . . without regard to the various dishes which were there preparing," both Thoreau and his traveling companion declined the eels.[58]

At the end of the century, Fannie Farmer disapproved of eels. Perhaps appropriately (in view of her name), Farmer had reservations about all fish: "Fish meat, with but few exceptions, is less stimulating and nourishing than meat of other animals." These concerns became a flat-out prohibition when it came to eels, which "should not be eaten by those of weak digestion." She offered only one recipe for fried eel, in which two-inch pieces were dipped in cornmeal and fried in pork fat. It was still the old spitchcock.[59]

By 1912, eels barely made it into Helen S. Wright's self-consciously traditional *The New England Cook Book*. But her one recipe was also for spitchcocked eels, fillets dipped in egg and cracker crumbs and fried in lard.[60]

Perhaps the best among the crop of nostalgic twentieth-century Yankee cookbooks was Imogene Wolcott's *The New England Yankee Cook Book*. (In Yankee style, many of these cookbooks had titles so unadorned that they were interchangeable.) Reminiscences were scattered throughout Wolcott's book. As part of a recipe for cornmeal-coated fried eels (a final gasp from the spitchcock tradition, taken from Norma Roberts of Bristol, New Hampshire, who attributed it to her grandmother), Wolcott offered another reason for the absence of the eel from the New England table: "Eels . . . were barred from many rivers years ago by impassable dams. In the early fall eels used to migrate up the rivers and were taken by means of sluiceways that ran into an 'eel pot.' Hauls of a hundred or more at night were not uncommon at the time of the year when they returned. At Amoskeag they were taken in such numbers that they became known as 'Derryfield Beef' after the old name for Manchester, N.H." The damming of rivers was essential to the growth of industry in New England but deadly for eels, salmon, and other migratory fish.[61]

Eel consumption had become a historical curiosity. This interview with an elderly Connecticut River fisherman in the early twentieth century indicated that even among rural people the love affair with eels had run its course: "When I go past a house where they're cookin' shad I can tell by the smell whether it's spawned. If they're cookin' eels I hold my nose till I get by. Yes, eels are pretty bad to my smeller. People say they are good eatin', but they ain't good for me."[62]

Clams

Though not an English mollusk, the clam was sufficiently similar to the English mussel and cockle to be readily adopted into the colonists' diet. On occasion, it was even admired. As William Wood reported, there were particularly large specimens that "would bee in good esteeme amongst the English." Mostly, however, the English sentiment—indeed the sentiment for the next two centuries among the English in New England—was that there were invariably "better fish" than clams.[63]

As the uncomplimentary remarks of John Winthrop and Edward Johnson indicate, clam-eating was associated with the deprivations of the early years of settlement and with occasional years of scarcity thereafter. In his early-eighteenth-century account of those first years, Cotton Mather too relegated clams to the lowest echelons when he complained that "the only food the poor had was acorns, ground-nuts, mussels, and clams."[64]

For the most part, then, a perception brought over from England that "except among very poor and backward groups of people shellfish were usually only a subsidiary source of food" predominated in the New England attitude toward clams, despite the more favorable tradition in which "shell fish were ... highly regarded as food and some traditional techniques for procurement when available from surrounding waters were a part of every husbandman's cultural repertory."[65]

There were practical reasons why there was little enthusiasm for shellfish. On the simplest grounds, the settlers, coming mostly from the middle levels of European society, would have considered a hardship any diet that relied exclusively on one food, if only seasonally. Also, while they employed Indians as shellfish gatherers, the English were sometimes forced to collect this resource themselves, and this was no easy task. Obtaining enough shellfish to sustain a family was exhausting work. Diana Muir points out just how thoroughly fantastic was William Wood's prospect of gathering clams by dancing a jig: "Remember that it takes four or five hundred oysters or quahogs to feed a family for a day, and that thousands more had to be gathered and dried over smoky fires in the hot summer sun for winter food. Stoop-labor. Sweaty, muddy, back-breaking, and often plagued by horseflies." This was a different proposition from buying cockles in the town market or harvesting mussels from local waters every so often as a supplement to the basic family food supply.[66]

Furthermore, procurement of shellfish in both settler and Indian society was largely women's work. William Wood's dancing squaw and Edward

Johnson's desperate female harvesters are both reminders of the gendered dimension of shellfish acquisition. According to one archaeologist, the "widely recognized identification of women with shellfishing . . . is responsible [in part] for the common reputation of shellfish and molluscs as a low priority foodstuff."[67]

Finally, the Indian enthusiasm for clams undoubtedly lowered their value in English eyes. All along the New England shoreline, from present-day Connecticut to Maine, Indian clam banks were, as we have noted, marked by great piles, or middens, of shells, sometimes centuries old, unmistakable evidence that clams were Indian food.[68]

However, such evidence of Indian clam consumption, and even of Indian feasting on clams, does not constitute evidence of the existence of any Indian tradition of the clambake as we understand that festival. Kathy Neustadt has demonstrated that, although it contained Indian elements, the Yankee clambake was not a direct descendant of any particular Indian ritual. It suited the Yankee participants in the eighteenth-century commemorative feasts that foreshadowed the clambake, such as the Plymouth Forefathers' Day banquets noted in chapters 1 and 2, to believe that the Indians had taught their ancestors about festive shellfish cookery. The clambake's development in the nineteenth century incorporated this romanticized view of the history of English-Indian relations.[69]

It was during the eighteenth century that the clam began to escape its old associations for the colonists and to assume a new identity as an agreeable food. But the process was a slow one. In 1720 the clam still represented the lean years of New England's founding, for in the "century festival" held at Plymouth that year, the meal consisted of "first a Wooden Dish of Indian Corn and Clams to represent how our Fathers fed in 1620, then an elegant Dinner to shew 1720." By the 1740s, however, Hannah Glasse could, as Kathy Neustadt notes, "include the clam within the edible and enjoyable category." After another two decades, with the founding in Plymouth of the Old Colony Club and the inauguration of the Forefathers' Day banquet, clams had secured a place within a key New England commemorative festival, placed on par with venison, apple pie, eels, and oysters.[70]

So the clam was becoming a symbol not of the scarcity of the early years but rather of the natural abundance that fed the revered founders. "In honor to the ancestors of the country, who were fed with clams, and other bounties of the sea, they called [the Forefathers' Day meal] a *feast of shells*," wrote one Boston journalist in 1806. In fact, many different seashells "were being incorporated regularly in physical as well as symbolic form in American commemorative celebrations by the end of the eighteenth century." The symbolic use of shells can be traced to medieval Catholic Europe, where the scallop shell became an emblem of pilgrimage to the supposed tomb of Saint James of Compostela in Spain. Now in Protestant North America, seashells were also doing service as symbols, this time in honor of Puritan saints. Because the clam shell is rather small and undistinguished, the more decorative and larger scallop and oyster shells often took its place. A particularly flamboyant example of the fad was the 1799 Forefathers' Day feast in Plymouth, where "a shell of uncommon size"—that of an oyster, weighing two hundred pounds—"adorned the head of the table." Even more evocative of cultural ripeness was the point during the 1820 Plymouth bicentennial when "at the ball in the evening some young ladies hung a shell suitably decorated on the breast of Mr. [Daniel] Webster, the orator of the day."[71]

The shell had thus become the symbol of the American cornucopia. By the unlikely marriage of a traditional Catholic icon and a traditional Indian food, two negative associations magically canceled each other out and a new Yankee symbol was born. In this era of American civic fervor, there was little place for the clam's earlier role as a reminder of lean Puritan beginnings.

As the nineteenth century progressed, the new notion of shellfish, especially clams, as symbols of bounty and celebration took firmer hold. By 1840, clams were established in their role as stars of the clambake. The political cast of these public feasts is recounted by Kathy Neustadt: "In his *Dictionary of Americanisms*, Bartlett recorded that 'the greatest feast of the kind that ever took place in New England' was 'that of a grand political mass-meeting in favor of General [and subsequently President William Henry] Harrison on the 4th of July, 1840[;] nearly 100,000 people assembled in Rhode Island . . . [and] a clambake and chowder were prepared.'"[72]

Somewhat earlier in the century, as new editions of English cookbooks took their lead from Amelia Simmons's *American Cookery* and began to include recipes for distinctly American products, clam recipes appeared alongside others firmly associated with American cuisine, such as pumpkin pie, squash, and maple. Clams were entering the cuisine in chowders, soups, stews, and pies.[73]

But clams also retained older associations with simple sustenance and were still eaten as inexpensive everyday fare. In 1829 Lydia Maria Child presented them in this way. One of her recipes, for boiled clams, amounted to nothing but clams and a spoonful of water. Another, for stewed clams, was only slightly more embellished, calling for the addition of flour and water to thicken the clam broth and the customary "dozen slices of toasted bread

"How New Englanders Eat Clams," sketched by J. Becker, in "Rhode Island—Rocky Point—the New England Veterans' Clambake," Frank Leslie's Illustrated Newspaper, *16 August 1873. (Courtesy Fall River Public Library)*

or cracker" upon which to serve them. We have seen this remnant of the medieval practice of serving "thin pottages . . . poured over 'brewes' or sops" before, in John Josselyn's seventeenth-century dish of eels.[74]

As Child's recipes illustrate, the lingering notion that clams were for poor people, poor times, or frugal living was hard to shake. Sandra L. Oliver sums up Sarah Anna Emery's observations as a resident of the fishing village and mill town of Newburyport, Massachusetts: "in the early nineteenth century, raw, whole, and cooked clams were peddled through the streets[,] and . . . they 'were considered a plebeian dish, from which many persons turned in disgust.'" One reason for such disgust may have been the continued use of clams as bait for cod and haddock.[75]

On the other hand, the linkage between clams and New England historical pieties that had been developing in Forefathers' Day observances began to trickle down into cookbooks by the 1830s. Mrs. Lee reported that "the pilgrims to Plymouth, it is said, could cook this shell fish and lobsters in nearly fifty different ways, and even as puddings, pancakes, &c."[76]

Catharine Beecher included clams in her 1846 cookbook, but only after a long section on the more desirable halibut, bass, blackfish, shad, mackerel, sturgeon, and traditional fish chowder. "To Cook Clams," in her recipe of that name, was to roast them. In Beecher's clam soup recipe, spices were first added and then, in a surprising but modern twist, subtracted: "two and a half spoonfuls of flour, worked into three of butter, with pepper, mace, and other spices to your taste. It is better without spice."[77] The styling of clams as an American political specialty and a classic New England dish was not yet apparent in Beecher, but there were hints of things to come in her call for minimal seasoning. Such an emphasis on plain-style cooking would be taken up by later promoters of New England as an expression of regional values.[78]

Mrs. Webster offered more clam recipes than Beecher. She concurred with Beecher about roasting: it was a "superior mode of cooking" clams. She also told how to "Pot Clams" and how to make "Clam Pancakes" and "Long Clams." For roasting, her advice was to "place them flatwise in an old tin or iron pan, so as to save the liquor, and set the pan over a furnace of ignited coal," after which "empty the liquor into your dish, then take out and add the clam, either cut in pieces or whole; add butter, salt and pepper; other seasoning to taste." Note that "a furnace of ignited coal," that is, a cookstove, had begun to replace open hearth cooking.[79]

Webster's recipes gave other indications of the modern spirit. Like Beecher, she made little use of spices. Her pot clams were not potted in the earlier preserved sense but rather steamed in a pot. After being opened, they were removed and served simply "with a little of the liquor, butter, salt and pepper." Then, "to a slice or two of toasted bread, soaked in the clam liquor, add the clams." The trenchers, manchets, sops, and sippets of earlier centuries had become the nineteenth century's ubiquitous toast.[80]

At the end of one of Webster's brief clam recipes was the caveat that "clams and oysters generally agree with those who like them. Lobsters may form an exception." Thus did suspicions about the suitability of shellfish linger.[81]

In keeping with old-fashioned tastes, fish chowders and stewed oysters were still in the ascendant in the 1881 *Aunt Mary's New England Cook Book*, penned anonymously and attributed to "a New England Mother." The double dose of familial identifiers in title and authorship is matched by the double use of New England on the title page; both were useful strategies for convincing the buying public of the book's sentimental value. (We shall discuss this motif further in chapter 7.) But for Aunt/Mother Mary, clams were still tangential to New England cooking. For example, her stewed clams recipe used an oyster dish as its point of reference: "Stew same as oysters, with less liquor." That was the entire recipe.[82]

A decade later, clams were featured in their own right in *Godey's Lady's Book and Magazine*. A recipe for "Soft Steamed Clams" presented a brick placed inside a saucepan of boiling water as the key to success. The clams, served in their shells, were to be accompanied by a modern sauce "composed of a little chopped onion, a little melted butter, salt, pepper, and the juice of a lemon."[83]

By the turn of the century, clams were undergoing more refined preparations. Mary J. Lincoln and Anna Barrows proposed in 1902 that steamed clams be served "hot or cold in cups with a garnish of whipped cream." They also saw fit to scallop clams and to use them as bouillon.[84]

The improvement in the clam's reputation, aided by the invention of the clambake tradition, coincided with the consolidation of various foods and preparations into a self-consciously regional Yankee cuisine. Whatever her Puritan forebears might have thought of them, by 1896 Fannie Merritt Farmer was thus able to say that "soft-shell clams are dear to the New Englander."[85]

As with the clambake, the promotion of a regional cuisine made a perfect fit with the emerging leisure and tourism industries. Food nostalgia was, in turn, aided by the publication throughout the first half of the twentieth century of a number of New England travelogues. In this vein, Hildegarde Hawthorne, rambling with her sister in 1916, reported this episode: "[In Beverly, Massachusetts,] hunger assailed us . . . and we found a place that advertised seafood and there lunched on a magnificent tureenful of steamed clams. 'There are places in this world where you can not get steamed clams,' I told Sister, 'and yet people live in them.' 'Exist!' We finished our clams in happy silence."[86]

No sooner had the clam fully arrived in polite society than the process of changing its history to improve its pedigree got underway. In the sentimental preface to *The New England Cook Book* of 1912, Helen S. Wright evoked the spirit of her Yankee ancestors by cataloging some of their possessions, which she claimed to have found in the proverbial old trunk in the attic. Wright seemed to fall into a trance when she encountered "the aroma of her [ancestor's] spice bag . . . sweet lavender and thyme . . . lace mitts and pattens . . . wedding-gown of softest muslin." And, naturally, "there is a book of recipes."[87]

Thus when we get to Wright's own recipes, we are to assume that they carried with them the imprimatur of the Yankee past. It is significant then that clams made an early appearance in her fish and shellfish section. Preceded only by fish consommé was "Clam Purée" and "New England Clam Chowder." The purée was essentially a rich chowder, using 1½ pints of cream, butter, water, flour, and breadcrumbs. The chowder, although in a butter and flour sauce, included tomatoes but omitted cream. We will discuss chowders, including clam chowders, at greater length below. Suffice it to say at this point that the inclusion of these two recipes indicated Wright's promotion of the clam as part of the New England dietary legacy.[88]

In the 1930s, Yankee culture was proclaiming itself, as seen in Wilbur L. Cross's preface to Imogene Wolcott's nostalgic cookbook: "Whence cometh the strength, physical and intellectual, of New Englanders?" In view of his chosen genre, Cross found the answer, unsurprisingly, in food. "It has come, along with their famous conscience, from the natural and sane diet which, except for the first hard years at Plymouth, has contained all the vitamins essential to sound bodies and sound minds," he wrote, sounding much like a Wonder Bread commercial. As for those first hard years, the Pilgrims managed with "mussels along the shore," and clams and oysters, which these hardy pioneers "soon discovered . . . in the waters of this paradise of the New World." No credit was given to their Indian tutors. The intervening centuries were easily elided: "oyster stew has since become a New England dish. . . . Most famous of all is clam chowder, without which no Friday dinner can be complete."[89]

There is no evidence, however, of clam chowder Fridays as a New England tradition. The Puritans sometimes selected Thursday as a day for religious observances, such as thanksgivings, in order to distance themselves from the Anglican church calendar's meatless Fridays, and possibly also because they considered Thursday, the day of the Last Supper, more biblical. Cross's clam chowder Fridays were a reversion to medieval fast day practices that Pilgrims and Puritans would have disliked.[90]

Cross's truncated retelling of New England history was offered to show the continuity of Yankee cuisine. The legacy of clam-eating moved seamlessly from "the first hard years at Plymouth" directly to Wolcott's array of clam recipes, many of which sounded like miniature New England travelogues: "Clam Chowder, Copley-Plaza" (Wolcott called for three quarts of "Duxbury" clams, although she gave no explanation for their superiority), "Rhode Island Clam Chowder," "Martha's Vineyard Quahog Fritters," and "Deep Sea Clam Pie (Cape Cod Style)." The clam now marked out a suitable pilgrimage to the holy places of Yankee heritage.[91]

Clams had been transformed from despised food into symbols of Yankee self-proclamation, even though, as Sandra L. Oliver points out, clams were "a recreational shellfish," appropriate for clambakes and other casual affairs, and not a "food to offer guests at an important meal." But perhaps it was precisely because clams were associated with informality that they managed to climb the social ladder. The ascendancy of the casual is so complete in American culture that it is difficult for us to appreciate the sense of freedom that Victorians felt at open-air occasions such as clambakes. However, the glorification of plainness was not accomplished without effort. To assist in its transformation from a necessity to a virtue, a Pilgrim clam lineage was invented.[92]

Chowder

We all know what ingredients go into making a chowder. Or do we? Is it best to begin with cod, haddock, clams, lobster, or scallops? For the broth, do we use water and flour, cod's head liquor, or fish stock? And how much broth is best — only a little to moisten the dry ingredients, or enough to make the solids swim? Is milk or cream added to the broth? Flour or crackers? Do we put the crackers in to thicken the chowder, or do we serve them alongside? Are potatoes essential? If added, should they be sliced and placed in alternating layers with fish and onions or diced and scattered throughout the liquid to cook? Should we put in salt pork? And what about tomatoes, that source of much contention in chowder debates? At different times and in different locales throughout New England, all of these ingredients have been endorsed by some, while others have as strenuously opposed their entry into the chowder bowl.[93]

The story of chowder is one of development, change, and cultural borrowing cloaked in a popular mythology that gives the dish a timeless air and a purer Anglo-American provenance than it deserves. Dip your ladle into the history of New England chowder, and you are apt to come up with French, English, Basque, and Celtic fishermen, medieval European cooks, a reversal in popularity between fish and seafood, perhaps a few Indian elements, and even one ingredient — the potato — that traveled from the New World to the Old and back again before arriving in the chowder pot via Scots-Irish immigrants.

The English word "chowder" probably derives from *chaudière*, cauldron, and from the name for a fisherman's stew, *la chaudrée*. The stew itself originated in sixteenth- and seventeenth-century Brittany, from whence it traveled to the coasts of England, Wales, and Ireland, and on to the European

North Atlantic fishing fleets. From the fishing camps of Newfoundland, Nova Scotia, and Maine it was but a short trip to New Brunswick and down the coast to the rest of New England.[94]

While the dish, as well as the pot in which it was cooked, undoubtedly originated in France, similar stewed fish preparations appeared independently on the other side of the channel at about the same time. According to a fifteenth-century manuscript, a dish made by English cooks involved "an haddock or codling" that was cooked in a "sauce of water and salt." By that time in England, the practice of "boiling or poaching fish was common." Sandra L. Oliver notes that a variation on the word chowder appeared in Cornwall as early as the mid-sixteenth century.[95]

As for its arrival in New England, chowder "need not have spread to New England from anywhere," Oliver asserts, "but could have come directly here with fishermen settlers." Indeed, a dish that made the most of ship's stores and ocean products—"hardtack[,] . . . salt pork, salt fish, and possibly some onions and other root vegetables"—could have arrived in coastal regions via many routes.[96]

While there is no direct evidence of an Indian contribution to the chowder pot, the workaday chowders of the European banks fishermen were similar to succotash when it included fish. Colin Calloway describes an exchange of fishing techniques and skills, amounting to "an amalgamation of Indian and European strategies for procuring and processing the region's maritime resources," that took place at "early fishing stations." It is at least possible that fish cooking techniques were also exchanged.[97]

Centuries later, in 1950s New England, the story had come full circle when Eleanor Early described chowder-making as she imagined it was practiced by the first settlers at Plymouth: "In Pilgrim days, women tossed whatever edibles were at hand (usually codfish and corn) into a pot called a *chaudière*." Early's remarks about Plymouth settler practice amounted to an unacknowledged description of the typical "standing dish" of the seventeenth-century New England natives, as we heard Daniel Gookin describe it in chapter 1: "generally boiled maize . . . mixed with kidney beans, or sometimes without. Also they frequently boil in this pottage fish and flesh of all sorts."[98]

By the middle of the eighteenth century, chowder, like clams, had lost its early ties to subsistence and become leisure fare. For example, a recipe was published in a Boston newspaper in 1751. In May 1760 the Reverend Ebenezer Parkman of Westborough, Massachusetts, in Boston for the annual elections, ministerial convention, and Harvard Commencement, was invited by "a number of Gentlemen & Ladies" to cruise Boston Harbor "in a Convenient Boat." After sailing out to the lighthouse and taking tea there, the party "re-embark'd—Eat our Chowder 'o board [aboard] in good order—returnd & landed just after nine at Eve."[99]

The subsequent inclusion of chowder in Hannah Glasse's standard cookbook, as well as its appearance in the second edition of Amelia Simmons's *American Cookery*, further reflected the way in which the dish had entered the culinary canon, as leisure food for the elite but also as proper sustenance for those "who could afford little meat" or who were simply interested in frugality.[100]

Typical of the practical chowders was Lydia Maria Child's substantial recipe—four pounds of fish to serve four or five people. She used the standard technique of first coating the bottom of the kettle with the fat that was "tried out" when salt pork was fried, then removing the pork pieces and alternately layering fish, crackers, sliced or small onions, and sliced potatoes, dotting the ingredients throughout with the fried pork, and seasoning with salt and pepper. To this dense combination she added a "bowl-full of flour and water, enough to come up even with the surface of what you have in the pot." Clams were merely an agreeable addition, as was a cup of "tomato catsup" or a cup of beer. In 1829 Child was still preparing her chowder in a kettle hung over a hearth fire, and she recommended that the cook "hang it high, so that the pork may not burn." Her recipe differed from other fish chowders of the time in its emphasis on steaming rather than boiling: "It should be covered so as not to let a particle of steam escape, if possible." Otherwise, it was virtually identical to any number of early-nineteenth-century fish chowders.[101]

So too (except for the omission of potatoes) was a chowder offered by Prudence Smith at about the same time. This milkless fish pottage Smith dubbed "New England Chowder":

Have a good haddock, cod, or any other solid fish, cut it in pieces three inches square, put a pound of fat salt pork in strips into the pot, set it on hot coals, and fry out the oil. Take out the pork and put in a layer of fish, over that a layer of onions in slices, then a layer of fish with slips of fat salt pork, then another layer of onions, and so on alternately until your fish is consumed. Mix some flour with as much water as will fill the pot, season with black pepper and salt to your taste, and boil it for half an hour.

Have ready some crackers soaked in water till they are a little softened; throw them into your chowder five minutes before you take it up. Serve in a tureen.[102]

In her first chowder recipe, Mrs. Lee displayed her usual high style and Anglophilia by paraphrasing Hannah Glasse's "Chouder." The recipe called for "thin slices of cod between pieces of pork belly," rather than the chunks of fish interspersed with salt pork scraps in more common chowders. The mixture was layered with sliced onions, then strewn with "sweet herbs" and covered with water. She put "a paste over the whole," before baking it for four hours "with fire above as well as below." Disdaining a chowder pot, Lee slow-baked her chowder in a stewpan. Before serving, she poured a glass of hot Madeira over it, then garnished it with stewed mushrooms, truffles, and oysters. Little of the soon-to-be-ascendant New England plain style was in evidence here.[103]

Lee's "Chowder for Ten or Twelve" was her bow to convention, a recipe virtually identical to Child's and Smith's. Lee made it clear that such simple fare was most appropriate for recreational occasions: "this Receipt is according to the most approved method, practised by fishing parties in Boston harbor." Her clam chowder was essentially the same recipe with clams substituted for cod.[104]

Despite its association with leisure dining, a decade after Lee published her work, chowder had become a standard dinner item in cookbooks. Only two issues remained: what type of fish was best, and what enrichments were to be added. Prudence Smith had begun her "New England Chowder" with "a good haddock, cod, or any other solid fish." Mrs. Webster asserted that "cod and bass make the best chowder," although she conceded that clams, and even blackfish, were "tolerably good." Catharine Beecher preferred haddock or bass. Webster, like Child, called for "a tumbler of wine, catsup, and spices," which would "improve" the chowder. In Beecher, this became "mushroom catsup and Port wine."[105]

The general similarity of these recipes indicates the emergence of a standard nineteenth-century New England chowder, one that was considerably thicker than our soupy modern variety. By midcentury, milk was occasionally being added, although it did not become a standard chowder ingredient until later in the century. Instead, it was treated like beer or wine as an enrichment, or, as in Mrs. Howland's "Chowder for Invalids," as medicinal.[106]

The subsistence world of pottages and standing dishes had become one in which more and more people were apt to participate in parties and picnics. Thus, although not all chowders were for leisure times, leisure times were for chowders. Sandra Oliver writes that "by the mid-nineteenth century, the word 'picnic' meant chowder party in some parts of coastal New England."[107]

Chowder now also began to appear in a sentimental light in fiction and memoirs. Harriet Beecher Stowe portrayed a romantic chowder party in her 1862 novel, *The Pearl of Orr's Island*, which was set in earlier nineteenth-century coastal Maine. In this story, the jaunty Captain Kittridge, cajoling the heroine out of a glum mood, suggested an impromptu chowder party, featuring in this instance a clam chowder: "Come, little Mara, get on your sun-bonnet. . . . we're goin' to dig some clams, and make a fire, and have a chowder; that'll be nice, won't it." His daughter Sally, the workaday counterpoint to the refined Mara, dug the clams, after which "the Captain leisurely proceeded to open the clams, separating from the shells the contents, which he threw into a pan, meanwhile placing a black pot over the fire in which he had previously arranged certain slices of salt pork, which soon began frizzling in the heat. 'Now, Sally, you peel them potatoes, and mind you slice 'em thin,' he said, and Sally soon was busy with her work." A bit later it was time to eat: "each one, receiving a portion of the savory stew in a large shell, made a spoon of a small cockle, and with some slices of bread and butter, the evening meal went off merrily."[108]

Genteel English travelers wryly expatiating on American customs constituted a major literary genre in the nineteenth century. Things American could also furnish amusement if the traveling transpired in the opposite direction and an American ventured into England. A case in point was Caroline Howard King's tale of "the semi-tragic experience of a friend of mine apropos of chowder." King's friend, Emelyn Story, was staying at a castle in the north of England, "when one morning, as the ladies of the party were sitting together, the conversation turned on different kinds of cookery. . . . 'We hear so much of your delicious American dishes, Mrs. Story,'" the hostess said. "'Is there not one, peculiar to your country, of which you could give the receipt to my housekeeper, and which could be made here?'" Rashly, the houseguest "mentioned 'chowder' as a fish soup belonging especially to New England. The ladies were interested at once. 'Chowder,' they repeated, 'how charmingly Indian that sounds!'"

Mrs. Story was prevailed upon to instruct the housekeeper in making the dish for dinner that evening. Although her chowders had been "praised and admired at her cottage at Nahant," when faced with the housekeeper's "contemptuous English face" she could only repeat the recipe "as well as she could." The housekeeper sniffed, "I will do my best, Mrs. Story, but I cannot think it will be nice."

At dinnertime, the gathered company excitedly awaited what they mistakenly labeled "a true Indian Dish." But they too were wondering, "Can it be nice?" The chowder that was served that evening was far from nice, made with freshwater fish from the estate's pond, soft bread, thick slices of ham, and whole onions, the entire mess boiled in milk. Only one gallant gentleman attempted a second spoonful, but Mrs. Story released him from his social duty, saying "Oh, General B., don't try to eat this horrible stuff, it is not in the least like a chowder."

The next day, the American lady attempted to explain the making of a real fish chowder to the English ladies, but the only response from her hostess was satisfied condescension: "I fancy it would always be difficult to reproduce an Indian dish in England, I have no doubt the chowder would be excellent in your own country." The American gave the whole subject up for lost, realizing that it would "be useless to try to enlighten her as to the Indian side of the question."[109]

In the late 1880s, before Cape Cod had been "'discovered' as a summer playground," the young A. Hyatt Verrill lived in the port town of Woods Hole, where there was "usually a whaling vessel or two, or several Banks fishing schooners, moored to the docks." Among the old salts who haunted the port was the improbably named Captain Finny, now retired, who nevertheless kept "a fully equipped whale boat moored to his little ramshackle wharf. . . . And when, on rare occasions, we would see the Captain removing the tarpaulin from his whale boat and stepping its mast, we knew that a fish chowder was about to be evolved."

The captain "regarded making a fish chowder as an almost holy rite and surrounded it with all the ceremony of a sacred feast." First, he went "sailing away down the Sound" to catch the fish for his chowder. Upon his return, "from somewhere among the old sails, oars and spars, coils of rope, tackle blocks and lobster pots, fish nets and miscellaneous maritime junk in his shed he would produce an enormous iron kettle," which, having probably first served for "b'ilin' ile" on a whaler's tryworks, now became the chowder kettle.

The young Verrill never did learn what went into the chowder, "for no one dared approach near enough to see." As the captain's nephew attested, "Unk's as tetchy as a bear with a sore head when he's a-makin' of a chowder." As one might guess, Verrill claimed that the end result of this mysterious process was sublimity itself: "Never, I am sure, were there such delectable fish chowders as those prepared with such rites and ceremonies by Captain Finny."

According to the formula for this type of story, these delicious chowders of old, like some magical dish once eaten on an enchanted isle, were no longer to be had anywhere on earth. Thus did Verrill conclude his 1936 recollection by decrying the hotel and summer cottages that had displaced the wonders of Finny and his chowder and destroyed "the Woods Hole of my boyhood." By now there are doubtless other accounts in which a new crop of old-timers reminisce in reverent tones about the hotel and cottages.[110]

By the early twentieth century, chowder recipes called for shellfish as often as fish. Both the fish and clam varieties might receive the "New England" designation, for example in a milkless fish version from 1905 and in a milkless clam chowder with both tomatoes and potatoes from 1912. These two cases were exceptions to the emerging norm that regional chowders should include milk, as in a fish chowder of 1905 made with haddock, potato, and a pint of milk; a lobster chowder from the same year made with milk and "six Boston crackers"; and a clam chowder with all of the standard ingredients (salt pork, onions, potatoes, pepper, and salt) and a teacup of milk.[111]

Around this time, Hildegarde Hawthorne was writing ecstatically about "the delectable seafood, [and] chowders" of the Central Hotel in Provincetown, Massachusetts, by then a vacation destination. Although the ingredients in the pot varied and the name New England was applied randomly, increasingly chowders were identified with the convention-breaking spirit of fishing and seafaring, now domesticated as seashore leisure times.[112]

By the third decade of the twentieth century, the practical associations of chowder had been subsumed within festive affiliations, and its unmannerly origins had been forgotten. Chowder could appear in church ladies' club cookbooks, as in the 1937 Thimble Club's "Fisherman's Chowder," or it could be marketed with greater sophistication, as in Imogene Wolcott's Nantucket scallop chowder and "Clam Chowder, Copley-Plaza." By this time, too, the clam had achieved primacy over fish in New England chowder. In his contribution to the Wolcott volume, "Yankee Doodle in a Kettle," Joseph C. Lincoln extolled one of Wolcott's recipes as "a genuine A No.1 New England clam chowder."[113]

The chowder pot had always been ingeniously adaptable. As potatoes made their way into American cuisine in the eighteenth century, they also made their way into the pot. As clams were canned in large numbers in New England in the latter part of the nineteenth century, they began to replace fish. Whether one had water, cod's head liquor, or milk; cod, haddock, bass, or clams; crackers, potatoes, or flour—with a little onion and salt pork it was possible to make a chowder.[114]

But perhaps the most ingenious combination in the chowder pot was that of New England images. On the one hand, there was the romantic notion of a "girl who lived near the sea [who] considered a chowder kettle as much a part of her 'setting out' as six patchwork quilts and a feather mattress." On the other hand, there was the rough-living North Atlantic fisherman, whether Basque, Celtic, English or Indian. The fisherman and the girl had been wed, as it were, in the myth that is New England chowder.[115]

Lobsters

In 1621 Edward Winslow reported to a friend back in England concerning the Plymouth settlement that "our Bay is full of Lobsters all the Summer." In Salem a few years later, Francis Higginson observed that "the least Boy in the Plantation may both catch and eat what he will of" lobsters. Lobsters were not only plentiful in early New England, they were large. Higginson reported some weighing twenty-five pounds.[116]

But lobsters were not always a welcome sight on early colonial tables. As noted above, in 1623 Governor Bradford complained of having only lobster to serve visitors, "without bread or anything else but . . . water." Early New Englanders would have been perplexed to find lobsters grouped, as they were by one twentieth-century writer, with caviar and filet mignon as foods that "carry high-status social cachet."[117]

No delicacy, American lobsters were nonetheless better received than many shellfish. They were soon being cooked much the same way as their smaller European counterparts, in sauces for other fish, or as accompaniments to roasts.[118]

Anne Gibbons Gardiner gave a recipe for "Fish Sauce with Lobster," to be served with salmon, turbot, broiled cod, or haddock: "To make the Lobster Sauce, Take a Lobster which has been boiled, bruse the Body in fine Butter melted thick, and cut the Flesh into little pieces. Stew it all together, and give it a Boil." If a richer sauce was desired, she suggested using half beef gravy to half lobster sauce. Beef and veal gravies often sauced fish. Of course, lobster sauce might also be used on lobster meat itself. Catharine Beecher provided an example, with a sauce consisting of vinegar, egg yolks, lobster spawn, mustard, salad oil, butter, salt, and pepper.[119]

Lobster could be potted, as another Gardiner recipe illustrated. The meat of the "Claws and Belly of a boiled Lobster" was pounded to a paste in a mortar with two blades of mace, a little white pepper, salt, and a lump of butter the customary "Size of an Egg." Half of this mixture was then put into a pot, the tail meat was added, the remaining lobster paste was used to cover it, and all was sealed with a quarter-inch of clarified butter.[120]

Forcemeat balls were featured in one of Mrs. Gardiner's two recipes for lobster pie. Consisting of lobster meat mixed with egg yolk, nutmeg, flour, pepper, and salt, the balls were browned in butter, put into a dish with oysters, anchovies, and more butter, baked, and finished with "a Layer of good rich Gravy."[121]

When not potting lobsters, baking them in pies, or using them in sauces, eighteenth- and nineteenth-century New England cooks were apt to stew or fricassee them. Both these methods, as applied to lobster, entailed simmering small pieces of meat in white wine or cream, seasoned with mace, cayenne, nutmeg, salt, and pepper.[122]

Boiled lobsters were served cold with dressing, not hot and "in the rough," as we are most likely to encounter them today. In the 1840s, Beecher and Webster both presented boiled lobster served in this fashion. Beecher's recipe was little more than a warning: "These must never be cooked after they are dead. Put them alive in boiling water, and boil them till the small joints come off easily." Webster recommended for both lobsters and crabs that they be eaten "cold with a dressing of vinegar, mustard, sweet oil, salt and cayenne."[123]

Perhaps because lobsters were congenial to Lydia Maria Child's emphasis on frugality, she had much to say about them. Although it appeared several years before Webster's and Beecher's, Child's recipe was more modern than theirs, amounting to a cold lobster salad, made with "hard" lettuce, the meat of one lobster, and a dressing of egg yolks, oil, vinegar, mustard, cayenne, and salt. The same novel treatment would work with chicken. By this time, lobsters were not to be had by the "least Boy." A trip to the market was necessary. Child gave tips for judging freshness: raise "the end of a lobster" with your hand, and if it "springs back hard and firm" it is fresh; "if they move flabbily, it is not a good omen."[124]

The American taste for lobster was on the rise. By 1842, Mrs. Webster could write: "It would be better for the health of those who do not labor, if they would use more fish and less flesh, for food. With the exception of salmon and lobsters, there is little danger, in our country, of this kind of aliment being taken to excess."[125]

When nineteenth-century canning methods, developed around 1840 and perfected during the Civil War, were redirected toward peacetime activities, lobsters were among the most popular canned products. By 1880, there were twenty-three lobster canneries in Maine. But increased regulation and limited supply brought an end to the canneries by the end of the century.[126]

Perhaps that was a good thing, if the observations made by Samuel Adams Drake during an 1875 visit to one cannery are to be given credence. Drake found that "a literally 'smashing' business was being carried on, but with an uncleanness that for many months impaired my predilection for this delicate crustacean. . . . Frequent boiling in the same water, with the slovenly appearance of the operatives, male and female, would suggest a doubt whether plain Penobscot lobster is as toothsome as is supposed." He maintained that "the whole process was in marked contrast with the scrupulous neatness with which similar operations are elsewhere conducted." One doubts that his readers were reassured.[127]

Nevertheless, lobsters were becoming ever more popular. Fresh lobsters, made more widely available by improved transportation, were increasingly preferred. In 1896 Fannie Farmer included two pages on this emerging delicacy in her famous *Boston Cooking-School Cook Book*. "Lobsters belong to the highest order of Crustaceans," she pronounced, as though knighting them.[128]

In 1916 Hildegarde Hawthorne saw Portland, Maine, fishing smacks unloading their lobster catch. Dozens of the creatures were packed into each barrel, and barrel after barrel filled barges moored at slips along the wharf. The cargo was headed for "N'York," a local bystander reported. This "burly, white-haired man, his face burned to a dark brick-red . . . laid a loving hand on one of the biggest" of the captured crustaceans.[129]

Recipes for stewed or fricasseed lobster were still appearing in twentieth-century cookbooks, but under modern names. Helen S. Wright's "Lobsters, or Crabs, Buttered," for instance, called for lobster, white wine, butter, lemon, and rich gravy—in other words, stewed lobster. By the mid-twentieth century, potted lobster and lobster forcemeat were things of the past. Now boiled or baked, served in a Newburg sauce (the updated version of fricassee), or in a salad or chowder, lobster had assumed its modern forms.[130]

Oysters

In Britain, oysters have been eaten, and undoubtedly loved, since prehistoric times. They were a particular favorite of the Romans. In fifteenth-century London, oysters were "plentiful, very popular and on the whole inexpensive." As noted earlier, a sixteenth-century traveler to England said that the oysters "which are cried in every street" were better than any he had seen in Italy. Oysters were brined by seventeenth-century husbandmen, who bought them fresh to insure their quality. The shells, rich in lime, were used as fertilizer. One eighteenth-century source maintained that only the shells were used, the oysters discarded. But given the number of pickled oyster recipes in cookbooks of the day, this practice must have been uncommon. As with other fish in medieval and early modern England, oysters were often baked in heavily spiced pies, or stewed.[131]

Like other small fish, fresh oysters were sometimes fried immediately to prevent spoilage, as in this 1715 recipe: "Take youre oysters and wett them in the yeolks of eggs and buter youre frying pann very well and fry them as quick as you cann." These instructions would work equally well today.[132]

Despite being inexpensive, oysters were enjoyed by all classes. A 1772 recipe by Susannah Carter, "To ragoo Oysters," illustrated the more elegant end of the spectrum, with pistachio nuts, white wine, butter, nutmeg, egg yolks, and cream flavoring four dozen of the largest Melton oysters, and the whole garnished with "Seville oranges cut in small quarters." The price of the main ingredient may have been low, but Carter's cookbook didn't earn its name, *The Frugal Housewife*, with this extravagant concoction.[133]

Oyster-eating quickly became an American pastime. In 1697 Labadist missionaries to Brooklyn were already writing: "Then was thrown upon the fire, to be roasted, a pail full of Gowanes oysters which are the best in the country. They are fully as good as those of England . . . large and full, some of them not less than a foot long." Foot-long oysters were corroborated by other travelers. Oysters were served in colonial taverns, along with the usual tavern fare of fowl, beefsteaks, ham, and hot bread.[134]

New England oysters were pickled for export to Barbados. The early bounty of this resource is evident not only in its commercial exploitation but also in such recipes as Mrs. Gardiner's pickled oysters, which began "Take two hundred Oysters, the freshest you can get."[135]

Oysters only became more popular in the nineteenth century. A French visitor found that "Americans have almost a passion for oysters, which they eat at all hours, even in the streets." They were sold in the streets as well as eaten there. In Boston in 1830 oystermen could be heard peddling their wares with the cry, "Oys! Oys!—Here's your fine, fresh Oys! Come, buy!" Boston's Revere House was said to serve one hundred gallons of oysters a week.[136]

Oyster houses, or saloons as they were often called, specialized in quick, fresh oyster meals. Richard Pillsbury states that they "began appearing in the late eighteenth century as some of the first freestanding restaurants in the nation." Advertised with red and white balloon-shaped signs, they were popular in every coastal city, frequented mostly by lunchtime crowds of men. Some oyster saloons did set aside curtained booths or special rooms for women and families. Commercial oyster eateries were organized along class lines. Establishments "resplendent with gilding, plate-glass mirrors, and pictures" catered to "judges, generals, and parsons." Meanwhile, "the carter or mechanic" could get oysters that would "satisfy a gourmand," but usually from a cart in the street.[137]

Nineteenth-century New England cookbooks abounded with "escalloped" oysters, oyster sauce, oyster soup, pie, and patties, stewed oysters, roasted oysters, and fried oysters. But oysters were also used in more esoteric recipes. For instance, Mrs. Lee offered "Oyster Attelets," which was a sweetbread, cut into small pieces, a slice or two of bacon, and oysters, seasoned with parsley, shallot, thyme, salt and pepper, then skewered, covered with bread crumbs, and broiled or fried.[138]

Oysters also became a condiment. Mrs. Lee recommended "Oyster Ketchup," made by boiling "one hundred oysters with their liquor, till the strength be extracted from them." In 1845 J. H. Prescott described an "Oyster Catchup" that called for a quart of oysters: "Press them through a sieve, then add white wine one pint, salt one ounce, spice to flavor. Boil for fifteen minutes, strain and bottle." Prescott even came up with an "Oyster Powder," made of equal parts oysters and wheat flour, reduced to a paste, rolled, dried, powdered, and kept in corked bottles. One ounce reconstituted made a pint of oyster sauce, he claimed. As with clams, oysters were sometimes folded into pancake batter. By the end of the century, they were also being folded into omelettes and combined with macaroni.[139]

Many recipes continued to call for large numbers of oysters. J. H. Prescott's fifty-oyster pie of 1845 was matched by Mrs. S. G. Knight's "Oyster Sauce for Turkeys, &c" of 1864, which began with the instruction to "strain fifty oysters." (This from someone who claimed to be an apostle of frugality, as we shall see in the next chapter.) An 1880 *Godey's* recipe for fish chowder stated that it would be "an improvement to add fifty salt oysters with the milk."[140]

Yankee tavern owners went to great lengths to have supplies of oysters on hand throughout the winter months. In late autumn they stocked their cellars with oysters (and sometimes clams), burying them in beds of damp sea sand mixed with cornmeal. To keep their buried treasures alive, they watered the beds twice a week. The mollusks would be dug out of the pile as needed. Oyster pies and patties were favorite ways of serving cellar oysters, perhaps because oysters that ascended from the tavern depths were not as fresh as those from the briny deep. However, some writers, such as Mrs. Lee, preferred older oysters: "Some piscivorous gourmands think that oysters are not best when quite fresh from their beds, and that their flavor is . . . much ameliorated by giving them a feed. . . . Cover them with clean water, with a pint of salt to about two gallons (nothing else, no oatmeal, flour, nor any other trumpery) . . . after they have lain in it twelve hours, change it for fresh salt and water, and in twelve hours more they will be in prime order for the mouth."[141]

At midcentury, oyster parties were the rage among the New England aristocracy, as they were in every sophisticated metropolis. Creamed and curried oysters served in fancy puff pastry shells were the highlight of late night suppers. Wealthy householders began to copy tavern owners, keeping oysters buried in sand in their cellars. Others, with less storage space, pickled smaller supplies to be served on special occasions. Pickled oysters and eggnog were a New England New Year's Eve specialty. The oyster and social seasons coincided—oysters were available from September to April, those months with "r" in the name.[142]

Ever since the colonists began to move inland, oysters had been in demand among the landlocked. Whether carried in saddlebags by lone traders on horseback or packed in kegs and loaded on spring wagons along with farm necessities, oysters made their way to the interior. Farm wives would swap their homemade butter, cheese, cloth, or yarn for a dozen or two fresh oysters. According to Harriet Beecher Stowe, the inland town (based on Natick, Massachusetts) where her novel *Oldtown Folks* was set, was at the turn of the nineteenth century located in "an oyster-getting district." That "charming bivalve was perfectly easy to come at" there, presumably through the good offices of peddlers.[143]

In the middle of the nineteenth century, foreign visitors continued to be impressed by the American passion for oysters. During a visit to Boston, William Thackeray ate a raw oyster while dining at the Parker House, then remarked that "he felt as though he had just swallowed a baby." Certainly, Thackeray had had oysters in England. Perhaps it was the size of the oyster that he found unusual. Charles Dickens also ate oysters in Boston. He described a typical Boston supper as featuring "at least two mighty bowls of hot stewed oysters, in any one of which a half-grown Duke of Clarence might be smothered easily."[144]

Like many popular foods, oysters were also considered medicinal, as Mrs. Lee attested: "in the catalogue of easily digestible and speedily restorative foods . . . the oyster certainly deserves the best character." To retain that character they were not to be overcooked; consequently, one late-century author advised cooks to use an old-fashioned spider, heavier than a stew pan, "and there will be less liability to burn."[145]

Despite the low price of oysters, recipes for mock oysters, made of salsify, the "vegetable oyster," as Lydia Maria Child called it, or of corn, often seasoned with mace, appeared in cookbooks throughout the nineteenth century. Catharine Beecher included three different ways of cooking vegetable oysters. J. H. Prescott offered a recipe for "Oyster Corn Cakes" that called for "green corn, rasped with a coarse grater," along with milk, flour, eggs, salt, and pepper. He assured his readers that "these cakes afford as good an imitation of the taste of oysters as can be made with salsify." Mock oysters were turning into mock mock-oysters.[146]

Harriet Beecher Stowe was bemused by such vistas of artifice. She had two of the "Oldtown" women discuss "the critical properties of *mace*, in relation to its powers of producing in corn fritters a suggestive resemblance to oysters." This conversation created a bit of a mystery, which Stowe proceeded to resolve: "As ours was an oyster-getting district, and as that charming bivalve was perfectly easy to come at, the interest of such an imitation can be accounted for only by the fondness of the human mind for works of art."[147]

Although by the early twentieth century they were becoming more costly, oysters continued to occupy many pages in New England cookbooks. In a 1903 church ladies' cookbook from Newport, New Hampshire, a section that was entitled "Fish and Oysters" indicated that the oyster was still the favorite among shellfish. The year before, Mary J. Lincoln and Anna Barrows included broiled and fried oysters, as well as "Oysters Supreme," a fricassee with cream, chopped mushrooms or chicken, eggs, and breadcrumbs. In 1912 Helen S. Wright gave directions for pickling, scalloping, stewing, frying, and spicing oysters and for putting them into soups and pies. As the century advanced, these traditional recipes persisted, partly owing to the deliberate promotion of nostalgia. Imogene Wolcott included such timeworn offerings as oyster fritters, oyster soup, oyster stew, and "Chicken Smothered in Oysters." She also threw in a fanciful "Chatham Oyster Shortcake," stewed oysters over unsweetened shortcake.[148]

The oyster's association with New England, while never exclusive to the region, was strong enough to endure in nostalgic cookbooks. But the oyster itself, long overfished, was becoming rare and too expensive to provide a quick midday meal or to fill a bowl large enough to smother a half-grown duke. By Wolcott's day, oysters had become a luxury food. For earlier generations it had not been so. While a lucky few can say that the world is their oyster, the Atlantic seaboard of the United States, as it was in the nineteenth century, must certainly be called the oyster's world.[149]

Other Fish to Fry

As we have noted, early English observers were impressed with the size, numbers, and variety of the fish and shellfish swimming in New England waters. Francis Higginson exclaimed that "the aboundance of Sea-Fish are almost beyond beleeving," specifically listing cod, bass, "Herring, Turbut, Sturgion, Cuskes, Hadocks, [and] Mullets," in addition to some of the species considered so far in this chapter.[150]

William Wood commented on some of these species from a more gustatory perspective:

> The Sammon is as good as it is in England and in great plenty. The Hollibut is not much unlike a pleace [plaice] or Turbut, some being two yards long and one wide: and a foot thicke; the plenty of better fish makes these of little esteeme, except the head and finnes, which stewed or baked is very good: these Hollibuts be little set by while Basse is in season. . . . The Basse is one of the best fishes in the countrey, and though men are soone wearied with other fish, yet they are never with Basse; it is a delicate, fine, fat, fast fish, having a bone in his head, which containes a sawcerfull of marrow sweet and good, pleasant to the pallat, and wholsome to the stomack.

Roger Williams implied that it was from the Indians that the English learned to "make a daintie dish" of the head of the bass, "the braines and fat of it being very much, and sweet as marrow."[151]

John Josselyn, imbued with the scientific spirit of the later seventeenth century, attempted to provide a comprehensive account of New England fish species to the Royal Society, devoting several pages to an annotated, descriptive list before throwing up his hands at the plenitude before him and merely giving the names of over sixty different additional kinds. As with previous observers, the unusual size and teeming abundance of the fish were Josselyn's primary impressions. He saw sturgeon that were sixteen feet long, and he also saw more than ten thousand alewives caught by two men in two hours, "without any Weyre at all, saving a few stones to stop the passage of the River."[152]

These accounts indicate that the settlers began immediately to catch and eat the fish that were so readily available to them, and they continued to do so. According to one historian, in 1740 fish figured regularly in the diet of the typical New Englander. Fifty to seventy-five years later, salted fish continued to be eaten year-round, while fresh fish were brought to the table whenever they were available.[153]

Reflecting these trends, in her first edition Amelia Simmons included instructions for purchasing fish and preparing salt fish, while in the second edition she offered an extensive collection of fish recipes. She began with a delectable bass:

> Season high with salt, pepper and cayenne, one slice salt pork, one of bread, one egg, sweet marjoram, summersavory and parsley, minced fine and well mixed, one gill wine, four ounces butter; stuff the bass — bake in the oven one hour; thin slices of pork laid on the fish as it goes into the oven; when done pour over dissolved butter: serve up with stewed oysters, cramberries, boiled onions or potatoes.

Simmons noted that "the same method may be observed with fresh *Shad*, *Codfish*, *Blackfish* and *Salmon*."[154]

In 1842 Mrs. Webster gave recipes for trout, perch, shad, halibut, blackfish, sturgeon, salmon, mackerel, and bass. Many of these were among the fish that were most widely consumed in New England. Nineteenth-century cookbooks often made no distinctions regarding methods of preparing different species, grouping them, as did Catharine Beecher, into one generic discussion: "Put fish into cold water to boil. Remove any mud taste by soaking in strong salt and water. It is cooked enough when it easily cleaves from the bone, and is injured by cooking longer." Later, she offered a few more specific tips, such as "halibut is best cut in slices, and fried, or broiled. Bass are good every way. Black fish are best broiled or fried." The exalted reputation of bass thus persisted from the seventeenth century into the nineteenth. Indeed, many today would echo the sentiments of Wood, Williams, Simmons, and Beecher on the subject of bass.[155]

Beecher also considered salt fish: "Salt shad and mackerel must be soaked over night for broiling." Salt fish was a staple whose storage required proper care: "Codfish is improved by changing it, once in a while, back and forth from garret to cellar." However, "some dislike to have it in the house anywhere." Beecher shed further light on this aversion with the comment that "salt fish barrels must not be kept near other food, as they impart a fishy smell and taste to it."[156]

Salt fish provided the basis for New England's ubiquitous fish cakes and fish hash. The bland taste of salt fish was sometimes enhanced by cream sauce. An early-twentieth-century Vermonter recalled that "cream was used by my grandmother as we would use milk. Creamed codfish was just that, creamed with real cream." The baking pan would sometimes be brought to the table along with the fish so that the cream could be scooped hot from the pan. Salted salmon was also prepared in this way.[157]

Daniel Vickers observes that "wherever colonists lived within the sound of the surf, they kept shallops, wherries, canoes, and other little craft haled up on the beach or moored in tidal streams." As for freshwater fishing, "youths and older men in particular rowed and sailed in the inshore waters . . . [fishing] for their own tables, for their neighbors, and for nearby markets." The popular attachment to amateur fishing may have its roots in memories of fishing with grandfathers and other elders. But this was also serious business. By-employments such as small-scale fishing were often crucial in helping New England farmers retain and pass on their ability to remain economically independent.[158]

Such incidental fishing could be found on all levels of society and in all periods from the eighteenth century to the twentieth. John Adams's diary, for example, includes an account of an afternoon in 1760 spent fishing and picnicking. In the early twentieth century Clifton Johnson heard from a Nantucketer about catching and cooking fresh fish: "[My wife]'s a good cook, and we have the best there is on our table as far as sea food is concerned. I'm tellin' you there's as much difference between fresh fish and those you get inland as between cheese and chalk. I bring in a fish I've caught that's hardly dead yet. 'Here you are, Ma,' I say; and she washes him up, rolls him in meal, and in a few minutes he's in the frypan. You can eat such a fish with relish. But the sweetness is all gone out of cold storage fish. It ain't worth a cuss." While this man equated inland fish with "cold storage," rivers and lakes also produced highly appetizing fresh fish.[159]

The place of fresh fish in the New England diet is difficult to quantify, as it supplemented stored and purchased foods. But the impact of this kind of fishing on the formation of Yankee mythology is easier to assess. Lore about fishing punctuated the regional literature. When an early-twentieth-century Yankee sportsman's instructions to cook brook trout by hanging it from a birch sapling over an open fire, or when a Nantucketer's recommendation to first "'sleever' your mackerel" were repeated in cookbooks, regional identity was the fish that was being fried.[160]

Shad

Shad is not much eaten today, but in earlier times, before damming and pollution decimated its numbers, this fish was among New England's most important. Like the eel, the shad is migratory, traveling from the Atlantic to inland lakes via rivers and streams. It spawns in fresh water and is in season in New England in April, May, and early June. For the cold climate of the Northeast, the spawning of the shad signaled the welcome coming of spring. The practice of prefixing "shad" to various flora and fauna that also emerge in spring along the spawning route, called the shad run, gave us the white-flowered shadbush, with its edible shadberries, the shad-blossom ("the pyrus, one of the most conspicuous early flowers," noted Henry David Thoreau), the shad-fly, and even the shad-frog. At the other end of the naming spectrum was the expression "she [or he] looks like a June shad," which was used, for instance, by one nineteenth-century letter writer to describe the worn-out state in which she found her sister.[161]

The plentiful shad was long used in New England as fertilizer. Edward Winslow provided the earliest evidence: "according to the manner of the *Indians*, we manured our ground with Herings or rather Shadds, which we have in great abundance and take with great ease at our doores." There is some dispute about whether native people used fish as fertilizer before contact with Europeans, but there is no dispute that shad became important for this purpose. Edwin Mitchell wrote that during the spring runs in the Connecticut River in the nineteenth century there were sometimes "fish jams," where one could find "Yankee farmers gathering the helplessly packed fish by the cartload for use as fertilizer on their fields."[162]

Perhaps because of its use as fertilizer, not to mention as hog feed, shad was considered by some to be disreputable. One family in Hadley, Massachusetts, was alleged to have hidden their dinner platter of the fish from an unexpected caller. But Sarah Josepha Hale called it a "delicate and delicious fish," and shad recipes were found in most nineteenth-century regional cookbooks. Broiling was the simplest method of preparation, with the same procedure described in book after book: the fish was to be cleaned, split, dried, cooked on a greased gridiron, turned occasionally, then dressed with salt, pepper, butter, and sometimes garnished with parsley. Mrs. Webster broke from the pack by suggesting that "a smoke of corn cobs while it is broiling, improves it much." Baked shad was often stuffed, as large fish frequently were, with forcemeat, breadcrumbs, and seasoning.[163]

But the main point about shad was its numbers. In the seventeenth century Edward Johnson noted that Watertown, Massachusetts, "aboundes" in shad and other fish. The enormous spring shad runs in the Connecticut River offered a major opportunity for by-employment. In 1879 the catch was said to be 436,000 fish. One early-nineteenth-century farmer who built a fishing pier at the mouth of the Connecticut valued it as much as his farm. While this may have been an extreme case, many farmers throughout the region, for instance those who caught shad in the Merrimack River, supplemented their farming with shad fishing.[164]

Their run being a veritable spring event, shad provided occasions for celebration. One of Edwin Mitchell's "old New England custom[s]" was "annual alfresco feasts of fishes." These fish fries were stag affairs, at which "the younger men usually spent part of the afternoon in impromptu athletic contests—running, jumping, wrestling, and the like—while the older men sat around, smoking, telling stories, quenching their thirst." This sounds remarkably like an Indian feast, from which Mitchell claimed the fish fry derived, although he gave no evidence for such a lineage. The fish were cooked "in a great long-handled frying pan, black from age and use," along with a "slice of salt pork the size of a man's hand." Although Mitchell's account was doubtless embellished, events of the sort probably did occur. Mitchell added that a street in Hartford, Connecticut, was named Fishfry, and that the city's first seal depicted a catch of salmon and shad.[165]

Frogs' Legs and Turtle Soup

In *Oldtown Folks* Miss Debby summed up a widespread American attitude toward French food and culture: "I never saw any good of the French language . . . nor, for that matter, of the French nation either; they eat frogs, and break the Sabbath, and are as immoral as the old Canaanites." Persistent as that strain has been, New Englanders also had a tradition of admiring the French, and of eating frogs' legs. John Adams regretted that the colonists "had been taught by their former 'absurd masters' to dislike Parisian cookery." After the American alliance with France in 1778, there was a vogue for French cooking, at least among the elite.[166]

But frogs' legs also had New England culinary associations. They appeared on lists of the aquatic foods eaten by native peoples, and in some rural areas into the twentieth century a plate of fried frogs' legs was a common summer dinner. A mid-twentieth-century Vermont cookbook treated a frogs' legs recipe as unexceptional: "Lay frogs' legs in a dish, cover with oil, salt, pepper and a little lemon juice, and leave for a half an hour. Rub the broiler with an onion. Broil five or six minutes on each side, pour melted butter over them and serve. If fried in butter, a little less time will be required." A New Hampshire collection of "cherished recipes" included frogs' legs "dipped in egg and crumbs and fried in deep fat," as well as a recipe for sautéing six pairs of legs "à la Provencal."[167]

Despite the efforts of patriots like Adams, the English propaganda that the French "lived on frogs and salad" was generally believed, and many Americans considered the French diet a subject for jest. Sometimes, however, the joke was on the Americans, as in this incident from the period of the American Revolution: "Nathaniel Tracy, to entertain properly the admiral and officers of the French fleet, had the swamps of Cambridge searched for green frogs, which were served whole in the soup at a formal dinner. The first officer who struck one with his spoon fished it out, held it up, and exclaimed, 'Mon Dieu! une grenouille!'" The French roared with laughter.[168]

Amelia Simmons copied Susannah Carter's detailed instructions for cooking a sea turtle. Seven substantial paragraphs were required—from hanging up "your Turtle" by its "hind fins" and cutting off the head, to separating "the callapach from the callapee" with a sharp knife, to putting "the guts into another vessel," and clearing away "the slime." Between "equal portions of the different parts of the Turtle" the cook was to strew sweet herbs. Then she was to divide the seasoned meat, along with the boiled blood of the turtle, veal forcemeat balls, and six eggs, among a number of dishes. The dishes were filled with water, Madeira, and parsley "to make it look green," and the soup was finally baked in a hot oven for two hours.[169]

Throughout the eighteenth and nineteenth centuries, New England ship captains returned from tropical waters with barrels of large sea turtles and of pickled limes to give as gifts or to sell. The complexity of the Carter/Simmons recipe indicates that turtle was considered top of the line cuisine, but all kinds of people liked turtle soup. Local freshwater turtles were used when tropical sea turtles were unavailable. The small, indigenous snapping turtles from the ponds of Cape Cod, New Hampshire, and Maine became the basis of "Snapper Soup." "One of Maine's tall tales is of a snapping turtle that was kept in a swill barrel until it grew to weigh eighty-six pounds," one writer reported, although the average size of these local turtles rarely exceeded ten pounds. As such tall tales and elaborate recipes illustrate, rarity and taste gained turtles and frogs a place on the New England table.[170]

Sacred Cod

Cod was the fish on which New England was founded and on which it prospered, so we conclude as well as begin this chapter with it. Bartholomew Gosnold considered the fish so important that he named the promontory whose waters were rich in the species Cape Cod. While King James I thought Cape James a more fitting name (several maps of the time so designated it), a century later Cotton Mather wrote that "Cape Cod is a name which [that part of New England] will never lose until shoals of codfish be seen on its highest hills."[171]

For their own victuals the English settlers considered cod "but coarse meate." But by the eighteenth century, the cash-producing fish had become a featured item on wealthy colonial tables. As noted in chapter 2, a visitor to Boston in 1744 was served a codfish dinner in a well-to-do home: "Saturday, July 21 . . . I was invited to dine with Captain Irvin upon salt cod fish, which here is a common Saturday's dinner, being elegantly dressed with a sauce of butter and eggs."[172]

Puritan New England's abstinence from meat on the Sabbath came with an elegant dressing. Saturday codfish dinners, "served . . . in the best families," had apparently begun to serve other cultural purposes. Several decades after the visitor's repast with "Captain Irvin," ritualized codfish dinners took place at the home of John Hancock. The Hancocks "served codfish every week, keeping open house for everybody who cared to attend." The representatives of the featured species were "arranged on crested pewter platters that were ordered from England expressly for the purpose." The pale flesh of the fish, "elegantly dressed," first in butter and egg sauces, next in custom-made and ornamented serving dishes, symbolized the confident civilization that codfish-based wealth had, by the second half of the eighteenth century, succeeded in erecting in New England's major seaports. Not only for the Hancocks was cod a signature dish.[173]

The codfish dinner was still holding its own in 1875, when Samuel Adams Drake wrote that "a fish dinner is eaten at least once a week by every family in New England. . . . In effect, the cod-fish is to New England what roast beef is to old Albion." Recognizing that the comparison of dried codfish to roast beef might seem far-fetched to some, Drake added that "a Yankee can fatten on it where an Englishman would starve." After a century of American independence, democracy, and ecclesiastical disestablishment, weekly cod dinners were eaten by everyone, not just by the elite; their association with Sabbath-day abstinence had weakened; and they provided yet another excuse to assert the superiority of all things American and Yankee. For Drake, offering his thoughts a decade after the Civil War, the former was synonymous with the latter.[174]

The eighteenth century's restrained cod with egg dressing devolved, in one nineteenth-century instance, into a riot of color and taste called "Cape Cod Turkey." The upper classes joined with the hoi polloi in eating Cape Cod Turkey, or at least it figured in the childhood recollections of the well-born Caroline Howard King. At the Kings, Cape Cod Turkey was made with salt cod (boiled "encased in a cloth between two thin fishes of the same variety"), beets, carrots, potatoes, cucumbers or lettuce, and egg sauce or "Essex sauce (made from little bits of fried salt pork)." Allegedly, this hodge-podge was as much an aesthetic experience as a meal: "The legitimate way of enjoying all these good things was to mix them together, making your plate look like a painter's pallet with the various colors of the vegetables, the whole amalgamated and softened by the pale yellow of the egg sauce." King maintained that "it was rarely that any one who once tasted this dainty mixture" didn't ask for "a second fare." Chacun à son goût.[175]

Along with Cape Cod Turkey, plainer versions of creamed salt cod dotted Yankee cookbooks well into the twentieth century. In the eighteenth and nineteenth centuries cookbooks also regularly gave instructions for preparing every part of the fish that was edible, including tongues, cheeks, and sounds. Mrs. Lee offered cod sounds boiled, broiled, roasted, and baked. Sandra L. Oliver reports that in the nineteenth century cod sounds fell out of favor, although *Godey's* published at least one recipe for them in 1881. It called for three large sounds to be boiled in milk and water until tender, cooled, spread over with an oyster forcemeat, then rolled "in the shape of a chicken," skewered, basted "as you would chicken," roasted "slowly," and finally served with a "fine oyster sauce." "Cod someway most every day" might have been the motto of Yankee cooks.[176]

As we have seen, the profitability of New England commercial fishing was crucially dependent on the sale of mediocre cod to the Catholics of southern Europe and of distinctly inferior cod to the slaveholding sugar plantation grandees of the West Indies. Ironically, the descendants of those who had been fed the dregs of the Yankee catch developed methods of cooking cod that have stood the test of time better than Yankee creamed cod: Portuguese *bacalhau* (salt cod baked with olive oil, olives, potatoes, and other savory ingredients) and Jamaican "Stamp and Go" (fried codfish cakes seasoned with hot pepper). At least in this small chapter of culinary history, the world has been turned upside down, to the benefit of all.

Sailing Ships

Cod was too important to New England to remain merely a case in point of culinary incompetence. A white pine carving of the "Sacred Cod" had already become the symbol of the region's economic success story (two previous carvings had been lost to fire and war) when the Massachusetts House of Representatives passed the following motion in 1784: "That leave may be given to hang up the representation of a cod-fish in the room where the House sit, as a memorial to the importance of the cod-fishery to the welfare of this Commonwealth." Moved to the new Bulfinch State House in 1798, the Sacred Cod oversaw legislative activity at that site for almost a century before being moved again in 1895 to the new House chamber, where it hangs today.[177]

There was ample reason for this reverence. The commercial fishing industry, the prime commodity of which was codfish, grew throughout the seventeenth and eighteenth centuries. Governor Winthrop noted in 1639 that "here was such store of exceeding large and fat mackerel upon our coast this season, as was a great benefit to all our plantations." This was because a three-man boat could catch "in a week, ten hogsheads, which was sold at Connecticut for £3.12 the hogshead." A couple of years later, Winthrop recorded in his journal that New Englanders had "followed the fishing so well, that there was about 300,000 dry fish sent to market."[178]

Over the next several decades, as the lucrative West Indian market began to be exploited, the catch increased tenfold, and four hundred boats and a thousand men were employed in "the coastal fisheries between Maine and Boston." In the 1670s, coastal shallops began to be replaced by deep-sea barks and ketches, then by larger sloops and schooners. During King Philip's War, fears of famine prompted the Massachusetts legislature to prohibit the export of food from Massachusetts. But the economically crucial cod and mackerel exports were specifically excluded from the ban.[179]

By the beginning of the American Revolution, New England's fish exports accounted for more of the region's total exports than any other commodity, almost 35 percent. Just under two-thirds of these fish were shipped to the West Indies, the remainder to Southern Europe. According to Stephen

Innes, "over 10 percent of the Massachusetts labor force derived the bulk of its income from work in the fisheries." Fishing figured in the peace negotiations that followed the Revolution. "Massachusetts man" John Adams lobbied for American fishing rights to the same grounds that, as British subjects, Massachusetts fishermen had long exploited, and for landing rights in Newfoundland in order that the fishermen could dry their catches.[180]

The fisheries spawned other enterprises. As early as the 1650s, it was clear that Boston would be the center of a shipbuilding industry that derived from and sustained the fisheries. The city was building "an impressive array of full-rigged ships, ketches, pinnaces, and yawls." Other Massachusetts towns, among them Salem, Medford, and Taunton, were also building ships. Throughout the colonial period, it was "salted fish and seagoing vessels" that were Massachusetts Bay's "most lucrative exports."[181]

Those vessels were stocked with the array of commodities that constituted the other 65 percent of exports on the eve of the Revolution. Fishing had begotten shipbuilding, which in turn begat the larger carrying trade — in salted meats, grains, molasses, sugar, rum, and slaves. We will have more to say in subsequent chapters about various aspects of this commerce, but it is worth emphasizing here that to trade in salt cod was to trade, indirectly or directly, in slaves. Not only was cod used to feed slaves, it was also among the commodities accepted in Africa in direct exchange for slaves. Some New England merchants, particularly several in Newport, Rhode Island, "deliberately pursued the [slave] trade as a part of their commercial enterprise."[182]

Despite John Adams's skilled negotiating, decreased fish stocks and the disruptions of trade caused by the Revolution precipitated a decline in New England commercial fishing from which it never recovered. But by then shipping was New England's primary business. After the war, American ships could buy and sell almost anywhere in the world without paying taxes to Britain. The profitable China trade opened up in the 1780s. During the quarter century of war in Europe beginning in 1792, New England interests even recaptured the lion's share of the West Indies trade, from which they had been excluded by the British once the former colonies became an independent and openly competitive nation. New England maritime commerce continued to expand throughout the first half of the nineteenth century, for example into the world-encircling whaling ventures made famous by Herman Melville's *Moby Dick*.[183]

This economic muscle-flexing was to have even more far-reaching effects when a large share of the wealth, urbanization, marketing and distribution networks, and financial expertise accumulated and created over nearly two centuries of fishing and seaborne trading was, in the early decades of the nineteenth century, redirected into the American Industrial Revolution. Until about 1860, New England was America's premier manufacturing region. There were of course a great many factors involved in such a major historical development as industrialization. But far from the least was the generations of experience that New England's maritime merchants had marshaled in capitalist methods of organizing economic life. The American economy as we know it today in part traces its origins to the fishing for cod and the selling of them for profit, no questions asked, at which New England early and continuously excelled.[184]

CHAPTER 4

Every Thing Is Moving & Changing

Cookbooks & Commerce

From the preceding chapter, it is clear that understanding the place of fish in New England food culture requires giving some consideration to New England's overall economic development. But those larger economic forces and trends influenced other departments of the world of New England food besides fish and fishing. Broadly speaking, the foods discussed in the first two chapters—grains and legumes—were primarily associated with an economics of subsistence, while those with which we have just dealt in chapter 3 and with which we shall deal henceforth—fish, meat, sugar-based preparations, and stimulant or alcoholic beverages—had diverse and increasingly essential ties to an economics of buying and selling in the marketplace. This chapter therefore seems an appropriate point to describe more systematically the evolving economic and social context within which New Englanders produced and consumed their foods.

Master of His Own Labor and Land

We begin with a summary of the scholarly debate about how capitalism rose to dominance in the English colonies and the United States. In this debate the meaning of the term "capitalism" has itself been contested. For our purposes, it is sufficient to define capitalism as any economic activity in which there is a conscious effort to increase production, in which the ownership of resources tends to become more concentrated and unequal, in which the exchange of goods is mediated by cash, and in which sellers and buyers need not abide in proximity to each other.

It is now generally agreed that in the 1620s and 1630s, at the time of the founding of New England, Old England was farther along in its own transition to capitalism than any other nation. A full survey of the emergence of

English capitalism would be beyond our scope. The most relevant aspects of the process from our point of view are that the population of England grew significantly in the course of the sixteenth and seventeenth centuries, that the growth rate was especially high in urban areas, that there was consequently a need for an increased food supply, and that the changes that took place in English agriculture in order for this demand to be supplied resulted in greater prosperity and power for a relatively few landowners and in declining fortunes for many other people. A significant proportion of the group that lost ground (literally as well as figuratively) were lesser yeomen and husbandmen who had heretofore enjoyed terms of tenancy that amounted to de facto land ownership. Such people now found themselves either managing to remain on the land only on much less secure and more dependent terms, or reduced to the condition of landless wage laborers.[1]

This particular ramification of the transition to capitalism in England was perhaps the single most significant of the economic (as opposed to the religious) factors encouraging the plantation of English colonies in North America. As Stephen Innes writes, "if, in an era of declining real wages, [wage labor] led only to poverty and dependency, then only men and women who controlled their own labor could be regarded as free. To lose control over one's labor was inevitably to compromise one's liberty and security along with everything else bound up in the ancient but potent notion of 'freeborn Englishman.'" In other words, what lured many English people to North America was freedom, the prospect of retaining it, recovering it, or gaining it for the first time. As John Smith declared in 1624, "here are no hard landlords to rack us with high rents or extorting fines. . . . Here every man may be master of his own labour and land . . . and if he have nothing but his hands he may set up his trade, and by industry grow rich."[2]

Among the inducements to immigration listed above—retaining freedom, recovering it, or gaining it for the first time—the immigrants to New England included a much higher proportion of people responding to the first inducement than to the second or third. Virginia, Pennsylvania, and other non–New England areas attracted many who were willing to undergo the explicit but temporary dependence of indentured servitude in order to escape the virtual certainty of lifelong wage-labor servitude in their homeland. In one or the other of these colonies, they anticipated recovering their freedom or obtaining it for the first time.

But the majority of the first settlers of New England came from relatively well fixed positions in the middle stratum of English society. They arrived in configurations of family units and groups of families from the same locale, possessed of sufficient resources to create almost immediately a society based on freehold land tenure shared among families whose circumstances were approximately equal. In short, when they emigrated, they had not yet lost the freedom and independence that land or other forms of property, wealth, and skills bestowed, and their removal to New England insured that they and their descendants would retain such freedom and independence far into the future.[3]

Harbored within the words we have quoted from John Smith is the crux of the debate over the transition to capitalism in the English New World. To live in America was to obtain or to make secure one's landed independence and thereby avoid becoming a victim of the transition to capitalism in England, trapped in economic servitude. On the other hand, living in America could also mean, even if one had nothing but one's own two hands, setting up one's trade and by industry growing rich. One could become a beneficiary rather than a victim of the transition to capitalism, securing not only independence but also prosperity and power. (That proceeding on to this phase of the process entailed locking others into the very same dependence one had migrated and labored in order to escape went unacknowledged in Smith's discussion.)

In *Creating the Commonwealth* Stephen Innes argues that the great majority of the first settlers of New England, certainly of its leaders, were steeped in the idea that to grow rich by laboring industriously with one's hands was not only a person's prerogative but also his duty. As Innes sees it, the transition to capitalism in New England had already occurred before the ships bringing the immigrants had set sail from England.

Innes provides abundant evidence from Puritan sermons and other early New England discourse to substantiate this view. John Winthrop, for example, argued that it was legitimate to dispossess the natives of North America because they "inclose noe Land, neither have they any setled habytation, nor any tame Cattle to improve the Land by." To justify the settlement of New England with the argument that it would lead to enclosure and improvement of the land was to suggest that one intended to reproduce in New England the very same process of capitalist agricultural change that was driving one from Old England to New England in the first place.[4]

On the other hand, in the same discourse containing this implicit endorsement of capitalist improvement, Winthrop also demonstrated an acute awareness of the manifold victimization and corruption that early English capitalism was generating:

This Land growes weary of her Inhabitants . . . it is come to passe, that children, servants & neighboures, especially if they be poore, are compted the greatest burthens, which if thinges weare right would be the cheifest earthly blessinges. . . . We are growne to that height of Intemperance in all excess of Riott [extravagant way of living], as noe mans estate allmost will suffice to keepe saile with his æquals: & he whoe failes herein, must live in scorne & contempt. Hence it comes that all artes & Trades are carried in that deceiptfull & unrighteous course, as it is allmost impossible for a good & upright man to mainetayne his charge & live comfortablie in any of them.

It might be expected that a society founded on the basis of these words would stress mastery by all over their own labor and land but would not stress setting up one's trade and by industry growing rich, insofar as this entailed poverty for others and conspicuous consumption and dishonesty for oneself.[5]

Of course the region's development did not turn out to be an either/or matter. The society that actually developed in New England both provided outlets for capitalist energies and managed to maintain for several generations an equilibrium in which there was for most people neither great wealth nor poverty but rather middling independence. The outlets for capitalist energies were most manifest, as we saw in the last chapter, in those merchants who cultivated the fishing industry, and the maritime trade based on it, to the point that they became "the Dutch of England's empire." Nor did New England's farmers remain aloof from the profits of such maritime trade. On the eve of the American Revolution, New England's second largest export was salted meat, produced from livestock that had been driven from inland farms to seaports for slaughter and processing. Most of the resulting salt pork and beef was then shipped, along with the fish that were the largest export, to the slavery-based West Indian sugar plantations, although an unknown amount was also traded domestically and along the coast to other colonies. We shall describe the colonial meat export trade more fully in the next chapter.[6]

Clearly, the farm families that comprised the majority of New England's population throughout the colonial period were involved as sellers in the transatlantic capitalist market that was the first British Empire. They were also involved as buyers. As we shall see in subsequent chapters, they increasingly consumed the molasses, sugar, coffee, tea, and rum that were exchanged along the Atlantic trade routes for their livestock and the merchants' fish.

Nevertheless, throughout the seventeenth and eighteenth centuries, most of these farm families lived as much as possible apart from these complex market transactions. They maintained freehold ownership of their farmsteads, managed inheritance patterns so that such landed security would prevail into the next generation, and produced and preserved for themselves a great deal of what they needed in the way of food and the other necessities of life through a "safety first" mixed rather than staple cash crop agriculture.

What they could not directly produce and preserve for themselves they undertook to obtain by bartering goods and labor with their neighbors. The husking bees described in chapter 1, the sharing of fresh meat from slaughtered livestock described in chapter 5, and the apple paring bees described in chapter 6 were the most visible manifestations of this system of "local exchange." The long-distance exchanges taking place in the early capitalist marketplace were resorted to only to meet those needs that could not be met more locally. The purpose of just about everything that took place on the New England family farm was to perpetuate what the first immigrants to New England had sought and secured: a landed freedom and independence that had seemed to be growing increasingly elusive or precarious back in the mother country.[7]

Full of the Fatness of the Past Season

One of the main activities that occurred on New England family farms in pursuit of this primary goal of independence was foodstuff preservation. Most of what was produced in farm households—whether from the pasture, the field, the garden, or the orchard—had to be preserved, if the family was to live reasonably well year-round. In later chapters we will describe in greater detail the preservation of such particular foods as meats, dairy goods, and fruits. Here, in an effort to give our sketch of New England subsistence farming a bit more shading and color, we offer a preservation overview.

In the standard study of the food culture of English rural households, as much attention is paid to preservation as to production and cooking. As far as field crops were concerned, legumes and milled grains were stored in sacks or barrels, either inside the house or outside in a separate granary, ready to be scooped out for daily or weekly use in breads and pottages. Much of the grain crop and much of the orchard yield were rescued from spoilage and saved for later consumption by being liquefied, as beer in the former case and as wine or cider in the latter.

Livestock—specifically cows, sheep, and goats—contributed to the year-round foodstuff supply not only by being slaughtered and salted but also by producing milk, which was then preserved by conversion into butter and cheese. Fish were more often purchased already cured than home-raised and processed, although some wealthy seventeenth-century yeomen built and stocked their own fish ponds. This catch was then subjected to the same treatments that the fish brought home from the market had already received—drying, salting, or pickling.

Vegetables and fruits were preserved by drying, pickling, or being converted into jams, jellies, pastes (such as apple butter), or wine. These items were dried by being spread out in an oven with sugar sprinkled over them; some methods involved soaking them in a syrup prior to placing them in the oven. Once dried, the fruits or vegetables were hung on strings, usually in the hall, the room which served as the kitchen and primary living area. Pickling involved parboiling and then placement in a liquid bath of salt, water, and verjuice.[8]

The earliest colonial probate inventories reveal the persistence of these preservation methods among immigrants to New England. Besides powdering tubs for salt meat, many households had churns and other implements for making butter and cheese, brewing apparatus, and barrels and sacks to store, among other things, grains and legumes. Remains of seventeenth-century houses show that hams, sides of bacon, or other meats were hung in the chimney for smoking, and that strings of dried apples, pumpkins, and ears of seed corn were suspended from the rafters.[9]

During the first several decades of settlement, these preservation resources and procedures, tried and true as they were, proved inadequate to insure protection from the annual prospect, if not the annual experience, of scarcity. Particularly in late winter and early spring, food supplies were apt to run low even in otherwise comfortable households. Laurel Thatcher Ulrich notes that in seventeenth-century Essex County, Massachusetts, cases of food theft were more likely to occur at this time of year than any other. These thefts were likely to be perpetrated because the thieves' own provisions had become alarmingly depleted; and such acts were likely to be detected because whatever was stolen constituted a higher proportion of the victims' total supply, making its absence more noticeable.[10]

In April of an unknown seventeenth-century year, one Ipswich, Massachusetts, woman wrote to her brother in Medford lamenting a scarcity of apples and worrying that the remaining carrots might well be rotten. Her concerns pointed to one particular type of limitation in the preservation capabilities of the first couple of generations in New England: fruits and vegetables all but disappeared from the diet after the early autumn.[11]

The scarcity of preserved fruits and vegetables is particularly anomalous and noteworthy, since most houses in seventeenth-century Massachusetts included underground cellars where provisions could remain cool but not freeze. Moreover, the presence of such cellars represented a departure from typical English farmhouse designs of the period. Yet surviving seventeenth-century probate inventories only occasionally list root vegetables located in this below-grade chamber, and even then only in small quantities. It appears that the first settlers of New England figured out how to build houses in which fruits and vegetables could be kept available and edible well past harvest time and then neglected to utilize their houses for this purpose. During those early years, apples and carrots were unlikely to be found in April in Ipswich or Medford or anyplace else in New England because not enough had been placed in storage below the frost line at the end of the previous summer.[12]

As noted in chapter 2 and as will be discussed in greater detail in chapter 5, fears of scarcity had largely disappeared by the middle of the eighteenth century. Salt meats, grains, and cider were by that time being stored away in sufficient quantities to last well into the summer, instead of approaching exhaustion in the spring. This improvement was partly the result of more efficient utilization of traditional storage and preservation technologies and partly of increased production, particularly, expanded apple cultivation.

Over the next hundred years, until the revolutionary emergence of canning and refrigeration in the second half of the nineteenth century, this trend continued and accelerated. Butter and cheese began to be available in most households during most of the year, and increasingly vegetables and fruits were now laid away in cellars, where they remained available to diversify the family diet through the winter and on into the spring and summer, right up to the next year's garden and orchard harvest.[13]

As stored and preserved provisions steadily increased in quantity and significance, so did discourse about the threats to which they were vulnerable. Farm diaries and daybooks from late-eighteenth- and early-nineteenth-century New England regularly described struggles with frost, flood, decay, vermin, and rodents. Both men and women had to spend time sorting through stores of beans, pumpkins, and apples, discarding those that were going bad in order to salvage those that remained good.[14]

Advice about how best to cope with the various hazards also proliferated. Lydia Maria Child explained in 1829 that cornmeal and rye meal were "in danger of fermenting" in the summertime and should therefore be stored in cool places with large stones placed in the middles of the barrels to make them even cooler. An occasional stirring was also good for the meal, she added. In 1846 Catharine Beecher urged frequent whitewashing of cellars to keep them "sweet and clean," echoing the opinion of an almanac half a century before. Making adequate allowance for ventilation was necessary to prevent decay in winter fruit, stated a farming periodical in 1850. Picking through items that had begun to spoil would be facilitated by arranging basement bins and shelves somewhere other than along the walls, the same journal argued in the same year. To avoid frost in cellars, building embankments around houses in winter was recommended. Scattering tubs of water among the vegetables in the cellar was another frost-prevention method offered by a Maine newspaper in 1810.[15]

It was claimed in 1798 and again in 1825 that fall harvesting and subsequent placement on a bed of sand in the cellar would extend the life of root vegetables. Lydia Maria Child disagreed with this advice, however, regarding at least one root vegetable, the parsnip, which she said should be dug up only in the spring and then kept in the cellar "covered up in sand, entirely excluded from the air." Child did endorse the practice adopted by "many farmers" of wintertime burial of cabbages and potatoes in holes in the ground outdoors. Unfortunately, at least some of the Maine farmers who made use of such methods found their cabbages and potatoes severely damaged by frost when they later checked on them.[16]

Cellar storage of apples on beds of sand was suggested to Maine farmers in 1854. In 1867 *Godey's Lady's Book and Magazine* called for straw instead of sand for apples. Another scheme for prolonging the viability of apples through the winter mentioned by a farm diarist in 1835 was to pick them before they were entirely ripe. Readers of a midcentury cookbook were told to keep apples outdoors in barrels as long as possible and then to move them to a back room, not consigning them to the cellar "until weather requires." Vigilance was counseled by the author not only in the search for spoiled apples but also in the wiping away of excess moisture.[17]

Improved methods and techniques were proposed for foods that were treated prior to storage as well as for those that were laid away more or less as they were. We learned in chapter 2 of Lydia Maria Child's ideas about a more effective way of drying pumpkin, first boiling and straining it, then spreading it out "thin in tin plates" and drying if "hard in a warm oven." Catharine Beecher said berries and most other fruits should be dried in the sun and then stored in bags "in a cool, dry place." Repeatedly from the 1770s into the mid-nineteenth century, writers offered best, approved, new, sure, and effectual procedures for pickling cucumbers or making butter or cider. The recipes would either lengthen the life or improve the flavor of the items thus treated, or both. Ways of rescuing previously preserved items that were beginning to spoil also regularly appeared in print. In chapter 5 a couple of formulas for best or long-lasting preservation of corned beef are described.[18]

From the types of sources upon which we have drawn for this account—not only farm diaries, daybooks, and periodicals, but also cookbooks and periodicals intended primarily for urban readers—it would appear that not only country but also village, town, and city households continued to avail themselves of food preservation traditions until relatively recent times. By the first half of the nineteenth century, the era of most of our sources, many New England households had become efficient food warehouses, designed with considerable thought and care. As Sandra L. Oliver states, "housewives matched up food storage with . . . in-house climates": vegetables, fruits, cider, and salted or pickled meats in the cellar; dried apples, pumpkins, peppers, herbs, and braided seed corn in the attic and kitchen; butter and cheese in any "dry, cool place"; and grains and beans wherever they would "stay free of mold."[19]

Memoirists of the day frequently expressed a sense that the house had been filled with the earth's bounty, top to bottom, end to end. Samuel G. Goodrich remembered in 1857 that "the cellar, extending under the whole house, was a vast receptacle," especially in the autumn, holding great barrels of beef, pork, and cider and "numerous bins of potatoes, turnips, beets, carrots, and cabbages." "The mellow flavor of [the harvest] seemed to pervade the whole house," wrote Ellen Chapman Rollins in recollections published in 1883. "The garret was crammed, and the kitchen beams were hung thick with earth-grown things. . . . The cellar beneath was full of the fatness of the past season."[20]

But it was Harriet Beecher Stowe who in 1869 articulated this theme most broadly: "The great abundance of *food* in our New England life is one subject quite worthy of reflection, if we consider the hardness of the soil, the extreme severity of the climate, and the shortness of the growing season between the late frosts of spring and those of early autumn. But, as matter of fact, good, plain food was everywhere in New England so plentiful, that at the day I write of nobody could really suffer for want of it." As Stowe wrote, the canning and refrigeration revolutions of the later nineteenth century were superseding the colonial preservation and provisioning improvements celebrated by her narrator.[21]

Work of Odd Moments

By the late eighteenth century, despite the trends of increased food production and more efficient preservation, population growth, land shortages, and other factors were combining to erode the family farm way of life. Sons could no longer be reasonably certain that at some point in early adulthood they would be settled on farmsteads adequate to sustain traditional independence. While some were able to migrate to the West and others to obtain college educations and launch professional careers, the majority found themselves attempting to piece together secure livelihoods by combining farming with what was hoped would be temporary engagement in other occupations such as fishing, craft trades, household manufacture, or, eventually, employment in the various types of industrial manufacturing enterprises that were founded with increasing frequency and success in New England from the 1790s onward. As these trends persisted and intensified, wage labor became an ever-more commonplace presence in households that had heretofore defined themselves by their avoidance and transcendence of it.[22]

When we speak of the paramount importance of independence to the inhabitants of New England family farms, we refer to the farm unit as a whole in relation to any outside institutions or forces that might be capable of exercising economic control over it. The only individual human beings who may properly be characterized as independent or free in these arrangements were the male heads of the farm households. By long-standing legal and customary traditions in both England and New England, the women (and children) within the household were dependent upon and subordinated to the husband and father. As Allan Kulikoff writes, "men decided what crops to produce, how to divide farm tasks among family members, when to send crops to distant markets."[23]

However, within an overall structure of formal and actual subordination, women were generally expected to act with considerable autonomy. In the English traditions with which the colonists were familiar, not only the kitchen and other areas within the house, but also the vegetable garden, livestock and poultry pens, and dairy barn, were considered the woman's domain. Jeanne Boydston points out that throughout the colonial heyday of the independent family farm, "women were responsible for providing fruits, vegetables, dairy products, and fowl; for manufacturing various goods needed by the family; for managing the distribution of goods in the household; for the daily care of the house proper, the home lot, and much of their own equipment; and for training and supervising infants, older daughters, and female servants."[24]

This summary list of farm wives' standard duties omits what was probably the most time-consuming and arduous of all: women "prepared all of the food for family consumption, collecting and chopping kindling and spending long (and dangerous) hours coaxing cooking fires to just the right temperature." As one Long Island farm mistress exclaimed in 1769, "O, I am dirty and tired almost to death cooking for so many people." To top it all off, "all colonial women were expected to be able to assume their husbands' responsibilities as need arose."[25]

Clearly, the traditional role of the New England farm wife was a classic case of labor and responsibility loaded onto the backs of subordinates, even as recognition and explicit authority are withheld or only partially conceded. Anyone with any experience at all in the contemporary American workplace is familiar with the pattern. This tendency was exacerbated by the fact that, as Christopher Clark points out, men's tasks tended to be "seasonally variable," whereas female jobs such as cooking, making, laundering, and mending clothes, and taking care of children "were a continuous process, not seasonal." In addition, the expectation that women would fill in for men as needed was not reciprocated. "Instances of men doing household tasks . . . were rarely recorded."[26]

The difficulties in maintaining independence experienced by farm households from the late eighteenth century onward only added to the already unequal labor burden borne by women. New kinds of work taken on by men in the effort to piece together secure livelihoods, such as "farm-based manufacturing" or "stall-feeding of beef cattle," were "timed to occupy periods when the demands of field work were not pressing," such as the winter months. In contrast, women's additional contributions to the family income, such as the production of textile and dairy goods in the home for sale outside the home, were taken on without any reduction in traditional household chores.[27]

Manufacture carried out in the home eventually evolved into "outwork," where the work itself continued to be done mostly by women in the home, but ownership of raw materials and finished products, along with profits, was relinquished to merchant owners and employers, leaving the female workers with nothing but wages. In Hampshire County, Massachusetts, in the 1840s, outworking women from farm and artisan households braided palm leaf hats. Commentators promoted hatmaking under this putting-out system as a remedy for idleness among women and children. The job would be the "work of odd moments which would otherwise be unimproved," thought one newspaper editor.[28]

The testimony of women actually engaged in such labor told a different story. One woman described how her mother, her sisters, and she had during one particular week "took up the carpets and cleaned house and made soap and cut five dresses and made two or three sun bonnets . . . all this besides braiding, [which] we won't say anything about." Another woman in the labor force referred with ironic quotation marks to the notion that there was any idleness available from which she needed to be rescued. Other family members had been away from home, and she had needed to take care of their chores: "I have to be Hannah and mother in the house and John at the barn, besides braiding double rim[m]ed hats when there is 'nothing else to do.'" Present-day women, holding down full-time paid employment without any particular diminution of their housekeeping and caregiving roles, can appreciate this woman's muted sarcasm.[29]

With the emergence of outwork, wage-labor dependency had become an integral part of the household labor routine. At the same time, other women, mostly daughters, were assisting the struggle for independence and security by wage employment in textile mills, which they expected, as we noted earlier, to be only temporary. Capitalist labor relations were both enveloping and penetrating rural households. And increasingly, as the first half of the nineteenth century wore on, people of rural background were being drawn into cities, where every aspect of their lives, from employment for wages to the purchase of goods and services with cash in shops and stores, was conducted within a capitalist framework.

In the context of the family farm, women's household labor and production had not for the most part been measured in cash terms. But neither had men's labor and production. Detachment from the market and cash economy had characterized most aspects of the family farm. As the market and cash economy became increasingly predominant, most forms of labor and production did begin to be defined by cash; women's housework, however, did not. In the new cash universe, it changed from being simply part of the labor that was needed for subsistence, well-being, and autonomy to being set apart as "unpaid" labor.

The complex cultural process that dictated that the labor required for the maintenance of the household must remain unpaid while all other forms of labor were assigned monetary value is not our primary concern here. The story of the sentimentalization of the nineteenth- and twentieth-century middle-class home as a refuge from the inhuman logic of the workplace and the cash nexus has been often told. What we wish to emphasize is that what was now called housework, transmuted from what had been the woman's portion of farm household production, had in the world of capitalist relations and wage labor become if anything even more necessary and valuable than it had been in the world of independent farm households.[30]

What we mean by this is that housework still retained the "use value" it had always had. Meals still needed to be prepared for eating and clothes made for wearing. To this was now added an indispensable, though unacknowledged, cash or "exchange value." By Jeanne Boydston's calculations, in the middle of the nineteenth century in a working-class family, the wife's unpaid household labor was what elevated the family's resources above subsistence level, in spite of the fact that her husband's wages were likely to remain below that level. From the point of view of the family, the wife's contribution was obviously crucial. From the point of view of employers, "this sizable but uncounted labor in the home" was what allowed them to keep wages below subsistence level in the first place, which means that it was also what allowed them to keep profit margins high. "The difference," Boydston concludes, "was critical to the development of industrialization in the antebellum Northeast."[31]

As for unpaid housework in middle-class families, Boydston argues that middle-class salaried incomes were generally sufficient for a comfortable day-to-day existence. However, they were not large enough to make possible the security against future vicissitudes that people on that level of society had come to expect, in part because of memories of the long tradition of freehold land ownership and the insulation from market fluctuations that it had bestowed. The middle-class wife's unpaid labor, exercised either directly in her own cooking, cleaning, doing the laundry, taking care of children, and making items for family use, or indirectly in vigilant oversight of purchases of commodity and labor (that is, that of servants), "created the surplus that could be translated into home ownership, an expanded business operation, savings, or investment." In other words, continued engagement by the middle-class urban housewife in many of the activities of her farm mistress forebears was what made possible her family's acquisition of the closest approximation to traditional nonmarket rural independence that a market-dominated urban world offered.[32]

The cookbooks and household manuals upon which this book relies were written primarily for readers living in the market-dominated urban world. The very first American cookbook, Amelia Simmons's *American Cookery* of 1796, began with advice on purchasing foods in the marketplace. Indeed, the identity that Simmons chose to proclaim on her title page, "an American Orphan," suggests the erosion of the family and the emergence of individualism as the basis of social structure that is always associated with capitalism. As Simmons stated in her preface, "the orphan, though left to the care of virtuous guardians, will find it essentially necessary to have an opinion and determination of her own."[33]

A primarily urban, market-oriented, money-income world was implicit in all nineteenth-century New England cookbooks. Lydia Maria Child recommended that her typical reader "get a friend in the country to procure you a quantity of lard, butter, and eggs, at the time they are cheapest, to be put down for winter use. You will be likely to get them cheaper and better than in the city market." The assumption was that the reader must usually have recourse to the city market. Sarah Josepha Hale pointed to the broader outlines of the economic context of her readers' lives in 1852: "The husband earns, the wife dispenses; are not her duties as important as his?" Here was a world in which husband and wife concentrated not on household production within their respective domains, but rather on the getting and spending of money. Hale's rhetorical question about the importance of the wife's spending role to the family's well-being begins to provide confirmation of Jeanne Boydston's analysis of the economics of antebellum housework.[34]

Hinted at in Hale's question was the central theme of the household advice literature of the day: the need for economy on the part of most people. Lydia Maria Child laid the greatest stress on this idea, not only calling her book *The American Frugal Housewife*, but also announcing on the title page that it was "dedicated to those who are not ashamed of economy." A few years later Mrs. N. K. M. Lee criticized the tendency to entertain guests "in a more expensive manner than is compatible with the general convenience of the family," a bad habit that brought along with it "an expense in dress, and a dissipation of time, from which [the family] suffers in various ways." The proper antidote to such lavishness was "a house fitted up with plain good furniture," including a dining table set "without ostentation" on which would be served "a well-dressed plain dinner." A household thus organized and presented would "bespeak a sound judgment and correct taste in a private family" that would "place it on a footing of respectability with the first characters in the country."[35]

In subsequent decades authors continued to sound this alarm. Mrs. E. A. Howland's *American Economical Housekeeper*, in great part plagiarized from Child, was "particularly recommended to the attention of those who would cook well at a moderate expense." The subtitle of Mrs. S. G. Knight's 1864 cookbook was "how to prepare a nice dish at a moderate expense," echoing Howland's stated intention almost verbatim. In the introduction Knight claimed (falsely) that her book was unique in this respect: "The universal cry among the less wealthy classes is, 'We can do nothing with Cook Books, the receipts are so *extravagant*!' . . . For the last twenty years the writer has been collecting receipts for her own private use. Many of these were so valuable, combining economy with excellence, she was constantly giving them to her friends. One lady remarked that one single receipt given her was worth five dollars to her."[36]

In the 1880s *Aunt Mary's New England Cook Book* was subtitled along the same lines as its predecessors: "a collection of useful and economical cooking receipts." The author also continued the tradition of claiming to have made a clearing for frugality in a forest of extravagance: "No claim is made for a collection of fancy or artistic formulas. . . . The majority of 'Cook Books' are filled with receipts, a large proportion of which are never used, being beyond the requirements and means of most families. These are within the reach of every housekeeper, and if carefully followed, satisfactory and beneficial results are certain."[37]

If Lydia Maria Child and those who followed were writing for "those who are not ashamed of economy," then their implicit antagonists were those who were ashamed of economy. Who were they? Child provided several clues. She thought she confronted a situation in the late 1820s in which "our wealthy people copy all the foolish and extravagant caprice of European fashion." Lamentably, "people of moderate fortune" were being misled into aping them: "I would ask, Is it *wise* to risk your happiness in a foolish attempt to keep up with the opulent?" Child echoed John Winthrop's indictment of England almost exactly two hundred years before. Then in England, as now in America, so it seemed, fashionable extravagance had tempted people to live beyond their means: "We are growne to that height of Intemperance in all excesse of Riott, as noe mans estate allmost will suffice to keepe saile with his æquals: & he whoe failes herein, must live in scorne & contempt."[38]

Just as Winthrop had reacted against aspects of the emergence of capital-

THE

AMERICAN

FRUGAL HOUSEWIFE.

DEDICATED TO

THOSE WHO ARE NOT ASHAMED OF ECONOMY.

BY MRS. CHILD,

AUTHOR OF " HOBOMOK," " THE MOTHER'S BOOK," EDITOR OF THE
" JUVENILE MISCELLANY," &c.

A fat kitchen maketh a lean will.—FRANKLIN.
" Economy is a poor man's revenue; extravagance a rich man's ruin."

TWELFTH EDITION.
ENLARGED AND CORRECTED BY THE AUTHOR.

BOSTON:
CARTER, HENDEE, AND CO.
1833.

Title page from American Frugal Housewife, *12th ed., 1833.*
(Courtesy American Antiquarian Society)

ism in England, so Child was appalled by the same phenomena accompanying the rise of market capitalism in New England. According to Richard L. Bushman, in the first half of the nineteenth century a culture of gentility and refinement was widely disseminated among the American middle class, having (as Child grasped) originated among the European aristocracy and been passed on to the colonial elite before coming to rest in modest American parlors and front yards. Not only did Child perpetuate a long Puritan tradition with her criticisms of the itch for gentility, she also echoed a number of other contemporary critics of the tendency to be "the servile and debased imitators of *courtly modes and forms*."[39]

While refinement was the "polar opposite" of capitalism, in that it encouraged leisure and consumption rather than thrift and the work ethic, Bushman notes that refinement and capitalism were partners, in that capitalism supplied the goods—carpets, furniture, silverware, stylish clothing, and so forth—that betokened a refined household. In inveighing against excessive expenditure on such goods, Child was taking note of one of the major fronts along which capitalism was making its advance into New England and the United States.[40]

But as Child continued on with her critique, she glanced at the more fundamental way that the advent of a society based on market capitalism had changed people's lives:

> Of what *use* is the effort [to keep up with the opulent] which takes up so much of your time, and *all* of your income? Nay, if any unexpected change in affairs should deprive you of a few yearly hundreds, you will find your expenses have *exceeded* your income; thus the foundation of an accumulating debt will be laid, and your family will have formed habits but poorly calculated to save you from the threatened ruin. Not one valuable friend will be gained by living beyond your means, and old age will be left to comparative, if not to utter poverty.

The most telling point here was not so much the concluding prospect of poverty, as the combination of factors that were posited as potentially bringing it on. Any unexpected change in affairs. Living beyond your means. In a market economy one was apt to be at the mercy of the market. One had to take the available steps to gain independence from it, just as New England farm families had learned to sustain their independence by utilizing preservation technologies as a precaution against environmental features, cycles, and unpredictable variations. Living beyond one's means in a market economy, as though changes in one's affairs were not to be expected, was the equivalent of a farm family who neglected to fill up its house with salt meats, butter, cheese, sacks of grains and beans, root vegetables, and dried fruits, as though there were no such thing as a New England winter.[41]

Child drove this point home again and again, nowhere more pointedly than when she said: "A few thousands in the bank are worth all the fashionable friends in Christendom." Here she counterposed a positive balance in the savings bank to what we now call networking. To us, as already to many in Child's day, cultivating marketable, potentially lucrative relationships is a form of investment, our way of making provision for the winter and beyond. But Child was unprepared to think in the liquefied, abstracted terms that capitalism encouraged. Where we might see investment, she saw only expense. She needed a sense of solid, tangible assets, "like money in the bank," that was more closely analogous to well-stocked farmhouse cellars and attics.[42]

Independence, or rather the threat of its loss, was on the minds of other household advisers besides Child. Sarah Josepha Hale had fewer reservations about the culture of gentility and refinement than did Child. She offered as a model housekeeper a friend of hers who was "capable of directing—even *doing* if necessary in the kitchen as well as shining in the drawing room." Nevertheless, Hale included in her 1839 cookbook a chapter of "Cheap Dishes," which was intended for "the rich, who intend to continue so, the thriving who mean to be rich, the sensible and industrious, who love comfort and independence, [and] the benevolent who wish to do good." In keeping with her inclination to smooth over tensions and oppositions, Hale linked economical cookery with as much of the New England tradition as possible. She promoted it as the mainstay of the independence that Captain John Smith had promised immigrants to New England and also of the wealth that Smith had additionally encouraged them to expect. She even included the charity that John Winthrop and other leaders had always insisted must accompany such wealth.[43]

On the other hand, Mrs. Mary Hooker Cornelius, writing a few years later, seemed to suggest that nothing was likely to be of much avail against rampaging market forces. After issuing the familiar warning that "it is much better to adopt a style of expenditure below your means than above them," and offering various pieces of more specific advice, she concluded her introductory discussion thus:

The writer cannot refrain from adding a few words of sympathy and encouragement for those who, having passed their youth in affluent ease, or in the delights of study, are obliged by the vicissitudes of life, to spend their time and strength in laborious household occupations. There are many such instances in this country, particularly in the great Western Valley [i.e., the Middle West]. Adversity succeeds prosperity like a sudden inundation, and sweeps away the possessions and the hopes of multitudes. The poor and uneducated are often rapidly elevated to wealthy independence, while the refined and highly educated are compelled to taste the bitterness of poverty; and minds capable of any attainment, and that would grace any station, are doomed to expend their energies in devising methods for the hands to earn a scanty livelihood.

As it seemed to Mrs. Cornelius, in the aftermath of several of the boom-and-bust sequences to which the antebellum economy was prone, the market had shattered the connections between prudence, virtue, or any other laudable characteristic and the attainment of independence. Independence had become the plaything of economic vicissitude, which bestowed it capriciously on the undeserving while holding the deserving in merciless thrall to wage servitude.[44]

Lydia Maria Child, who inaugurated for nineteenth-century New England the genre of the frugal household manual and formulated the polemic against extravagance in the pursuit of refinement more fully than her successors, had offered more hope. That she was concerned with the perils surrounding traditional household independence in the capitalist milieu was more broadly hinted at by her cautionary tale of "a farmer's daughter, who had lately married a young physician of moderate talents, and destitute of fortune." This young woman, disregarding the traditions in which she was reared, spent her entire dowry on furnishing her house "with as much splendor as we usually find among the wealthiest." She would have been better served, Child suggested, had she adapted the tradition of household production, with "tasteful vases of her own making," and the tradition of household resource preservation, by saving half of her dowry and allowing it to earn "six per cent." This income "would have clothed her as well as the wife of any man, who depends merely upon his own industry, ought to be clothed." By combining resources and techniques from the noncapitalist world of New England's and her own rural past with capitalism's magic power of making cash money produce more cash money, she could have aided in reproducing for the household of her industrious professional husband the insulation from marketplace fluctuations enjoyed (presumably) in the household of her industrious farmer father.[45]

If Child is to be believed, then Jeanne Boydston is correct. The middle-class wife's success or failure at contributing to the family's resources by shrewd household management made the difference between whether the family became secure and independent or barely stayed afloat, if not sinking outright into poverty. Child told one other story that made this point even more explicitly. A "young, pretty, and very amiable girl" was brought up in ignorance of household skills and management. She married "a young lawyer, without property, but with good and increasing practice." Not knowing how to take care of the house, "her wastefulness involved him in debt" and eventually poverty.

After a term in purgatory, in which the husband had to teach school in "a remote town in the Western States," he imparted to his wife the household lore her mother had shortsightedly withheld. "And the change in her habits gradually wrought such a change in her husband's fortune, that she might bring up her daughters in idleness, had not experience taught her that economy, like grammar, is a very hard and tiresome study, after we are twenty years old." Here Child outlined the exact connections Boydston has plotted. No household labor from the wife, and the family could acquire no property. (Since this is a middle-class rather than a working-class family, wasteful expenditure must be added to the equation to cause a drop below subsistence level.) Well-focused household labor from the wife, and the family had all the resources it needed.[46]

In this story, the woman did not come from a farm background. Yet the tradition upon which Child drew to provide lessons in frugality for women living in a marketplace world was the tradition of the nonmarketplace farm household. Her recipes for salting pork or beef, drying pieces of pumpkin, or making jelly or Johnny cake as cheaply yet tastily as possible amounted to bits and pieces of traditional technique salvaged from the precapitalist past and brought to bear on the capitalist present.

That such was her overall procedure she announced at the outset: "The true economy of housekeeping is simply the art of gathering up all the fragments, so that nothing be lost. I mean fragments of *time*, as well as *materials*." She proceeded to offer "Odd Scraps for the Economical":

See that the beef and pork are always *under* brine; and that the brine is sweet and clean. . . . See that the vegetables are neither sprouting nor decaying: if they are so, remove them to a drier place, and spread them.

Examine preserves, to see that they are not contracting mould; and your pickles, to see that they are not growing soft and tasteless.

It was presumably by learning how to heed and act on advice such as this that the lawyer-reduced-to-schoolteacher's wife was enabled to bring about "such a change in her husband's fortune." The premise and promise of the farm grandmother's scrapbook that Child pieced together was that longer-lasting supplies of salt pork, root vegetables, fruit preserves, and pickles would translate into that "few thousands in the bank" that was "worth all the fashionable friends in Christendom." By such traditional economies, new forms of servitude to economic forces would be avoided, and a new form of freehold tenure of economic resources would be achieved.[47]

Catharine Beecher (eventually with the assistance of her world-famous, novel-writing sister) was probably the single most influential contributor to the corpus of nineteenth-century domestic advice and instruction literature. Beecher sounded all the themes upon which we have touched. Here she was on the avoidance of extravagance:

> Do not begin housekeeping in the style in which you should end it, but begin on a plain and small scale, and increase your expenditures as your experience and means are increased.
>
> Be determined to live within your income, and in such a style that you can secure time to improve your own mind, and impart some of your advantages to others.
>
> Try to secure *symmetry* in your dress, furniture, style of living, and charities. That is, do not be profuse in one direction, and close and pinching in another.

Already we begin to see the difference between Beecher and her compeers. She was more careful and systematic in her thinking. In this instance, she took the principle of financial prudence—living only as stylishly as one's resources permitted—and extended it into a more generalized portrayal of personal self-sufficiency and integrity—in effect, inner independence.[48]

But Beecher was well aware of the forces that were making the achievement of such a condition heroically difficult. American society had in many essential respects come unglued:

> Every thing is moving and changing. Persons in poverty, are rising to opulence, and persons of wealth, are sinking to poverty. The children of common laborers, by their talents and enterprise, are becoming nobles in intellect, or wealth, or station; while the children of the wealthy, enervated by indulgence, are sinking to humbler stations. . . . all gradations . . . are placed side by side.[49]

MISS BEECHER'S

DOMESTIC RECEIPT BOOK:

DESIGNED AS A

SUPPLEMENT

TO HER

TREATISE ON DOMESTIC ECONOMY

NEW YORK:

HARPER & BROTHERS, 82 CLIFF STREET.

1846.

Title page from Miss Beecher's Domestic Receipt Book, *1846.*
(Courtesy The Schlesinger Library, Radcliffe Institute, Harvard University)

To the overall upheaval caused by the unimpeded operation of market forces was added the utter wrongheadedness of the system of educating young women. (This was a theme that Child had already emphasized.) The housekeeping wisdom of their mothers, grandmothers, and great-grandmothers was not being passed on to them. The young woman of the mid-nineteenth century in the northern United States, faced with the task of managing a household, was "like a young, inexperienced lad, who is required to superintend all the complicated machinery of a manufactory, which he never was trained to understand, and on penalty of losing reputation, health, and all he values most." The new economic and social realities seemed alien, impossibly burdensome. It was as though our typical young woman, stripped of New England farm household lore, had become her brother, stripped of the Yankee ingenuity to which such lore had famously given birth.[50]

Most women thus felt overwhelmed. Having lost their place in the independent farm household, they also lost any sense of mastery that such an environment had encouraged, even among those occupying subordinate positions within it. Women were now "driven along by the daily occurrences of life . . . the mere sport of circumstances." But, Beecher insisted, seconded by her sister Harriet Beecher Stowe, "there is nothing which so distinctly marks the difference between weak and strong minds as the question whether they control circumstances or circumstances control them."[51]

With the attainment of a strong mind, controlling circumstances, rather than being controlled by them, became possible, and the first step toward developing a strong mind was for a woman in charge of a modern household to understand that her work was "dignified, important, and difficult." Beecher expanded upon this point in the most grandiloquent fashion:

A man who feels that the destinies of a nation are turning on the judgement and skill with which he plans and executes, has a pressure of motive, and an elevation of feeling, which are great safeguards from all that is low, trivial, and degrading. So an American mother and housekeeper, who . . . rightly estimates the long train of influences which will pass down to hundreds, whose destinies, from generation to generation, will be modified by those decisions of her will, which regulated the temper, principles, and habits, of her family, must be elevated above petty temptations which would otherwise assail her.

Here indeed did the ignorant, the helpless, the sports of circumstance, become strong-minded. The household tradition of men and women cooper-

Fig. 7.

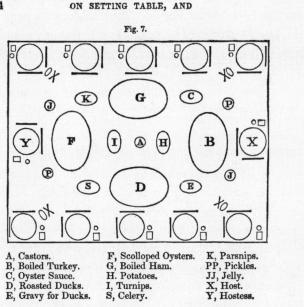

A, Castors.
B, Boiled Turkey.
C, Oyster Sauce.
D, Roasted Ducks.
E, Gravy for Ducks.

F, Scolloped Oysters.
G, Boiled Ham.
H. Potatoes.
I, Turnips.
S, Celery.

K, Parsnips.
PP, Pickles.
JJ, Jelly.
X, Host.
Y, Hostess.

"The proper mode of setting a dinner-table," from Miss Beecher's Domestic Receipt Book, *1846. (Courtesy The Schlesinger Library, Radcliffe Institute, Harvard University)*

ating in mastery of land and labor was transmuted into a transgendered exercise of will and control on the grandest possible scale.[52]

In a more practical vein, such imposition of will and taking of control meant managing the affairs of the household according to "*a habit of system and order.*" Beecher invoked this principle again and again in her works: "Nothing secures ease and success in housekeeping so efficiently as *system* in arranging work." And she followed up on such general endorsements of planned coherence with systematic inventories of essential kitchen implements, highly detailed descriptions and diagrams of menus and table settings for formal dinners, indeed with room-by-room analyses of every space and function of the household and organ-by-organ consideration of the parts of the human body, their requisite care, and maintenance. It all contrasted distinctly with Lydia Maria Child's methodology. The scrapbook drawn from the agrarian past had become the steadily more complete and comprehensive treatise bespeaking the rational and professional present, with all the augmented sense of independence, mastery, and control that such a transformation implied.[53]

But while Beecher was more self-consciously rational and modern than Child, she had by no means jettisoned the rural New England heritage. We have reproduced a number of her highly traditional recipes and preservation techniques. In the following passage, Beecher and her sister combined their commitment to coherence and plan with crucial elements drawn from the world of their forefathers. The words date from 1869, just after the "Yankee" victory in the Civil War:

> Let us suppose a colony of cultivated and Christian people, having abundant wealth, who now are living as the wealthy usually do, emigrating to some of the beautiful Southern uplands, where are rocks, hills, valleys, and mountains as picturesque as those of New-England, where the thermometer but rarely reaches 90° in summer, and in winter as rarely sinks below freezing-point, so that outdoor labor goes on all the year, where the fertile soil is easily worked, where rich tropical fruits and flowers abound, where cotton and silk can be raised by children around their home, where the produce of vineyards and orchards finds steady markets by railroads ready made; suppose such a colony, with a central church and school-room, library, hall for sports, and a common laundry, (taking the most trying part of domestic labor from each house,) — suppose each family to train the children to labor with the hands as a healthful and honorable duty; suppose all this, which is perfectly practicable, would not the enjoyment of this life be increased, and also abundant treasures be laid up in heaven, by using the wealth thus economized in diffusing similar enjoyments and culture among the poor, ignorant, and neglected ones in desolated sections where many now are perishing for want of such Christian example and influences?

We have here the beginnings of a Yankee South, in complement to the "Yankee West" that had been mostly settled within the lifetimes of the Beecher women, and where they had themselves both lived. The little colony was to be planted by people with ample resources who had presumably experienced a moral and spiritual change of heart — the same type of people who had originally planted New England.[54]

There would be the church and the school from colonial days and the more recent innovation of the public library. In relation to our present concerns, the production of cotton would be removed from the system of slave labor and integrated into a world of families combining the efforts of all their members in household production. The proportion of foodstuffs and textiles to be sent off for sale in distant marketplaces would be much greater than it had been in colonial New England, in the days before the transportation revolution. These market sales, along with unspecified reductions in expenditure the colony would achieve, would generate the surplus wealth that was capitalism's signal triumph. But in contrast to what was actually happening in the dawning age of the robber baron, this surplus wealth, the fruit of traditional New England industry and frugality, would be devoted to equally traditional New England charity.

Catharine Beecher and Harriet Beecher Stowe were proposing that the newly reunited United States become colonial New England on a transcontinental scale, that it be "knitt together in this worke as one man," supplying the necessities of some out of the superfluities of others, just as John Winthrop had insisted to his fellow passengers while crossing over from Old to New England in 1629 must be the norm for life in the new society. In thus extending the influence and sway of "a Christian house" (the title of the chapter which this passage concluded), Beecher and Stowe offered concrete literary realization of their claim that "she, who is the mother and housekeeper in a large family, is the sovereign of an empire." Women, superbly independent in their domestic sovereignty, were to show everyone the royal road to recovery of New England household independence and village uprightness.[55]

It was a noble dream, but it was no better suited to serve as a model for the industrialized, urbanized, fully capitalized America that was taking shape in 1869 than was the idealized recall of the rural and village New England Thanksgiving that Harriet Beecher Stowe presented in *Oldtown Folks*, a novel she published that same year (analyzed here in chapter 6). The literature of household instruction, no matter how thoughtful and thorough and masterful, could not turn back the clock.

What it could do and did, however, was contribute to a cultural climate in which that portion of the New England past consisting of subsistence family farms was remembered with particular affection and respect. At the end of the previous chapter, we stressed the important role in the growth of a market economy in New England played by a very different portion of the New England past, the merchants based in Boston and other urban seaports such as Salem and Newport. Those speaking from the family farm perspective, while acknowledging that a certain degree of refinement was acceptable and even desirable, held simplicity and plainness in the highest esteem. Conversely, those speaking from the urban and mercantile perspective, while certainly not discountenancing simplicity and plainness, counterbalanced them with a rather greater proportion of refinement. Such propensities were reflected in Mrs. Lee's statement, just a few short pages after her exhortations to frugality, that "a good cook is as anxiously attentive to the appearance and color of her roasts, as a young beauty is to her complexion at a birthday ball."[56]

The heightened refinement—the urbanity—of the urban merchants was reflected in their foodways. As we have noted, Mrs. Lee, the "Boston House-keeper" of 1832, stood out among the New England cookbook authors of her day for the complexity of her recipes and the luxury of her ingredients—for example, lemon rind, truffles, and morels. Similarly, a woman who grew up in a Salem merchant family around this same time repeatedly referred in her memoirs to such things as mangoes, "Malaga grapes," Madeira and other imported wines, and olives.[57]

In such circles, dining unashamedly from a menu enriched by delicacies was nothing new. The Gardiners of mid-eighteenth-century Boston, their prosperous way of life funded in large part by the sale of imported drugs and medicines to apothecaries throughout New England, supplied their table with such fine imported foods and spices as lemons, vermicelli, red wine, "Troufles and Morels," "Chyan Pepper," "Jamaica Pepper," and "the best of Olive Oyl." A couple of generations earlier, Samuel Sewall, centrally involved in the Boston export-import trade in its initial phases, inhabited a food world filled with "China Oranges," marmalade, Canary wine, and sugared almonds.[58]

Imported spices, fruits, and wines had long been on sale in the countryside as well. That was part of the urban merchants' cycle of transactions. Nevertheless, most New Englanders away from the coast geographically and down from the top socially did not have such items very often. For them, the largely self-contained family farm had been the primary socioeconomic milieu. But in the first half of the nineteenth century the family farm was displaced as such by the marketplace. And urban merchants certainly played an important part in this displacement.[59]

For a variety of reasons—Puritan enshrinement of austerity and plainness, the steady emergence of democracy—the sophistication and refinement of seaports and cities could not be put forward as a cultural model for the emergent marketplace world. Acceptance of the marketplace way of life could be more effectively facilitated if the homespun, homegrown, home-stored, and home-cooked democracy of the family farm way of life that the marketplace was dislodging could be incorporated into it.

In the early phases of this process, until 1850 or so, the marketplace world's recall of the family farm world, as seen in the household and kitchen advice literature, contained a significant quotient of practicality. Family farm subsistence practices were passed along to marketplace households because they could still be useful. Also, it was hoped that family farm independence might somehow be adapted and recreated within the marketplace context.

As time and continuing social and technological change placed the family farm world at an ever greater distance, however, the practical element in recollections of it steadily diminished. And as practicality retreated, nostalgia advanced. In the second half of the nineteenth century, the family farm way of life as a whole receded out of reach and was replaced as the primary object of recall by the particular foods associated with it. The era in which we still live had begun: one in which the image of old-time New England is formed not by the Federal-style mansion of the Salem merchant and the "haunch of venison cooked in claret wine" savored in its formal dining room, but rather by the unadorned residence of the Plymouth Pilgrim or the Concord Minuteman and the baked beans and Indian pudding thought to have been contentedly eaten at its hearthside.[60]

CHAPTER 5

Fresh & Sweet Pasture

Fowl, Game, & Meat

*T*he two distinctive practices of Britain's first farmers, who had come to the island in the fourth millennium B.C.E., were grain cultivation and husbandry of domesticated animals. Over the thousands of years separating this migration from that of the English to New England in the seventeenth century C.E., livestock husbandry had not changed all that much. Significant improvements in feeding, for example, did not take place until after the middle of the seventeenth century. To a nineteenth- or twentieth-century English farmer, the cows possessed by his sixteenth-century predecessor "would look like dwarf bags of bones, misshapen through ill-feeding and casual breeding."[1]

Jay Allan Anderson calculates that an average English husbandman in the years just before the immigration to New England would have owned "three horses, four cows, five pigs, twenty-five sheep, and numerous goats, poultry, rabbits, pigeons, and bee hives," as well as an ox or two that served primarily as beasts of burden. Within this collection, the pigs were the "most significant source of meat." Cattle were generally considered more valuable for dairy products (often called "white meat") than for beef. They were slaughtered and consumed directly only when they had become too weak to survive the winter on the limited supplies of available fodder. The sheep, goats, poultry, rabbits, and pigeons provided supplementary sources of flesh food, mostly eaten fresh, with the poultry additionally yielding eggs and the sheep and goats dairy products.[2]

Domesticated animals were not the only source of flesh meat in the English diet. During the Middle Ages, average English people had eaten game animals in significant amounts. By the early seventeenth century they ate them somewhat less frequently, partly as a result of the fact that "as the forest receded . . . beasts of prey became rarer," and partly because of laws restricting the right to hunt certain species to the gentry and aristocracy. The best

"A Perfect Cow," in "A New England Dairy and Stock Farm," Harper's New Monthly
Magazine, *October 1878. (Courtesy Fall River Public Library)*

known of such laws were those making deer hunting an exclusively upper-
class privilege, in consequence of which venison was regarded as "a high
status food, rarely eaten but continually craved."[3]

Nevertheless, the game laws were not yet as strictly enforced as they would
be later in the seventeenth century and thereafter. Commoners remained
free to pursue hare and such varieties of fowl as plover, teal, mallard, quail,
woodcock, partridge, and pheasant.

Above and beyond the licit forms of hunting, many people ventured into
deer parks and other game preserves for a bit of poaching, although it is not
known exactly how much traffic in illicit game there was. The existence of
popular fowling manuals, the prevalence in cookbooks of recipes for wild
hare (as opposed to domesticated rabbits or coneys), and the emphasis in

literature promoting immigration to America on the abundance of deer in the new land—all these indicate that game flesh remained, on the eve of the Great Migration to New England, a type of food that English people valued. It was "a minor but nevertheless significant portion" of their diet.[4]

For the native peoples, the flesh meat that they obtained from hunting the animals in their environment was much more than a minor part of their diet. In the northern part of the region, where climatic conditions kept horticulture to a minimum, people largely lived on fish, migratory birds, and such forest animals as beaver, caribou, moose, deer, and bear. During the winter season that stretched from October through March, success in killing large forest animals made the difference between survival and starvation, and even in good years, February and March were likely to be marked by hunger, as by that point in the year animal prey was "lean and relatively scarce."[5]

Winter was also the hunting season for the native groups farther south whose primary sustenance was derived from the corn-and-bean horticulture described in chapters 1 and 2. According to William Cronon, a typical season's hunt for a southern New England inland village would bring in about forty pounds per person of deer and bear meat, these two animals providing more than 75 percent of the total seasonal meat supply. For these southern people, who also had their stored corn and beans to rely upon, game animals were as important for their hides as for their flesh, if not more important. Animal skins were their sole source of clothing.[6]

The New England Indians did not keep livestock in any sense recognized by Europeans. However, it is now generally understood that the distinction between domesticated farm animals and "wild" forest or woodland animals simplifies the variety of relationships that have existed between human groups and their environments. The Algonquians' practice of periodic burning of the forests surrounding their homes and encampments "created ideal habitats for a host of wildlife species." Most especially, as the turn-of-the-nineteenth-century clergyman and president of Yale Timothy Dwight noted, "the object of these conflagrations was to produce fresh and sweet pasture for the purpose of alluring the deer to the spots on which they had been kindled."[7]

As we now understand the environmental effects of native firing of woodlands, it created a landscape full of "boundary areas between forests and grasslands." Such areas were conducive to patterns of plant growth that turned them into rich feeding grounds for deer and other animals. This increased supply of fodder led to larger populations of the game and fowl that lived upon it, which in turn led to larger populations of predators that lived upon them. As Timothy Dwight seemed to grasp with his use of the term "pasture," native burning of the forest was a form of animal husbandry, just as the native hunt for game was a form of harvest, the gathering of a foodstuff "which [the native people] had consciously been instrumental in creating."[8]

Among the elements that the English introduced into the New England environment, their animal husbandry had the most radical consequences. English livestock trampled down Indian crops, ultimately forcing the Indians to fence the crops in and move toward an English mode of tillage. Livestock were a threat to English crops as well, but the measures taken to protect those crops essentially placed all Indian foodstuff milieus, not only the plots of hilled corn and beans, but also the shellfish-gathering sites and the hunting terrain, in even greater jeopardy.

Roger Williams told of a wolf being deprived of a deer it had caught by "two *English* Swine," who proceeded to gorge themselves on their contraband prey. The anecdote aptly summarized many aspects of the intrusion of English livestock into the New England environment. Between direct hunting by the English, competition from their livestock, and habitat alteration, the wildfowl and deer that the Indians had husbanded and that had impressed early European observers with their abundance were greatly reduced in New England by the end of the seventeenth century and were approaching non-existence in the region a century after that.[9]

Above all, the English settlers needed land to feed their livestock, and this necessity drove them constantly to enlarge the territory under their control. In many towns ten times as much land was devoted to pasture as to tillage. The tendency was self-perpetuating. Livestock contributed to the creation of agricultural surpluses. The sale of these surpluses generated additional wealth, which encouraged investment in yet more grazing land. And as the craving for land persisted, the pressure correspondingly increased to remove the natives from whatever areas they still inhabited and to convert those areas from native horticulture and game husbandry to English tillage and livestock husbandry.

Such livestock-driven land hunger on the part of the English was the proximate cause of King Philip's War in the 1670s. But well before this, in the 1640s, a Narragansett chieftain, Miantonomo, had seen clearly that the importation of the English way of life onto his people's land meant that his people's way of life was being driven off the land: "our fathers had plenty of deer and skins, our plains were full of deer, as also our woods, and of turkies, and our coves full of fish and fowl. But these English having gotten our land, they with scythes cut down the grass, and with axes fell the trees; their cows and horses eat the grass, and their hogs spoil our clam banks and we shall all be starved."[10]

Thus, like fishing, farming was involved from the outset in the relationships and expansionist tendencies dictated by a capitalist economy. Nevertheless, as described in the last chapter, after the initial dispossession of the natives there did ensue two centuries when New England's family farms were involved only marginally in marketplace relationships. These farms were primarily devoted to the production of "a comfortable subsistence." It was during this historical eddy that there developed notions of family farming as being uniquely hospitable to virtuous living, as opposed to the trading that took place in towns and cities and the fishing that was launched from seaports. It was also during this period that New England's food culture was created. Within this culture, flesh foods became increasingly prominent.[11]

Wildfowl

The consumption of wildfowl was another way in which Indian and English foodways resembled each other. Southern New England Indians ate partridge, heath cock, pigeon, owl, and such waterfowl as crane, swan, goose, brant, duck, and cormorant. During the annual migratory periods, groups of Indians lived at marshland encampments for the purpose of taking the waterfowl as they passed through.[12]

Similarly, the medieval English ate swan, crane, heron, bustard, quail, snipe, mallard, partridge, plover, sparrow, finch, lark, and blackbird. Pigeons were domesticated by yeomen, while peacocks, pheasants, partridges, and swans were "reared and cherished" by people higher up on the social scale. The swans, in particular, were maintained on rivers by the owners of especially large estates.[13]

Birds provided fresh meat at times when it was otherwise unavailable and variety at all times. For many common people, fowl was the only fresh meat they ever ate. Swans and peacocks served as banquet fare for the gentry and aristocracy, while those who were less well off but who nevertheless had the resources to mark special occasions made do with herons and bustards. The principal cooking methods were roasting and boiling or stewing.[14]

Probably bird-eating also conferred the pleasures of freshness and variety upon the New England Indians. Dean R. Snow estimates that at the time of contact, meat and fowl together constituted 10 percent of the diet in southern areas. Since the preponderance of this consumption was allocated to deer, bear, and other large game, the sense of variety imparted, in the midst of many smoked venison repasts, by a fresh-cooked crane may have been particularly marked. There is little testimony regarding native methods of cooking fowl, beyond William Wood's mentioning it as a component of succotash. Howard S. Russell states that "birds were sometimes roasted whole, with bear oil to baste them."[15]

By the seventeenth and eighteenth centuries, the range of British fowl considered good eating was beginning to narrow. Cranes, gulls, and herons were now thought to taste too much like fish. Some large land birds, in particular the bustard, were declining in both numbers and popularity. In addition, "fewer of the small wild birds were now accepted as a regular part of the diet." However, pigeons continued in great demand, and seventeenth- and eighteenth-century cookbooks included recipes for the potting of pigeons as well as woodcocks, swans, geese, and some smaller birds. The trend toward domestication of prized species such as partridges and pheasants also continued. Some eighteenth-century gentry created their own pond habitats for duck, mallard, teal, widgeon, and goose. The birds would be sent to London, either to supply the tables of their own townhouses or to be sold.[16]

New England was settled just before more restricted notions of fowl consumption had fully taken hold, and in any case such ideas would doubtless not have withstood the North American bird cornucopia. During the first years in Plymouth, there were so many wildfowl in the area "that one man at six shoots hath killed 400." Within fifty years such hunting excesses greatly reduced the population of wildfowl in New England. Nevertheless, larger game birds such as partridges, songbirds of all kinds, and waterfowl continued to be hunted, cooked, and eaten, particularly in frontier areas. According to Thomas Robinson Hazard, in the early nineteenth century the salt ponds, marshes, and hills of southern Rhode Island continued to teem with duck, teal, plover, curlew, meadowlark, partridge, and snipe.[17]

Hazard's explanation for the persistence of such an abundance of wildfowl in a settled portion of New England at such a relatively late date was that all other birds had been eclipsed as candidates for the table by "the superlative flavor of a well-fattened, well-killed, well-picked, well-dry-dressed Rhode Island turkey." Nevertheless, he enthusiastically praised the virtues of the roasted ducks prepared by his grandfather's female African American cook, and he claimed that the local teal, when roasted by this same cook, excelled "the boasted wild, celery-fed canvas-back [duck] of the Chesapeake."

Around this same time, Ella Shannon Bowles and Dorothy S. Towle report, the teal preparations of housewives in the Hampton, New Hampshire, area were also in high repute.[18]

Such gems of wildfowl cookery were becoming increasingly isolated phenomena, however. Many kinds of birds continued to be found in different parts of the United States, of course, and some of them found their way to urban and eastern markets. It was doubtless at the market that the "ducks and partridges or quail according to season" were obtained for the course consisting of those birds that formed part of the sequence of formal dining in the King household in Salem, Massachusetts, in the second quarter of the nineteenth century. Less exalted folk may also have occasionally bought game birds in the marketplace. Lydia Maria Child and Sarah Josepha Hale, both seeking to appeal to readers in average circumstances, told how to cook partridge, and another antebellum writer added recipes for widgeon, canvasback duck, quail, woodcock, snipe, and reed bird.[19]

Nevertheless, for the most part nineteenth-century New England cookbooks did not bother to identify particular types of birds, other than chicken, turkey, and the occasional duck or goose, in their poultry recipes. Although Amelia Simmons, who wrote around the time of Thomas Robinson Hazard's childhood, offered tips on the purchasing of specific wildfowl, she referred only to generic "fowl" when it came to actual cooking. Similarly, Lydia Maria Child wrote of how "to curry fowl" and Catharine Beecher of how "to stew birds."[20]

Mrs. N. K. M. Lee did supplement her discussions of "fowl" and "fowl, wild" with entries on partridge, wild duck, and other species. But very few of her successors followed her lead. It was not until self-conscious antiquarianism emerged in the last decades of the nineteenth century that New England cookbooks took note again of the likes of snipe, partridge, pheasant, quail, lark, plover, and woodcock.[21]

Behind the species that was the exception to this rule of diminishing wildfowl cookery there hangs a particularly appalling tale of environmental depredation. The passenger pigeon had not only served as food for the Indians but had also provided them with oil for cooking other foods. The most significant fact about the passenger pigeon, however, was that it easily outnumbered all other varieties of North American fowl. Acknowledging that his readers would find it difficult to believe him, William Wood wrote in the 1630s that in spring and autumn, one would see "neyther beginning nor ending, length, or breadth" of the flocks of "Millions of Millions" of migrating passenger pigeons. The rest of the year, their nests would be so

"Netting Wild Pigeons in New England," Frank Leslie's Illustrated Newspaper,
21 September 1867. Note stool pigeons on the ground.
(Courtesy Fall River Public Library)

thick in a certain spot a few miles from the English settlements "that the
Sunne never sees the ground in that place."[22]

In fact, there were so many passenger pigeons that their own foraging
for food sometimes created major problems for the colonists. Winter famine was feared in Plymouth in 1643 because passenger pigeons had eaten up
most of the grain crop. That same year, John Winthrop attributed a region-
wide grain scarcity partly to pigeons. They were also known to have cleaned
out entire districts of their acorns, thus depriving the colonists' hogs of one
of their primary food sources.[23]

At its height, the North American passenger pigeon population is estimated to have been between three and five billion. But the colonists soon
set about to destroy them, particularly during their migrations. In 1648 John
Winthrop reported that "it was ordinary for one man to kill . . . five or six
dozen at one shoot [shot]." A. W. Schorger concludes that hunting with
guns was the most significant cause of the birds' demise. Trapping with nets,
however, was also of major importance. As early as 1674, John Josselyn wrote
that "of late" pigeons were "much diminished" in New England, "the *English* taking them with nets." In the perfected method, blinded pigeons—
"stool pigeons—were staked to the ground to serve as decoys, luring flocks

from the sky to be ensnared in the nets. The trapped birds were then beaten to death by anyone who could swing a club. For weeks afterward, pigeon would be the staple of the daily diet.[24]

Another variety of pigeon slaughter was observed by a traveler passing through Rhode Island in 1760. During the evening roosts of the "prodigious" migratory flocks, the birds sitting "one upon another in such crouds, as sometimes to break down the largest branches," people would "go out with long poles, and knock numbers of them on the head." The pigeons made little effort to escape, being "either . . . fatigued by their flight, or terrified by the obscurity of the night." The traveler subsequently "met with scarcely any other food" than pigeon at the inns where he stayed. The massacre continued unabated for the next century and a half, until the death of the last passenger pigeon in a Cincinnati zoo in 1914.[25]

In contrast to other wildfowl, pigeon was as omnipresent in nineteenth-century cookbooks as on eighteenth-century tavern menus. Here is a typical recipe, for "Alamode Pigeons":

Wash them very clean; make a stuffing of bits of salt pork, pounded biscuit, thyme, or summer savory, a little salt, and one or two eggs. Stuff the breasts sufficiently to make them look plump, lay them in a stew pan or pot, cover them with water, add a little thyme, and half a pint of red wine.

If young, two and a half hours moderate stewing is sufficient; if old, three or four hours. Add more seasoning before you take them off, if required.[26]

Chicken

The chicken originated in southeast Asia. After domestication, it was introduced into the Roman world via Persia and Greece, reaching Britain by the first century B.C.E. and becoming fairly common shortly thereafter in those parts of the island under Roman occupation. In the Middle Ages, chicken was an established part of the British diet. Monastic orders that forbade the eating of animals exempted chicken and other fowl from prohibition. Among those in the secular world, "most families kept hens," especially in rural areas, "since they had a long life [sic] as egg producers before they were consigned to the pot."[27]

In the course of the sixteenth century, as one minor manifestation of the transition to capitalism in England, the price of chicken more than doubled, making it too expensive for many people for whom it had previously been standard fare. Nevertheless, live chickens and other fowl remained among the most widely held possessions of average rural families, "so common that frequently [they were] not itemized in inventories." In such husbandman households, it began to be more advantageous to abstain from eating the chickens (and eggs) that were available in one's own yard and instead to take them to town for sale to those who could afford them.[28]

In New England widespread chicken-keeping was in evidence early on. In a 1627 assessment of the animal resources of the Plymouth settlement, "chickens were considered," along with swine, "too numerous to list." By the turn of the eighteenth century, colonial probate inventories, like those in England, ignored chickens not because they were scarce but rather because they were plentiful.[29]

At midcentury in Deerfield, Massachusetts, store sales of chicken occurred but only infrequently. In a study of the distribution and sale of food in colonial Boston, it is stated that in the eighteenth century farmers and peddlers sold "small meats," including poultry, but no information is offered regarding the volume of such transactions. During the colonial period, as New England lagged well behind the mother country in the degree to which marketplace relationships had become definitive, it is likely that most farm families reverted to the medieval pattern of eating their own chickens, once egg production went into decline, rather than selling them.[30]

Harriet Beecher Stowe provided evidence on this point in both directions. In her novel *The Minister's Wooing*, which took place in an urban setting (Newport, Rhode Island) at the turn of the nineteenth century, a farm household's African American cook and foodstuff steward stated that she had "come down" into town "'fore light to sell my chickens an' eggs,—got a lot o' money for 'em, too." But if an outlying farm household sold its chickens and eggs in the neighboring town, a small urban household in that same town nevertheless could supply its chicken and egg needs without a trip to the market. Struggling with the news of the apparent death at sea of her male cousin and childhood chum, the novel's heroine, Mary Scudder, was sent into the family barn to get some eggs and feed the chickens. As she watched the bright and sprightly hens and cocks "pecking the corn, even where it lodged in the edge of her little shoes," Scudder said to herself, "'Poor things, I am glad they enjoy it!'—and even this one little act of love to the ignorant fellowship below her carried away some of the choking pain which seemed all the while suffocating her heart." Unfortunately, the retrieval of the eggs recalled to her mind the times that she and her departed cousin had fetched eggs together, "and she sat down with a faint sickness, and then turned and walked wearily in." Whatever Stowe may have meant to indicate about the emergence of a marketplace economy in New England, she certainly made it clear that keeping one's own barnyard creatures offered rich possibilities for spiritual experience.[31]

The trend in England by which chicken came to be consumed primarily by the upper classes was reproduced to some extent in New England. In Essex County, Massachusetts, in the seventeenth century, chicken was one of the luxury items stolen from gentry households. One member of the colonial elite, a minister's wife, allegedly brought about her own death by consuming, a few days after childbirth, a repast of roast chickens accompanied by "strong beer flip." "Wonderful that in learned and elevated situations among the great, should be such ignorance," was the reflection of the Boston physician who recorded this unfortunate occurrence in his diary.[32]

Chicken pie was another way of cooking chicken favored by the well-off of colonial New England. Mistress Anne Gibbons Gardiner, whose pumpkin pie and fish and seafood dishes we have already sampled, also recorded a recipe for chicken pie in her manuscript cookbook. The chicken pieces were to be supplemented by ham or bacon, beefsteak, and anchovy and seasoned with salt, pepper, and "a little beaten Mace. . . . Put in a full pint of water and cover the Pie; bake it well, and when it comes from the Oven, fill it with good Gravy."[33]

Half a century later "the feast began with a chicken pie" more often than not, when a wealthy Salem, Massachusetts, family chose to engage in formal dining. However, chicken pie was not an exclusively upper-class dish. On all levels of society, it was a standard component of Thanksgiving dinners, supplementing the roasted turkey. Through the nineteenth century, even the largest of turkeys weighed no more than eight pounds and could not satisfy the main course needs of most families. We will have more to say about chicken pie in the next chapter.[34]

Harriet Beecher Stowe's New England novels focused on the middling levels of society. The social range of chicken consumption was indicated in *Oldtown Folks*. On the one hand, there was the scene late in the novel in which the narrator, from a middling background but with connections to the Boston mercantile elite, was served chicken along with "oyster-*paté*" by his Boston friends. On the other hand, there was the simple cold chicken he and his friends were given from their own more modest households for sustenance on their journey to the college preparatory educational establishment they would be attending. In two other novels Stowe depicted cold chicken, and "cold fowl and tongue delicately prepared, and shaded with feathers of parsley," as part of the menu for festive occasions observed by average New Englanders.[35]

The amount of chicken consumption among the general population in the nineteenth century is uncertain. One writer has inferred from agricultural census statistics and other factors that "the role of chicken in the daily eighteenth- and nineteenth-century diets has been overemphasized." We are not in a position to assess this statement, but we do note an earlier writer's citation of the fact that poultry sales in Boston in 1848 totaled $1 million, with sales of eggs adding another $1 million.[36]

Popular cookbooks of the era included instruction in the purchasing of chicken, along with other types of poultry. Amelia Simmons recommended "yellow leg'd" chickens as having the sweetest taste, going on to explain that for all poultry "a tight vent" was a sign that a bird was "fresh killed" rather than stale, and that legs that were "smooth" rather than "rough" and "speckled" showed that it was young. Child added checks of the feet (which should not be "hard, stiff, and worn") and the bottom of the breastbone (if "soft, and gives easily, it is a sign of youth; if stiff, the poultry is old"). Beecher gave the fullest advice, further adding tests for limber joints, full, bright eyes, and thin, tender skin, easily torn with a pin. The most desirable birds were those that were "full grown, but not old."[37]

Once the nineteenth-century housewife got her chicken home from the market, what did she do with it, besides make the chicken pies we have already mentioned? New England chicken cookery consisted primarily of roasting or boiling. Simmons lumped together the roasting of "fowl" with that of turkey. In her case, as in that of later writers who addressed themselves more specifically to the roasting of chicken, the advice regarding stuffing was to use the same mixture for all other poultry as for turkey. We shall therefore defer our discussion of poultry stuffing to the turkey section.

Stuffing aside, there wasn't a whole lot more to say about roasting a chicken. Simmons advised suspending the stuffed bird upside down "to a steady solid fire, basting frequently with salt and water, and roast until a steam emits from the breast." She also called for dusting with flour and a further basting with gravy prior to serving. Child and Beecher added little to these instructions, except for a roasting time recommendation of one hour.[38]

Child recommended an hour for boiling a chicken as well. She may have assumed that her readers would be utilizing older, and therefore cheaper, birds because her contemporary Mrs. Lee stated that twenty minutes was enough boiling time even for a large chicken. Lee included an elaborate boiled chicken recipe that involved two hours' soaking in skim milk, heating in initially cold water until the boiling point was reached, removal from the fire and remaining "in the water close covered for half an hour," and being served with white sauce. Three decades later Mrs. S. G. Knight split the difference on boiling time, stating that a young chicken that had been "stuffed as for roasting" would be done in forty-five minutes.[39]

Among other chicken recipes, broiling was occasionally mentioned. As usual, Mrs. Lee came up with several curiosities, such as sugared chicken fritters and "Chickens in a Minute." There were recipes for chicken soup and, after chowder came to be considered one of the hallmarks of Yankee cuisine, chicken chowder. Beecher remarked that chicken, along with veal, was the "most suitable" flesh food for curries, and several other cookbooks, beginning with Child, did indeed contain recipes for curried chicken or fowl.[40]

The chicken dish that was mentioned the second most frequently in our cookbook sample, after chicken pie, was fricasseed chicken. Instances appeared beginning with Child in the 1820s through to the early twentieth century. Child featured both a "brown" and a "white" version, the latter with egg yolks, cream, nutmeg, and lemons. While Beecher presented "Fricassee Chickens" only in a simple brown version, Mrs. Lee's "Chickens Fricasseed" were, as might be expected, quite white and quite rich:

> Prepare and cut up two chickens; put them in a stewpan with some butter, parsley, a bay-leaf, thyme, basil, two cloves, mushrooms, and a slice of ham; let them stew till scarcely any sauce remains, then add a little flour, warm water, salt and pepper; stew it again and reduce the sauce. When nearly done put in the yolks of three eggs beaten up with a little cream or milk; thicken it over the fire, but do not let it boil; a small quantity of lemon-juice or vinegar may be added. Place the breasts and bones of the chickens on a dish, lay the legs and wings over them, and then pour the sauce over the whole; garnish with the mushrooms. Take off the skins before you cut up the chickens if you wish the fricassee very white.

One hopes that those who wished for the extra whiteness read the recipe through to the end before beginning to implement it.[41]

A 1963 cookbook devoted to the cuisine of northern New England offered a glimpse of how farm housewives had utilized their hens for eating after egg production had ceased. In "Great-Grandmother's Scalloped Chicken," the pieces of the bird were subjected first to long simmering in seasoned broth, then to baking. The baking was to take place amid layers of dressing and a sauce consisting of ground skin from the chicken, milk, chicken broth, fat reserved from the broth, flour, salt, and eggs. "This will serve a dozen people well," the author claimed. "To serve 12 from one old hen—what more could a thrifty housewife ask? And serve them deliciously, too."[42]

Turkey

The turkey straddles the dividing line between wild and domesticated fowl. First domesticated by the Indians of Central America, turkeys were brought to Spain in the 1520s, whence they made their way to France, England, and other European nations. The first mention in any English source occurred in 1541. By 1575 they had become "rather common Christmas fare" for many English people, including husbandmen who were keeping them in their farmyards. However, as with chickens, the primary purpose of English turkey-keeping was not home consumption but market sale. Data on turkey prices are available from 1560 onward. In the seventeenth and eighteenth centuries turkeys were driven to the London market in the autumn.[43]

"Tame turkeys" were on the list of items to be sent to Massachusetts Bay as early as 1629. Seven years later they were plentiful enough in Cambridge, Massachusetts, to be regulated as a potential nuisance. The same year, John Winthrop Jr. had a domestic turkey cock and hen with him in Saybrook, Connecticut, so early on conditions were propitious for the propagation of the species in that colony. In the late eighteenth century, domestic turkeys were reported as being numerous in Newport, Rhode Island.[44]

By the 1790s commercialized farming of domestic turkeys existed in New as in Old England. Thousands of turkeys were driven from New Hampshire farmyards to market in Boston. Reportedly, they had minds of their own regarding the rhythms of their travels: "When the shades of evening had reached a certain degree of density, suddenly the whole drove with one accord rose from the road and sought a perch in the neighboring trees. The drover was prepared for such a halt and drew up his wagon beside the road, where he passed the night." How widespread such turkey marketing was before the nineteenth century is uncertain. In 1802 one diarist noted it as a "singular circumstance" that several hundred turkeys had been driven to market in Salem, Massachusetts.[45]

The importation of Central American turkeys into New England by way of Spain and England was a distinct case of coals to Newcastle. Turkeys, of larger size and different coloring than the type that had been domesticated in Central America, were among the "wild" species that had been encouraged to increase and multiply in New England by Indian environmental management. William Wood stated that they could be found year-round in groups of a hundred or more. Thomas Morton was told by Indians he queried that as many as a thousand wild turkeys might be found in the nearby woods on any given day.[46]

The turkey found in the New England region had "the use of his long legs so ready, that he can runne as fast as a Dogge," wrote William Wood. The earliest colonists therefore sometimes had trouble hunting them down, unless they shot them in the legs. Indians were also asked to assist in English turkey hunts. According to Roger Williams, one Indian method of capturing turkeys was by laying nets under oak trees, where the birds would come to eat acorns. At seasons of major turkey abundance, collective hunts would be organized, with hundreds of hunters "spread over such a great scope of ground, that a turkey could hardly escape them."[47]

The New England turkey was prized by the Indians not only for its flesh but also for its plumage. Several seventeenth-century observers spoke of native coats or cloaks "curiously made of the fairest feathers of their ... Turkies, which commonly their old men make; and is with them as Velvet with us." According to John Josselyn, such turkey-feather coats were primarily made for Indian children. One of the uses the colonists proceeded to find for the wings of wild turkeys was as hearth brushes.[48]

Although the ground speed of New England wild turkeys was an obstacle that English hunters had to overcome, overcome it they did. William Wood and Thomas Morton noted some of the other factors that made New England turkeys easy rather than difficult to hunt. For example, if one turkey in a group was shot down, the others would "sit fast neverthelesse," seemingly awaiting their own turns in the gunners' sights. Additionally, in winter, turkeys fed on "Shrimps, & such smal Fishes" that they found in coastal tidal flats. The tracks they made in the snow in their passage to these sites were easily followed, with the frequent result that hunters "killed ten or a dozen in halfe a day."[49]

Wild turkeys were generally held to taste better than domestic ones. People of refined palate were the most apt to register a preference. At the invitation of "an old farmer," the great French gourmet Anthelme Brillat-Savarin went hunting for wild turkey near Hartford, Connecticut, in 1794. He succeeded in bagging, along with several squirrels and partridges, a bird that had let him get within ten paces. The subsequent dinner Brillat-Savarin put together for his American companions featured partridge wings "*en papillottes*," squirrels "stewed in Madeira," and roasted wild turkey that was "delightful to look upon, delightful to smell, and delicious to taste; . . . until the last morsel was eaten, you could hear all around the table, 'Very good! Exceedingly good! Oh, my dear Sir, what a glorious bit!'"[50]

After Brillat-Savarin, not many would be in a position to dine on a wild turkey that had been living in New England at the time it was killed. In 1813 the last wild turkey in Connecticut would meet its end. Already in 1672 John Josselyn was noting that in eastern Massachusetts, hunters had been so successful "that 'tis very rare to meet with a wild *Turkie* in the Woods." The turkeys persisted in western Massachusetts, with numbers constantly dwindling, through the eighteenth century, but they were extinct there by 1851. The wild turkeys on sale in the markets of eastern cities in the nineteenth century were mostly shipped in from the ever-retreating areas beyond the edge of pioneer advance.[51]

At the time of American independence, the wild turkey had been all but eliminated from New England and other settled regions. It continued to be plentiful, however, in the territories farther west that the founders of the new nation coveted, and Benjamin Franklin, James Madison, and others urged that it, rather than the bald eagle, be designated the national bird. The debate was conducted in terms of imputed character traits. Franklin argued that the bald eagle was "of bad moral Character," stealing its food from other more "diligent" birds. The turkey was "a much more respectable Bird, and withal a true original Native of America," so courageous that it "should not hesitate to attack a Grenadier of the British Guards, who would presume to invade his FarmYard with a *red* Coat on." Franklin conceded that the turkey might be "a little vain and silly." But proponents of the eagle found the turkey not merely vain and silly but cowardly and stupid, and such qualities were apparently worse than to be a thief, because the eagle was selected for this honor.[52]

There were some reports of New England wild turkeys being domesticated by the colonists, so that they "remain about their Houses as tame as ours in *England.*" William Bentley of Salem, Massachusetts, for example, had tamed wild turkey for dinner one evening in 1798. A more frequent occurrence was interbreeding, at first by accident and increasingly by design. The hybrids tended to be larger, healthier, and more vigorous than their domestic, though not than their wild, parents.[53]

Before proceeding to turkey cookery, we feel obliged to include a few remarks on the name of this bird. A. W. Schorger notes how incongruous it would have been for the United States to have a national bird that bore the name of a foreign nation. But how did the turkey get its name in the first place? As with Johnny cake, there have been any number of fanciful theories. Among the more absurd have been that the blue on the head of the bird resembled turquoise, which "was once called Turkey stone," or that "the name was derived from the ... call notes *turk, turk, turk*." Another suggestion was that the name given to the peahen and peacock on the Indian subcontinent, *togi* or *togei*, somehow not only evolved into "turkey" but also got transferred from peafowl to the bird brought to Spain from Central America.[54]

A more likely explanation is that the name derives from the fact that "in the Middle Ages nearly everything exotic was obtained in or through Turkish, or Arabian territories." In the sixteenth century, after Columbus's voyages began the process of food exchanges between the two hemispheres, maize from the New World was called "Turkey wheat" in most European languages. In the early fourteenth century, almost two hundred years before the Columbian exchange brought both maize and turkeys to Europe, the peacocks depicted on one Englishman's coat of arms were described as "three Turkey-cocks in their pride proper."[55]

In keeping with the tendency to associate new commodities of all kinds with trade with the East, and perhaps because the "Turkey merchants" of the Mediterranean basin first acquired the Central American fowl and subsequently brought it to England, the label turkey got affixed to the new import. Whatever its origins, the name stuck. Samuel Johnson's 1755 *Dictionary* defined the turkey as "a large domestic fowl brought from Turkey." This erroneous understanding of the bird's origins was widely disseminated, transmitted to people in New England through at least one popular farming handbook.[56]

Thomas Robinson Hazard, it will be remembered, considered the "well-fattened, well-killed, well-picked, well-dry-dressed Rhode Island turkey" to be supreme among birds that qualified as fit for human consumption. Hazard would no doubt have insisted that the wild turkey slain and cooked by Brillat-Savarin was, the French chef's unimpeachable gastronomic credentials notwithstanding, inferior to this particular strain of domesticated turkey. Hazard offered detailed amplification of every part of the above description.

Well-fattened: "He eats plentifully of milk curdled with rennet when in infancy, and in boyhood feeds largely on grasshoppers. . . . The curdled milk . . . keeps the infant turkey from the gasps and the bowel complaint." The grasshopper diet was succeeded by "hard, sound Rhode Island corn," which was (of course) "incomparably richer and more oily in quality than the western chaffy stuff." Apples, "Tallman sweetings," were a useful dietary supplement, adding to the "juiciness and flavor of the flesh." Hazard mentioned that many of the turkeys thus fed were destined for the Boston market, and the account is indeed reminiscent of the seventeenth-century English writer Sir Kenelm Digby's description of chickens that were raised for the market being crammed with a paste of crushed raisins, breadcrumbs from the highest quality wheat bread, and milk. "The delight of this meat will make them eat continually," commented Digby, "and they will be so fat . . . that they will not be able to stand, but lie down upon their bellies to eat."[57]

But to continue with Hazard on Rhode Island turkeys, the remainder of the process of preparing them for the table was to make sure that they were "well-killed, well-picked, well-dry-dressed": First the "sacred creature" was to be deprived of food for eighteen hours, then suspended from a "spike," head down. "Reverently but quickly cut asunder the jugular vein, and just as soon as the breath leaves pluck off the feathers before the body gets cold. This done, remove the crop and entrails without loss of time, restoring the liver and gizzard, when the latter is cleansed of the gravelly contents and its inside skin. Then tie a string around the body and both wings and also around both legs, and hang him up in a cool, dry place for from two to three days." If such care were taken throughout the turkey's life and with the manner of its death, it would be well worth it, for "you will then have a superior dish, if properly seasoned and roasted, to any other known animal, fowl, or fish, whether wild game or domestic, on this or any other terraqueous globe within the scope of man's knowledge."[58]

Hazard offered no guidance on proper seasoning and roasting, although he did tell a story about a South County magnate, Rowland Brown, who had occasion to provide, after a day of fox hunting, a dinner for a venerable Irishman who went by the name of Slauter. Slauter was apparently well known for his politeness, and Brown had decided to put this admirable characteristic to the test:

The table was quickly spread, but nothing but a huge Indian bran pudding appeared on it. Mr. Brown helped Master Slauter to a goodly portion with repeated apologies for the extreme meagreness of the fare, to all of which the old gentleman replied, "Very good, Mr. Brown, very good," suiting the action to his word by occasionally conveying a morsel to his mouth. After the experiment had been fully tested without Master Slauter indicating by word or look any disapprobation, Mr. Brown ordered a couple of splendid roast turkeys and fixings to be brought in, to which he bountifully helped his Irish guest, who, after taking a mouthful, turned urbanely to his host and remarked, "A very great addition to the supper, Mr. Brown."[59]

As the anecdote indicates, turkey was considered appropriate for special occasions besides Thanksgiving. We have noted the place it achieved in British Christmas celebrations, and more generally it "replaced the old celebratory birds of the Middle Ages, the peacocks and swans of the rich, the bustards and herons of the poor." In New England in 1661 a turkey stolen from the Andover, Massachusetts, household of Simon and Anne Bradstreet was being saved for the wedding of one of the master and mistress's daughters. Similarly, in Harriet Beecher Stowe's representation of early national Newport, Rhode Island, "an indefinite series" of turkeys were to be baked in the morning for the engagement party that evening of the minister, Samuel Hopkins, and his intended, Mary Scudder.[60]

Nevertheless, the special occasion with which turkey has come primarily to be associated is of course Thanksgiving. The connection between the holiday that we now observe and the so-called first Thanksgiving held in Plymouth in 1621 exists only mythically, not historically, having been invented no sooner than the second half of the nineteenth century. In any case, turkey played only a minor part, if any, in that 1621 feast, which was indeed one of the first celebrations in America of the traditional English harvest home. One of the two available accounts mentioned only that enough "fowle" had been hunted down in the woods in one day to supply "the Company almost a weeke," along with five deer contributed by the native chief Massasoit and the ninety warriors who accompanied him to the party. The other account, that of William Bradford, did speak specifically of "great store of wild turkeys," but Bradford was writing less about a specific harvest festival than about the overall stock of provisions that the colonists had managed to accumulate "as winter approached."[61]

The leading authority on turkey, A. W. Schorger, found only scattered references in colonial sources to the bird in connection with Thanksgiving. "It is doubtful that a turkey became a common adjunct to a Thanksgiving dinner until about 1800," he concluded. Shortly after 1800 William Bentley did indeed state that turkey was indispensable to Thanksgiving, and in 1828 an English visitor to Boston found "the quantity of turkeys in relation to other kinds of food" on sale in the market the evening before Thanksgiving "quite extraordinary." His amazement was dispelled when he was told that "on thanksgiving days persons of every condition have a roasted turkey at dinner."[62]

The year before, in Sarah Josepha Hale's fictional Thanksgiving dinner, "the roasted turkey took precedence . . . being placed at the head of the table." The trend toward nationalization of this New England holiday, to come to fruition during the Civil War in great part through Hale's efforts, was apparent by 1835, when President Andrew Jackson issued a Thanksgiving proclamation: "We thank thee for the bountiful supply of wildlife with which Thou has blessed our land; for the turkeys that gobble in our forests." But of course by this time, at least in Thanksgiving's New England homeland, the gobblers that were served up were far more likely to have come from the farmyard or the market than the forest.[63]

Although turkey was important to the nineteenth-century Thanksgiving, a case can be made that until the twentieth century, pie was at least as important. We make such a case in our next chapter and therefore defer our primary discussion of Thanksgiving until then.[64]

For now, we content ourselves with taking note of Caroline Howard King's recollection that in early-nineteenth-century Salem, Massachusetts, "many old-fashioned people" of the upper classes resisted the introduction of the cookstove for as long as possible, maintaining that "meats had a wholly different flavor and relish when they were roasted before an open fire." One such person, a "very energetic and spirited lady," went so far as to "roast the family Thanksgiving turkey herself, in a tin-kitchen, before the fire, in her back parlor." A bird fit to set before her favorite nephew was not to be left to the servants. "She is lovingly remembered now by her daughters, shrouded in a large white apron with her elegant silk dress carefully pinned up, making frequent visits to the assembling family party in the front parlor on Thanksgiving Day, flourishing her basting ladle in one hand, and often interrupting herself in some interesting family tale, to run and see if 'Cousin John's' turkey was getting burned."[65]

The recipes for roast turkey found in New England cookbooks were all derived from standard English practice. Hannah Glasse had offered two stuffings and three sauces (bread, onion, and oyster) to go with roast turkey. The sauces were themselves supplementary to gravy made from the bird's own drippings, which, Glasse stressed, should always be included as well, especially in the case of one of the sauces: "Serve this [sauce] up in a basin by itself, with good gravy in the dish, for every body don't love oyster sauce."[66]

Amelia Simmons gave a stuffing recipe similar to one of Glasse's, with "soft wheat bread," beef suet, eggs, and herbs; "some add a gill of wine; . . . others omit the sweet herbs, and add parsley done with potatoes." In another of Simmons's stuffings, we find an intriguing variation on our own

Thanksgiving menu: mashed potatoes, which, "wet" with butter and seasoned with salt, pepper, and sweet herbs, constituted the stuffing. As for the turkey itself, the generic instructions for all fowl already quoted in the chicken section were all that Simmons included. Despite Hannah Glasse's hesitations about oysters, Simmons also included a recipe for turkey or other fowl, "To smother a Fowl in Oysters," in which oysters were to be found wherever one turned. The bird was to be boiled rather than roasted, and the oysters were to be prime constituents of both stuffing and sauce.[67]

Lydia Maria Child was relatively laconic on the subject of turkey. Two-and-a-half to three hours was her recommended time for both boiling and roasting "a good sized turkey." Her stuffing was quite similar to a salt pork version Simmons had included, down to the particular herbs to be utilized (sage, summer savory, sweet marjoram). "An egg worked in makes the stuffing cut better; but it is not worth while when eggs are dear." She also gave detailed carving instructions.[68]

Mrs. Lee called for fancier roasted and boiled turkeys than Child, as one would expect. The stuffing for a roasted turkey was to consist primarily of sausage meat, with "a few bread crumbs and a beaten egg." Following Glasse and no doubt other English authorities, Lee said to serve the turkey "with gravy in the dish, and bread sauce in a sauce tureen." With boiled turkey she recommended the use of "a floured cloth to make it very white." Whiteness, which she also emphasized in her recipe for fricasseed chicken, seems to have been a particular concern of Lee's. Whiteness was to be further accentuated by pouring over the turkey "some oyster sauce made rich with butter, a little cream, and a spoonful of soy."[69]

Most subsequent turkey recipes exhibited only minor variation from the main themes drawn from English cooking that we have already described. All boiled turkeys down to the early twentieth century involved oysters in a major way. Not long after the turn of the twentieth century, however, boiled turkeys were as rarely found on New England and American dinner tables as were wild turkeys in New England and American forests.[70]

As for roast turkey, the basic options for stuffing—breadcrumbs, egg, salt pork, butter, sausage meat, salt, pepper, herbs—mostly persisted into the middle of the twentieth century and beyond. The same selection of sweet herbs recommended by Simmons and Child—sage, sweet marjoram, summer savory—was still featured in 1905.[71]

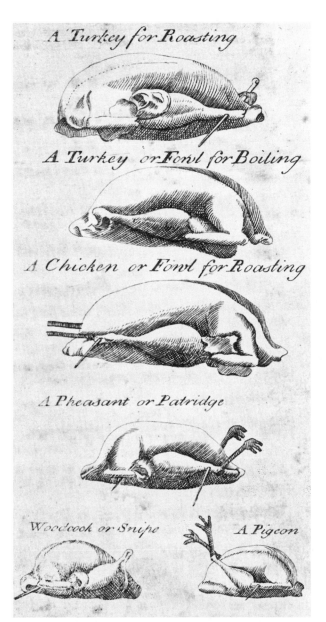

Engraving by Paul Revere, in Susannah Carter, The Frugal
Housewife, *1772. (Courtesy American Antiquarian Society)*

William Wood's catalog "of the Beasts that live on the land" in New England consisted of "Lyons," bears, moose, deer, porcupines, raccoons, squirrels, rabbits, hares, ferrets, foxes, ounces, wolves, otters, beavers, and muskrats. Most of these animals, but especially bears and deer, were indispensable to the subsistence of the Indians living in the north and important, though not crucial, to that of those living in the south.[72]

The English settlers certainly used many of these creatures for food as well. Those in Plymouth gladly accepted the five deer brought by Massasoit to the 1621 harvest feast. Governor Bradford's wedding banquet in the summer of 1623 featured venison. In the next decade Wood was happy to note that "there be a great many" deer in New England, "and more in the Massachusetts bay, than in any other place, which is a great helpe and refreshment to these planters." Deer were not the only game animals that Wood commended as sources of food. Bears were "accounted very good meate, esteemed of all men above Venison," and the colonists would have a larger supply of such top-of-the-line fare were it not for the wolves that preyed upon New England's bear population. Thus did Wood intimate that the natives' two primary sources of flesh meat might play a comparable part for the English.[73]

Such a scenario was not improbable, especially in regard to deer, which Wood rated as gastronomically inferior to bear but which had long been the most prestigious of all English flesh foods. This noble beast that was reserved for noble people back in England was found all over the place in New England, as many as a hundred on view within a mile in springtime.[74]

Although as of 1627 the Plymouth colonists had not yet acquired sufficient expertise or firepower to hunt deer on their own, this situation did not long persist. Deer hunting was pursued energetically in the territories of all English settlements, so much so that as early as 1646 it had to be regulated and restricted in Portsmouth, Rhode Island. Massachusetts enacted its first limitations on deer hunting in 1694 and adopted additional measures through the eighteenth century. But all to no avail. As noted above, by the end of the seventeenth century the game population of New England had already been greatly reduced by hunting and habitat alteration. A century later deer, elk, bear, and lynx survived only on the northernmost fringes of the region.[75]

In view of the success of the great seventeenth-century game hunt, the early colonists presumably ate a great deal of venison and other game flesh.

The further presumption that they must have experienced satisfaction over this prolonged feasting on aristocratic food is at first sight plausible. Yet there are no traces in the record of any expressions of special triumph in this regard. William Wood's statement that the abundance of deer in Massachusetts was "a great helpe and refreshment" to the first planters sounds more like an acknowledgement of subsistence needs than a boast about feasting in a world turned upside down. Beyond such relatively neutral remarks, New Englanders had little to say about the forest creatures that were there for the taking and that they did indeed take. They were as close-mouthed about high-status venison as they were about no-status maize. Why should this have been the case?

Part of the explanation may be that the very availability of game in general and of deer in particular stripped it of its prestige. Having formerly been rare, deer had been highly valued. Having now become common, it was valued hardly at all. But there was an even more potent factor at work. Writing twenty years after Wood in the 1650s, Edward Johnson referred to "Venson," bear, and other indigenous species only as food for the Indians. As we saw in chapter 1, Johnson contrasted the natives' reliance on "the flesh of a few wild creatures and parch't Indian corn" with the settlers' success in building traditional English farmsteads and recreating a traditional English food culture. The previous association of hunting and venison with the aristocracy was thus outweighed by their present association with the Indians. Like "parch't Indian corn," game and venison were not viewed by the Puritan spokesmen for New England as part of the way of life they were building. They were only a necessary and temporary evil.[76]

Because game was in short order rendered all but extinct in New England, these expectations of a merely transitory presence in cookery and diet were fulfilled in the case of game as they were not in that of corn. Archaeological evidence from various eighteenth-century New England sites indicates only a minimal presence of wild animal species among the flesh meats that were consumed. This was true even in the frontier area of Deerfield, Massachusetts.[77]

Game did remain a trace element in the world of New England food. After it became scarce, it reverted to its old role as party food for the upper classes. Samuel Sewall, a leading figure among the Boston elite at the turn of the eighteenth century, had venison on a number of occasions—once when he breakfasted with the lieutenant governor of Massachusetts. More than a century after this, at Caroline Howard King's wealthy home in Salem, Massachusetts, the "*pièce de résistance*" of the family's formal dining would usually be "a haunch of venison cooked in claret wine, or partly cooked only, for each guest had a plated silver chafing dish standing before him, on which he was expected to cook his slice or slices according to his own taste."[78]

There was a recipe for roast venison in one nineteenth-century cookbook intended for readers interested in "economy," but the fullest discussion of venison, and of other game animals, was that provided by Mrs. Lee. She told not only how to roast a haunch of venison but also how to make venison "collops," venison hash, and venison pasty or pie. Hare she included as well—roasted, hashed, or "jugged." Otherwise, the presence of game in our cookbook sample is thin indeed. Simmons gave tips on the purchase of hare, leveret, and rabbit, and a century later a cookbook offered a recipe for squirrel. That Mrs. Lee, the most refined and gourmandizing of all antebellum cookery authors of New England origin, gave the most ample consideration to game animals is consistent with our suggestion that game's upper-class cachet had been largely restored in eighteenth- and nineteenth-century New England.[79]

Early in the twentieth century, game recipes were found in self-consciously antiquarian cookbooks, one of which copied many of its recipes from Lee. Later, they were offered from the opposite end of the social spectrum—from areas that represented themselves as maintaining ties to the rugged simplicities of the frontier. This is then the second of the two ways in which game persisted in New England food culture—as an accoutrement of extreme rusticity as well as of extreme urbanity.

The historical validity of this second provenance is indicated by the glimpse Harriet Beecher Stowe gave of the daily fare in a mountain village at the end of the eighteenth century. It regularly featured "game and fish brought in by the united woodcraft" of the minister and the schoolmaster. Such a frontier tradition lay behind the fact that a 1939 cookbook with regionalized subdivisions included squirrel pie from New Hampshire and muskrat stew from Maine. Similarly, the "Yankee Hill-Country" volume of 1963 had roast venison, baked coon, and baked rabbit among its offerings. "There is no better eating than a young coon properly baked," the author averred. "The meat tastes like the most delicate roast pork."[80]

As late as 1915 even the most awesome of all New England forest creatures could figure in backwoods uses of game for food. In that year a New Hampshire man offered this testimonial to bear meat: "Yes, I caught a bear this summer. . . . I've caught eight bears . . . in the last five years. This one was fat as a pig. He weighed two hundred and fifty pounds. I gave considerable of the meat away to the neighbors. It was tender and a lot of 'em e't it."

Despite overhunting, environmental transformation, and cultural permutation, William Wood's seventeenth-century assessment of bear meat as "very good . . . esteemed of all men" appears to have stood the test of time.[81]

Domesticated Meat Animals

We will mostly confine ourselves to pork and beef, which provided the preponderance of the flesh meat in the diet of the average New Englander. In Carole Shammas's survey of seventeenth- and eighteenth-century probate inventories for rural Massachusetts, well over a majority of households owned cattle and pigs, and in urban areas of the same colony just before the American Revolution, over 20 percent did. Less than half of these same rural households, and only a negligible portion of the urban ones, had any sheep. A quantitative study of Deerfield, Massachusetts, covering most of the eighteenth century found that together pork and beef accounted for 80 percent of the meat consumed there. The remaining 20 percent was veal, lamb, and mutton. These served, like poultry, as occasional sources of fresh meat.[82]

Nineteenth-century cookbooks certainly included recipes for these other meats. Nevertheless, the story of meat in New England was a story of pork and beef. Further, it was a story of pork and beef cooked and eaten only after they had been subjected to various treatments designed to preserve them. We devote the next several pages to New England meat preservation technology, a subset of the overall preservation ethos described in chapter 4.

The Hog Weighed 280

In farm households the process by which livestock was transformed into a consumable foodstuff (as opposed to its uses in tillage and dairy production) began at slaughtering time. According to English tradition, this period commenced in November and continued into February, although most of the activity was concentrated toward the beginning. This tendency to slaughter early was accentuated in New England. Scarcities of fodder had always made it difficult to keep cattle alive and well through an English winter, and the colder New England winters only exacerbated the problem. On the other hand, slaughtering during the warm months was limited by the danger that the meat would spoil before preservation techniques had taken full effect; once again this became even more of an issue in New England summers that were generally warmer than those of Old England.[83]

Slaughtering did not take place only on farms. Livestock husbandry "flourished" in Portsmouth, New Hampshire, "until fairly recent times," and butchering waste and implements have been found at Portsmouth archaeological sites dating from the eighteenth century. In western Massachusetts toward the end of that century, pigs and cattle "were owned by many non-farm families as well as farmers." Colonial Bostonians also "kept cattle or hogs." And livestock slaughter was as long-lasting as it was widespread. Into the 1850s "most slaughtering was done by farmers in winter, who, after satisfying their own demands, sold the remainder of the carcass to a neighboring storekeeper or small packer, who cured it for the market." English practice, perpetuated in New England, was to dispatch first those animals least likely to survive the winter.[84]

In *Oldtown Folks*, which featured a prosperous New England farm family at the end of the eighteenth century, Harriet Beecher Stowe represented the farm wife, the narrator's kindly grandmother, as objecting to the impending slaughter of a calf on grounds of sympathy and identification with the calf's distressed mother. While we may doubt that such remonstrances took place with any frequency, it is true that livestock slaughter was men's work. Sometimes, though, due to the absence or incapacity of the resident male, women were forced to engage in it. On such occasions they tended to regard it as a "business which I dislike," in the words of a nineteenth-century Maine diarist.[85]

An entry in the diary of Persis Sibley Andrews, another Maine woman, from the same year provided details of the slaughtering process: "On Monday we had a swine & a beef slaughtered. . . . We took care of the fat of the entrails & cleaned the tripe that day. Tuesday I stood by the man who cut & salted the meat — & saved such as we wanted fresh — then we cared for the sause — & the cows feet (I like the dish call'd 'cow-heels') — then we tried and strained all the tallow and lard. The hog weighed 280."[86]

This hog was presumably thrown into boiling water after having been cut open and bled. Such at least was the method John Josselyn recorded as having been in use in Cambridgeshire, England, in the first half of the seventeenth century. Harriet Beecher Stowe also indicated the centrality of kettles of boiling water in the hog slaughter techniques prevalent in the Natick, Massachusetts, area at the end of the eighteenth century.

The man who cut and salted the meat for the Maine diarist could conceivably have been an African American. Stowe depicted a "vigorous old negro" as being "famed as a sort of high-priest in all manner of butchering operations for miles around" in the Natick area. As we shall see in the next chapter, Stowe also placed an African American in charge of the slaughtering operations done in preparation for the Thanksgiving observance of the novel's principal farm family.[87]

Most aspects of the disposition of the parts of slaughtered animals were referred to in the above diary entry. A small portion was set aside to be eaten fresh in the immediate days ahead. If the slaughter was on a large enough scale, some of it would be shared with neighbors. Such gifts or loans would be reciprocated when the neighboring household slaughtered its own livestock. Martha Ballard was given 6½ pounds of beef, along with a mincemeat pie, by one of her Hallowell, Maine, neighbors in 1808. The entrails and tripe (beef cattle stomach) trimmed and cleaned by the diarist may also have been eaten fresh. Such at least had been the practice in sixteenth- and seventeenth-century England. Between dining on one's own livestock and on that bestowed by one's neighbors, New England farm families annually experienced anew the mood evoked by the Elizabethan rhymester Thomas Tusser when he stated that after "slaughter time entereth in . . . then doth the husbandman's feasting begin."[88]

But most of the slaughtered beef cattle and swine from that December 1844 day on the Andrews farm in Maine was not eaten fresh but rather preserved through various forms of salting. The methods commonly practiced in sixteenth- and seventeenth-century English yeoman households included dry salting, soaking in brine or pickling, and smoking. Judging from the advice offered by Lydia Maria Child, these methods were successfully transplanted to New England.

For salt pork, Child said to "scald coarse salt in water and skim it, till the salt will no longer melt in the water." Then, "pack your pork down in tight layers; salt every layer; when the brine is cool, cover the pork with it, and keep a heavy stone on the top to keep the pork under brine." More salt was to be added as needed. Child claimed that brine made this way would "continue good twenty years." Such procedures were similar to Stuart-era recipes that "instruct the cook to boil the meat in a brine, allow it to cool, and then pour the corned pork into a barrel or crock for storage under a weighted cover."[89]

Brined pork that was intended to be kept for only a brief time was called "'collared,' while that put away for the winter was known as 'soused.'" Some seventeenth-century recipes for soused pork advised seasoning with pepper, mace, ginger, nutmegs, and lemon and for the addition of wine to the liquid. These flavors covered up "the unpleasantness of mild tainting." Persis

Sibley Andrews, our nineteenth-century Maine farm wife, mentioned that she "cared for the sause" as part of her slaughtering and preserving activities.[90]

To us, the most flavorful form of preserved pork is ham. Hams were made by an essentially two-stage process. First, salt, applied either by rubbing (that is, "dry") or immersion in salted liquid (that is, a pickle), reduced the water content of the meat. It was then "ready for slow drying," either in the attic or "a smoke-filled chimney."[91]

The recipe Lydia Maria Child gave as "the old-fashioned way for curing hams" was a form of dry salting in which the hams were first basted with molasses, then rubbed with saltpeter (potassium nitrate), and finally rubbed "very thoroughly" with "common salt." "They must be carefully turned and rubbed every day for six weeks," Child continued; "then hang them in a chimney, or smoke-house, four weeks." A seventeenth-century English recipe differed only in calling for coarse sugar instead of molasses and requiring only two weeks of turning and rubbing prior to hanging in the attic or chimney.[92]

A recipe included in a Rhode Island cookbook from the first half of the twentieth century and said to have been "used successfully for five generations" provided an example of a ham made by pickling prior to smoking. It varied from a standard seventeenth-century English recipe only in adding sugar or molasses to the pickle and stipulating six weeks of pickling instead of three.[93]

Bacon was usually made in the same ways as ham. Actually, the distinction between ham and bacon was not always kept clear. Child and Amelia Simmons both referred to them interchangeably. At any rate, there were numerous references in the diaries of eighteenth- and nineteenth-century New England farm wives to hanging bacon up in the chimney to smoke six weeks or so after placing it in a pickle.[94]

Jay Allan Anderson states that "barrels of corned beef frequently appear in inventories" of the English yeomen he studied, "but recipes rarely occur in cookbooks, probably because everyone was thoroughly familiar with the process." If recipes had been published at that time, they probably would have resembled one offered by Child, calling for "six pounds of coarse salt, eight ounces of brown sugar, a pint of molasses, and eight ounces of salt-petre" to be boiled in four gallons of water. "Skim it clean while boiling. Put it to the beef cold; have enough to cover it; and be careful your beef never floats on the top," she concluded. Additional salt, rescalding, and reskimming were the remedies "if it does not smell perfectly sweet." Half a century earlier, in

1778, a writer in the *New England Almanac* claimed that the same measures against noisomeness proposed by Child would allow pickled or corned beef to last through the summer. Another almanac recipe from 1791 was trumpeted as "a sure way of putting up beef to remain good and fit . . . for the space of years."[95]

Although the internal organs of the slaughtered beasts mentioned by Persis Sibley Andrews may have been eaten fresh, they may also have been added to the sausage that was usually made a week or so after hogs were slaughtered. Farm wives' diaries spoke often of cutting sausage meat, cleaning the intestinal skin tissue that would provide the casings, and filling the casings with the cut or shredded meat. These women may have followed a procedure similar to that recommended in 1615 in Gervase Markham's *The English Housewife*: Alternately lean and fat shreds of pork were to be scored with a sharp knife, mixed "all well together," seasoned with salt, pepper, and sage, blown into casings, turned into links with pieces of thread, and hung in the chimney for a few days. In some New England households, a sausage gun was used to inject the meat into the casings.[96]

The final aspect of the 1844 Maine diary entry on beef and swine slaughter to notice is the reference to trying and straining "all the tallow and lard." Every conceivable constituent of the beast was put to use. Animal fat was made into lard for cooking and tallow for candles. Whiskers and bristles were turned into brushes, while hides and skins "found extensive use in households."[97]

As discussed in chapter 4, seventeenth-century New England meat preservation technology was generally adequate, though not foolproof, as a protection against scarcity. While about two-thirds of the probate inventories taken in that century during the winter months indicated the presence of salt pork and beef, only 15 percent of those taken at the end of the summer indicated such a presence. "By late spring and early summer, many families were reaching the bottom of their meat barrels," writes Sarah F. McMahon. A housewife in seventeenth-century Essex County, Massachusetts, for example, was suspected of food theft on the basis of her statement that she had substantial amounts of pork and beef on hand toward the end of the winter. It was assumed that everyone except those at the highest levels of society "would have reached the end of their provisions" by that point in the year.[98]

In the eighteenth century, preservation methods, though remaining basically unchanged, came to be utilized with increased efficiency to the point that even the fear of scarcity significantly receded. By 1790, 81 percent of winter probate inventories included salt meats, while the proportion of late summer inventories containing them had climbed to 43 percent. Per capita amounts of meat provided to widows in wills rose from 120 pounds in the early eighteenth century to 200 pounds in the early nineteenth century. With preserved meats remaining available for consumption well into the summer, the role of such fresh summertime fare as fish, fowl, and small game changed from contributing seasonally to subsistence to providing variety "in an otherwise monotonous diet."[99]

Cattle and Pigs: Keeping Them and Selling Them

We have noted that for English yeomen of the seventeenth century, their own pigs were the principal source of the meat in their diet. Cattle were kept primarily for dairy production and were slaughtered and eaten only when they could no longer be maintained through the winter.

This pattern was long established. In the eleventh century Domesday survey, pigs outnumbered cattle in eastern England three to one. Archaeological evidence from the other side of the island indicates that even earlier, pigs were the main food animal. Swine reproduced at high rates, with sows bearing litters of as many as eight piglets a couple of times a year or more. Most medieval peasants could "keep two or three hogs, and could afford to kill one at least once a year." Less salt was needed to preserve the flesh of swine, and its taste was also less compromised by the process. Pork consumption thus primarily occurred within the orbit of subsistence farming, although a market trade in particularly esteemed regional breeds began to emerge in the sixteenth century.[100]

As for cattle, during the sixteenth century much of the common-field acreage on which lesser peasants had grazed such cattle as they had was enclosed and allocated by landowners to more profitable uses. Loss of access to grazing land aroused fears of loss of the creatures that grazed on them; and in food terms, the fear was that dairy products not meat would be lost: "my cow is a commonwealth to me, for . . . she allows me, my wife and son, for to banquet ourselves withall, butter, cheese, whey, curds, cream, sod [boiled] milk, raw-milk, sour-milk, sweet-milk, and butter-milk."[101]

On the other hand, C. Anne Wilson contends that in the Middle Ages beef "emerged as the Englishman's favourite fleshmeat." In the thirteenth century the demand for beef was strong enough to generate procedures for satisfying it by market purchase rather than consumption from one's own herds. Farmers raised cattle in the north and west of England and drove them long distances to "lowland markets." By the sixteenth century, the beef cattle trade had become systematized. The animals were driven to grazing grounds closer to the point of sale, where they were sold to middlemen graziers, who fattened them up before reselling them to butchers in London and other urban centers. The next two centuries saw the system further refined, as specialized meat, as opposed to dairy, breeds of cattle were developed.[102]

This mixed pattern of meat economics, demand being supplied through a combination of subsistence resource exploitation and market transaction, continued to prevail in New England. We have already cited evidence that subsistence living was not characteristic of farm families only. Townspeople kept cattle and pigs and occasionally slaughtered and ate them. Yet the marketing of livestock also developed early in the region. Livestock husbandry was central to the type of farming that the settlers were determined to practice, partly because it was what they were used to and partly because it required less labor than raising grain crops. Those who could afford to brought livestock with them on their transatlantic voyages. Those who came later and hadn't been able to bring their own animals bought cattle or pigs from their predecessors whose herds had multiplied sufficiently to provide a marketable surplus. As early as 1638 live cattle were driven to Boston, where they commanded high prices.[103]

Of course, selling live animals to other settlers did not constitute a market in meat. But it did demonstrate the desirability of obtaining disposable income through the raising of farm animals for sale. As Edward Johnson wrote, it had become "the common practice of those that had any store of Cattel, to sell every year a Cow or two, which cloath'd their backs, fil'd their bellies with more varieties then the Country of it self afforded, and put gold and silver in their purses beside."[104]

When the immigration to New England, and with it the supply of purchasers of living farm animals, came to an end in 1640, farmers were prepared to participate in the export trade with the West Indies that opened up shortly thereafter. Once again, live animals were driven to market in Boston, but now an apparatus for selling them not as animals but rather as meat developed. Somebody had to butcher the beasts, salt down and pack the resulting flesh meat, and inspect the shipments before they were sent off. The export of salt meat to the West Indies was carried on successfully throughout the colonial period. Just before the American Revolution, meat was second only to fish among New England exports, accounting for 20 percent of the total (versus 35 percent for fish). Ninety-nine percent of meat exports went to the West Indies.[105]

Meat sold on the international trading circuits was not meat sold to the people of New England. But the industrial and marketing structures that developed to supply this trade eventually found domestic customers. Thus we read of a man who in 1671 brought home from a Boston butcher shop a leg of mutton and a piece of beef, and of another man who in January 1704 bought a whole hog and a quarter of beef from two different vendors and the next day salted them both away. In Boston in the 1730s and 1740s, the domestic market in meat was large enough to generate complaints about the high prices butchers were charging.[106]

From the farmer's point of view, the disposition of his livestock between home consumption and sale was not an either/or proposition. There were a variety of options available to him, depending upon circumstances. Christopher Clark's description of what tended to happen on Connecticut River Valley farmsteads toward the end of the eighteenth century probably reflects the situation that also prevailed elsewhere in New England and at other times.

When there was more than enough grain to feed the family, some of it would go, along with the hay that was likely to be plentiful at the same time, to fatten the livestock. The portion of this fattened livestock that was not needed for home consumption might be sent on the hoof to market. When grain for the family and fodder for the animals were in shorter supply, more of the animals might have to be slaughtered to meet the family's needs, but the farmer might still sell some of his holdings, not on the hoof but directly as salted and dried meat. Animals that might be killed and eaten in a severe winter might be kept alive through a mild one, to be, in another year, either eaten at home or sold, either as live animals or as dried meat. All in all, people living on farms both ate their own pork and beef and sold them to others, while people not living on farms both ate their own pork and beef and bought them from others.[107]

Beef and Pork in the New England Diet

By the nineteenth century, the United States was as famous for meat-eating as England had already become by the seventeenth century. Timothy Dwight stated that the norm in New England, even among poor people, was to have meat two or three times a day; "a breakfast without . . . an addition [of meat, fish, or cheese] is considered scarcely worth eating." An English traveler later in the century was more sardonic. He substantiated his remark that "as a flesh-consuming people, the Americans have no equal in the world" by noting that he had seen "gentlemen choose as many as seven or eight differ-ent kinds of animal food from the bill of fare, and after having all arranged before him in a row, . . . commence at one end and eat his way through in half a dozen minutes."[108]

The English were only taking out on the Americans their own experience of having been skewered (so to speak) by the French for their exhibitions of this same meat-eating trait. One F. M. Misson claimed that the English people who had come within his ken in the 1690s would tend only to "nibble a few crumbs" of bread, "while they chew the meat by whole mouthfuls." Sarah Josepha Hale was doubtless not the only spokesperson for Anglo-American civilization who justified the two nations' love of meat with re-marks along such lines as "forty thousand of the beef-fed British, govern and control ninety millions of the rice-eating natives of India."[109]

There has been some discussion among scholars as to whether pork or beef predominated among these vigorous meat-eaters. Sandra L. Oliver cites evidence that puts beef in the lead, but most other writers conclude in favor of pork. Sarah F. McMahon finds that in eighteenth-century Middlesex County, Massachusetts, there was more pork than beef. On the other hand, another quantitative study indicates that in one eighteenth-century western Massachusetts town equal amounts of pork and beef were consumed. The evidence cited earlier from Carole Shammas regarding livestock holdings in Massachusetts in colonial times shows a higher rate of ownership of cattle than pigs, although this may reflect a tendency to keep more of the cattle alive for dairy production.[110]

In the end it does not matter whether it was pork or beef that was eaten the most. The more important trend is that salt meat of both kinds steadily became more prominent in the New England diet. In the seventeenth cen-tury, people primarily ate succotash or bean porridge with a bit of salt meat in it, the amount of meat decreasing in inverse proportion to the distance in time from the previous autumn's slaughter. A hundred and fifty years later, the "ample depths" of the "huge dinner-pot" in which people's daily meals were prepared contained "beets, carrots, potatoes, and turnips" boiling "in jolly sociability with the pork or corned beef which they were destined to flank at the coming meal." Pottage fare had thus been displaced by boiled dinner.[111]

Again and again, Harriet Beecher Stowe depicted the daily food of low- and middling-level New Englanders in the first decades of American inde-pendence as consisting of variations on boiled dinner. The estimable and the execrable alike partook of "the beef, pork, and vegetables of our daily meal." Breakfast, if not boiled dinner, featured another product of the meat preservation effort: "the smoking hot brown bread, the beans and sausages, which formed our morning meal."[112]

Stowe's sense that preserved meat had come to play as central a part in the New England diet as grains and legumes is confirmed by Christopher Clark's description of how Connecticut Valley farm families would increase their supplies of meat when grain ran low. In Northampton, Massachusetts, in 1816—the famous "year without a summer"—one of the school districts had decided that no school could be offered that year because with grain so scarce, no family had enough to take on the schoolteacher as a boarder. However, a farmer donated a heifer that he could not afford to feed. It provided the means of subsistence when grain could not, and the schoolhouse opened for business after all. To some degree, in other words, meat had by this point become a more reliable everyday food source than its legume and grain predecessors.[113]

Beef Cookery

In the nineteenth and twentieth centuries New Englanders continued to live on boiled dinner. An octogenarian living in Bristol, Rhode Island, in 1915 recalled that when he was a boy, "Mother would hang the pots on the crane and put in beef, pork and cabbage and other vegetables, and you'd have a dinner that would do you some good, and that would stand by you so you could go out and swing an ax or a sledge-hammer." This "old-fashioned but favorite dish" was included in cookbooks throughout the period under study.[114]

In chapter 1 we described a version of succotash that amounted to boiled dinner and that has been said to date from 1869, the centennial of the first Plymouth Forefathers' Day banquet. Such a tradition is consistent with boiled dinner's inclusion on the menu for the 1876 centennial observances in Mystic, Connecticut. As with baked beans, chowder, Indian pudding, Johnny cake, and many other dishes, it was in the concluding decades of the nineteenth century that this humdrum subsistence food began its transformation into a New England cultural icon. And the mystique of Yankee cooking that was being created in the 1870s had entered into a mature phase by 1939, when it was claimed that the entire meal regularly served to "radio and movie star" Nelson Eddy on his visits to his mother in Rhode Island consisted of such icons: a main course of "New England" boiled dinner, followed by a dessert of Indian pudding.[115]

Boiling was indeed the method of cooking beef that was called for more frequently than any other in the Yankee cookbooks of the first half of the nineteenth century. We might expect this, given that these cookbooks reflected generations of experience with the necessities arising not only from open hearth cookery but also from the low quality of the all-too-well-aged cattle flesh available to most New England farm families.

But the cookbooks tried to make a virtue of necessity, offering visions of tough old beasts transformed into Continental elegance by long simmering. Back in the 1720s E. Smith had told how "To Stew a Rump of Beef." The cut was first stuffed with a forcemeat, then subjected to successive simmerings in ever more enriched liquid—seasoned water, beer, and gravy, which was then thickened with breadcrumbs and supplemented by "some oysters, mushrooms, and ox's palate." Six or seven hours was required, an indication that the recipe was devised with some fairly unpromising raw material in mind.[116]

Virtually every New England cookbook of the first half of the nineteenth century offered recipes of this sort, most often dressing them up with the French expression "à la mode." Amelia Simmons gave three versions of à-la-moded beef, calling for a round instead of a rump and for elevating the meat within the pot using skewers or bones. In two versions the simmering liquid included claret or other wine. Even the austere Lydia Maria Child presented a version of "Alamode Beef." Her more luxurious contemporary Mrs. Lee provided not only "Beef Alamode" in three forms, but also "Beef Alabraise," "Beef Aladaube," and "Beef Alanglaise." The dish continued to be featured until early in the twentieth century.[117]

Catharine Beecher weighed in with two alamodes, one of which will serve to represent the genre as it took shape in New England:

If you have about five pounds of beef, take one pound of bread, soak it in water, pour off the water and mash it fine, adding a bit of butter the size of a hen's egg, salt, mace, pepper, cloves, half a teaspoonful each, pounded fine.

Mix all with a tablespoonful of flour and two eggs.

Then cut holes through the beef and put in half of this seasoning, and put it in a bake pan with boiling water enough to cover it.

Put the pan lid, heated, over it, and a few coals on it, and let it stew two hours, then take it up and spread the other half of the dressing on the top, and add butter the size of a hen's egg, heat the pan lid again hot enough to brown the dressing, and let it stew again an hour and a half.

When taken up, if the gravy is not thick enough, add a teaspoonful of flour wet up in cold water, then add a couple of glasses of white wine to the gravy, and a bit of butter as large as a walnut.

The purpose of the stuffing in this and other such recipes was to make the meat more tender. In some versions of "Beef Alamode," the tenderizing effect was accomplished more simply by larding—filling up holes of the sort seen in Beecher's recipe with seasoned pork or bacon fat.[118]

In 1902 Mary J. Lincoln and Anna Barrows presented a simplified method of stewing beef. Gone were stuffing, seasonings, wine, and the French nomenclatural adornment. Their dish, seared and then simmered in water only, was called merely "Pot Roast or Braised Beef." "Beef Alamode" having been thus killed off, it was now ready to be reinvented as yet another edible symbol of the New England way of life. All that was needed was to create a plainer seasoning mixture, throw some root vegetables into the pot, and arrange them "around the meat" on the serving platter "à la" New England Boiled Dinner. The result was "Yankee Pot Roast," such as the recipe contributed to a cookbook in 1939 by a Massachusetts woman who (no surprise here) traced it back three generations to her New Hampshire farm great-grandmother.[119]

Roasting meat over or in front of a fire is among the most venerable of all cooking methods. Despite a chronic scarcity of fresh and tender flesh, there had developed in the great households of medieval times the tradition of "the roast beefs of old England." As fireplace technology evolved, open fire roasting was transferred from the outdoors or from indoor central hearths to the interior wall hearth-and-chimney arrangement that was the English norm at the time of the immigration to New England and that quickly became standard in colonial New England as well.[120]

Open fire roasting requires some method of turning the meat so that it is evenly cooked on all sides. In both Britain and the colonies, those with limited means (and thus also with limited roasting opportunities and occasions) got along by hanging the meat on a string in front of the fire and manually initiating a twisting and untwisting process that the heat and draughts of the fire would also facilitate. More comfortably situated people, again on both sides of the Atlantic, had spits, some resting on andirons, some involving suspension from above. Clockwork or pulley mechanisms were developed to enable movement that would insure equal exposure to the fire. Children would be called upon to keep such machinery in motion. In chapter 2, Lucy Larcom recalled how eager she was to perform this task. In some households, children would be replaced by a dog, who kept the roasting works in action by running, rat-race fashion, in a wheeled cage connected to the spit.

C. Anne Wilson states that in Britain before the nineteenth century "meat was seldom oven-roasted" in the home. In the eighteenth century the less well off would take their joints along with their bread dough to the village baker to be baked in his oven. In the colonies this implied distinction between roasted and baked meats was blurred by the adoption of the device known variously as the roasting oven, roasting kitchen, or tin kitchen. Enclosed on all sides except the front, which was turned toward the fire, and with a spit running through it on which the joint (or bird) was impaled, the tin kitchen maximized the advantages and minimized the disadvantages of both roasting and baking. On the one hand, the danger of drying posed by oven baking was avoided by the device's curved bottom for catching drippings and its backdoor access for basting. On the other hand, the necessity of continuous attention imposed by open fire roasting was reduced by the fact that since cooking was being carried out in a partially enclosed space, it went forward more uniformly, even without frequent turning.

Standard English roasting techniques included attaching a piece of buttered paper to the meat, basting with anything from salted water to mixtures of wine and vinegar, dredging with flour, oatmeal, or fine breadcrumbs, and serving with garnishes that could range from horseradish to a sauce of "burnt butter, gravy, mushrooms, oysters," and thin slices of boiled beef tongue. The purpose of both the dredging and the basting was to keep the meat from getting too dry, that of the buttered paper to prevent scorching.[121]

New England authors offered little additional detail. Amelia Simmons mentioned only the simplest form of basting, with salt and water. Papering she recommended only for roast veal, not for roast beef. She gave a general guideline of a quarter of an hour of roasting time per pound with a "brisk hot fire," adding the usual caveat that this would vary with the age and tenderness of the cut. It was better "to hang down rather than to spit," she also stated. "Pricking with a fork will determine you whether done or not," Simmons instructed, and her definition of "done" was "rare," which was "the healthiest and the taste of this age."[122]

In spite of the virtues of the tin kitchen, Simmons did not mention it. Among the cookbooks we consulted, only the non–New Englander Eliza Leslie specifically touted it, although Catharine Beecher's general roasting instructions proceeded on the assumption that the reader would be making use of a "tin oven."[123]

As implied by Simmons's and Beecher's use of the term "baking" in connection with "à la mode" methods of beef cookery, until 1850 or so baked beef was understood to be more akin to stewed than to roast beef. For Mrs. Lee, Eliza Leslie, and Beecher, whenever a piece of beef was to be baked in an oven—either old-fashioned brick or new-fangled range—it was to be placed in a pan with water. Baked beef "is a plain family dish, and is never provided for company," Leslie warned.[124]

But as the cookstove became predominant, baked beef came to be conflated with roasted rather than stewed beef. The "Roast Beef" presented by "Aunt Mary" in 1881 was, in accordance with beef roasting traditions, to be dredged with flour and protected against scorching with buttered paper. But in accordance with beef baking traditions, it was to be cooked in an oven in a pan with water. Twenty years later Mary J. Lincoln and Anna Barrows placed the meat on a rack in a pan in an oven and were thereby able to "roast" it using a minimal amount of water. Fannie Farmer had already judged even this method to be "not desirable." Water would be seldom needed, she said, "if size of pan is adapted to size of roast." Nevertheless, the ambiguity between baking and roasting persisted, for Farmer advised readers that "for roasting, consult Time Table for Baking Meats." Similarly, Lincoln and Barrows said in the text of their "Roast Beef" recipe to "bake twelve to fifteen minutes to each pound."[125]

Other aspects of New England beef cookery require only brief consideration. Broiling of beefsteaks was described by eighteenth-century English authors. "The quicker beef-steak can be broiled the better," counseled Lydia Maria Child. However, on the North American side of the Atlantic in the eighteenth and nineteenth centuries, beefsteak was more likely to be fried. It was also likely to be eaten at any time of the day. At Charles Dickens's hotel in Boston in the 1840s, "breakfast would have been no breakfast unless the principal dish were a deformed beef-steak with a great flat bone in the centre, swimming in hot butter, and sprinkled with the very blackest of all possible pepper." This was the T-bone steak, which was then unfamiliar to most Europeans.[126]

As long as food preservation remained a paramount concern, people were not particularly squeamish about the parts of animals that they ate. Persis Sibley Andrews, the nineteenth-century Maine farm housewife who had to supervise a livestock slaughter mentioned, particularly, that she liked "the dish call'd 'cow-heels.'" Eighteenth-century English cookbooks proposed a variety of ways of cooking the heads, tongues, udders, feet, and brains of calves and oxen. This tradition was carried forward in New England into the twentieth century, principally focusing on calf's head, but also encompassing the tongue, stomach, heart, and thymus or pancreas.[127]

Here's a little something along these lines from the woman who, in a rather different mode, also gave us "Over the river and through the wood":

> Calf's head should be cleansed with very great care; particularly the lights [lungs]. The head, the heart, and the lights should boil full two hours; the liver should be boiled only one hour. It is better to leave the wind-pipe on, for if it hangs out of the pot while the head is cooking, all the froth will escape through it. The brains, after being thoroughly washed, should be put in a little bag; with one pounded cracker, or as much crumbled bread, seasoned with sifted sage, and tied up and boiled one hour. After the brains are boiled, they should be well broken up with a knife, and peppered, salted, and buttered. They should be put upon the table in a bowl by themselves. Boiling water, thickened with flour and water, with butter melted in it, is the proper sauce; some people love vinegar and pepper mixed with the melted butter; but all are not fond of it; and it is easy for each one to add it for themselves.

In the case of calf's head, Catharine Beecher outdid Child in concern for economy, as she recommended saving the cooking liquid and using it "for a soup the next day." Beecher noted that removing "all the bones" would allow the dish to be presented "more handsomely" at the table.[128]

As we have seen, a domestic market for meat existed in colonial times, so it is not surprising that advice on purchasing beef was a feature of nineteenth-century cookbooks. As might be expected, Child went into considerable detail, not only specifying which cuts were best for which types of cooking, but also adding money-saving tips: "Bones from which roasting pieces have been cut, may be bought in the market for ten or twelve cents, from which a very rich soup may be made. . . . A bullock's heart is very profitable to use as a steak. Broiled just like beef. . . . Some people stuff and roast it." Mrs. Lee and Beecher were more organized than Child, providing illustrated explanations of the different cuts of beef and how to cook them.[129]

Dairy Products

Since cattle were prized on the farmsteads of both Old and New England more for dairy products than for meat, we insert here a few words on them. Toward the close of the sixteenth century, average English people were becoming fearful of being deprived of "white meats," long an essential component of their farm economy and diet. And in the view of historians, dairy products, along with flesh meat, did indeed become less readily available to most English people for a hundred years or so after the middle of the sixteenth century.[130]

Nevertheless, during this period dairy farming remained integral to the yeoman way of life. Jay Allan Anderson estimates that the cows, ewes, and goats owned by a middling seventeenth-century English farmer produced about a thousand gallons of milk annually. It was the farmstead mistress who was primarily responsible for preserving the bulk of this output by converting it into butter and cheese. Everywhere cows predominated over ewes and goats. Much of the butter produced in yeoman households was sold for cash rather than consumed at home.

A higher proportion of the milk output was devoted to cheese than butter, cheese being more of a staple food. Cheese came in green, "spermyse," soft, and hard varieties—essentially cream cheese, herbed cream cheese, cottage cheese, and the many firm varieties that the word cheese usually denotes today. By the seventeenth century, hard cheeses from the vicinity of the town of Cheddar, in the west of England, had won a high reputation.[131]

Dairying was carried across the Atlantic. Five of the sixteen head of cattle in Plymouth in 1627 were producing milk. On into the eighteenth century, the majority of the ceramic objects owned by Plymouth people were used for dairy-related activities. Elsewhere in colonial New England, there was widespread and increasing possession not only of butter and cheese but also of the equipment needed to make them. We noted in chapter 4 the appearance in standard seventeenth-century New England house designs of a "milk room" for making and storing dairy goods. Sarah F. McMahon concludes that by the early nineteenth century, butter and cheese were available year-round even to families of "moderate wealth." A generation or so before this, a traveler judged Rhode Island butter and cheese to be "excellent."[132]

In the household of Ezra Stiles, the late-eighteenth-century president of Yale, about a pound of cheese a day was consumed. In 1728 a Boston newspaper stated that a typical "genteel" family would be likely to have dairy products at every meal—milk for breakfast and supper and cheese for dinner. Harriet Beecher Stowe depicted cheese being eaten in a variety of contexts, from an elegant Boston wedding reception, to the festivities accompanying the provision of wood for the minister of a mountain village, to Sunday lunch between the morning and afternoon church services on an island in Maine.[133]

It was the mistress who made the butter and cheese in wealthy as well as middle-class households. The wife of Christopher Gore, proprietor of a large estate in Waltham, Massachusetts, in the early nineteenth century, "was an authority on the dairy." On a more middling level, in Hampshire County, Massachusetts, in 1840, farm women regularly bartered or sold their cheese and butter. One historian estimates that between 14 percent and 23 percent of all New England farm income in that year was earned by dairying. In Hampshire County in 1860, women's dairy earnings were just under half a full-time laborer's annual wages and between 10 percent and 20 percent of "total farm earnings."[134] Buttermaking tended to be concentrated in the fall and spring, cheesemaking in the summer. This pattern is consistent with the fact that in mid-eighteenth-century Deerfield, Massachusetts, exchanges of butter took place primarily in the summer, those of cheese in the fall.[135]

Sarah F. McMahon provides evidence that some women made butter on through the winter. At least two nineteenth-century cookbooks included recipes for winter buttermaking. But other sources warned against winter butter as inferior and even unhealthy. From Child's advice that "butter is sweetest in September and June," it appears that butter was sometimes made in the summer.[136]

In this area as in others, the cookbooks indicate that throughout the first half of the nineteenth century New England remained poised between subsistence and market modes of economic functioning. Just before the beginning of the century, Amelia Simmons was explaining to her readers how to shop for butter and cheese. Fifty years later, Catharine Beecher was telling hers how to make them at home.[137]

The early-nineteenth-century Salem, Massachusetts, diarist William Bentley reflected prevailing upper-class opinion when he stated that "in most of our towns the cheese is of an inferior quality and unfit for exportation." In these elite circles, bringing in dairy products from elsewhere was the order of the day. "The best families" were "expecting their cheese from England," said Bentley. Merchants in Boston and Portsmouth, New Hampshire, catered to such sentiment by importing Cheshire cheese and Irish butter.[138]

Anathemas from the likes of Bentley notwithstanding, cheesemaking flourished in western Connecticut, western Massachusetts, Vermont, and the Yankee-settled belt of New York State. A late-eighteenth-century French traveler stated that he had found "American cheese equal to the best Cheshire of England, or the Roquefort of France." Quality was matched by quantity. In 1860 one aged Vermont widow was claimed to have made 97 cheeses weighing all told over 4,000 pounds. Others in the neighborhood produced over 5,000 pounds apiece. Ten years earlier, 2,750,000 pounds of cheese were made in Litchfield County, Connecticut.[139]

People in the region took pride in their cheesemaking prowess, evincing this memorably at the turn of the nineteenth century. That was when Elder John Leland persuaded farmers in the vicinity of a village in the Berkshire region of western Massachusetts with the uncannily appropriate name of Cheshire "to contribute the milk from one day's milking for the purpose of making a colossal cheese to be presented to" Thomas Jefferson, in celebration of his election as president of the United States. The cheese was duly manufactured. Weighing 1,450 pounds, it was transported by boat and wagon (drawn by "six horses with beribboned bridles") to Washington, where it was presented to Jefferson on New Year's Day, 1802. It is pleasant to conclude this brief account of dairy goods in New England by noting that two centuries after Elder Leland's "Big Cheese," the cheddars sent forth from Yankee cheese districts remain highly edible, if less spectacularly proportioned.[140]

Pork Cookery

According to C. Anne Wilson, in Britain from medieval times "pork was almost as well liked as beef." This was fortunate since, as we have seen, swine was the nation's principal source of meat. Souse, pickled for long keeping, was through the eighteenth century the form of salted pork that figured most largely in the British diet, both for everyday eating and Christmas feasting. As time went on, the meaning of souse got attached less to all the parts of the pig and more to the head, ears, cheeks, snout, feet, and entrails only.[141]

More significant for the Christmas feast was brawn, which in the Middle Ages had been made with soused wild boar meat. By the sixteenth century, wild boars having mostly disappeared, domesticated boar or sometimes simply pig was used to make brawn. By the eighteenth century Hannah Glasse found it necessary to explain to her readers how to tell "true boar pig's brawn" from "that of a barrow-hog or sow."[142]

Another way of cooking pork that was, at least among average people, reserved almost exclusively for festive occasions was roasting the whole pig. In 1615 Gervase Markham described how to slaughter, decapitate, and quarter the beast, then take it directly to the fire. He recommended that, prior to spitting, lemon peel be sprinkled over two of the porker's quarters, "tops of" thyme over the other two. "The head requires more roasting" than the brains, Markham noted, adding that gravy seasoned with sage would constitute a suitable sauce. A typical seventeenth-century stuffing might be made with sweet herbs, bacon, lemon peel, anchovies, minced liver, beef suet, and seasoned bread crumbs.[143]

In the eighteenth century Hannah Glasse offered a recipe for pig roasted whole rather than quartered ("keep flouring it till the eyes drop out"), along with brief instructions on ways of cooking (mostly roasting) particular cuts and on preparing a great many "different sorts of sauce for a pig." "If you should be in a place where you cannot roast a pig," you could bake one, according to Glasse. Earlier in the eighteenth century, E. Smith gave a recipe for fricasseeing a whole pig ("the head must be roasted whole, and set in the middle, and the fricasee round it"). Other forms of pork cookery found in eighteenth-century English cookbooks, such as Susannah Carter's boiled leg of pork that had to have been "in salt six or seven days" before being put in the kettle, were more representative of the soused meat that constituted the bulk of pork consumed by most people.[144]

The tendency to confine the meaning of souse to what would be, for us, the funkier parts of the pig was evidently well developed by the time the New England cooking tradition began to make its way into cookbooks. Child's recipe was intended for "pigs' feet, ears, &c." Otherwise, as with other aspects of meat preservation, her instructions amounted to a variation on traditional English practice: soaking; boiling; placing in cold water; reboiling of "the jelly-like liquor in which [the meat] was cooked with an equal quantity of vinegar," along with salt, cloves, allspice, and cinnamon; and pouring of this pickling blend "scalding hot" over the boiled meat in cold water. Mrs. Lee likewise spoke of sousing only in connection with pig's head, ears, and feet. Beecher further narrowed its scope to just the feet.[145]

Imogene Wolcott's 1939 cookbook claimed that "Souse Meat" was another name for "Hog's Head Cheese." These were actually two different things, however, which Wolcott's recipe synthesized. Nineteenth-century recipes for "the famous 'Pig's Head Cheese'" involved cleaning and boiling the head, mincing and seasoning the separated meat, tightly packing it, and pressing it with a heavy weight for twenty-four hours or more.[146]

Sarah Josepha Hale offered a more complex treatment of "Pork Cheese." The head was to be cured in salt and saltpeter for four days, in company with four pig tongues, and the resulting ensemble of pig body parts was then to be washed, tied in "a clean cloth," and boiled "until the bones will come easily out of the head." Next the cook was told to take the skin off the head "as whole as possible." Two strips of cloth, "long enough to fold over the top when the shape is full," were to be laid "across each other" in the bottom of a "round tin, shaped like a small cheese." The skin that had been preserved as a unit was next put "round the tin." Meanwhile, the skinless head had been chopped into small pieces and "highly seasoned" with pepper, cayenne, and salt. This chopped and seasoned head meat was now to join the four tongues cut into slices to make a layered filling for the skin on the strips of cloth in the tin. The concluding steps were to "draw the cloth tightly across the top," press with a weighted plate, "till it be quite cold," and serve "with vinegar and mustard . . . for luncheon or supper."[147]

Mrs. Lee gave a recipe for collaring pig's head. (This, the reader may recall, was the name for short-term pork preservation.) First, the hair, snout, eyes, and brain were removed. What remained of the head was soaked overnight and drained, then salted "extremely well" and left to itself for five days. On the sixth day it was boiled, and the bones were removed. From this point it was subjected to convoluted presentation maneuvers: "then lay it on a dresser, turning the thick end of one side of the head toward the thick end of the other, to make the roll of an equal size; sprinkle it well with salt and white pepper, and roll it with the ears; and, if you think proper, put the pig's feet round the outside, when boned, or the thin parts of a couple of cowheels." What now remained was to swaddle it, bind it with tape, boil it, and press it down under a weight "until it is quite cold." After all that, Lee concluded on an ominous note: "If likely to spoil, slice and fry it, either with or without batter."[148]

Other parts of the pig that are less likely to be regarded favorably today but that received particular notice in our cookbook sample were the cheeks (which Child judged "better than any other pieces of pork to bake with beans"), feet, liver, heart, and lungs.[149]

The standard treatment for boiled ham was on view in Catharine Beecher's 1846 cookbook: long boiling, skinning, partial baking, covering with "pounded rusk or bread crumbs," and final baking. "Boiled ham is always improved by setting it into an oven for near an hour, till much of the fat fries out, and this also makes it more tender," Beecher concluded, appending an injunction to save the fat from the baking process "for frying meat."[150]

Roasted whole pig, which has now passed into the realm of culinary exotica, was included in New England cookbooks throughout the nineteenth and early twentieth centuries. In the versions offered in the first half of the nineteenth century, most of the details regarding methods of cooking and presentation resembled those found in eighteenth-century English sources. Thus, Mrs. Lee, like Hannah Glasse, emphasized the need for a hotter fire at the two ends than in the middle. Child, like Glasse, mentioned the eyes dropping out as a test of the progress of the roasting. And when roasting was completed, Child and Lee both followed Glasse in chopping off the head, splitting both the carcass and the head in two, laying the carcass in a dish, and placing the bisected head on each side of it. Lee went along with Glasse's further advice to cut the ears off the head and put them "one at each end," stressing that the ears must be "nice and crisp."[151]

Possibly belaboring the obvious, Lee began her recipe by noting that pig was "in prime order for the spit when about three weeks old." She added that "a sucking-pig, like a young child, must not be left for an instant," inadvertently associating her roast pig festivities with the satirical visions of the culinary uses of Irish babies found in Jonathan Swift's *A Modest Proposal*. Since, as she reiterated at the close of her recipe, "a pig is a very troublesome subject to roast, most persons have them baked. Send a quarter of a pound of butter, and beg the baker to baste it well." But no sooner had this last flourish made its way into the text than, following Glasse once again, Lee added a recipe for baking a pig at home.[152]

A few years later Catharine Beecher perpetuated this tradition with her recipe for "Baked, or Roasted Pig." As with roast beef, the distinction between roasting and baking became more elusive as the cookstove and range came to supersede the open hearth. While one of the early-twentieth-century recipes for roast pig in our sample spoke of roasting "over a bright fire," the other, from the no-nonsense domestic scientists Mary J. Lincoln and Anna Barrows, envisioned cooking "in moderate heat," which bespoke an oven.[153]

Beginning with Child, a theme that did not bode well for pork's future reputation was sounded in the cookbooks. Child stressed that "fresh pork should be cooked more than any other meat" and went on to refer to "the slight sickness occasioned by eating roasted pork." Similarly, Beecher warned that "pork must be cooked slowly and very thoroughly." And Eliza Leslie, one of the few antebellum authors to mention pork chops (which she also called pork steaks) included the following in her recipe for them: "They require much longer broiling than beef-steaks or mutton chops." Such cautionary notes were being sounded more stridently by the early twentieth century. "If this meat be not thoroughly well-done, it is disgusting to the sight and poisonous to the stomach," wrote an author in 1905. "Other meats under-done may be unpleasant, but pork is absolutely uneatable."[154]

The perils of pork consumption loomed even larger in the cookbooks' marketing advice. "Pork made by still house slops is almost poisonous, and hogs that live on offal never furnish healthful food," wrote Beecher. Hale agreed: "This meat is . . . *dangerously* unwholesome when ill fed, or in any degree diseased." The same 1905 author who thought undercooked pork "disgusting" stated that "the pig, from its gluttonous habits, is particularly liable to disease, and if killed and eaten when in an unhealthy condition, those who partake of it will probably pay dearly for their indulgence."[155]

This last author's moralistic terminology (disgusting, gluttonous, indulgence) indicates that by the end of the nineteenth century, it was not only considerations of health that were affecting perceptions of pork. As we have noted, a major strand in the cultural fabric of the nineteenth century was the propagation of aristocratic conceptions of refinement among large portions of the American middle class. One form this development took was the installation of white picket fences in front of middle-class homes. Richard L. Bushman sums up the cultural significance of such front yards: "Fences served the practical purpose of keeping animals out of the foreyard, but an inexpensive field fence would have been equally effective. . . . The painted fence kept out animality as well . . . and established the realm [of] taste and gentility."[156]

No New England animal embodied free-ranging animality more than the hog. From the dawn of English presence in the region, "swine were weed creatures . . . breeding . . . quickly." They swarmed over the landscape, since they were "willing to eat . . . anything . . . and were . . . able to hold their own against wolves and bears." That the hog remained ubiquitous even as late as 1846 is indicated by the fact that it was the only animal that Catharine Beecher told her readers how to slaughter.[157]

Yet the very town in which Beecher had lived as a girl, Litchfield, Connecticut, epitomized the impact of "the refinement of America" on pigs and pork. Whereas in the eighteenth century "geese, turkeys, and ringed hogs still ran free in the streets" of Litchfield, after 1780 and on into the time of Beecher's residence as the minister's daughter, Litchfield civilized itself with, among other things, "white houses with fenced front yards."[158]

In the rougher-and-readier life of colonial times, everyone had owned a hog. As that life was superseded and its acceptance of "animality" brought under restraint, the hog and its flesh were likewise labeled taboo. For aristocratic Caroline Howard King in the 1820s and 1830s, pork could still be part of her family's cuisine. The treats she remembered included "'scraps,' which were brought to us from one especial farm in Danvers. They were little bits of pork, prepared in some mysterious way with sage or sweet marjoram." Fifty to seventy-five years later, after the culture of refinement had had time to have a fuller impact, King's enjoyment of "scraps" would be countenanced

"Pigs" and "The Pig-Tight Gate," Harper's New Monthly Magazine, *September 1860 and January 1858. (Courtesy Fall River Public Library)*

less and less. The era had arrived in which a "growing prejudice against pork in all its varieties . . . pervades our best classes."[159]

In 1846 Catharine Beecher could still state that "corn-fed pork is best." Like her "directions for cutting up a hog," this was a link to the New England past. We have quoted in chapter 1 Henry Adams's statement that as of 1800, "Indian corn was eaten three times a day in another form as salt pork." The pigs ate the corn, and the people ate the pigs. Pork was ubiquitous in colonial and early national New England. When cash disappeared during Shay's Rebellion, salt pork served as currency. During the American Revolution, a captured British officer who boarded with a family in Pepperell, Massachusetts, stated that dinner every day consisted of "fat salt pork and sauce." Here was boiled dinner once again, made in this family with pork.[160]

The same 1905 author who used terms like "disgusting" and "gluttonous" in connection with pigs and pork controverted Beecher's judgment that the best pork was fed on corn. Now it was "dairy-fed pork" that had become "the best." To the extent that it could be accepted at all, it had to be felt that pork had emerged from an environment of special handling. As boiled dinner was being turned into "New England Boiled Dinner," it certainly would not do to retain as its core component a meat saddled with so many negative associations. Such is the explanation for the fact that twentieth-century boiled dinner was always made with corned beef, never with salt pork.[161]

But in yet another spin of the cultural wheel, the very denigration of pork eventually begat its revival in ostentatiously rustic forms. Lydia Maria Child had noted that "fried salt pork and apples is a favorite dish in the country; but it is seldom seen in the city." She went on to give instructions on how to make it, but few if any among city-dwelling cookbook authors and readers took up her suggestion until well into the twentieth century. After "the refinement of America" had run its course and become orthodoxy rather than innovation, it became possible for a salt pork vogue of sorts to arise. Cookbooks began to include recipes for "Pork Stew," "Baked Salt Pork," "Roast Salt Pork," "Pan-Fried Salt Pork," "Salt Pork in Egg Batter," and "Salt Pork and [Salt] Codfish."[162]

The Way of All Flesh

"I hold a family to be in a desperate way when the mother can see the bottom of the pork barrel," James Fenimore Cooper had a frontier housewife declare in an 1845 novel. "My children I calkerlate to bring up on pork with just as much bread and butter as they may want." This woman's outlook comes down to us today as though from a foreign country. The revolution in meat taste brought about by the campaign against pork remains basically in effect, affecting far more than the composition of New England Boiled Dinner. Twenty-first-century fast food restaurants offer a bit of fish or chicken and beef, beef, beef.[163]

But in a larger sense, our food world is quite similar to that of this fictional female pioneer. The technological and transportation resources to deliver fresh vegetables to vast numbers of people have been available for a century and more, and, dating from before the time that Cooper's novel was published, there have been repeated attempts to convince people of the nutritional (and from some quarters the moral) superiority of a diet based on vegetable matter rather than animal flesh. Nevertheless, what this woman stated her children would be raised on—meat and starch—is what American children today, by a huge majority, continue to be raised on. The only major component of our diet that Cooper's character failed to mention was sugar, the rise of which to a central position was already well along in 1845, as we shall see in the next chapter.

The economics of meat consumption, and its environmental consequences as well, have not changed much from what they were at the time of the English immigration to the North American colonies. That immigration was in many ways an early manifestation of what is now called globalization. The kinds of things that happened in the seventeenth and eighteenth centuries in the meat department of the global supermarket also happen now. Then, salt meat was sent from New England southward. Now, the fast food industry maintains its live animal resources in South America and sends the product to North America. And just as English livestock permanently altered the ecosystems of the New England region, so are the efforts to supply the contemporary demand for meat comparably altering South American ecosystems. Plus ça change . . .

CHAPTER 6

Of a Fruity Flavor

Apples, Preserves, & Pies

Roger Williams declared of the strawberry that it was "the wonder of all the Fruits growing naturally" in New England. After quoting "one of the chiefest Doctors of *England*" to the effect that "God could have made, but God never did make a better Berry," Williams went on to speak, confusingly, of "some parts where the *Natives* [had] planted" strawberries. Indeed, he recalled that in one particular area they had planted so many "within a few miles compasse . . . as would fill a good ship."[1]

Many Europeans were impressed by the abundance of fruits and berries in the New World, especially strawberries. It was possible to find on the Atlantic coast of North America, said one, "fields and woods that are died red." The first settlers of what is now known as Portsmouth, New Hampshire, apparently thought that was what they were seeing, for they named the place Strawberry Bank. American strawberries were also admired for their strikingly large size, "some being two inches about," according to William Wood.[2]

In speaking of native plantings, perhaps Williams simply meant that in places where the Indians grew the corn-bean-pumpkin triumvirate, naturally growing strawberries were particularly noticeable. Until recently the prevailing view was that "no fruits were cultivated by the Indians." Raspberries, blackberries, blueberries, huckleberries, currants, grapes, cherries, and plums were noted along with strawberries in seventeenth-century accounts as growing in North America. But all species of New World fruit were believed to be, as William Wood stated of the cherries he had tasted, "as wilde as the Indians."[3]

The idea that the literal fruit-fulness of the New England landscape had come into existence without human intervention formed part of the colonists' rationale for taking possession of the land, as evidenced by John Winthrop's claim that the natives "inclose noe Land." One obvious form of land enclosure was the planting of fruit and vegetable gardens, the edge of the garden being frequently understood to represent the boundary between the realm of cultivation and civilization and that of wilderness and savagery.

In the settlement of Massachusetts Bay, seed for garden produce was brought over in quantities far out of proportion to the requirements of subsistence. According to Jonathan Beecher Field, this indicated the settlers' determination to assert their right to ownership. By planting as many gardens and orchards as they could, they would dot the landscape with unmistakable symbols of the opposition between civilized and savage. Thus, an island in Boston harbor was granted to Winthrop and his heirs in perpetuity, but only on the condition they maintain a vineyard and orchard there.[4]

The ideological function of the gardens planted by the English would have been compromised, if not destroyed, had it been understood that the Indians were already cultivators of garden produce. But with fruit as with corn, beans, pumpkins, and game, the Indians managed their environment in order to make it produce what they needed. According to one estimate, fruits and vegetables constituted approximately 4 percent of the native diet in the seventeenth century. Among the seasonal special-purpose camps to which native groups are thought to have repaired during the summer were "plant collecting localities."[5]

The place the English dubbed Strawberry Bank was probably one such site: "The practice of burning off the forests created a 'parklike' landscape, where game animals could move freely and fruit-bearing bushes could thrive." What these conclusions of present-day scholarship indicate is that the fields and woods appeared to the first Europeans to be dyed red because the Indians had in fact dyed them red. William Wood spoke truer than he knew when he referred to fruits that were "as wilde as the Indians." The fruits, like the Indians, were not wild.[6]

That said, it is also true that the colonists borrowed little from the Indians in the realm of fruit cookery. Evidence regarding Indian use of fruit as an ingredient is sparse. As seen in chapter 1, Roger Williams noticed that the Narragansetts made bread with dried strawberries and cake with dried currants. Edward Johnson described a Narragansett diplomatic banquet at which the English emissaries were served corn puddings to which a "great store of black berryes, somewhat like Currants" had been added. Other observers simply noted the consumption of "all sorts of Berries," especially in the summer. Such seasonal patterns suggest that fruit was mainly eaten fresh. Some, however, was dried and stored for use in the breads, cakes, and puddings seen by Williams and Johnson.[7]

Except for the noteworthy dimensions of the strawberries, there was little that was unfamiliar to the English settlers about the types of fruit they encountered in New England. Wild berries had been eaten in Britain since prehistoric times, cherries and grapes were introduced by the Romans, and plums were known since at least the immediate post-Roman era. By the seventeenth century, sixty-one varieties of plums and thirty-five types of cherries were being cultivated in Britain.[8]

The same source also recorded sixty-two varieties of pears and seventy-seven types of apples, and these two fruits, which were not native to North America (except for crabapples), had long been the most popular in Britain. The literal meaning of the Anglo-Saxon word for orchard was apple-tree enclosure, and in medieval and Renaissance literary sources, apples and pears were the fruits most frequently mentioned. To assist in evoking the lusty vitality of the female protagonist of his "Miller's Tale," for example, Geoffrey Chaucer likened the sweetness of her breath to that of a "hoord of apples laid in hay or heeth." At the festive climax of William Shakespeare's *Love's Labour's Lost*, winter was epitomized as a time "when roasted crabs [crabapples] hiss in the bowl," creating an island of warmth and cheer within the rustic cottage against the hanging icicles and blowing wind without it.[9]

Although there was an element of denial in the first settlers' perceptions of Indian uses of fruit, their own uses of fruit were indeed more developed. The most significant thing that New England offered to the immigrants in this regard was an environment that was even more hospitable to their favorite types of fruit than their homeland had been.

Apples

Of one type was this statement particularly true. We shall be considering some specific types of apple preparations—preserves, pies, cider—later in this chapter and in chapter 8. But apples have been sufficiently prominent in New England food culture to deserve a section all to themselves.

Peregrine White, the first child of English parents born in New England (on the *Mayflower*, as it sat in Cape Cod harbor in November 1620), planted an apple orchard from seed when he was twenty-eight years old. But by this time, there were many apple orchards in the Massachusetts Bay and Plymouth colonies. The array of fruit and vegetable seeds stowed in the first ships had of course included apple seeds. Indeed, the first apple orchard in the

Massachusetts Bay region had been planted even before organized settlement began—in 1625 on a slope of what was to become Beacon Hill in Boston by the clergyman William Blaxton. According to Ann Leighton, "the first universally recognized New England apple" was the Blaxton's Yellow Sweeting, grown by the reverend gentleman on a homestead in what is now Cumberland, Rhode Island, where he moved after leaving Boston. Two trees of that orchard were still bearing fruit in 1830.[10]

Time only increased the popularity of apples among New Englanders. In the eighteenth century it was generally acknowledged that apples grew better in America, and "the fruit-growing world look[ed] to the central Atlantic states and New England for what was flourishing in apple culture." A case in point dating from 1826 was provided by Dr. Joseph Stevens of Castine, Maine. Stevens described the "names and Situations of Apple Trees set out in our garden . . . Baldwin—7 paces N.W. of Great Apple Tree. Ribstone Pippin—7 paces N.W. of Baldwin . . . A fine fall apple. Pumpkin Sweet—7 paces N.W. of Ribstone—21 of G. A. Tree. . . . R. Island Greening—7 paces N.W. of Baldwin . . . very fine apple—Keep till January. Hubbardstown Nonsuch. . . ." And so on through several more varieties documented with equal care and precision.[11]

Apple orchards such as that of Dr. Stevens could be maintained with relatively little effort, and this fact was of considerable significance in the creation of the agricultural surpluses that had been achieved in the region by the middle of the eighteenth century. Since it took less work to grow apples than it did to grow the barley from which beer was made, cider gradually replaced beer as the staple beverage. As beer consumption declined, much of the land formerly allocated to barley was utilized for "bread-grain crops." Moreover, on land where grain could not grow, an apple orchard could flourish, thereby increasing the total area under cultivation. This trend was further accentuated by the fact that "when orchards [did occupy] good land . . . grain could be planted among the trees." More cider and less beer meant more bread and vegetables—an increase in both the total amount and the kinds of food produced.[12]

Amelia Simmons recommended in 1796 that apples, which "are highly useful in families, . . . ought to be more universally cultivated, excepting in the compactest cities." "There is not a single family but might set a tree in some otherwise useless spot," she went on, confirming Sarah F. McMahon's analysis of how orchards were utilized to reclaim marginal land. Simmons also felt that "the intrusions of boys" into orchards were "too common in America." Her remedy for this early republican reenactment of the drama of original sin was to give "free access into orchards" to the types of boys who would plant and tend apple trees, while barring the types who would be "neglectful." The result would be that "millions of fruit trees would spring into growth. . . . The net saving would in time extinguish the public debt, and enrich our cookery." Simmons identified the same benefits of expanded apple cultivation as McMahon—increased prosperity in general and a more varied and tasty diet.[13]

Actually, Simmons's recommendations were being implemented even as she wrote. New England's experience of the facilitation of all agriculture by apple culture was being carried westward by an alumnus of Simmons's apple-tree planting fraternity: John Chapman (1774–1845) from Leominster, Massachusetts, better known, of course, as Johnny Appleseed. By the late 1790s, Chapman had established an apple tree nursery in northwestern Pennsylvania. In the early decades of the nineteenth century, he moved on across northern and central Ohio and eastern Indiana, "shrewdly judging along what routes pioneers would be likely to settle and planting apple seedlings just ahead of settlements from which homesteaders could start their orchards."[14]

John Chapman's modus operandi suggests that he understood apples and cider to be indispensable parts not only of "the frontier diet" but also of frontier farming as a whole, just as they had been in colonial New England. This socioeconomic reality underlay his transformation into Johnny Appleseed, a major American folk hero whose real and imaginary exploits are still retold for twenty-first-century American children.[15]

In the nineteenth century New England apple cultivation yielded a bountiful crop of legend and recollection besides the Johnny Appleseed myth. Lucy Larcom's wealthy childhood neighbor had an apple orchard "from which we caught glimpses and perfumes of unknown flowers. Over its high walls hung boughs of splendid great yellow sweet apples, which, when they fell on the outside, we children considered as our perquisites. When I first read about the apples of the Hesperides, my idea of them was that they were like the Colonel's 'pumpin-sweetings.'" Apparently, the children of Beverly, Massachusetts, presumably not all of them girls, were better behaved than the boys Amelia Simmons complained about, as they waited for other people's apples to fall into their laps rather than barging in and taking them. Nevertheless, the aroma and allure of forbidden fruit that always seems to be associated with an apple orchard, especially one with walls around it, was certainly present here, as it was in Simmons's complaints about transgressive boys.[16]

Around the same time that Larcom was composing her memoirs, Thomas Robinson Hazard was singing the praises of a variety of southern Rhode Island apple. He alleged that eighteenth-century Newport merchant Metcalf Bowler was presented by a potentate of Persia, "from his own garden, situated on the site of the ancient Garden of Eden," with "a young apple tree growing in a porcelain tub, which was declared to be one of the few lineal descendants of the tree of knowledge." At first, Bowler planted the seedling in a greenhouse, but he "was admonished in a dream by an angel, claiming to be Mother Eve, to do no such thing, as the climate of southern Rhode Island was, if anything, a little more favorable to its growth than that of southern Assyria, from whence it was removed. Mr. Bowler had such faith in the vision that he had the tree carefully removed from the tub or vase with the earth attached and transplanted into Rhode Island soil, where it grew and flourished beyond his most sanguine expectations, and finally developed into what has ever since been called the Rhode Island greening."[17]

With his forthright introduction of "Mother Eve" into his tale, Hazard highlighted the connections between apples and original sin that Simmons and Larcom only hinted at. But he did so in order to turn those connections upside down. He depicted a member of the expanding class of urban merchants importing not merely a luxurious food from the distant, exotic realms with which he trafficked, but something directly descended from the source of luxury itself, the tree of knowledge. But Mother Eve proved to be the agent of reconversion from commerce and sophistication to rustic simplicity and innocence, commanding Bowler to dispense with the artifice of a greenhouse and sink the tree (and himself) into good plain "Rhode Island soil."

Other varieties of apple told the stories of their growers' or eaters' adoration straightaway in their names. Old England offered such examples as Winter Queening, Love's Pearmain, Slack-my-Girdle, and Lady's Finger. To these, New England added Ladies Sweeting, Danver's Winter Sweet, The Melon, Winter Banana, Juicy Bite, Missing Link, Large Never Fail, Westfield Seek-No-Further, Autumn Strawberry, Red Astrakhan, The Mother, and many others. There were also names with a bit of an edge to them, such as the Bushwacker, Sparhawk, Bullet, Sops of Wine, Cabbage Head, and Sheepnose. Sweet this and that, happy evocations of other fruits, claims for hardiness, bits of banter and teasing: Yankee ingenuity in the naming of apples rivaled that of the Indians in the naming of corn.[18]

Among the many methods of cooking apples, those of Old England included "ffrutours" [fritters], usually made during Lent, apple and almond milk purees, and puddings of rice and chopped apples. The combination of meat and applesauce was made much more intimate in a medieval soup in which apple puree was thinned with meat broth. Apples that had been boiled and put through a sieve were made into a pottage known as "appulmos."[19]

Roasting of apples was transported to New England, along with Shakespeare's association of it with protective and reviving warmth. In Harriet Beecher Stowe's *Oldtown Folks*, Harry and Tina Percival, orphan children who had run away from unworthy guardians, took shelter from a Massachusetts autumn rainstorm in a manor house that had been abandoned by its pre-Revolutionary gentry owners. After finding "a nice little room full of pretty things," they succeeded in getting a fire going, "the brightest, most hopeful companion a mortal could ask for in a chill, stormy day in autumn." Before long, Tina proposed to "roast some apples for dinner,—I saw ever so many out here on the tree. Roast apples with our corn bread will be so good!"[20]

Roasted apples bore a close resemblance to baked apples, one of New England's most durably popular apple dishes. In 1846 Harriet Beecher Stowe's sister offered several recipes, prefacing them with the remark that "pippins are the best apples for cooking." Apples baked whole were to be tested with a fork for doneness (sweet apples needed "much longer" baking), covered with white sugar "if sour fruit," and served with cream "or a thin custard."[21]

Apples were also commonly served in the form of pudding. One of the best known of these, Bird's Nest Pudding, bore a distinct resemblance to baked apples. Apples were peeled and cored, a custard of eggs, milk, sugar, and flavoring was poured on top of them, and they were baked. Variations mostly involved either the custard or the ingredient used to fill the holes in the cored apples. As far as the latter was concerned, the choices ranged from nothing (Child) to sugar (Beecher) to raisins (mid-twentieth century). As for the custard, there were any number of possibilities. The custard for Mrs. E. A. Howland's 1845 Bird's Nest Pudding was composed of nothing but sago (a starch made from the leaves of the sago palm tree) and water.[22]

In the nineteenth century distinctions between apple puddings, apple dumplings, and what we might now consider forms of apple pie were imprecise. The name of one of Amelia Simmons's recipes encapsulated this imprecision: "*An apple Pudding Dumplin*: Put into paste, quartered apples, lie in a cloth and boil two hours, serve with sweet sauce." This is a dumpling dish in that the apples were boiled inside a paste or crust; it was also a boiled bag pudding. Lydia Maria Child replicated this recipe, calling it simply "Apple Pudding." She noted that "some people like little dumplings, made by rolling up one apple, pared and cored, in a piece of crust, and tying them up in spots all over the bag."[23]

One early-twentieth-century author followed Child by giving her version of this dish the name "Boiled Apple Pudding." On the other hand, Imogene Wolcott's was called "Apple Dumplings." Wolcott specified baking, although "Grandmother's recipe" involved boiling in a bag. "Dumplings may be steamed, too, but modern Yankee cooks usually prefer theirs baked," she concluded. Apparently, the history of "apple Pudding Dumplin" paralleled that of Indian pudding.[24]

In nostalgic contexts, dumplings rather than pudding was the preferred nomenclature. Caroline Howard King remembered that "apple dumplings were a very favorite dish with children" in early-nineteenth-century upper-class Salem. According to Thomas Robinson Hazard, this had also been true in southern Rhode Island a few decades before. "Aunty Phillis," his grandfather's cook, had made apple dumplings "with a thin crust, and a cat-head apple quartered and cored, in each of them, as big as a good sized pumpkin. For Phillis used to say there was 'nothing on airth she so 'spised as an apple dumpling with a crust as thick and hard as a jonny-cake board, with no cat-head in it.'" Hazard still vividly recalled how as a child he "used to lie with my eyes on the ceiling just at the south-east corner of the chamber, and fancy to myself a great platter of apple dumplings, almost swimming in sugar sauce, standing there on a shelf, all of which I devoured, each one at one mouthful!"[25]

Child mentioned a variation on apple pudding/dumplings in which the holes left by the departed cores were filled up with washed rice. Thus had the rice-and-chopped-apples pudding of medieval England crossed the Atlantic. Rice and apples were combined in a variety of ways in New England. If Child proposed rice in apples, Mrs. Lee offered several versions of "Apples in Rice." An alternative form of the early-twentieth-century "Boiled Apple Pudding" mentioned earlier utilized rice instead of crust. This "makes a very good pudding, called an *Avalanche*," the author asserted.[26]

Let's return to Amelia Simmons. Here is the dish upon which she bestowed the name "Apple Pudding":

One pound apple sifted, one pound sugar, 9 eggs, one quarter of a pound butter, one quart sweet cream, one gill rose-water, a cinnamon, a green lemon peel grated (if sweet apples,) add the juice of half a lemon, put on to paste No. 7. Currants, raisins and citron some add, but good without them.

By "sifted" Simmons probably meant grated. To us, this concoction, baked (one supposes) with a bottom crust ("paste No. 7"), would be a pie rather than a pudding. And indeed, with its eggs, sugar, cream, and spices, it distinctly resembled Simmons's "Pompkin" preparation which we have identified as the prototype of modern pumpkin pie. But obviously a custardized apple pie filling such as Simmons's was not the prototype of modern apple pie.[27]

Catharine Beecher presented a similar recipe without the crust, making something more like what we would now call a pudding. Peeled and grated apples were combined with grated stale bread and a custard of eggs, milk, sugar, and "rose water, or grated lemon, or orange peel." The resulting mixture was then baked.[28]

This stale-bread-and-apple pudding was not far removed from the dish known as Brown Betty. One early-twentieth-century Brown Betty recipe called for "one loaf of stale bread crumbled fine, one-half cupful of milk, and twelve apples. Alternate layers of bread and sliced apples, sugared, buttered, and spiced. Moisten with the milk. Bake in a tin pudding-pan for three hours."[29]

A close relation of Brown Betty was Apple Pandowdy. Although as Evan Jones says, this name "has a fine Yankee ring to it," the dish was also known under a number of aliases, stretching from "Apple Jonathan and Apple Potpie . . . to Yankee Apple John and Apple Betty," the last evoking its resemblance to Brown Betty. Caroline Howard King remembered pandowdy as "a dark brown mixture of baked bread and apple, rich with spices and sweetened with molasses."[30]

A recipe for Apple Pandowdy from 1880 (according to Imogene Wolcott, who reprinted it without more specific attribution in 1939) was sweetened with sugar as well as molasses and spiced with cloves and cinnamon. It used "baking powder biscuit crust." Another recipe known definitely to be from the 1880s, as well as one from the 1850s, made use of pie crust. The health food advocate of the 1850s who offered a crustless pumpkin pie likewise offered a pandowdy, which he called "Apple Pudding," featuring a spartan paste made with unbolted wheat flour, cornmeal, and water. A Maine pandowdy of unknown date utilized salt pork and "dumplings as for soup." It was to be simmered in a "dinner kettle."[31]

Catharine Beecher offered more "modes of preparing apples for the table" than just about anyone else. These included directions for two forms of long-term fruit preservation—apple butter and "Fruit Cheese." Long boiling in syrup or cider was to be followed by storage in pans or jars "in a dry, cool place." The butter would keep a year "if well boiled," Beecher promised. The cheese could be "cut in slices for the tea table." These recipes return us to the world of traditional food preservation, which we now explore in relation to fruit more fully than we could in chapter 4.[32]

Preservation and Preserves

The native people of New England probably ate the majority of their fruit fresh and only a minority preserved and/or cooked. Among the colonists, the situation was reversed. European tradition stretching back to the Greco-Roman physician Galen had held that fresh fruit was unhealthy. The medieval opinion that "raw pears a poison, baked a medicine be" was still being echoed in a seventeenth-century English medical treatise: "And all manner of fruit generally fill the blood with water, which boileth up in the body as new wine doth in the vessel, and so prepareth and causeth the blood to putrify, and consequently bringeth in sickness."[33]

Such views often went unheeded. Among the well-born and wealthy, fresh plums, cherries, grapes, and berries were regularly consumed. Upper-class schoolboys of the fifteenth century avidly ate plums, pears, pomegranates, and oranges. As for the common people, they ate fresh fruit "as and when they could get it," joining eagerly in cherry feasts or fairs "held in the orchards when the crop was ripe," and creating sufficient demand for fresh strawberries and cherries to support London street hawkers.[34]

But it is likely that fear of fresh fruit consumption was intensified, rather than eased, by the consumption itself. With harvests uncertain, people gorged themselves on fresh fruit in summers when the crop was abundant. But the wages of such excess was diarrhea, which was easily conflated with the symptoms of dysentery, also prevalent in the summertime: "the popular fancy saw a relation between the diarrhoeas and dysenteries of the hot months and the laxative effect of a liberal diet of fruit." People's very flouting of medical orthodoxy thus paradoxically secured their agreement with it.[35]

The colonists brought this heritage with them to New England. They certainly partook, straight from the bushes, of the impressive stock of berries produced by Indian burning-off procedures, just as they enjoyed plenty of apples straight from the trees that they themselves planted. But the preponderance of the yield from orchard and native-cleared forest was not directly consumed. Partly because of age-old health concerns, most fruits were not eaten, even in season, until after they had been cooked.

Objections to fresh fruit for health reasons were overcome to some extent in the eighteenth century, as notions of a balanced diet began to gain acceptance. But traces of the traditional fears were still to be discerned in persistent warnings against the health hazards of fruit gluttony. "Fruit, moderately eaten, is wholesome, particularly as correcting the grossness of animal food," conceded Mrs. Lee. "But an excess of it, and especially of unripe fruit, is productive of many diseases."[36]

But most fruit would not have been eaten fresh even had medical opposition never developed. Not surprisingly, ideas about what was healthy coincided with the requirements of subsistence. The bulk of the fruit crop was necessarily subjected to treatments designed to preserve it for later consumption.

In the sketch in chapter 4, we gave several examples of the storage of fresh apples in the cellar. It appears from the testimony of Lydia Sigourney, who grew up in Connecticut at the turn of the nineteenth century, that the best apples from the harvest were the ones that were thus stored fresh. They were "thoroughly wiped, and wrapped in paper" before they were laid away. Pears were also "comfortably accommodated" down below. A woman who grew up in Massachusetts later in the century stated that in the autumn dried apples "were put away to use for pies, sauce, and cake the next summer when the fresh apples were gone." This implied that fresh apples sufficient to supply pie-, sauce-, and cake-making during the autumn, winter, and spring were simultaneously being put away.[37]

Apple drying, usually accompanying sorting, was mentioned in the records of many households. Apples that were less than perfect were peeled, cut, and strung. Sometimes apple drying was turned into a ritual analogous to the husking bee for corn: "The bee was held in the barn . . . there were a number of tables set out with pans and knives, and needles and strings. Bushel baskets of apples stood around the tables. . . . The men pared the apples and some of the women pared and some strung."[38]

Harriet Beecher Stowe emphasized the similarity of the occasion to the husking bee as far as courtship and sexuality were concerned. At an apple bee in her fictionalized early-nineteenth-century Connecticut village, "the young people around the tubs of apples were having the very best of times. The apple, from the days of Mother Eve and the times of Paris and Helen, has been a fruit full of suggestion and omen in the meetings of men and maidens; and it was not less fruitful this evening."[39]

Apple bees were also times to make applesauce. According to Alice Morse Earle, after paring, quartering, and coring, the apples were placed in brass kettles, "sweet and sour in proper proportions, the sour at the bottom since they required more time to cook," with quinces "to give flavor" and molasses "for sweetening." When enough applesauce had been made to last through the winter, it was placed in barrels in the cellar, and "when slightly frozen was a keen relish."[40]

In seventeenth-century English yeoman households fruit drying sometimes involved the use of sugar. One sugar syrup method remained in use through the eighteenth century in both Old and New England. Amelia Simmons copied from Susannah Carter a recipe "to dry peaches," calling for as much sugar as would be equal in weight to the peaches. Half the sugar was used to make a syrup in which the peaches were boiled. After being split and stoned, the peaches were boiled again and drained. The other half of the sugar was boiled "almost to a candy." The peaches were soaked in the sugar candy overnight, then placed on a glass in a heated box to dry.[41]

One late-eighteenth-century Salem, Massachusetts, woman mentioned placing her quinces in a syrup made of the fruit's own cores and parings. In a similar recipe "for preserving quinces," Amelia Simmons called for a syrup of this kind, but she also said to add sugar in a weight ratio to the quinces of five to four.[42]

The Salem housewife also referred to preserving damson plums, noting that she was "a week too late." She no doubt followed a procedure, involving neither sugar nor syrup, similar to what a standard modern cookbook calls "canning in a boiling-water bath." Simmons's version of this method stated that newly ripe damsons should be used. They were to be placed in air- and watertight bottles, which were in turn to be placed over the fire in a kettle of cold water. After slow heating, half an hour of slow boiling, and a period of cooling, the bottles were to be removed from the kettle and deposited in a cold place. If the seals on the bottles were properly maintained, the plums would keep for a year.[43]

In Maine in the 1860s, a diarist recorded that she canned and bottled those fresh blueberries that she did not immediately use in pies. She probably used a method similar to that just described, which Simmons (this time following Carter) stated would work for gooseberries as well as plums.[44]

Another Maine woman referred to the preservation of strawberries. Although she indicated no specific methods, and may have relied on oral tradition, strawberry preservation recipes would have been available to her in contemporary cookbooks. Catharine Beecher said to layer strawberries and sugar, in a one-to-one ratio by weight, in a preserving kettle, to boil the mixture for fifteen minutes, to place it in sealed bottles, and to place the bottles in a box filled with dry sand. "The flavor of the fruit is preserved more perfectly, by simply packing the fruit and sugar in alternate layers, and sealing the jar, without cooking," Beecher added. Unfortunately, strawberries stored away uncooked did not "look so well."[45]

Distinctions between fruit preserved in sugared syrup and the "preserves" that we think of as synonymous with jams and jellies were elusive before the canning revolution of the late nineteenth century. Cookbooks placed recipes "for preserving" fruit in the same section with those for jams, jellies, and preserves. According to C. Anne Wilson, British fruit preserves traditions were derived from quince marmalade, which migrated to Britain from Portugal in the Middle Ages. By the sixteenth century, marmalades were being made with plums, prunes, pears, apples, and strawberries. The fruit was boiled, coarsely sieved, and reboiled with sugar. Traditional marmalades were "dense and solid, to be cut with a knife rather than lifted up on a spoon." Jam, a term not used in English cookbooks until the early eighteenth century, was originally distinguished from marmalade by the lesser degree of refinement involved in preparing it. The bruised soft fruit was simply boiled once in sugared syrup, without being passed through a sieve or strainer.[46]

Although Lydia Maria Child disapproved of preserves as being "unhealthy, expensive, and useless to those who are well," she included a recipe for raspberry jam that was to be made in the manner just described. She stated that "a pound of sugar to a pound of fruit is the rule for all preserves." This indeed had long been the recommended proportion, and it continued to be in later cookbooks. Catharine Beecher added other directives, such as picking fruit when it was relatively dry and avoiding "long boiling," which "hardens the fruit." After cooking, preserves should remain uncovered in their storage containers for three days, then be sealed either with paper soaked in brandy or with a "split bladder" similarly soaked. Beecher also provided tips for rescuing preserves that were beginning to spoil. Sarah Josepha Hale emphasized that the preserves would burn if the preserving pan were placed "flat upon the fire," that constant stirring was necessary after the sugar was added, and that the heat should be carefully regulated to avoid altering the texture, color, or flavor of the fruit for the worse.[47]

The emergence of jam eventually eroded the distinctiveness of marmalade. In a Carter/Simmons quince marmalade recipe, straining of the fruit was omitted, as it was in Child's quince and apple marmalades. Catharine Beecher's quince marmalade did fit the traditional pattern, the quinces being stewed, strained, and restewed with sugar. In an 1820s servants' manual, a recipe for "liquid currant jam, of the first quality" hovered between jam and marmalade. Some of the currants were to be strained, but prior to the two boilings rather than between them.[48]

Home preparation of jams, preserves, and marmalades remained widespread at the turn of the twentieth century, although by this time the categories were hopelessly confused. Some things that were called preserves were made like jam, some like marmalade. For example, in preparations called quince marmalade, the syrup of boiled parings and cores that we have seen in quince preservation techniques from the eighteenth century was utilized. There were even some marmalades that were made like marmalade. And self-conscious traditionalists made jams and marmalades more elaborately than they had ever been made before.[49]

The genealogy of jelly is even more complex than that of preserves, marmalade, and jam. As we shall see with pies, jelly encompassed types of foodstuffs that for us have come to stand in stark opposition. In fact, "jelly of flesh" and fish jelly are older than fruit-based jellies. In the fourteenth century meat jellies were made by simmering calves' feet or pigs' feet, snouts, or ears in wine, vinegar, and water, straining and seasoning the liquor, and pouring it over pieces of meat, where it would solidify and could be decorated with laurel leaves. Chefs were advised to test their meat jelly broth by plunging their hands into it, "and if thy hand be clammy, it is a sign that it is good."[50]

In early modern England, jellies based on calves' feet liquor were served as delicacies at the conclusions of banquets, the liquor being mixed, in one typical example, with wine, sugar, spices, and egg whites. The fascinating consistency of jelly led to its being molded and sculpted into representations of fruit and other still-life forms. Jellies based on real fruit were introduced around this time but were at first regarded as a dubious innovation.[51]

Calves' feet jellies much like those of the sixteenth century remained in vogue into the nineteenth century. Child's recipe, for four feet boiled in a gallon of water, called for wine, sugar, and egg whites as above, replacing the spices with lemon juice.[52]

Beecher included a similar recipe, but she noted that "the American gelatine, now very common, makes as good jelly, with far less trouble, and in using it you only need to dissolve it in hot water, and then sweeten and flavor it." The development Beecher noted meant that the use of jelly for conspicuous food display would no longer be the exclusive preserve (so to speak) of the wealthy. As Sandra L. Oliver explains, after calves' feet or isinglass jellies were replaced in the second half of the nineteenth century by manufactured

"American gelatine," virtually anyone could use such gelatin in conjunction with ready-made "fancy molds" to produce jellied flowers, grape clusters, or whatever else struck one's fancy.[53]

We found only two fruit jelly recipes in which fruit juice was to be mixed with another jelling substance, whether isinglass jelly, calves' feet jelly, or ready-made gelatin. Throughout the period under study, fruit jellies were made by boiling the fruit, generally in just enough water to cover it, straining the resultant juice through a sieve or jelly bag, adding sugar in the standard pound-for-pound ratio, boiling the sugar-juice mixture, and pouring it into jars or glasses for cooling and setting. In some sources toward the end of the period, it was recommended that the sugar be heated in the oven prior to being mixed with the strained fruit juice. Various authors cautioned against squeezing the jelly bag while the juice was being strained through it, since, as Hale stated, this allowed "thicker particles" through and kept the jelly from being "brilliantly clear." Another author argued that squeezing was permissible "after the clear juice has been obtained."[54]

The fruit jelly that was virtually ubiquitous was currant jelly or, as it came to be popularly known, "currant jell." Child was merely voicing the common wisdom when she stated that "currant jelly is a useful thing for sickness." Her recipe, along with others of the era, called for the currants to be boiled in a jar placed in a pot, then strained through a sieve. Beecher recommended that the juice thus obtained be further filtered through a jelly bag. Juice and sugar were to be, as usual, in equal proportions.[55]

Many nineteenth-century cookbooks included chapters or sections on "receipts for food and drink for the sick," and various other jellies besides "currant jell" were included. Child noted that rice jelly was "very nourishing and beneficial to invalids." Beecher featured "American Isinglass," tapioca, sago, rice, and sassafras jellies. In one of her novels, Beecher's sister spoke of "jelly of Iceland moss sent across" by a neighbor lady for the benefit of the main character during what proved to be the young woman's final illness. "I'm a-goin' to make her some jelly this very forenoon," promised another good-hearted soul, knowing full well the invalid would not survive.[56]

Jellies, and jams as well, were also present during moments of health and heightened well-being. Caroline Howard King remembered the "damsons, and quinces and raspberry jam" that her family regularly had "for preserves." On state occasions the table would be adorned with "moulds of cranberry and currant jellies" standing "at the corners" and, during the dessert course, "calf's foot jelly not made in moulds but broken up and glittering in cut glass jelly glasses."[57]

Jams and jellies could betoken the good life further down the social scale as well. When Harriet Beecher Stowe depicted the "faultless" tea served up by a respectable housewife in Newport, Rhode Island, at the end of the eighteenth century—the scene took place in a household that embodied "the simple, dignified order of a true New England home"—she included "jellies of apple and quince quivering in amber clearness" among the items offered. In such ways did Yankee mistresses turn foodstuff preservation for subsistence into high culinary art.[58]

White Sugar Every Day

Most of the dishes we have just been describing were comprised of close to 50 percent sugar. It was the "preservative properties" of this magical ingredient that made it possible to keep these fruit preparations for "many months, if stored in tightly sealed boxes or jars where damp air could not reach them." Since we have just considered a type of food that was crucially dependent on sugar, and since we intend to devote the balance of this chapter and all of the next one to other foods that also came to rely on sugar, it seems appropriate to say a few words at this point about how sugar—among the many available sources of sweetness—came to exemplify sweetness itself. The emergence and triumph of sugar entailed not only the eclipsing of such competitors in the provision of sweetness as honey and maple, but also the reconfiguration of the Anglo-American meal.[59]

Beekeeping is known to have flourished in Britain well before the Roman conquest. Much of the honey that was produced was used in mead or metheglin, an alcoholic beverage. The Romans brought a tradition of more diverse culinary uses of honey, along with an opinion that sugar from the sugarcane that was native to India was fit for use only as a medicine.

Gradually sugarcane and sugar made their way to Persia. Brought further westward first by Arabs then by Europeans, sugar arrived in Britain as part of the medieval trade in oriental spices. In the thirteenth and fourteenth centuries both sugar and honey were used as sweeteners in British aristocratic and gentry households. Honey was still a lot cheaper and remained the only sweetener in use for the majority of the British population. At the time of the colonization of North America, sugar continued to be expensive, and yeoman households included beehives among their array of food resources.[60]

The colonists brought honeybees to New England. One eighteenth-century visitor to the colonies reported that the Indians of the region called the bees English flies. Whether the Indians had used any other sweetener, before the English came, has been debated. The prime candidates for this role are maple syrup and sugar, made from the sap of the sugar maple trees that were abundant in the northern portions of New England but scarce in the southern areas where Indian settlement was more densely concentrated.[61] While conclusive evidence is lacking, the inference of most of those who have looked into the question is that there had been a tradition of maple production in the north but not in the south. Such production would have been greatly facilitated for the Abenaki of the north by the metal pots and kettles that they began acquiring in trade with Europeans during the years prior to English colonization.[62]

By the early eighteenth century the English living in the region filled with maple trees were producing maple syrup and sugar. Some scholars are convinced that they learned maple sugaring from the Abenaki, just as in Canada the French learned it from the Iroquois.[63]

However these uncertainties may eventually be resolved, by the time New Hampshire Yankees took up maple sugaring, the forces that would marginalize not only maple but also honey had already been at work for several decades. In 1634 an English proponent of honey in quince marmalade was forced to admit that many people seemed determined to use sugar instead. In the 1660s people were told that "honey sops," a traditional potion of beer, honey, spices, white bread, and currants, could also be made with sugar. These were straws in a wind of sugar predominance that was to blow ever more strongly over the next three centuries.[64]

Planting of sugarcane had proceeded during the medieval centuries across the Mediterranean basin and had been extended into the Atlantic with cultivation in the Azores and Canary Islands. Christopher Columbus's maritime activities, including his Atlantic crossings, took place within the milieu of the Mediterranean and Atlantic islands sugar trade, controlled by Genoese merchants. One of the Spanish monarchy's major goals for the colony Columbus planted on Hispaniola during his second voyage was to develop a sugarcane industry there.[65]

However, it would not be Columbus or the Spanish but rather the British who would succeed in realizing this goal, and in spectacular fashion. British colonies established on Barbados in 1627 and on Jamaica in 1655 came to be devoted almost exclusively to sugar production, with the requisite labor provided by slaves imported from Africa. For centuries sugar had been made by pressing short lengths of sugarcane stalks through a roller mechanism until syrup was exuded. The syrup was then evaporated by boiling—one, two, or several times depending on the degree of refinement desired—and poured into loaf-shaped vessels to cool and harden. During the cooling stage, "the emerging 'raw sugar' [would leave] behind it molasses, or treacle, which [could not] be crystallized further by conventional methods," but which could be consumed. Proving to be a great deal cheaper than crystallized sugar, molasses was in fact consumed in vast quantities.[66]

In the Caribbean, sugar was produced in an integrated fashion. To insure maximum output, cultivation and harvesting in the field were coordinated with grinding and boiling in the mill. "Very early in its career," states Sidney W. Mintz, the West Indian sugarcane plantation was functioning as "an industrial enterprise."[67]

As might be expected, the working conditions for the African slave labor force anticipated in most essential respects those prevailing during the English Industrial Revolution a century and a half later. Mintz quotes an observer at the turn of the eighteenth century who stated that the slaves "broil as it were, alive, in managing the fires" that kept the great kettles of cane syrup "constantly boiling." Extreme discomfort was combined with the constant danger of industrial accidents. The workers who fed the stalks into the mill "were liable, especially when tired or half-asleep, to have their fingers caught between the rollers. A hatchet was kept in readiness to sever the arm, which in such cases was always drawn in."[68]

As in later mill towns, workers were also ill-fed. In many cases, planters gave their slaves no food at all, only allowances of rum with which to purchase food or weekend time off in which to grow it. One historian summarized the resulting situation: "The rum was drunk, the Saturdays or Sundays encroached upon or wasted, and the slaves starved. . . . When I think of the colossal banquets of the Barbados planters . . . and remember that the money was got by working African slaves twelve hours a day on such a diet, I can only feel anger and shame."[69]

Later industrialism was anticipated in constantly increasing production as well as in grim conditions for the laborers. During the first decades of the plantation system, output rose at a "headlong" rate, such that sugar prices fell by 70 percent between 1645 and 1680. The drop in price made sugar "a constant presence in the lives of a significant number of English men and women before 1700." By 1800 sugar had become a much more constant presence, as yearly consumption per person had increased to over twenty-four pounds from about four pounds in 1700.[70]

In New England sugar appears in the records from an early date. It was purloined from gentry households in Essex County, Massachusetts, in the seventeenth century. In 1651 a farmer from Andover swapped rye for sugar

"Sugar Boiling," in "Three Weeks in Cuba," Harper's New Monthly Magazine, *January 1853. (Courtesy Fall River Public Library)*

with a Salem storekeeper. In the eighteenth century sugar was regularly advertised in Boston newspapers, and it was on sale in other communities as diverse as coastal and mercantile Portsmouth, New Hampshire, and interior and agricultural Deerfield, Massachusetts. In fact, it "may have been . . . the most important sweetener" in frontier Deerfield. In the second half of the century, Essex County fishing families were apt to have sugar on their kitchen shelves.[71]

Seventeenth-century immigrants to the colonies "were advised to defer their sugar purchases" until reaching their destinations, because sugar would be cheaper there than it had been at home. Estimated annual per capita consumption in Boston in the 1720s was ten pounds of crystallized sugar and a gallon of the much cheaper molasses. The degree to which sugar had by this time entered into New England consciousness, at least that of the more genteel element, was indicated in the diary of Samuel Sewall. He noted that the minister presiding at a wedding he had attended had said that "Love was the Sugar to sweeten every Condition in the married Relation."[72]

Sidney W. Mintz sums up the demand for sugar that was created in the English population by the proto-industrial, slavery-based production system: "During the period 1750–1850 every English person, no matter how isolated or how poor, and without regard to age or sex, learned . . . to like [sugar] enough to want more than they could afford. . . . A rarity in 1650, a luxury in 1750, sugar had been transformed into a virtual necessity by 1850." The account would be just as accurate if the terms "colonial" and "American" were substituted for the term "English." By the 1770s colonial per capita consumption of sugar and molasses was almost double that of England. Three-quarters of the colonial demand for refined white sugar was supplied from twenty-six domestic refineries located in port cities, half of them in New England.[73]

Until 1850, the cycle of increasing production, decreasing prices, and increasing consumption was sustained without major technological change. When such change did finally occur, it ushered in the era of true mass consumption of sugar. Improved cane growing and new machinery and forms of transportation "eventuated in vast new agro-industrial complexes, completely different from the smaller enterprises that preceded them." Prices fell as dramatically as they had at the outset of the plantation system, and the English and American people could now afford to have sugared tea and coffee and sugar-based jam, pie, and cake at every meal. Annual American per capita sugar consumption shot up from the twenty to thirty pound range in 1855–1865 to the ninety to one hundred pound range in 1920–1940.[74]

Before turning to the ramifications of the sugar revolution for Anglo-American cooking and eating, we should note that among sugars a hierarchy of preferences prevailed that was analogous to that for grains and breads. Sugar ranged in color from brown to white, depending on the degree of refining to which it had been subjected, just as breads ranged from black to white depending on the grains, and degrees of refinement thereof, with which they were made. Probably as sugar usage became more widespread, preferences among its grades were simply assimilated to ancient grain and bread attitudes. In Stowe's *Oldtown Folks* a Massachusetts farm boy visualized the highest style of life that he could bestow upon his mother as one in which she would "sit in [her] satin gown and drink . . . tea with white sugar every day."[75]

Such ideas persisted into the late nineteenth century. Average Americans took advantage of reduced sugar prices to purchase increased amounts of the best sugar. "I give my wife fifty cents . . . with which to buy sugar for the week . . . and, as she finds that fifty cents will now buy as many pounds of the white as we once could get of yellow sugars, she buys the white," a worker in a sugar refinery told his employer in 1883.[76]

These developments resulted not only in more widespread sugar consumption, but also in new conceptions about the flavors of food and the designs of meals. Before the seventeenth century, sugar was deployed in aristocratic cookery simply as one spice among many. It contributed as often to preparations of flesh, fowl, or fish as to anything else. In one of the few medieval recipes in which the quantities of ingredients were specified, chicken in sage sauce for forty people, the amount of sugar was equal to the amount of powdered cinnamon. The "aim of the medieval cook," states Bridget Ann Henisch, was that food be "poynante [sharp] and also doucet [sweet]."[77]

Just as sugar was mingled with what were thought of as other spices within individual dishes, so were savory and sweet dishes (to the extent that the distinction had any validity at all) mingled within each course. Strawberries and sugar came with both the first and second courses of a 1497 supper party. Obviously such customs militated against any progression from savory to sweet over the course of the meal. In medieval banquets, "the place assigned to the dessert, insofar as it existed, appears to have been a matter of indifference."[78]

The idea that the meal would culminate in a dish that was defined by its sweetness—by the dominating presence of sugar in it—gained currency among the upper classes only in the late seventeenth century, after the sugar-cane plantation system had begun to work its miracles of production. Thereafter it sifted downward through society along with the sugar upon which it was dependent. Sweetness was thereby set off as the basis of a category of taste and flavor worthy of special attention and treatment.[79]

That sugar now constituted a new universe of "sweets" and dessert cookery that was becoming broadly accessible was signaled by the wide readership, some of it no doubt in the colonies, of Hannah Glasse's *The Compleat Confectioner*, published in 1760. Glasse told middle-class readers how to make custards, creams, and pastries to be served in various situations, but especially at the end of the meal. *The Compleat Confectioner*'s success in the period just before Yankee cookbooks began to be published is an indication that, as a distinct entity, Yankee cooking was born into a gustatory world defined by sugar. It was perhaps the first cuisine in which the opposition between savory and sweet dishes and the importance of dessert could be taken for granted.[80]

A Pie in the House

Pies evolved from "the Roman idea of sealing meat inside a flour and oil paste as it cooked." Butter and lard, the cooking fats of northern Europe, could be used to make such pastes plastic enough, and water could make them strong enough, so that they could become "free-standing container[s]; and thus, at an unknown date and place, the pie was invented." Appropriately, such containers of animal flesh were dubbed "coffins." The name "pie" may be associated with the magpie, a bird noted for its habit of collecting miscellaneous objects. Certainly, a variety of ingredients were mixed together within the freestanding pie shells of the Middle Ages. Indeed, in that it was a medley of what are now considered heterogeneous elements, medieval pie epitomized medieval cuisine.[81]

The shell or crust of a pie was not always eaten, as in a fifteenth-century recipe for eel pie in which the eels and sauce were spooned out of the crust and served atop slices of white bread. Since the pies of that day could be both large and elaborate, strength was often a more important consideration than taste and texture in the making of a crust. "Take strong dough" (meaning no fat, only flour, water, and seasoning) was the advice offered in one cookbook.[82]

Fish pies such as the eel pie just mentioned arose as a way of coping with fast days and seasons. The rest of the time, pies made with flesh or fowl were more common. In all types the basic faunal component was combined with spices (including but not highlighting sugar), wine, and dried fruits. In spite of the use of "strong dough," special measures were needed to keep the top crust from falling during baking. The instructions for another eel pie said to leave a hole in the top crust "and at that hole, blow in the coffin with thine mouth a good blast of wind. And suddenly stop the hole, that the wind abide within . . . and when he is a little harded in the oven, prick the coffin with a pin stuck on a rod's end."[83]

The pies so far described would have been found mostly in aristocratic or gentry households. Pie, however, was also to be found in less august circles. The expression "humble pie" refers both to an ingredient—the entrails of animals, called "umbles," from which pies (and also pottages) were made—and also to a consumer—the "lesser folk" who ate such pies. In early modern yeoman households "pies were the most important dishes prepared from cereals" after breads, pottages, and puddings.[84]

The hierarchy of grain use in pie crusts replicated that for breads. Quality wheat went into the pies for quality people, while less refined wheat or wheat mixed with inferior grains went into the pies for inferior people. In some cases, the lower orders had to be content with pies made from the miller's barely ground leftovers.[85]

The pies made by prosperous yeoman goodwives could be as elaborate as anything from kitchens higher up the social ladder. In an eighteenth-century "battalia pye," chickens or pigeons were seasoned with pepper, salt, and nutmeg "pritty high" and placed in the crust along with "whole" larks, sausage balls, spinach, oysters raw or pickled, "blades of large mace," and pickled barberries. A pie like this, which manifestly might contain "anything that happened to be perched or swimming around," showed the persistence among the yeomanry of mélanged medieval cooking preferences.[86]

Pie could be a form of preservation. Cold pies were made to keep longer by filling them up with clarified butter, "which set and excluded the air." The type of crust that was used also made a difference in how long a pie would keep. In the 1615 *English Housewife*, by Gervase Markham, crust made from rye flour was recommended for "standing dishes, which must be kept long," such as pies made with game or "gammons of bacon." For pies made with most types of fowl or young flesh "which are to come to the table more than once, (yet not many days)," an intermediate grade of crust made from coarse wheat was specified. "The finest, shortest, and thinnest crust," made from the most refined wheat flour, was to be reserved for pies made either with the highest quality meats and poultries or with sweet potatoes and quinces.[87]

As sugar became more widely available, its use in flesh, fish, and fowl pies diminished, and these came to be classified as savory. There was no sugar, for example, in the yeoman battalia pie. That a greater emphasis on sugar in pie entailed a reduced emphasis on meat, fish, or poultry is illustrated in the evolution of mince or mincemeat pie. Minced pies developed from small tarts or pasties filled with minced meat or fish. As with other medieval pies, the mincemeat was combined with spices and dried fruits. By the sixteenth century, mincemeat pie had become a Christmas treat.[88]

Gervase Markham's recipe for mince pie used a leg of mutton, mutton suet, currants, raisins, prunes, dates, orange peel, and spices. The top crust was to be opened and sugar to "a good thickness" strewn upon the mixture only during the final few moments before serving. In the course of the seventeenth century, calf's tongue came to be preferred as the meat used in mincemeat. Then it was found that the suet, spices, and fruits could be combined months in advance and mixed with the shredded meat only as the pie was being made. The meat had become an afterthought in a filling consisting essentially of fruit, spices, and fat. It was only a matter of time before the meat was sometimes omitted altogether, sugar became the primary seasoning, and the mince pie without meat that we now know emerged.[89]

Thus, in her directions for the filling of her "mince-pies the best way," which would "keep good four Months," Hannah Glasse called for half a pound of sugar to half an ounce (plus two large nutmegs) of other seasonings, while leaving shredded meat as merely a last-minute possibility. Over in New England a few years later, Mrs. Gardiner of Boston specified sugar in approximately the same dominating ratio to other spices as Glasse, but she forthrightly entitled her recipe "mince pies, without flesh meat."[90]

As the basis for pie, instead of as a supplement, fruit began to come into its own in the sixteenth century. Generally, pastries with a fruit or vegetable filling were called tarts instead of pies, although this was not always the case. We have heard Edward Johnson, for example, referring to pumpkin pies and apple, pear, and quince tarts. By whatever name, enclosure in a pastry shell was "far and away the most important way of preparing fruit" in English yeoman households. The belief that the more thorough the cooking the more the threat of sickness from fresh fruit would be minimized may have been the reason that many fruit tarts involved boiling and straining the fruit into a puree.[91]

On the other hand, in Gervase Markham's recipe for a pippin tart, the crust was filled with solid ingredients: cored and halved "pippins of the fairest," whole cloves, sticks of cinnamon, butter, and enough sugar both to cover the apple halves "all clean over" and also to apply, along with melted butter and rose water, to the top crust during the last few minutes of baking. Tarts filled with spinach or young peas, even flower petals, continued to be made throughout the seventeenth century. The same residually medieval sweet/savory seasoning blend was utilized in fruit, vegetable, and flower-petal tarts alike. It was not until the eighteenth century that such blends were abandoned in favor of "simple sweetening with sugar."[92]

A great many colonial pies were made with the stronger forms of pie crust described by Markham, utilizing rye, mixtures of rye and wheat, or wheat that was less than fully bolted. An observer of mid-eighteenth-century Delaware stated that the crust for "house-pie, in country places . . . is not broken if a wagon wheel goes over it."[93]

Since wheat was less readily available in New England, Yankee pie crusts were probably at least as sturdy as this. In *Oldtown Folks* Harry and Tina Percival, the orphan protagonists, had various items of food secretively bestowed upon them by a kindly farmhand as part of the preparations for their escape from their unfit guardians. Among these was "a minced pie, with a rye crust of a peculiarly solid texture, adapted to resist any of the incidents of time and travel." According to Sandra L. Oliver, until the opening of the Erie Canal in 1825, rye was used in average Yankee families to "extend" the wheat in pie crusts.[94]

However, from its very first appearance in print, Yankee cooking conducted itself as if these plebeian pie crusts scarcely existed. All of Simmons's nine pastes were to be made with wheat exclusively, most of them being explicitly denominated the puff pastes which required what Markham had called "the finest wheat flower." Variation came about by varying the proportion of butter (in some cases combined with lard or suet) to flour, although the quantity of eggs or egg whites also made a difference. Since these were puff pastes, some of the butter or other fat was added to the flour during an initial mixture, the rest incorporated a little at a time during successive rollings. Simmons's lowest fat to flour ratio was 3:7, her highest 1:1. Her "Royal Paste" consisted of half a pound of butter, one pound of flour, two ounces of "fine sugar," four egg whites "beat to a foam," and two egg yolks.[95]

As for pie fillings, besides pumpkin pie, Simmons offered an array that looked both backward and forward. Her "Sea Pie" resembled the "battalia pye" described above, and her chicken pie was equally savory. All three of her mince pies retained the meat component—one with calf's foot, one with calf's tongue, and one with boiled beef. Mince pies required "a hotter and brisker oven than fruit pies."[96]

Fruits that Simmons identified as appropriate for pie filling included apples, currants, plums, raspberries, blackberries, and peas (possibly a misprint for peaches). The rise of sugar was reflected in the comment that "every species of fruit" utilized for pie filling might be "only sweetened, without spices." For her two apple pies, Simmons gave no indications of sugar quantities. For currant pie, she called for a proportion of sugar to fruit of one to three, much less than the fruit preservation norm.[97]

Yankee pie crusts developed little in the nineteenth century. Child felt that "a quarter of a pound of butter is enough for a half a pound of flour." In Beecher's "very plain paste," the proportion of butter was only half that, although she also offered richer crusts, the richest with equal amounts of butter and flour. Beecher disapproved of pie crust as it was usually made. She offered as "healthful" alternatives crusts in which boiled mealy potatoes were to be mixed with flour, sour milk or cream, and saleratus. Twenty years later in the 1860s, Mrs. S. G. Knight went back to Child's 1:2 ratio of butter to flour, although she added a spoonful of lard.[98]

Similar recommendations continued to appear. "If economy [was] not needed," butter was called for. If it was, lard would serve. The ultimate in economy was reached by a recipe using one tablespoon of lard to sixteen of flour. In 1939 the winning recipe in a New England apple pie contest showed its commitment to economy with a 1:3 ratio of lard to flour. Beecher's healthier version surfaced again in 1881 in a crust made with flour, cream, and salt: "It will not look so inviting, but will taste very good."[99]

As for meat, poultry, and fish pies, the formula was simple and remained essentially unchanged. The dish or pan was lined with the bottom crust; pieces of the flesh or fish, salt pork and other seasoning, and gravy were inserted; and the mixture was covered with a top crust and baked. In the case of chicken, the gravy was usually made from the liquid in which the bird was boiled, and the gizzards, livers, hearts, and necks were often included. Sometimes eggs were added. Seasoning was usually salt and pepper only, although nutmeg, mace, parsley, thyme, shallots and other herbs and spices were occasionally to be found. Catharine Beecher sought to encourage the use of her potato crust in her meat and chicken pies.[100]

In spite of the fact that in both England and New England mince pie without meat had become an accepted option by the middle of the eighteenth century, most nineteenth-century Yankee mince pie recipes followed Simmons in continuing to call for shredded meat. Child said to use "a tender, nice piece of beef—any piece that is clear from sinews and gristle." Hale used a calf's tongue in her "rich mince meat," lean beef in her "family" or "plain" varieties. In our sample from before the Civil War, about half the authors offered mincemeats without meat as well as with it. The pattern continued in the second half of the nineteenth century and on into the twentieth, with meatless versions usually labeled as "mock mince pie."[101]

The essentials of Yankee fruit pie cookery are contained in Child's recipe for apple pie:

Apple Pie
    When you make apple pies, stew your apples very little indeed; just strike them through, to make them tender. Some people do not stew them at all, but cut them up in very thin slices, and lay them in the crust. Pies made in this way may retain more of the spirit of the apple; but I do not think the seasoning mixes in as well. Put in sugar to your taste; it is impossible to make a precise rule, because apples vary so much in acidity. A very little salt, and a small piece of butter in each pie, makes them richer. Cloves and cinnamon are both suitable spice. Lemon-brandy and rosewater are both excellent. A wine-glass full of each is sufficient for three or four pies. If your apples lack spirit, grate in a whole lemon.

The fruit pie had come to the fore as a result of the sugar revolution, but there was nevertheless an effort to balance the sweetness imparted by sugar with the inherent sweetness and "spirit" of the fruits with which it was used.[102]

Some recipes did specify amounts of sugar—four ounces to eight quartered apples, four ounces to a pint of currants, a cup to a dozen "good-sized"

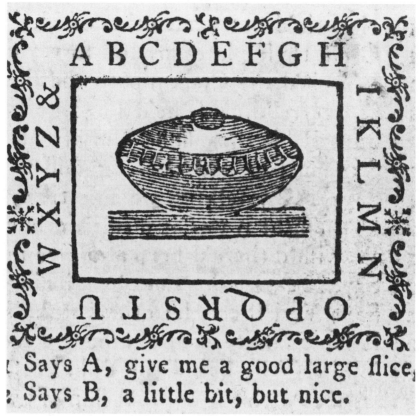

Alphabet sampler, in The Tragical Death of A, Apple-Pie, *1791.*
(Courtesy American Antiquarian Society)

stewed apples, two tablespoonfuls to enough moist berries to fill a standard pie plate, in recipes respectively from Mrs. Lee, Mrs. A. L. Webster, Mrs. S. G. Knight, and "Aunt Mary." Some fruit pies were made by alternating layers of the fruit with layers of brown or white sugar, with or without additional seasoning. Sarah Josepha Hale advised that when making pies from "ripe summer fruits, such as raspberries, blueberries, cherries, damsons, &c. always take a deep plate, line it with paste, place a teacup, inverted in the middle and fill the pie with fruit, [and] a good quantity of brown sugar, with very little spice or seasoning." The fruit juice released during baking would "settle under the cup" instead of oozing out the sides of the pie.[103]

There were those who objected to pie. Hale castigated mince pie as "rich, expensive and exceedingly unhealthy" and also thought it "a pity" that people insisted on making "ripe fruits into pies; they would be so much healthier eaten with bread then [*sic*] pie-crust." However, fruit pies were "harmless compared with *meat pies, which should never be made*" (Hale's emphasis). Beecher introduced her discussion of pie crust with the comment that "this is an article which, if the laws of health were obeyed, would be banished from every table." Uniting "the three evils of animal fat, *cooked* animal fat, and heavy bread," rich pie crust was the most indigestible item in "the whole range of cooking." As a result, she offered "healthful" alternatives.[104]

Some years before, a French traveler had provided evidence in support of Hale's and Beecher's views, calling the type of pie he had seen consumed at New England supper tables "nothing but a greasy paste, never sufficiently baked." According to a writer for *Harper's Monthly* in 1866, to be as American as apple pie was to have been incapacitated for the enjoyment of life: "How can a person with a pound of green apples and fat dough in his stomach feel at ease?"[105]

The pie naysayers got nowhere, as we know. Pie has retained its popularity in New England up to the present day. It came to be viewed as an exclusively dessert dish not only late in its history but also late in the history of the sugar revolution. Mince, apple, and cranberry pies were part of the dessert course at the banquets of Caroline Howard King's Salem childhood in the 1820s and 1830s. But for a long time after that, pie continued to play less glamorous dietary parts. Mince pie was supper fare for a farmhand in *Oldtown Folks*. A young man was served pumpkin pie for breakfast at a Stonington, Connecticut, farm in 1846. Three years before, Richard Henry Dana was given apple pie for both breakfast and supper while sojourning on the Isles of Shoals, off the coast of New Hampshire. Pie was a regular part of the breakfast menu in the households of both Ralph Waldo Emerson and Oliver Wendell Holmes.[106]

Later in the century breakfast pie began to fall out of fashion in elite circles. Members of the faculty of Phillips Academy in Andover, Massachusetts, were embarrassed in the 1890s when Matthew Arnold's letters home from an 1883 trip to America were published, and it was revealed that the breakfast repast they had laid out for him had included mince pies. In rural districts, however, the fondness for pie around the clock held on. A Vermont woman made 421 pies in 1877, slightly more than one a day. Around this time, Mark Twain's friend Charles Dudley Warner concluded that "all the hill and country towns" of New England "were full of women who would have felt ready to sink in mortification through their scoured kitchen floors if visitors caught them without a pie in the house. The absence of pie would have been more noticeable . . . than a scarcity of the Bible."[107]

Seventy-five years later "eating pie for breakfast" had become something "of which Vermonters have been accused." The custom was justified by the fact that most of these people had to put in "several hours of heavy farm labor" before breakfast and therefore needed hearty sustenance. Thus did this 1941 writer feel called upon to defend her neighbors against imputations of rusticity. Since then, the country has become an escape from decaying cities and overcrowded suburbs, and nothing seems more appealing than a breakfast of warm apple pie and hot coffee on a crisp autumn morning in Vermont.[108]

Thanksgiving

We have already quoted Gervase Markham on the relationship between types of pastry crusts and the keeping times for pies. The coarser the flour the longer the pie would remain good. After wheat became more widely available, the New England climate made it possible to make pies that would keep for a while even if more refined flour was used for the crust. (In a colder climate, there was also less danger that the fats in the crusts would turn rancid.) So in the nineteenth century, after the autumn harvest came the time for making "all manner of pies."[109]

Apple and pumpkin pies, especially, would be made by the dozens. The majority were not eaten right away but were stored in pantries, pie closets, or odd corners of the house where the winter weather would keep them cool or even freeze them, allowing them to keep for weeks or months. This was also the season for making mincemeat, a means by which part of the slaughtered livestock would be preserved. Some of the mincemeat went straightaway into pies, while the rest, given that mincemeat was made to last, would be stored for later pie making.[110]

As discussed in chapter 5, Thanksgiving evolved, not from some alleged first event at Plymouth in 1621, but from the traditional English harvest home festival that came to be widely celebrated in the colonial period. By the nineteenth century, Thanksgiving had become the primary New England holiday. During the days before Thanksgiving, housewives reportedly made batches of thirty, seventy, even a hundred pies at a time—apple, pumpkin, mince, and others.[111]

The story is no doubt apocryphal that in at least two towns Thanksgiving was officially postponed because of a shortage of molasses for pie making. But the fact that such a tale made the rounds testifies to the importance of pie in New England Thanksgivings. As Harriet Beecher Stowe summarized the matter, "the making of *pies* at this period assumed vast proportions that verged upon the sublime. Pies were made by the forties and fifties and hundreds, and made of everything on the earth and under the earth."[112]

Turkey was also featured in Thanksgiving accounts, of course, autumn being the time of slaughter as well as harvest. "What a sight of pigs and geese and turkeys and fowls and sheep must be slaughtered to gratify the voraciousness of a single day," enthused a Connecticut man in 1784. An 1842 evocation of a farm Thanksgiving spoke of "turkies, chickens in pairs, geese, ducks, all ready for the spit." Caroline Howard King remembered "a cold outer kitchen" in her family's Salem house, "hung round with chickens, turkeys, geese, and ducks" purchased from farmers who brought them into town to sell during the week before Thanksgiving.[113]

Thanksgiving dinner at the Kings "was always the same, chicken-pie, boiled turkey and oyster sauce, ducks and partridges," along with plum pudding, pies, and fruits. Another account tells of "the dinner with its turkey, big chicken pie, and Thanksgiving cake . . . and a plentiful supply of nuts and raisins." We have noted in chapter 5 some of the testimony that turkey "took precedence" in Thanksgiving dinner. Nevertheless, what the above recollections had in common was that the turkey, whether in the slaughtering, purchasing, or eating, appeared together with other poultry.[114]

The poultry portion of the menu, moreover, was infiltrated by pie, especially in the form of "big chicken pie." Pie was at least as important as turkey in the Yankee Thanksgivings of the nineteenth century. "Thanksgiving Day absolutely no restraint was put upon us. The food was of the richest [kind] and varied and abundant, and morning, noon and night we stuffed and stuffed." Thanksgiving betokened the plenty "which independent husbandry can produce." Certainly the turkey and other birds that were eaten for Thanksgiving beyond the point of satiety were suggestive of such plenty.[115]

In spite of Caroline Howard King's statement that her family's poultry provisions "lasted for many weeks into the winter," most poultry was eaten fresh. The majority of families could not afford enough fowl both to load the Thanksgiving table and meet household needs through the winter. Among other considerations, chickens were too valuable as sources of eggs.[116]

A food that could be consumed unstintingly on Thanksgiving Day and still remain plentifully on hand months later would be an even fitter symbol of bounty than chickens and turkeys. According to Harriet Beecher Stowe, who represented the colonial and nineteenth-century Yankee Thanksgiving more compellingly than anyone else, such a food was pie. In the weeks leading up to Thanksgiving, Stowe wrote, the brick oven "brooded over successive generations of pies and cakes, which went in raw and came out cooked, till butteries and dressers and shelves and pantries were literally crowded with a jostling abundance."[117]

Stowe made it seem as if the entire house was turned into a pie closet for Thanksgiving. But the Thanksgiving pie cornucopia was no fleeting thing. Every year it contributed to family security and prosperity until the next growing season. "A great cold northern chamber, where the sun never shone, and where in winter the snow sifted in at the window-cracks, and ice and frost reigned with undisputed sway, was fitted up to be the storehouse of these surplus treasures. There, frozen solid, and thus well preserved in their icy fetters, they formed a great repository for all the winter months; and the pies baked at Thanksgiving often came out fresh and good with the violets of April." In this mythic description of the Yankee household, such opposites as the cycles of nature and the ingenuities of culinary art, present indulgence in excess and prudent care for the morrow, were paradoxically united on an annual basis.[118]

Stowe's rendition of Thanksgiving warrants further analysis. She had a lot more to say about pie in connection with the holiday:

> The pie is an English institution, which, planted on American soil, forthwith ran rampant and burst forth into an untold variety of genera and species. Not merely the old traditional mince pie, but a thousand strictly American seedlings from that main stock, evinced the power of American housewives to adapt old institutions to new uses. Pumpkin pies, cranberry pies, huckleberry pies, cherry pies, green-currant pies, peach, pear and plum pies, custard pies, apple pies, Marlborough-pudding pies, — pies with top crusts, and pies without, — pies adorned with all sorts of fanciful flutings and architectural strips laid across and around, and otherwise varied, attested the boundless fertility of the feminine mind, when once let loose in a given direction.

In Stowe's hands, pie became an occasion to celebrate women's domestic creativity.[119]

The household utilized for the representation of Thanksgiving in *Oldtown Folks* was the central venue of the novel, the home of the narrator's grandfather, "a well-to-do farmer." Stowe began by disputing the stereotype that the Puritans and their Yankee descendants were killjoys. "There was an abundance of sober, well-considered merriment" in New England, and Thanksgiving was a prime case in point. Not only did people fearlessly eat, sing, joke, laugh, play, and dance on the day itself, the womenfolk of the family engaged in unrestrained self-expression for weeks and weeks beforehand. Even the faintest hint of drudgery was absent from the labor of pie making. It was entirely pleasurable.[120]

Stowe's Thanksgiving household depicted the independent family farm, the basic social unit of colonial New England. In Old England as well as New, such farmsteads were understood to be places in which independence and freedom flourished as nowhere else. Self-sufficient farmers enjoyed "the true independence which burdened fields and fatted herds will always give to a life of honesty and continued labor."[121]

Such independence was the prerogative of the male head of the household only. Stowe, in contrast, offered a benign version of life on the Yankee farm, in which gender inequalities counted for naught. As Thanksgiving approached, the females reveled in a kitchen creativity that no male authority figure sought to restrict and to which the male narrator paid wholehearted tribute.

As with gender politics, so with every other potential source of conflict. In "How We Kept Thanksgiving at Oldtown," conflict did not exist. Anglicans from Boston, ex-Tories at that, came calling in the evening, but the narrator's Congregationalist grandmother, the presiding spirit of the occasion, remained "so full of motherliness, that she could have patted the very King of England on the head, if he had been there, and comforted his soul with the assurance that she supposed he meant well, though he didn't exactly know how to manage. . . . And I think she would have done exactly the same by the Pope of Rome himself, if that poor heathen sinner had presented himself on Thanksgiving evening."[122]

Just as the struggle with Great Britain in the recent past of the novel's action had apparently been resolved, so the more remote clashes between English settlers and Indians were seen from the benevolent vantage point of feminized Yankee dominion: "All the poor, loafing tribes, Indian and half-Indian, who at other times wandered, selling baskets and other light wares, were sure to come back to Oldtown a little before Thanksgiving time, and report themselves in my grandmother's kitchen. The great hogshead of cider in the cellar, which my grandfather called the Indian Hogshead, was on tap at all hours of the day; and many a mugful did I draw and dispense to the tribes that basked in the sunshine of our door."[123]

Nor was the group whose victimization had occasioned the national upheaval contemporaneous with Stowe's writing of *Oldtown Folks* excluded from the Thanksgiving embrace. The household servant, "black Caesar," was an enthusiastic participant in the festivities. During the preparations, his "efforts in slaughtering, picking, and dressing" kept "the great pile of chickens and turkeys . . . daily supplied." During the climactic evening's dancing, there was "black Caesar, full of turkey and pumpkin pie, and giggling in the very jollity of his heart," having "rosined his bow, and tuned his fiddle, and practised jigs and Virginia reels, in a way that made us children think him a perfect Orpheus."[124]

Other descriptions of Yankee Thanksgiving painted a more realistic picture. Caroline Howard King referred with traditional aristocratic contempt to the beggars at her mother's door at Thanksgiving time as all coming with "the same whining request." Even the sentimental John Carver noticed out of the corner of his eye the economic forces that were eroding yeoman independence, as he daydreamed that the thought of Thanksgiving had "brought health to the home-sick heart of the noble boy, toiling in the city, for enough to raise the mortgage from the widowed mother's dower."[125]

But Stowe was not striving for realism. If we wish to view her effort in a positive light, we can say that shortly after Sarah Josepha Hale had, in the midst of the Civil War, persuaded Abraham Lincoln to nationalize the Yankee ritual of Thanksgiving, Stowe sought to persuade the nation that the new holiday meant—now that the war had removed the last impediment— liberty, justice (or at least charity), and prosperity for all. Everyone, female as well as male, Catholic as well as Protestant, Indian as well as English, black as well as white, was now to inhabit a coast-to-coast, top-to-bottom Yankee social order. To adapt Stowe's language at the commencement of the Thanksgiving chapter, in a nation cleansed from the blemish of slavery, "the means of securing the goods of life" were now to become "so free to all, that everybody should find abundant employment for his faculties in a prosperous seeking of his fortunes."[126]

If we wish to cast a colder eye, however, we would say that Stowe's description of a Yankee Thanksgiving proposed as a model for the world of emergent corporate capitalism (the world in which *Oldtown Folks* was published) the same past society that such capitalism was already well along in destroying. The New England farm and village, characterized by household production, consumption, and close-knit community, had been undermined by such prosperous seeking of fortunes as had sent pioneers westward and dotted the Yankee homeland with factories and ever more populous towns and cities. Dependence on international markets for the sugar and molasses in Thanksgiving pies was about to be expanded into dependence on and enmeshment in markets of every degree and description—commodity, labor, you name it.[127]

In chapter 4 we emphasized that for many of the original colonists, removal to New England had been an effort to secure landed independence and thereby escape the wage labor dependence that early capitalism was generating at a rapid rate in the England of the seventeenth century. At the time *Oldtown Folks* was published, the wheel had turned full circle. The vast majority of the descendants of the original immigrants (along with a whole new set of immigrants who were removed from view by Stowe's nostalgic choice of setting and subject) were destined to enter into the wage labor dependence that more mature forms of capitalism were generating in the New England and United States of the second half of the nineteenth century.

Stowe and her sister Catharine Beecher proposed a form of resistance to these trends with the household production utopia they presented in *The American Woman's Home*, published contemporaneously with *Oldtown Folks*. With the fictional representation of Thanksgiving, however, Stowe did something different. Rather than offering an alternative, however unrealistic, to the emergence into the world of 1869 of capitalism as a system, she came to capitalism's assistance by propagating the notion that there were no strings attached to American abundance. In this version of utopia, neither compromise of freedom nor erosion of community was entailed by a seat at the modern American table.

CHAPTER 7

The Cake Came Out Victorious

Gingerbread, Election Cake, & Doughnuts

*H*arriet Beecher Stowe's cakes were as rich as her pies. Toward the end of *Oldtown Folks*, she described a New England community celebration called "The Minister's Wood-Spell," now long forgotten and even at the time Stowe wrote a relic of earlier days. Nevertheless, she went to some lengths to explain the festivity to her readers: "'What is a wood-spell?' you say. Well, the pastor was settled on the understanding of receiving two hundred dollars a year and his wood; and there was a certain day set apart in the winter . . . when every parishioner brought the minister a sled-load of wood; and thus, in the course of time, built him up a mighty wood-pile."[1]

Using several rhetorical devices, Stowe indicated that the quaint wood-spell was more than an old-fashioned party. In the slow pace of the practiced storyteller, she set the scene by answering the reader's imagined question: "'What is a wood-spell?' you say. Well, . . ." The occasion demanded heightened speech ("thus, in the course of time") of almost biblical proportions ("built him up a mighty wood-pile"). She was aware that it was comical to describe an essentially trivial event (this was, after all, only building a woodpile) in such ponderous terms. Nevertheless, as her detailed explanation of the minister's support implied, she was at the same time endorsing the Yankee position that careful attention to moral injunctions, even when the arena was small, was of ultimate significance. It was not the Yankees' fault that their salvation was to be worked out on the puny material of salaries and woodpiles rather than on the heroic scale of the Old Testament. Neither the inherent humor nor the high seriousness of the Yankee situation were slighted in Stowe's masterful depiction.

After the wood was gathered, the assembled party celebrated its accomplishment with food, and the star of the board was "the wood-spell cake, which was to be made in quantities large enough to give ample slices to every

parishioner." This "certain day set apart," with its overt religious association (helping to pay the minister's salary), underlying spiritual meaning, and
communal meal, amounted to a Yankee feast day. By such feasting, as by
fasting on the Sabbath with codfish and baked beans, New Englanders reproduced the substance of the medieval Catholic traditions that they had
outwardly and formally proscribed.[2]

Despite the practical reason for the festivity and the carefully egalitarian
distribution ("ample slices to every parishioner"), the massive wood-spell
cake seems an oddly luxurious centerpiece for a Yankee church gathering.
And the name of the event—wood-*spell*—conjures up a feeling of mystery
ordinarily off limits to Yankees. If Stowe sensed any contradiction between
the Puritan legacy of opposition to mystical feasting and an annual Yankee
celebration capped off by the secularized but nevertheless ritualized consumption of a superior type of bread, she didn't let on about it.

Why wasn't this literal daughter of Calvinist minister Lyman Beecher
and figurative daughter of the entire New England Puritan tradition made
uneasy by feasting on rich cakes on certain days set apart? Why did she
muster her considerable narrative talents to mythologize the event as a Yankee triumph of biblical proportions? The answer lies in part in Stowe's re-
jection of Calvinist rigidity and embracing of a more nurturing (and nourishing) Christianity.[3]

In this respect, Stowe participated in the liberalizing of Puritan theology
that was a central feature of New England intellectual life in the nineteenth
century. But something more material, with deeper historical roots, was also
involved. This was the longing of the English and their Anglo-American
descendants to eat wheat of the best quality. This ancient struggle had been
won by 1869, when this novel was published. But the victory was in its infancy and worth celebrating. Stowe invited her readers to revel in the material as well as spiritual successes of New England society.

The feeling of accomplishment, indeed of victory, that attended the eating of cake for most people before the late nineteenth century is difficult for
us to understand because in various forms and derivatives cake now appears
on the American table around the clock. We are so accustomed to having it
and eating it too that only in its most elaborate dress, say as a wedding cake,
does it command notice.

But, as we shall see in this chapter, to cut cake "without end," as the "emi-
nently serviceable" Miss Nervy Randall was prepared to do at the wood-
spell, represented the fulfillment of the heart's desire not only of New England for two centuries but of Old England for two millennia. Therefore, as

Stowe grasped, the abundance symbolized by lavish communal consumption of cake was an achievement worthy to be cast in heroic terms. It was truly appropriate to declare, when the wood-spell cake emerged in all its glory from the bake oven, that "the cake came out victorious."[4]

In chapter 1 we discussed the difficulties the colonizing English faced in adding wheat in appreciable amounts to their diet. Corn became their staple grain and Indian pudding, Ryaninjun, and Johnny cake their staple dishes. But their ongoing reluctance to acknowledge the Indian origins of this grain and some of these dishes bespoke their ongoing desire for wheat. Such a desire was not easily set aside because it long antedated the colonization of North America. In order to comprehend the significance of cake in nineteenth-century New England, we must amplify our earlier sketch of the history of grain preferences in England.

Thereafter we will look at cake's emergence from bread. Finally, we will focus on three New England cakes—gingerbread, election cake, and doughnuts. But long before these and other cakes graced Yankee tables from Marblehead to the Midwest, the bread from which cake was derived began life as a rough lump of coarse-grained dough baked before the fire. It is there that our story begins.[5]

Grains in Britain

Cereal crops have been grown in Britain since Neolithic farmers "grew their corn in forest clearings." During the Bronze Age, barley became "the predominant cereal of Britain," although wheat was grown to some extent. Better varieties, those more easily threshed and capable of being made into bread, were sown during the Roman period, although the damp, uncertain climate made the Roman passion for wheat difficult to fulfill. Wheat was also imported from the Mediterranean, where "during the whole of the classical period wheat was gradually replacing barley as the food of man."[6]

When Germanic tribes replaced the Romans, they grew barley as their main crop and saw little reason to bother with wheat. The Germanic invasions had a profound effect on agriculture, as on society in general, but this was not the only cause of the decline in wheat consumption after the Romans left Britain. Beginning in the seventh century, the commerce and trade that had for centuries included an active wheat market were curtailed with the Muslim domination of the Mediterranean. Along with the rest of Europe, Britain was forced to rely on its own agriculture. Throughout the Middle Ages and into the early modern period, barley, as the safest crop, "was planted extensively all over the country." Also, it "was grown universally because it was the brewing corn."[7]

Oats reached Britain during the Iron Age. At least from the Roman occupation, and perhaps earlier, the Scots grew oats extensively in the "wetter reaches of the highland zone," making this grain what it long remained— the basis of the daily bread of Scotland.[8]

Oats were eaten as bread and pottage in other parts of Britain as well, especially in the cold north of England. However, as noted in chapter 1, by the sixteenth and seventeenth centuries most English people could get by without oats, and the association of oat-eating with social inferiority began to take hold, more distinctly in relation to bread than pottage. This attitude was expressed by a sixteenth-century traveler who reported after a visit to a Scottish knight's household that "they vulgarly eate harth cakes of oates." In the early nineteenth century Scotland was ridiculed by Sydney Smith as "that knuckle-end of England,—that land of Calvin, oat-cakes, and sulphur."[9]

Rye was not so despised as oats, possibly because there was no comparable ethnic-superiority hook upon which such sentiments could be hung, but it was always considered most palatable when combined with wheat. Sometimes rye was grown separately, then combined with wheat or some other grain; at other times, it was "part of a mixed crop." In either case, it was known as maslin, or monkcorn. Elizabeth David says that it was introduced "by the Saxon and Scandinavian conquerors who came from areas where rye had already for centuries been the predominating bread grain." A durable and useful combination, maslin was grown in Britain throughout the Middle Ages and into the seventeenth century, especially in "the sandy lands of eastern England."[10]

In chapters 1 and 2 we noted that utilization of beans and peas in breadmaking was universally deplored. Everyone agreed that "peas made an illtasting bread, and beans one still worse." Nevertheless, grain supplies were never secure enough completely to rule out supplementation with legumes. It probably would have little cheered British pea- and bean-eaters to know that this practice had also been followed, and equally disliked, in Greece and Rome. In fact, Gervase Markham's seventeenth-century instructions for making bread that included beans and peas probably varied little from the practice of the classical world: "You shall take of barley two bushels, of pease two pecks, of wheat or rye a peck, a peck of mault: these you shall grind together, and dress it through a meal sieve, then putting it into a sowr trough . . . and bake it into great loaves with a very strong heat."[11]

When the Romans left Britain and the trade routes of the Mediterranean closed, wheat agriculture may have been curtailed, but the association of wheat with high living remained. While "the poore man . . . eateth browne bread . . . made of . . . grosse graines," he nevertheless wished to be eating, as Elizabeth David has stated, "the finest part of the wheat flour," that was "reserved for the rich and the religious houses."[12]

On the Continent, the Roman wheat-eating tradition persisted among the aristocratic Goths and Franks, who in turn influenced Norman France. With the Norman Conquest, Roman ways were carried back to Britain. In terms of wheat, the Norman Conquest was a Roman Reconquest.[13]

In the late Middle Ages, several factors converged to extend wheat-eating from the aristocracy to the gentry and eventually to the middling classes, even to the poor. By the fourteenth century, the best milled, bolted, and baked wheat bread, known as manchet bread, was widely desired. In essence manchet bread differed little from the best breads of ancient Greece and Rome: "hot rolls, made of the best wheat and as white as milk." The passion for it was attested to by sixteenth-century physician-writer Andrew Boorde: "I do love manchet breade, and great loves [loaves] the whiche be well mowlded and thorowe baken, the brande abstracted and abjected."[14]

Manchet was also known as wastel bread, "from the Norman French *gastel* or cake." Chaucer's Prioress, whom we encountered in chapter 1, was in the habit of feeding "wastelbreed" to her lap dogs. This top-grade bread was also called pandemain. The term probably derived either from "*panis domini*, the sacramental bread," or from "*panis dominicus* . . . demesne bread." The sacramental meaning is more likely, in that the bread "was often stamped with a figure of Our Saviour." By the fifteenth century it mostly went by the name manchet, although the "panis domini" affiliation, linking the best breads or cakes with religious feasts, was deeply rooted in English tradition.[15]

Now that wheat was part of the English diet, its manifest superiority for making glutinous soft bread and rich smooth pottage could not forever be kept from the lower echelons. Their exposure to the grain occurred in a number of ways—from receiving it as alms at the gates of monasteries and manor houses, to being given it as leftovers after feasts, to being paid with it at harvest time "when the quality of the food was apt to be rather good in order to encourage the tenant-workers to greater efforts."[16]

Yet into the early modern period, wheat yields continued to be low because "much land which would not in its natural state bear wheat had to be worked and enriched and persuaded to do so." It was certainly "not worth the labour of the small peasant to dig, cart and spread the clayey marl on his strips of open field, when these would shortly be reallotted to neighbours." But the demand for wheat made the labor and expense of such measures increasingly worth the effort.[17]

The grain aspirations of the common people occasioned negative comment from their betters (who, of course, ate wheat bread themselves). In the fourteenth century, for example, the poet John Gower complained that "labourers of old were not wont to eat of wheaten bread; their meat was of beans or coarser corn. . . . Then was the world ordered aright for folk of this sort." To informal social disapproval was added explicit governmental regulation. Restrictions on the sale of white bread, such as mandating that "bakers were only allowed to make [spiced white loaves] for Good Fridays, Christmas Day and funerals," were analogous to the enforcement of fish days in order to limit the consumption of meat.[18]

But neither tongue-clicking nor official prohibition could dissuade the majority of people from wanting to eat wheat. R. A. McCance and E. M. Widdowson point out that this demand was based as much on social dynamics as gustatory preference: "The person who is sure of his position in society can . . . eat the plainest fare without loss of caste, but those who are conscious of a social inferiority are often the most exacting about their food and clothes. It was so over bread."[19]

Seventeenth-century diarist Sir Symonds d'Ewes noted that "the poorer sort traversed the markets to find out the finest wheats, for none else would now serve their use, though before they were glad of the coarser rye bread." In 1616, according to a report of the London Grocers' Company, "the poor would not buy barley or rye, either alone or even if mixed with two-thirds wheat." The blend they approved now had to be four-fifths wheat. Thirty years later one of Oliver Cromwell's officers stated that he had been "forced to make the soldiers' bread of some old rye . . . and to buy as much wheat to mix with it, the soldiers not being able to eat the rye bread without a mixture of wheat in it."[20]

Slowly but surely, more wheat was grown to satisfy this preference. In the early fourteenth century there were thirty-two brown bread bakers in London and only twenty-one white. By 1574, the proportions were tilted differently—sixty-two white and thirty-six brown. A century later, "the separate guild of the brown bakers disappeared altogether." In order for this to have happened, wheat had to be produced in greater quantities. According to Jay Allan Anderson, by the early years of the seventeenth century, wheat accounted for 38 percent of the grain grown, as compared to rye at 27 percent, barley at 19 percent, and oats at 16 percent.[21]

"The Wheaten Loaf and the Family Circle," Harper's New Monthly Magazine, *August 1857. (Courtesy Fall River Public Library)*

During the first half of the eighteenth century, improvements in agriculture further increased wheat yields, and wheat bread finally became plentiful. There was a string of bad harvests later in the century, but "by that time the wheaten bread habit had become so firmly established that it could not be checked." The grain of choice had to be imported to meet demand.[22]

G. M. Trevelyan summarized all these developments: "in the course of the eighteenth century, Englishmen of all classes became so dainty as to insist on refined wheat bread." At century's end, the idea that everyone deserved to eat "white wheaten bread" received official recognition in the Speenhamland poor relief system, which based the amounts doled out on the price of such bread. The working people of Nottinghamshire felt secure enough in their status as wheat eaters to joke that they had "lost their *rye teeth.*"[23]

We can now see more fully that what we discussed in chapter 1—the complicated response of the settlers of New England and their descendants to Indian corn, their desire to acknowledge their reliance on it as little as possible and to maximize their consumption of wheat bread—was a reenact-ment, condensed in time, of the struggle of their ancestors to procure wheat in order to find not only physical enjoyment but also social elevation. Such was the background to the New England fondness for cake.[24]

From Bread to Cake

The knowledge that wild yeast, ale barm ("a frothy liquid from the top of ale" that was also known as brewer's yeast), and even wine must would raise dough was far from new when wheat became more widely available in the first half of the seventeenth century. As discussed in chapter 1, the use of natural leavens in Britain probably predated the Iron Age. But these agents were "temperamental" and so were often left out of the breadmaking process.[25]

Changed attitudes about leavening coincided with the increased access to wheat. It began to be thought that leavening was essential to the making of "fine" bread and desirable in everyday bread. Lowland Britons in particular looked down on unleavened hearth cakes. Wheat was becoming the daily bread and its texture was improving.[26]

In a familiar pattern, claims about the health advantages of leavened bread kept pace with "rising" demand. Soon medical experts were warning against ingesting the unleavened bread that had fed their ancestors. It would, they cautioned, "produce 'slymy humours' in the stomach."[27]

Although leavening was most often applied to wheat breads, it was also claimed to improve the taste of breads made of inferior grains, even those made with peas and beans. A "sour trough," a large wooden mixing drum in which residual pieces of yeasted dough (in essence sourdough) were left to be incorporated into the next batch, might be used in such situations, as Gervase Markham recommended: "'sowre leaven . . . saved from a former batch' is broken into bits in warm water, strained, mixed with flour into a sponge 'as thicke as pancake batter,' let sit all night, mixed with a little more water, *barme* . . . , 'salt to season it,' enough flour to make it 'stiffe, and firme,' then kneaded and turned into loaves."[28]

In the fifteenth and sixteenth centuries the manchets of the striving mid-dle classes were usually made without leavening. But whenever possible, people wanted these breads "raised with the best beer barm and thoroughly kneaded." With the greater need to knead (so to speak), additional tech-niques and devices came into widespread use. Large batches of dough might be kneaded by foot, and bakers used a device known as a brake to assist with hand-kneading. By the eighteenth century the transition to yeasted bread was complete. Breads now had to be "white, light and relishing." It would be a horror for anyone to have "bread put before him which is not kneaded, not leavened, made of the dregs of beer; bread like lead."[29]

Doughs in which prodigious amounts of fat coat the flour go back to ancient Rome. Among the earliest was the *libum*, made with two pounds of cheese to one pound of flour and "baked on the hearth under a crock." In Roman-British towns, similar enriched breads, in which fat entered the dough in the form of cheese, butter, or lard, were baked in decorative pottery molds. One surviving mold "carries a representation of four figures standing around a tripod which has been interpreted as the emperor Septimius Severus, his wife and two sons celebrating a Roman victory over the Caledonians."[30]

In early modern Britain the wealthy were increasingly likely to fold the enrichments on offer in their kitchens—milk, butter, cream, eggs, sugar, spices, and "plums"—into their bread doughs. Among the earliest examples is a 1596 recipe for "fine biscuit bread" made with four eggs "beaten together for two hours." Gervase Markham gave a similar recipe, which he called "fine bread." It was made of "a quarter of a pound of fine sugar, and the same of sifted flour, aniseeds and two eggs, beaten well together and baked in a single buttered mould."[31]

While Markham and others considered eggs enrichments for fine breads, along the same lines as animal fats, spices, fruits, and sugar, the addition of eggs, either alone or together with yeast, also leavened the bread. Within a few decades, the leavening of these richer breads tended in the direction of using eggs alone.

Cooks who had worked only with yeast-raised doughs, that is most cooks, now required retraining. Essential to the success of eggs in raising dough was the creation of a "foam." Novices were warned in particular about the speed with which egg foams deflate. To maintain volume, full heat had to be applied to the batter as soon as the eggs were beaten, both to encourage further expansion as hot air entered the mixture and to set the cake before the whipped eggs fell.

The techniques of yeast baking—for instance, giving the sponge plenty of time to rise and waiting until the dough was mixed to heat the oven— were the opposite of those required for egg foams, as the following directions indicated: "you must keep beating your cake till . . . the oven is ready," and "it must not stand to rise." Or, to contradict Milton, when it came to the new methods of baking, it didn't serve only to stand and wait. Toward the end of the seventeenth century, with new cake mixtures now considerably less manageable than yeast doughs, "the tin hoop . . . [came] into use as a means of holding the cake in shape and helping it to rise evenly." With the advent of the egg foam, fine, sweetened bread had completed its evolution into a separate species known as cake.[32]

These fashionable English cakes were soon gracing colonial and early national tables. By 1786, there were at least two commercial cake bakers in Boston. Simmons's *American Cookery* included a "Plumb" cake, two "Plain" cakes (made not with less butter or fewer eggs, but without raisins), five loaf cakes (including another "plain" one calling for three pounds of sugar, three pounds of "shortning," eighteen eggs, nine pounds of flour, and "3 pints emptins," along with "allspice and orange to your taste, or fennel, carroway or coriander seeds"), a "cheap" seed cake, a Queens cake, a Shrewsbury cake, cupcakes, and pound cakes. Yeast continued to be used, but eggs had become indispensable.[33]

Simmons's cautionary note preceding the Shrewsbury cake recipe outlined the procedures she considered essential to the new mode: "N.B. In all cases where spices are named, it is supposed that they be pounded fine and sifted; sugar must be dryed and rolled fine; flour, dryed in an oven; eggs well beat or whipped into a raging foam." Sugar and butter were preferred over honey and oil, raw flour over bread crumbs (more on this in our discussion of gingerbread), and care was taken to ensure the quality of all three. Yeast was supplemented or replaced by eggs, which were used lavishly, while spices were used with restraint. In the effort to produce "much whiter and lighter" cakes, cake making had become "a matter not undertaken lightly."[34]

To some extent, the difference between yeasted and egg-leavened cakes was a distinction between large and small. Despite the fact that the Anglo-Saxon term "cake" is "glossed with the Latin *pastillus* (little cake) in one of the later word lists," throughout the eighteenth century, cakes—especially those made for important occasions—were often quite large. For instance, plum cakes might contain as much as fourteen pounds of flour and three or four pounds of butter and sugar. Enormous special occasion cakes were still being made in nineteenth-century New England. An 1816 wedding cake "exceeded 130 pounds." Such cakes, filled with heavy fruit and nuts, required "a considerable amount of ale-barm."[35]

By the late sixteenth century, the advantages of the smaller cakes—they were baked in less heat, in smaller ovens, and leavened more quickly, with eggs—tipped the balance in their favor as everyday fare. Though large cakes dominated banquet tables, the small cakes that had become fashionable among the gentry were, with the help of commercial bakers, also becoming quotidian fare for the rest of the population.[36]

The new small cakes provided light fare. One variety known as "wigs" were favored for Lenten suppers among the "fasting" gentry. Among other favorites were currant buns, Bath buns and "Lun's cake" (both made famous by the baker Sally Lunn of Bath), and muffins (first popular in the north of England and known elsewhere by the old Anglo-Saxon term crumpet).[37]

Toward the end of the seventeenth century, cakes became an alternative to traditional breakfasts of "ale, bread[,] and meat or fish pottage." Eating sweet rolls for breakfast, accompanied by (or it might be more accurate to say accompanying) the newly fashionable hot drinks—chocolate, coffee, and tea—caught on quickly. One recipe from 1727 described "an ordinary cake . . . good to eat with butter for breakfasts."[38]

One more step remained before cake in the form in which we now know it could emerge. In some of her gingerbreads, Amelia Simmons relied on a new leavening agent—pearlash. That this refined form of potash, obtained from wood ashes, could be used to raise doughs was a recent American discovery. Simmons offered the first instance of its use in print.[39]

Thirty-three years after Simmons, Lydia Maria Child used not a single egg nor a bit of yeast in her gingerbreads. The pearlash that was new in Simmons's day had become cheap, and Child took to it with a vengeance. She was aware of at least one of its disadvantages, however. Even more so than with eggs, "every thing mixed with pearlash should be put in the oven immediately," lest it deflate.[40]

Pearlash leavened more quickly than yeast and more cheaply than eggs, but when it was used alone it could produce a heavy final product. It was superseded by another refinement of potash, saleratus (from *sal aeratus*, "literally, aerated salt"), which released more carbon dioxide and thereby more effectively stretched the wheat fibers and raised the mixture. With either saleratus or pearlash, acid and liquid had to be mixed into the batter to begin the chemical reaction. These could be the same ingredient—lemon juice, sour milk, honey, molasses—or dry acid in the form of cream of tartar could be mixed with the liquid.[41]

Cooking chemicals had been around for a couple of generations before methods to stabilize and market them were perfected in the 1850s. Among the decisive accomplishments were the mass production of cream of tartar and the development of baking powder, which is "sodium bicarbonate and salts plus some starch to keep the mixture dry."[42]

Commercial baking powder took the risk out of combining the right amounts of chemicals, but some cooks continued to blend their own, while others even persisted in making pearlash from wood ashes. Then there was the true old guard, who abstained from chemicals because they detected a "coarse texture, dark color, and . . . unpleasant flavor." Nevertheless, most cooks accepted the new cost- and labor-saving products.[43]

Chemical leavens had one other use: they could disguise the sour flavor of baked goods that had gone bad. Catharine Beecher deployed "saleratus dissolved in warm water, enough to sweeten it" in this way. She went on to suggest ways to recreate the process; it was "so much liked that some persons allow bread to turn sour for the purpose. Bread can be kept on hand for this use any length of time." Saleratus sourdough brought leavens full circle, back to the sour trough.[44]

In the nineteenth century the derivation of cake from bread culminated in a profusion of names and presentations. Ella Shannon Bowles and Dorothy S. Towle explain: "Cakes were frequently named for war heroes and the political figures of the times. Harrison cake honored Old Tippecanoe. Nor was the naming limited to the masculine gender. Molly Stark, wife of the hero of Bennington, gave hers to a somewhat heavy cake that was leavened with pearlash."[45]

America's premier political figure was associated not only with cherry pie, but also with "Washington Cake . . . so called because it was a favorite at the table of General Washington," according to an 1843 New Hampshire paper. The health food craze begun by Sylvester Graham undoubtedly inspired a Graham Cake (made without graham flour). Before the temperance movement, there was the delightful Tipsy Cake. The recipe began, "pour over a sponge cake, made in the form of a porcupine, as much white wine as it will absorb, and stick it all over with blanched sweet almonds, cut like straws." After the temperance movement, there was only the larded Temperance Cake. The economizing housewife used salt pork for shortening in various bluntly named Pork Cakes. Bible-ridden New England produced Vermont Scripture Cake with directions such as "Judges 5:25" and "Jeremiah 6:20."[46]

Stowe's *The Minister's Wooing* included a reference to "the great Mont-Blanc loaf-cake, with its snowy glaciers of frosting." *Godey's Lady's Book and Magazine* was probably translating the name of this cake, rather than referring to a region of New Hampshire, when in the 1880s it published two recipes for "White Mountain Cake." Together, the two recipes added up to Stowe's description—one was a loaf cake, the other had white frosting.[47]

The *Godey's* cake with white frosting was not a loaf cake but rather a coconut layer cake. Today, layer cake is what the word "cake" primarily denotes. According to Bowles and Towle, it was in the 1880s that layer cakes became "the masterpieces of cake making." Richard J. Hooker mentions that "a cookbook of 1885 listed thirty kinds." Such cakes, "gave the American housewife a new way to offer . . . showy creations to her family and friends."[48]

Having surveyed the development of cake in English and American cuisine, we turn now to three cakes of particular importance to New Englanders.

Gingerbread

During the medieval and early modern periods, moistened bread and breadcrumbs were used in many dishes, from sauces, broths, and pottages to fried fish and roasts. While the bread that added bulk to most stews and pottages was stale and of low quality—"branny brown breadcrumbs"—finely grated wheat crumbs seasoned the gentry's roasts and baked fish, and "bulked out [its] . . . light-coloured pottages . . . until they were 'standing.'" Such crumbs were a treasure to be "kept locked away along with the spices."[49]

Although the colonists at first had little bread that warranted special security measures, they too used crumbs and stale bread in sauces for meat, sometimes softening them with milk. In time the crumbs were transferred to the top of the roasting fish or meat. (We described such uses in our chapter on fish; breadcrumbs still enter our cuisine this way, in gratinéed dishes.)[50]

As we mentioned in chapter 6, sweet and savory ingredients were intermixed in medieval cuisine. The earliest English gingerbreads, mixtures of sweetener (usually honey), spices, and breadcrumbs, emerged from a combination of the fine breadcrumbs and the mingled sweets and spices traditions. To elaborate, "the grated crumb of stale manchet" was mixed with pepper, saffron, cinnamon, aniseed, and ginger, sweetened with honey, colored red with "sanders" (sandalwood), moistened with red wine, worked into a dough, rolled thin, cut into cakes, and dried in a cool oven until it became a crisp sweetmeat. These first red and spicy gingerbreads more resembled modern gingerbread-man cookies than modern cakelike gingerbreads.[51]

Gingerbread's development into a cake began in the seventeenth century. Flour replaced breadcrumbs in the standard mixture, which was "made up stiffly into cakes and baked in the oven." It was this still relatively firm cake that was early in the century "your Gingerbread used at the Court" and later on "made for King Charles II."[52]

As gingerbread evolved into its modern baked forms, the sweetening agent began to dominate over the other spices. As we saw in chapter 6, into the Elizabethan period honey was the main English sweetener; and naturally, it sweetened early gingerbreads. In the sixteenth- or early-seventeenth-century manuscript cookbook now in print as *Martha Washington's Booke of Cookery*, the recipe most resembling the medieval breadcrumb gingerbreads called for "a gallon of ye purest honey." Yet it was during the period of this manuscript that sugar began to replace honey as the upper-class sweetener of choice. Thus, although there was one recipe that called for honey, the book included four gingerbreads with sugar, in amounts ranging from "6 pound of good loaf sugar beat small" to "3 pound of sugar" to "a pound of searced sugar" to "a little rose water & sugar."[53]

One recipe in *Martha Washington's Booke of Cookery* for what is arguably a gingerbread (although it was given the name "Pepper Cakes") was made with "treakle 4 pound." This ingredient is what became known in America as molasses. Molasses (as we noted in chapter 6) was a cheap by-product of the process of producing sugar from sugarcane that played a crucial role in rum manufacture (as we shall describe in chapter 8). Eventually, in America and in England, the cheapness of treacle/molasses, along with its ties to the rum industry, would damage this sweetener's reputation. In Bernard Shaw's *Major Barbara*, when Undershaft wished to convey his opinion that the kind of charity engaged in by Major Barbara of the Salvation Army was ineffective at best and dangerous at worst, he exclaimed: "You gave them bread and treacle and dreams of heaven." In other words, pie in the sky sweetened with molasses.[54]

But in the early seventeenth century, all that lay in the future. Treacle or molasses remained what it had long been—a valued commodity used to concoct antidotes to poison. At the same time, these medicinal uses were being complemented by culinary ones, as in the "Pepper Cakes" recipe above. One of the gingerbreads claimed to have been fit for a king, that for Charles II, was made with treacle.[55]

Treacle remained sufficiently respectable in the eighteenth century for E. Smith to use it as the principal sweetener in one of her gingerbreads. However, Smith's array of recipes casts doubt on Karen Hess's assertion that treacle "came to characterize" English gingerbread. The recipe in question included sugar as well as treacle, and two others were made with sugar only.

Similarly, Hannah Glasse called for equal amounts of sugar and treacle. It appears that sugar remained at least as important as treacle to the making of gingerbread in England.[56]

There remained plenty of room for variation in gingerbreads. Sometimes they were spiced with ginger only, sometimes with pepper, mace, aniseed, coriander seeds, caraway seeds, cloves, cinnamon, nutmeg, or all of the above, along with the ginger. They might contain raisins, candied lemon or orange peel, or citron. Yet the broad outline of a crisply baked, sweetened, and butter-, egg-, or cream-enhanced spice cake was set. In this form gingerbread crossed the Atlantic and soon became a colonial favorite.[57]

In 1720 Samuel Sewall was served "Ginger-Bread" along with some other unspecified type of "Cake" at the home of the governor of Massachusetts. He was given some of each to take home with him, and the next day he passed along his cake and gingerbread, "wrapped up in a clean sheet of Paper," to a widow he was courting. He must have considered both items valuable to bestow them as love tokens.[58]

Colonial soldiers were fond of a simple variety of gingerbread, which provided refreshment on muster days and "quasimartial" occasions. Benjamin Franklin nibbled such a gingerbread on his youthful way from Boston to Philadelphia. For fancier occasions there were fancier gingerbreads, such as the "Ginger Bread Royall" in the Martha Washington volume, made with blanched almonds.[59]

As in so many areas, the trail of evidence for the more coherent story of gingerbread in New England begins several decades after Samuel Sewall and Ben Franklin with Amelia Simmons. Simmons offered five gingerbread recipes in *American Cookery*. The one she called "Soft Gingerbread to be baked in pans" took the cake when it came to eggs, requiring twenty. This was the debut of an American favorite—soft, cakelike gingerbread. Like many other early American cakes, it was small by medieval standards and large by ours: "Rub three pounds of sugar, two pounds of butter, into four pounds of flour, add 20 eggs, 4 ounces ginger, 4 spoons rose water, bake as No. 1" (15 minutes). As its name indicated, another of Simmons's gingerbreads, "Molasses Gingerbread," called for molasses rather than sugar. This version was to be leavened exclusively with pearlash.[60]

Lydia Maria Child's emphasis on frugality meant that her gingerbreads were smaller and less rich than Simmons's. Besides her elimination of eggs and reliance on pearlash, Child made only limited use of butter or any other shortening. Her gingerbread baking was not entirely threadbare, however. She used roughly the same amounts of sugar as molasses. We give her first

Gingerbread molds from Old Stimpson Bakery, ca. eighteenth century.
(Courtesy Peabody Historical Society; photograph by Jeffrey R. Dykes)

molasses gingerbread recipe in full because it epitomized plain-style New England baking before the onset of self-conscious traditionalism:

> Gingerbread. A very good way to make molasses gingerbread is to rub four pounds and a half of flour with half a pound of lard and half a pound of butter; a pint of molasses, a gill of milk, tea-cup of ginger, a tea-spoonful of dissolved pearlash stirred together. All mixed, baked in shallow pans twenty or thirty minutes.

This recipe, along with her others for hard and soft gingerbread, represented the standard types of the nineteenth century.[61]

As with so much else so with gingerbread: where Child counseled austerity, Mrs. Lee offered refinement. Lee's elegant marzipan-type gingerbread was one such example. She restored Simmons's eggs to the recipes, although not back to Simmons's level. Pearlash was kept to a minimum. Lee revived the custom of mixing dried fruits, such as orange peel, lemon peel, or candied citron, into gingerbread batter. Like Child, she employed almost equal amounts of sugar and molasses, using the English word treacle.[62]

Sarah Josepha Hale and Catharine Beecher represented the mean of antebellum Yankee gingerbread cookery. Both made considerable use of pearlash or saleratus and somewhat less use of eggs. Hale made sugar more prominent than molasses in her recipes, while Beecher clearly separated molasses- from sugar-based recipes. Embodying both moderation and plenty, their gingerbreads could have been made by Polly Shubel, the "driving, thrifty, doctrinal and practical female" domestic in *Oldtown Folks*, who, the narrator reported, "gave me many a piece of good advice, sweetened with ginger-bread." (Didactic responsibilities, to the extent that they were assigned to females, were often discharged in the kitchen.)[63]

When we move ahead a couple of decades to Mrs. S. G. Knight, we encounter another avowed apostle of culinary frugality. Knight offered eleven gingerbread recipes, indicating gingerbread's sure place in the Yankee kitchen. But Knight was not, in fact, particularly economical. She called for a great deal more sugar than molasses (sugar in nine recipes, molasses in two) and also for lots of butter (in ten recipes) and eggs (in eight recipes). Baking soda was utilized in seven recipes—the three without eggs, and four of those with eggs. There were no dried fruits and hardly any spices besides ginger. Relatively few ingredients, a copious use of dairy products, and a predominance of sugar for sweetening marked Knight's gingerbreads as typical of the home baking done by prosperous midcentury Yankee women. These recipes were less parsimonious than Child's, or even Hale's or Beecher's.[64]

In combining a narrow range of permissible ingredients (a standard formula) with an assertion (made by the sheer number of recipes) that gingerbread should be made at home, Mrs. Knight's collection amounted to an early response to an emerging threat to Yankee gingerbread's status. Baked by commercial establishments and popular with the masses of immigrants who were beginning to alter and literally "alienate" the Yankee landscape, gingerbread was becoming a fast food in our sense. As a result, it was losing its place in the traditional precincts of the household and town and was joining the anonymous world of the marketplace. This challenge to gingerbread's Yankee identity was met most directly in the vigorous rhetoric of Thomas Robinson Hazard, who made a career of reburnishing the reputations of many symbolic Yankee foods.[65]

Hazard began his reverie by calling to mind the gingerbread of the village baker, pointing a contrast with "the vile stuff now sold at bakers' and restaurants." This newer stuff was "molded into little toad-stool-shaped patties, made of sour flour, rancid grease butter, and spoiled lard, disguised with a thousand poisonous compounds, and only half baked at that!" Hazard was quite effective in intimating rottenness, or at least dampness and darkness, with his description of "little toad-stool-shaped patties." In objecting to the bakers' use of "a thousand poisonous compounds" to camouflage an "off" taste, however, he was objecting to stratagems that went back centuries.[66]

Although "it raises my gorge," as Hazard said, to think about this kind of gingerbread, he had an alternative to put forward. A gingerbread once made by "old Stephen Greene," a baker of his acquaintance, "ought to have been, if peradventure it was not, famed throughout the world." So delicious was this gingerbread that "it used to be thought" Greene "had possessed himself by some occult means, or magic arts, of the recipe . . . used by the purveyors of the gods and goddesses." These were suggestive phrases. Hazard's association of Greene's superior gingerbread with the food of the gods and goddesses is reminiscent of the link made in the Middle Ages between fine quality wheat bread and divinity (as in the Christ-image-stamped pandemain). The difference was that Hazard offered his identification, as well as his allusion to baker Greene's possible "occult means, or magic arts," in jest.[67]

With all this talk of occult means, magic arts, and gods and goddesses, however, a reader may begin to think of another art besides that of baking for which New England was famous—the black art of witchcraft. If so, Hazard anticipated such thoughts, for he proceeded to state that the magical and/or divine origin of Greene's recipe was "rendered the more probable" by the fact that a "sibyl or spirit medium" even greater than the witches of Salem had lived not far from Greene's bakery.[68]

Hazard's humorous tone was part of a rhetorical strategy for turning something lowly (in this case gingerbread) into a Yankee icon. This conversion of the ordinary into the honored we have already analyzed in relation to Johnny cake, baked beans, codfish, boiled dinner, and other dishes. But now, with the godly allusion as a clue, we begin to guess that something larger than the creation of a food tradition was going on in the Hazard passage.

The process Hazard described with baker Greene's gingerbread had antecedents far older than New England. Reenacted here in terms that were secular and seemingly lighthearted but that nevertheless conveyed a depth of cultural feeling for Yankee New Englanders was the dynamic of the lowly becoming godly at the heart of the Christian myth. After more careful consideration, perhaps it is not surprising to find that the food mythology of a people descended from a pious but outcast sect would have its roots in their understanding that the more socially marginal a people (or a food), the better suited they were for glorification. Hazard thus used gingerbread as Stowe used the wood-spell cake—to adapt the New England tradition, developing a Yankee form of eucharistic ritual.[69]

The cultural use of gingerbread took another, rather surprising form in the late nineteenth century. Between the publication of Mrs. Knight's *Tit-Bits* in 1864 and the turn of the twentieth century, the roles of molasses and sugar in New England gingerbreads came to be reversed.

The reputation of molasses had declined from the seventeenth century, after it became a surplus commodity in the processing of West Indian sugar. As an article of diet, it was thereafter identified with the lower classes of England and America, and its negative image was reinforced by its role in the manufacture of rum. But since molasses was cheap compared to sugar, it remained in daily, if moderate, use among the middle classes (and, as with any sweet thing, delighted children). In an 1823 Vermont deed, a farmer promised to support his aging parents with an annual "ten pounds of brown sugar, two pounds of loaf sugar, [and] one gallon of molasses." (Converted to liquid measure, this was approximately 200 ounces of sugar versus 128 of molasses.)[70]

Though sugar was more highly prized, good cooks transformed molasses into everyday treats, such as dense and glossy molasses gingerbread. Until the last quarter of the nineteenth century, however, Anglo-American cooks considered baking with molasses a challenge, at times recommending that dishes including molasses be enhanced with sugar. It is striking, therefore, that just when sugar was becoming less expensive, molasses overtook it in New England gingerbread cookery. Why did late-nineteenth-century Yankees overturn the traditional sugar-molasses, white-dark hierarchy?

For evidence of this change, we turn to *Aunt Mary's New England Cook Book*, published in 1881. As we pointed out when we analyzed this volume in our discussion of clams, the region was identified twice on the title page, in both the pseudonymous author and title. This dual assertion of regional affiliation was accompanied by a dual assertion of familial association: "Aunt Mary's New England Cook Book . . . by a New England Mother." Thus had a generic Yankee domesticity superseded authorial individuality. The emphasis was repeated in the introduction, which also began: "A New England mother." Lest the reader had somehow missed the point, the introduction also struck a number of aesthetic and moral chords associated with Yankee values, such as: "No claim is made for a collection of fancy or artistic formulas . . . Plain, clear, and simple language is used."[71]

The recipes and rhetoric of *Aunt Mary's* appear to have been devised not simply to preserve the Yankee past but to assert it. By comparison, the New England authors of the popular cooking manuals of the first few decades of the century—the triumvirate of Child, Hale, and Beecher—displayed no comparable need to pledge regional allegiance. Remaining unself-conscious participants in New England society and culture, these earlier Yankee authors were content with their individual identities, and they used broad, inclusive, almost generic terms in their titles—American, domestic, housekeeper.

In light of the insistent Yankee tenor of *Aunt Mary's*, it is especially interesting that all of the gingerbreads in the collection were sweetened with molasses, and only molasses. This was a break with the tradition of including some sugar gingerbread recipes, and indeed with the tradition of considering the finer gingerbreads to be those made with sugar. This change further required the invention of new categories to distinguish gingerbreads, such as "Gingerbread (Milk)," "Gingerbread (Water)," and "Gingerbread (Sour Milk)." So important was molasses to "a New England Mother" that she concluded her "Gingerbread" section with a recipe for "Molasses Cookies."[72]

Molasses would henceforth dominate Yankee gingerbreads. In one New Hampshire community cookbook of 1898, two gingerbreads were presented, one a molasses-only variety, the other made with molasses and sugar. Both were called "Molasses Gingerbread." In another cookbook, also from New Hampshire and dating from 1903, of the five gingerbread recipes only one used sugar. All of the gingerbreads in the 1905 region-invoking *New England Cook Book* contained molasses.[73]

In her 1910 *Our New England Family Recipes*, five hundred limited-edition, signed copies of which were published by the prepositionless National Society New England Women, Mrs. Francis Jarvis Patten struck a high note reminiscent of Mrs. Lee. She identified herself by all three of her husband's names, and she quoted John Ruskin on "What does Cookery mean?" But such refinement was now combined with Yankee neo-boosterism, so it was not sugar but molasses that sweetened all three of her gingerbreads. The sugar gingerbread, formerly the choice of such refined ladies, seemed to be going the way of the passenger pigeon.[74]

In yet another "New England" cookbook, this one published in 1912 by an author who specialized in both traditionalism and plagiarism, there was one recipe for gingerbread and two for ginger cookies. The cookie recipes, "Gingernuts" and "Ginger Snaps," were lifted from Catharine Beecher, and their inclusion meant that two-thirds of the sample reflected the fashionable emphasis on molasses. In 1918 a Boston-area church group provided only one gingerbread, but it was sweetened with molasses. And finally, in Imogene Wolcott's 1939 "New England Yankee" cookbook (two regional monikers were now required), molasses was featured in three of the four gingerbreads.[75]

In spite of the fact that the previously preferred sugar had gotten much cheaper, noticeably more molasses and less sugar were called for in Yankee gingerbread recipes published between 1880 and 1940 than in those published between 1829 and 1865, when the world was first introduced to practical, frugal Yankee cooking. Molasses gingerbread had entered the Yankee canon.

Although the addition of another "classic" to the roster of New England foods might be taken to indicate cultural expansion, it is more plausible to regard it as a sign of contraction. By the end of the nineteenth century, New England's influence was on the wane. The foreign-born had virtually taken over New England cities. Family farming, the anchor of Puritan and Yankee independence from wage labor, was a thing of the past. And New England's industrial and economic dominance was receding as industries moved to other regions. Suffering an identity crisis, Yankees discovered that they could overlook molasses's image problems and use it to evoke a revered past when Yankee cultural and economic power dominated American life. The assertive flavor of molasses aptly corresponded to the defiant assertion of a cultural heritage that was felt to be slipping from preeminence.[76]

Election Cake

Realizing the commercial potential of New England nostalgia, *Godey's* published a number of cakes with regional names in the 1880s. Although the "White Mountain" cakes were probably not intended to appeal on these grounds, as mentioned previously, other recipes clearly were. "Boston Cake," an egg-raised spice cake featuring a "saltspoonful" of powdered cardamom, had no discernible culinary connection to Boston.[77]

Two recipes for "Connecticut Loaf Cake" did have strong ties to the New England cake making tradition. They return us to Harriet Beecher Stowe's wood-spell cake, with which we began this chapter. Stowe's description of the ministerial wood-spell was probably based in part on her sister Catharine's account of such a festival as it was observed in their father's Litchfield, Connecticut, parsonage in the winter of 1817. In the aftermath of the death of Lyman Beecher's wife, oldest daughter, Catharine, had been placed in charge of the food preparations. From her partial description, it appears that the cake she made for the wood-spell festivities was *Godey's* "Connecticut Loaf Cake."

Catharine began with the "preliminaries, . . . the spices . . . pounded, the sugar . . . rolled, the flour . . . sifted." Then, "the cake was duly made [i.e., mixed], and placed in large stone pots or earthen jars set around the kitchen fire, and duly turned and tended till the proper lightness was detected." Next came "the baking of the loaves . . . and were I to tell the number of loaves I put into and took out of the oven, . . . I fear my credit for veracity would be endangered."[78]

Lyman Beecher's parishioners proceeded to arrive with their offerings of wood, and "before sundown the yard, street, and the lower rooms of our house were swarming with cheerful faces." The paterfamilias greeted his people, "adroit in detecting and admiring the special merits of every load [of wood] as it arrived." His sons passed around cider and flip, the beverages of the day, while his daughters "were as busy in serving" slices of cake, doughnuts, and cheese.[79]

The staff writer at *Godey's* who wrote the copy accompanying one of its versions of "Connecticut Loaf Cake" may well have had in mind either Harriet's fictional description or Catharine's recollection of the Beechers' wood-spell cake, when she wrote: "This is an excellent, rich and nourishing cake, well worth all the care, time and labor needful to have it in perfection. To those who taste it for the first time it is a new revelation in the art of the cake baker, though well known to old New England housewives."[80]

The ingredients were two pounds of raisins, the same amount of currants, half a pound of citron, a pint of milk, two pounds each of butter and sugar, six eggs, half a pint of "fresh baker's yeast," four grated nutmegs, half an ounce of powdered mace, and three pounds of well-sifted flour. The dough was mixed in stages, beginning with dredging the fruit and preparing the ingredients "the day before." The next morning, half the butter, sugar, and eggs were mixed with the flour, milk, and yeast and set to rise all day. In the evening, the rest of the butter, sugar, and eggs were added, and the dough was left to rise all night. "Early" the next morning, the fruit and spices were added, and the dough was set to rise for a *third* time (which *Godey's* emphasized), for two or three hours. The cake was baked in a deep pan in an oven "which must be very hot at first, and allowed to cool so as to bake rather slowly, say three or four hours." Finally, it could be "iced or not, as fancy may decide."[81]

With its fussy instructions to be followed for three days with "care, time and labor" and its fretful concern "to have it in perfection," *Godey's* loaf cake recipe epitomized the refinement of the late nineteenth century, asserting the letter of affiliation with New England but leaching out the spirit. The tenor of these instructions little resembled the happy reminiscences of Catharine Beecher, whose loaves (not one mere loaf) were "duly made," "duly turned and tended," and baked amid all the other anticipatory activity.

If only as a prim ghost of itself, Connecticut loaf cake was retained because its roots went back to New England's beginnings. It was identical to election cake, whose name referred to the day when it was traditionally served. Since the 1630s in Massachusetts, Election Day had been observed in May; it was the day that executive and legislative leaders were elected and one of the ministers of the established church delivered the election sermon. The name Election Day also referred to a key Puritan notion that only the theologically "elect" were allowed to vote in the first Massachusetts elections.[82]

In the eighteenth century, May became a kind of triple-threat holiday season, with the Harvard commencement and annual meetings of clergymen coinciding with Election Day. In Stowe's depiction in *Oldtown Folks* of Election Day as it was celebrated in New England in the 1790s, its definitive characteristics were that "the Governor took his seat with pomp and rejoicing, and all the housewives outdid themselves in election cake."[83]

Earlier, Stowe had elaborated on the notion of all the housewives outdoing themselves in election cake: "Hadn't the receipt for election cake been in the family for one hundred years? And was not Polly [the family domestic] the sacred ark and tabernacle in which that divine secret resided? Even Miss Mehitable [Polly's mistress] had always been politely requested to step out of the kitchen when Polly was composing her mind for this serious work."[84]

Just as the minister retired to his study in the seventeenth and eighteenth centuries for the "serious work" of composing the election sermon, the cook retired to her kitchen in the nineteenth century for the equally serious work of composing and baking the election cake. Stowe's wood-spell cake was the same cake as election cake, so it is fitting that the same suggestions, only apparently tongue-in-cheek, of holy ritual enveloped both of them. And the "divine secret" of Stowe's two ceremonial cakes closely resembled Thomas Robinson Hazard's Yankee-made "divine" gingerbread.[85]

The secularized eucharistic role that election cake played in the Yankee community was also a theme in the reminiscences of John Howard Redfield, whose Connecticut boyhood was contemporaneous with the Beecher wood-spell:

> In preparation for [Election week] every family baked ovenfuls of what was called "election cake," which was a delicious loaf cake, too sacred to be used for anything but weddings, high teas, and Election week. [For weddings] it was usually made extra rich, and covered with very ornate and appropriate frostings. [For Election week] it was prepared as a somewhat more plain and digestible compound, but the supply had to be abundant, for the whole juvenile population expected to feast upon it through the week. And what feasts! Was every cake so delicious? The delicate frostings of white of egg and sugar, the rich, sweet, and spicy substance of the cake itself, and the raisins which were embedded in the toothsome compound were joys which no Connecticut boy could ever forgo or forget.[86]

Redfield's ejaculations—"And what feasts! Was every cake so delicious? . . . joys which no Connecticut boy could ever forgo or forget"—were similar to those of Catherine of Siena as she meditated on the Holy Eucharist: "the food of the sacrament that I have set up for you in the hostel of the mystical body . . . the food to strengthen the pilgrim travelers who go the way of my Truth's teaching, so that weakness will not cause them to fall." Election cake and Yankee gingerbread, evoking ecstasy and hinting at divine secrets, were not so different in their effects on the spiritual life of the community, in their ability to "feed" the town, from the mystical food that strengthened this medieval Roman Catholic saint's pilgrim travelers—though of course noting such a similarity would have offended a nineteenth-century Yankee.[87]

Admittedly, the contexts of Catherine of Siena's fourteenth-century writings and Stowe's and Redfield's recollections were vastly different. The tone of the Stowe and Redfield pieces was one of self-congratulatory contentment with the largely egalitarian abundance that was the decided achievement of rural and small town New England in the early national and antebellum era. Yet, as we saw in chapter 4, forces from both within and without were already beginning to rend the fabric of Yankee social harmony. The making of literal fabric in the region's cotton mills was tearing at the social cohesion that had been New England's ideal since John Winthrop had encouraged the earliest Puritan immigrants to be "knite together in this worke as one man." Nevertheless, election cake remained the culinary correlative of a golden era.

Election cake's importance in the celebration of communal life resulted in many mentions in cookbooks and reminiscences of the nineteenth century, as well as in the later nostalgic literature. Caroline Sloat agrees that it was "one of those . . . foods that figured in people's childhood memories." Yet from this distance the cake itself appears to be little more than what Sandra L. Oliver describes as "a richer version of modern yeasted coffee cake." Lucy Larcom admitted as much in her description of it: "''Lection cake' . . . was nothing but a kind of sweetened bread with a shine of egg-and-molasses on top; but we thought it delicious."[88]

As might be expected, Lydia Maria Child's version was more straightforward in both tone and preparation than *Godey's* Connecticut loaf cake, yet its simplicity better expressed the homely abundance the old cake was baked to celebrate: "Old-fashioned election cake is made of four pounds of flour; three quarters of a pound of butter; four eggs; one pound of sugar; one pound of currants, or raisins if you choose; half a pint of good yeast; wet it with milk as soft as it can be and be moulded on a board. Set to rise over night in winter; in warm weather, three hours is usually enough for it to rise. A loaf, the size of common flour bread, should bake three quarters of an hour."[89]

Fried Cakes

Such was the name given locally to the splendid doughnuts that were to be had in the 1950s from a little shop in the little town in the Yankee belt of upstate New York where the grandparents of one of us lived. Doughnuts were among the most ubiquitous of nineteenth-century New England's many sweetened, fatted breads. Child's recipe was typical: "take one pint of flour, half a pint of sugar, three eggs, a piece of butter as big as an egg, and a tea-spoonful of dissolved pearlash. When you have no eggs, a gill of lively emptings will do; but in that case, they must be made over night." She suggested flavoring with "cinnamon, rose-water, or lemon-brandy." Later authors concurred with Child's advice that "the more fat they are fried in, the less they will soak fat," usually specifying lard as the frying (or boiling) medium. Where Child mentioned yeast as an alternative to eggs, others said to use both. Her pearlash, or its derivatives, was rarely called for. Mace, nutmeg, and ground orange peel were additional flavoring options.[90]

Doughnuts were particularly popular for times when less than a full meal was appropriate, such as the Sabbath. Thus an 1845 cookbook recommended doughnuts, along with cheese, pie, and bread and butter, for the Sunday noon portion of a "course of dinners for a week." The cheese that Harriet Beecher Stowe's Maine islanders had between Sunday church services was accompanied by doughnuts. On other days, doughnuts were part of the mid- or late-morning refreshment known increasingly as lunch. A Maine ship-builder's wife gave them to her servants for "a luncheon, in the middle of the forenoon of a washing day."[91]

Doughnuts were also comfort food. Feeling sorry for the little heroine Tina, who was forced to live with a cruel guardian, a character in Stowe's *Oldtown Folks* "toddled to her milk-room, and, with a melting heart, brought out a doughnut" for her. Later, the girl was again offered a doughnut in solace, this time by the guardian's kindly hired hand: "When the child rose up in the bed and showed her swelled and tear-stained face, Sol whispered: 'There's a doughnut I saved for ye.'" Tina certainly appreciated the gesture. She "went to sleep hugging the doughnut."[92]

Special occasions could also feature doughnuts. Another character in *Old-town Folks* was reported to be happily "bilin' up no end o' doughnuts" to mark her nephew's return home from Harvard for spring vacation. In *The Pearl of Orr's Island*, a woman upheld "her reputation as a forehanded house-wife" by finding time "to rush to her kitchen, and make up a loaf of pound cake and some doughnuts," upon learning that the minister would be paying a call the next day. The tea party with which *The Minister's Wooing* commenced, mentioned in chapter 6 in connection with its jellies, also featured a "loaf of faultless cake, a plate of crullers and wonders, as a sort of sweet fried cake was commonly called."[93]

Stowe mentioned another gala event that offered an excuse to eat doughnuts when she described the children in *The Pearl of Orr's Island* arranging "some bread and cheese and doughnuts on a rock on the shore," thus imitating "the collation usually spread . . . at a ship launch." When the time came for "the festive preparations" for an actual ship launch, the aforementioned "forehanded housewife" remained concerned about "her housewifely reputation." It had been "a disputed point in the neighborhood whether she or Mrs. Pennel made the best doughnuts." Once launched, ships could serve as doughnut-eating venues. On whalers "the try-works were equipped for doughnut making."[94]

In *The Minister's Wooing*, doughnuts also figured in the abolitionist subplot. Candace, the Marvyn family's slave when the story began, was frying doughnuts when she heard of her cousin's manumission, accomplished through the efforts of the minister of the novel's title, Samuel Hopkins: "'He do dat ar'?' said Candace, dropping the fork wherewith she was spearing doughnuts. 'Den I'm gwine to b'liebe ebery word *he* does.'"[95]

A bit later, Candace was "sitting before the ample fireplace in the kitchen, with two iron kettles before her." One contained coffee, the other "puffy doughnuts, in shapes of rings, hearts, and marvellous twists, which Candace had such a special proclivity for making, that Mrs. Marvyn's table and closets never knew an intermission of their presence."[96]

Candace was summoned from her kettles to the drawing room, to be asked by Hopkins whether she thought slavery was right, and by her master if she would prefer to be free. She answered "no" to the first question and "yes" to the second, whereupon she was immediately released from bondage. Leaving the room in a state of high agitation, she returned shortly to explain how the change in her condition would affect her doughnut cookery: "I want ye all to know . . . dat it's my will and pleasure to go right on doin' my work jes de same; an' Missis, please, I'll allers put three eggs in de crullers, now."[97]

Doughnuts also played a part in the resolution of the main love plot of *The Minister's Wooing*. In turn-of-the-nineteenth-century Newport, Rhode Island, it was customary "when a wedding was forthcoming" for "all intimate female friends of the bride, old and young," to hold a quilting party. After the engagement of Mary Scudder, the novel's heroine, to Samuel Hopkins, such a party was duly held, and Candace brought to it a multitude of picnic baskets, one of which contained the "great Mont-Blanc loaf-cake" discussed above. It was also filled with other "cakes of every species," including "the twisted cruller and puffy doughnut."[98]

Despite Candace's vow to "b'liebe ebery word *he* does," she proved instrumental in seeing to it that Hopkins's marriage to the beautiful Mary did not take place. Her former master and mistress's son, Jim Marvyn, had declared his total devotion to Mary before shipping out as a sailor. Mary had not explicitly reciprocated, but Stowe made it clear that Mary did indeed return the young man's affections. Alas, word came that he had been lost at sea. It was only after coming to a resigned acceptance of the loss of Marvyn that Mary consented to become the wife of the heroically antislavery but also ultra-Calvinistic (not to mention middle-aged and stiff) Hopkins.

But it turned out that Marvyn was not dead after all, and soon he returned and renewed his entreaties to Mary. Clearly she loved him and not Hopkins, but she felt obliged to proceed with the marriage to Hopkins.

Enter Candace and her doughnuts. Candace was present when Hopkins presided over a service of "solemn fasting and prayer" for the liberation from slavery of an individual whose aspiration in life was to become a missionary to Africa. She sat "where she could see Mary and James in the singers' seat," and she had "certain thoughts planted in her mind which bore fruit afterwards in a solemn and select consultation held with Miss Prissy [a scatterbrained, but good-hearted seamstress] at the end of the horse-shed by the meeting-house, during the intermission between the morning and afternoon services." As in *The Pearl of Orr's Island*, the menu for this weekly Sabbath midday picnic was "rich slices of cheese, and a store of . . . favorite brown doughnuts."

Candace opened the deliberations by observing that "'dar's *reason* in all tings, an' a good deal *more* in some tings dan der is in oders. Dar's a good deal more reason in two young, handsome folks comin' togeder dan der is in'— Candace finished the sentence by an emphatic flourish of her doughnut."

In the ensuing conversation Miss Prissy divulged her inclination to tell Hopkins that he ought to release Mary from her engagement to him. Candace responded by offering decisive encouragement: "'Well now, honey,' said Candace, authoritatively, 'ef you's got any notions o' that kind, I tink it mus' come from de good Lord, an' I 'dvise you to be 'tendin to't, right away. You jes' go 'long an' tell de Doctor yourself all you know, an' den le's see what'll come on't. I tell you, I b'liebe it'll be one o' de bes' day's works you eber did in your life.'"[99]

Stowe meant it when she said that Candace spoke "authoritatively." This African American kitchen genius was the person whom Stowe primarily counterposed to Samuel Hopkins and his extreme, if laudably abolitionist, Calvinism. Candace had already given explicit expression to her theological views, in which immediate inspiration superseded the finespun reasoning to which Hopkins was addicted. But the core of Candace's theology and humanity, seen in action throughout the novel, consisted of the instincts and arts of mothering, concisely, superbly, and climactically summarized in this "emphatic flourish of her doughnut" that allowed everyone to go home happy.[100]

CHAPTER 8

Delicious Draught

Cider, Rum, Tea, & Coffee

One of the beverages New Englanders drank—cider—was central to the economics of subsistence; three others—rum, tea, and coffee—were equally central to the economics of emergent capitalism. Detailed consideration of mead (or metheglin), beer and ale, and water we must forego. Mead was the earliest British alcoholic drink. It was brought to the colonies right away—William Bradford mentions a shipment that didn't make it across the Atlantic because those on board drank it all up "under the name leakage"—and it was still making cookbook appearances in the nineteenth century. Beer was the staple beverage of English yeomen, but in New England it was replaced in this role by cider. A tradition distinctive to New England did develop of utilizing trees, such as spruce, sassafras, or birch, in the brewing of beer. It manifested itself in nineteenth-century cookbooks and, being particularly strong in northern New England, in Harriet Beecher Stowe's novel *The Pearl of Orr's Island*, set in Maine. As for water, that darling of the nineteenth-century temperance movement, it became safe to drink only toward the end of the period under study.[1]

Cider

Cider was brought to Britain from Normandy a century after the Norman Conquest and spread rapidly. In the seventeenth century cider production thrived, especially in southern England. Sometimes it was made from a mixture of apples and pears, sometimes from pears alone, in which case it was called perry. A variety made from the finest quality fruit and subjected to more elaborate distillation and fermentation, so that it was three or four times as strong as ordinary cider, came to be known as "Royal Cider."[2]

In chapter 6 we outlined the factors—reduced labor requirements, the release of acreage and grains for other foodstuff purposes—that led to increased apple cultivation relative to barley tillage and to the consequent replacement of beer by cider as the region's primary drink. Sarah F. McMahon's statistics from Middlesex County, Massachusetts, covering the years 1635 to 1835, show a steady increase in cider possession compared to beer possession.[3]

The figures confirm anecdotal testimony regarding the central place of cider in New England life. At the topmost social level, an eighteenth-century president of Harvard "was in the habit of laying in each year thirty or more barrels of cider as he had to provide for much entertaining. Late in the winter he would draw off part of his stock and into each barrel he would pour a bottle of spirit and a month later some of this blend would be bottled for use on special occasions." Perhaps this was President Edward Holyoke's method of producing "Cider Royal," the regulated tavern price of which in 1729 (in New Jersey, at least) was double that of ordinary cider.[4]

According to another source, ministers, who might be faced with ceremonial obligations equivalent to those of a Harvard president, "often stored forty barrels of cider for winter use." In the parson's household in Harriet Beecher Stowe's Maine novel, the reverend gentleman was wont to sip in the evening from a silver cup filled with "clear amber" cider, accompanied by "just the crispest, nicest square of toast." The sister who kept house for him "had conceived the idea that some little ceremony of this sort was absolutely necessary to do away with all possible ill effects from a day's labor, and secure an uninterrupted night's repose."[5]

But apart from these genteel situations, cider was also the beverage everyday people chose for everyday consumption. An English visitor to Boston in 1740 stated that "the generality of the people" had cider "with their victuals." According to Alice Morse Earle, it was drunk morning, noon, and night by infants, college students, "delicate women," and laborers. John Adams's tankard upon rising every day was apparently typical, for according to the estimate of one agricultural historian, in Massachusetts in 1767 (when Adams was a young man), each inhabitant drank on the average more than an entire barrel of cider in the course of the year. In *Oldtown Folks*, set in Massachusetts a few decades later, cider, like boiled dinner, was constantly consumed by the lovable and hateful alike. Moreover, we saw in chapter 6 that Stowe represented cider's dispensation to Indians as a symbol of traditional New England charity.[6]

According to Earle, "Connecticut cider soon became especially famous." As evidence, she quotes a passage from a 1660 letter Roger Williams wrote to John Winthrop Jr., who was governor of Connecticut at the time. The "lo. [loving] lines" from Winthrop to which Williams was replying prompted Williams to compare them with "a Cup of your Conecticut Cydar (wch we are glad to heare abounds with you)." More than a century later, French exile Anthelme Brillat-Savarin drank at a Connecticut farmhouse from "vast jugs" of cider. It was, he said, "so excellent that I could have gone on drinking it for ever."[7]

One scholar presents statistics that indicate that few colonial New England households had the equipment to make cider themselves. Nevertheless, the cider that everyone was drinking did get made. The cider mill was frequently built on a hillside, so that carts could unload the apples "on the upper level and take away the barrels of cider on the lower." A cylindrical mechanism, powered by a horse "walking in a small circle" first crushed the apples. The resulting "pomace" would remain in a vat overnight and then be put into the cider press the next day. Spread out within the press between layers of straw, the pomace would be compressed "very slowly at first, then harder, until the mass was solid and every drop of juice had trickled into the channels of the platform and thence to the pan below."[8]

Such emphasis by Alice Morse Earle on the glacial pace of cider pressing calls to mind John Keats's picture of the personified spirit of autumn, who "by a cyder-press, with patient look, . . . / [watches] the last oozings hours by hours." It is unlikely that many of the family members or farmhands employed in cider making maintained patient looks as they watched the last oozings of the cider press hours by hours, but we hope that at least a few of them felt at least a small portion of what Keats so memorably evoked.[9]

Rum and Flip

In our survey of sugar and molasses in chapter 6, we did not particularly emphasize their close connection with certain beverages. International trade in sugar, molasses, rum, chocolate, tea, and coffee all arose and flourished interdependently. Demand for refined white sugar was crucially linked to its use as a sweetener in chocolate, tea, and coffee. What concerns us now is the principal use of sugar's cheaper cousin, molasses. From the very beginnings of the West Indian sugar cane industry, molasses was made the basis of "Rumbullion, alias Kill-Devil, . . . a hot, hellish, and terrible liquor."[10]

In 1651, when this characterization was made, rum was already being distilled in the North American colonies—and especially in New England—

as well as in the sugar islands themselves. By 1770 there were 144 rum distilleries in the colonies, 98 (or 68 percent) of them in New England. The 5 million gallon output of these domestic distilleries in that year supplied about 60 percent of the total colonial consumption of 8.5 million gallons. In view of the particularly high incidence of distilleries in New England, an even higher proportion of the total rum consumption there may have been of domestic rum.[11]

Domestically distilled rum was "an inexpensive alternative" to West Indian rum, say John J. McCusker and Russell R. Menard. In the 1770s, at a tavern in Holden, Massachusetts, famed for making especially good flip, a mug of flip made with New England rum cost nine pence, and one made with the "West India" product cost eleven pence. Rum had already by 1686 become cheap enough and widely enough consumed to come to the attention of a leading New England clergyman, Increase Mather. "It is an unhappy thing that in later [recent] years a kind of drink called rum has been common among us," Mather complained. "They that are poor and wicked, too, can for a penny make themselves drunk."[12]

In the eighteenth century Edmund Burke stated that New Englanders were "more famous for the quantity and cheapness than for the excellency of their rum." Such judgments were as little heeded as those of our own day on, say, the beer produced by major American breweries. Half a century later, a Yankee herbalist conceded that when New England rum was fresh from the distillery, "the odour and taste is so disagreeable that it is not fit to be drunk by the human species." However, the writer had found by his "own observation" that if New England rum was allowed to age, and especially if it was "carried to sea" for a good long spell (eighteen months in the example given), it would emerge "free from any disagreeable smell" and would also have "a very pleasant taste." Not quite a ringing endorsement.[13]

The figure given above for overall rum consumption in the colonies in 1770 works out, at the least, to slightly more than one-eighth of a pint (2.5 ounces) per inhabitant per day—more than four times the amount drunk in the same year by the average inhabitant of Great Britain. This assumes that everyone drank rum, which is a safe assumption. While rum was handed out with particular liberality to laborers, "as a source of energy while performing hard manual work," it was also readily available to women. In one community, Deerfield, Massachusetts, in the eighteenth century, rum arrived mostly from Boston, though at what ratio of domestic to West Indian is unknown. Once it arrived, it was exchanged so commonly among the people of the area that a historian attempting to keep track of it states that references to it, along with those to cider, "could not be fully recorded" in her database. Other scholars state that rum "was bought by every class of Deerfielders in amazing quantity." One seventy-six-year-old woman purchased three quarts in the year of her death, 1754.[14]

So Baron Friedrich von Riedesel, commander of German mercenaries in the Revolutionary War and later a prisoner of war, was perhaps guilty of understatement when he restricted to the male inhabitants the "strong passion for strong drink, especially rum" that he observed among New Englanders. And maybe John Adams wasn't being all that hyperbolic when during his tenure as U.S. president he observed regarding the Greek and Roman cult of the god of wine that "if the ancients drank wine as our people drink rum and cider, it is no wonder we hear of so many possessed with devils." We have already noted that, with cider, Adams made his own contributions to New England bibulousness.[15]

The herbalist who damned Yankee rum with faint praise claimed that "good *rum* properly diluted with water, sweetened with sugar, and drank with moderation, strengthens the lax fibres, incrassates the thin fluids, and warms the habit. It proves the most beneficial to those exposed to heat, moisture, corrupted air, and putrid diseases." So if you want your lax fibers strengthened and your thin fluids incrassated, get yourself a hogshead or two of Medford rum, send it around the world a couple of times on a Yankee clipper, and bottoms up![16]

A form of spirits so universally consumed was bound to give birth to various mixed drinks. One of these was "black-strap," made with rum and yet more molasses. Tavern keepers would hang a piece of salt cod in proximity to their supplies of black-strap, in hopes that the customer who ate some of the cod would get thirsty and call for another round of the black-strap. In the opinion of Josiah Quincy, "this black-strap was truly the most outrageous . . . of all the detestable American drinks on which our inventive genius has exercised itself."[17]

The most popular mixed drink made with rum was flip. It is a toss-up whether to designate flip as a derivative of rum or of its other principal ingredient, beer. It was made by mixing sugar, molasses, or dried pumpkin with "strong beer" and a gill (quarter pint) of rum. A red-hot iron poker (called variously a "loggerhead," "flip-dog," or "hottle") was thrust into the liquor, making it "foam and bubble and mantle high," and giving it "the burnt bitter taste so dearly loved." At one tavern, if not more, the custom was to enhance the flip with a compound of cream, eggs, and sugar. An additional fresh egg beaten in after the loggerhead had worked its magic would cause the froth to spill out over the top of the mug. Such a spectacle warranted a special name—"bellows-top."[18]

Flip-dogs were in such constant use that they frequently had to be sent to the village blacksmith for repair. One such repair demonstrates how the colonial New England economy was comprised of an interplay between long-distance exchange via the international markets and local exchange or barter. In compensation for his labors, the blacksmith received not cash but goods from his neighbor the tavern keeper's available resources. But the goods were an imported commodity—two gills of "West India Rum at 4d" apiece.[19]

Known in diverse incarnations and under diverse names, flip also earned a place in song and story. It was primarily a wintertime potion. Thus the entry for December in the 1704 *New England Almanac* called to mind a scene in which "By tavern fires tales are told. / Some ask for dram when first come in, / Others with flip and bounce begin." In the era of the American Revolution, patriotic significance was conferred on flip by the Connecticut versifier John Trumbull: "While briskly to each patriot lip / Walks eager round the inspiring flip: / Delicious draught! whose powers inherit / The quintessence of public spirit." These lines were published in 1776, thus preceding by a couple of decades Joel Barlow's tribute to hasty pudding as the sustenance of a nation of "sturdy freemen." By James Russell Lowell's day, flip participated in nostalgic conjurations of colonial tavern atmospherics: "Here dozed a fire of beechen logs, that bred / Strange fancies in its embers golden-red, / And nursed the loggerhead whose hissing dip, / Timed by nice instinct, creamed the mug of flip."[20]

If Harriet Beecher Stowe is to be believed, flip was not consumed exclusively in taverns. In *The Minister's Wooing*, Candace, the strong-minded and authoritative African American cook, used a mug of flip as a medicament (as well as a management tool) for her husband Cato, both easing him of his coughing fit and keeping him quiet in the corner. In *Oldtown Folks*, at the ministerial wood-provisioning festivities, "the minister himself heated two little old andirons red-hot in the fire, and therewith from time to time stirred up a mighty bowl of flip, which was to flow in abundance to every comer." It was subsequently shown being dispensed to every comer indeed— from a Paul Bunyanesque farmer who "sipped his mug of flip, looking, with his grizzly beard and shaggy hair and his iron features, like a cross between a polar bear and a man," to the deacon, "a mournful, dry, shivery-looking man, with a little round bald head," who "sipped his tumbler of flip and ate his cake and cheese as if he had been at a funeral."[21]

A possible real-life instance of home flip consumption, and another in-dication of flip's cold weather utility, comes from the recollections of John Marsh, a nineteenth-century temperance advocate. During Marsh's Con-necticut childhood, flip "was a usual drink on the Sabbath, in the winter months, on returning from church. Well do I remember crying in meeting from the cold (there were then no stoves), and holding on to my chair after drinking the Flip till my head became steady."[22]

No discussion of the role of rum in colonial New England society would be complete without a recapitulation of the drink's entanglement in slavery. The rum produced and consumed in New England was dependent on slave labor, either for the molasses from which it was made or for that portion of the rum itself that was distilled in the West Indies. Molasses and rum came into New England, and domestically distilled rum was sent forth from it, as part of the "triangular" trading circuit of the eighteenth century, in which, along with the molasses and rum, cod, salt meat, slaves, and other commodi-ties were exchanged between New England, southern Europe, the west coast of Africa, and the sugar islands.[23]

The rum distilled in New England that was reserved for export was used to help maintain the system as a whole. It was shipped to West Africa, where it purchased more slaves for the sugar industry labor force. "New England rum replaced . . . French brandy all along the African coast" in the direct slave trade. Overall, this maritime commerce was indispensable to New En-gland's prosperity in the eighteenth century and, as we noted at the end of chapter 3, provided much of the capital that was in the nineteenth century invested in the American Industrial Revolution, in the forefront of which New England remained until the Civil War. And at the heart of it all was slavery.[24]

"Grocery" Drinks

The slave labor system and the expansion of international trade that brought sugar, molasses, and rum into prominence also led to the rise of three new nonalcoholic drinks: chocolate, tea, and coffee. "Groceries" was the term used in the seventeenth and eighteenth centuries for newly imported con-sumable commodities from distant places. The category embraced tobacco, spices, and dried fruits, as well as sugar products and the new beverages. Whereas in 1559 groceries accounted for about 9 percent of all imports into England and Wales (and chocolate, tea, coffee, and tobacco contributed nothing to this 9 percent), by the second half of the seventeenth century their share had risen to almost 17 percent. A century later, just before the American Revolution brought about a reconfiguration of the early modern trading system, the portion of English and Welsh imports that was groceries had doubled again, to almost 36 percent. It was the spectacular increase in chocolate, tea, coffee, sugar, and tobacco imports that was mainly responsible.[25]

Tea

First imported from China by the Portuguese in the sixteenth century, tea began coming into Britain in large amounts in the later seventeenth century. It came in two categories: black (such as Bohea or Souchon) and green (such as Imperial or Hyson). Its acceptance was facilitated by the fact that Catherine of Braganza, the Portuguese wife of Charles II, added tea-drinking to the ceremonial routine of life at court. The idea that a hostess could "brew and serve tea herself in the presence of her guests . . . had great appeal," and soon the mistresses of aristocratic and gentry households were following Queen Catherine's example.[26]

High import duties were imposed on the new drink, which meant that smuggling probably supplied anywhere from half to three-quarters of total British consumption through most of the eighteenth century. Respectable people did not shrink from participating in the illegal tea trade. In 1779 a parson received a bag of tea in the dead of night from "Andrews the Smuggler." It has been estimated that when illegal supplies are incorporated into the calculations, British tea intake had reached the level of one pound per person per year by the 1740s, enough for almost everyone to have at least a bit every day.[27]

An early license for the sale of tea in New England was issued in Boston in 1690. According to Caroline Howard King, "the first tea used in New England" was that sent to the family of the appropriately named Philip English of Salem, Massachusetts, though at what date King does not say. "The only direction that came with it was that it was to be boiled. So boiled it was, the water in which it was cooked being carefully thrown away, and then it was served as greens. It is needless to say that the English family did not much relish their new dainty, to partake of which they had invited their neighbors and friends." Alice Morse Earle says that some people in Salem sought to make boiled tea leaves more acceptable as table greens by enhancing them with butter and salt.[28]

After these unpromising beginnings, colonial tea consumption reached significant levels by 1720 and flourished until the beverage became entangled in Revolutionary-era politics. In 1740 an English traveler reported that tea-drinking was all the rage among New England tradesmen's wives. But tea never caught on in North America as fully as it had in Britain. Again taking the smuggling factor into account, annual per capita consumption in 1773, just prior to the Boston Tea Party, has been estimated at a little more than half of what it was in Britain at the same time.[29]

Still, tea had many devotees among the colonials. When nonimportation covenants became part of the Revolutionary strategy and abstention from tea was therefore a sign of fealty to the cause, many found it difficult to remain firm. John Adams hoped that the tea he was served by John Hancock in 1771 had come from Holland and was therefore not tainted by British imperial impositions. But whether it was or not, he went ahead and drank it. Later, Adams asked the proprietress of a tavern in Falmouth, Massachusetts, for a cup of tea, "provided it has been honestly smuggled or paid no duties." The landlady refused him, however, insisting that he content himself with coffee. "I must be weaned, and the sooner the better," Adams wrote penitently to his wife, Abigail.[30]

Tea consumption was in fact significantly reduced during the Revolutionary War, but afterward it made a comeback and remained the second nonalcoholic beverage of choice throughout the nineteenth century and indeed on into our own day. It was considered particularly suitable in certain venues. One of these was the sick room. We referred in chapter 6 to the final illness of the heroine of Stowe's *The Pearl of Orr's Island*. Tea was, like jelly, part of the caregiving repertoire. "'Hadn't you better wake her?' said Miss Ruey," one of the kindly old women attending upon the fatally afflicted young woman; "'a cup of hot tea would do her so much good.'" Stowe proceeded to comment that "Miss Ruey could conceive of few sorrows or ailments which would not be materially better for a cup of hot tea. If not the very elixir of life, it was indeed the next thing to it."[31]

Some cookbook authors dissented from Miss Ruey's opinion. Mrs. Lee declared that "the frequent drinking of a quantity of strong tea, as is the general practice, relaxes and weakens the tone of the stomach, whence proceeds nausea and indigestion, with a weakness of the nerves, and flabbiness of the flesh, and very often a pale wan complexion." As if that were not alarming enough, she added that "persons of weak nerves ought to abstain from [tea] as carefully as from drams and cordial drops; as it causes the same kind of irritation on the tender delicate fibres of the stomach, which ends in lowness, trembling, and vapors." Lee did concede that mixing milk into one's cup of tea "in some quantity" would mitigate these evils, and she allowed that healthy people, "those who are strong and live freely," might have it for breakfast to good effect, as it would "cleanse the alimentary passages, and wash off the salts from the kidneys and bladder."[32]

Lee also cautioned, strangely, that tea "should never be drank hot by any body." There is no sign of agreement with this notion on the part of any other author, except perhaps for Catharine Beecher's remark that "black tea improves by boiling, but green is injured by it." In 1881 the perspective on this question that has become universal was vigorously expressed by "Aunt Mary": "all tea lovers are pleased with *hot* tea."[33]

There is little evidence in our sample to support Miss Ruey's idea that tea would actually make ill people well. One tried and true home remedy that went under the name of tea was not tea at all, but rather a concentrate made from the juice left over after boiling beef or beef bones. People thought this beef tea was "good for what ails you." Catharine Beecher presented a recipe for beef tea in her chapter of recipes for sick people: "Broil a pound of tender, juicy beef ten minutes, salt and pepper it, cut it in small pieces, pour on a pint of boiling water, steep it half an hour, and then pour it off to drink. Another way is slower, but better. Cut the beef in small pieces, fill a junk bottle with them, and keep it five hours in boiling water. Then pour out, and season the juice thus obtained." In the first method, the small pieces of high-grade beef functioned as loose tea leaves, in the second, as tea leaves placed in a tea ball.[34]

The principal part played by tea in nineteenth-century New England society was as a lubricant of female socializing. A few pages back, we introduced the minister in *The Pearl of Orr's Island*, along with his sister Emily, at the point she was serving him a nightcap of cider. This particular evening, Miss Emily had suspected her brother of harboring a secret, and she had attempted to pry it out of him, but to no avail.

Stowe later provided a view of the reverend brother's perspective on the matter, and tea figured largely in his rationale for not taking his sister into his confidence: "he reflected with dismay on the number of women in his parish with whom Miss Emily was on tea-drinking terms,—he thought of the wondrous solvent powers of that beverage in whose amber depths so many resolutions yea, and solemn vows, of utter silence have been dissolved like Cleopatra's pearls. He knew that an infusion of his secret would steam up from every cup of tea Emily should drink for six months to come, till gradually every particle would be dissolved and float in the air of common fame. No; it would not do."[35]

In this respect, as the focus and catalyst of woman-centered social interaction, tea-drinking in the early days of the American nation reproduced the context in which tea-drinking had first arisen in Britain a century before. Stowe conjured up such tea-table scenes in both everyday and formal situations. The "faultless" tea party at the outset of *The Minister's Wooing* was an instance of the latter.[36]

Coffee

The coffee tree is native to northeast Africa. A drink produced by the infusion of the roasted beans of this tree in water was consumed in the Muslim world, making its way to Europe in the seventeenth century. Coffeehouses were established in Britain by the 1650s, their men's club ambience imported from the East along with the beverage for which they were named. By the 1680s coffee was being consumed in many gentry households. In one, the two or three pounds a year bought in 1685 became the two or three pounds a month bought eight years later.[37]

As any contemporary American traveler to Britain instantly experiences, coffee did not ultimately take hold in that nation, losing out to tea in the eighteenth century. The history of "grocery" beverages developed rather differently in North America. The first license in New England for the sale of coffee (and chocolate) was granted in 1670 to a Boston woman. Coffeehouses soon followed. There were two in Boston by 1690. In the course of becoming an item for consumption in the home, coffee was subjected to initiation-by-ignorance rituals of a sort similar to those in the case of tea. People "boiled the whole coffee-beans in water, ate them, and drank the liquid." As enthusiastic participants in a coffee-drinking culture, we consider this less forgivable than imagining that tea leaves might serve as spinach.[38]

We have no statistical information on the level of coffee consumption in North America in colonial times. In the first half of the nineteenth century, partly no doubt because during the Revolution coffee came to be associated with patriotism and tea with the reverse, but also because it was a lot cheaper, coffee emerged as the American national beverage. As of 1830, annual American coffee consumption per capita was almost six times that of tea, just under three pounds versus just over half a pound. Thirty years later, coffee consumption had more than doubled and was almost nine times as much as that of tea.[39]

Like tea, coffee elicited mixed reactions from those concerned with health. Writing in 1801 before coffee's full ascendancy, the comical New Hampshire herbalist Samuel Stearns stated that, on the plus side, "some call it good for the head-ache, a weak stomach, and disorders arising from intemperance and hard study. It moderates internal fermentation, and does service in corpulent and phlegmatic habits. . . . In some it assists digestion, promotes the natural secretions, prevents sleepiness, and relieves the spasmodic asthma." On the other hand, alas, "in delicate constitutions, [coffee] sometimes produces headaches and other nervous symptoms." It was "hurtful to thin habits, the bilious, melancholic, hypochondriac, and those subject to haemorrhages." With such large potencies for both good and ill, coffee was best handled with care. One authority had informed Stearns "that coffee should be boiled from eight to twelve hours before it is drank [!], and also mixed with an equal quantity of milk."[40]

Three decades later, despite, or perhaps because of, coffee's newly commanding position among American beverages, Mrs. Lee took a sterner position. She was even harder on coffee than tea: "Coffee affords very little nourishment, and is apt to occasion heat, dryness, stimulation, and tremors of the nerves, and for these reasons is thought to occasion palsies, watchfulness, and leanness. Hence, it is very plain that it must be pernicious to hot, dry, and bilious constitutions. If moderately used it may be beneficial to phlegmatic persons, but, if drank very strong, or in great quantities, it will prove injurious even to them."[41]

Such opinions were totally beside the point, in that New Englanders continued to down cup after cup of their favorite drink. Cookbook authors, including Lee, were therefore obliged to include instruction in coffee preparation or risk being judged less than comprehensive. Then as now, and as with cereal grains, coffee ran the gamut as far as quality and prestige were concerned. At the bottom end were substitutes for coffee beans, such as potatoes, pumpkins, peas, or parched rye.[42]

But even Lydia Maria Child, ever on the lookout for additional ways of saving a few pennies, frowned on ersatz coffee. "As substitutes for coffee, some use dry brown bread crusts, and roast them; others soak rye grain in rum, and roast it; others roast peas in the same way as coffee," she noted. But "none of these are very good; and peas so used are considered unhealthy." In extreme cases, such as "where there is a large family of apprentices and workmen, and coffee is very dear, it may be worth while to use the substitutes, or to mix them half and half with coffee." But even in such situations, "the best economy is to go without."[43]

Sarah Josepha Hale voiced the same reservations as Child about coffee substitutes, but she did allow that the best of this bad lot was "toasted crust of bread." Sure enough, "Crust Coffee" turned up in a cookbook as late as 1881. This was to be made with Ryaninjun, pieces of which were to be dried in the oven "slowly and hard," steeped in boiling water for fifteen minutes, and served with milk or cream and sweetener, as desired. The author stated that "many prefer this to imported coffee; it is nutritious and more healthy, especially for children and aged people." At this distance, such a claim already appears audacious. It became breathtakingly so with the additional comment that "if the pot is kept in a cold place the coffee left in it can be used several times." Wake up and smell the reheated crust coffee.[44]

Such substitutes were appealing on grounds (so to speak) of convenience as well as economy. Until the twentieth century, making a merely average quality pot of genuine coffee involved several laborious steps. To begin with, coffee beans did not come into the household preroasted. As might be expected, it was Mrs. Lee, wearing for this purpose her gourmet rather than her health-maven hat, who provided the most complete instruction in roasting:

> Roasting coffee is by far the most difficult operation of the housekeeper; when carried far enough, an aromatic oil is formed by the heat and forces itself out upon the surface of the grains, giving them a glossy appearance, and an odor which is considered their perfection; yet too little roasting prevents the aroma from appearing, and too much completely volatilizes it, leaving nothing but a flat bitter taste. The heat should be strong and the operation shortened as much as possible without burning the grains. The roaster should be close or well covered all the time, and in order to improve the looks and flavor, a small piece of butter may be added to the coffee, while parching.[45]

Once the beans were roasted, they had to be ground and made to act in concert with hot water in such a way as to produce liquid drinking coffee. Some of the methods of filtering water through ground beans with which we are familiar were known in the nineteenth century but were not yet in general use. Cooks therefore had to resort to placing the grounds in the water, boiling the mixture, and then somehow encouraging the grounds to settle. For this last—obviously crucial—step, the white, yolk, and shell of an egg might be mixed with the grounds (this was also claimed to improve the flavor), or pieces of dried fish skin might be added during boiling, or a small amount of cold water might be added at boiling's conclusion, or a combination of some or all of the above might be utilized.[46]

The fact that coffee-making procedures were so complex helps to explain why even the fastidious Mrs. Lee did not share our aversion to reheating. Her brew would be "of the finest flavor, and may be kept three days in summer, and four or five in winter; when ordered for use, it only requires heating in the coffee-pot, and may be served up at two minutes' notice."[47]

Then as now, some appreciated coffee of the highest quality. We have referred several times to Caroline King's description of the typical banquet of her Salem childhood days. The banquet would terminate in coffee: "I must not forget to mention the delicious coffee made from the pure Mocha bean which ended the feast. An old Salem sea-captain had presented my father with a bag of the choicest variety, and it was only used on great occasions, enriched by cream so thick that it had to be taken from the cream pitcher with a ladle, and by the sparkling loaf sugar of those days, and served hot and fragrant, in my grandmother's delicate old India china mugs."[48]

Catharine Beecher agreed that "Mocha," along with "Old Java," made the best coffee. But more often in cookbooks it was a method of preparation rather than a variety of bean that defined gourmet coffee. Surprisingly, it was Child who first explained how to make what we now call French roast coffee. "French coffee is now so celebrated," she said, that she felt compelled to talk about it, though she could not refrain from commenting, with a crassness that would have made true connoisseurs cringe, had any such people read her book, that "no prudent housekeeper will make it, unless she has boarders, who are willing to pay for expensive cooking."[49]

But whether French roast was to be made in shabbily genteel Boston boardinghouses or Salem mansions, Child proceeded to explain how to make it:

> The coffee should be roasted more than is common with us; it should not hang drying over the fire, but should be roasted quick; it should be ground soon after roasting, and used as soon as it is ground. Those who pride themselves on first-rate coffee, burn it and grind it every morning. The powder should be placed in the coffee-pot in the proportions of an ounce to less than a pint of water. The water should be poured upon the coffee boiling hot. The coffee should be kept at the boiling point; but should not boil. Coffee made in this way must be made in a biggin. It would not be clear in a common coffee-pot.[50]

The most fulsome celebration of good coffee in the annals of nineteenth-century New England was penned by Thomas Robinson Hazard. We have had many occasions to describe Hazard's lavish tributes to the masterpieces

—the Johnny cake, wildfowl, and other dishes—prepared by Phillis, his grandfather's African American cook. But the long-deferred climax of the *Jonny-Cake Papers* pertained to Phillis's coffee.

Phillis would have been just as scornful of the housekeepers of the late nineteenth century "who, to save a little trouble, buy their coffee ready burnt at the grocery shops" as Hazard was of the people who ate late-nineteenth-century commercialized gingerbread. Phillis roasted the beans herself, having previously "made" her master "get the best Old Mocha coffee." Not until "all the 'gret-room' folks were up, washed, and dressed, and ready to sit down to the table" would she "put her coffee into her long-handled iron pan" and hold it "over the fire, herself stirring it all the time with a sweet-scented white *wannut* stick that she called her coffee stirrer. It was very seldom that Phillis allowed any of her coffee to get burned, but if a grain did chance to, she always picked it out and threw it into the fire; for Phillis used to say that if there was anything on airth she 'spised, it was bitter, burned coffee."[51]

After the roasting, the grinding: "The very minute the coffee was done parching, Phillis put it in the coffee-mill and made Abe grind it as quick as he could, for she said the very best part of the coffee began to mount up toward heaven (from whence she said the Gods brought it to Narragansett) the moment it was parched enough, and continued to do so through all its stages of preparation until it was drank." Since time was of the essence, the drinkers were summoned to the table during the grinding, while at the same time sugar and cream were put into the cups, "which were always full twice the size of tea-cups, so as to keep the coffee hot."[52]

Hazard's account of the brewing, as those in the "gret-room" waited expectantly, was short on technical details, but Phillis did not bother with a biggin or any other newfangled or French methods: "Just as soon as Abe had ground the last grain of coffee, Phillis always put it in her coffee-pot and set it over the fire for a prescribed time known best to herself, and settled it with an egg-shell."[53]

The moment of truth, and poetry, had arrived. The coffee was taken "immediately in to the breakfast table to be drank without delay, the whole house, besides a considerable portion of out-doors, being so thoroughly impregnated with the delightful aroma of the precious decoction that all the horses, cattle, pigs, sheep, and poultry on the farm used to draw near from all the quarters to snuff the delightful perfume, and even whole flocks of passing birds have been known to light upon the chimney and roof of the house before breakfast was over."[54]

Phillis's coffee made a lasting impression on Phillis's master's grandson.

"Cheerfulness," Harper's New Monthly Magazine, *June 1860.*
(Courtesy Fall River Public Library)

He "would rather have a good cup of coffee for breakfast, accompanied with nothing else but a good jonny-cake . . . than to have everything else on earth beside, minus good coffee." Moreover, good taste in coffee was the touchstone for discrimination in all things: "I may say further that in my experiences, I have ever found that those people who have a fine taste in coffee, have a cultivated taste in everything else, including not only articles of food and drink, but all the works of nature and art, of whatever degree and kind, including sculpture and painting, poesy and love-making."[55]

Coffee was key not only to the development and refinement of the individual but also to a crucial event in modern history. Throughout *The Jonny-Cake Papers*, Hazard had repeated the tantalizing proposition "that Phillis, his grandfather's never-to-be-forgotten unparalleled colored cook" was "the remote cause of the French Revolution, and the death of Louis XVI and Marie Antoinette." Now, in the last few pages he explained what he meant by this.[56]

It seems that a "forlorn-looking critter" was taken in for the night by Hazard's grandfather. This person perked up the next morning at breakfast, upon smelling "the parfoom of Aunt Phillis' coffee." The mystery guest was none other than the "Dolphin," or crown prince, of France, who had been rejected by Marie Antoinette in favor of "Whales" of England, because Whales had offered her a sweeter-smelling perfume, "Hotto o' Roses." The Dolphin had been carrying a vial of Hotto o' Roses around the world, in hopes of replacing it with an aroma superior to it. One whiff of Phillis's coffee and he knew that he had found what he was looking for. He emptied the vial, filled it up with Phillis's supremely aromatic potion, sped back to France, interrupted the wedding of Antoinette and Whales, and won her hand for himself.[57]

But beware of getting what you wish for. "When 'Ria got to be Queen she sent all over Paris to find some French cook that could make coffee like Phillis', but she couldn't find any that could hold a dipped candle to Phillis. This spiled 'Ria's temper and made her so mad that she cut such didoes that Bonaparte came along . . . and hanged Louis and 'Ria with a green grape-vine, across a ten foot Varginny zig-zag rail fence, Louis on one side and 'Ria on t'other."[58]

Phillis's coffee proved to be vastly superior to the "Coffee, French Method of Preparing" extolled in Mrs. Lee's and other cookbooks. More broadly, Hazard concluded his ruminations on New England and nineteenth-century food and life with down-home New England cutting the super-sophisticated French down to size. It was a vein of humor that many before Hazard had mined and that Mark Twain would soon also dig into in *Huckleberry Finn*. It is not much of a stretch to call Thomas Robinson Hazard the Rhode Island Yankees' answer to Twain.[59]

Writing also of early national Rhode Island, Harriet Beecher Stowe depicted another African American cook, Candace in *The Minister's Wooing*, as a coffee maker par excellence. Candace did not need special procedures or new technology to make great coffee. In the episode discussed in chapter 7 in connection with doughnuts, the point at which Candace was summoned by her mistress to speak with Reverend Hopkins about slavery was also a critical point in the process of roasting coffee beans. Candace was not pleased to be interrupted in the delicate operation of stirring her kettleful of beans "vigorously with a pudding stick." "'Bress his [Hopkins's] heart!' said Candace, looking up perplexed. 'Wants to see me, does he? Can't nobody hab me till dis yer coffee's done; a minnit's a minnit in coffee;—but I'll be in dereckly,' she added in a patronizing tone. 'Missis, you jes' go 'long in, an' I'll be dar dereckly.'"[60]

The moment was richly ironic. To review the overall situation: slavery had not been abolished in Newport, and merchants were still profiting from the slave trade. Stowe's fictional Hopkins was modeled on the historical Samuel Hopkins, a Newport clergyman of the late eighteenth century, who denounced slavery, against the interests of many of his parishioners; Stowe's character was preparing to do the same thing. He had come to call on two of those parishioners, Candace's owners, in an effort to convince them of the rightness of his proposed course of action. As his conversation with them proceeded, he decided to ask Candace to come into the drawing room and state whether or not she desired to be liberated. Candace answered that she would indeed prefer not to be enslaved.

Between Candace's poised focus on her roasting coffee beans and her queenly condescension to her nominal mistress, it was already clear that the need to ask the question at all underscored the absurdity of slavery. Candace's command of housewifely activities was on a par with that of the heroine's mother herself, who, we were told at the start of the book, was possessed of "faculty":

> To her who has faculty nothing shall be impossible. She shall scrub floors, wash, wring, bake, brew, and yet her hands shall be small and white; she shall have no perceptible income, yet always be handsomely dressed; she shall have not a servant in her house,—with a dairy to manage, hired men to feed, a boarder or two to care for, unheard-of pickling and preserving to do,—and yet you commonly see her every afternoon sitting at her shady parlor-window behind the lilacs, cool and easy, hemming muslin cap-strings, or reading the last new book. She who hath faculty is never in a hurry, never behindhand. She can always step over to distressed Mrs. Smith, whose jelly won't come,—and stop to show Mrs. Jones how she makes her pickles so green,—and be ready to watch with poor old Mrs. Simpkins, who is down with the rheumatism.[61]

Candace lacked small white hands and other appurtenances of Caucasian independence and refinement. But that, exactly, was the irony. Faculty was a psychological and spiritual quality, that inner integrity and command of circumstance that Stowe and her sister emphasized in their contributions to household advice and instruction literature. In the assurance of her commitment to her roasting kettle, Candace evinced faculty in this sense to the utmost. As we see her throughout the novel giving off the outward and visible, housewifely signs of an inward and spiritual graciousness, we are not surprised that it was Candace who articulated the theology that Stowe considered the proper alternative to the rigid Calvinism of Samuel Hopkins. With Candace and coffee, Stowe used New England food and drink to show New England civilization overcoming its worst tendencies and beginning to realize its best ones.

Conclusion

*T*hat cuisines have the power to transmit culture and that they reflect not only material reality but also social aspiration are insights that have recently led to an avid interest in culinary history. A belief in the power of cuisine to tell a good, and complex, story has informed our study of New England cooking, from a look into the first pots placed over the fire in the English settlements of the seventeenth century to a look into the pages of the last "real Yankee" cookbooks of the early twentieth century.

The results of our efforts can be viewed from both wide and narrow angles — the wide angle including all the rich lore, anecdote, recipe variation, and social commentary that make up the bulk of this book. But what of the narrow angle? How do we summarize the social meaning of the Yankee table and the social consequences of provisioning it?

First, New England food was tied to England and Puritan New England, not least because Yankee New England valued its connection to its own history above all else. But along with acknowledgement of a condoned history, we must now recognize the suppressed connection of the cuisine to Indian foodways. We know also that New England's cuisine was standardized by those who believed in a "timeless tradition" in which they and their ancestors were the central characters. Such rhetoric served to cast many culinary changes, even reversals in the estimation of various foods, as evidence of seamless continuity. The resulting social construct has been accepted at face value into our own time.

We now know as well that New England's signature dishes evolved, in part, to enshrine the foodways of the independent farm family, even as the independent farm itself was succumbing to the economic dislocations of early capitalism. As the relations and values of the market spread from coastal cities into the countryside, the cookbooks and domestic manuals of the day told their readers how to act in their new role as consumers. In emphasizing frugality and restraint, this literature helped effect a reconciliation between the new world of increased production and wealth, on the one hand, and, on the other, Puritan and agrarian traditions of self-discipline and simplicity. And so, even as the Yankee was cast out of the paradise of the family farm, whether exiled to the expanding West or swallowed up in the city, the remembered farm family foods were sanctified. With their very plainness now redefined as their glory, they provided communion with that former cohesive society. They became, as it were, a taste of paradise lost.

Thus did subsistence foods, even some formerly "savage" foods, become the nectar and ambrosia of the gods. In creating a glorious New England culinary past and, more importantly, in asserting that past as the definitive guide to the future, the descendants of New England's first settlers constructed rituals such as Thanksgiving, narratives such as *The Jonny-Cake Papers* and the festive meals of Stowe's novels, and how-to manuals such as Child's and Beecher's cookbooks. In foods as in so many other cultural expressions, the domineering, once-dominant Yankees, through their own unique blend of myth and magic—brilliantly disguised as an aversion to myth and a disavowal of magic—attempted to create normative America out of plain, frugal New England.

What does this close look at such culinary contradictions, evasions, ambiguities, revisions, and assertions mean? It means that food has social significance. A "pots and pans" history, as one historian disparagingly called it, relying on the Yankees' own tales and myths about themselves and on the largely untapped resource of cookbooks, is another legitimate way to gather evidence with which to illuminate, sometimes critically, sometimes appreciatively, the ambitious Yankee endeavor that contributed so much to the expression of American culture.[1]

Since the awakening to social history that occurred in the mid- to late twentieth century, the formerly controlling narratives produced by the highly literate English settlers of New England have been in a sense turned against their creators as evidence of their duplicitous, if ingenious, social mastery. In some respects, our history of New England cooking is merely an extension of that profound insight about the usefulness of looking at nontraditional historical material, extended to the long-neglected female arena of domestic cookery. We can now say that the story of New England's food is not the story that the Yankees alone told. It is a tale that extends from the suppression of native contributions to an immigrant Anglo-American cuisine to the nativizing of that cuisine in response to the immigration from the Catholic countries of Europe to the new industrial cities. Those cities and their factories had been created in large part by Yankee ingenuity combined with, in a sense powered by, the surplus capital of the New England trading empire that was only one of the many remarkable but not always saintly legacies of the Puritan and Yankee world.

Notes

INTRODUCTION

1. Early, *New England Cookbook*, 58; Fischer, *Albion's Seed*, 135–36.

CHAPTER ONE

1. McManis, *Colonial New England*, 27; Bradford, *Of Plymouth Plantation*, 62. For a discussion of some of the promotional literature about New England specifically, see Cressy, *Coming Over*, 1–36.

2. To be more precise about those "thousands of native people": according to one estimate, the Indian population of the area now defined as New England at the beginning of the seventeenth century was 112,000, according to another, 139,000. Snow, *Archaeology of New England*, 33; Salisbury, *Manitou and Providence*, 22–30.

3. *Journal of the Pilgrims at Plymouth*, 34. As originally published, the title of this work was *A Relation or Iournall of the beginning and proceedings of the English Plantation settled at Plimoth in New England* (London, 1622). It is commonly known as *Mourt's Relation*. The primary author was probably Winslow.

4. Bradford, *Of Plymouth Plantation*, 66, 72. A few years before the Pilgrims set forth, the tribes along the Massachusetts coast suffered mortality rates of 80 to 90 percent from an attack of plague, chicken pox, or measles (the exact nature of the disease is still debated by historians). See Wilkie and Tager, *Historical Atlas of Massachusetts*, 13; and Snow, *Archaeology of New England*, 40.

5. Russell, *Long, Deep Furrow*, 7; Rutman, *Husbandmen of Plymouth*, 4–5. The difficulties of the first winter are a central feature of the Pilgrim story, mentioned by virtually every historian. The major source has been Bradford, *Of Plymouth Plantation*, 77.

6. Bradford, *Of Plymouth Plantation*, 62; Rutman, *Husbandmen of Plymouth*, 42, 44. For a discussion of adaptation by the English to the climate of North America in the course of the seventeenth century, see Kupperman, "Climate and Mastery of the Wilderness in Seventeenth-Century New England." For a discussion of English and Indian methods of clearing land, see Cronon, *Changes in the Land*, 48, 108, 116, 128–29.

7. *Journal of the Pilgrims at Plymouth*, 63.

8. Bradford, *Of Plymouth Plantation*, 81, 85. The idea that Squanto learned about fertilizing with fish from the English had become a scholarly consensus. See Ceci, "Fish Fertilizer"; Snow, *Archaeology of New England*, 75–76; and Hurt, *Indian Agriculture in America*, 38–39. More recently, however, the view that such a method of fertilization was a traditional native practice has been vigorously defended. See Nanepashemet, "It Smells Fishy to Me." In 1636 John Winthrop Jr.

wrote to his father about the native peoples of the Narragansett group, through whose territory in what is now southern Rhode Island he had just traveled, that "the ground there seemeth to be farre worse then the ground of the massachusett[,] being light sandy and Rocky[,] yet they have good Corne without fish; but I understand that they take this course[:] they have every one 2 feilds which after the first 2 yeares they lett one feild rest each yeare, and that kepes their ground continually in hart [fertile]." Winthrop Jr. to John Winthrop, 7 April 1636, *Winthrop Papers*, 3:246 (punctuation added).

9. Hurt, *Indian Agriculture in America*, 1–10. According to John Winthrop Jr., writing in 1662, "some English" (but by implication not all) had adopted the native practice of planting beans, pumpkins, and squashes amid their corn crop. Winthrop also described how the colonists planted corn with ploughs rather than with the hoes utilized by the natives, laying out the furrows in a grid pattern and dropping the corn kernels at the points where the furrows crossed. Mood, "John Winthrop, Jr., on Indian Corn," 127–28. See also Hardeman, *Shucks, Shocks, and Hominy Blocks*, 64–65, 75, 77–78. For an early description of native corn-bean-pumpkin tillage, see below, chap. 2, n. 1.

10. Fussell, *Story of Corn*, 203–4. Fussell erroneously calls niacin an amino acid.

11. Root and de Rochemont, *Eating in America*, 16–17; Fussell, *Story of Corn*, 176, 202–3. For a survey of the native diet, see Russell, *Indian New England before the Mayflower*, 73–95 (nutritional summary on 92–94).

12. Smith, *Popped Culture*, 10, 12–13; Columbus, *Log*, 105; *Shorter OED*, 1:1190. Corn, now the name of this grain in American English, was originally a generic term for any important cereal crop of a region or country. Thus "Indian corn" designated the primary grain of that people, although as often as not, especially in cookery contexts, Indian corn was called "Indian meal" or simply "Indian." Eventually in the United States, "corn" came to refer exclusively to this particular grain.

13. Hurt, *Indian Agriculture in America*, 1–10; Hardeman, *Shucks, Shocks, and Hominy Blocks*, 4. Although Snow, in *Archaeology of New England*, 262, 279, states that corn horticulture may have commenced in southern New England as early as 2,700 years ago, more recent writers think that this happened no more than 900–1,000 years ago. See Dincauze, "Capsule Prehistory of Southern New England," 29–30; and Smith, *Popped Culture*, 14.

14. Hardeman, *Shucks, Shocks, and Hominy Blocks*, 112; Verrill, *Foods America Gave the World*, 3–4, 20. For the food storage technology of the native peoples of southern New England, see Bennett, "Food Economy of the New England Indians," 376–78; and Hardeman, *Shucks, Shocks, and Hominy Blocks*, 112–13.

15. Early, *New England Cookbook*, 58; Verrill, *Foods America Gave the World*, 10–17.

16. Higginson, *New-Englands Plantation*, B2; Johnson, *Johnson's Wonder-Working Providence*, 114.

17. Martha Johanna Lyon to John Winthrop Jr., 23 March 1649, *Winthrop Papers*, 5:323; Johnson, *Johnson's Wonder-Working Providence*, 115.

18. Field, "'Peculiar Manuerance,'" 18; Johnson, *Johnson's Wonder-Working Providence*, 210.

19. Johnson, *Johnson's Wonder-Working Providence*, 85. For another passage in which corn is presented as a necessary evil, see Bradford, *Of Plymouth Plantation*, 122.

20. Panschar, *Economic Development*, 8.

21. McCance and Widdowson, *Breads White and Brown*, 4 (quoting Plautus).

22. Wilson, *Food and Drink in Britain*, 233; Henisch, *Fast and Feast*, 157; Chaucer, *Chaucer's Poetry*, 370 (line 24), 10 (lines 147, 146); both Chaucer quotations are also found in McCance and Widdowson, *Breads White and Brown*, 20. See also Slack, *Northumbrian Fare*, 5.

23. Anderson, "'Solid Sufficiency,'" 163–64 (Harrison quotation), 173.

24. Braudel, *Structures of Everyday Life*, 137; Wilson, *Food and Drink in Britain*, 246, 260–61.

25. For a discussion of the economic developments in sixteenth- and seventeenth-century England that encouraged immigration to North America, see below, chap. 4, nn. 1–5. For the dietary consequences of these largely adverse economic circumstances, see Braudel, *Structures of Everyday Life*, 194–96; Drummond and Wilbraham, *Englishman's Food*, 49–51, 55, 157; and Shammas, *Pre-Industrial Consumer in England and America*, 129. For the difficulties encountered in growing wheat, see McMahon, "Comfortable Subsistence," 31–33, 52–54; Russell, *Long, Deep Furrow*, 22–23, 68; and McManis, *Colonial New England*, 89, 91–92. In a quantitative study of food consumption in Deerfield, Massachusetts, in the eighteenth century, the author states that "wheat transactions [were] by far the most extensive" of the exchanges of grains recorded in the residents' account books and daybooks that provide most of her evidence. Derven, "Wholesome, Toothsome, and Diverse," 52. This finding conflicts with those of McMahon and others cited above. McMahon provides abundant evidence from Middlesex County, Massachusetts, probate inventories and widows' portions in support of her conclusion that Indian corn "remained the standard bread grain for two hundred years" (32). Derven's conclusion that wheat was consumed in much greater quantity than corn and other grains arises in part from the nature of her evidence. Transactions involving a commodity that was considered more valuable, wheat, are more likely to have been recorded in account books than those involving one that was considered less valuable, Indian corn. In addition, Derven's own evidence supports her conclusion only shakily at best. Almost 400 pounds worth of Indian corn transactions (more than 8.75 bushels) were recorded over an eighteen-year period in her sources, whereas thirty-nine years, or more than twice as many, were required to record more than 550 pounds of wheat transactions. Presumably, something on the order of twice the quantity of corn, or almost 800 pounds, was exchanged during the same thirty-nine years. See Derven, "Wholesome, Toothsome, and Diverse," 62 (table 1, grain section). Calculation of the weight of a bushel of cornmeal is based on the estimate in Rombauer and Becker, *Joy of Cooking*, 594, that three cups of cornmeal weigh one pound.

26. Winthrop, *Life and Letters of John Winthrop*, 1:312. Additional versions of Winthrop's essay are found in *Winthrop Papers*, 2:106–41.

27. This polarized ideology, which we shall be emphasizing, did not of course pre-

clude daily, sometimes amicable, interaction between English and Indians, as well as many other forms of cultural interchange besides the one by which the English came to utilize maize in their cookery. On the colonists' struggles to maintain an English identity, see Lepore, *Name of War*, 5–8. Some people did speak up in favor of Indian corn. In 1662 John Winthrop Jr. was asked by the chemist and agricultural reformer Robert Boyle to provide the Royal Society with information about "Indian Corne." Winthrop complied with a brief essay that was filled with genuine appreciation. He spoke of "this Beautifull noble Eare of Corne" and stated that "much Experience" had proven such corn to be "wholesome and pleasant for Food of which great Variety may be made out of it." Mood, "John Winthrop, Jr., on Indian Corn," 125. But Winthrop was in general far more curious and open-minded than the average New Englander, and the entire context of his discussion was one of advanced, scientific, reform-minded thought—in other words, of a distinctly minority perspective.

28. On gluten see *Cambridge World History of Food*, 1:1013, 2:1878.

29. Wilson, *Food and Drink in Britain*, 308, 310–11, 315; Anderson, "'Solid Sufficiency,'" 214.

30. Wilson, *Food and Drink in Britain*, 315–16. The boiling of pudding in bags was not unknown prior to the seventeenth century; see Henisch, *Fast and Feast*, 123; and McCance and Widdowson, *Breads White and Brown*, 11.

31. Bowles and Towle, *Secrets of New England Cooking*, 175, 177. The name "whortleberry" continued in usage into the nineteenth century, as in the recipe for whortleberry pudding in Child, *American Frugal Housewife*, 64.

32. Many descriptions of the colonial New England kitchen and hearth are available. See for example Earle, *Home Life in Colonial Days*, 56–61; Dow, *Every Day Life in the Massachusetts Bay Colony*, 34–35, 39–41, 91; Gould, *Early American House*, 24–25; Bowles and Towle, *Secrets of New England Cooking*, 64–65; Whitehill, *Food, Drink, and Recipes of Early New England*, 8–9; Doudiet, "Coastal Maine Cooking," 215–19; and Oliver, *Saltwater Foodways*, 7–11. The sixteenth- and seventeenth-century English hearthside, from which that of colonial New England before long became indistinguishable, is described in Hess, *Martha Washington's Booke of Cookery*, 20–21. For a discussion of the place of the hearth and fireplace within the typical New England house plan of the seventeenth century, see Cummings, *Framed Houses of Massachusetts Bay*, 28–29. See also Bacon, *Forgotten Art of Building and Using a Brick Bake Oven*, 12–13. According to Braudel, *Structures of Everyday Life*, 298, the use of a chimney and fireplace set in the wall for cooking, as opposed to an open hearth with a smokehole in the ceiling, emerged everywhere in Europe in approximately the twelfth century. In Britain, it took "another four hundred years before wall fireplaces were constructed in every home." Thus, William Harrison spoke of this change as having occurred, at least among English yeomen, only a generation or two before 1577. See Wilson, *Food and Drink in Britain*, 84; and Anderson, "'Solid Sufficiency,'" 158–59 (quoting Harrison). For a discussion of bake ovens, see below, chap. 2, nn. 21–26, 37.

33. Bowles and Towle, *Secrets of New England Cooking*, 176.

34. Ibid., 177. For an instance of chilled and solidified boiled bag pudding, see Webster, *Improved Housewife*, 77. For the persistence of boiled bag puddings, see, for example, ibid., 75, 77; Simmons, *American Cookery* (introduction by Wilson), 26; Child, *American Frugal Housewife*, 61; Hale, *Good Housekeeper*, 105–6; Beecher, *Miss Beecher's Domestic Receipt Book*, 104, 113; Knight, *Tit-Bits*, 45, 120; *Godey's*, March 1882, 281; and Wright, *New England Cook Book*, 156. Mrs. Knight stated (*Tit-Bits*, 45) that she "much prefers the *tin* pudding boiler," which according to Oliver (*Saltwater Foodways*, 38) had become standard kitchen equipment by the 1870s. Metal containers for boiling puddings had been in use at least since the late eighteenth century. Amelia Simmons mentioned them, as well as bags and stoneware, in her boiled Indian pudding recipe given below, n. 37.

35. Bowles and Towle, *Secrets of New England Cooking*, 175–76.

36. Ibid., 176; King, *When I Lived in Salem*, 98. For a discussion of the emergence in general of the dessert course, see below, chap. 6, nn. 77–80. According to Andrew F. Smith, "serving pudding first was intended to check the appetite for meats, but as puddings increasingly became sweet, they were usually reserved for the end of the meal." Smith, "In Praise of Maize," 198.

37. Simmons, *American Cookery* (introduction by Wilson), 26. These recipes appeared verbatim in Emerson, *New-England Cookery*, 47, which was largely cribbed from Simmons. It is outside the scope of this book to discuss the issues involved in arriving at a definitive edition of *American Cookery* from among the myriad revisions and claims for authorship of the many early versions of the work. The author of the second edition corrected errors in the first edition, inserted additional recipes, and even disavowed and removed an entire section on purchasing foodstuffs. However, from its first appearance, *American Cookery* was a best-seller, and all versions and editions were frequently reprinted. For that reason, and also in the interest of constructing a readable narrative, we refer to "Simmons" as the author of all the material in both the first (Hartford) and the second (Albany) editions. For further discussion see Simmons, *American Cookery* (introduction by Wilson), xvii–xix; and Simmons, *American Cookery* (introduction by Hess), ix–xii.

38. Hazard, *Jonny-Cake Papers*, 53.

39. Child, *American Frugal Housewife*, 61. Child is now primarily remembered as the author of the Thanksgiving poem "Over the River and through the Wood"; see chap. 2. Sweeteners are further discussed in chaps. 6 and 7.

40. Lee, *Cook's Own Book*, 161; Hale, *Good Housekeeper*, 105–6. Authorship of *The Cook's Own Book* was attributed on the title page to "a Boston Housekeeper," who was subsequently identified as Mrs. N. K. M. Lee. No evidence confirming the existence of such a person has ever been found, but, as with Simmons, for the sake of narrative convenience we shall continue to give the name "Lee" to the author of this collection. Many of the recipes in the collection were copied from other cookbooks. Such a practice was typical at the time. However, it was untypical of Lee to have copied from Child, since as we shall see, her culinary inclinations generally stood in stark contrast to those of Child. Hale is best

remembered as the person most responsible for the establishment of Thanksgiving as a national holiday (see below, chaps. 2 and 6) and as the author of "Mary Had a Little Lamb."

41. Leslie, *Directions for Cookery*, 302–3; Prescott, *Valuable Receipts*, 19; Webster, *Improved Housewife*, 77–78. In another of her many publications, Eliza Leslie turned Indian pudding into a variation on traditional English plum pudding; see "Peach Indian Pudding" in *Lady's Receipt Book*, 115. Midcentury Indian pudding recipes may also be found in Mann, *Christianity in the Kitchen*, 65–66; Hunt, *Good Bread*, 16; and Mendall, *New Bedford Practical Receipt Book*, 46–47. The Indian puddings in Allen, *Housekeeper's Assistant*, 50–51, were copied, with slight variation, from Simmons.

42. Bowles and Towle, *Secrets of New England Cooking*, 64–65; Stowe, *Minister's Wooing*, 156 (chap. 16).

43. Stowe, *Minister's Wooing*, 263 (chap. 30).

44. Knight, *Tit-Bits*, 49–50, 120; *Godey's*, June 1880, 561; *Godey's*, March 1882, 281; Turner, *New England Cook Book*, 161; Wright, *New England Cook Book*, 155–56. There is a recipe for boiled Indian pudding, bag and all, in Wright's volume (156); her cookbook is marked by self-conscious antiquarianism.

45. Early, *New England Cookbook*, 136.

46. Wolcott, *New England Yankee Cook Book*, 177, 72. According to Thomas Robinson Hazard, there was more than nostalgia and mythmaking involved in the insistence that corn be "slowly ground between fine grained stones of Rhode Island granite." Coarse-grained millstones produced a coarser "round" cornmeal, whereas "Narragansett granite rock, most of which is of a peculiarly fine grain," produced a finer "soft feeling flat meal." Hazard went on to contrast the millers of the later nineteenth century with those of his childhood and youth. Whereas in the hands of the former the grain was "rolled, re-rolled, tumbled, and mumbled over and over again, until all its life and sweetness had been vitiated or dispelled," those earlier millers had been true artists: "See the white-coated old man now first rub the meal, as it falls, carefully and thoughtfully between his fingers and thumb, then graduate the feed and raise or lower the upper stone, with that nice sense of adjustment, observance, and discretion that a Raphael might be supposed to exercise in the mixing and grinding of his colors for a Madonna, or a Canova in putting the last touch of his chisel to the statue of a god, until, by repeated handling, he had found the ambrosia [cornmeal] to have acquired exactly the desired coolness and flatness—the result of its being cut into fine slivers by the nicely-balanced revolving stones." Hazard, *Jonny-Cake Papers*, 18–20. While heavily nostalgic, Hazard's 1879 account offered a lucid culinary and gastronomic rationale for a particular type of cornmeal milling—by slow grinding with a carefully specified variety of rock. When this tradition was reinvented in 1939, such nuances of food production had vanished and there remained only sentimental evocation of old-time New England.

47. Anderson, "'Solid Sufficiency,'" 177–78; Wilson, *Food and Drink in Britain*, 213; Smith, *Compleat Housewife*, 133; Glasse, *Art of Cookery Made Plain and Easy* (glossary and notes by Davidson), 111, 187.

48. Child, *American Frugal Housewife*, 65.

49. Beecher, *Miss Beecher's Domestic Receipt Book*, 108; Knight, *Tit-Bits*, 104; *Aunt Mary's New England Cook Book*, 55–56 (the dish is there called "Fried Indian Pudding"); Lincoln and Barrows, *Home Science Cook Book*, 20–21; Wolcott, *New England Yankee Cook Book*, 164–65. Child's recipe reappeared verbatim in Hale, *Good Housekeeper*, 106. Eliza Leslie complained that "Indian mush . . . is seldom made properly, or rather *wholesomely*" in *More Receipts*, preface. She was well advised to avoid the name hasty pudding, since in her own recipe for Indian mush she stated unequivocally that the dish was "exactly the reverse" of "wholesome and nutritious . . . if made in haste. It is not too long to have it altogether three or four hours over the fire; on the contrary it will be much the better for it." Leslie, *Directions for Cookery*, 301–2.

50. Barlow, "Hasty Pudding," 88. For native methods of utilizing cornmeal in conjunction with boiling water, see Bennett, "Food Economy of the New England Indians," 380.

51. Barlow, "Hasty Pudding," 96. Waldo Lincoln, the first bibliographer of American cookbooks, defended his listing of twenty-three printings of Barlow's poem on the grounds that "it describes quite meticulously the preparation of this once popular and quite important dish"; see Smith, "In Praise of Maize," 203.

52. Barlow, "Hasty Pudding," 97–98. Thomas Robinson Hazard revived Barlow's pedantry about hasty pudding consumption techniques, stating in 1879 that "people nowadays don't know how to eat hasty pudding and milk. A spoon should be dipped into the milk before it lifts the pudding, to keep it from sticking, which should then be dropped into the porringer of milk, so as each mouthful shall remain separate." Hazard, *Jonny-Cake Papers*, 54.

53. Deetz, *In Small Things Forgotten*, 83–87, 168–70; Bushman, *Refinement of America*, 76–78.

54. Barlow, "Hasty Pudding," 91. For descriptions of other corn poetry, see Hardeman, *Shucks, Shocks, and Hominy Blocks*, 43, 220–23; and Smith, "In Praise of Maize," 195. The English pamphleteer William Cobbett, who had lived for a time on Long Island, published a book about Indian corn in 1828 that included several pages in praise of what he called mush. Cobbett was attempting to encourage widespread consumption of corn in Britain, as a nutritious alternative for working people to potatoes, oats, and bread. He railed against the resistance to his campaign on the part of people who had "such a *prejudice* against any sort of meal or flour, that does not proceed from wheat"; see Cobbett, *Treatise on Cobbett's Corn*, 208. The advocacy of corn consumption by Cobbett and others paid dividends in the 1840s when, in an unexpected reenactment of the situation of the first settlers of New England, corn imports from America provided some relief to those suffering from the famine in Ireland; indeed, corn had already been imported into Ireland during an early period of dearth in 1830. See Miller, *Emigrants and Exiles*, 205, 283, 284, 301. The famine had an impact on the world of cookbook publishing. Eliza Leslie's *The Indian Meal Book: Comprising the Best American Receipts for the Various Preparations of that Excellent Article*, was reprinted in London and Dublin in 1846, supplementing its original purpose of

assisting "strangers newly arrived in the British-American provinces, and consequently unacquainted with the various modes" of corn cookery, with that of encouraging "the introduction of Indian Meal into Great Britain and Ireland" (Leslie, *Corn Meal Cookery*, xix). Another contribution along these lines was a pamphlet written by a namesake of one of the present authors: Staveley, *American Indian Meal and Hominy Receipt Book*.

55. Williams, *Key into the Language of America*, 11–12; Mood, "John Winthrop, Jr., on Indian Corn," 130.

56. Bowles and Towle, *Secrets of New England Cooking*, 4; Fussell, *Story of Corn*, 196, 198; Mariani, *Dictionary of American Food and Drink*, 195–96; Orcutt, *Good Old Dorchester*, 33 (quoting Clap).

57. Fussell, *Story of Corn*, 196–97. See also Hardeman, *Shucks, Shocks, and Hominy Blocks*, 142.

58. Mood, "John Winthrop, Jr., on Indian Corn," 130. For virtually identical methods offered almost two centuries later, see Alcott, *Young House-Keeper*, 408–9.

59. Lincoln and Barrows, *Home Science Cook Book*, 19–20. In 1879 Thomas Robinson Hazard had distinguished between "your modern tasteless western corn, hulled with potash" and "the hulled corn of old . . . hulled in the nice sweet lye made from fresh hard oak and maple-wood ashes." Hazard, *Jonny-Cake Papers*, 57. On potash, soda, and similar chemicals, see below, chap. 7, nn. 39–44. Instructions on the use of lye in hulling were also presented in Wolcott, *New England Yankee Cook Book*, 106; and Rombauer and Becker, *Joy of Cooking*, 200. See also Hardeman, *Shucks, Shocks, and Hominy Blocks*, 142–43.

60. Cobbett, *Treatise on Cobbett's Corn*, 210–12. There was another strain of Yankee corn pudding that was based on neither cornmeal nor hulled corn but rather on the more tender incarnations of the grain—either the particular variety known as sweet corn, or green corn ("the unripe and tender ears" of any variety [*Shorter OED*, 1:828]). For typical recipes see Beecher, *Miss Beecher's Domestic Receipt Book*, 114; Knight, *Tit-Bits*, 46, 58; Inman, *Rhode Island Rule Book*, 18; Lincoln and Barrows, *Home Science Cook Book*, 152; Bowles and Towle, *Secrets of New England Cooking*, 188.

61. Oliver, *Saltwater Foodways*, 12; Rutman, *Husbandmen of Plymouth*, 43–45. See also Sedgwick, *Hope Leslie*, 61 (vol. 1, chap. 5): "The meadows were, for the first time, enriched with patches of English grain, which the new settlers had sown, scantily, by way of experiment, prudently occupying the greatest portion of the rich mould, with the native Indian corn."

62. McManis, *Colonial New England*, 91–92; Russell, *Long, Deep Furrow*, 22–23; Rutman, *Husbandmen of Plymouth*, 46; McMahon, "Comfortable Subsistence," 32; Dow, *Every Day Life in the Massachusetts Bay Colony*, 157; Butler, *Becoming America*, 60. For a discussion of the availability of wheat flour and bread in colonial Boston, see Friedmann, "Victualling Colonial Boston," 193–95.

63. McMahon, "Comfortable Subsistence," 32; Rutman, *Husbandmen of Plymouth*, 46; below, chap. 6, n. 12, chap. 8, n. 3; McManis, *Colonial New England*, 91; Drummond and Wilbraham, *Englishman's Food*, 43 (quoting Johnson, *Dictionary*, 1st ed. [1755]).

64. Mood, "John Winthrop, Jr., on Indian Corn," 130.

65. David, *English Bread and Yeast Cookery*, 90, 94, 98, 99, 101; Wilson, *Food and Drink in Britain*, 231. Simmons gave a recipe for emptins; see Simmons, *American Cookery* (introduction by Wilson), 47, and Simmons, *American Cookery* (introduction by Hess), 64, 69 (glossary).

66. Bowles and Towle, *Secrets of New England Cooking*, 68; Earle, *Home Life in Colonial Days*, 67.

67. Earle, *Home Life in Colonial Days*, 67; Bowles and Towle, *Secrets of New England Cooking*, 68.

68. Hazard, *Jonny-Cake Papers*, 27.

69. Child, *American Frugal Housewife*, 76–77, 78; Hale, *Good Housekeeper*, 28. John Winthrop Jr. had also mentioned the inclusion of wheat back in 1662, before the blast had made wheat more scarce in New England.

70. Hale, *Good Housekeeper*, 27–30; Child, *American Frugal Housewife*, 77, 79–80; Beecher, *Miss Beecher's Domestic Receipt Book*, 85–86. See also *Cook Not Mad*, 34; Hunt, *Good Bread*, 8–9; and Chadwick, *Home Cookery*, 3. To appreciate the magnitude of Hale's eight-pound loaf, involving a total of six quarts of meal, it is worth noting that in Thomas Robinson Hazard's grandfather's household, three quarts of meal, in the same proportions specified by Hale, were sufficient to make "large round loaves of the size of a half-peck measure." Hazard, *Jonny-Cake Papers*, 27. Regarding yeast, Elizabeth David writes that at this time "there had been many attempts to produce a form of solidified yeast which would be more stable and less bitter than ale or beer yeasts and more efficient than those obtained from a solution or wort," made with the types of ingredients listed above in the text. David, *English Bread and Yeast Cookery*, 94. Beecher, in *Miss Beecher's Domestic Receipt Book*, 86, included two recipes for solidified yeast cakes, one made with cornmeal, the other with wheat flour.

71. Beecher, *Miss Beecher's Domestic Receipt Book*, 89; Prescott, *Valuable Receipts*, 16. For molasses in later nineteenth-century recipes, see for example "Yankee Brown Bread," in *Godey's*, February 1880, 178. For saleratus, see below, chap. 7, n. 41.

72. Crawford, *Old New England Inns*, 221–22 (quoting Adam Hodgson); Hazard, *Jonny-Cake Papers*, 28.

73. Quincy, *Life of Josiah Quincy*, 26. Quincy's recollections help to explain the otherwise anomalous fact that as of 1745, the family of the Reverend Jonathan Ashley of Deerfield, Massachusetts, was "expected to consume almost four times as much wheat as Indian corn"; see Coe and Coe, "Mid-Eighteenth-Century Food and Drink on the Massachusetts Frontier," 41. Note Quincy's acknowledgement of New England's reliance on the importation of wheat from regions farther south.

74. Stowe, *Oldtown Folks*, 224 (chap. 22).

75. Oliver, *Saltwater Foodways*, 49.

76. Nissenbaum, *Sex, Diet, and Debility in Jacksonian America*, 3 (quoting Emerson); Hale, *Good Housekeeper*, 27; Beecher, *Miss Beecher's Domestic Receipt Book*, 90–91. Beginning in the 1740s, "Brown Bread," containing varying proportions

of cornmeal, was included among the types subjected to price regulation; see Brayley, *Bakers and Baking in Massachusetts*, 94, 96.

77. Knight, *Tit-Bits*, 35. Hess, *Martha Washington's Booke of Cookery*, 451, notes that the practice of naming recipes after those from whom one learned them goes back to the era of manuscript cookbooks. For varying nomenclatures and proportions of grains but a fairly consistent proportion of sweetener, see, for example, *Aunt Mary's New England Cook Book*, 25; *Meriden Cook Book*, 63; Turner, *New England Cook Book*, 129–30; and Wright, *New England Cook Book*, 184–86. The use of coffee cans as steaming containers, later to become a widespread practice, was recommended in a 1902 cookbook; see Lincoln and Barrows, *Home Science Cook Book*, 38 (baking powder cans were also given as an option). Knight's recipe did not specify the container.

78. Bowles and Towle, *Secrets of New England Cooking*, 139; Hazard, *Jonny-Cake Papers*, 28.

79. Hazard, *Jonny-Cake Papers*, 28. There was an additional type of leavened bread made with cornmeal (but not with rye), which was known variously as "Amadama" and "Anadama" bread. Each of these names was accompanied by a myth of origin. In the first case, "the story goes that [this corn bread] was named for the woman [from Rockport, Massachusetts] who first made it. If she ever was away from home when her husband arrived, you could hear him booming, 'Where am 'er, damn 'er?' Finally she was known as Amadama." Bowles and Towle, *Secrets of New England Cooking*, 140–41. "Anadama" bread was supposedly first prepared "by a fisherman who had a lazy wife and often had to do his own cooking." He named his creation "after his wife, 'Anna, damn her.' Polite society modified this to Anadama Bread." Wolcott, *New England Yankee Cook Book*, 145.

80. The origin of the street name in Chelsea, Vermont, was related as follows by one of the traditionalist writers: a peddler, arriving in the town at noon, walked down the street to sell his wares. At every house he came to, the people were eating Johnny cake. "Tarnation, if 'tain't Johnnycake Lane!" he is said to have exclaimed. Early, *New England Cookbook*, 107. The story is told slightly differently in Wolcott, *New England Yankee Cook Book*, 133.

81. Wood, *New Englands Prospect*, 71; Karr, *Indian New England*, 77 (Champlain), 81 (Gookin); Williams, *Key into the Language of America*, 96–97, 114.

82. Bragdon, *Native People of Southern New England*, 104; Pillsbury, *No Foreign Food*, 26–27. Bragdon's statement that the New England Algonquians made "fried" bread is perhaps open to question. M. K. Bennett found "no mention . . . of frying" in the sources he examined on cooking techniques utilized by those groups, although he notes the instance in Mary Rowlandson's captivity narrative in which the Indian leader, King Philip himself, fed her with "a pancake about as big as two fingers; it was made of parched wheat, beaten and fried in bear's grease, . . . I thought I never tasted pleasanter meat in my life." See Bennett, "Food Economy of the New England Indians," 379; and Rowlandson, "Sovereignty and Goodness of God," 47. Bennett's further inference that possibly "frying came to be used late in the [seventeenth century], after iron

pans could be had from the English" is not entirely valid. As noted below (chap. 6, n. 62), several scholars have concluded that the North American Indians began obtaining metal cooking vessels through trade with Europeans early in the seventeenth century, if not earlier.

83. The contortions to which the early colonists subjected themselves in order to avoid native or Scottish open-hearth bread cookery is illustrated by John Winthrop Jr.'s description of their efforts to oven-bake a bread made with glutenless cornmeal alone: "if it be mixed into a stiff past, it will not be good as when it is made into a thinner mixture a little stiffer then the Battar for Pancakes, or puddings, and then baked in a very hott oven, standing all day or all Night therein, therefore some use to bake it in panns like puddings. But the most ordinary way is this, the Oven being very hott they have a great Wooden Dish fastened to a long staff, which may hold the quantity of a Pottle [half a gallon], and that being filled, they empty it on an heape in the Oven, upon the bare floore thereof cleane Swept, and so fill the Oven, and usually lay a second laying upon the top of the first, because the first will otherwise be too thinn for the proportion of a Loafe because it will spread in the oven at the first pouring of it in: . . . some will fill the whole floore of the Oven as one intire Body and must then cut it out in greate peices; In just such manner handled it wilbe (if baked enough) of a good darke yellow Colour, but otherwise white which is not so wholesome nor pleasant, as when well baked of a deeper Colour." That these gargantuan oven-baked corn pancakes amounted to an exercise in futility, attempting to treat corn as though it were wheat or rye, is further indicated by Winthrop's statement that yeast or other leavening was used in preparing them. Mood, "John Winthrop, Jr., on Indian Corn," 129-30. The minority that chose to bake their cornmeal batter or dough "in panns like puddings" were on the right track, of course. Although what Winthrop described sounds similar to some of the methods of baking Ryaninjun that we have just encountered, the crucial difference was the presence of a grain containing gluten in the latter and its absence from the former. Dumping what was essentially the substance of Johnny cake onto the oven floor and leaving it to fend for itself was not a procedure that was destined to endure.

84. Wood, *New Englands Prospect*, 71; Williams, *Key into the Language of America*, 11. Laurel Thatcher Ulrich states, in *Age of Homespun*, 45, that native "parched maize" was called "*nokake* in some dialects and *yohicake, yoheag, yokeg*, or *nokehick* in others." John Winthrop Jr. provided additional detail on how Nocake or Nókehick was made: "a very Common way of dressing of it [by the natives] is by parching it among the Ashes, which they do so artificially, by putting it amongst the hott Embers, and continually stirring of it that it wilbe thoroughly parched without any burneing, but be very tender, and turned almost quite the inside outward, which wilbe almost white and flowry, this they sift very cleane from the Ashes, and then beate it in their wooden Mortars with a long Stone for a pestle, into fine meale, which is a constant food amongst them, both at home, and especially when they travell, being putt up into a Bagg for their Journey, being at all times ready, and may be Eaten either drie, or mixed with water."

Mood, "John Winthrop, Jr., on Indian Corn," 129. Smith, in *Popped Culture*, 19, thinks that Winthrop's phrase "turned almost quite the inside outward, which wilbe almost white and flowry" was a description of popped corn. The earliest English references to Nókehick were probably those in *Journal of the Pilgrims at Plymouth*, 46, 59. According to Hardeman, *Shucks, Shocks, and Hominy Blocks*, 141, "when parched grains were recooked they had much of the original flavor of fresh, green corn."

85. Henisch, *Fast and Feast*, 99; Wilson, *Food and Drink in Britain*, 244 (quoting Froissart); Wood, *New Englands Prospect*, 72.

86. Hazard, *Jonny-Cake Papers*, 32–33.

87. *Shorter OED*, 1:1068. In *Dictionary of American Biography*, 10:17, doubt is cast on the connection of the expression "Brother Jonathan" specifically with Jonathan Trumbull. But the author acknowledges that the British did use this phrase "to designate the Americans as early as March 1776."

88. Simmons, *American Cookery* (introduction by Wilson), 34.

89. Hazard, *Jonny-Cake Papers*, 28–30, described the "jonny-cake" prepared in his grandfather's household at roughly the same time that Simmons published her cookbook. The cornmeal was first scalded with boiling water. Fluid was then added, "sometimes new milk, at other times pure water, to make it of a proper consistence." After kneading, the dough was placed on a "jonny-cake board," which had to be "a red oak board taken from the middle part of the head of a flour barrel." Before baking, the cake was "well dressed on the surface with rich sweet cream to keep it from blistering when placed before the fire. . . . The cake was next placed upright on the hearth before a bright, green hardwood fire. This kind of fire was indispensable also. And so too was the heart-shaped flat-iron that supported it, which was shaped exactly to meet every exigency. First the flat's front smooth surface was placed immediately against the back of the jonny-cake to hold it in a perpendicular position before the fire until the main part of the cake was sufficiently baked. Then a slanting side of the flat-iron was turned so as to support the board in a reclining position until the bottom and top extremities of the cake were in turn baked, and lastly, the board was slewed round and rested partly against the handle of the flat-iron, so as to bring the ends of the cake in a better position to receive the heat from the fire. . . . When the jonny-cake was sufficiently done on the first side, a knife was passed between it and the board, and it was dextrously turned and anointed, as before, with sweet, golden-tinged cream, previous to being placed again before the fire."

90. Simmons, *American Cookery* (introduction by Wilson), x.

91. Axtell, *European and the Indian*, 51.

92. Cummings, *Framed Houses of Massachusetts Bay*; Cronon, *Changes in the Land*, 128–32. For a discussion of the environmental impact of English livestock, see below, chap. 5, nn. 9–10. And for a discussion of Roger Williams's partial dissent from this approach to native/English relations, see Stavely, "Roger Williams and the Enclosed Gardens of New England." Hazard, *Jonny-Cake Papers*, 57–58, discussed "the great Indian dish called no-cake" as something entirely distinct from Johnny cake. He noted that it was used by the natives as a traveling

food, but he did not link this function to the emergence of the names journey cake and Johnny cake. Karen Hess links Johnny cake not only culinarily but
also linguistically to the oat breads of the north of Britain: "The name comes
from *jannock*, a word from northern England, especially Lancashire, referring
to 'oaten bread.'" Simmons, *American Cookery* (introduction by Hess), xiii. See
also Hess, introduction to *English Bread and Yeast Cookery*, v. This explanation
does not take account of the fact that, as noted above (n. 23), "oat cake" had
not been part of the diet of the "southern lowland" emigrants to New England.
Anderson, "'Solid Sufficiency,'" 173.

93. Mariani, *Dictionary of American Food and Drink*, 382; Child, *American Frugal
Housewife*, 75; Cutler, *O Brave New Words*, 21; Bowles and Towle, *Secrets of New
England Cooking*, 139, 144; Hooker, *Food and Drink in America*, 32.

94. *Shorter OED*, 1:248; Wilson, *Food and Drink in Britain*, 250, 246.

95. Root and de Rochemont, *Eating in America*, 106; Hardeman, *Shucks, Shocks,
and Hominy Blocks*, 145; Mariani, *Dictionary of American Food and Drink*, 282;
Barlow, "Hasty Pudding," 92. Also appearing on Barlow's list of lesser dishes
were boiled bag puddings and "all of Indian that the bake-pan knows," a category which presumably included baked Indian pudding. Hazard, *Jonny-Cake
Papers*, 51, referred to "them pumpkin jonny-cakes."

96. Child, *American Frugal Housewife*, 75–76.

97. Hale, *Ladies' New Book of Cookery*, 390; Beecher, *Miss Beecher's Domestic Receipt
Book*, 292–93, 98.

98. Beecher, *Miss Beecher's Domestic Receipt Book*, 292. See also Howland, *American
Economical Housekeeper*, 18. Thomas Robinson Hazard remembered eating "half
and half flour and Indian jonny-cake . . . very delightful for a change," at his
grandfather's house well before the opening of the Erie Canal. This indicates
the grandfather's relatively high social position. Hazard also ate "jonny-cakes"
made with a mixture of rye and cornmeal and even some made with rye meal
only. Hazard, *Jonny-Cake Papers*, 49, 51.

99. Webster, *Improved Housewife*, 133. For additional midcentury Johnny cake
recipes, see *Cook Not Mad*, 36; Alcott, *Young House-Keeper*, 402–3; *Roger Cookery*, 11; Bliss, *Practical Cook Book*, 112–13; and Hunt, *Good Bread*, 11–12.

100. Hazard, *Jonny-Cake Papers*, 203.

101. Oliver, *Saltwater Foodways*, 45, 404 n. 37.

102. Ibid., 160–61; Wolcott, *New England Yankee Cook Book*, 132; Inman, *Rhode
Island Rule Book*, 8.

103. Fussell, *Story of Corn*, 222–23; Mariani, *Dictionary of American Food and Drink*,
282. If Thomas Robinson Hazard is to be believed, the dispute between Newport and South Counties was a fairly recent development in the 1890s. In 1879
Hazard began the first of his *Jonny-Cake Papers* with an unequivocal declaration
uniting Washington (or South) and Newport Counties as the only two places
in the entire world where genuine Rhode Island white corn meal could be obtained (17). In *Echoes from South County Kitchens*, 102–8, "Johnny" was spelled
with an "h" in seven Johnny cake recipes; four were baked (including one called
"Old Rhode Island Johnny Cakes"), two were fried, and one was fried and then

baked. Nevertheless, the distinctive value of the Rhode Island Johnny cake tradition was upheld in these recipes. The serving instructions in "Lippitt Hill Johnny Cakes" (104) concluded with an exhortation to "thank God for R.I. flint corn."

104. Knight, *Tit-Bits*, 38–39; Patten, *Our New England Family Recipes*, 54. For additional late-nineteenth- and early-twentieth-century Johnny cakes exemplifying the tradition here outlined, see *Godey's*, May 1881, 472, and February 1882, 185; and Turner, *New England Cook Book*, 133.

105. Early, *New England Cookbook*, 107–8. "A spider is a black frying pan that once had legs and sat on the hearth. Spiders haven't legs now and no longer sit on the hearth. They are excellent things to cook in because the heat spreads evenly over their broad black bottoms." Ibid., 110–11. See also Booth, *Hung, Strung, and Potted*, 19. For other nineteenth-century corn bread recipes, besides that of Child (above, n. 96), calling for baking in a griddle or spider, see Howland, *American Economical Housekeeper*, 26; and *Godey's*, April 1880, 370. Regarding the warnings against cutting hot bread, compare the admonition in the recipe for "Steamed Boston Brown Bread" in Bowles and Towle, *Secrets of New England Cooking*, 144, that "brown bread should never be cut with a knife, it should be sliced with the aid of a string."

106. Child, *American Frugal Housewife*, 76; Hale, *Ladies' New Book of Cookery*, 389–90. See also Wright, *New England Cook Book*, 196–97.

107. Johnson, *Highways and Byways of New England*, 215–16; Early, *New England Cookbook*, 110. Thomas Robinson Hazard's recollection of bannock, "made of eggs, milk, and fine Indian meal, mixed thin and baked in a pan over the fire," incorporated the basics of Child's recipe. Hazard, *Jonny-Cake Papers*, 49. The anonymous Nantucket miller's term "corn cake" was used frequently in recipes of the nineteenth and early twentieth centuries, as in "Sachem's Head Corn Cake" (Beecher, *Miss Beecher's Domestic Receipt Book*, 99), "Indian Corn Cakes" (Webster, *Improved Housewife*, 132), "Corn Cakes" (*Meriden Cook Book*, 68), and "Boston Corn Cake" (Wright, *New England Cook Book*, 181–82).

108. Cutler, *O Brave New Words*, 21; *Echoes from South County Kitchens*, 107, 110; Vaughan, *Yankee Hill-Country Cooking*, 100–101. Mariani, in *Dictionary of American Food and Drink*, 382, states that no recipes for spoon bread were published until 1906. However, a recipe for "Soft Corn-Bread" that ended with the instruction to "serve it with a spoon from the same dish in which it is baked" was included in a section of "Distinctively Southern Dishes" in Ronald, *Century Cook Book*, 247–48 (first published in 1895).

109. Russell, *Indian New England before the Mayflower*, 77; Hazard, *Jonny-Cake Papers*, 52. For a mid-twentieth-century recipe in which berries were added to Johnny cake, see Bowles and Towle, *Secrets of New England Cooking*, 143.

110. Wolcott, *New England Yankee Cook Book*, 154; Bowles and Towle, *Secrets of New England Cooking*, 143; *Echoes from South County Kitchens*, 114. In *Cook's Own Book*, 85–86, Lee did include "Gingerbread, Indian."

111. Karr, *Indian New England*, 80 (Gookin); Josselyn, *John Josselyn, Colonial Traveler*, 93; Bennett, "Food Economy of the New England Indians," 380. John Win-

throp Jr. did not mention beans in his description of native boiled corn cookery: "When the Corne in the Eare is full, whiles it is yet greene it hath then a very sweete tast, this they gather and boyle a convenient time, and then they drie it, and put it up into Baggs or Basketts, for their store, and so use it as they have occasion boyleing of it againe either by it selfe, or amongst their Fish or Venison or Beavers Flesh, or such as they have, and this they account a principall Dish, either at their ordinary Meales or Feastivall times, they boyle it whole, or beaten Gross." Mood, "John Winthrop, Jr., on Indian Corn," 131.

112. Wilson, *Food and Drink in Britain*, 199 (quoting Andrew Boorde, from 1542); Wood, *New Englands Prospect*, 72. Wood was probably wrong about how many kinds of things were included in the same pot. Daniel Gookin's more careful account mentioned fish and flesh (though not necessarily put in at the same time) but not fowl. Karr, *Indian New England*, 80. According to Sally Smith Booth, in *Hung, Strung, and Potted*, 76–77, "one widespread belief [of the Atlantic coast Indians] was that if a dinner pot contained both the beasts of the ground and the birds of the air, then the forest gods would be provoked into driving away all game."

113. Wilson, *Food and Drink in Britain*, 200–203, 216–17, 219–20; Anderson, "'Solid Sufficiency,'" 203–6 (quoting Markham).

114. McMahon, "Comfortable Subsistence," 45; Pillsbury, *No Foreign Food*, 27, 37. On both sides of the Atlantic, pottage was sometimes known as "spoon-meat," with the "meat" half of the expression denoting not animal flesh but rather food in general; see Anderson, "'Solid Sufficiency,'" 180; and Earle, *Home Life in Colonial Days*, 87.

115. Bowles and Towle, *Secrets of New England Cooking*, 4; Verrill, *Foods America Gave the World*, 89; Root and de Rochemont, *Eating in America*, 34; Neustadt, *Clambake*, 32. Forefathers' Day was December 22, believed to be the date the Pilgrims reached not just Plymouth harbor, but Plymouth Rock; see Deetz and Deetz, *Times of Their Lives*, 14. The authors provide, pp. 14–16, a concise account of the Plymouth Rock tradition, which is based more on legend than fact.

116. Barlow, "Hasty Pudding," 91; Hazard, *Jonny-Cake Papers*, 51.

117. Stowe, *Oldtown Folks*, 135 (chap. 14). Evan Jones offers one more piece of succotash lore: "Indian women . . . would freeze their winter succotash (made of dried vegetables) and use an idle tomahawk to chop off chunks to melt over a fire as needed." Aside from the dubious reference to "an idle tomahawk," Jones's description is similar to what a twentieth-century cookbook called a "very old" recipe for "Frozen Bean Porridge," in which the preparation was "set out to freeze. Small amounts are cut . . . as needed and 'het' boiling hot. An iron kettle is best but any heavy kettle will do. . . . Without doubt, much of New Hampshire was 'settled' on frozen bean porridge." See Jones, *American Food*, 6; and Wolcott, *New England Yankee Cook Book*, 104.

118. Beecher, *Miss Beecher's Domestic Receipt Book*, 77.

119. Bliss, *Practical Cook Book*, 97; Knight, *Tit-Bits*, 108; *Meriden Cook Book*, 48; Turner, *New England Cook Book*, 95; Wright, *New England Cook Book*, 61.

120. Bowles and Towle, *Secrets of New England Cooking*, 9–10; Jones, *American Food*, 6; Wolcott, *New England Yankee Cook Book*, 74.

121. Deetz, *In Small Things Forgotten*, 170.

122. Hardeman, *Shucks, Shocks, and Hominy Blocks*, 43; Barlow, "Hasty Pudding," 96.

123. Weeden, *Economic and Social History of New England*, 1:230.

124. Booth, *Hung, Strung, and Potted*, 46, 48; Dow, *Every Day Life in the Massachusetts Bay Colony*, 117–18 (quoting Bailey). One New England farmer took a dim view of husking bees: "If you love fun and frolic, and waste and slovenliness more than economy and profit, then give a husking," he opined. Ears husked to the tune of "dirty songs for the entertainment of the boys" would be "mixed, crumbled, and dirty; some husked, some half husked, and some not at all"; quoted in Hardeman, *Shucks, Shocks, and Hominy Blocks*, 44.

125. On the connections between corn and sexuality in Indian culture, see Hardeman, *Shucks, Shocks, and Hominy Blocks*, 69–70.

126. Ibid., 46, 169–83; Elverson and McLanahan, *Cooking Legacy*, 5–6.

127. Adams, *History of the United States*, 45.

128. Bradford, *Of Plymouth Plantation*, 77.

129. Rowlandson, "Sovereignty and Goodness of God," 45.

130. Ibid., 45.

131. Cronon, *Changes in the Land*, 34–53, 108–56.

132. Rowlandson, "Sovereignty and Goodness of God," 45. The sight of wheat, relatively rare and precious in New England even in the best of circumstances, must have been particularly painful for Rowlandson. Squakeag was in Northfield, Massachusetts. The groundnut plant, sometimes also called the Indian potato (*Apios tuberosa*), is a wild vine of the bean family that once grew abundantly along the eastern seaboard but is now quite rare. See *Shorter OED*, 1:837; Russell, *Indian New England before the Mayflower*, 81; and Gibbons, *Stalking the Wild Asparagus*, 107.

133. Rowlandson, "Sovereignty and Goodness of God," 47, 60. In one fictional captivity account, parched corn also formed part of the diet. See Sedgwick, *Hope Leslie*, 76 (vol. 1, chap. 6).

134. Rowlandson, "Sovereignty and Goodness of God," 68–69. On scorched-earth tactics and corn, see Hardeman, *Shucks, Shocks, and Hominy Blocks*, 113, 205–8.

135. Rowlandson, "Sovereignty and Goodness of God," 69.

136. Stowe, *Oldtown Folks*, 11 (chap. 1). Stowe's Oldtown was based on Natick, Massachusetts, which John Eliot founded in the seventeenth century as a home for some of the Indians he had succeeded in converting, and where Stowe's husband, Calvin Stowe, had grown up. A more sympathetic understanding of Indian culture is found in Catharine Sedgwick's *Hope Leslie* and Lydia Maria Child's *Hobomok*. For an analysis of the romanticized portrayals of Indians that became prevalent in the first half of the nineteenth century, see Lepore, *Name of War*, 191–226. According to Laurel Thatcher Ulrich, in *Age of Homespun*, 354, "the theme of the disappearing Indian is laced through early-nineteenth-century literature"; for extended discussion, see 353–66. And for the ongoing

presence of Indians in New England, see Lepore, *Name of War*, 227–40; Simmons, *Spirit of the New England Tribes*; and Robinson, "Narragansett History."

CHAPTER TWO

1. Karr, *Indian New England*, 82 (Champlain).
2. Wilson, *Food and Drink in Britain*, 201–2; *Cambridge World History of Food*, 1:277–80, 2:1728, 1830.
3. *Cambridge World History of Food*, 1:271; Henisch, *Fast and Feast*, 103; Anderson, "'Solid Sufficiency,'" 163–64 (quoting Harrison); Mennell, *All Manners of Food*, 41 (quoting Langland); Cobbett, *Treatise on Cobbett's Corn*, 210.
4. Anderson, "'Solid Sufficiency,'" 45–48, 87–89; Wilson, *Food and Drink in Britain*, 201–3.
5. *Cambridge World History of Food*, 2:1729, 1:273–76; Columbus, *Log*, 102, 105.
6. *Cambridge World History of Food*, 2:1729; Anderson, "'Solid Sufficiency,'" 258; Simmons, *American Cookery* (introduction by Wilson), 15 (this is the first of several references we shall make to the shopping recommendations that were later removed in the second [Albany] edition); Bliss, *Practical Cook Book*, 90.
7. For a description of Boston commercial bean baking in the first decade of the twentieth century, confirming the aptness of this nickname, see Brayley, *Bakers and Baking in Massachusetts*, 172–75.
8. Pillsbury, *No Foreign Food*, 37; Drummond and Wilbraham, *Englishman's Food*, 25; Henisch, *Fast and Feast*, 112; Wilson, *Food and Drink in Britain*, 88, 202; Anderson, "'Solid Sufficiency,'" 221–22.
9. Earle, *Home Life in Colonial Days*, 145; Booth, *Hung, Strung, and Potted*, 132; Russell, *Indian New England before the Mayflower*, 80.
10. Hooker, *Food and Drink in America*, 230; Neustadt, *Clambake*, 40–42. A recipe dating from 1923 for "Baked Beans, Maine Lumbercamp Style" was included in Wolcott, *New England Yankee Cook Book*, 102–3.
11. Bragdon, *Native People of Southern New England*, 103 (quoting Gookin); Bennett, "Food Economy of the New England Indians," 379. Baking under inverted pots covered with coals was a method utilized in Britain since before the birth of Christ. See Wilson, *Food and Drink in Britain*, 230. New Englanders of colonial and early national times used the Dutch oven (also called a bake kettle) to achieve the same results. Most modern descriptions of the Dutch oven are based on that found in Earle, *Home Life in Colonial Days*, 66.
12. Driver, *Indians of North America*, 67; Russell, *Indian New England before the Mayflower*, 80; Snow, *Archaeology of New England*, 324.
13. Bowles and Towle, *Secrets of New England Cooking*, 64–65.
14. Larcom, *New England Girlhood*, 21.
15. Ibid., 21–22.
16. Ibid., 22. For the tin kitchen, see below, chap. 5, nn. 120–21. In Nathaniel Hawthorne's *House of the Seven Gables*, 85 (chap. 7), the heroine Phoebe also attested to the unique virtues of her mother's "Indian cake . . . possessing a richness, and . . . a delicacy, unequalled by any other mode of breakfast-cake." Made with

corn ("Indian"), this would presumably have been a Johnny cake. On the other hand, the "'nimble cake' . . . baked on a board before the open fire" in the Salem household of Caroline Howard King was probably not a Johnny cake, given that King characterized it as "light and flaky." King, *When I Lived in Salem*, 99.

17. Larcom, *New England Girlhood*, 23; Larkin, *Reshaping of Everyday Life*, 51–52. Compare Brewer, "Home Fires," 68: "In the colonial and early national periods, American women cooked in cavernous, drafty, and often dangerous fireplaces which served as primary heat sources as well. Equipment was unsophisticated, cumbersome, and often difficult to manage. . . . All . . . techniques were fuel consumptive, dirty, and labor intensive, requiring periodic but close attention and a great deal of stooping and heavy lifting."

18. Larcom, *New England Girlhood*, 23, 21, 22.

19. Ibid., 23.

20. Among other expressions of nostalgia for the traditional fireside and/or kitchen, see Hawthorne, "Fire Worship" (though it has only limited reference to cooking); Stowe, *Minister's Wooing*, 12–13 (chap. 2); Stowe, *Pearl of Orr's Island*, 61 (chap. 8); Stowe, *Oldtown Folks*, 57–61 (chap. 6); King, *When I Lived in Salem*, 23–25; and Johnson, *Highways and Byways of New England*, 236–37. Brewer, "Home Fires," surveys the cultural as well as the practical dimensions of the transition to cookstoves.

21. Anderson, "'Solid Sufficiency,'" 159–60; Gould, *Early American House*, 52; Oliver, *Saltwater Foodways*, 18.

22. Beecher, *Miss Beecher's Domestic Receipt Book*, 83; Earle, *Home Life in Colonial Days*, 67; Dow, *Domestic Life in New England*, 17; Dow, *Every Day Life in the Massachusetts Bay Colony*, 93; Booth, *Hung, Strung, and Potted*, 16.

23. Child, *American Frugal Housewife*, 79.

24. Beecher, *Miss Beecher's Domestic Receipt Book*, 83–84. For an appreciation of the unique capabilities of the brick oven, see Hess, *Martha Washington's Booke of Cookery*, 19; and Hess, introduction to *English Bread and Yeast Cookery*, xiii. For a detailed account of the brick oven's development from the seventeenth century to the nineteenth, see Bacon, *Forgotten Art of Building and Using a Brick Bake Oven*.

25. Larcom, *New England Girlhood*, 51–52; Oliver, *Saltwater Foodways*, 18 (quoting Mary Elizabeth Weaver Farnsworth, "Reminiscences of a Nonagenarian").

26. Ulrich, *Midwife's Tale*, 85; Anderson, "'Solid Sufficiency,'" 159–60; Gies and Gies, *Life in a Medieval Village*, 48; Booth, *Hung, Strung, and Potted*, 132; Gould, *Early American House*, 49.

27. Larcom, *New England Girlhood*, 38–39.

28. Simmons, *American Cookery* (introduction by Wilson), 15; Child, *American Frugal Housewife*, 51. Hanging the dry beans over the fire overnight indicated that this was a recipe for the hearthside. See also Howland, *American Economical Housekeeper*, 69; and Bliss, *Practical Cook Book*, 90. These recipes did not represent the ultimate in baked bean austerity. For a version without pork or any other source of fat, see Hunt, *Good Bread*, 17.

29. Oliver, *Saltwater Foodways*, 79. The idea that pepper would enhance the health-

fulness of baked beans may hearken back to the premodern, Galenic conception of a proper diet, according to which the coldness of pulses needed to be balanced by the warmth of pepper. See Laudan, "Birth of the Modern Diet," 76–79; and Scully, *Art of Cookery in the Middle Ages*, esp. 40–53. Another health issue in connection with beans was that they were, as Catharine Beecher delicately put it, "slower of digestion" than many other foods (*Treatise on Domestic Economy*, 83). Sarah Josepha Hale, in *Good Housekeeper*, 107, similarly cautioned that "Pork and Beans . . . does not agree with weak stomachs."

30. *Aunt Mary's New England Cook Book*, 20; DuSablon, *America's Collectible Cookbooks*, 46–47 (quoting *The Buckeye Cook Book* [1883]); *Meriden Cook Book*, 45; Wright, *New England Cook Book*, 104; Thimble Club, *Choice Recipes from Old New England*, 56–57; Lincoln and Barrows, *Home Science Cook Book*, 148; Inman, *Rhode Island Rule Book*, 19; Wolcott, *New England Yankee Cook Book*, 100. Mary J. Lincoln was a leader, along with Fannie Merritt Farmer, in the domestic science movement, for which see Shapiro, *Perfection Salad*; and Levenstein, *Revolution at the Table*, esp. 72–85. For a discussion of the increased presence of molasses in gingerbread at this same time, see below, chap. 7, nn. 70–76.

31. *Aunt Mary's New England Cook Book*, 20; DuSablon, *America's Collectible Cookbooks*, 46–47; Lincoln and Barrows, *Home Science Cook Book*, 148.

32. Child, *American Frugal Housewife*, 51; *Aunt Mary's New England Cook Book*, 20; Beecher, *Miss Beecher's Domestic Receipt Book*, 78; Hale, *Good Housekeeper*, 107; *Meriden Cook Book*, 45; Wolcott, *New England Yankee Cook Book*, 100; Lincoln and Barrows, *Home Science Cook Book*, 148; Wright, *New England Cook Book*, 104.

33. Early, *New England Cookbook*, 57–58; above, n. 8.

34. Whitehill, *Food, Drink, and Recipes of Early New England*, 9 (quoting New Hampshire historian William Little). Little continued in a way that sheds light on the "Frozen Bean Porridge" recipe mentioned in chap. 1, n. 117: "When the good man was going away in winter to work, with his team, the wife would make a bean porridge, freeze it with a string in it so he could hang it on one of the sled stakes, and when he was hungry he would break off a piece and melt and eat it."

35. Larcom, *New England Girlhood*, 38; Booth, *Hung, Strung, and Potted*, 132; Doudiet, "Coastal Maine Cooking," 226.

36. McMahon, "Comfortable Subsistence," 48.

37. Gould, *Early American House*, 52; above, n. 26.

38. Knappen, *Tudor Puritanism*, 442–50; Hamilton, *Gentleman's Progress*, 108. For further discussion of Saturday codfish dinners, see below, chap. 3, nn. 172–73.

39. Hill, *Society and Puritanism in Pre-Revolutionary England*, 145–218. In New England, fast days were also observed when repentance was required of the entire society, although the total number remained well below what was characteristic of Catholic countries: 166 fast days were observed in seventeenth-century France, according to Braudel, *Structures of Everyday Life*, 214. For more on fast day traditions, see below, chap. 3, nn. 21, 37.

40. Neustadt, *Clambake*, 30–32.

41. The scholarly literature on the jeremiad is enormous; the pioneering discussion is in Miller, *New England Mind*, 28–51. For a book-length treatment, see Bercovitch, *American Jeremiad*.

42. Buell, *New England Literary Culture*, 193–213 (Webster quotation at 199).

43. Carver, *Sketches of New England*, 15–16.

44. Stowe, *Minister's Wooing*, 156–57 (chap. 16).

45. *Meriden Cook Book*, 45; above, n. 33.

46. Gould, "Baked Beans," 33–34.

47. Ibid., 335–36.

48. Ibid., 336–37.

49. The individuality of the bean was also stressed in another piece of Maine commentary. Each one "should be treated like a voter in an election. You must understand each bean to bake a collection of them." In a true Maine beanpot, the beans "never wholly assimilate or mash." As for Boston Baked Beans, it was to this Down East spokesman merely "a sort of brown paste with nubbly particles in it, dejected in appearance"; quoted in Jones, *American Food*, 10. As seen in the previous chapter, Rhode Islander Thomas Robinson Hazard commented in a similar vein regarding Boston Brown Bread (chap. 1, n. 79). Babylon-on-the-Charles was evidently vulnerable to attack from every rural New England direction. For the harvesting methods of premigration English yeomen, see Anderson, "'Solid Sufficiency,'" 87.

50. Wilson, *Food and Drink in Britain*, 343; Drummond and Wilbraham, *Englishman's Food*, 30; Anderson, "'Solid Sufficiency,'" 52–53 (the last two sources both quote Harrison).

51. Wood, *New Englands Prospect*, 71; Williams, *Key into the Language of America*, 101; Karr, *Indian New England*, 81 (Gookin).

52. Russell, *Indian New England before the Mayflower*, 80–81; Bragdon, *Native People of Southern New England*, 103; Trigger, *Handbook of North American Indians*, 15:273; University of Illinois Extension, "Pumpkins and More," <http://www.urbanext.uiuc.edu/pumpkins/history.html>. Indians may also have baked pumpkins whole. See Root and de Rochemont, *Eating in America*, 40.

53. Johnson, *Johnson's Wonder-Working Providence*, 85, 115.

54. Dow, *Every Day Life in the Massachusetts Bay Colony*, 98; Wolcott, *New England Yankee Cook Book*, 171; Booth, *Hung, Strung, and Potted*, 131; Root and de Rochemont, *Eating in America*, 40; Wilson, *Food and Drink in Britain*, 343. In the novel she published a few years before *The American Frugal Housewife*, Lydia Maria Child supplied the breakfast table of the earliest colonists with both "roasted pumpkin" and "pumpkin and milk"; see Child, *Hobomok*, 9 (chap. 1), 98 (chap. 13).

55. Knight, *Journal*, 69; Beecher, *Miss Beecher's Domestic Receipt Book*, 160. Another recipe for pumpkin preserves appeared in 1912 in Wright, *New England Cook Book*, 288. For more on fruit preservation and preserves, see below, chap. 6, nn. 37–49.

56. Doudiet, "Coastal Maine Cooking," 220; above, chap. 1, nn. 95–96; Wright, *New England Cook Book*, 184.

57. Beecher, *Miss Beecher's Domestic Receipt Book*, 91; Knight, *Journal*, 46. See also Prescott, *Valuable Receipts*, 15; and Turner, *New England Cook Book*, 133.

58. Earle, *Home Life in Colonial Days*, 143, 163; Earle, *Stage-Coach and Tavern Days*, 108; University of Illinois Extension, "Pumpkins and More," <http://www.urbanext.uiuc.edu/pumpkins/history.html>; Dow, *Every Day Life in the Massachusetts Bay Colony*, 98. Regarding the drying of pumpkin, Lydia Maria Child proposed an alternative to the traditional method of cutting and stringing, "like apples. It is a much better way to boil and sift the pumpkin, then spread it out thin in tin plates, and dry hard in a warm oven." Child, *American Frugal Housewife*, 115. This advice was repeated almost verbatim in Howland, *American Economical Housekeeper*, 42. We learn from Sloat, *Old Sturbridge Village Cookbook*, 9, that Howland "included a number of Mrs. Child's recipes without giving credit."

59. Wilson, *Food and Drink in Britain*, 349. A recipe of this type was included, with only minor variation, in two different seventeenth-century English cookbooks; see *Compleat Cook*, 14–15; and Woolley, *Gentlewoman's Companion*, 145–46. The pumpkin pie recipe in *Compleat Cook* was reproduced in *Godey's*, September 1889, 234–35.

60. Wilson, *Food and Drink in Britain*, 349; Johnson, *Johnson's Wonder-Working Providence*, 210.

61. Gardiner, *Mrs. Gardiner's Family Receipts*, 55, v–vii. After the war the Gardiners returned to America, some to the lands in Maine in which Anne Gibbons Gardiner's husband had invested. The manuscript cookbook was first published in Hallowell, Maine, in 1938. That in their social and cultural makeup New England and the other colonies came to resemble Old England more closely in the eighteenth century than they had in the seventeenth century has become the accepted view in recent scholarship. For summary descriptions of this development and the reasons for it, see Greene and Pole, *Colonial British America*, 15, 221–23.

62. Simmons, *American Cookery* (introduction by Wilson), x, 28. Karen Hess states that American pumpkin pie is "purely English," evidencing the same Hannah Woolley apple/pumpkin pie recipe from which, as we have shown, the Simmons recipe sharply diverged. See Glasse, *Art of Cookery Made Plain and Easy* (introduction by Hess), x; and Simmons, *American Cookery* (introduction by Hess), xiv–xv. The glossary included with the Wilson edition of Simmons defines a "dough spur" as "an instrument used for ornamenting pastry, in the form of a toothed wheel, set in a handle, frequently a product of the carving (scrimshaw) done on whaling vessels" (xxix). Other names for the same instrument were "jagging iron" and "jagger wheel." See also Early, *New England Cookbook*, 113. The Whaling Museum in New Bedford, Massachusetts, has an extensive collection of jagger wheels.

63. Child, *American Frugal Housewife*, 66–67.

64. Hale, *Good Housekeeper*, 84; Beecher, *Miss Beecher's Domestic Receipt Book*, 110, 125. See also Gilman, *Lady's Annual Register . . . for 1840*, 39; Bliss, *Practical Cook Book*, 159; and Mann, *Christianity in the Kitchen*, 80. As with his recipe for

baked beans, Hunt, in *Good Bread*, 16, went to extremes of plainness with his pumpkin pie, which was to be made either without a crust altogether, or with a crust of "fine or unbolted flour and shortened with potato."

65. *Godey's*, October 1882, 377; January 1883, 185; November 1887, 413; November 1890, 426; December 1891, 537.

66. Smith, *Modern American Cookery*, 10; Hale, *Good Housekeeper*, 84; Oliver, *Saltwater Foodways*, 69, 319 (on both pages quoting *Mystic Press*); Hazard, *Jonny-Cake Papers*, 51. James Whitcomb Riley (1849–1916) more famously colloquialized pumpkin in his poem, "When the Frost is on the Punkin." The expression "some pumpkins" dates from the middle of the nineteenth century. Originally, it was used to describe a person or matter of importance. Thomas Robinson Hazard used it in 1879 to describe what to him was a matter of supreme importance when he acknowledged that the white cornmeal ground at a certain Rhode Island mill "must have been some pumpkins." *Shorter OED*, 2:1619; Hazard, *Jonny-Cake Papers*, 35.

67. Child, "New England Boy's Song about Thanksgiving Day," <http://eir.library .utoronto.ca/rpo/display/poem473.html>; Hale, *Northwood*, 1:110. For Hale's efforts to nationalize Thanksgiving, see Smith, "First Thanksgiving," 81–84. For more on pie and Thanksgiving, see below, chap. 6, nn. 109–27.

CHAPTER THREE

1. Vickers, *Farmers and Fishermen*, 249–50, 251, 158–59, 261–64.

2. Anderson, "'Solid Sufficiency,'" 80.

3. McManis, *Colonial New England*, 10; Innis, *Cod Fisheries*, 71 (quoting Gosnold).

4. Innis, *Cod Fisheries*, 71 (quoting Pring); Earle, *Home Life in Colonial Days*, 115 (quoting Smith).

5. Innis, *Cod Fisheries*, 75; Vickers, *Farmers and Fishermen*, 90 (quoting Winthrop and White). See also Wood, *New Englands Prospect*, 34.

6. Innis, *Cod Fisheries*, 73–75.

7. Ibid., 75.

8. Vickers, *Farmers and Fishermen*, 87–88, gives the best explanation of the Atlantic fish trade.

9. Ibid., 99; Weeden, *Economic and Social History of New England*, 2:641, 245. Vickers defines refuse fish: "Cod that was broken, undersized, oversalted, left out in the rain, or damaged in any other way Europeans termed 'refuse' and unfit for consumption by free men" (99).

10. Vickers, "Work and Life on the Fishing Periphery," 84–85.

11. Vickers, *Farmers and Fishermen*, 89–90.

12. Vickers, "Work and Life on the Fishing Periphery," 99, 98; Oliver, *Saltwater Foodways*, 351.

13. Vickers, "Work and Life on the Fishing Periphery," 99 (quoting the records of the Massachusetts General Court for 1674).

14. Ibid., 112–13; Vickers, *Farmers and Fishermen*, 93.

15. Vickers, "Work and Life on the Fishing Periphery," 113–15.

16. Vickers, *Farmers and Fishermen*, 95–96.

17. Vickers, "Work and Life on the Fishing Periphery," 87.

18. Bailyn, *New England Merchants in the Seventeenth Century*, 81–82.

19. Oliver, *Saltwater Foodways*, 332.

20. Drummond and Wilbraham, *Englishman's Food*, 47 (quoting the *Polycronycon* [1357]); Root and de Rochemont, *Eating in America*, 51–52; Wood, *New Englands Prospect*, 37–38.

21. Drummond and Wilbraham, *Englishman's Food*, 63 (quoting William Harrison, *Description of England* [1577]).

22. Bradford, *Of Plymouth Plantation*, 130; Johnson, *Johnson's Wonder-Working Providence*, 77–78; Winthrop, *Winthrop's Journal*, 2:91. Bradford seemed to indicate a few pages earlier (122–23) that shellfish stood at the very bottom of the pecking order. People "went to seeking of shellfish" at low tide only when their forays into deeper waters in search of "bass and such like fish" resulted in an inadequate catch.

23. Henisch, *Fast and Feast*, 35; Wilson, *Food and Drink in Britain*, 34, 44 (quoting dried cod cooking instructions from *The Goodman of Paris* [ca. 1393]).

24. Karr, *Indian New England*, 80 (Gookin); Williams, *Key into the Language of America*, 17.

25. Snow, *Archaeology of New England*, 72; Bennett, "Food Economy of the New England Indians," 385.

26. Wood, *New Englands Prospect*, 94–95; Josselyn, *John Josselyn, Colonial Traveler*, 80–81. Unfortunately, Wood reverted to standard European racism in his description of Indian ice-fishing: "they wil sit like so many apes" around their fishing holes.

27. Snow, *Archaeology of New England*, 66, 334; Bennett, "Food Economy of the New England Indians," 385–86; Bragdon, *Native People of Southern New England*, 110–12, 116–17; Russell, *Indian New England before the Mayflower*, 91–92.

28. Above, chap. 1, n. 81; Bragdon, *Native People of Southern New England*, 110; Russell, *Indian New England before the Mayflower*, 73, 75; Snow, *Archaeology of New England*, 324; Josselyn, *John Josselyn, Colonial Traveler*, 93, 79; Root and de Rochemont, *Eating in America*, 35.

29. Wood, *New Englands Prospect*, 34–35.

30. Ibid., 38; *Journal of the Pilgrims at Plymouth*, 48. John Josselyn, like Wood before him, marveled at oysters that had to be "cut into three pieces" before they would fit into the mouths of those who would dine upon them. Josselyn, *John Josselyn, Colonial Traveler*, 79; Wood, *New Englands Prospect*, 37.

31. Wilson, *Food and Drink in Britain*, 17, 21, 28, 43, 54; Anderson, "'Solid Sufficiency,'" 117 (quoting Langland).

32. Wilson, *Food and Drink in Britain*, 48, 54–55; Drummond and Wilbraham, *Englishman's Food*, 39 (quoting Jacob Rathgreb, *A True and Faithful Narrative* [1604]).

33. Wilson, *Food and Drink in Britain*, 21, 29, 35, 48, 53; Drummond and Wilbraham, *Englishman's Food*, 38 (quoting Andrew Boorde, *Dyetary of Helth* [1542]); Anderson, "'Solid Sufficiency,'" 79, 81.

34. *Columbia Encyclopedia*, s.v. "Eels," <www.bartleby.com/65>.

35. *Journal of the Pilgrims at Plymouth*, 97; Snow, *Archaeology of New England*, 66, 72; Earle, *Home Life in Colonial Days*, 117.

36. Anderson, "'Solid Sufficiency,'" 79–81 (citing Harrison, *Description of England* [1577]); Wilson, *Food and Drink in Britain*, 29, 25, 37.

37. Wilson, *Food and Drink in Britain*, 30–31. Some weeks, there might be as many as four fast days. Both Friday and Saturday were fast days until 1585, and only Friday thereafter. Some Mondays, and until the beginning of the fifteenth century many Wednesdays, were also fast days. Abstention from meat marked the forty days of Lent. During some periods in the Middle Ages, as many as half the days of the year were designated as fast days. Well into the seventeenth century, at least in France, more than 160 fast days continued to be observed. On this kind of regimen, it is not surprising that most fish found a place in the cuisine. Anderson, "'Solid Sufficiency,'" 81. See also Scully, *Art of Cookery in the Middle Ages*, 60–61.

38. Baker, "Seventeenth-Century English Yeoman Foodways at Plimoth Plantation," 107.

39. Josselyn, *John Josselyn, Colonial Traveler*, 79–80 (also quoted in Anderson, "'Solid Sufficiency,'" 216; and in Leighton, *Early American Gardens*, 110).

40. Wilson, *Food and Drink in Britain*, 53, 241–43. Our discussion of the grain and bread hierarchy, begun in chapter 1, is continued in chapter 7. For a fifteenth-century example of eels served over bread, see below, chap. 6, n. 82.

41. Wilson, *Food and Drink in Britain*, 164, 221: "it was only in Tudor times that an emerging middle class, which did not despise butter as the food of the poor, began to use it liberally" (164). Even in pastry and cakes, butter was only gradually accepted in place of cream. By the eighteenth century, butter's earlier associations with poverty would be forgotten, and the butter-and-flour sauce would come to eclipse the many sweet, acidic, and spicy sauces of the Middle Ages. See also Hess, *Martha Washington's Booke of Cookery*, 9.

42. Smith, *Compleat Housewife*, 5, 36, 46; Wilson, *Food and Drink in Britain*, 57, 105, 134, 183; Scully, *Art of Cookery in the Middle Ages*, 86. For collaring of meat, see below, chap. 5, n. 90; and for savory pies, see below, chap. 6, nn. 83–86, 96, 100.

43. Glasse, *Art of Cookery Made Plain and Easy* (glossary and notes by Davidson), table of contents. Regarding the "Eel Soop" (77), Glasse stated that with "a Piece of Carrot to brown it," it could be made to look like meat stew. Alan Davidson, in his glossary to the cited edition, explains "To pitchcock Eels": "Pitchcock. Properly spitchcock, a verb referring to a way of preparing eels by cutting them into pieces, dressing them with breadcrumbs and chopped herbs and then grilling or frying them. . . . Hannah Glasse . . . omits the herbs and takes the word to mean grilling pieces of eel, since she gives a similar but separate recipe for frying eel." That one of its modes of preparation commanded a verb of its own in the English language is evidence that the eel was no bit player in English cuisine. Davidson also remarks parenthetically: "There was another word, spatchcock, apparently of Irish origin and meaning a way of grill-

ing pieces of fowl." Glasse, *Art of Cookery Made Plain and Easy*, 194. It seems to us that the close culinary connection between wild fowl and wild fish—the fact that the "cock" is retained in the word spitchcock—together with the obvious similarity of spitchcock to spatchcock make a good case for Irish origin.

44. DuSablon, *America's Collectible Cookbooks*, 3; Carter, *Frugal Housewife*, 53. Scully, in *Art of Cookery in the Middle Ages*, 205, says that in France and Italy, "pepper lost favour in aristocratic cookery" toward the end of the Middle Ages. On anchovies see Wilson, *Food and Drink in Britain*, 23–24, 49: "Mediterranean anchovies, pickled in brine, were occasionally imported during Elizabeth's reign . . . [and] they were added to sauces or made dishes" (49).

45. Above, chap. 2, n. 61; Gardiner, *Mrs. Gardiner's Family Receipts*, 64, 67.

46. Gardiner, *Mrs. Gardiner's Family Receipts*, 15.

47. Ibid., 22, 27, 55, 51. For more on medieval pies and pie crusts, including one example from the fifteenth century of an eel pie whose crust was not intended to be eaten, see below, chap. 6, nn. 81–83.

48. Simmons, *American Cookery* (introduction by Wilson), 6–7, xxx. Thoreau similarly referred to eels as "still squirming in the pan" in *Week on the Concord and Merrimac Rivers*, 28.

49. Lee, *Cook's Own Book*, 68.

50. Ibid., 68–69. Fish recipes constituted part of the material added to the second (Albany) edition of Simmons, *American Cookery*; two are discussed below. For the gridiron see Earle, *Home Life in Colonial Days*, 61–62; and Gould, *Early American House*, 77–78.

51. Webster, *Improved Housewife*, 67–74.

52. Allen, *Housekeeper's Assistant*, 129–30. See also *Roger Cookery*, 18; and Bliss, *Practical Cook Book*, 39.

53. Beecher, *Miss Beecher's Domestic Receipt Book*, 65.

54. Hale, *Ladies' New Book of Cookery*, 29.

55. Ibid., iv.

56. Ibid., 28–60 (quotations on 54).

57. Ibid., 54, 31.

58. Thoreau, *Walden and Other Writings*, 463. A less well known chronicler, Joseph Anthony of New Bedford, Massachusetts, had "a grand supper of broiled eels" in November 1823; see Oliver, *Saltwater Foodways*, 376 (quoting *Life in New Bedford 100 Years Ago . . . in a Diary Kept by Joseph R. Anthony*). The Thoreau anecdote is also quoted in Oliver, *Saltwater Foodways*, 68, but the juicy part of the story is omitted.

59. Farmer, *Boston Cooking-School Cook Book*, 135, 155.

60. Wright, *New England Cook Book*, 25.

61. Wolcott, *New England Yankee Cook Book*, 45. For more on the impact of dams on fish, see below, n. 161.

62. Johnson, *Highways and Byways of New England*, 264. According to Thomas Robinson Hazard, as early as the turn of the nineteenth century, the "laboring people" of southern Rhode Island "abhorred the idea of eating fresh-water fish, with the exception of trout." Presumably this aversion encompassed eels. See

Hazard, *Jonny-Cake Papers*, 345. Such attitudes were of course never prevalent in the Connecticut River watershed area where Clifton Johnson's informant lived. The shad that he mentioned figured prominently there, not only in the cuisine, but also in the culture; see below, nn. 161–65.

63. Wood, *New Englands Prospect*, 38.

64. Above, n. 22; Neustadt, *Clambake*, 25 (quoting Mather).

65. Wilson, *Food and Drink in Britain*, 17; Anderson, "'Solid Sufficiency,'" 79.

66. Muir, *Reflections in Bullough's Pond*, 10; above, n. 29.

67. Wood, *New Englands Prospect*, 34–35; Johnson, *Johnson's Wonder-Working Providence*, 77–78 (and above, n. 22); Bragdon, *Native People of Southern New England*, 110 (quoting Cheryl P. Claassen, "Gender, Shellfishing, and the Shell Mound Archaic").

68. Russell, *Indian New England before the Mayflower*, 92. Although it is common to speak of New England clams, there are in fact several species involved, and the nomenclature, based on both size and species, can cause confusion. The round or hard-shelled clams are also known as quahogs (pronounced "koehogs"), a name that may derive from the Narragansett word "poguauhock." It is from quahog shells that the Narragansetts made their famous wampum. By a process of rubbing and polishing, they turned the clam shells into cylindrical beads that were traded as currency and used for ornament throughout Indian New England. The small quahog is known as a cherrystone clam. The young quahogs are called littlenecks. The largest quahogs, which are less delicately flavored, are often used in soups and chowders or mixed in a breadcrumb stuffing. They are sometimes called chowders. Soft shell clams are also called long clams or long-necks. They are the species one often sees stooped clammers raking from mud flats at low tide. Soft shell clams may be eaten raw but are most often served steamed, from which they get their common name, steamers. See Oliver, *Saltwater Foodways*, 370; Root and de Rochemont, *Eating in America*, 22; Bowles and Towle, *Secrets of New England Cooking*, 28; *Shorter OED*, 2:2382; and Farmer, *Boston Cooking-School Cook Book*, 140.

69. Neustadt, *Clambake*, 19–69, and passim. We do not have space to discuss all aspects of this complicated subject. Neustadt's book is a nuanced account of both the Indian elements in the Yankee clambake and the Yankee influence on collective Indian memory.

70. Ibid., 32 (quoting Ezra Stiles), 26, 31–32. An indication of the improved fortunes of the clam is this somewhat farcical story from the 1740s, around the same time that Hannah Glasse was helping to make the bivalve more respectable: "[Friday, June 15] Narrows Ferry [which ran from Staten Island to Long Island]: I came to the Narrows att two o'clock and dined att one Corson's [Jacob Corsen] that keeps the ferry. The landlady spoke both Dutch and English. I dined upon what I never had eat in my life before—a dish of fried clams, of which shell fish there is abundance in these parts. As I sat down to dinner I observed a manner of saying grace quite new to me. My landlady and her two daughters put on solemn, devout faces, hanging down their heads and holding up their hands

for half a minute. I, who had gracelessly fallen too without remembering that duty according to a wicked custom I had contracted, sat staring att them with my mouth choak full, but after this short meditation was over, we began to lay about us and stuff down the fryed clams with rye-bread and butter. They took such a deal of chawing that we were long att dinner, and the dish began to cool before we had eat enough. The landlady called for the bedpan. I could not guess what she intended to do with it unless it was to warm her bed to go to sleep after dinner, but I found that it was used by way of a chaffing dish to warm our dish of clams. I stared att the novelty for some time, and reaching over for a mug of beer that stood on the opposite side of the table, my bag sleeve catched hold of the handle of the bed pan and unfortunately overset the clams, at which the landlady was a little ruffled and muttered a scrape of Dutch of which I understood not a word except mynheer, but I suppose she swore, for she uttered her speech with an emphasis." Hamilton, *Gentleman's Progress*, 39–40.

71. Neustadt, *Clambake*, 32–33 (quoting evidence from Albert Matthews, "The Term Pilgrim Fathers and Early Celebrations of Forefathers' Day" [1915]). For a snippet of Webster's oration on this occasion, see above, chap. 2, n. 42.

72. Neustadt, *Clambake*, 45–46.

73. Simmons, *American Cookery* (introduction by Wilson), xix.

74. Child, *American Frugal Housewife*, 58–59; Wilson, *Food and Drink in Britain*, 247. For Josselyn's eel recipe, see above, n. 39. By the end of the eighteenth century, clams, along with oysters, served as ordinary fare as far inland as Deerfield, Massachusetts. See Derven, "Wholesome, Toothsome, and Diverse," 52.

75. Oliver, *Saltwater Foodways*, 351 (quoting Emery, *Reminiscences of a Nonagenarian* [1879]), 370.

76. Lee, *Cook's Own Book*, 51.

77. Beecher, *Miss Beecher's Domestic Receipt Book*, 60.

78. The movement away from spiced foods was occurring in many places besides New England, however. See Mennell, *All Manners of Food*, 53–54.

79. Webster, *Improved Housewife*, 73; Mrs. Webster's clam pancakes began with a basic pancake batter, and then added either whole stewed or finely chopped clams. She warned against cutting corners with the batter by using clam liquor, which "does not make them so light as milk." Simplest of all were her "Long Clams," which were shelled, then broiled or stewed, and seasoned "to the liking." The modern categories, in accordance with which long clams are usually steamed, were clearly not yet in place.

80. Ibid. See also Bliss, *Practical Cook Book*, 41.

81. Webster, *Improved Housewife*, 73.

82. *Aunt Mary's New England Cook Book*, 19.

83. *Godey's*, April 1891, 365.

84. Lincoln and Barrows, *Home Science Cook Book*, 122–23. Lincoln and Barrows called for several changes of fresh water. They seem to have been concerned about cleanliness to the point of obsession. There were countless other examples of the rising popularity of the clam. Among the early-twentieth-century cook-

books containing "traditional" clam recipes were Turner, *New England Cook Book*, 53, 115; Patten, *Our New England Family Recipes*, 78, 82–83; and Thimble Club, *Choice Recipes from Old New England*, 20.

85. Farmer, *Boston Cooking-School Cook Book*, 140.

86. Neustadt, *Clambake*, 19–39, and passim; Hawthorne, *Old Seaport Towns of New England*, 117–18.

87. Wright, *New England Cook Book*, xxix–xxx.

88. Ibid., 20–21.

89. Wolcott, *New England Yankee Cook Book*, xiii–xiv.

90. Neustadt, *Clambake*, 36–37. Although, as discussed in chapter 2, a tradition of a meatless Sabbath did emerge in colonial New England, the point here is that Friday was the one day in particular that the Puritans would not have set aside for food abstinence practices.

91. Wolcott, *New England Yankee Cook Book*, 4, 5, 61.

92. Oliver, *Saltwater Foodways*, 373. The association of clams with leisure was also evident in the naming of clam dishes. For instance, on Cape Cod in the early twentieth century, clam fritters were playfully called Fannie Daddies. See Early, *New England Cookbook*, 28; and Wolcott, *New England Yankee Cook Book*, 59. Myths about clams achieved gargantuan proportions by the middle of the twentieth century, as in Eleanor Early's tale of the Cape Cod sea clam, four of which would fill a pie. Early, *New England Cookbook*, 27. This recipe also appeared in Wolcott, *New England Yankee Cook Book*, 61.

93. Oliver, *Saltwater Foodways*, 301, points out that corn chowder is not a New England dish, so we leave it out of our discussion here. For the twentieth-century tomatoes-in-chowder controversy, see Smith, *Souper Tomatoes*, 72–73.

94. Hooker, *Book of Chowder*, 1–2; Oliver, *Saltwater Foodways*, 293–94.

95. Anderson, "'Solid Sufficiency,'" 215; Oliver, *Saltwater Foodways*, 293.

96. Oliver, *Saltwater Foodways*, 294; Hooker, *Book of Chowder*, 3.

97. Hooker, *Food and Drink in America*, 114; Calloway, *Dawnland Encounters*, 179. Calloway acknowledges that such a synthesis of fishing strategies would have been developed only in the realm of subsistence fishing, not in that of "commercial dry cod fishing."

98. Early, *New England Cookbook*, 3; above, chap. 1, n. 111. Gookin continued on to provide considerable detail about the fish presence in succotash: "fish and flesh of all sorts, either new taken or dried, as shads, eels, alewives, or a kind of herring, or any other sort of fish. But they dry mostly those sorts before mentioned. These they cut in pieces, bones and all, and boil them in the aforesaid pottage. I have wondered many times that they were not in danger of being choked with fish bones; but they are so dextrous to separate the bones from the fish in their eating thereof that they are in no hazard." Karr, *Indian New England*, 80.

99. Hooker, *Book of Chowder*, 27; Parkman, Diary, 30 May 1760, American Antiquarian Society. The lingering Puritan ambivalence about a day devoted exclusively to pleasure was indicated by the words Parkman appended just after the passage quoted in the text: "landed just after nine at Eve: having met with no

remarkable Evil." For Election Day in the eighteenth century (in connection with Election Cake), see below, chap. 7, n. 83.

100. Smith, *Souper Tomatoes*, 71; Hooker, *Book of Chowder*, 3, 28; Simmons, *American Cookery* (introduction by Hess), 22–23; Oliver, *Saltwater Foodways*, 295. The date of the first appearance of chowder in an edition of the Glasse cookbook is given variously in these sources as 1768, 1763, and 1789. Under the title "To Make Chouder, a Sea Dish," it was included in the first American edition in 1805. See Glasse, *Art of Cookery Made Plain and Easy* (introduction by Hess), 274–75. Here is the Simmons recipe: "Chouder. Take a bass weighing four pounds, boil half an hour; take six slices raw salt pork, fry them till the lard is nearly extracted, one dozen crackers soaked in cold water five minutes; put the bass into the lard, also the pieces of pork and crackers, cover close and fry for 20 minutes; serve with potatoes, pickles, apple sauce or mangoes; garnish with green parsley." Richard J. Hooker comments that "strange as this very dry chowder might seem, it was acceptable to two other compilers of cookbooks who in 1805 and 1831 copied the recipe without comment or acknowledgment." Hooker, *Book of Chowder*, 4–5. These two cookbooks were *New American Cookery, or Female Companion* (New York, 1805) and *Cook Not Mad*. The latter even included Simmons's suggestions for condiments (20). Elsewhere, Hooker makes the point that this earliest American chowder recipe was unusual in another respect, "that it was fried, rather than stewed" (29). Although Simmons called her recipe a chowder, perhaps in oblique acknowledgement of the growing popularity of the dish, it was in essence potted bass.

101. Child, *American Frugal Housewife*, 59.

102. Smith, *Modern American Cookery*, 21–22.

103. Lee, *Cook's Own Book*, 51; Glasse, *Art of Cookery Made Plain and Easy* (introduction by Hess), 274–75.

104. Lee, *Cook's Own Book*, 51. In 1842 Daniel Webster declared that a chowder made with the cod and haddock caught during "a long morning spent in the most exhilarating sport" would "make you no longer envy the gods." Hooker, *Book of Chowder*, 38 (quoting S. P. Lyman, *The Public and Private Life of Daniel Webster*).

105. Smith, *Modern American Cookery*, 21–22; Beecher, *Miss Beecher's Domestic Receipt Book*, 62–63; Webster, *Improved Housewife*, 68–69. While nineteenth-century cookbooks were apt to use the terms cod and haddock interchangeably, they are different, though closely related, species. The great commercial advantage of cod—it takes well to drying and salting—was not shared by haddock. For that reason, haddock appeared throughout the culinary record but never attained the status of cod. See, for instance, Child, *American Frugal Housewife*, 57; and Farmer, *Boston Cooking-School Cook Book*, 136–37. On Finnan Haddie (from the Scottish port Findhorn and Scottish colloquial for haddock), a haddock dish not native to New England but very popular there, see Mariani, *Dictionary of American Food and Drink*, 117.

106. Smith, *Souper Tomatoes*, 71; Oliver, *Saltwater Foodways*, 296; *Roger Cookery*, 18; Gilman, *Lady's Annual Register . . . for 1838*, 61; Howland, *American Economi-

cal Housekeeper, 62; Prescott, *Valuable Receipts*, 9; Bliss, *Practical Cook Book*, 35; Chadwick, *Home Cookery*, 84–85, 89–90. Four of these chowders included milk.

107. Oliver, *Saltwater Foodways*, 295.

108. Stowe, *Pearl of Orr's Island*, 138, 142, 144 (chap. 14).

109. King, *When I Lived in Salem*, 100–102.

110. Verrill, *Along New England Shores*, 126–31. See also Abbott, *Old Paths and Legends of the New England Border*, 122–23.

111. Turner, *New England Cook Book*, 51–53, 59–60; Wright, *New England Cook Book*, 21. See also *Godey's*, May 1880, 465 (fish chowder); August 1881, 184 (lobster chowder); November 1881, 473 (clam chowder); and *Aunt Mary's New England Cook Book*, 16–18. What is today called "Rhode Island Clam Chowder" does not contain milk; however, the only chowder recipe in our sample from a Rhode Island source does contain milk. See Inman, *Rhode Island Rule Book*, 10.

112. Hawthorne, *Old Seaport Towns of New England*, 222.

113. Thimble Club, *Choice Recipes from Old New England*, 28–29; Wolcott, *New England Yankee Cook Book*, 4–5, 12, 125–28.

114. Oliver, *Saltwater Foodways*, 295–96, states that the onion was the crucial ingredient, quoting in substantiation a passage from a story by Sarah Orne Jewett. On canned clams, see ibid., 344. Common crackers eventually became the standard accompaniment for chowder. In New England the most popular were Kennedy's Commons and Bent's Water-Crackers. Accounts of origin can be found in Brayley, *Bakers and Baking in Massachusetts*, 140–41; Panschar, *Economic Development*, 3; Early, *New England Cookbook*, 5–6, 8; and G. H. Bent Co., "History of Bent's," <www.bentscookiefactory.com/history.htm>. Common crackers derived from the English sea biscuit, known on land as hardtack. Home recipes for them appeared in cookbooks from the eighteenth to the early twentieth centuries, although commercial production predominated. Early on, crackers were big business. According to John Winthrop Jr., New England was exporting them in the 1660s. See Weeden, *Economic and Social History of New England*, 1:204. In Britain they retained their original name, biscuit. For biscuit origins, see Hess, *Martha Washington's Booke of Cookery*, 335; Panschar, *Economic Development*, 31–32; and Martin, *Standard of Living in 1860*, 26–27, 54. For English recipes, see Smith, *Compleat Housewife*, 181–82; for American, see Beecher, *Miss Beecher's Domestic Receipt Book*, 92–93; Lee, *Cook's Own Book*, 55; Webster, *Improved Housewife*, 130–31; and Patten, *Our New England Family Recipes*, 17. Crisp breads produced by soaking in water prior to baking went back at least as far as the sixteenth century. See Hess, *Martha Washington's Booke of Cookery*, 349, and recipe C144.

115. Early, *New England Cookbook*, 3.

116. *Journal of the Pilgrims at Plymouth*, 96–97; Higginson, *New-Englands Plantation*, B3.

117. Above, n. 22; Pillsbury, *No Foreign Food*, 14. Of course, we might find lobster no more palatable than did Bradford were it served to us unseasoned, unsauced, and with nothing to accompany it but water.

118. Carter, *Frugal Housewife*, 181; Oliver, *Saltwater Foodways*, 332; Hooker, *Food and Drink in America*, 53.

119. Gardiner, *Mrs. Gardiner's Family Receipts*, 19, 15; Beecher, *Miss Beecher's Domestic Receipt Book*, 71. See also the recipe for lobsters "neatly dressed" in lobster sauce in Webster, *Improved Housewife*, 72.

120. Gardiner, *Mrs. Gardiner's Family Receipts*, 23–24. For similar recipes a century later, see Allen, *Housekeeper's Assistant*, 130.

121. Gardiner, *Mrs. Gardiner's Family Receipts*, 54. See also Lee, *Cook's Own Book*, 75, 112; Allen, *Housekeeper's Assistant*, 130–31; Bliss, *Practical Cook Book*, 41; and Mendall, *New Bedford Practical Receipt Book*, 13. Some lobster "pies" consisted of little more than lobster and a breadcrumb and butter topping.

122. Stewed and fricasseed lobster recipes appeared in Allen, *Housekeeper's Assistant*, 130; Chadwick, *Home Cookery*, 94; and Mendall, *New Bedford Practical Receipt Book*, 12. For stewed lobster patties, see Lee, *Cook's Own Book*, 112.

123. Beecher, *Miss Beecher's Domestic Receipt Book*, 64–65; Webster, *Improved Housewife*, 72; Oliver, *Saltwater Foodways*, 344. Cold boiled lobster was not invented in New England. In the mid-fifteenth century, "crab and lobster were . . . boiled and eaten cold with vinegar." Wilson, *Food and Drink in Britain*, 44.

124. Child, *American Frugal Housewife*, 120, 60. Cold dressed lobster was included in a few other nineteenth-century sources. See, for example, Chadwick, *Home Cookery*, 94.

125. Webster, *Improved Housewife*, 65. Webster's implied reservations about excessive lobster consumption surfaced in her recipe for lobsters "neatly dressed" in lobster sauce (cited in n. 119). She warned the reader to "*eat but little* of the lobster" (Webster's emphasis).

126. Oliver, *Saltwater Foodways*, 344.

127. Drake, *Nooks and Corners of the New England Coast*, 84. Drake went on to discuss both the effort to regulate lobstering and its inadequacy: "In order to arrest the wholesale slaughter of the lobster, stringent laws have been made in Maine and Massachusetts. The fishery is prohibited during certain months, and a fine is imposed for every fish exposed for sale of less than a certain growth. Of a heap containing some eight hundred lobsters brought to the factory, not fifty were of this size; a large proportion were not eight inches long" (84–85).

128. Farmer, *Boston Cooking-School Cook Book*, 141–42. When she added that they "live exclusively in sea-water, near rocky coasts," we get the impression she meant *exclusively*.

129. Hawthorne, *Old Seaport Towns of New England*, 28–29.

130. Wright, *New England Cook Book*, 27, 132, 236; Wolcott, *New England Yankee Cook Book*, 10, 48–50. Lobster chowder was sometimes called stew, as in Bowles and Towle, *Secrets of New England Cooking*, 60, but this was not the same as stewed lobster.

131. Wilson, *Food and Drink in Britain*, 21; Drummond and Wilbraham, *Englishman's Food*, 39 (quoting Jacob Rathgreb, *A True and Faithful Narrative* [1604]); Anderson, "'Solid Sufficiency,'" 117–18, 216–17.

132. Anderson, "'Solid Sufficiency,'" 217 (quoting Evelyn A. Benson, *Penn Family Recipes* [1715]).

133. Carter, *Frugal Housewife*, 113.

134. Neustadt, *Clambake*, 25; Earle, *Home Life in Colonial Days*, 118–19 (quoting Labadist missionaries); Crawford, *Old New England Inns*, 221.

135. Booth, *Hung, Strung, and Potted*, 115; Gardiner, *Mrs. Gardiner's Family Receipts*, 32.

136. Hooker, *Food and Drink in America*, 53 (quoting French traveler Moreau de Saint Méry), 115, 145–46. The "Oys!" cry is reported in slightly different form and with the much later date of the 1880s in Oliver, *Saltwater Foodways*, 386. The Revere House, not to be confused with the house where Paul Revere resided in the late eighteenth century, was a Boston hotel whose menu in the 1850s "retained the New England tradition." See Hooker, *Food and Drink in America*, 143.

137. Pillsbury, *No Foreign Food*, 24; Martin, *Standard of Living in 1860*, 50; Hooker, *Food and Drink in America*, 145–46.

138. Lee, *Cook's Own Book*, 128–31. For examples of some of the more popular oyster preparations, see Child, *American Frugal Housewife*, 120; *Cook Not Mad*, 16; *Roger Cookery*, 16–17; Beecher, *Miss Beecher's Domestic Receipt Book*, 60; Webster, *Improved Housewife*, 73–74; Bliss, *Practical Cook Book*, 28, 39–40; Mann, *Christianity in the Kitchen*, 80–81; Chadwick, *Home Cookery*, 91–93; and Mendall, *New Bedford Practical Receipt Book*, 12–13.

139. Lee, *Cook's Own Book*, 129; Prescott, *Valuable Receipts*, 10, 26; Webster, *Improved Housewife*, 74; *Durham Cook Book*, 26, 24–25. For an acknowledgement of the great variety of foods that were pickled or made the basis of ketchups, see below, chap. 4, n. 18.

140. Prescott, *Valuable Receipts*, 10; Knight, *Tit-Bits*, 20, 5–6; *Godey's*, May 1880, 465. For oysters as basic ingredients in sauce for poultry, see chap. 5, nn. 66–67, 69–70. By the middle of the nineteenth century, some northern oyster beds were becoming depleted, and efforts to replant them with southern oysters were undertaken. In the 1850s, investors brought Chesapeake Bay oysters to Narragansett Bay. The same practice was followed in Long Island Sound. See Muir, *Reflections in Bullough's Pond*, 209–10; Bowles and Towle, *Secrets of New England Cooking*, 29; Oliver, *Saltwater Foodways*, 385.

141. Bowles and Towle, *Secrets of New England Cooking*, 29; Oliver, *Saltwater Foodways*, 386–87; Jones, *American Food*, 18; Lee, *Cook's Own Book*, 128.

142. Leslie, *Lady's Receipt Book*, 393, described an oyster supper: "It is customary at oyster suppers to have a great portion of oysters roasted in the shell and brought in on large dishes 'hot and hot.' Near every two chairs should be placed a small bucket to receive the shells. An oyster knife, and a clean coarse towel must be laid beside every plate, for the purpose of opening the oysters; an office that is usually performed by the gentlemen. . . . Besides those that are roasted, there should be other dishes of them, fried, stewed, and pickled. Also, oysters in pies and patties;—cold-slaw; beets; pickles; and celery; bread in the form of rolls, and butter . . . Ale and porter." For examples of pickled oyster recipes, see

Beecher, *Miss Beecher's Domestic Receipt Book*, 65; and Bliss, *Practical Cook Book*, 40–41.

143. Bowles and Towle, *Secrets of New England Cooking*, 29; Muir, *Reflections in Bullough's Pond*, 109; Stowe, *Oldtown Folks*, 284 (chap. 27).

144. Bowles and Towle, *Secrets of New England Cooking*, 29 (quoting Thackeray); Dickens, *American Notes*, 78 (chap. 3). For more on Dickens's Boston oyster adventures, see Payne, *Dickens Days in Boston*, 48, 58.

145. Lee, *Cook's Own Book*, 128–29; *Aunt Mary's New England Cook Book*, 18–19.

146. Child, *American Frugal Housewife*, 121; Beecher, *Miss Beecher's Domestic Receipt Book*, 81; Prescott, *Valuable Receipts*, 23. See also Webster, *Improved Housewife*, 87; Hunt, *Good Bread*, 17; and *Meriden Cook Book*, 48. Child spoke of salsify almost in the accents of myth or legend: "This vegetable is something like a parsnip; is planted about the same time, and requires the same cooking. It is said to taste very much like real oysters."

147. Stowe, *Oldtown Folks*, 284 (chap. 27).

148. Whatsoever Circle, *King's Daughters . . . Cook Book*, 38–39; Lincoln and Barrows, *Home Science Cook Book*, 121–22; Wright, *New England Cook Book*, 6, 32–36, 243–44; Wolcott, *New England Yankee Cook Book*, 8, 9, 51, 52, 53, 54, 55, 56, 85, 91. See also Thimble Club, *Choice Recipes from Old New England*, 26; and *Echoes from South County Kitchens*, 57–59.

149. Now considered an integral part of New England seafood cuisine, scallops only became so in the twentieth century and are therefore omitted here. For information, see Hart, "Sea Scallops," <www.nefsc.noaa.gov/sos/spsyn/iv/scallop>; Oliver, *Saltwater Foodways*, 390; and Mariani, *Dictionary of American Food and Drink*, 355–56. For examples of the few scallop recipes in nineteenth-century cookbooks, see Webster, *Improved Housewife*, 72–73; Beecher, *Miss Beecher's Domestic Receipt Book*, 65; and *Aunt Mary's New England Cook Book*, 19.

150. Higginson, *New-Englands Plantation*, B3.

151. Wood, *New Englands Prospect*, 35–36; Williams, *Key into the Language of America*, 112.

152. Josselyn, *John Josselyn, Colonial Traveler*, 75–82 (sturgeon on 76, alewives on 77).

153. Weeden, *Economic and Social History of New England*, 2:540–41; Oliver, *Saltwater Foodways*, 13–14. Of course fresh fish were also acquired at the market, a process that involved as much skill as fishing. On buying and storing fish in the colonial period, see Pillsbury, *No Foreign Food*, 24–25.

154. Simmons, *American Cookery* (introduction by Hess), 21–22.

155. Webster, *Improved Housewife*, 65–68, 70–71; Oliver, *Saltwater Foodways*, 46; Beecher, *Miss Beecher's Domestic Receipt Book*, 62.

156. Beecher, *Miss Beecher's Domestic Receipt Book*, 62, 222–23.

157. Oliver, *Saltwater Foodways*, 13; Jones, *American Food*, 96; Webster, *Improved Housewife*, 72; Pixley, *Green Mountain Cook Book*, 17–18.

158. Vickers, *Farmers and Fishermen*, 147, 313–14.

159. Booth, *Hung, Strung, and Potted*, 72; Johnson, *Highways and Byways of New England*, 223.

160. Bowles and Towle, *Secrets of New England Cooking*, 16–17. The authors ex-

plained that "in off-island speech [sleever] means to cut each side of the fish away in one piece from head to tail."

161. *Columbia Encyclopedia*, s.v. "Shad," <www.bartleby.com/65>; Hale, *Ladies' New Book of Cookery*, 42; Thoreau, *Week on the Concord and Merrimac Rivers*, 79 ("Sunday"); Clark, *Roots of Rural Capitalism*, 133; Mitchell, *It's an Old New England Custom*, 55. Thoreau was among the first to note how dams, canals, and factories had "put an end to [the] migrations" into interior New England of shad and other fish. Thoreau, *Week on the Concord and Merrimac Rivers*, 29 ("Saturday"), 79 ("Sunday").

162. *Journal of the Pilgrims at Plymouth*, 95; Mitchell, *It's an Old New England Custom*, 54. For the debate over the use of fish as fertilizer, see above, chap. 1, n. 8.

163. Oliver, *Saltwater Foodways*, 391; Earle, *Home Life in Colonial Days*, 123–24; Hale, *Ladies' New Book of Cookery*, 42–43; *Cook Not Mad*, 16; Bliss, *Practical Cook Book*, 37; Patten, *Our New England Family Recipes*, 83; Turner, *New England Cook Book*, 47; Wright, *New England Cook Book*, 40; Webster, *Improved Housewife*, 68. Sometimes shad were salted; Mitchell, *It's an Old New England Custom*, 56.

164. Johnson, *Johnson's Wonder-Working Providence*, 74; Clark, *Roots of Rural Capitalism*, 110; Mitchell, *It's an Old New England Custom*, 54, 59; Oliver, *Saltwater Foodways*, 6; Vickers, *Farmers and Fishermen*, 313–14.

165. Mitchell, *It's an Old New England Custom*, 52–53, 58–59, 62. West Springfield, Massachusetts, also named a street after shad.

166. Stowe, *Oldtown Folks*, 250 (chap. 24); Cummings, *American and His Food*, 30 (quoting Adams).

167. Pixley, *Green Mountain Cook Book*, 19; Thimble Club, *Choice Recipes from Old New England*, 54, and title page.

168. Cummings, *American and His Food*, 30–31 (paraphrasing *Recollections of Samuel Breck* [1877]).

169. Simmons, *American Cookery* (introduction by Wilson), 20–22; Carter, *Frugal Housewife*, 29–32.

170. Bowles and Towle, *Secrets of New England Cooking*, 48.

171. Early, *New England Cookbook*, 3–4 (quoting Mather); McManis, *Colonial New England*, 10; Langdon, *Everyday Things in American Life*, second illustration following page 581. One of the "Cape James" maps belonged to Captain John Smith. The word cod derives from the Middle English for bag, which the large, rather shapeless fish was thought to resemble. See Mariani, *Dictionary of American Food and Drink*, 116–17.

172. *Journal of the Pilgrims at Plymouth*, 96; Hamilton, *Gentleman's Progress*, 108.

173. Above, chap. 2, nn. 38–39; Bowles and Towle, *Secrets of New England Cooking*, 16.

174. Drake, *Nooks and Corners of the New England Coast*, 314.

175. King, *When I Lived in Salem*, 98. See also Bliss, *Practical Cook Book*, 33; Bowles and Towle, *Secrets of New England Cooking*, 15; and Early, *New England Cookbook*, 19.

176. Bliss, *Practical Cook Book*, 34; Brown, *Recipes From Old Hundred*, 40; Pixley,

Green Mountain Cook Book, 17; Rombauer and Becker, *Joy of Cooking*, 405; Lee, *Cook's Own Book*, 53; Oliver, *Saltwater Foodways*, 368, 346; *Godey's*, March 1881, 277. See also Mosser, *Foods of Old New England*, 68. The tongue is the throat; the cheeks are the small rounds of flesh on either side of the head. The sound is a tube that runs along the backbone and is filled with varying amounts of gas, by which the fish modulates its swimming depth. Mark Kurlansky writes that cod sounds are boiled for the production of isinglass, an industrial clarifying agent and component of glue. See Kurlansky, *Cod*, 34.

177. Innis, *Cod Fisheries*, 5; Drake, *Nooks and Corners of the New England Coast*, 314. The carving was briefly "cod-napped" by Harvard Lampoon staffers in 1933.

178. Winthrop, *Winthrop's Journal*, 1:310, 2:42.

179. Innes, *Creating the Commonwealth*, 299.

180. McCusker and Menard, *Economy of British America*, 108–9; Innes, *Creating the Commonwealth*, 300; Root and de Rochemont, *Eating in America*, 101.

181. Innes, *Creating the Commonwealth*, 292, 298.

182. Ibid., 295, 298; McManis, *Colonial New England*, 105–6, 108–10; Root and de Rochemont, *Eating in America*, 85; Weeden, *Economic and Social History of New England*, 1:245, 364, 371–72; 2:641; Butler, *Becoming America*, 38, 72. Among the Newport slave traders was Abraham Redwood, whose fortune helped to found the oldest lending library in the United States, the Redwood Library and Athenaeum. For a mid-eighteenth-century description of New England's "circular commerce," see Burnaby, *Travels through the Middle Settlements in North-America*, 70–71, 79.

183. Weeden, *Economic and Social History of New England*, 2:820–21, 824–26; North, *Economic Growth of the United States*, 36–45; Henretta and Nobles, *Evolution and Revolution*, 222–25.

184. North, *Economic Growth of the United States*, 160–65, 168–76; Dalzell, *Enterprising Elite*, 61–67.

CHAPTER FOUR

1. The most convenient overview of this and other aspects of economic and social change in sixteenth- and seventeenth-century England is Wrightson, *English Society*, esp. 121–48. See also Hill, *Reformation to Industrial Revolution*, 61–71; Stone, *Causes of the English Revolution*, 67–76; Kulikoff, *Agrarian Origins of American Capitalism*, 34, 36–38, 64–65, 187–90; and Innes, *Creating the Commonwealth*, 65–68.

2. Innes, *Creating the Commonwealth*, 65, 80–83; Cressy, *Coming Over*, 99 (quoting Smith, "The general historie of Virginia, New England and the Summer Isles" [1624]). See also Hill, "Pottage for Freeborn Englishmen."

3. Kulikoff, *Agrarian Origins of American Capitalism*, 194, 200; Innes, *Creating the Commonwealth*, 61–63; Vickers, *Farmers and Fishermen*, 14. For demographic profiles of the migration to New England in the 1630s, along with various positions in the ongoing debate regarding the migrants' motives, see Cressy, *Coming Over*, 63–106; Anderson, "Migrants and Motives"; and Archer, "New England Mosaic."

4. Innes, *Creating the Commonwealth*, 56, and passim; Winthrop, *Life and Letters of John Winthrop*, 1:312 (see also above, chap. 1, n. 26). For enclosure and various initiatives to improve the land, along with their profitability for some and adverse consequences for others, see Wrightson, *English Society*, 132–39.

5. Winthrop, *Life and Letters of John Winthrop*, 1:309–10.

6. McCusker and Menard, *Economy of British America*, 108; Innes, *Creating the Commonwealth*, 278–87, 296–300. Estimates of the value of the coastal trade among the thirteen colonies vary. According to one, exports from New England along the coast totaled 70 percent of those to the rest of the world. However, this figure may well underestimate the value of New England exports to the region that became Atlantic Canada. When these additional exports are taken into account, the coastal trade may turn out to have been more valuable than trade with the rest of the world. Evidence on this point is surveyed in McCusker and Menard, *Economy of British America*, 109.

7. This summary of the nature and goals of colonial New England farm households is based primarily on Henretta, *Origins of American Capitalism*, 48–54, 57–58, 59–62, 69–70, 87–93, 97–103, 106–8; Clark, *Roots of Rural Capitalism*, 21–58; and Vickers, *Farmers and Fishermen*, 1, 15, 16, 76, 244–46. For arguments that stress the emergence of market relations and values, rather than a reluctance to engage in them, see especially Rothenberg, *From Market Places to a Market Economy*; and Wood, "Enemy Is Us." For an overview of the debate, see Gilje, "Rise of Capitalism in the Early Republic," esp. 13–15 n. 4. In *Age of Homespun*, 105, Laurel Thatcher Ulrich summarizes scholarship that stresses varying degrees of participation in market production during the eighteenth century, not only between regions, but even within households.

8. This summary of the preservation traditions the colonists brought with them is drawn from Anderson, "'Solid Sufficiency,'" 85–147. Anderson describes yeoman verjuice as "a simple vinegar made from tart apples" (140–41). For verjuice as it was made in other milieus, see Scully, *Art of Cookery in the Middle Ages*, 79–81.

9. Dow, *Domestic Life in New England in the Seventeenth Century*, 19–20; Dow, *Every Day Life in the Massachusetts Bay Colony*, 43–44; Gould, *Early American House*, 24–25, 28; Booth, *Hung, Strung, and Potted*, 24–26; Cummings, *Framed Houses of Massachusetts Bay*, 28–29; Hardeman, *Shucks, Shocks, and Hominy Blocks*, 71, 114. In 1662 John Winthrop Jr. provided a description of early settler techniques of storing corn: "where they have Roome enough to spread the Eares thin, and keepe them dry, they onely pull off the huske, and lay the Eares thin in their Chambers and Garretts, but the Common way is to weave it together in long traices by some parts of the husks left upon the Eare (this worke they call traicing) and these traices they hang upon Stayes or other bearers without doors, or within, for it will keepe good and sweete hung in that manner all the Winter after, though it be in all weather without." Mood, "John Winthrop, Jr., on Indian Corn," 127.

10. Ulrich, "It 'Went Away Shee Knew Not How,'" 98.

11. Ibid., McMahon, "Comfortable Subsistence," 39, 58.

12. Cummings, *Framed Houses of Massachusetts Bay*, 29; McMahon, "Comfortable Subsistence," 39.

13. McMahon, "Comfortable Subsistence," 33, 36–41, 45, 52–59; McMahon, "'All Things in Their Proper Season,'" 132–33. Butter was generally made in the autumn and spring, cheese in the summer; see McMahon, "'All Things in Their Proper Season,'" 148.

14. McMahon, "Laying Foods By," 174–75; McMahon, "'All Things in Their Proper Season,'" 143.

15. Child, *American Frugal Housewife*, 9; Beecher, *Miss Beecher's Domestic Receipt Book*, 223; McMahon, "Laying Foods By," 172–73, 174; Doudiet, "Coastal Maine Cooking," 222.

16. McMahon, "Laying Foods By," 175–77; Child, *American Frugal Housewife*, 33. The very presence of potatoes in New England had been an early manifestation of the long-term trend toward improvements in the food supply. They were not introduced into the region until the 1720s; by the end of the eighteenth century, they ranked "first for universal use, profit, and easy acquirement," according to Amelia Simmons. Shortly thereafter, in the early decades of the nineteenth century, they constituted "the major portion of vegetable stores recorded in [probate] inventories." Mary Ellen Chase wrote that during her childhood in 1890s Maine "ninety-nine families out of a hundred would have stared, incredulous, at a potato-less dinner." Simmons, *American Cookery* (introduction by Wilson), 10; McMahon, "Comfortable Subsistence," 40; and McMahon, "'All Things in Their Proper Season,'" 144–45 (quoting Chase, *A Goodly Heritage* [1939]).

17. McMahon, "Laying Foods By," 173 n. 9, 177; Doudiet, "Coastal Maine Cooking," 222; Cornelius, *Young Housekeeper's Friend*, 227.

18. Child, *American Frugal Housewife*, 115; Beecher, *Miss Beecher's Domestic Receipt Book*, 224–25; McMahon, "Laying Foods By," 179–80; below, chap. 5, n. 95. Recipes for pickling cucumbers and many other vegetables, fruits, nuts, birds, fish, and shellfish, as well as for making ketchups, relishes, and other such condiments, were included in almost all New England cookbooks of the nineteenth century. Ketchup long antedated the popularity of the tomato and was until the early twentieth century regularly based upon other ingredients, for example walnuts. Pickle and condiment recipes were mostly derived from eighteenth-century English sources. The design of this book does not permit a discussion of these preparations. Suffice it to say that virtually every English and New English cookbook we examined included a section on pickles and/or ketchups.

19. Oliver, *Saltwater Foodways*, 8–9; Child, *American Frugal Housewife*, 14; Beecher, *Miss Beecher's Domestic Receipt Book*, 222. Dairy products were often both made and stored in a "milk room," generally located on the north or northeast side of the house and with a floor lowered to the point that it was "halfway between the cellar and the ground floor." Cummings, *Framed Houses of Massachusetts Bay*, 31; Doudiet, "Coastal Maine Cooking," 223.

20. Sloat, *Old Sturbridge Village Cookbook*, 123 (quoting Samuel G. Goodrich, *Recollections of a Lifetime* [1857]); McMahon, "'All Things in Their Proper Season,'" 140 (quoting Ellen Chapman Rollins, *New England Bygones* [1883]). See

also Stowe, *Poganuc People*, 167–68, 169, 175–76 (chap. 16). The warnings in nineteenth-century cookbooks and household manuals concerning the "bad smell" of stored cabbages and turnips were obscured in the mists of Samuel Goodrich's nostalgia; see, for example, Beecher, *Miss Beecher's Domestic Receipt Book*, 223.

21. Stowe, *Oldtown Folks*, 223 (chap. 22).

22. We are here summarizing and simplifying a complex process of social change. For more detailed accounts see Henretta, *Origins of American Capitalism*, 115–20, 262–70; Clark, *Roots of Rural Capitalism*, chaps. 3, 5, 7; Vickers, *Farmers and Fishermen*, 249–53, 258–59, 261–63, 290–91, 313–14, 323–24; and Gross, *Minutemen and Their World*, 74–94.

23. Wrightson, *English Society*, 92; Kulikoff, *Agrarian Origins of American Capitalism*, 34, 36. See also Clark, *Roots of Rural Capitalism*, 25–26; and Boydston, *Home and Work*, 7.

24. Gies and Gies, *Life in a Medieval Village*, 144–46; Anderson, "'Solid Sufficiency,'" 29–31; Boydston, *Home and Work*, 11–12.

25. Boydston, *Home and Work*, 12–14.

26. Clark, *Roots of Rural Capitalism*, 26.

27. Ibid., 132.

28. Ibid., 186. For a description of palm leaf hatmaking that emphasizes continuities with household production traditions, see Ulrich, *Age of Homespun*, 398–99.

29. Clark, *Roots of Rural Capitalism*, 188. The Hampshire County newspaper editor was not the first man to extol textile-related labor as a remedy for feminine idleness. In 1814, Berkshire County, Massachusetts, orator Elkanah Watson stated that expanded production of woolen textiles would "confine the younger class of females to habitual industry." Even earlier, in 1753, as part of a campaign in Boston to employ the poor in spinning schools and a linen factory, the Rev. Samuel Cooper preached that "spinning was 'peculiarly adapted to prevent idleness.' It could be fitted into 'those little Vacancies of Time, that necessarily intervene between other Kinds of Business.'" See Ulrich, *Age of Homespun*, 331–32 (quoting Elkanah Watson, "Address Delivered before the Berkshire Agricultural Society"), 157–61, 165 (quoting Samuel Cooper, *Sermon Preached in Boston . . . August 8, 1753*).

30. Boydston, *Home and Work*, 142–63, is an excellent account of the sentimentalized understanding of the home as detached from labor and money. The pioneering study is Cott, *Bonds of Womanhood*.

31. Boydston, *Home and Work*, 130–33, 134–36, 137.

32. Ibid., 133–34, 136–37.

33. Simmons, *American Cookery* (introduction by Wilson), 5–10, 3.

34. Child, *American Frugal Housewife*, 14–15; Hale, *Ladies' New Book of Cookery*, iii.

35. Lee, *Cook's Own Book*, viii, ix. Lee's recipes, however, were usually not in keeping with this outlook. For an appreciation of Child on the score of frugality, see Sloat, *Old Sturbridge Village Cookbook*, 24: "Mrs. Child in her Frugal Housewife has won unfading laurels in producing that which is calculated to benefit

the greatest number" (quoting *The Farmer's Monthly Visitor* [New Hampshire, 1843]).

36. Howland, *American Economical Housekeeper*, 9; Knight, *Tit-Bits*, 5.

37. *Aunt Mary's New England Cook Book*, 3.

38. Child, *American Frugal Housewife*, 88; Winthrop, *Life and Letters of John Winthrop*, 1:309–10 (and above, n. 5).

39. Bushman, *Refinement of America*, 412 (quoting critic John Fanning Watson of Philadelphia), and passim.

40. Ibid., xvii–xix.

41. Child, *American Frugal Housewife*, 89–90.

42. Ibid., 110.

43. Hale, *Good Housekeeper*, 134, 105. The first quotation also appeared in Hale, *Ladies' New Book of Cookery*, 439.

44. Cornelius, *Young Housekeeper's Friend*, 12, 20.

45. Child, *American Frugal Housewife*, 90–91.

46. Ibid., 97.

47. Ibid., 3, 8.

48. Beecher, *Miss Beecher's Domestic Receipt Book*, 276.

49. Beecher, *Treatise on Domestic Economy*, 16–17.

50. Beecher, *Miss Beecher's Domestic Receipt Book*, 278.

51. Beecher and Stowe, *American Woman's Home*, 225.

52. Beecher, *Treatise on Domestic Economy*, 136–37.

53. Ibid., 144; Beecher and Stowe, *American Woman's Home*, 222; Beecher, *Miss Beecher's Domestic Receipt Book*, 247. For inventories of kitchen implements, see Beecher, *Treatise on Domestic Economy*, 369–71; and Beecher, *Miss Beecher's Domestic Receipt Book*, 252–68; for formal dining description and layout, see Beecher, *Miss Beecher's Domestic Receipt Book*, 243–46. For systematic analysis of the house and the human body, see Beecher and Stowe, *American Woman's Home*, passim. Similar contrasts between Beecher and Child are drawn in Beecher, *Treatise on Domestic Economy*, vi (introduction by Sklar); and Sklar, *Catharine Beecher*, 154, 166.

54. Beecher and Stowe, *American Woman's Home*, 41–42.

55. Winthrop, "Modell of Christian Charity," 198; Beecher, *Treatise on Domestic Economy*, 144. For a more comprehensive discussion of Catharine Beecher's ideology of domesticity, see Sklar, *Catharine Beecher*, 155–67. Regarding *American Woman's Home* specifically, Sklar states that in it Beecher presented "the family as a small-scale model of how the society as a whole should function" (264).

56. Lee, *Cook's Own Book*, xx. The stresses and strains attendant upon producing refined meals in the open hearth kitchen were also apparent in Lee's complaint that "the patience of cooks is exhausted" by the constant need of "attendance to prevent the accident" of things "catching fire." "Kitchen fireplaces . . . are seldom light enough for the nicer operations of cookery," she further fretted (xxi). Putting refinement in its place, but not disapproving of it altogether, was indicated in Child's case by, for example, her statement (above, n. 45) that it would have been proper for the extravagant farmer's daughter to have had "tasteful

vases," so long as she had made them herself. For indications that refinement had spread from coastal towns into the rural interior of New England in the late eighteenth and early nineteenth centuries and that ambivalence about it persisted, see Ulrich, *Age of Homespun*, 291–305, 309, 317–39. Catharine Beecher's interest in simultaneously expressing and controlling aspirations to refinement was evident in her formal dining advice that laid everything out according to a strictly predefined pattern; see above, n. 53, and illustration, p. 143. In her commentary on this diagram, Beecher made such remarks as: "There are modes of *garnishing dishes*, and preparing them for table, which give an air of taste and refinement, that pleases the eye." Beecher, *Miss Beecher's Domestic Receipt Book*, 246. While working as a schoolmistress in Hartford, Connecticut, in the 1820s, Beecher worked out her own synthesis of traditional feminine refinement and evangelical activism. See Sklar, *Catharine Beecher*, 61–77.

57. Lee, *Cook's Own Book*, 11, 12; King, *When I Lived in Salem*, 26–27, 105.

58. Gardiner, *Mrs. Gardiner's Family Receipts*, v, 12, 13, 2, 3, 4, 8, 23, 21, 66; Sewall, *Diary*, 1:32; 2:768 (31 August 1714), 2:959 (10 October 1720), 2:961 (12 October 1720), 2:962 (18 and 19 October 1720), 2:965 (2 November 1720), 2:966 (7 November 1720).

59. Coe and Coe, "Mid-Eighteenth-Century Food and Drink on the Massachusetts Frontier," 44; Derven, "Wholesome, Toothsome, and Diverse," 49, 53–55. Lucy Larcom stated that in Beverly, Massachusetts, during her childhood in the 1820s and 1830s "jars of preserved tropical fruits, tamarinds, gingerroot, and other spicy appetizers" were to be found "in the cupboards of most housekeepers." However, Beverly is next door to Salem, and Larcom's passage was part of her evocation of the "spirit" of "our Massachusetts coast towns." Larcom, *New England Girlhood*, 94–95, 117.

60. King, *When I Lived in Salem*, 25. For similar comments see Pillsbury, *No Foreign Food*, 218. And for the nineteenth-century invention of the "traditional" New England landscape, see Wood, *New England Village*.

CHAPTER FIVE

1. Wilson, *Food and Drink in Britain*, 62–63, 78, 103; Drummond and Wilbraham, *Englishman's Food*, 24, 25; Anderson, "'Solid Sufficiency,'" 63 (quoting G. E. Fussell, *The English Dairy Farmer, 1500–1900* [1966]).

2. Anderson, "'Solid Sufficiency,'" 58, 60, 68, 64, 66, 100; Drummond and Wilbraham, *Englishman's Food*, 24, 25, 29; Wilson, *Food and Drink in Britain*, 78. The sheep also provided wool, of course.

3. Wilson, *Food and Drink in Britain*, 81–84, 96; Drummond and Wilbraham, *Englishman's Food*, 24, 25; Anderson, "'Solid Sufficiency,'" 79.

4. Wilson, *Food and Drink in Britain*, 108; Anderson, "'Solid Sufficiency,'" 77–79.

5. Cronon, *Changes in the Land*, 39–40.

6. Ibid., 46–48.

7. Ibid., 51; Dwight, *Travels in New England and New York*, 4:38.

8. Cronon, *Changes in the Land*, 51; Dwight, *Travels in New England and New York*, 4:38. See also Muir, *Reflections in Bullough's Pond*, 19.

9. Cronon, *Changes in the Land*, 128–31, 135–37, 100–101; Williams, *Key into the Language of America*, 174; Muir, *Reflections in Bullough's Pond*, 144.

10. Cronon, *Changes in the Land*, 138–41, 162 (quoting Miantonomo). Miantonomo is also quoted in Innes, *Creating the Commonwealth*, 34. Cronon cites "Leift Lion Gardener His Relation of the Pequot Warres," *Massachusetts Historical Society Collections*, 3d ser., 3 (1833): 154–55; Innes uses a recent anthology: "Miantonomo's Call for Indian Unity, 1642," in *Major Problems in American Colonial History: Documents and Essays*, ed. Karen Ordahl Kupperman (Lexington, Mass.: D. C. Heath, 1993), 135.

11. McMahon, "Comfortable Subsistence."

12. Bennett, "Food Economy of the New England Indians," 386; Snow, *Archaeology of New England*, 76.

13. Wilson, *Food and Drink in Britain*, 118–20.

14. Ibid., 120–26. Roasting methods are discussed below, n. 120.

15. Snow, *Archaeology of New England*, 334; Wood, *New Englands Prospect*, 72 (see also, above, chap. 1, n. 112); Russell, *Indian New England before the Mayflower*, 75.

16. Wilson, *Food and Drink in Britain*, 126–28, 134–35; Thirsk, "Patterns of Agriculture in Seventeenth-Century England," 48. For an example of potted swan in an eighteenth-century cookbook, see Smith, *Compleat Housewife*, 72.

17. Hooker, *Food and Drink in America*, 21 (quoting Sidney V. James, ed., *Three Visitors to Early Plymouth* [1963]); Baker, "Seventeenth-Century English Yeoman Foodways at Plimoth Plantation," 107; McMahon, "Comfortable Subsistence," 34; Earle, *Home Life in Colonial Days*, 110; Booth, *Hung, Strung, and Potted*, 93; Hazard, *Jonny-Cake Papers*, 76–78. Hazard stated that, as with freshwater fish (see chap. 3, n. 62), eating "small birds" such as blackbirds and robins would have been, to the working people of this Rhode Island neighborhood at this time, "as repugnant . . . as the eating of rats and mice" (345–46).

18. Hazard, *Jonny-Cake Papers*, 76, 69, 77; Bowles and Towle, *Secrets of New England Cooking*, 80–81. For the Chesapeake canvasback duck, see Hooker, *Food and Drink in America*, 111, 224. A cookbook published in 1939 that strove to perpetuate New England culinary tradition included a recipe for "Coot Stew," accompanied by another "recipe" from Maine. In order to assist the reader in appreciating the latter, the author remarked that "fifty goose shot will rattle off a coot as though his feathers were made of steel." Here is the Maine "recipe": "Place the bird in a kettle of water with a red building brick free of mortar and blemishes. Parboil the coot and brick together for 3 hours. Pour off water, fill the kettle, and again parboil for 3 hours. Once more throw off the water, refill the kettle, and this time let the coot and brick simmer together overnight. In the morning throw away the coot and eat the brick." Wolcott, *New England Yankee Cook Book*, 99.

19. Martin, *Standard of Living in 1860*, 13; King, *When I Lived in Salem*, 26; Child, *American Frugal Housewife*, 121; Hale, *Good Housekeeper*, 54; Bliss, *Practical Cook Book*, 84–86. See also Prescott, *Valuable Receipts*, 6.

20. Simmons, *American Cookery* (introduction by Wilson), 7–8, 18–19; Child,

American Frugal Housewife, 54–55; Beecher, *Miss Beecher's Domestic Receipt Book*, 41.

21. Lee, *Cook's Own Book*, 78–79, 83–84, 67, 133–34; Turner, *New England Cook Book*, 66–67; Wright, *New England Cook Book*, 110, 116, 118–20, 124–26. This last author copied many of her wildfowl recipes from Lee, a practice she also followed for domesticated fowl.

22. Schorger, *Passenger Pigeon*, 133–34; Wood, *New Englands Prospect*, 30. The Indians also used duck and goose oil in cooking; see Russell, *Indian New England before the Mayflower*, 91.

23. Matthiessen, *Wildlife in America*, 56, 200–201; Winthrop, *Winthrop's Journal*, 2:92.

24. Schorger, *Passenger Pigeon*, 204, 170–98; Winthrop, *Winthrop's Journal*, 2:348; Booth, *Hung, Strung, and Potted*, 97; Josselyn, *John Josselyn, Colonial Traveler*, 71.

25. Burnaby, *Travels through the Middle Settlements in North-America*, 76–77 (also cited in Hooker, *Food and Drink in America*, 54–55); Schorger, *Passenger Pigeon*, 27–30.

26. Knight, *Tit-Bits*, 19. See also ibid., 22; Child, *American Frugal Housewife*, 56; Beecher, *Miss Beecher's Domestic Receipt Book*, 42; Mann, *Christianity in the Kitchen*, 137; and *Aunt Mary's New England Cook Book*, 12–13. "Alamode Pigeons" is an example of a "made dish." Although this terminology has fallen out of use in America, it remains current in Britain. Essentially, it refers to "either a more elaborate mode of cookery than plain broiling or roasting, or else some combination of those elementary processes, — as for example half roasting and finishing in the stew pan, which is a very common way of dressing a *ragout*." Made dishes usually involved some degree of variety and complexity in the ingredients and seasonings included, and there was often an indication of French influence, as the terms "ragout" and "alamode" suggest. Such French-influenced preparations were condemned as "too highly seasoned, to be wholesome, and too expensive to be available for a family dinner" on the one hand. On the other hand, they were regularly included, as with Mrs. Knight, in cookbooks aimed at a middling, "family" readership. Such ambivalence had also been seen in Hannah Glasse's cookbook in the mid-eighteenth century. Glasse counterposed the sophistication and "tricks" of "a *French* booby" to the honest plainness of "a good *English* cook," but she also devoted an entire lengthy chapter to "*Made-Dishes*." Many of the recipes in the chapter included either "à la" or "the French way" in their titles. See Hooker, *Food and Drink in America*, 77–78 (quoting *The Cook and Housewife's Manual* [1826], and *The Housekeeper's Book* [1838]); and Glasse, *Art of Cookery Made Plain and Easy* (glossary and notes by Davidson), ii and "Contents, Chap. II." For a discussion of English attitudes toward French culinary complexity in the seventeenth century, see Mennell, *All Manners of Food*, 84–95. Many of the recipes mentioned or described in the remainder of this chapter would have been considered made dishes.

27. *Cambridge World History of Food*, 1:496; Wilson, *Food and Drink in Britain*, 113–

14, 116, 119; Scully, *Art of Cookery in the Middle Ages*, 29. A songwriter of the 1990s agreed with medieval monastic authorities. Chicken should not be proscribed by vegetarians, since it was a "cusp species, kind of like broccoli walkin' around"; see Brown, "Canned Goods."

28. Wilson, *Food and Drink in Britain*, 130–31; Anderson, "'Solid Sufficiency,'" 71–72.

29. Hooker, *Food and Drink in America*, 29; Baker, "Seventeenth-Century English Yeoman Foodways at Plimoth Plantation," 107; Booth, *Hung, Strung, and Potted*, 91.

30. Coe and Coe, "Mid-Eighteenth-Century Food and Drink on the Massachusetts Frontier," 42; Friedmann, "Victualling Colonial Boston," 197.

31. Stowe, *Minister's Wooing*, 83 (chap. 9), 188 (chap. 21).

32. Ulrich, "It 'Went Away Shee Knew Not How,'" 97; Dow, *Every Day Life in the Massachusetts Bay Colony*, 77–78.

33. Gardiner, *Mrs. Gardiner's Family Receipts*, 56.

34. King, *When I Lived in Salem*, 25; Sloat, *Old Sturbridge Village Cookbook*, 22–23. For chicken pie recipes besides those cited below in chap. 6, nn. 96, 100, and 115, see Bliss, *Practical Cook Book*, 83–84; Knight, *Tit-Bits*, 25; *Durham Cook Book*, 32–33; and Wright, *New England Cook Book*, 108–9.

35. Stowe, *Oldtown Folks*, 429 (chap. 40), 346 (chap. 32); Stowe, *Minister's Wooing*, 257 (chap. 30); Stowe, *Pearl of Orr's Island*, 297 (chap. 30).

36. Pillsbury, *No Foreign Food*, 24; Martin, *Standard of Living in 1860*, 49.

37. Simmons, *American Cookery* (introduction by Wilson), 7–8; Child, *American Frugal Housewife*, 53; Beecher, *Miss Beecher's Domestic Receipt Book*, 30. See also Prescott, *Valuable Receipts*, 4.

38. Simmons, *American Cookery* (introduction by Wilson), 18; Child, *American Frugal Housewife*, 53; Beecher, *Miss Beecher's Domestic Receipt Book*, 47.

39. Child, *American Frugal Housewife*, 53–54; Lee, *Cook's Own Book*, 48–49; Knight, *Tit-Bits*, 21. Catharine Beecher, in *Miss Beecher's Domestic Receipt Book*, also mentioned stuffing in her recipe "To Stew Birds" (41).

40. Child, *American Frugal Housewife*, 53–55; Lee, *Cook's Own Book*, 50; Bliss, *Practical Cook Book*, 82–83; Turner, *New England Cook Book*, 62; Knight, *Tit-Bits*, 28; Wolcott, *New England Yankee Cook Book*, 21; Beecher, *Miss Beecher's Domestic Receipt Book*, 39–40; *Meriden Cook Book*, 23.

41. Child, *American Frugal Housewife*, 54; Beecher, *Miss Beecher's Domestic Receipt Book*, 50–51; Lee, *Cook's Own Book*, 49–50. Lee offered equally rich brown fricassees, such as "Chickens Chiringate" (49); there had been a similar recipe in Glasse, *Art of Cookery Made Plain and Easy* (glossary and notes by Davidson), 39. See also Bliss, *Practical Cook Book*, 82; and Mann, *Christianity in the Kitchen*, 142. Later fricassee recipes in our sample were of the brown persuasion. See *Aunt Mary's New England Cook Book*, 10; and Patten, *Our New England Family Recipes*, 13–14. Wright, *New England Cook Book*, 108, reprinted Lee's recipe verbatim and without acknowledgement. Plagiarism had remained standard practice among cookbook authors in the eighteenth and early nineteenth centuries

but was no longer so in Wright's day. Perhaps she was inspired by antiquarianism in this respect as in others.

42. Vaughan, *Yankee Hill-Country Cooking*, 50, 53–55. Another intriguing preparation claimed to be "excellent for tough fowl" was "South County Chicken," which could be made with rabbit as well as chicken. See *Echoes from South County Kitchens*, 25.

43. Schorger, *Wild Turkey*, 3, 478–79, 369, 468–69; Wilson, *Food and Drink in Britain*, 128–30.

44. Schorger, *Wild Turkey*, 479–80, 219.

45. Ibid., 480 (quoting Edgar Gilbert, *History of Salem, N.H.* [1907], and William Bentley, *Diary* [1905–14]).

46. Cronon, *Changes in the Land*, 51, 23; Wood, *New Englands Prospect*, 30; Schorger, *Wild Turkey*, 50 (quoting Morton, *New English Canaan* [1632]).

47. Wood, *New Englands Prospect*, 30; Cronon, *Changes in the Land*, 190 n. 17; Williams, *Key into the Language of America*, 91. See also Schorger, *Wild Turkey*, 377; Cronon, *Changes in the Land*, 64.

48. Williams, *Key into the Language of America*, 119; Wood, *New Englands Prospect*, 101; Schorger, *Wild Turkey*, 357; Josselyn, *John Josselyn, Colonial Traveler*, 70; Mitchell, *It's an Old New England Custom*, 26.

49. Wood, *New Englands Prospect*, 30–31; Cronon, *Changes in the Land*, 23 (quoting Morton).

50. Cronon, *Changes in the Land*, 23; Schorger, *Wild Turkey*, 142, 370; Mitchell, *It's an Old New England Custom*, 26–27 (quoting Brillat-Savarin, *Physiologie du Goût* [1826]). Cotton Mather must have been served a turkey that was old as well as wild when he complained in 1717 in a letter to the Royal Society that the bird's flesh was "tough and hard"; see Schorger, *Wild Turkey*, 371, 572.

51. Mitchell, *It's an Old New England Custom*, 28; Josselyn, *New England's Rarities Discovered*, 42 (also quoted in Cronon, *Changes in the Land*, 100); Hooker, *Food and Drink in America*, 54, 109.

52. Franklin, *Writings*, 1088; Booth, *Hung, Strung, and Potted*, 94. Given the turkey's failure to run when its companions were shot and killed, the accusation of stupidity was perhaps difficult to dispute. On the other hand, to the Indians the turkey had been "a prized bird because it had the powers of quickness and cleverness." The Indian use of turkey feathers for apparel and ornament, noted above, had spiritual significance: "By putting turkey feathers in a hair knot or coat, the individual is incorporating the turkey's keen abilities"; see Weinstein, Passas, and Marques, "Use of Feathers in Native New England," 183.

53. Josselyn, *New England's Rarities Discovered*, 42; Schorger, *Wild Turkey*, 139, 142–43.

54. Schorger, *Wild Turkey*, 16.

55. Ibid., 16, 3; Crosby, *Columbian Exchange*, 188.

56. Tannahill, *Food in History*, 253; Wilson, *Food and Drink in Britain*, 129; Schorger, *Wild Turkey*, 16 (quoting Johnson, *Dictionary* [1755]); Cronon, *Changes in the Land*, 100 (the handbook was Samuel Deane, *The New England Farmer* [1790]).

57. Hazard, *Jonny-Cake Papers*, 72–73; Wilson, *Food and Drink in Britain*, 130 (quoting Digby, *The Closet Opened* [1669]).

58. Hazard, *Jonny-Cake Papers*, 73–74.

59. Ibid., 323.

60. Wilson, *Food and Drink in Britain*, 129–31; Ulrich, "It 'Went Away Shee Knew Not How,'" 97; Stowe, *Minister's Wooing*, 260–61 (chap. 30). The household from which the wedding turkey was stolen was that of *the* Anne Bradstreet, the poet.

61. Smith, "First Thanksgiving," 81, 84–85; Deetz and Deetz, *Times of Their Lives*, 22; *Journal of the Pilgrims at Plymouth*, 95–96; Bradford, *Of Plymouth Plantation*, 90.

62. Schorger, *Wild Turkey*, 368–69 (Boston market quotation from J. Stuart, *Three Years in North America* [1833]).

63. Hale, *Northwood*, 1:109; Schorger, *Wild Turkey*, 369 (Schorger was unable to verify the Jackson proclamation). On the place of turkey in Thanksgiving dinner, see Oliver, *Saltwater Foodways*, 242–43; and Smith, "First Thanksgiving," 80.

64. See below, chap. 6, nn. 109–27.

65. King, *When I Lived in Salem*, 24–25. For the tin kitchen, see the discussion below, nn. 120–21.

66. Glasse, *Art of Cookery Made Plain and Easy* (glossary and notes by Davidson), 34. For another roast turkey recipe in an English source known to have circulated in the colonies, see Smith, *Compleat Housewife*, 22.

67. Simmons, *American Cookery* (introduction by Wilson), 18–19.

68. Child, *American Frugal Housewife*, 55, 122–23.

69. Lee, *Cook's Own Book*, 227. Catharine Beecher agreed that the bird "looks nicer if wrapped in a cloth dredged with flour"; see Beecher, *Miss Beecher's Domestic Receipt Book*, 42. See also *Roger Cookery*, 15; and Bliss, *Practical Cook Book*, 80. As with "Chickens Fricasseed," Wright, in *New England Cook Book*, 123–24, plagiarized Lee's recipe for "Turkey, Roasted."

70. For other boiled turkey recipes, see Knight, *Tit-Bits*, 20; and Turner, *New England Cook Book*, 61–62.

71. Turner, *New England Cook Book*, 61. For other roast turkey and/or stuffing recipes, see Beecher, *Miss Beecher's Domestic Receipt Book*, 46–47; and *Durham Cook Book*, 33. Salt pork stuffing, in a version more austere than those of Simmons and Child, had one final moment in the spotlight; see Vaughan, *Yankee Hill-Country Cooking*, 63. On the page facing the 1905 stuffing recipe in the Turner volume was an advertisement for "Bell's Spiced Seasoning," now known as Bell's Seasoning. This product of the William G. Bell Company of Boston, consisting of rosemary, oregano, sage, ginger, marjoram, thyme, and pepper, had first been concocted in 1867, when Bell had been a mere lad; see Early, *New England Cookbook*, 39.

72. Wood, *New Englands Prospect*, 20.

73. Cressy, *Coming Over*, 8; Wood, *New Englands Prospect*, 23, 21.

74. Cronon, *Changes in the Land*, 24.

75. Baker, "Seventeenth-Century English Yeoman Foodways at Plimoth Plantation," 107; Booth, *Hung, Strung, and Potted*, 69; Cronon, *Changes in the Land*,
101.

76. Johnson, *Johnson's Wonder-Working Providence*, 85, 210; Field, "'Peculiar Manuerance,'" 20.

77. Pendery, "Archeology of Urban Foodways in Portsmouth, New Hampshire,"
21–22; Coe and Coe, "Mid-Eighteenth-Century Food and Drink on the Massachusetts Frontier," 42; Derven, "Wholesome, Toothsome, and Diverse," 56.

78. Martin, *Standard of Living in 1860*, 49; Sewall, *Diary*, 1:380 (20 October 1697);
King, *When I Lived in Salem*, 25. Venison, either roasted or cooked at the table in
the manner described by King, was sometimes served for Thanksgiving dinner
in the later nineteenth century; see Hooker, *Food and Drink in America*, 223.

79. Howland, *American Economical Housekeeper*, 11; Lee, *Cook's Own Book*, 83, 238,
94; Simmons, *American Cookery* (introduction by Wilson), 8–9; *Meriden Cook
Book*, 24.

80. Turner, *New England Cook Book*, 67–68; Wright, *New England Cook Book*, 114–
15, 120–21 (plagiarizing from Lee); Stowe, *Oldtown Folks*, 357 (chap. 33); Wolcott, *New England Yankee Cook Book*, 98, 280; Vaughan, *Yankee Hill-Country
Cooking*, 46–48.

81. Johnson, *Highways and Byways of New England*, 55.

82. Shammas, *Pre-Industrial Consumer in England and America*, 54; Derven,
"Wholesome, Toothsome, and Diverse," 56. Mutton achieved one macabre moment in the spotlight. In the Borden household in the textile manufacturing
city of Fall River, Massachusetts, on the sweltering morning of 4 August 1892,
the breakfast menu included mutton soup with potatoes and cold leftover boiled
mutton. The day before, there had been the same boiled mutton (though served
piping hot this time) and mutton soup for the midday meal, and the soup had
been warmed up again for supper. Steaming mutton soup three times in a row in
the steaming August heat. Not long after the diners adjourned from a breakfast
table that must rank as one of the most bizarre in New England history, an axe
murder that certainly does rank among the most famous and gruesome in New
England history was perpetrated upon two of them, the master and mistress of
the household. The next year during the trial of Lizzie Borden for this murder,
Bridget Sullivan, the Borden family domestic and crucial witness to the events
of that day, "laughed at the mutton and cold mutton, and mutton broth, just
as others have laughed at the same thing. Lizzie laughed, too, at the mutton."
Rebello, *Lizzie Borden Past and Present*, 90–93.

83. Anderson, "'Solid Sufficiency,'" 99–100; Wilson, *Food and Drink in Britain*,
78; McMahon, "Comfortable Subsistence," 35–36; Sloat, *Old Sturbridge Village Cookbook*, 22. For a discussion that places less emphasis on the tendency in
England to slaughter early, see Gies and Gies, *Life in a Medieval Village*, 146–47.

84. Pendery, "Archeology of Urban Foodways in Portsmouth, New Hampshire,"
23–25; Clark, *Roots of Rural Capitalism*, 77; Friedmann, "Victualling Colonial
Boston," 197; Martin, *Standard of Living in 1860*, 13; Anderson, "'Solid Sufficiency,'" 100; Drummond and Wilbraham, *Englishman's Food*, 24–25.

85. Stowe, *Oldtown Folks*, 144–45 (chap. 16); McMahon, "Laying Foods By," 187 (quoting a November 1844 entry from the diary of Hannah Buxton).

86. McMahon, "Laying Foods By," 187–88 (quoting a December 1844 entry from the diary of Persis Sibley Andrews of Freeport, Maine).

87. Anderson, "'Solid Sufficiency,'" 101 (citing Josselyn, *Account of Two Voyages to America* [London, 1673]); Stowe, *Oldtown Folks*, 124–25 (chap. 13), 290 (chap. 27).

88. Dow, *Every Day Life in the Massachusetts Bay Colony*, 91; Clark, *Roots of Rural Capitalism*, 79, 88; McMahon, "'All Things in Their Proper Season,'" 138 (quoting a January 1808 entry from the diary of Martha Moore Ballard); Anderson, "'Solid Sufficiency,'" 102 (quoting Thomas Tusser).

89. Child, *American Frugal Housewife*, 40–41; Anderson, "'Solid Sufficiency,'" 102, 107. Evan Jones evokes "the pork barrel in the cellar . . . where red-streaked creamy slabs of sidemeat had been laid down in brine thick enough to let the pork pieces float when the heavy hewn-oak cover was lifted. This is an image of treasury . . . dipping into the pork barrel still turns up in accounts of lawmakers' machinations"; see Jones, *American Food*, 12.

90. Anderson, "'Solid Sufficiency,'" 107–8; McMahon, "Laying Foods By," 188 (quoting Andrews).

91. Anderson, "'Solid Sufficiency,'" 103–4.

92. Child, *American Frugal Housewife*, 41–42; Anderson, "'Solid Sufficiency,'" 103–4.

93. *Echoes from South County Kitchens*, 23; Anderson, "'Solid Sufficiency,'" 103.

94. Child, *American Frugal Housewife*, 41–42; Simmons, *American Cookery* (introduction by Wilson), 5–6; McMahon, "Laying Foods By," 189 n. 31. Anne Gibbons Gardiner recorded in her manuscript cookbook a recipe for "Hams to cure, the New England Way" that confusingly combined techniques of dry salting and pickling. Gardiner first spoke of rubbing the hams with the same ingredients Child called for and then hanging them up to smoke, the rubbing phase to last for six weeks, the hanging and smoking for four, again just as in Child's dry salting procedure. Although Gardiner called the blend of salt, saltpeter, and molasses that was repeatedly to be rubbed in the meat a "Pickle," it did not function as such until later on in the recipe. There she spoke of the hams as though they had been left to soak in the waterless "Pickle" she had called for earlier. Probably she jotted down notes about genuine pickling and forgot to insert any transition to what was essentially a different recipe. Gardiner added a few details regarding the smoking process, stating that the best smoke was obtained either from "Tanners Bark" or "Horse Dung." Gardiner, *Mrs. Gardiner's Family Receipts*, 42. Simmons, in *American Cookery* (introduction by Wilson), 6, recommended "cobs or malt fumes" as the smoking agent. Preservation techniques for pork and ham are discussed together in *Cook Not Mad*, 7–8; and Gilman, *Lady's Annual Register . . . for 1840*, 108.

95. Anderson, "'Solid Sufficiency,'" 113; Child, *American Frugal Housewife*, 41; McMahon, "Laying Foods By," 180 (quoting Nathan Daboll, *New England Almanack* [1778]); McMahon, "'All Things in Their Proper Season,'" 143 n. 34 (quot-

ing Isaiah Thomas, *New England Almanac* [1791]). A contemporary of Child's cautioned that "although the same brine will answer for pickling beef, as that for hams, and the lean parts of pork, yet the two kinds of meat should not be in the brine at the same time. A small piece of beef placed in a barrel where there is pork, would spoil the latter quickly. A beef barrel, likewise, should never be used for pork, no matter how thoroughly scalded or cleansed." *Cook Not Mad*, 8.

96. McMahon, "'All Things in Their Proper Season,'" 143 n. 33; McMahon, "Laying Foods By," 189 n. 31; Anderson, "'Solid Sufficiency,'" 104–5; Earle, *Home Life in Colonial Days*, 154 (sausage gun: "much like a tube-and-piston . . . syringe"). Earle states that in colonial New York farmhouses, sharpened spades were used to cut sausage meat (154–55).

97. Anderson, "'Solid Sufficiency,'" 102; McMahon, "Laying Foods By," 189 n. 31; Clark, *Roots of Rural Capitalism*, 77.

98. McMahon, "Comfortable Subsistence," 36; Ulrich, "It 'Went Away Shee Knew Not How,'" 98.

99. McMahon, "Comfortable Subsistence," 36–38.

100. Wilson, *Food and Drink in Britain*, 75–76, 88; Gies and Gies, *Life in a Medieval Village*, 147–48; Anderson, "'Solid Sufficiency,'" 69.

101. Drummond and Wilbraham, *Englishman's Food*, 29 (quoting Thomas Lodge and Robert Greene, *A Looking Glasse, for London and England* [1598]).

102. Wilson, *Food and Drink in Britain*, 79, 96.

103. Friedmann, "Victualling Colonial Boston," 191; Innes, *Creating the Commonwealth*, 279–81.

104. Johnson, *Johnson's Wonder-Working Providence*, 209. See also Bradford, *Of Plymouth Plantation*, 302: from the sale of cattle at high prices to later immigrants, "the ancient planters which had any stock, began to grow in their estates."

105. Innes, *Creating the Commonwealth*, 281; Friedmann, "Victualling Colonial Boston," 195–97; McCusker and Menard, *Economy of British America*, 108.

106. Friedmann, "Victualling Colonial Boston," 197, 196.

107. Clark, *Roots of Rural Capitalism*, 77–78.

108. Dwight, *Travels in New England and New York*, 4:249 (also quoted in Oliver, *Saltwater Foodways*, 17); Martin, *Standard of Living in 1860*, 46 (quoting Horace P. Batcheler, *Jonathan at Home* [1864]).

109. Wilson, *Food and Drink in Britain*, 97 (quoting F. M. Misson, *Memoirs* [1719]); Hale, *Good Housekeeper*, 21. In the introductory "Custom-House" section of *The Scarlet Letter*, 20–21, Nathaniel Hawthorne described the elderly chief official as having noteworthy powers of recalling "the good dinners which it had made no small portion of the happiness of his life to eat." His memories of flesh foods were particularly vivid: "A tenderloin of beef, a hind-quarter of veal, a spare-rib of pork, a particular chicken, or a remarkably praise-worthy turkey, which had perhaps adorned his board in the days of the elder Adams, would be remembered."

110. Oliver, *Saltwater Foodways*, 15; McMahon, "Comfortable Subsistence," 37, 55, 56; Derven, "Wholesome, Toothsome, and Diverse," 56; Shammas, *Pre-Indus-*

trial Consumer in England and America, 54, 58. Others who have discussed the issue, all of whom place pork in the lead, include Cummings, *American and His Food*, 15–16; Martin, *Standard of Living in 1860*, 49; Russell, *Long, Deep Furrow*, 149–50; Hooker, *Food and Drink in America*, 56, 112–13; Coe and Coe, "Mid-Eighteenth-Century Food and Drink on the Massachusetts Frontier," 41, 42; Ross, "Patterns of Diet and Forces of Production," 190–92; and Pillsbury, *No Foreign Food*, 24.

111. McMahon, "Comfortable Subsistence," 45–48; Stowe, *Pearl of Orr's Island*, 61 (chap. 8).

112. Stowe, *Oldtown Folks*, 309 (chap. 29), 223 (chap. 22). See also ibid., 80 (chap. 7), 99 (chap. 9), 168 (chap. 18), 199 (chap. 20), 402 (chap. 37); and Stowe, *Minister's Wooing*, 189 (chap. 22).

113. Clark, *Roots of Rural Capitalism*, 77–78. If the cook at a fictional late-nineteenth-century Maine logging camp is to be believed, legumes, in the form of baked beans, remained the staple food in such a rough-and-ready locale, while boiled dinner was served less often, as "a kind of delicacy." See Howells, *Modern Instance*, 84, 86 (chap. 9).

114. Johnson, *Highways and Byways of New England*, 236; *Aunt Mary's New England Cook Book*, 8; *Roger Cookery*, 13; Mendall, *New Bedford Practical Receipt Book*, 20; Inman, *Rhode Island Rule Book*, 13; *Echoes from South County Kitchens*, 78–79; Wolcott, *New England Yankee Cook Book*, 72; Vaughan, *Yankee Hill-Country Cooking*, 18–19. We omit pies made with beef from this section and refer the reader to the section on pie in chapter 6, esp. n. 100.

115. Above, chap. 1, nn. 120, 46; Oliver, *Saltwater Foodways*, 319.

116. Smith, *Compleat Housewife*, 32.

117. Simmons, *American Cookery* (introduction by Wilson), 19–20, 45; Child, *American Frugal Housewife*, 49; Lee, *Cook's Own Book*, 11–12; Knight, *Tit-Bits*, 8; Turner, *New England Cook Book*, 72; Wright, *New England Cook Book*, 65–67.

118. Beecher, *Miss Beecher's Domestic Receipt Book*, 37–38; Simmons, *American Cookery* (introduction by Wilson), 20. See also Gilman, *Lady's Annual Register . . . for 1838*, 102; and Bliss, *Practical Cook Book*, 52–53. For the medieval "larded-boiled dish," see Scully, *Art of Cookery in the Middle Ages*, 47, 91.

119. Lincoln and Barrows, *Home Science Cook Book*, 126–27; Wolcott, *New England Yankee Cook Book*, 70. The elements of Yankee Pot Roast had been found scattered among Mrs. Lee's many "Ala" stewed beef recipes, most of which had not involved stuffing or forcemeat, and one of which had had onions, carrots, and turnips cooked along with the meat. But Lee's seasoning blends were relatively complex; the root vegetables were to be added in conjunction with "the rind of a lemon," for example. See Lee, *Cook's Own Book*, 11.

120. For fireplace architecture, see above, chap. 1, n. 32. The following survey of roasting technology in Britain and New England is based on Wilson, *Food and Drink in Britain*, 84, 98, 100; Earle, *Home Life in Colonial Days*, 62–66; Gould, *Early American House*, 70–74; and Oliver, *Saltwater Foodways*, 11. For the healthfulness of roasting according to Galenic theory, see Scully, *Art of Cookery in the Middle Ages*, 95, 102. And for an appreciation of open fire roast-

ing's distinctive gastronomic value, see Hess, *Martha Washington's Booke of Cookery*, 21–22.

121. Smith, *Compleat Housewife*, 17, 32; Glasse, *Art of Cookery Made Plain and Easy* (glossary and notes by Davidson), 3, 69, 183; Wilson, *Food and Drink in Britain*, 98–99.

122. Simmons, *American Cookery* (introduction by Wilson), 17–18. See also Child, *American Frugal Housewife*, 48; and Lee, *Cook's Own Book*, 11, 13. Simmons drew at many points upon Carter, *Frugal Housewife*, and it may be that her phrase "brisk hot fire" echoed Carter's phrase "small brisk fire" in Carter's "General Rules to be observed in Roasting" (*Frugal Housewife*, 1).

123. Leslie, *Directions for Cookery in Its Various Branches*, 69; Beecher, *Miss Beecher's Domestic Receipt Book*, 43.

124. Simmons, *American Cookery* (introduction by Wilson), 45; above, nn. 117–18; Lee, *Cook's Own Book*, 13; Leslie, *Directions for Cookery in Its Various Branches*, 71–72; Beecher, *Miss Beecher's Domestic Receipt Book*, 41–42. Ambiguities in this respect were underscored by the fact that Beecher placed her recipe "To Bake Beef" in her chapter on "Boiled Meats," even though this chapter was immediately followed by one on "Roasted and Baked Meats."

125. *Aunt Mary's New England Cook Book*, 13; Lincoln and Barrows, *Home Science Cook Book*, 126; Farmer, *Boston Cooking-School Cook Book*, 179.

126. Smith, *Compleat Housewife*, 23; Glasse, *Art of Cookery Made Plain and Easy* (glossary and notes by Davidson), 6; Child, *American Frugal Housewife*, 48; Hooker, *Food and Drink in America*, 56, 111, 113; Dickens, *American Notes*, 79 (chap. 3). See also Lee, *Cook's Own Book*, 18.

127. Smith, *Compleat Housewife*, 47, 58; Glasse, *Art of Cookery Made Plain and Easy* (glossary and notes by Davidson), 8, 13, 14, 71; Carter, *Frugal Housewife*, 17, 81; Simmons, *American Cookery* (introduction by Wilson), 24; Child, *American Frugal Housewife*, 52; Lee, *Cook's Own Book*, 18; Howland, *American Economical Housekeeper*, 68; Knight, *Tit-Bits*, 8, 9–10; Turner, *New England Cook Book*, 74–75; Inman, *Rhode Island Rule Book*, 14; *Meriden Cook Book*, 6; Lincoln and Barrows, *Home Science Cook Book*, 138.

128. Child, *American Frugal Housewife*, 47–48; Beecher, *Miss Beecher's Domestic Receipt Book*, 39. Simmons provided more elaborate instructions in how to "dress a Calve's Head. Turtle fashion" in *American Cookery* (introduction by Wilson), 22. See also Gilman, *Lady's Annual Register . . . for 1838*, 71–72; *Roger Cookery*, 41; and Mann, *Christianity in the Kitchen*, 138–39.

129. Child, *American Frugal Housewife*, 44, 45; Lee, *Cook's Own Book*, xxxii–xxxiii; Beecher, *Miss Beecher's Domestic Receipt Book*, 26, 27–28. In our sample the earliest occurrence of beef shopping advice is Simmons, *American Cookery* (introduction by Wilson), 5; and the latest is Knight, *Tit-Bits*, 7.

130. Drummond and Wilbraham, *Englishman's Food*, 49–50, 99; Wilson, *Food and Drink in Britain*, 155, 159–60, 163, 165.

131. Anderson, "'Solid Sufficiency,'" 118–37; Wilson, *Food and Drink in Britain*, 144, 158–63, 178–79, 181–82. Gies and Gies estimate, in *Life in a Medieval Village*, 149, that milk was produced at the rate of between 120 and 150 gallons per

cow a year on the typical peasant farmstead during the later Middle Ages. This is roughly consistent with Anderson's figure for the seventeenth century of a thousand gallons for a farmstead having four cows and many goats.

132. Baker, "Seventeenth-Century English Yeoman Foodways at Plimoth Plantation," 107; Deetz, *In Small Things Forgotten*, 77–80; above, chap. 4, n. 19; McMahon, "Comfortable Subsistence," 39; Burnaby, *Travels through the Middle Settlements in North-America*, 70. For evidence on possession of dairy products and equipment, see Dow, *Every Day Life in the Massachusetts Bay Colony*, 35, 42, 44; Cummings, *Framed Houses of Massachusetts Bay*, 29; Ulrich, "It 'Went Away Shee Knew Not How,'" 96, 97, 99; Shammas, *Pre-Industrial Consumer in England and America*, 54; and McMahon, "Comfortable Subsistence," 57.

133. Hooker, *Food and Drink in America*, 58, 67; Stowe, *Oldtown Folks*, 468 (chap. 45), 402–3 (chap. 37); Stowe, *Pearl of Orr's Island*, 277 (chap. 28). For additional discussion of the ministerial wood-provisioning festivities, see below, chap. 7, nn. 1–4, 78–79, 93; and chap. 8, n. 21.

134. Hammond, "Producing, Selecting, and Serving Food at the Country Seat," 90; Clark, *Roots of Rural Capitalism*, 145 (citing Joan Jensen, "Cloth, Butter, and Boarders," *Review of Radical Political Economics* [1980], for the 14–23 percent estimate), 275–76.

135. Above, chap. 4, n. 13; Derven, "Wholesome, Toothsome, and Diverse," 51.

136. McMahon, "'All Things in Their Proper Season,'" 148; Leslie, *Lady's Receipt Book*, 249–50; Howland, *American Economical Housekeeper*, 95; Cornelius, *Young Housekeeper's Friend*, 225; Hale, *Good Housekeeper*, 16; Child, *American Frugal Housewife*, 14–15.

137. Simmons, *American Cookery* (introduction by Wilson), 9–10; Beecher, *Miss Beecher's Domestic Receipt Book*, chap. 21.

138. Whitehill, *Food, Drink, and Recipes of Early New England*, 17 (quoting Bentley); Friedmann, "Victualling Colonial Boston," 199; Pendery, "Archeology of Urban Foodways in Portsmouth, New Hampshire," 12. For Ireland as an exporter of butter, see Braudel, *Structures of Everyday Life*, 197.

139. Whitehill, *Food, Drink, and Recipes of Early New England*, 17 (quoting French traveler Jean Pierre Brissot de Warville); Mitchell, *It's an Old New England Custom*, 42.

140. Mitchell, *It's an Old New England Custom*, 43–44.

141. Wilson, *Food and Drink in Britain*, 79, 90, 104–5; Anderson, "'Solid Sufficiency,'" 107–8.

142. Wilson, *Food and Drink in Britain*, 88–90, 103–4; Anderson, "'Solid Sufficiency,'" 109–11; Glasse, *Art of Cookery Made Plain and Easy* (glossary and notes by Davidson), 161.

143. Anderson, "'Solid Sufficiency,'" 192–93 (quoting Markham).

144. Glasse, *Art of Cookery Made Plain and Easy* (glossary and notes by Davidson), 4–5; Smith, *Compleat Housewife*, 78–79; Carter, *Frugal Housewife*, 16–17.

145. Child, *American Frugal Housewife*, 52; Lee, *Cook's Own Book*, 145; Beecher, *Miss Beecher's Domestic Receipt Book*, 29. See also *Cook Not Mad*, 60; and *Roger Cookery*, 16.

146. Wolcott, *New England Yankee Cook Book*, 78–79; Knight, *Tit-Bits*, 12.

147. Hale, *Ladies' New Book of Cookery*, 159. See also Allen, *Housekeeper's Assistant*, 100; Bliss, *Practical Cook Book*, 75; and *Godey's*, May 1881, 472. A mid-twentieth-century recipe for "Old-Fashioned Head Cheese" that did not confuse it with souse was found in Vaughan, *Yankee Hill-Country Cooking*, 40.

148. Lee, *Cook's Own Book*, 145. Child, in *American Frugal Housewife*, 46, suggested more economical ways of utilizing pig's head.

149. Child, *American Frugal Housewife*, 46, 44; Lee, *Cook's Own Book*, 144, 145; Hale, *Ladies' New Book of Cookery*, 159; Knight, *Tit-Bits*, 11–12.

150. Beecher, *Miss Beecher's Domestic Receipt Book*, 36–37. If Beecher's recipe sounds familiar, this is because a similar sequence of cooking procedures is still commonly utilized. The bridge between Beecher and our own day may be found in early-twentieth-century cookbooks with recipes for boiled ham similar to hers, though with variations on the coating of the ham during baking, ranging from whole cloves and "as much brown sugar as possible," to blends of cracker crumbs, white sugar, and cloves, or of cracker crumbs, brown sugar, pepper, tarragon, and melted butter. See Turner, *New England Cook Book*, 87–88; Inman, *Rhode Island Rule Book*, 12; Farmer, *Boston Cooking-School Cook Book*, 210; and Lincoln and Barrows, *Home Science Cook Book*, 138–39.

151. Glasse, *Art of Cookery Made Plain and Easy* (glossary and notes by Davidson), 4; Child, *American Frugal Housewife*, 50; Lee, *Cook's Own Book*, 143–44. See also *Roger Cookery*, 15–16; and Allen, *Housekeeper's Assistant*, 101.

152. Lee, *Cook's Own Book*, 143–44.

153. Beecher, *Miss Beecher's Domestic Receipt Book*, 45–46; Turner, *New England Cook Book*, 86; Lincoln and Barrows, *Home Science Cook Book*, 140.

154. Child, *American Frugal Housewife*, 49–50; Beecher, *Miss Beecher's Domestic Receipt Book*, 46; Leslie, *Directions for Cookery in Its Various Branches*, 120–21; Turner, *New England Cook Book*, 86.

155. Beecher, *Miss Beecher's Domestic Receipt Book*, 31; Hale, *Ladies' New Book of Cookery*, 159; Turner, *New England Cook Book*, 85.

156. Bushman, *Refinement of America*, 258–59.

157. Cronon, *Changes in the Land*, 135, 129; Beecher, *Miss Beecher's Domestic Receipt Book*, 31.

158. Bushman, *Refinement of America*, 372. Ringing swine through the nose to keep them from rooting up crops was a measure that had been adopted during the early years of English settlement; see Cronon, *Changes in the Land*, 137; and Innes, *Creating the Commonwealth*, 282.

159. King, *When I Lived in Salem*, 99; Hooker, *Food and Drink in America*, 221 (quoting Mary Terhune, in Marion Harland, *Common Sense in the Household* [1880]).

160. Beecher, *Miss Beecher's Domestic Receipt Book*, 31; Adams, *History of the United States of America*, 45; Abbott, *Old Paths and Legends of the New England Border*, 346; Booth, *Hung, Strung, and Potted*, 34 (quoting the diary of British officer Thomas Hughes).

161. Turner, *New England Cook Book*, 85. See also Knight, *Tit-Bits*, 10. There may have been some rural New Englanders who shared the sentiments of an elderly

Englishwoman interviewed in 1902: "We kep' a pig then—so did everyone; and the pork and brawn it were good, not like what we buy now. We put it mostly in brine, and let it be for months; and when we took it out and boiled it, it were red as a cherry and white as milk, and it melted just like butter in your mouth." Anderson, "'Solid Sufficiency,'" 186 (quoting a woman interviewed by the novelist W. H. Hudson).

162. Child, *American Frugal Housewife*, 60; Inman, *Rhode Island Rule Book*, 15; Wolcott, *New England Yankee Cook Book*, 75; Vaughan, *Yankee Hill-Country Cooking*, 20–23. As we have already seen with baked beans and clam chowder and as we shall see again with cakes, no particular stigma was ever attached to the use of salt pork in preparing nonpork dishes.

163. Cummings, *American and His Food*, 12 (quoting Cooper's frontier housewife in *The Chainbearer* [1845]). On the menu at McDonald's, for example, pork is seen only in breakfast sausage.

CHAPTER SIX

1. Williams, *Key into the Language of America*, 96. Williams's "chiefest Doctor" was identified by Edward Everett Hale as "Dr. Boteler" in *Tarry at Home Travels*, 207–8.

2. Hooker, *Food and Drink in America*, 12; Muir, *Reflections in Bullough's Pond*, 18; Wood, *New Englands Prospect*, 14.

3. Bennett, "Food Economy of the New England Indians," 390; Snow, *Archaeology of New England*, 66; Williams, *Key into the Language of America*, 97; Wood, *New Englands Prospect*, 15, 19.

4. Winthrop, *Life and Letters of John Winthrop*, 1:312 (see also, above, chap. 1, n. 26); Field, "'Peculiar Manuerance,'" 16–17. For a discussion of the garden/wilderness polarity that stresses its place in the religious thought of seventeenth-century New England, see Stavely, "Roger Williams and the Enclosed Gardens of New England." The symbolism of the garden edge as the border of civilization should not be taken literally. Obviously, the settlers thought of their fields and pastures as part of the realm of civilization. Nevertheless, the garden and its boundary constituted the clearest outward and visible sign of the entire domain of cultivation and civilization, which was comprised more literally of the farmstead as a whole.

5. Snow, *Archaeology of New England*, 334, 76.

6. Bragdon, *Native People of Southern New England*, 128.

7. Williams, *Key into the Language of America*, 96–98; Johnson, *Johnson's Wonder-Working Providence*, 162; Wood, *New Englands Prospect*, 70; Russell, *Indian New England before the Mayflower*, 84. John Josselyn, for example, wrote that "they feed likewise upon . . . divers sorts of Berries" in *John Josselyn, Colonial Traveler*, 93.

8. Wilson, *Food and Drink in Britain*, 324, 325, 328, 341.

9. Ibid., 341, 328; Henisch, *Fast and Feast*, 114; Chaucer, *Chaucer's Poetry*, 110 ("Miller's Tale," line 76); Shakespeare, *Love's Labour's Lost* (V.ii.935), in Harrison, *Shakespeare*, 429. According to Jay Allan Anderson, Shakespeare was re-

ferring to apples roasted in mead, a popular evening snack among sixteenth- and seventeenth-century English yeomen; see Anderson, "'Solid Sufficiency,'" 224.

10. Helfman, *Apples, Apples, Apples*, 23; Leighton, *American Gardens in the Eighteenth Century*, 227; Russell, *Long, Deep Furrow*, 47–48. For the birth of Peregrine White, see *Journal of the Pilgrims at Plymouth*, 41.

11. Leighton, *American Gardens in the Eighteenth Century*, 225; Doudiet, "Coastal Maine Cooking," 221–22 (quoting Stevens).

12. McMahon, "Comfortable Subsistence," 42, 43, 47, 59. For more on this topic, see below, chap. 8, n. 3.

13. Simmons, *American Cookery* (introduction by Wilson), 16; McMahon, "Comfortable Subsistence," 47–48.

14. *American National Biography*, 4:705–6.

15. Haley, "Johnny Appleseed" did more than any other single piece of writing to create the Johnny Appleseed myth. In her old age Lydia Maria Child contributed a poem on the subject: see Child, "Apple-seed John."

16. Larcom, *New England Girlhood*, 37. The classic case of youthful fruit theft, along with analysis of it as the archetype of sin, is found in Augustine's *Confessions*, 2:4–10. The medieval English poet John Lydgate remembered that as a boy he "ran into gardens" and "apples there I stole"; quoted in Henisch, *Fast and Feast*, 113.

17. Hazard, *Jonny-Cake Papers*, 90. According to Hazard's 1915 editor, Bowler was a conscientious, "improving" agriculturalist who did indeed introduce the Rhode Island Greening into America. Ibid., 392.

18. Glasse, *Art of Cookery Made Plain and Easy* (glossary and notes by Davidson), 164; Helfman, *Apples, Apples, Apples*, 72, 74; Russell, *Long, Deep Furrow*, 160–61. The presence on this list of a "Red Astrakhan" variety of apple is intriguing. The city of Astrakhan is located at the point where the Volga River drains into the Caspian Sea, within the general area of "Southwest Asia and the region around the Mediterranean" where "cultivated apples . . . are believed to have originated"; see *Cambridge World History of Food*, 2:1720. In 1920 a travel writer encountered the aging novelist William Dean Howells dispensing "red astrakhans, almost too perfect to be real," to his fellow passengers on a trolley in southern Maine. "Do have some," he was heard to say as he passed them out. "The children love my red apples, perhaps you will too. There will be enough for us all." Whiteside, *Touring New England*, 274, 276.

19. Henisch, *Fast and Feast*, 116–17; Wilson, *Food and Drink in Britain*, 334.

20. Stowe, *Oldtown Folks*, 139–40 (chap. 15). See also John Greenleaf Whittier, "Snow Bound," in *Complete Poetical Works*, 401: "And, for the winter fireside meet, / Between the andirons' straddling feet, / The mug of cider simmered slow, / The apples sputtered in a row." For a medieval instance, see Henisch, *Fast and Feast*, 114 (quoting *A Fifteenth Century Schoolbook* [1956]): "sytt or stonde be the fyre a litell while. . . . The nyghtes be pretty and colde now. A roste apple ye shall have, and fenell seede. Mor we wyl not promyse youe."

21. Beecher, *Miss Beecher's Domestic Receipt Book*, 115. See also Lee, *Cook's Own*

Book, 3; and Lincoln and Barrows, *Home Science Cook Book*, 7. As usual, Lee's recipe was more complex than Beecher's, while Lincoln and Barrows said merely to "Wipe, put in a granite pan, and bake in moderate heat until tender." Baked apples could also take a savory rather than a sweet form. See, for example, Vaughan, *Yankee Hill-Country Cooking*, 74–75; and Bowles and Towle, *Secrets of New England Cooking*, 123–24.

22. Child, *American Frugal Housewife*, 63; Beecher, *Miss Beecher's Domestic Receipt Book*, 108–9; Vaughan, *Yankee Hill-Country Cooking*, 134–35; Howland, *American Economical Housekeeper*, 35. An early-twentieth-century Bird's Nest Pudding omitted the apples altogether and strove instead for a more realistically sculpted facsimile of a bird's nest, with cornstarch or blancmange serving for "the foundation of the nest" and strips of sugared and boiled lemon peel representing the straw. To reproduce the bird's eggs housed in the nest, the part usually played by the apples, the reader was instructed to "extract the contents of four eggs through a small hole, and fill the shells with hot blanc-mange or corn-starch. When cold, break off the shells, and lay the molded eggs in the nest." Turner, *New England Cook Book*, 163–64. Two of Beecher's baked apple recipes were virtually identical to Bird's Nest Pudding, except that the custard was poured on after rather than before baking. There were several later versions of this recipe. See Beecher, *Miss Beecher's Domestic Receipt Book*, 115–16; Lincoln and Barrows, *Home Science Cook Book*, 7, 8; and Pixley, *Green Mountain Cook Book*, 79.

23. Simmons, *American Cookery* (introduction by Wilson), 27; Child, *American Frugal Housewife*, 63.

24. Wright, *New England Cook Book*, 153; Wolcott, *New England Yankee Cook Book*, 179. Mrs. Lee had allowed for apple dumplings to be either bag-boiled or baked in *Cook's Own Book*, 4.

25. King, *When I Lived in Salem*, 98; Hazard, *Jonny-Cake Papers*, 108–9.

26. Child, *American Frugal Housewife*, 63; Lee, *Cook's Own Book*, 5–6; Wright, *New England Cook Book*, 153–54. See also Beecher, *Miss Beecher's Domestic Receipt Book*, 116.

27. Simmons, *American Cookery* (introduction by Wilson), 27; above, chap. 2, n. 62. Simmons did not specify a cooking method for her apple pudding, but the puddings before and after it were both to be baked. Mrs. Lee proposed baking a richer apple custard, with butter and egg yolk rather than milk or cream and eggs, in a "puff crust," calling the result "Apple Cheesecakes" in *Cook's Own Book*, 3.

28. Beecher, *Miss Beecher's Domestic Receipt Book*, 116. In 1963 this recipe reappeared as "Apple Bread Pudding," with applesauce standing in for the grated apples; see Vaughan, *Yankee Hill-Country Cooking*, 134.

29. Turner, *New England Cook Book*, 162. See also Weston, *Practical Cook Book*, 70; and Pixley, *Green Mountain Cook Book*, 57.

30. Jones, *American Food*, 11; King, *When I Lived in Salem*, 99.

31. Wolcott, *New England Yankee Cook Book*, 178; *Godey's*, February 1886, 213; Mann, *Christianity in the Kitchen*, 78–79; Hunt, *Good Bread*, 13. See also Thim-

ble Club, *Choice Recipes from Old New England*, 139; and Early, *New England Cookbook*, 139.

32. Beecher, *Miss Beecher's Domestic Receipt Book*, 116–17. Mrs. Lee provided various specimens of apple exotica, such as five versions of apple fritters (perhaps derived from medieval Lenten apple "ffrutours"), "Apples Festooned," and "Apple Poupeton." Lee, *Cook's Own Book*, 4–5. Apple fritters also appeared in Mendall, *New Bedford Practical Receipt Book*, 47.

33. Drummond and Wilbraham, *Englishman's Food*, 68; Wilson, *Food and Drink in Britain*, 334 (quoting *School of Salernum* [ca. 12th or 13th century]), 348 (quoting Thomas Cogan, *Haven of Health* [1612]). See also Laudan, "Birth of the Modern Diet," 77–79.

34. Wilson, *Food and Drink in Britain*, 333–34; Henisch, *Fast and Feast*, 113.

35. Wilson, *Food and Drink in Britain*, 334; Drummond and Wilbraham, *Englishman's Food*, 69.

36. Wilson, *Food and Drink in Britain*, 359; Lee, *Cook's Own Book*, xxxi. See also Hale, *Good Housekeeper*, 87–89, where there were warnings about the unhealthfulness of over- as well as underripe fruit.

37. McMahon, "'All Things in Their Proper Season,'" 141 (quoting Lydia Sigourney, *Letters of Life* [1866]), 149 (quoting Mary Philinda Dole, *A Doctor in Homespun* [1941]).

38. McMahon, "'All Things in Their Proper Season,'" 142–43; Doudiet, "Coastal Maine Cooking," 223 (quoting Mary E. Wilkins, *The People of Our Neighborhood* [1898]).

39. Stowe, *Poganuc People*, 243–45, 247–48 (chap. 22).

40. Doudiet, "Coastal Maine Cooking," 223; Earle, *Home Life in Colonial Days*, 146–47. Note that Earle disagreed with Beecher (above, n. 21) regarding which type of apple required longer cooking. Earle also gave a recipe for apple butter. For more on applesauce, see *Aunt Mary's New England Cook Book*, 57; Turner, *New England Cook Book*, 204; Wright, *New England Cook Book*, 154; Lincoln and Barrows, *Home Science Cook Book*, 8; and Bowles and Towle, *Secrets of New England Cooking*, 263, 259.

41. Above, chap. 4, n. 8; Carter, *Frugal Housewife*, 162; Simmons, *American Cookery* (introduction by Wilson), 43–44. Catharine Beecher recommended a simpler method of sun drying and bag storage of berries and other fruit, akin to stringing apples and pumpkins. Beecher, *Miss Beecher's Domestic Receipt Book*, 224–25 (see also, above, chap. 4, n. 18).

42. McMahon, "'All Things in Their Proper Season,'" 150; Simmons, *American Cookery* (introduction by Wilson), 39.

43. McMahon, "'All Things in Their Proper Season,'" 150; Rombauer and Becker, *Joy of Cooking*, 804–5; Simmons, *American Cookery* (introduction by Wilson), 43.

44. McMahon, "'All Things in Their Proper Season,'" 150; Simmons, *American Cookery* (introduction by Wilson), 41; Carter, *Frugal Housewife*, 159–60.

45. McMahon, "Laying Foods By," 185; Beecher, *Miss Beecher's Domestic Receipt Book*, 157–58. For similar strawberry preservation recipes, see Simmons, *American Cookery* (introduction by Wilson), 39; Hale, *Ladies' New Book of Cookery*,

331–32; and Knight, *Tit-Bits*, 92–93. For additional recipes for preserving fruits of various kinds, see Bliss, *Practical Cook Book*, 232–33; Chadwick, *Home Cookery*, 71; and Mendall, *New Bedford Practical Receipt Book*, 65.

46. Wilson, *Food and Drink in Britain*, 301, 337, 354–55. In at least some eighteenth-century cookbooks, the term was not "jam" but rather "giam": see Glasse, *Art of Cookery Made Plain and Easy* (glossary and notes by Davidson), 145; and Carter, *Frugal Housewife*, 152.

47. Child, *American Frugal Housewife*, 81, 118; Beecher, *Miss Beecher's Domestic Receipt Book*, 158–59, 153; Knight, *Tit-Bits*, 92–93; Hale, *Ladies' New Book of Cookery*, 329–30. In her promotion of frugality, Child commended such a gustatorily dubious concoction as "barberries preserved in molasses" (81).

48. Carter, *Frugal Housewife*, 159; Simmons, *American Cookery* (introduction by Wilson), 40; Child, *American Frugal Housewife*, 118; Beecher, *Miss Beecher's Domestic Receipt Book*, 159; Roberts, *House-Servant's Directory*, 97. This last author, who was of African descent and came from Antigua in the West Indies, was butler at Gore Place, the Waltham, Massachusetts, country seat of Christopher Gore, a wealthy lawyer, diplomat, and Federalist. See Hammond, "Producing, Selecting, and Serving Food at the Country Seat," 88–89. Various fruit jams were also offered in *Roger Cookery*, 27; and Mendall, *New Bedford Practical Receipt Book*, 70–71.

49. *Meriden Cook Book*, 58–59; Turner, *New England Cook Book*, 211; Wright, *New England Cook Book*, 274–75, 289–90.

50. Wilson, *Food and Drink in Britain*, 91–92.

51. Ibid., 106–7.

52. Child, *American Frugal Housewife*, 31. Other forms of meat jelly remained in use. Child noted that "some people like the jelly obtained from a boiled hand of pork, or the feet of pork, prepared the same way as calf's foot jelly" (119). For a recipe see Chadwick, *Home Cookery*, 69.

53. Beecher, *Miss Beecher's Domestic Receipt Book*, 155; Oliver, *Saltwater Foodways*, 36. Calf's-foot jelly recipes continued to appear in cookbooks of the 1850s. See Bliss, *Practical Cook Book*, 230; and Chadwick, *Home Cookery*, 66. Isinglass is made from the air bladders of large fish such as cod or sturgeon (see also above, chap. 3, n. 176).

54. Child, *American Frugal Housewife*, 119; *Roger Cookery*, 27; Bliss, *Practical Cook Book*, 229–32; Chadwick, *Home Cookery*, 66–70; Mendall, *New Bedford Practical Receipt Book*, 70–71; *Aunt Mary's New England Cook Book*, 58; *Meriden Cook Book*, 58; Wright, *New England Cook Book*, 275; Beecher, *Miss Beecher's Domestic Receipt Book*, 153; Hale, *Ladies' New Book of Cookery*, 345; Turner, *New England Cook Book*, 208. This last source stipulated that the jelly bag, which "should be in every kitchen," ought to be made of flannel, "pointed at the bottom, so that the jelly will run out chiefly at one point."

55. Child, *American Frugal Housewife*, 81–82; Simmons, *American Cookery* (introduction by Wilson), 43; Beecher, *Miss Beecher's Domestic Receipt Book*, 159; Bliss, *Practical Cook Book*, 230–31; Chadwick, *Home Cookery*, 66–67; Mendall, *New Bedford Practical Receipt Book*, 70–71; *Aunt Mary's New England Cook Book*, 58.

56. Beecher, *Miss Beecher's Domestic Receipt Book*, xi; Child, *American Frugal Housewife*, 118; Stowe, *Pearl of Orr's Island*, 374, 376 (chap. 39). There was a "Moss Jelly" recipe in Chadwick, *Home Cookery*, 67.

57. King, *When I Lived in Salem*, 99, 25, 26.

58. Stowe, *Minister's Wooing*, 35 (chap. 4), 156–57 (chap. 16). See also above, chap. 2, n. 44.

59. Wilson, *Food and Drink in Britain*, 302.

60. Ibid., 278, 281, 284–85; Braudel, *Structures of Everyday Life*, 224; Scully, *Art of Cookery in the Middle Ages*, 52; Anderson, "'Solid Sufficiency,'" 75–77.

61. Earle, *Home Life in Colonial Days*, 111.

62. Nearing and Nearing, *Maple Sugar Book*, 22–39; Bennett, "Food Economy of the New England Indians," 383–84; Russell, *Indian New England before the Mayflower*, 86–88; Trigger, *Handbook of North American Indians*, 15:138–39, 153, 298; Snow, *Archaeology of New England*, 46, 58, 72; Calloway, *Dawnland Encounters*, 6–7, 180. Evidence regarding native possession of metal cooking vessels is cited in several of these sources. For an example of primary evidence on this point, see Wood, *New Englands Prospect*, 70: "For the ordering of their victuals, they boile or roast them, having large Kettles which they traded for with the French long since, and doe still buy of the English as their neede requires, before they had substantiall earthen pots of their owne making."

63. Russell, *Indian New England before the Mayflower*, 87; Hooker, *Food and Drink in America*, 62–63; Trigger, *Handbook of North American Indians*, 15:298; Calloway, *Dawnland Encounters*, 13.

64. Wilson, *Food and Drink in Britain*, 307.

65. Mintz, *Sweetness and Power*, 37; Braudel, *Structures of Everyday Life*, 224; Fernández-Armesto, *Columbus*, 9–11, 18, 136.

66. Wilson, *Food and Drink in Britain*, 281. For the role of molasses in the manufacture of rum, see below, chap. 8, nn. 10, 23–24.

67. Mintz, *Sweetness and Power*, 50.

68. Ibid., 48 (quoting Thomas Tryon, *Friendly Advice to Gentlemen-Planters of the East and West Indies* [1700]), 50 (quoting W. L. Mathieson, *British Slavery and Its Abolition* [1926]).

69. Ibid., 169 (quoting R. Pares, *Merchants and Planters* [1960]). Between the American Revolution and the Civil War, maple sugar was advocated by some Americans as an antislavery alternative to cane sugar; see Nearing and Nearing, *Maple Sugar Book*, 18–20.

70. Mintz, *Sweetness and Power*, 159–60; Shammas, *Pre-Industrial Consumer in England and America*, 82.

71. Ulrich, "It 'Went Away Shee Knew Not How,'" 97; Dow, *Domestic Life in New England in the Seventeenth Century*, 17–18; Friedmann, "Victualling Colonial Boston," 199–200; Pendery, "Archeology of Urban Foodways in Portsmouth, New Hampshire," 12; Coe and Coe, "Mid-Eighteenth-Century Food and Drink on the Massachusetts Frontier," 44; Derven, "Wholesome, Toothsome, and Diverse," 57–59; Vickers, *Farmers and Fishermen*, 169.

72. Hooker, *Food and Drink in America*, 33; Friedmann, "Victualling Colonial Boston," 200; Sewall, *Diary*, 2:730 (22 October 1713; also quoted in Earle, *Stage-Coach and Tavern Days*, 136). A family consuming at the rate of the ten-pounds-a-year-per-person 1720s Boston average would have used in the course of the year several of the "great loaves or cones" weighing nine or ten pounds in which sugar was commonly purveyed in colonial times. Such loaves were reduced to powder with sugar shears or cutters; see Earle, *Home Life in Colonial Days*, 155. A century later a wealthy Salem, Massachusetts, family had a "row of tall conical shaped pyramids of loaf sugar" on hand in its store closet, along with barrelfuls of both white and brown sugar. In this household, sugar was turned into powder with a mortar and pestle. In this same memoir it appears that molasses, though cheap, could fascinate and excite well-born children. The store closet contained "jugs of molasses, of a kind that has vanished from the earth now, rich, dark, and thick, of a fruity flavor, with a glow of red like a gem in the heart of it, which we children infinitely preferred to any preserve, on our rice or hasty pudding, and which even on bread alone made a dessert not to be despised." King, *When I Lived in Salem*, 109-10. For a boyish recollection of childhood molasses consumption, also from an elite source, see Hazard, *Jonny-Cake Papers*, 220: "There was a motley brown, red, and yellow colored molasses jug in [my grandfather's great-room] closet which, notwithstanding the dim light, I was not slow to discover. I remember it now with its cob stopple just as well as if it was but yesterday I saw it. Now I had in my pocket a sort of an old broken-pointed hacked bladed jack-knife that I traded a big hunk of gingerbread for with Pete Allen. After taking the cob stopple out of the jug, I opened my jack-knife and found I could just reach the molasses by holding the end of the handle between my thumb and finger, but not so deep as to afford a good lick of molasses. So I took the handle between my fore and middle finger and pushed the knife down as far as it would reach, with both my fingers thrust into the neck of the jug. I got five or six good licks in this way, but unfortunately in endeavoring to get my fingers a little too far in the nozzle of the jug, the knife handle slipped from between them and fell, blade and all, cajunct to the bottom of the inside of the jug." Later Hazard stated that in South County, Rhode Island, a district long involved in trade with the West Indies and Africa, molasses remained "a great medium of barter" in the early nineteenth century: "The South Kingstown town records show that many large farms in that town were exclusively sold for molasses." Ibid., 338.
73. Mintz, *Sweetness and Power*, 148; Shammas, *Pre-Industrial Consumer in England and America*, 83; McCusker and Menard, *Economy of British America*, 290, 292-93.
74. Mintz, *Sweetness and Power*, 69, 126; Martin, *Standard of Living in 1860*, 36, 72.
75. Mintz, *Sweetness and Power*, 22, 87; Stowe, *Oldtown Folks*, 110-11 (chap. 10).
76. Cummings, *American and His Food*, 80-81. The paleness hierarchy existed in the world of maple syrups and sugars as well. In spite of the overall dominance of cane sugar, maple was produced on a significant scale in northern New England

in the eighteenth and nineteenth centuries. The highest "Fancy" rating was accorded to syrup that was lightest in color and most neutral in taste. With the turn toward "natural" flavors and colors in recent years, these categories have become outmoded. See Russell, *Long, Deep Furrow*, 171; and Brown and Segal, "Sugaring Off," 249, 251.

77. Wilson, *Food and Drink in Britain*, 290; Henisch, *Fast and Feast*, 117; Hess, *Martha Washington's Booke of Cookery*, 11–12. Sugar was also used in the Middle Ages for medicinal purposes and, like jelly, for sculptured representations of animals, objects, or buildings. Such sugar "subtleties" were utilized for display and dramatic effect at royal and aristocratic festivals and banquets; see Mintz, *Sweetness and Power*, 45, 87–96. On its medicinal uses, see also Scully, *Art of Cookery in the Middle Ages*, 52–53, 189–90.

78. Henisch, *Fast and Feast*, 146; Mintz, *Sweetness and Power*, 131–32 (quoting W. E. Mead, *The English Medieval Banquet* [1931]).

79. Mintz, *Sweetness and Power*, 131–33. Even before the conquest of the sugar islands, the English upper classes stood out among other Europeans for their special fondness for sugar. One sixteenth-century traveler noted "the blackness of Queen Elizabeth's teeth 'a defect the English seem subject to, from their too great use of sugar.'" Wilson, *Food and Drink in Britain*, 300 (quoting Paul Hentzner, *Travels in England* [1612]).

80. Mintz, *Sweetness and Power*, 117–18. Glasse's book went through at least twelve editions. Mintz speculates that the so-called taste tetrahedron is of relatively recent origin: "Sweet could only be a countertaste to salt/bitter/sour when there was a plentiful enough source of sweetness to make this possible" (18). The argument offered here runs counter to Rachel Laudan's view that sugar lost prestige in consequence of the "Birth of the Modern Diet" (80).

81. Wilson, *Food and Drink in Britain*, 253–54. According to Scully, in *Art of Cookery in the Middle Ages*, 38, toward the end of the medieval period eggs were used to enrich pie crusts. Karen Hess equates the term "coffin" with "coarse pastries"; see Hess, *Martha Washington's Booke of Cookery*, 8.

82. Wilson, *Food and Drink in Britain*, 42; Henisch, *Fast and Feast*, 129.

83. Wilson, *Food and Drink in Britain*, 42, 86, 135, 254 (quoting *The Forme of Cury* [ca. 1390]). For a discussion of eel cookery that includes other examples of eel pie and eels served over bread sops, see above, chap. 3, nn. 34–62.

84. Wilson, *Food and Drink in Britain*, 86, 94; Anderson, "'Solid Sufficiency,'" 197, 178.

85. Wilson, *Food and Drink in Britain*, 271–72; Anderson, "'Solid Sufficiency,'" 178.

86. Anderson, "'Solid Sufficiency,'" 198 (quoting Thomas Newington, *Manuscript Recipe Book* [1719]). For another eighteenth-century battalia pie, see Smith, *Compleat Housewife*, 35.

87. Wilson, *Food and Drink in Britain*, 42, 109, 136; Anderson, "'Solid Sufficiency,'" 196 (quoting Markham). In Galenic theory, pie crust protected the "moist temperaments" of the foods it enclosed; Scully, *Art of Cookery in the Middle Ages*, 45. For the use of butter in connection with another form of preservation, potting, see above, chap. 3, n. 42.

88. Wilson, *Food and Drink in Britain*, 254; Scully, *Art of Cookery in the Middle Ages*, 204.

89. Anderson, "'Solid Sufficiency,'" 197 (quoting Markham); Wilson, *Food and Drink in Britain*, 273.

90. Glasse, *Art of Cookery Made Plain and Easy* (glossary and notes by Davidson), 74; Gardiner, *Mrs. Gardiner's Family Receipts*, 56. Gardiner claimed that her meatless mincemeat would keep for six months. "There is no mode of making mince pies, yet known, superiour, if equal, to this," she stated. Wilson, in *Food and Drink in Britain*, 94, notes the existence of a sixteenth-century recipe for mince pie made with umbles or entrails.

91. Wilson, *Food and Drink in Britain*, 349, 351; Anderson, "'Solid Sufficiency,'" 178, 224; Johnson, *Johnson's Wonder-Working Providence*, 210 (see also above, chap. 2, n. 60). As in New England, so in Old England "great care was taken to dry or cold store fruit specifically for [the] purpose" of making pies. See Anderson, "'Solid Sufficiency,'" 224.

92. Anderson, "'Solid Sufficiency,'" 224–25 (quoting Markham); Wilson, *Food and Drink in Britain*, 351–52.

93. Earle, *Home Life in Colonial Days*, 146. The filling of such house pie was "made of apples neither peeled nor freed from their cores." Earle's source, also quoted and cited in Hooker, *Food and Drink in America*, 63, 372, was Israel Acrelius, *A History of New Sweden* (1759).

94. Stowe, *Oldtown Folks*, 123 (chap. 13); Oliver, *Saltwater Foodways*, 12–13.

95. Anderson, "'Solid Sufficiency,'" 179–80 (quoting Markham); Simmons, *American Cookery* (introduction by Wilson), 29–30.

96. Simmons, *American Cookery* (introduction by Wilson), 23–24.

97. Ibid., 24–25.

98. Child, *American Frugal Housewife*, 69; Beecher, *Miss Beecher's Domestic Receipt Book*, 128; Knight, *Tit-Bits*, 61. See also Bliss, *Practical Cook Book*, 149–51 (ten crusts, including "Potato Paste" and "Suet Paste"); and Gilman, *Lady's Annual Register . . . for 1838*, 137–38 (puff paste).

99. *Aunt Mary's New England Cook Book*, 29–30; Inman, *Rhode Island Rule Book*, 40; Wolcott, *New England Yankee Cook Book*, 218. The cream pie crust could be made to look "brown and flaky" by dipping a napkin fringe in milk or cream and drawing it over the top crust before baking; *Aunt Mary's New England Cook Book*, 30. See also Wright, *New England Cook Book*, 164–65.

100. See, for example, Child, *American Frugal Housewife*, 56–57; Lee, *Cook's Own Book*, 140; Hale, *Good Housekeeper*, 87; Webster, *Improved Housewife*, 99; Beecher, *Miss Beecher's Domestic Receipt Book*, 38–39, 42, 48; *Aunt Mary's New England Cook Book*, 10. Helen S. Wright persisted in the antiquarian mode in this department as well, offering in 1912 an elaborate recipe for pigeon pie in *New England Cook Book*, 116–17.

101. Child, *American Frugal Housewife*, 66; Hale, *Good Housekeeper*, 86–87; Lee, *Cook's Own Book*, 141; *Roger Cookery*, 25–26; Webster, *Improved Housewife*, 92–94; Beecher, *Miss Beecher's Domestic Receipt Book*, 126; Bliss, *Practical Cook Book*, 157–58; Chadwick, *Home Cookery*, 53; Knight, *Tit-Bits*, 62–63; *Aunt Mary's New*

England Cook Book, 31; *Durham Cook Book*, 97–98; Whatsoever Circle, *King's Daughters . . . Cook Book*, 53; Wright, *New England Cook Book*, 169; Wolcott, *New England Yankee Cook Book*, 221.

102. Child, *American Frugal Housewife*, 67–68. See also the recipes for cherry and whortleberry pie. In 1909 apple pie was called "the democratic pie. . . . It is estimated that of all the pies consumed in this country the year round at least forty per cent. is apple pie." Brayley, *Bakers and Baking in Massachusetts*, 132.

103. Lee, *Cook's Own Book*, 139; Webster, *Improved Housewife*, 98; Knight, *Tit-Bits*, 63; *Aunt Mary's New England Cook Book*, 30; Beecher, *Miss Beecher's Domestic Receipt Book*, 110; Hale, *Good Housekeeper*, 84. See also *Roger Cookery*, 26; Bliss, *Practical Cook Book*, 151–60; Mann, *Christianity in the Kitchen*, 77–79; and Chadwick, *Home Cookery*, 54–56. The prizewinning 1939 apple pie had a cup of sugar to "6 to 8 tart apples"; see Wolcott, *New England Yankee Cook Book*, 218. Sugar beneath and above or interspersed with the fruit had been standard eighteenth-century practice; see Glasse, *Art of Cookery Made Plain and Easy* (glossary and notes by Davidson), 114, which Mrs. Gardiner copied into her manuscript cookbook (*Mrs. Gardiner's Family Receipt Book*, 57). Webster, in *Improved Housewife*, 98, copied Hale's tip about the teacup. One type of fruit pie that remained in vogue until surprisingly recently was cranberry pie. As Child noted in *American Frugal Housewife*, 68, such pies "need a great deal of sweetening." Nevertheless, recipes for cranberry pie or tart were brought forward as late as 1912. See *Durham Cook Book*, 99–100; and Wright, *New England Cook Book*, 166. Wolcott, in *New England Yankee Cook Book*, 219, mentioned the use of salt pork in apple pie filling, as did Bowles and Towle in *Secrets of New England Cooking*, 160–61, 159; and Vaughan, in *Yankee Hill-Country Cooking*, 145. If there was a tradition of utilizing salt pork in apple pie cookery, we found only one instance of it in the nineteenth-century portion of our cookbook sample; see Chadwick, *Home Cookery*, 55 ("Apple and Pork Pie").

104. Hale, *Good Housekeeper*, 85, 84; Beecher, *Miss Beecher's Domestic Receipt Book*, 127.

105. Cummings, *American and His Food*, 12 (quoting Constantin Volney, *View of the Soil and Climate of the United States of America* [1804]); Hooker, *Food and Drink in America*, 248 (quoting *Harper's*).

106. King, *When I Lived in Salem*, 26; Stowe, *Oldtown Folks*, 123 (chap. 13); Oliver, *Saltwater Foodways*, 17, 68; Mitchell, *It's an Old New England Custom*, 4; Martin, *Standard of Living in 1860*, 57 n. 40.

107. Mitchell, *It's an Old New England Custom*, 19, 21–22 (paraphrasing Warner, *Backlog Studies* [1872]); Hooker, *Food and Drink in America*, 248.

108. Pixley, *Green Mountain Cook Book*, 15.

109. McMahon, "'All Things in Their Proper Season,'" 141 (quotation from Joel Munsell, *Reminiscences of Men and Things in Northfield [Mass.] as I Knew Them from 1812 to 1825* [1876]).

110. Ibid.; McMahon, "Laying Foods By," 185; Oliver, *Saltwater Foodways*, 244; Stowe, *Oldtown Folks*, 287 (chap. 27).

111. Above, chap. 5, n. 61; McMahon, "'All Things in Their Proper Season,'" 141;

McMahon, "Laying Foods By," 185; Oliver, *Saltwater Foodways*, 243–44; Wolcott, *New England Yankee Cook Book*, 220. Colonial Thanksgiving days were also often observed after events deemed felicitous.

112. Mitchell, *It's an Old New England Custom*, 31–32; Stowe, *Oldtown Folks*, 285 (chap. 27).

113. Oliver, *Saltwater Foodways*, 242 (quoting Connecticut resident Shubael Breed); Carver, *Sketches of New England*, 27; King, *When I Lived in Salem*, 111.

114. King, *When I Lived in Salem*, 112; McMahon, "'All Things in Their Proper Season,'" 142 (quoting Sarah K. Bolton [b. 1841], *Pages from an Intimate Autobiography* [1923]); above, chap. 5, nn. 62–63. "Thanksgiving Cake" was included in *Aunt Mary's New England Cook Book*, 51.

115. McMahon, "'All Things in Their Proper Season,'" 142 (quoting Charles Oliver Howe [1822–1915], *What I Remember* [1928]); Carver, *Sketches of New England*, 31; Hale, *Northwood*, 1:109. For "Connecticut Thanksgiving Chicken Pie," see Webster, *Improved Housewife*, 99. As noted above (chap. 5, n. 34), with turkeys being relatively small, chicken pie was needed to insure that food quantities would be adequate for a festival.

116. King, *When I Lived in Salem*, 111–12; Anderson, "'Solid Sufficiency,'" 71–74, 114.

117. Stowe, *Oldtown Folks*, 287 (chap. 27).

118. Ibid.

119. Ibid., 285–86 (chap. 27). The entire chapter, "How We Kept Thanksgiving at Oldtown," covers 282–97. This passage, along with those quoted earlier regarding the baking and storage of pies, is used by David Hackett Fischer to illustrate the point that "the austerity of New England's food ways was softened by its abundance of baked goods." Fischer, *Albion's Seed*, 134–39 (quotation on 139). We have no major quarrel on this score, although Fischer's description of New England food austerity is overdrawn. He errs in speaking of Stowe's novel as though it were a memoir. But our primary dispute involves Fischer's contention that the Yankee love of baked goods was derived from an "East Anglian taste for baking." The book which Fischer cites as evidence for this claim, Allen, *British Tastes*, a compendium of mid-twentieth-century market research data, is of little value in identifying the food preferences of seventeenth-century people. We have found no evidence that baking characterized the East Anglian region to any outstanding degree in the sixteenth and seventeenth centuries. It seems from Fischer's source that in the mid-twentieth century, baking traditions were stronger in Yorkshire than East Anglia. Compare Allen, *British Tastes*, 75, and 162–63.

120. Stowe, *Oldtown Folks*, 23 (chap. 3), 282–87 (chap. 27).

121. Carver, *Sketches of New England*, 25. For an overview of celebrations of the family farm between the American Revolution and the Civil War, see Kulikoff, *Agrarian Origins of American Capitalism*, 60–95.

122. Stowe, *Oldtown Folks*, 295 (chap. 27).

123. Ibid., 298 (chap. 27). In *Age of Homespun*, 361, Laurel Thatcher Ulrich retells an Indian folk tale about an old basket maker who "went to a Yankee house beg-

ging cider." The owner "told him he could have as much as he could carry in his basket. Fortunately, it was a very cold day. The Indian went to the brook and dipped his basket in the water, taking it out and letting it freeze, then repeated the process again and again until it was lined with a thin coating of ice. Then he went back for the cider and carried it home."

124. Stowe, *Oldtown Folks*, 290, 293 (chap. 27).

125. King, *When I Lived in Salem*, 110–11; Carver, *Sketches of New England*, 40.

126. Stowe, *Oldtown Folks*, 283 (chap. 27). On how Thanksgiving became a national holiday, see Smith, "First Thanksgiving," 81–84.

127. The return of family members from distant points was a standard theme in portrayals of nineteenth-century Thanksgivings. See Carver, *Sketches of New England*, 30–31; King, *When I Lived in Salem*, 112–14; and Oliver, *Saltwater Foodways*, 239–40. That the time at which *Oldtown Folks* was published was one of emergent corporate capitalism is clear from such contemporaneous developments as transcontinental railroad expansion and consolidation, Andrew Carnegie's early maneuvers in the creation of his steel enterprises, and John D. Rockefeller's founding of the Standard Oil Company. During the period 1870–1916, "the business boom triggered a sharp increase in investments in the stocks and bonds of corporations"; *World Book*, 1998, CD-ROM ed., s.v. "Railroad," "Vanderbilt, Cornelius," "Hill, James Jerome," "Carnegie, Andrew," "Rockefeller, John Davison," and "United States, History of the: Industrialism and Reform (1870–1916)."

CHAPTER SEVEN

1. Stowe, *Oldtown Folks*, 397–98 (chap. 37).

2. Ibid.

3. On this, see the introductory essays to ibid., esp. xxii–xxxvi; and Stowe, *Minister's Wooing*, esp. ix–xxi. Both Stowe and her sister, Catharine Beecher, were drawn to Episcopalianism, Catharine actually becoming "an Episcopal convert." See Stowe, *Minister's Wooing*, xx; and Sklar, *Catharine Beecher*, 260.

4. Stowe, *Oldtown Folks*, 398 (chap. 37). Stowe's wood-spell menu included cheese and the alcoholic beverage known as flip as well as cake. For the cheese, see above, chap. 5, n. 133; for the flip, see below, chap. 8, n. 21. The wood-spell description as a whole was based on recollections of Stowe's own childhood experiences in the household of her father, Lyman Beecher. Perhaps her memory was refreshed by the description of a typical "*minister's wood-spell*," as it was conducted in Litchfield, Connecticut, that her sister Catharine Beecher contributed to their father's *Autobiography*, first published in 1864, a few years before the publication of *Oldtown Folks*. See Lyman Beecher, *Autobiography*, 1:238–39.

5. Fulfillment of the popular desire for wheat, especially in bread, was primarily made possible by improvements in agriculture. Although space does not permit consideration of them, improvements in milling and baking also played a significant part. On milling, see Wilson, *Food and Drink in Britain*, 188, 232, 235–36, 240; and David, *English Bread and Yeast Cookery*, 13–44. On baking, see Wilson, *Food and Drink in Britain*, 230, 232, 236, 240–41, 262; Panschar, *Eco-*

nomic Development, 18–23; and McCance and Widdowson, *Breads White and Brown*, 14–15.

6. Wilson, *Food and Drink in Britain*, 186–87, 232–34; McCance and Widdowson, *Breads White and Brown*, 11, 1; David, *English Bread and Yeast Cookery*, 9. The breads Roman bakers made from the famed "soft white wheats" of Italy were considered "far superior to the breads of the early Egyptians and Greeks." About Egyptian varieties we know little, but the breads, "all lovely and white," eaten by rich Athenians were also famous in their time. Antiphanes, writing before 350 B.C.E., wondered "how . . . any gentleman [could] go away when he sees those rows of lovely white loaves filling the oven." The Romans copied and improved upon these Greek creations. As discussed in chapter 1, "the kind of bread served was used to emphasize class, wealth and power." Lighter meant higher, darker lower. Petronius complained of a band of young Roman aristocrats: "if the bread they got wasn't the very whitest, they boxed the people's ears and put the fear of God into them." These attitudes taken to the extreme caused a reaction among some Greeks and Romans. Thus, "the poet in Horace's epistle to Augustus was happy to live on beans and brown bread." Plato advocated a diet based on a mixture of grains. But for every Horace, Seneca, or Plato, there was a Hippocrates asserting that those with chronic diarrhea should eat white bread, or a Galen claiming nutritional value for white bread. The preference for lightness in food thus went back to the Greeks and Romans. See McCance and Widdowson, *Breads White and Brown*, 5–6, 7–9; Panschar, *Economic Development*, 14; and Wilson, *Food and Drink in Britain*, 233.

7. Gies and Gies, *Life in a Medieval Village*, 21; Panschar, *Economic Development*, 17; McCance and Widdowson, *Breads White and Brown*, 11. Evidence of barley's extensive planting includes "the stores of barley in the monasteries on the eve of their dissolution [in the sixteenth century, which] exceeded those of wheat and rye put together." Medieval nursery rhymes attested to its popularity: "When good King Arthur ruled this land / He was a goodly king. / He stole three pecks of barley-meal / To make a bag pudding." Barley was as apt to be turned into pottage as bread. Oliver Cromwell favored barley broth with dried raisins or currants, white wine, rose water, butter, and sugar. Similar recipes appeared in the manuscript cookbook owned by Martha Washington, which was roughly contemporaneous with Cromwell. The first New Englanders ate a simpler pottage prepared with barley and hominy. See McCance and Widdowson, *Breads White and Brown*, 11; Wilson, *Food and Drink in Britain*, 211, 239; Hess, *Martha Washington's Booke of Cookery*, 5, 136; and Whitehill, *Food, Drink, and Recipes of Early New England*, 9–10. For barley broth as a "sick-dish," see Scully, *Art of Cookery in the Middle Ages*, 186–88.

8. Wilson, *Food and Drink in Britain*, 192, 196, 233; McCance and Widdowson, *Breads White and Brown*, 11–12.

9. Wilson, *Food and Drink in Britain*, 197, 199–200; above, chap. 1, nn. 23, 112; McCance and Widdowson, *Breads White and Brown*, 20 (quoting sixteenth-century traveler Fynes Moryson); *Bartlett's Familiar Quotations*, <www.bartleby .com/100/330.2.html> (quoting Sydney Smith). For Samuel Johnson's defini-

tion of oats by way of disparagement of Scots, see above, chap. 1, n. 63. For people of "the upland oatgrowing regions of Wales, [and] northern England," as for the Scots, oat cakes were often a preferred food. Such devotion was manifested in the making of a particular kind of oat cake, called clapbread, that was popular in Lancashire and Westmorland: "and so they clap it round and drive it to the edge in a due proportion till drove as thin as a paper, and still they clap it and drive it round, and then they have a plate of iron same size with their clap board and so shove off the cake on it and so set it on coals and bake it . . . not too hot but just to make it look yellow, it will bake and be as crisp and pleasant to eat as any thing you can imagine." And in the eighteenth century the farmers of northwest England were said to be so fond of their oat cakes that when they traveled to market they brought "their own coarse heavy bread to prevent their being forced to eat our Hertfordshire wheaten bread, saying—They do not like such a corky, bitter sort." See Wilson, *Food and Drink in Britain*, 257, 258 (quoting Celia Fiennes, *Journeys* [ca. 1680s–1710s]), 258–59 (quoting William Ellis, *The Country Housewife's Family Companion* [1750]).

10. Wilson, *Food and Drink in Britain*, 231, 199, 192, 197; McCance and Widdowson, *Breads White and Brown*, 12, 20; David, *English Bread and Yeast Cookery*, 6, 9. On the name itself: maslin, massledine, or "miscellin, mestlyng or some variant of this," was derived "from *miscelin*, its name in the Merovingian and Carolingian domains of France," and probably ultimately "from the French *miscere*, to mix." While maslin was usually sown and reaped as a mixture of grains, this practice tended to produce a mixture that was more rye than wheat and "soon degenerated, after a few poor seasons, into something approaching pure rye." Rye also ripens earlier than wheat, making the harvest even more problematic. Thus the versified warning: "But sow it not mixed, to grow so on land, / Lest rye tarry wheat, till it shed as it stand." Rye was also mixed with grains other than wheat, for instance with barley, but the conventional maslin was of rye and wheat. See McCance and Widdowson, *Breads White and Brown*, 17–18; Wilson, *Food and Drink in Britain*, 238–39; Anderson, "'Solid Sufficiency,'" 164 n. 4.

11. Above, chap. 1, n. 23, chap. 2, n. 3; Wilson, *Food and Drink in Britain*, 244; David, *English Bread and Yeast Cookery*, 6; McCance and Widdowson, *Breads White and Brown*, 7, 17 (quoting Markham). During years of poor harvests, governmental coercion was required to get British bakers to mix pulses in with their rye and barley, thereby extending the supply of brown bread for the common people. Whatever one thought of barley, oats, rye, maslin, or legumes, they were not the worst things of which medieval bread was made. Grinding weed seeds with meal, one of the world's oldest if least appetizing agricultural techniques, was common in Britain. Weeds were not merely tolerated, they were encouraged to grow amid stands of grain. This was a more reasonable practice than it at first sounds: "The large weed seeds, roughly ground, had a food content comparable to that of the ears of corn. The weeds were hardier than the cereals, and their presence was an insurance, for they were more likely to survive in a bad season when the true crop failed." At the end of the eighteenth century,

Orkney Islanders were still eating "breakfast bannocks made of barley which had been ground in their hand-querns; mingled with the barley were seeds of all manner of weeds which had been carefully retained." Wilson, *Food and Drink in Britain*, 189, 260.

12. Wilson, *Food and Drink in Britain*, 245; McCance and Widdowson, *Breads White and Brown*, 27 (quoting Philip Stubbes, *Anatomie of Abuses* [1585]); Hess, *Martha Washington's Booke of Cookery*, 18 (quoting Elizabeth David). As far as tillage of different grains was concerned, regions became known for their specialties. Place-names sometimes indicated an area's principal grain crop, as in "Barlow in Lancashire, Ryhall in Rutland, Wheathampstead in Hertfordshire and Oteley in Shropshire." McCance and Widdowson, *Breads White and Brown*, 10.

13. Wilson, *Food and Drink in Britain*, 237–38; Hess, *Martha Washington's Booke of Cookery*, 208.

14. Drummond and Wilbraham, *Englishman's Food*, 42; McCance and Widdowson, *Breads White and Brown*, 20, 1, 10 (quoting Boorde). As with the ancients, early modern British opinion did not speak with one voice on the bread question. Most agreed with Boorde about the superiority of white bread. The turn-of-the-eighteenth-century travel writer Celia Fiennes stated that rye bread "so disagrees with me as always to make me sick." Wilson, *Food and Drink in Britain*, 260–61 (quoting Fiennes, *Journeys* [ca. 1680s–1710s]). As we saw in chapter 1, the clergyman with whom Josiah Quincy boarded as a boy was of the same mind. Brown bread gave him heartburn. Quincy, *Life of Josiah Quincy*, 26; see also above, chap. 1, n. 73. On the other hand, barley bread was believed to be good for the gout. As the Elizabethan physician Thomas Cogan observed, "poor men," who regularly ate barley bread, "seldome" had the gout; see Drummond and Wilbraham, *Englishman's Food*, 74 (quoting Cogan, *Haven of Health* [1584]). On the origins of these opinions, see Hess, *Martha Washington's Booke of Cookery*, 207.

15. Drummond and Wilbraham, *Englishman's Food*, 42–43; Wilson, *Food and Drink in Britain*, 241; McCance and Widdowson, *Breads White and Brown*, 16; above, chap. 1, n. 22. Terminology became even more various as one moved down the bread hierarchy. For instance, William Harrison in the sixteenth century talked of the manchet, the cheat loaf, the ravelled cheat loaf, and bran bread. In another sixteenth-century source the terms were manchet, yeoman's bread, and carter's bread. The Assize of Bread, the system of price regulation in effect from the thirteenth century until 1815, used "penny white," "penny wheaten," and "household penny." While the names differed, the things named remained fairly consistent. The farther down the ladder one went, the coarser the grain, the higher the proportion of bran, and the darker the color. See McCance and Widdowson, *Breads White and Brown*, 16; Hess, *Martha Washington's Booke of Cookery*, 18, 17. Modern scholars have not always agreed on terminology. See Drummond and Wilbraham, *Englishman's Food*, 43; and Wilson, *Food and Drink in Britain*, 241–42.

16. Wilson, *Food and Drink in Britain*, 246; Gies and Gies, *Life in a Medieval Vil-*

lage, 140. Giving wheat bread as alms persisted into the eighteenth century, as seen in Daniel Defoe's comments regarding a hospital outside Winchester: "Every traveller that knocks at the door of this house, in his way, and asks for it, claims the relief of a piece of white bread and a cup of beer; and this donation is still continued"; see McCance and Widdowson, *Breads White and Brown*, 22–23.

17. Wilson, *Food and Drink in Britain*, 238. While acknowledging the difficulties twelfth- and thirteenth-century peasants encountered in fertilizing their fields, Gies and Gies, in *Life in a Medieval Village*, 16, nevertheless maintain that "the peasant villagers who formed the vast majority of the population cultivated wheat above all other crops." This assertion is not consistent with the majority of our evidence that wheat did not begin to dominate cultivation until several centuries later.

18. McCance and Widdowson, *Breads White and Brown*, 19, 23; Wilson, *Food and Drink in Britain*, 245–46 (quoting Gower); above, chap. 3, n. 21. See also above, chap. 1, n. 24.

19. McCance and Widdowson, *Breads White and Brown*, 23. All grades of bread were based on how finely the grain was ground and the extent to which the coat, or bran, of the kernel had been removed by sieving or bolting. See Drummond and Wilbraham, *Englishman's Food*, 42–43; Wilson, *Food and Drink in Britain*, 241; and McCance and Widdowson, *Breads White and Brown*, 16.

20. McCance and Widdowson, *Breads White and Brown*, 23 (quoting d'Ewes), 18 (quoting the Cromwellian general Lockhart); above, chap. 1, n. 24. Other upper-class voices implicitly conferred legitimacy on the popular preference for white bread when they denounced the practice of giving rye bread as alms: "If we give them a peece of browne bread . . . it is counted meritorious, . . . when we fare full delicately our selves." Ibid., 21 (quoting Stubbes, *Anatomie of Abuses* [1585]).

21. Wilson, *Food and Drink in Britain*, 246; Anderson, "'Solid Sufficiency,'" 163.

22. Wilson, *Food and Drink in Britain*, 261. Classical Athens and Rome had similarly been importers of wheat; McCance and Widdowson, *Breads White and Brown*, 3.

23. David, *English Bread and Yeast Cookery*, 6 (quoting Trevelyan); Wilson, *Food and Drink in Britain*, 263, 261 (quoting *Annals of Agriculture* [1796]). Note the residual disapproval in Trevelyan's "dainty."

24. New England's wheat cultivation difficulties meant that the people of the region did not gain full access to the preferred grain until a few decades after the English had done so. With the opening of the Erie Canal in 1825, "even the stores in rural communities offered wheat from New York State's Genesee Valley," and there finally began to be enough wheat to allow average people to have it as daily fare. Supplies became even more plentiful as agriculture developed in the Middle West and railroads replaced canals. See Sloat, *Old Sturbridge Village Cookbook*, 20; and Oliver, *Saltwater Foodways*, 12. According to Jane Whitehill, in *Food, Drink, and Recipes of Early New England*, 13, wheat abundance was not achieved in New England until "after the Civil War."

25. Panschar, *Economic Development*, 36, 19; David, *English Bread and Yeast Cookery*, 98, 94; Wilson, *Food and Drink in Britain*, 231; See also above, chap. 1, n. 65.

26. Anderson, "'Solid Sufficiency,'" 173. See also above, chap. 1, n. 23. For "fine" bread, see below, n. 31.

27. Drummond and Wilbraham, *Englishman's Food*, 74 (quoting Cogan, *Haven of Health* [1584]). Centuries later, Henry David Thoreau equated the lightness produced by leavening with digestibility: "Especially the transcendental philosophy needs the leaven of humor to render it light and digestible." Thoreau, "Thomas Carlyle and His Works," 227.

28. Wilson, *Food and Drink in Britain*, 259; Hess, *Martha Washington's Booke of Cookery*, 18 (quoting Gervase Markham). See also the mention of a "sowr trough" in the Markham recipe for bread that included peas, above, n. 11.

29. Wilson, *Food and Drink in Britain*, 255, 262; McCance and Widdowson, *Breads White and Brown*, 17.

30. Wilson, *Food and Drink in Britain*, 234. For New England cakes based on the same principle as these Roman doughs, see Child, *American Frugal Housewife*, 70; and Simmons, *American Cookery* (introduction by Wilson), 36. Having fat completely coat the flour "acts to keep the starch grains in the flour separate from each other so that when the liquid is added it does not form lumps." See Barham, *Science of Cooking*, 156–57. The same chemistry underlies the standard directions for making flour and butter roux, although not all cooks look kindly upon roux. See Hess, *Martha Washington's Booke of Cookery*, 4.

31. Wilson, *Food and Drink in Britain*, 234, 270; Panschar, *Economic Development*, 17–19. By the eighteenth century, the plum, or plumb, of the English cake of that name would cease to refer literally to a dried plum or prune and come to signify any preserved fruit in the cake such as raisins. *OED*, 10:1072–73.

32. Wilson, *Food and Drink in Britain*, 269–70. The protein in eggs coagulates during baking, helping to give cake its firmness. But first, when beaten together, the eggs form a stable foam that creates the basis for a fine-textured sponge. As Peter Barham explains, "a good sponge cake is moist and light. . . . To prepare a good sponge, you will need to make a foam of many small bubbles." Barham, *Science of Cooking*, 151–52. According to Karen Hess, in *Martha Washington's Booke of Cookery*, 335, the "sponge cake technique . . . was made possible by more efficient whisks."

33. Brayley, *Bakers and Baking in Massachusetts*, 114; Simmons, *American Cookery* (introduction by Wilson), 33–37.

34. Simmons, *American Cookery* (introduction by Wilson), 37, 34; Bowles and Towle, *Secrets of New England Cooking*, 219.

35. Wilson, *Food and Drink in Britain*, 250, 269; Whitehill, *Food, Drink, and Recipes of Early New England*, 11. Wilson argues that oven-baking was the cause of cakes becoming large (250). In the eighteenth century there were some large cakes—first seed cakes, then traditional plum wedding cakes—that began to be raised with eggs alone. The plum wedding cake in Lee, *Cook's Own Book*, 33–34, appears to have been based on eighteenth-century precedent. See Wilson, *Food and Drink in Britain*, 270.

36. Wilson, *Food and Drink in Britain*, 269–70; Hess, *Martha Washington's Booke of Cookery*, 19–20.

37. Wilson, *Food and Drink in Britain*, 270, 266.

38. Ibid., 265–66; Hess, *Martha Washington's Booke of Cookery*, 12–13. For chocolate, tea, and coffee, see below, chap. 8, nn. 25–61.

39. Simmons, *American Cookery* (introduction by Wilson), 36, xiv–xv.

40. Child, *American Frugal Housewife*, 70–71.

41. Rombauer and Becker, *Joy of Cooking*, 555–56; Sloat, *Old Sturbridge Village Cookbook*, 23. Saleratus was renamed baking soda; see Mariani, *Dictionary of American Food and Drink*, 23.

42. Barham, *Science of Cooking*, 156.

43. Jones, *American Food*, 78, 126; Smallzried, *Everlasting Pleasure*, 57–60; Pillsbury, *No Foreign Food*, 26; Whitehill, *Food, Drink, and Recipes of Early New England*, 11. Those who preferred the old ways continued to be represented in home baking. See, for example, "My Grandmother's Recipe for Loaf Cake," which called for "1 pt. of home made yeast," in *Echoes from South County Kitchens*, 199.

44. Beecher, *Miss Beecher's Domestic Receipt Book*, 84, 93. See also Child, *American Frugal Housewife*, 70–71. Karen Hess observes that "with stiff doughs, these baking powders do not so much leaven the dough as render the finished cake somewhat porous in texture." Hess, *Martha Washington's Booke of Cookery*, 200–201. Rombauer and Becker, in *Joy of Cooking*, 555, describe the effects of chemical leavens differently: "Sodium Bicarbonate or Baking Soda . . . used in combination with some acid ingredients such as sour milk or molasses . . . gives one of the very tenderest crumbs." For a fuller discussion of the chemistry of yeast, eggs, and chemical leavens, see Barham, *Science of Cooking*, 107–16, 151–66.

45. Bowles and Towle, *Secrets of New England Cooking*, 219–21, 224. "Bennington" refers to the battle of Bennington in the American Revolution. "You would not be satisfied with [the Molly Stark] cake," Bowles and Towle decided, "so we are not giving the directions."

46. Sloat, *Old Sturbridge Village Cookbook*, 20 (quoting *Farmer's Monthly Visitor* [1843]); Howland, *American Economical Housekeeper*, 31, 28; Lee, *Cook's Own Book*, 222; Knight, *Tit-Bits*, 72; Inman, *Rhode Island Rule Book*, 55; *Echoes from South County Kitchens*, 188; Wolcott, *New England Yankee Cook Book*, 253, 257.

47. Stowe, *Minister's Wooing*, 256 (chap. 30); *Godey's*, January 1891, 86, and May 1883, 470.

48. Bowles and Towle, *Secrets of New England Cooking*, 221; Hooker, *Food and Drink in America*, 249. The White Mountain Cake in Knight, *Tit-Bits*, 109, was a loaf cake without frosting; those in Turner, *New England Cook Book*, 193, and Patten, *Our New England Family Recipes*, 42–43, were layer cakes with white frosting. Cake wasn't to everyone's liking. One Bristol, Rhode Island, octogenarian opined that "now there are hundreds of persons who can't eat a piece of pork; or of beef, either, if it's got any fat on it. . . . Those same folks that can't eat pork will eat any quantity of sweet things to sweeten 'em up . . . But what's the good of cake and pie? They ain't nawthin' only windgalls. And this 'ere sugar stuff all colored up, and the chocolate candies—we didn't have no

such stuff when I was a boy." Johnson, *Highways and Byways of New England*, 236–37.

49. Wilson, *Food and Drink in Britain*, 246.

50. Booth, *Hung, Strung, and Potted*, 173. As a dish in its own right, pieces of bread in milk was known as "brewis." See Anderson, "'Solid Sufficiency,'" 175; and Oliver, *Saltwater Foodways*, 19. Caroline Howard King described the brewis she had as a child as "little crusty bits of brown bread stewed in cream" in *When I Lived in Salem*, 99.

51. Above, chap. 6, n. 77; Wilson, *Food and Drink in Britain*, 247, 264, 305; Simmons, *American Cookery* (introduction by Wilson), xv. Karen Hess propounds an alternative theory of the origins of gingerbread, according to which it derived, through terminological confusion, from *gingibrati*, a medicine made by taking "well cooked parsnips, minc[ing] them and cook[ing] them with clarified honey . . . aromatic powders, *gimigibre*, pepper, nutmeg, and galingale"; see Hess, *Martha Washington's Booke of Cookery*, 342–43.

52. Wilson, *Food and Drink in Britain*, 264; Simmons, *American Cookery* (introduction by Wilson), xv (quoting Sir Hugh Plat, *Delightes for Ladies* [1602]); Hess, *Martha Washington's Booke of Cookery*, 200 (quoting William Salmon, *The Family Dictionary* [1705]).

53. Above, chap. 6, nn. 60, 64; Hess, *Martha Washington's Booke of Cookery*, 342 (S186), 345–48 (S187–90).

54. Hess, *Martha Washington's Booke of Cookery*, 199–200 (C205); above, chap. 6, n. 66; below, chap. 8, nn. 10, 23–24; Shaw, *Major Barbara*, 310. Karen Hess explains the origins of the interchangeable terms treacle and molasses: "the first citing by OED is 'molassus or common Treacle,' 1694. Molasses was the earlier term in England, having been in use for well over a century at that point, and was brought to the colonies, where it persisted." However, by Hess's own dating of the Martha Washington manuscript, the term "treakle," appearing as it did in the Pepper Cakes recipe in that cookbook, had by 1694 also been in use for somewhat more or somewhat less than a century. Hess, *Martha Washington's Booke of Cookery*, 201.

55. Wilson, *Food and Drink in Britain*, 305; Hess, *Martha Washington's Booke of Cookery*, 200.

56. Smith, *Compleat Housewife*, 175; Hess, *Martha Washington's Booke of Cookery*, 200; Glasse, *Art of Cookery Made Plain and Easy* (glossary and notes by Davidson), 139.

57. Wilson, *Food and Drink in Britain*, 305; Smith, *Compleat Housewife*, 175; Hooker, *Food and Drink in America*, 63.

58. Sewall, *Diary*, 2:958–59 (5 and 6 October 1720).

59. Simmons, *American Cookery* (introduction by Wilson), xv; Hess, *Martha Washington's Booke of Cookery*, 348 (S190). There was a "Muster Day Gingerbread" in Wolcott, *New England Yankee Cook Book*, 161. Stowe described militia musters as "training days, when all the children were refreshed, and our military ardor quickened, by the roll of drums, and the flash of steel bayonets, and marchings and evolutions" in *Oldtown Folks*, 283 (chap. 27). One of E. Smith's three

gingerbreads (above, n. 56) was also made with blanched almonds. In *Martha Washington's Booke of Cookery*, 348, Hess states that this almond-based variety "hardly qualifies as gingerbread; it is more of a fruited spiced marchpane." On marzipan gingerbread, see also Wilson, *Food and Drink in Britain*, 264. For a New England marzipan gingerbread, see "Almond Brown Gingerbread," in Lee, *Cook's Own Book*, 1–2.

60. Simmons, *American Cookery* (introduction by Wilson), 36. One other feature of Simmons's "Molasses Gingerbread" worth noting is that it omitted ginger altogether (as did "Gingerbread Cake No. 3"). This is not as strange as it may seem. Ginger was also omitted from the earliest known gingerbread recipe. This may reflect a widely held medieval opinion that ginger was a coarse spice. See Wilson, *Food and Drink in Britain*, 247; Hess, *Martha Washington's Booke of Cookery*, 343; and Henisch, *Fast and Feast*, 102. "To Make Pepper Cakes" from the Martha Washington manuscript cookbook (above, n. 54) offered a similarly bemusing anomaly. The name highlighted pepper, but the recipe included ginger and left out the pepper.

61. Child, *American Frugal Housewife*, 70–71. As depicted by Karen Hess, the "lavishness" prevalent in the seventeenth-century "golden age of the English kitchen" was the polar opposite of the frugality recommended by Child. Hess, *Martha Washington's Booke of Cookery*, 4. Aspects of the earlier lavishness remained on display in Simmons, *American Cookery*.

62. Lee, *Cook's Own Book*, 1–2, 36, 85. See also, above, n. 59. In "American Gingerbread" (2), Lee omitted the dried fruits.

63. Hale, *Good Housekeeper*, 99–100; Beecher, *Miss Beecher's Domestic Receipt Book*, 134–35, 137–38; Stowe, *Oldtown Folks*, 64 (chap. 6). For additional antebellum gingerbreads, see *Cook Not Mad*, 39–40; Allen, *Housekeeper's Assistant*, 17–18; Prescott, *Valuable Receipts*, 22; Howland, *American Economical Housekeeper*, 23–24; and Bliss, *Practical Cook Book*, 175–77. The last offered no fewer than ten gingerbreads, encompassing the types offered by both Child and Lee. Bliss also included ginger cookies, gingersnaps, and ginger nuts (*Practical Cook Book*, 177–78), as did Beecher (*Miss Beecher's Domestic Receipt Book*, 134, 141–42).

64. Knight, *Tit-Bits*, 74, 77, 79, 81, 84, 114. For Knight and economy, see above, chap. 4, n. 36. For other gingerbreads contemporaneous with those of Knight, see Chadwick, *Home Cookery*, 16, 17, 19; Mendall, *New Bedford Practical Receipt Book*, 62–64; and Cornelius, *Young Housekeeper's Friend*, 58–59.

65. For additional recollections of colonial gingerbread, see Brayley, *Bakers and Baking in Massachusetts*, 128–29.

66. Hazard, *Jonny-Cake Papers*, 160. For similar stratagems see, for example, Wilson, *Food and Drink in Britain*, 262; and Brayley, *Bakers and Baking in Massachusetts*, 126–28.

67. Hazard, *Jonny-Cake Papers*, 160.

68. Ibid., 160–61.

69. In an appropriate twist for a Rhode Islander, Hazard referred not only to the alleged "witches and wizards" of Salem, but also to "the four Quakers who were hung by the wicked Puritans on Boston Common." The "pious but outcast

sect" being elevated in the passage along with Stephen Greene's consummate gingerbread was thus made up of some of the most famous victims of the early Massachusetts theocracy. *Jonny-Cake Papers*, 161.

70. Sloat, *Old Sturbridge Village Cookbook*, 13 (quoting Dummerston, Vermont, *Deeds*, vol. 8); measurement conversion based on Rombauer and Becker, *Joy of Cooking*, 590. For recollections of childhood molasses consumption, see above, chap. 6, n. 72. Apparently, even molasses was too expensive for some. Instructions on how to make a substitute for molasses from apples were reprinted from an Ohio agricultural periodical in Gilman, *Lady's Annual Register . . . for 1839*, 48–49.

71. *Aunt Mary's New England Cook Book*, title page and 3–4; above, chap. 3, n. 82, and chap. 4, n. 37.

72. *Aunt Mary's New England Cook Book*, 53–54.

73. *Durham Cook Book*, 170; Whatsoever Circle, *King's Daughters . . . Cook Book*, 87–88; Turner, *New England Cook Book*, 181–82. A strange choice of advertisement for a book written to teach cooking was the verse that appeared on the title page of the *King's Daughters* volume: "Cookin's like religion is— / Some's 'lected and some aint."

74. Patten, *Our New England Family Recipes*, 5, 56–57.

75. Wright, *New England Cook Book*, 194–95; Measuring Cup Group, *Cook Book*, 11–12; Wolcott, *New England Yankee Cook Book*, 160–62. For Beecher's gingersnaps and ginger nuts, see above, n. 63.

76. For a discussion of some aspects of New England's loss of leadership in the American Industrial Revolution after the middle of the nineteenth century, see Dalzell, *Enterprising Elite*, 109–12.

77. *Godey's*, April 1884, 401.

78. Lyman Beecher, *Autobiography*, 1:238–39.

79. Ibid., 1:239. The detail in Stowe's parallel account that matches Catharine's version most closely is that "the fire was besieged with a row of earthen pots, in which the spicy compound was rising to the necessary lightness." Stowe, *Oldtown Folks*, 398 (chap. 37).

80. *Godey's*, November 1890, 427.

81. *Godey's*, March 1884, 297. The second recipe (*Godey's*, November 1890), which made the connection with "old New England housewives," was identical with the earlier one except for calling for half as much powdered mace.

82. Morison, *Builders of the Bay Colony*, 85–87. Morison writes that after 1644 the centerpieces of our first two chapters, corn and beans, figured in the Massachusetts election process. If the voter agreed with the officially recommended choices for governor and deputy-governor, he used a kernel of corn to signify his assent. If he disagreed, he used a bean to indicate his dissent. This places the whimsical comment by a Maine resident—that in making baked beans, each individual bean "should be treated like a voter in an election"—in a somewhat more interesting light. Jones, *American Food*, 10 (see also above, chap. 2, n. 49).

83. Stowe, *Oldtown Folks*, 283 (chap. 27). For the combined late-May observances in eighteenth-century Massachusetts, see, for example, Parkman, *Diary*, 12 (27

May 1726), 137 (30 May 1746), 237 (30 May 1751), 289 (29 May 1755); and Parkman Diary, 28 May 1764, 31 May 1769, 25 and 26 May 1773, American Antiquarian Society.

84. Stowe, *Oldtown Folks*, 228 (chap. 22).

85. Ebenezer Parkman, the pastor of Westborough, Massachusetts, preached the election sermon in 1761; Parkman Diary, 28 May 1760, 19 May 1761, 28 May 1761, American Antiquarian Society.

86. Oliver, *Saltwater Foodways*, 22 (quoting Redfield from *Life in the Connecticut River Valley, 1800–1840, from the Recollections of John Howard Redfield* [1988 ed.]).

87. Catherine of Siena, *Dialogue*, 123.

88. Sloat, *Old Sturbridge Village Cookbook*, 17, 20; Oliver, *Saltwater Foodways*, 21; Larcom, *New England Girlhood*, 98–99 (also quoted in Sloat, *Old Sturbridge Village Cookbook*, 20).

89. Child, *American Frugal Housewife*, 71. Mrs. E. A. Howland cribbed this recipe from Child, although she inexplicably left out the currants; see Howland, *American Economical Housekeeper*, 20. There were five election cakes in Chadwick, *Home Cookery*, 18–19. Amelia Simmons added election cake to her second edition. See Simmons, *American Cookery* (introduction by Hess), 43–44, xiii–xiv. *Godey's* published a recipe called "Election Cake" in 1881, but it was unyeasted and, its name aside, was less like a traditional election cake than the magazine's Connecticut loaf cake; *Godey's*, April 1881, 375. Wolcott, *New England Yankee Cook Book*, 252, covered all the bases by giving four names, "Connecticut Raised Loaf Cake," "Election Cake," "March Meeting Cake," and "Dough Cake," to the same recipe.

90. Child, *American Frugal Housewife*, 73; Allen, *Housekeeper's Assistant*, 15–16; Beecher, *Miss Beecher's Domestic Receipt Book*, 139; Bliss, *Practical Cook Book*, 172–73; Hale, *Ladies' New Book of Cookery*, 372; Knight, *Tit-Bits*, 77, 83. David, in *English Bread and Yeast Cookery*, 422–23, states that doughnuts "were evidently a great speciality of the Isle of Wight." She gives examples from 1845 and 1930. These dates indicate that this may have been a case of culinary influence traveling back across the Atlantic. Early-nineteenth-century editions of standard English cookbooks, such as those of Carter, Glasse, and Maria Rundell, included distinctively American dishes, among them doughnuts. See Simmons, *American Cookery* (introduction by Wilson), xix. On the other hand, Karen Hess's insistence (in Glasse, *Art of Cookery Made Plain and Easy* [introduction by Hess], ix–x) that "there is nothing specifically American" about doughnuts and many other American foods is substantiated, as far as doughnuts are concerned, in Scully, *Art of Cookery in the Middle Ages*, 217. It may well be that by the nineteenth century, the European lineage of doughnuts was only dimly remembered, and that they became popular anew on the supposition that they were exotic imports from America. We have seen such a pattern with chowder.

91. Hooker, *Food and Drink in America*, 249; Howland, *American Economical Housekeeper*, 71 (also cited in Oliver, *Saltwater Foodways*, 18); Stowe, *Pearl of Orr's Island*, 277 (chap. 28) (see also above, chap. 5, n. 133); Doudiet, "Coastal Maine Cooking," 225 (quoting Noah Brooks, *Lem, a New England Village Boy* [1901]).

92. Stowe, *Oldtown Folks*, 90 (chap. 8), 115–16 (chap. 11).

93. Ibid., 435 (chap. 42); Stowe, *Pearl of Orr's Island*, 87 (chap. 10); Stowe, *Minister's Wooing*, 35 (chap. 4). The combination of pound cake and doughnuts seen in these last two examples was also offered at Catharine Beecher's wood-spell. The "bushels of doughnuts" that Beecher "boiled over the kitchen fire" that day were as much a danger to her "credit for veracity" as "the number of loaves [of cake she] put into and took out of the oven." Lyman Beecher, *Autobiography*, 1:239. Eleanor Early reports that "wonders" were doughnuts without a hole, "frilled on the edge." One Nantucket family "had Wonders for breakfast, for noonday dinner and for tea." Like Stowe's Tina, a little boy in the family took them "to bed with him." Early, *New England Cookbook*, 113–14.

94. Stowe, *Pearl of Orr's Island*, 174 (chap. 17), 296 (chap. 30); Oliver, *Saltwater Foodways*, 103–4. According to Early in *New England Cookbook*, 117, whaling ship doughnuts were called Seventy-Fours "because . . . a sailor once ate 74."

95. Stowe, *Minister's Wooing*, 83 (chap. 9).

96. Ibid., 103 (chap. 11).

97. Ibid., 104 (chap. 11). We discuss this episode from a coffee point of view below, chap. 8, nn. 60–61.

98. Ibid., 252 (chap. 29), 256 (chap. 30). Here again was the party combination of loaf cake and doughnuts.

99. Ibid., 312–13 (chap. 39).

100. Ibid., 201–3 (chap. 23). In the last half century, doughnuts have lost their social standing (and their "ugh"). An episode exemplifying their decline occurred in Cambridge, Massachusetts. As longtime residents of that city, we have observed that those concerned to "defend" the "historic character" of Harvard Square have not objected when any number of pizza or French bakery chains have established themselves there. But the cultural elite thought differently when a chain of donut shops wanted to open an outlet. The line in the sand was drawn at donuts. There is no question that the do(ugh)nut represents the culinary heritage most fittingly consumed in New England's educational hub. But having lost all prestige and having been reduced to fast food, the donut could enter the sacred precincts of Harvard Square only after its corporate purveyors agreed to conceal its identity. For this location only, the corporate awning color and name were relinquished, and the pretentious and un-Yankee alias "café" was adopted. In a cosmopolitan age, the cheap and common donut is without honor in its own country. See *Cambridge Chronicle*, 5 December 1974, 11 September 1975, 18 June 1992, 10 December 1998.

CHAPTER EIGHT

1. For mead, see Wilson, *Food and Drink in Britain*, 366; Bradford, *Of Plymouth Plantation*, 228; and Lee, *Cook's Own Book*, 115. For beer and ale, see Wilson, *Food and Drink in Britain*, 369–70, 372, 376; Anderson, "'Solid Sufficiency,'" 89, 91, 98; Burnaby, *Travels through the Middle Settlements in North-America*, 69; Simmons, *American Cookery* (introduction by Wilson), 47; Child, *American Frugal Housewife*, 86; Hale, *Good Housekeeper*, 113–14; and Stowe, *Pearl of*

Orr's Island, 137 (chap. 14), 335 (chap. 34). For water, see Wilson, *Food and Drink in Britain*, 383–84; Hooker, *Food and Drink in America*, 128–29; Brown, *Early American Beverages*, 95; Hale, *Good Housekeeper*, 115–16; and Martin, *Standard of Living in 1860*, 38–42. As with doughnuts, Karen Hess disputes the American origin of spruce beer, stating that it is "from Prussia, and has been in the literature as such . . . since 1500." See Glasse, *Art of Cookery Made Plain and Easy* (introduction by Hess), x.

2. Wilson, *Food and Drink in Britain*, 382, 404–5; Anderson "'Solid Sufficiency,'" 51, 143, 146. For a cider recipe in an eighteenth-century English cookbook, see Smith, *Compleat Housewife*, 251.

3. McMahon, "Comfortable Subsistence," 42, 43, 47, and esp. 59. (See also above, chap. 6, n. 12.) Some of the benefits of apple cultivation and cider manufacture were anticipated by English observers and realized in English practice. See Anderson, "'Solid Sufficiency,'" 144–45; and Wilson, *Food and Drink in Britain*, 383.

4. Dow, *Every Day Life in the Massachusetts Bay Colony*, 108; Earle, *Stage-Coach and Tavern Days*, 118.

5. Earle, *Stage-Coach and Tavern Days*, 128; Stowe, *Pearl of Orr's Island*, 98–99 (chap. 10). The traditional beverage, syllabub, which could be made with either wine or cider, was in New England increasingly made with cider. See Wilson, *Food and Drink in Britain*, 170; Glasse, *Art of Cookery Made Plain and Easy* (glossary and notes by Davidson), 146; Carter, *Frugal Housewife*, 147–48; Simmons, *American Cookery* (introduction by Wilson), 31; Brown, *Early American Beverages*, 16; and Field, *Colonial Tavern*, 142.

6. Earle, *Stage-Coach and Tavern Days*, 128, 125–27; Earle, *Home Life in Colonial Days*, 161; Whitehill, *Food, Drink, and Recipes of Early New England*, 17; Stowe, *Oldtown Folks*, 70–71 (chap. 6), 78 (chap. 7), 99 (chap. 9), 157 (chap. 17), 168 (chap. 18), 283, 288, 295 (chap. 27), 300 (chap. 28), 328 (chap. 30), 384 (chap. 35), 439 (chap. 42); see also above, chap. 6, n. 123.

7. Earle, *Stage-Coach and Tavern Days*, 128; Roger Williams to John Winthrop Jr., 6 February 1660, in Williams, *Correspondence*, 2:494; Hooker, *Food and Drink in America*, 83–84 (quoting Brillat-Savarin).

8. Shammas, *Pre-Industrial Consumer in England and America*, 54; Earle, *Home Life in Colonial Days*, 161–62. According to Hardeman, *Shucks, Shocks, and Hominy Blocks*, 135, during slack seasons, mills devoted primarily to grinding corn were adapted for cider pressing.

9. Keats, *Complete Poems*, 377 ("To Autumn," ll.21–22).

10. Earle, *Stage-Coach and Tavern Days*, 100 (quoting a 1651 description of Barbados).

11. McCusker and Menard, *Economy of British America*, 290–91. Hooker, *Food and Drink in America*, 86, gives a higher figure of 159 distilleries in New England in 1763. The difference may reflect the measures taken by Great Britain during the 1760s to bring the colonies into compliance with its system of imperial economic regulation.

12. McCusker and Menard, *Economy of British America*, 290; Earle, *Stage-Coach*

and Tavern Days, 111–12, 102 (quoting Mather). According to John Hull Brown, for most of the eighteenth century the difference in price between New England and West Indian rum was not all that great—only two pence a gallon; see Brown, *Early American Beverages*, 17–18. This would help to explain the 1770 colonial consumption figures. The volume of rum imports from the West Indies, 3.5 million gallons, though smaller than the figures for domestic production and consumption, was nevertheless quite substantial. It is unlikely that an expensive commodity would have been imported and purchased on such a scale. On the other hand, Brown's mere tuppence differential for a gallon of rum is inconsistent with the evidence of a tuppence difference in the price of a single mug of flip, depending on whether the rum in it came from New England or the West Indies.

13. Earle, *Stage-Coach and Tavern Days*, 103 (quoting Burke); Samuel Stearns, *The American Herbal, or Materia Medica* (Walpole, N.H., 1801), excerpted in Brown, *Early American Beverages*, 98.

14. Shammas, *Pre-Industrial Consumer in England and America*, 63, 83 (per capita rum consumption); Derven, "Wholesome, Toothsome, and Diverse," 49; Coe and Coe, "Mid-Eighteenth-Century Food and Drink on the Massachusetts Frontier," 45. We have inserted the phrase "at the least" into the opening sentence of the paragraph because Shammas probably underestimated per capita colonial consumption. Her calculations are based on an overall figure of 7.5 million gallons, which she draws from John J. McCusker's 1970 Ph.D. dissertation. But McCusker himself, working with Russell R. Menard, is the source of the 8.5 million gallon total given above in our text. That figure appears in a book published in 1985 that used McCusker's dissertation "as supplemented by later research." McCusker and Menard, *Economy of British America*, 291.

15. Earle, *Stage-Coach and Tavern Days*, 103 (quoting Riedesel and Adams).

16. Stearns, *American Herbal*, in Brown, *Early American Beverages*, 98. Stearns further claimed that "strong grog, poured down a sailor's throat, when he was apparently dead with the yellow fever in the year 1798, restored him to life and health." On the eve of the temperance movement, Lydia Maria Child promoted the use of rum in yet another context: "New England rum, constantly used to wash the hair, keeps it very clean, and free from disease, and promotes its growth a great deal more than Macassar oil. Brandy is very strengthening to the roots of the hair; but it has a hot, drying tendency, which N.E. rum has not." Child, *American Frugal Housewife*, 12.

17. Earle, *Stage-Coach and Tavern Days*, 104–5.

18. Ibid., 108–9, 112. Another version of flip was "calibogus" or "callabogus." According to one source (Brown, *Early American Beverages*, 20), this was simply rum and beer without the sweeteners; according to another (Stearns, *American Herbal*, in Brown, *Early American Beverages*, 98), it was flip made with spruce rather than malt beer. Flip could also be made with cider; see Earle, *Stage-Coach and Tavern Days*, 112.

19. Field, *Colonial Tavern*, 135–36.

20. Earle, *Stage-Coach and Tavern Days*, 108 (quoting the 1704 almanac); Hooker,

Food and Drink in America, 38 (quoting Trumbull, *M'Fingal* [1776]); Barlow, "Hasty Pudding," 91; Lowell, *Poetical Works*, 417 ("Fitz Adam's Story"; also quoted in Earle, *Stage-Coach and Tavern Days*, 113). Bounce was "made by pouring spirits such as rum or brandy over fruit, adding sugar, citrus fruit, spices, and water"; see Mariani, *Dictionary of American Food and Drink*, 51. Eliza Leslie included a recipe for "Cherry Bounce" in *Miss Leslie's Complete Cookery* (1839), reprinted in Brown, *Early American Beverages*, 54. It was made with cherries, sugar, and whiskey, and it had to be aged for at least three months. The variety to which the almanac bard referred was doubtless made with rum rather than whiskey.

21. Stowe, *Minister's Wooing*, 161, 163 (chap. 17); Stowe, *Oldtown Folks*, 398, 400, 402 (chap. 37). As noted in the last chapter, Stowe probably based the wood-spell account partly on the recollections of her sister that Catharine Beecher contributed to their father's *Autobiography*. Beecher mentioned gathering "the materials for beer for the flip" and the subsequent brewing "on a scale of grandeur befitting the occasion." As she told it, it was not the minister but rather his sons who "heated the flip-irons, and passed around the cider and flip," with a zeal and dedication equal to that exhibited by the minister's daughters "in serving the doughnuts, cake, and cheese." Lyman Beecher, *Autobiography*, 1:238–39.

22. Appleby, *Inheriting the Revolution*, 208 (quoting Marsh). This is only a possible instance of home flip consumption because people often repaired to the neighboring inn after church. See Earle, *Stage-Coach and Tavern Days*, 13–14.

23. A succinct summary of the pattern of the New England export-import trade in the eighteenth century is found in McManis, *Colonial New England*, 108–10. For the first outlines of the pattern a hundred years earlier, see Bailyn, *New England Merchants in the Seventeenth Century*, 84–86.

24. McManis, *Colonial New England*, 109–10; Brown, *Early American Beverages*, 17–18.

25. Shammas, *Pre-Industrial Consumer in England and America*, 77–78. Less important in New England than tea and coffee, chocolate is not discussed here. See Wilson, *Food and Drink in Britain*, 408–11; and for recipes, see Child, *American Frugal Housewife*, 83–84; Lee, *Cook's Own Book*, 51; Hale, *Good Housekeeper*, 113; Beecher, *Miss Beecher's Domestic Receipt Book*, 188; *Aunt Mary's New England Cook Book*, 61; and Turner, *New England Cook Book*, 236.

26. Wilson, *Food and Drink in Britain*, 411–13.

27. Ibid., 412, 415; Shammas, *Pre-Industrial Consumer in England and America*, 84–85, 64. The same elderly Englishwoman of the early twentieth century who stoutly defended the keeping of pigs (see above, chap. 5, n. 161), also commented that "we didn't drink no tea then . . . we had beer for breakfast then, and it did us good. It were better than all those nasty cocoa stuffs we drinks now." Anderson, "'Solid Sufficiency,'" 186 (quoting a woman interviewed by the novelist W. H. Hudson).

28. Earle, *Home Life in Colonial Days*, 164–65; King, *When I Lived in Salem*, 102.

29. Hooker, *Food and Drink in America*, 90–91; Shammas, *Pre-Industrial Consumer in England and America*, 64, 84–85.

30. Cummings, *American and His Food*, 34 (citing Charles Francis Adams's edition of his grandfather's *Works*); Hooker, *Food and Drink in America*, 91.

31. Above, chap. 6, n. 56; Stowe, *Pearl of Orr's Island*, 357 (chap. 37).

32. Lee, *Cook's Own Book*, xxix. Sarah Josepha Hale agreed with Lee. Hale and Child, like Lee, felt that among the two major types of tea, black was "less deleterious" than green—the reverse of the modern consensus. See Hale, *Good Housekeeper*, 18, 113; and Child, *American Frugal Housewife*, 84.

33. Lee, *Cook's Own Book*, xxix; Beecher, *Miss Beecher's Domestic Receipt Book*, 189; *Aunt Mary's New England Cook Book*, 63.

34. Beecher, *Miss Beecher's Domestic Receipt Book*, 196–97. See also Turner, *New England Cook Book*, 251–52. Other non-tea, hot steeped drinks were occasionally offered for sick people. Beecher included cranberry and apple "teas," as did Mrs. Bliss (*Practical Cook Book*, 251). Hale, *Good Housekeeper*, 143, stated that mint tea was "useful in allaying nausea and vomiting," while Knight, *Tit-Bits*, 105, claimed that "Hop Tea" was "most excellent for nervous headache."

35. Stowe, *Pearl of Orr's Island*, 113 (chap. 12).

36. Stowe, *Minister's Wooing*, chap. 4. For a nonfictional recollection of early-nineteenth-century New England tea parties, see King, *When I Lived in Salem*, 103–8.

37. Wilson, *Food and Drink in Britain*, 405–6.

38. Ibid., 407; Hooker, *Food and Drink in America*, 92; Earle, *Home Life in Colonial Days*, 165.

39. Cummings, *American and His Food*, 35, 34; Martin, *Standard of Living in 1860*, 42–43.

40. Stearns, *American Herbal*, in Brown, *Early American Beverages*, 97.

41. Lee, *Cook's Own Book*, xxix. Once again, Hale agreed; see *Good Housekeeper*, 18.

42. Hooker, *Food and Drink in America*, 130.

43. Child, *American Frugal Housewife*, 82.

44. Hale, *Good Housekeeper*, 113; *Aunt Mary's New England Cook Book*, 62.

45. Lee, *Cook's Own Book*, xxx. See also *Cook Not Mad*, 61; Beecher, *Miss Beecher's Domestic Receipt Book*, 187–88; and Hale, *Ladies' New Book of Cookery*, 391.

46. For variations on this basic outline, see Child, *American Frugal Housewife*, 83 (Child was the only author to suggest using "rind of salt pork" for settling coffee grounds); Lee, *Cook's Own Book*, 53; Hale, *Good Housekeeper*, 112–13; Prescott, *Valuable Receipts*, 24 (verbatim copy of Hale); Beecher, *Miss Beecher's Domestic Receipt Book*, 188; Webster, *Improved Housewife*, 215; *Aunt Mary's New England Cook Book*, 61–62; and Turner, *New England Cook Book*, 235. In the last, published in 1905, we begin to enter our universe of coffee preparation. The basic nineteenth-century method was described, and then an alternative procedure, "using a percolating coffee pot," was also included.

47. Lee, *Cook's Own Book*, 53. See also Hale, *Good Housekeeper*, 112.

48. King, *When I Lived in Salem*, 27.

49. Beecher, *Miss Beecher's Domestic Receipt Book*, 187; Child, *American Frugal Housewife*, 83.

50. Child, *American Frugal Housewife*, 83. A biggin was essentially a drip-grind coffee pot. The grounds were placed in a separate canister fitted into the mouth of the pot and the boiling water poured into the canister, whence, having been alchemically transformed by contact with the fresh-roasted and -ground powder, it dripped through into the main chamber. The biggin was contrived by an Englishman bearing that name. But Mrs. Lee gave the credit to a Frenchman, "Monsieur de Belloy." His (or Mr. Biggin's) original drip coffee pot had been made of tin, but that wasn't good enough for Lee: "Particular care should be taken not to make coffee in a tin vessel; it should be made either in a China vessel, or one of Delft ware, or in one of silver." See *OED*, 2:184; and Lee, *Cook's Own Book*, 53–54. See also Hale, *Ladies' New Book of Cookery*, 391, where there is a recipe for "Coffee Made in a French Filter or Grecque." This device was apparently similar to the French press which is nowadays in use among such English coffee-drinkers as there are.

51. Hazard, *Jonny-Cake Papers*, 363–64.

52. Ibid., 364.

53. Ibid., 365.

54. Ibid., 365–66.

55. Ibid., 366. The text accompanying the original of the illustration on p. 275 reads, "hail, soul-inspiring bean of Yemen, soother of the troubled, strengthener of the weary, dispeller of shadows, dispenser of cheerfulness, child of Araby the Blest, I give you welcome!" Strother, "Summer in New England," 2. In *House of the Seven Gables*, Nathaniel Hawthorne imagined coffee working similar magic on one of his characters: "In a little while the guest became sensible of the fragrance of the yet untasted coffee. He quaffed it eagerly. The subtle essence acted on him like a charmed draught, and caused the opaque substance of his animal being to grow transparent, or, at least, translucent; so that a spiritual gleam was transmitted through it, with a clearer lustre than hitherto. 'More, more!' he cried, with nervous haste in his utterance, as if anxious to retain his grasp of what sought to escape him. 'This is what I need! Give me more!'" Hawthorne, *House of the Seven Gables*, 92–93 (chap. 7).

56. Hazard, *Jonny-Cake Papers*, 362.

57. Ibid., 382–86.

58. Ibid., 386–87.

59. On attitudes toward the French, see above, chap. 3, nn. 166, 168; chap. 5, n. 26. Like Hazard, Twain would call the French crown prince "the Dolphin." As part of a conversation with Jim, the runaway slave with whom he was floating down the Mississippi on a raft, Huck Finn "told about Louis Sixteenth that got his head cut off in France long time ago; and about his little boy the dolphin, that would 'a' been the king, but they took and shut him up in jail, and some say he died there." Twain, *Adventures of Huckleberry Finn*, 83 (chap. 14).

60. Stowe, *Minister's Wooing*, 103 (chap. 11). Candace's friend Miss Prissy accused

another African American cook of incompetence: "Dinah, she wouldn't have put near enough egg into the coffee, if it hadn't been for me; why, I just went and beat up four eggs with my own hands and stirred 'em into the grounds" (Ibid., 140 [chap. 15]).

61. Ibid., 4 (chap. 1).

CONCLUSION

1. Rutman, *Husbandmen of Plymouth*, 77.

Bibliography

Abbott, Katharine M. *Old Paths and Legends of the New England Border: Connecticut, Deerfield, Berkshire.* New York: Putnam, 1907.

Adams, Henry. *History of the United States of America during the First Administration of Thomas Jefferson.* 2 vols. New York: Scribner's, 1889.

Alcott, William A. *The Young House-Keeper.* Boston: George W. Light, 1838.

Allen, Ann H. *The Housekeeper's Assistant.* Boston: James Munroe, 1845.

Allen, David Ellerton. *British Tastes: An Inquiry into the Likes and Dislikes of the Regional Consumer.* London: Hutchinson, 1968.

American National Biography. Vol. 4. Edited by John A. Garraty and Mark C. Carnes. New York: Oxford University Press, 1999.

Anderson, Jay Allan. "'A Solid Sufficiency': An Ethnography of Yeoman Foodways in Stuart England." Ph.D. diss., University of Pennsylvania, 1971.

Anderson, Virginia DeJohn. "Migrants and Motives: Religion and the Settlement of New England, 1630–1640." *New England Quarterly* 58 (September 1985): 339–83.

Appleby, Joyce. *Inheriting the Revolution: The First Generation of Americans.* Cambridge, Mass.: Harvard University Press, 2000.

Archer, Richard. "New England Mosaic: A Demographic Analysis for the Seventeenth Century." *William and Mary Quarterly*, 3d ser., 47 (October 1990): 477–502.

Aunt Mary's New England Cook Book. Boston: Lockwood, Brooks, 1881.

Axtell, James. *The European and the Indian: Essays in the Ethnohistory of Colonial North America.* New York: Oxford University Press, 1981.

Bacon, Richard M. *The Forgotten Art of Building and Using a Brick Bake Oven: A Practical Guide.* Dublin, N.H.: Richard M. Bacon and Yankee, Inc., 1977.

Bailyn, Bernard. *The New England Merchants in the Seventeenth Century.* Cambridge, Mass.: Harvard University Press, 1955; New York: Harper Torchbooks, 1964.

Baker, James W. "Seventeenth-Century English Yeoman Foodways at Plimoth Plantation." In *Foodways in the Northeast*, edited by Peter Benes, 105–13. Boston: Boston University, 1984.

Barham, Peter. *The Science of Cooking.* New York: Springer-Verlag, 2001.

Barlow, Joel. "The Hasty Pudding" (1793). In vol. 2 of *The Works of Joel Barlow*, edited by William K. Bottorff and Arthur L. Lord, 85–99. Gainesville, Fla.: Scholars' Facsimiles and Reprints, 1970.

Bartlett's Familiar Quotations. 10th ed. Boston: Little, Brown, 1919. <http://www.bartleby.com/100>. 24 February 2004.

Beecher, Catharine. *Miss Beecher's Domestic Receipt Book: Designed as a Supplement to Her Treatise on Domestic Economy.* New York: Harper, 1846.

———. *A Treatise on Domestic Economy* (1841). Edited by Kathryn Kish Sklar. New York: Schocken, 1977.

Beecher, Catharine E., and Harriet Beecher Stowe. *The American Woman's Home: Or, Principles of Domestic Science.* 1869. Reprint, Hartford, Conn.: Stowe-Day Foundation, 1985.

Beecher, Lyman. *The Autobiography of Lyman Beecher.* Edited by Barbara M. Cross. 2 vols. Cambridge, Mass.: Harvard University Press, 1961.

Bennett, M. K. "The Food Economy of the New England Indians, 1605–75." *Journal of Political Economy* 63 (October 1955): 369–97.

Bercovitch, Sacvan. *The American Jeremiad.* Madison: University of Wisconsin Press, 1978.

Bliss, Mrs. [of Boston]. *The Practical Cook Book.* Philadelphia: Lippincott, Grambo, 1850.

Booth, Sally Smith. *Hung, Strung, and Potted: A History of Eating in Colonial America.* New York: Clarkson N. Potter, 1971.

Bowles, Ella Shannon, and Dorothy S. Towle. *Secrets of New England Cooking.* New York: M. Barrows, 1947.

Boydston, Jeanne. *Home and Work: Housework, Wages, and the Ideology of Labor in the Early Republic.* New York: Oxford University Press, 1990.

Bradford, William. *Of Plymouth Plantation, 1620–1647.* Edited by Samuel Eliot Morison. New York: Random House, 1952.

Bragdon, Kathleen J. *Native People of Southern New England, 1500–1650.* Norman: University of Oklahoma Press, 1996.

Braudel, Fernand. *The Structures of Everyday Life—The Limits of the Possible.* Vol. 1 of *Civilization and Capitalism, 15th–18th Century.* Translated by Siân Reynolds. New York: Harper and Row, 1981.

Brayley, Arthur W. *Bakers and Baking in Massachusetts.* Boston: Master Bakers' Association of Massachusetts, 1909.

Brewer, Priscilla J. "Home Fires: Cookstoves in American Culture, 1815–1900." In *House and Home,* edited by Peter Benes, 68–88. Boston: Boston University, 1990.

Brown, Bonnie, and David Segal. "Sugaring Off: A Glimpse of New England Maple Sugaring." In *National and Regional Styles of Cookery,* edited by Alan Davidson, 247–54. London: Prospect, 1981.

Brown, Greg. "Canned Goods." On *The Live One.* St. Paul, Minn.: Red House Records, 1995.

Brown, John Hull. *Early American Beverages.* Rutland, Vt.: Charles E. Tuttle, 1966.

Brown, Nellie I. *Recipes From Old Hundred: 200 Years of New England Cooking.* New York: M. Barrows, 1939.

Buell, Lawrence. *New England Literary Culture: From Revolution through Renaissance.* Cambridge: Cambridge University Press, 1986.

Burnaby, Rev. Andrew. *Travels through the Middle Settlements in North-America in the Years 1759 and 1760.* London: T. Payne, 1775. Available online at <http://gdz.sub.uni-goettingen.de/en/index.html>, Early North Americana link. 24 February 2004.

Bushman, Richard L. *The Refinement of America: Persons, Houses, Cities.* New York: Knopf, 1992.

Butler, Jon. *Becoming America: The Revolution before 1776.* Cambridge, Mass.: Harvard University Press, 2000.

Calloway, Colin G., ed. *Dawnland Encounters: Indians and Europeans in Northern New England.* Hanover, N.H.: University Press of New England, 1991.

Cambridge (Mass.) Chronicle, 5 December 1974, 11 September 1975, 18 June 1992, 10 December 1998.

Cambridge World History of Food, The. Edited by Kenneth F. Kiple and Kriemhild Corneè Ornelas. 2 vols. Cambridge: Cambridge University Press, 2000.

Carter, Susannah. *The Frugal Housewife; or Complete Woman Cook.* London: F. Newbery, 1795.

Carver, John. *Sketches of New England: Or, Memories of the Country.* New York: E. French, 1842.

Catherine of Siena. *The Dialogue.* Edited and translated by Suzanne Noffke. New York: Paulist Press, 1980.

Ceci, Lynn. "Fish Fertilizer: A Native North American Practice?" *Science,* 4 April 1975, 26–30.

[Chadwick, Mrs. J.]. *Home Cookery: A Collection of Tried Receipts both Foreign and Domestic.* Boston: Crosby, Nichols, 1859.

Chaucer, Geoffrey. *Chaucer's Poetry: An Anthology for the Modern Reader.* Edited by E. T. Donaldson. New York: Ronald Press, 1958.

Child, Lydia Maria. *The American Frugal Housewife.* 12th ed. Boston: Carter, Hendee, 1833. Reprint, Worthington, Ohio: Worthington Historical Society, 1980.

———. "Apple-seed John." *St. Nicholas,* June 1880, 604–605. Reprinted in *Our Holidays in Poetry,* compiled by Mildred P. Harrington and Josephine H. Thomas, 144–47. New York: Wilson, 1929.

———. *Hobomok and Other Writings on Indians* (1824). Edited by Carolyn L. Karcher. New Brunswick, N.J.: Rutgers University Press, 1986.

———. "The New England Boy's Song about Thanksgiving Day." In *Representative Poems On-line,* edited by I. Lancashire. Toronto: Web Development Group, Information Technology Services, University of Toronto Library, 2000. <http://eir.library.utoronto.ca/rpo/display/poem473.html>. 24 February 2004.

Clark, Christopher. *The Roots of Rural Capitalism: Western Massachusetts, 1780–1860.* Ithaca, N.Y.: Cornell University Press, 1990.

Cobbett, William. *A Treatise on Cobbett's Corn* (1828). In *Cobbett's Country Book: An Anthology of William Cobbett's Writings on Country Matters,* edited by Richard Ingrams, 205–15. Newton Abbot, Eng.: David and Charles, 1975.

Coe, Michael D., and Sophie D. Coe. "Mid-Eighteenth-Century Food and Drink on the Massachusetts Frontier." In *Foodways in the Northeast,* edited by Peter Benes, 39–46. Boston: Boston University, 1984.

Columbia Encyclopedia. 6th ed. New York: Columbia University Press and Bartleby.com, 2002. <http://www.bartleby.com/65>. 24 February 2004.

Columbus, Christopher. *The Log of Christopher Columbus*. Translated by Robert H. Fuson. Camden, Maine: International Marine Publishing, 1987.

Compleat Cook, The. 1671. Reprint, London: Prospect, 1984.

Cook Not Mad, The. Watertown, N.Y.: Knowlton and Rice, 1830.

[Cornelius, Mrs. Mary Hooker]. *The Young Housekeeper's Friend*. Rev. and enl. ed. Boston: Frederick A. Brown, 1862.

Cott, Nancy F. *The Bonds of Womanhood: "Woman's Sphere" in New England, 1780–1835*. New Haven: Yale University Press, 1977.

Crawford, Mary Caroline. *Old New England Inns*. 1907. Boston: L. C. Page, 1924.

Cressy, David. *Coming Over: Migration and Communication between England and New England in the Seventeenth Century*. Cambridge: Cambridge University Press, 1987.

Cronon, William. *Changes in the Land: Indians, Colonists, and the Ecology of New England*. New York: Hill and Wang, 1983.

Crosby, Alfred W., Jr. *The Columbian Exchange: Biological and Cultural Consequences of 1492*. Westport, Conn.: Greenwood Press, 1972.

Cummings, Abbott Lowell. *The Framed Houses of Massachusetts Bay, 1625–1725*. Cambridge, Mass.: Harvard University Press, 1979.

Cummings, Richard Osborn. *The American and His Food: A History of Food Habits in the United States*. Chicago: University of Chicago Press, 1941.

Cutler, Charles L. *O Brave New Words! Native American Loan Words in Current English*. Norman: University of Oklahoma Press, 1994.

Dalzell, Robert F., Jr. *Enterprising Elite: The Boston Associates and the World They Made*. Cambridge, Mass.: Harvard University Press, 1987.

David, Elizabeth. *English Bread and Yeast Cookery*. 1977. Newton, Mass.: Biscuit Books, 1994.

Deetz, James. *In Small Things Forgotten: An Archaeology of Early American Life*. Rev. ed. New York: Anchor, 1996.

Deetz, James, and Patricia Scott Deetz. *The Times of Their Lives: Life, Love, and Death in Plymouth Colony*. New York: W. H. Freeman, 2000.

Derven, Daphne L. "Wholesome, Toothsome, and Diverse: Eighteenth-Century Foodways in Deerfield, Massachusetts." In *Foodways in the Northeast*, edited by Peter Benes, 47–63. Boston: Boston University, 1984.

Dickens, Charles. *American Notes for General Circulation, Pictures from Italy* and *Christmas Books*. Vol. 14 of *The Works of Charles Dickens*. New York: Bigelow, Brown, [1920s?].

Dictionary of American Biography. Vol. 10. New York: Scribner's, 1936.

Dincauze, Dena F. "A Capsule Prehistory of Southern New England." In *The Pequots in Southern New England: The Rise and Fall of an American Indian Nation*, edited by Laurence M. Hauptman and James D. Wherry, 19–32. Norman: University of Oklahoma Press, 1990.

Doudiet, Ellenore W. "Coastal Maine Cooking: Foods and Equipment from 1760." In *Gastronomy: The Anthropology of Food and Food Habits*, edited by Margaret L. Arnott, 215–32. The Hague: Mouton, 1975.

Dow, George Francis. *Domestic Life in New England in the Seventeenth Century.* Topsfield, Mass.: Perkins Press, 1925.

———. *Every Day Life in the Massachusetts Bay Colony.* 1935. Reprint, New York: Arno Press, 1977.

Drake, Samuel Adams. *Nooks and Corners of the New England Coast.* 1875. Reprint, Detroit: Singing Tree Press, 1969.

Driver, Harold E. *Indians of North America.* Chicago: University of Chicago Press, 1961.

Drummond, J. C., and Anne Wilbraham. *The Englishman's Food: A History of Five Centuries of English Diet.* Rev. ed. London: Jonathan Cape, 1957.

Durham Women's Club. *The Durham Cook Book: A Collection of Tested and Approved Recipes.* Concord, N.H.: Rumford Press, 1898.

DuSablon, Mary Anna. *America's Collectible Cookbooks: The History, the Politics, the Recipes.* Athens: Ohio University Press, 1994.

Dwight, Timothy. *Travels in New England and New York.* Edited by Barbara Miller Solomon. 4 vols. Cambridge, Mass.: Harvard University Press, 1969.

Earle, Alice Morse. *Home Life in Colonial Days.* 1898. Reprint, Williamstown, Mass.: Corner House, 1975.

———. *Stage-Coach and Tavern Days.* New York: Macmillan, 1900.

Early, Eleanor. *New England Cookbook.* New York: Random House, 1954.

Echoes from South County Kitchens. Wickford, R.I.: The Farm Home and Garden Center, n.d. [ca. 1940s].

Elverson, Virginia T., and Mary Ann McLanahan. *A Cooking Legacy: Over 200 Recipes Inspired by Early American Cooks.* New York: Walker, 1975.

Emerson, Lucy. *The New-England Cookery.* Montpelier, Vt.: Josiah Parks, 1808.

Farmer, Fannie Merritt. *The Boston Cooking-School Cook Book.* 1896. Reprint, New York: Weathervane Books, n.d.

Fernández-Armesto, Felipe. *Columbus.* New York: Oxford University Press, 1991.

Field, Edward. *The Colonial Tavern.* Providence, R.I.: Preston and Rounds, 1897.

Field, Jonathan Beecher. "'Peculiar Manuerance': Puritans, Indians, and the Rhetoric of Agriculture, 1629–1654." In *Plants and People,* edited by Peter Benes, 12–24. Boston: Boston University, 1996.

Fischer, David Hackett. *Albion's Seed: Four British Folkways in America.* New York: Oxford University Press, 1989.

Franklin, Benjamin. *Writings.* New York: Library of America, 1987.

Friedmann, Karen J. "Victualling Colonial Boston." *Agricultural History* 47 (July 1973): 189–205.

Fussell, Betty. *The Story of Corn.* New York: Knopf, 1992.

G. H. Bent Co. "History of Bent's." <http://www.bentscookiefactory.com/history.htm>. 24 February 2004.

Gardiner, Anne Gibbons. *Mrs. Gardiner's Family Receipts from 1763, Boston.* Edited by Gail Weesner. Boston: Rowan Tree Press, 1988.

Gibbons, Euell. *Stalking the Wild Asparagus.* New York: David McKay, 1969.

Gies, Frances, and Joseph Gies. *Life in a Medieval Village.* New York: HarperPerennial, 1991.

Gilje, Paul A. "The Rise of Capitalism in the Early Republic." In *Wages of Independence: Capitalism in the Early American Republic*, edited by Paul A. Gilje, 1–22. Madison, Wis.: Madison House, 1997.

Gilman, Caroline. *The Lady's Annual Register and Housewife's Memorandum Book for 1838*. Boston: T. H. Carter, 1838.

———. *The Lady's Annual Register and Housewife's Memorandum Book for 1839*. Boston: Otis, Broaders, 1839.

———. *The Lady's Annual Register and Housewife's Almanac for 1840*. Boston: Otis, Broaders, 1840.

Glasse, Hannah. *The Art of Cookery Made Plain and Easy*. London, 1747. Reprint, with glossary and notes by Alan Davidson. London: Prospect, 1983.

———. *The Art of Cookery Made Plain and Easy*. Alexandria, Va., 1805. Reprint, with introduction by Karen Hess. Bedford, Mass.: Applewood Books, 1997.

Godey's Lady's Book and Magazine. February 1880–December 1891.

Gould, John. "Baked Beans." Excerpted from *The House That Jacob Built* (1945). In *White Pine and Blue Water: A State of Maine Reader*, edited by Henry Beston, 333–37. New York: Farrar, Straus, 1950.

Gould, Mary Earle. *The Early American House: Household Life in America, 1620–1850*. Rev. ed. Rutland, Vt.: Charles E. Tuttle, 1965.

Greene, Jack P., and J. R. Pole, eds. *Colonial British America: Essays in the New History of the Early Modern Era*. Baltimore: Johns Hopkins University Press, 1984.

Gross, Robert A. *The Minutemen and Their World*. New York: Hill and Wang, 1976.

Hale, Edward Everett. *Tarry at Home Travels*. New York: Macmillan, 1906.

Hale, Sarah Josepha. *The Good Housekeeper*. Boston: Weeks, Jordan, 1839.

———. *The Ladies' New Book of Cookery*. New York: H. Long and Brother, 1852.

———. *Northwood: A Tale of New England*. 2 vols. Boston: Bowles and Dearborn, 1827.

Haley, W. D. "Johnny Appleseed: A Pioneer Hero." *Harper's New Monthly Magazine*, November 1871, 830–36. Also available online at <http://mason.gmu.edu/~drwillia/apple>. 24 February 2004.

Hamilton, Alexander. *Gentleman's Progress: The Itinerarium of Dr. Alexander Hamilton, 1744*. Edited by Carl Bridenbaugh. Chapel Hill: University of North Carolina Press, 1948.

Hammond, Charles A. "Producing, Selecting, and Serving Food at the Country Seat, 1730–1830." In *Foodways in the Northeast*, edited by Peter Benes, 80–93. Boston: Boston University, 1984.

Hardeman, Nicholas P. *Shucks, Shocks, and Hominy Blocks: Corn as a Way of Life in Pioneer America*. Baton Rouge: Louisiana State University Press, 1981.

Harrison, G. B., ed. *Shakespeare: The Complete Works*. New York: Harcourt, 1948.

Hart, Dvora. "Sea Scallops." Northeast Fisheries Science Center, National Oceanic and Atmospheric Administration, 2001. <http://www.nefsc.noaa.gov/sos/spsyn/iv/scallop>. 24 February 2004.

Hawthorne, Hildegarde. *Old Seaport Towns of New England*. New York: Dodd, Mead, 1916.

Hawthorne, Nathaniel. "Fire Worship" (1843). In *Nathaniel Hawthorne: Selected Tales and Sketches*, edited by Hyatt H. Waggoner, 493–501. New York: Holt, Rinehart, and Winston, 1970.

———. *The House of the Seven Gables* (1851). Introduction by Philip Young. New York: Holt, Rinehart, and Winston, 1957.

———. *The Scarlet Letter* (1850). Edited by Harry Levin. Boston: Houghton Mifflin, 1960.

Hazard, Thomas Robinson. *The Jonny-Cake Papers of "Shepherd Tom."* Introduction by Rowland Gibson Hazard. Boston: Merrymount Press, 1915.

Helfman, Elizabeth. *Apples, Apples, Apples*. Nashville: Thomas Nelson, 1977.

Henisch, Bridget Ann. *Fast and Feast: Food in Medieval Society*. University Park: Pennsylvania State University Press, 1976.

Henretta, James A. *The Origins of American Capitalism: Collected Essays*. Boston: Northeastern University Press, 1991.

Henretta, James A., and Gregory H. Nobles. *Evolution and Revolution: American Society, 1600–1820*. Lexington, Mass.: D. C. Heath, 1987.

Hess, Karen. Introduction to *English Bread and Yeast Cookery*, by Elizabeth David, v–xv. New York: Viking, 1980.

———, ed. *Martha Washington's Booke of Cookery*. New York: Columbia University Press, 1981.

Higginson, Francis. *New-Englands Plantation*. 1630. Reprint, New York: Burt Franklin, 1971.

Hill, Christopher. "Pottage for Freeborn Englishmen: Attitudes to Wage-Labour." In *Change and Continuity in Seventeenth-Century England*, 219–38. Cambridge, Mass.: Harvard University Press, 1975.

———. *Reformation to Industrial Revolution*. Harmondsworth, Eng.: Penguin, 1969.

———. *Society and Puritanism in Pre-Revolutionary England*. 2d ed. New York: Schocken, 1967.

Hooker, Richard J. *The Book of Chowder*. Harvard, Mass.: Harvard Common Press, 1978.

———. *Food and Drink in America: A History*. Indianapolis: Bobbs-Merrill, 1981.

Howells, William Dean. *A Modern Instance* (1882). Edited by William M. Gibson. Boston: Houghton, Mifflin, 1957.

Howland, Mrs. E. A. *The American Economical Housekeeper, and Family Receipt Book*. 2d ed. Cincinnati: H. W. Derby, 1845.

Hunt, William. *Good Bread: How to Make It Light without Yeast or Powders*. 2d ed. Boston, 1858.

Hurt, R. Douglas. *Indian Agriculture in America: Prehistory to the Present*. Lawrence: University Press of Kansas, 1987.

Inman, LeValley A. *A Rhode Island Rule Book*. Edited by Leah Inman Lapham. Providence, R.I., 1939.

Innes, Stephen. *Creating the Commonwealth: The Economic Culture of Puritan New England*. New York: Norton, 1995.

Innis, Harold A. *The Cod Fisheries: The History of an International Economy*. Rev. ed. Toronto: University of Toronto Press, 1978.

Johnson, Clifton. *Highways and Byways of New England*. New York: Macmillan, 1915.

Johnson, Edward. *Johnson's Wonder-Working Providence, 1628–1651* (1654). Edited by J. Franklin Jameson. New York: Scribner's, 1910. Reprint, New York: Barnes and Noble, 1959.

Jones, Evan. *American Food: The Gastronomic Story*. New York: Dutton, 1975.

Josselyn, John. *John Josselyn, Colonial Traveler: A Critical Edition of "Two Voyages to New England."* Edited by Paul J. Lindholdt. Hanover, N.H.: University Press of New England, 1988.

———. *New England's Rarities Discovered*. 1672. Boston: William Veazie, 1865.

Journal of the Pilgrims at Plymouth [Mourt's Relation], The. Edited by George B. Cheever. New York: Wiley, 1848.

Karr, Ronald Dale, ed. *Indian New England, 1524–1674: A Compendium of Eyewitness Accounts of Native American Life*. Pepperell, Mass.: Branch Line Press, 1999.

Keats, John. *Complete Poems and Selected Letters*. Edited by Clarence DeWitt Thorpe. New York: Odyssey Press, 1935.

King, Caroline Howard. *When I Lived in Salem, 1822–1866*. Edited by Louisa L. Dresel. Brattleboro, Vt.: Stephen Daye Press, 1937.

Knappen, M. M. *Tudor Puritanism: A Chapter in the History of Idealism*. Chicago: University of Chicago Press, 1939.

Knight, Mrs. S. G. *Tit-Bits: Or, How to Prepare a Nice Dish at Moderate Expense*. Boston: Crosby and Nichols, 1864.

Knight, Sarah Kemble. *The Journal of Madam Knight*. Edited by George Parker Winship. New York: Peter Smith, 1935.

Kulikoff, Allan. *The Agrarian Origins of American Capitalism*. Charlottesville: University Press of Virginia, 1992.

Kupperman, Karen Ordahl. "Climate and Mastery of the Wilderness in Seventeenth-Century New England." In *Seventeenth-Century New England*, edited by David D. Hall and David Grayson Allen, 3–37. Boston: Colonial Society of Massachusetts, 1984.

Kurlansky, Mark. *Cod: A Biography of the Fish That Changed the World*. New York: Walker, 1997.

Langdon, William Chauncy. *Everyday Things in American Life, 1607–1776*. New York: Scribner's, 1937.

Larcom, Lucy. *A New England Girlhood: Outlined from Memory*. Boston and New York: Houghton Mifflin, 1889.

Larkin, Jack. *The Reshaping of Everyday Life, 1790–1840*. New York: Harper, 1988.

Laudan, Rachel. "Birth of the Modern Diet." *Scientific American*, August 2000, 76–81.

[Lee, Mrs. N. K. M.]. *The Cook's Own Book: Being a Complete Culinary*

Encyclopedia. Boston: Munroe and Francis, 1832. Reprint, New York: Arno Press, 1972.

Leighton, Ann. *American Gardens in the Eighteenth Century: "For Use or for Delight."* Boston: Houghton Mifflin, 1976. Reprint, Amherst: University of Massachusetts Press, 1986.

————. *Early American Gardens: "For Meate or Medicine."* Boston: Houghton Mifflin, 1970. Reprint, Amherst: University of Massachusetts Press, 1986.

Lepore, Jill. *The Name of War: King Philip's War and the Origins of American Identity*. New York: Knopf, 1998.

Leslie, Eliza. *Corn Meal Cookery . . . Originally Published as the "Indian Meal Book" by Eliza Leslie of Philadelphia*. 1846. Reprint, Hamilton, Ohio: Lawrence D. Burns, 1998.

————. *Directions for Cookery in Its Various Branches*. 31st ed. Philadelphia: Carey and Hart, 1848. Reprint, New York: Arno Press, 1973.

————. *The Lady's Receipt Book*. Philadelphia: Carey and Hart, 1847.

————. *More Receipts*. Philadelphia: A. Hart, 1854.

Levenstein, Harvey A. *Revolution at the Table: The Transformation of the American Diet*. New York: Oxford University Press, 1988.

Lincoln, Mary J., and Anna Barrows. *The Home Science Cook Book*. 1902. Boston: Whitcomb and Barrows, 1911.

Lowell, James Russell. *Poetical Works of James Russell Lowell*. Edited by Marjorie R. Kaufman. Boston: Houghton Mifflin, 1978.

Mann, Mrs. Horace. *Christianity in the Kitchen: A Physiological Cook Book*. Boston: Ticknor and Fields, 1857.

Mariani, John F. *Dictionary of American Food and Drink*. New York: Ticknor and Fields, 1983.

Martin, Edgar W. *The Standard of Living in 1860*. Chicago: University of Chicago Press, 1942.

Matthiessen, Peter. *Wildlife in America*. New York: Viking, 1959.

McCance, R. A., and E. M. Widdowson. *Breads White and Brown: Their Place in Thought and Social History*. Philadelphia: Lippincott, 1956.

McCusker, John J., and Russell R. Menard. *The Economy of British America, 1607–1789*. Chapel Hill: University of North Carolina Press, 1985.

McMahon, Sarah F. "'All Things in Their Proper Season': Seasonal Rhythms of Diet in Nineteenth Century New England." *Agricultural History* 63 (Spring 1989): 130–51.

————. "A Comfortable Subsistence: The Changing Composition of Diet in Rural New England, 1620–1840." *William and Mary Quarterly*, 3d ser., 42 (January 1985): 26–65.

————. "Laying Foods By: Gender, Dietary Decisions, and the Technology of Food Preservation in New England Households, 1750–1850." In *Early American Technology: Making and Doing Things from the Colonial Era to 1850*, edited by Judith A. McGaw, 164–96. Chapel Hill: University of North Carolina Press, 1994.

McManis, Douglas R. *Colonial New England: A Historical Geography*. New York: Oxford University Press, 1975.

Measuring Cup Group. *Cook Book*. West Somerville, Mass.: West Somerville Baptist Church, ca. 1918.

Mendall, P. H. *The New Bedford Practical Receipt Book*. New Bedford, Mass.: Charles Taber, 1862.

Mennell, Stephen. *All Manners of Food: Eating and Taste in England and France from the Middle Ages to the Present*. 2d ed. Urbana: University of Illinois Press, 1996.

Meriden Hospital Women's Executive Committee. *Meriden Cook Book*. Meriden, Conn., [1898?].

Miller, Kerby A. *Emigrants and Exiles: Ireland and the Irish Exodus to North America*. New York: Oxford University Press, 1985.

Miller, Perry. *The New England Mind: From Colony to Province*. Cambridge, Mass.: Harvard University Press, 1953.

Mintz, Sidney W. *Sweetness and Power: The Place of Sugar in Modern History*. New York: Viking, 1985.

Mitchell, Edwin Valentine. *It's an Old New England Custom*. New York: Vanguard, 1946.

Mood, Fulmer. "John Winthrop, Jr., on Indian Corn." *New England Quarterly* 10 (March 1937): 121–33.

Morison, Samuel Eliot. *Builders of the Bay Colony*. 1930. Reprint, Boston: Northeastern University Press, 1981.

Mosser, Marjorie. *Foods of Old New England*. New York: Doubleday, 1957.

Muir, Diana. *Reflections in Bullough's Pond: Economy and Ecosystem in New England*. Hanover, N.H.: University Press of New England, 2000.

Nanepashemet. "It Smells Fishy to Me: An Argument Supporting the Use of Fish Fertilizer by the Native People of Southern New England." In *Algonkians of New England: Past and Present*, edited by Peter Benes, 42–50. Boston: Boston University, 1993.

Nearing, Helen, and Scott Nearing. *The Maple Sugar Book*. 1950. Reprint, New York: Schocken, 1970.

Neustadt, Kathy. *Clambake: A History and Celebration of an American Tradition*. Amherst: University of Massachusetts Press, 1992.

Nissenbaum, Stephen. *Sex, Diet, and Debility in Jacksonian America: Sylvester Graham and Health Reform*. Westport, Conn.: Greenwood Press, 1980.

North, Douglass C. *The Economic Growth of the United States, 1790–1860*. Englewood Cliffs, N.J.: Prentice-Hall, 1961.

Oliver, Sandra L. *Saltwater Foodways: New Englanders and Their Food, at Sea and Ashore, in the Nineteenth Century*. Mystic, Conn.: Mystic Seaport Museum, 1995.

Orcutt, William Dana. *Good Old Dorchester: A Narrative History of the Town, 1630–1893*. Cambridge, Mass.: John Wilson and Son, 1893.

Oxford English Dictionary. 20 vols. 2d ed. Oxford: Clarendon Press, 1989.

Panschar, William G. *Economic Development*. Vol. 1 of *Baking in America*. Evanston, Ill.: Northwestern University Press, 1956.

Parkman, Ebenezer. Diary, 1723–78. In Parkman Family Papers, American Antiquarian Society, Worcester, Mass.

———. *The Diary of Ebenezer Parkman*. Edited by Francis G. Walett. 3 vols. in 1. Worcester, Mass.: American Antiquarian Society, 1974. Covers the years 1719, 1723–34, and 1737–55.

Patten, Mrs. Francis Jarvis. *Our New England Family Recipes*. New York: Tobias A. Wright, 1910.

Payne, Edward F. *Dickens Days in Boston: A Record of Daily Events*. Boston: Houghton Mifflin, 1927.

Pendery, Steven R. "The Archeology of Urban Foodways in Portsmouth, New Hampshire." In *Foodways in the Northeast*, edited by Peter Benes, 9–27. Boston: Boston University, 1984.

Pillsbury, Richard. *No Foreign Food: The American Diet in Time and Place*. Boulder, Colo.: Westview Press, 1998.

Pixley, Aristene [Helen Elizabeth Tyler]. *The Green Mountain Cook Book: Yankee Recipes from Old Vermont Kitchens*. Brattleboro, Vt.: Stephen Daye Press, 1941.

Prescott, J. H. *Valuable Receipts*. Boston: Mead and Beal, 1845.

Quincy, Edmund. *Life of Josiah Quincy of Massachusetts*. Boston: Fields, Osgood, 1869.

Rebello, Leonard, comp. *Lizzie Borden, Past and Present*. Fall River, Mass.: Al-Zach Press, 1999.

Roberts, Robert. *The House-Servant's Directory*. 2d ed. Boston: Munroe and Francis, 1828.

Robinson, Paul A. "A Narragansett History from 1000 B.P. to the Present." In *Enduring Traditions: The Native Peoples of New England*, edited by Laurie Weinstein, 79–89. Westport, Conn.: Bergin and Garvey, 1994.

Roger Cookery, The: Being a Collection of Receipts, Designed for the Use of Private Families. Boston: Joseph Dowe, 1838.

Rombauer, Irma S., and Marion Rombauer Becker. *The Joy of Cooking*. Indianapolis: Bobbs-Merrill, 1975.

Ronald, Mary. *The Century Cook Book*. New York: Century, 1899.

Root, Waverley, and Richard de Rochemont. *Eating in America: A History*. New York: Morrow, 1976.

Ross, Eric B. "Patterns of Diet and Forces of Production: An Economic and Ecological History of the Ascendancy of Beef in the United States Diet." In *Beyond the Myths of Culture: Essays in Cultural Materialism*, edited by Eric B. Ross, 181–225. New York: Academic Press, 1980.

Rothenberg, Winifred Barr. *From Market Places to a Market Economy: The Transformation of Rural Massachusetts, 1750–1850*. Chicago: University of Chicago Press, 1992.

Rowlandson, Mary. "The Sovereignty and Goodness of God." In *Puritans among the Indians: Accounts of Captivity and Redemption, 1626–1724*, edited by Alden T.

Vaughan and Edward W. Clark, 29–75. Cambridge, Mass.: Harvard University Press, 1981.

Russell, Howard S. *Indian New England before the Mayflower*. Hanover, N.H.: University Press of New England, 1980.

———. *A Long, Deep Furrow: Three Centuries of Farming in New England.* Abridged ed. Hanover, N.H.: University Press of New England, 1982.

Rutman, Darrett B. *Husbandmen of Plymouth: Farms and Villages in the Old Colony, 1620–1692.* Boston: Beacon Press for Plimoth Plantation, 1967.

Salisbury, Neal. *Manitou and Providence: Indians, Europeans, and the Making of New England, 1500–1643.* New York: Oxford University Press, 1982.

Schorger, A. W. *The Passenger Pigeon: Its Natural History and Extinction.* 1955. Reprint, Norman: University of Oklahoma Press, 1973.

———. *The Wild Turkey: Its History and Domestication.* Norman: University of Oklahoma Press, 1966.

Scully, Terence. *The Art of Cookery in the Middle Ages.* Woodbridge, Eng.: Boydell Press, 1995.

Sedgwick, Catharine Maria. *Hope Leslie; Or, Early Times in the Massachusetts* (1827). 2 vols. in 1. Edited by Mary Kelley. New Brunswick, N.J.: Rutgers University Press, 1987.

Sewall, Samuel. *The Diary of Samuel Sewall, 1674–1729.* Edited by M. Halsey Thomas. 2 vols. New York: Farrar, Straus, and Giroux, 1973.

Shammas, Carole. *The Pre-Industrial Consumer in England and America.* Oxford: Clarendon Press, 1990.

Shapiro, Laura. *Perfection Salad: Women and Cooking at the Turn of the Century.* New York: Farrar, Straus, and Giroux, 1986.

Shaw, Bernard. *Bernard Shaw's Saint Joan; Major Barbara; Androcles and the Lion.* New York: Modern Library, 1956.

Shorter Oxford English Dictionary, The. 2 vols. 3d ed. Oxford: Clarendon Press, 1959.

Simmons, Amelia. *American Cookery.* 1st ed. Hartford, Conn., 1796. Reprint, with an introduction by Mary Tolford Wilson, New York: Dover, 1958.

———. *American Cookery.* 2d ed. Albany, N.Y., [1796]. Reprint, with an introduction by Karen Hess, Bedford, Mass.: Applewood Books, 1996.

Simmons, William S. *Spirit of the New England Tribes: Indian History and Folklore, 1620–1984.* Hanover, N.H.: University Press of New England, 1986.

Sklar, Kathryn Kish. *Catharine Beecher: A Study in American Domesticity.* New Haven: Yale University Press, 1973.

Slack, Margaret. *Northumbrian Fare.* Newcastle, Eng.: Frank Graham, 1981.

Sloat, Caroline, ed. *Old Sturbridge Village Cookbook.* Chester, Conn.: Globe Pequot Press, 1984.

Smallzried, Kathleen Ann. *The Everlasting Pleasure: Influences on America's Kitchens, Cooks, and Cookery, from 1565 to the Year 2000.* New York: Appleton-Century-Crofts, 1956.

Smith, Andrew F. "The First Thanksgiving." *Gastronomica* 3 (Fall 2003): 79–85.

———. "In Praise of Maize: The Rise and Fall of Corny Poetry." In *Food in the Arts*, edited by Harlan Walker, 194–205. Devon, Eng.: Prospect, 1999.

———. *Popped Culture: A Social History of Popcorn in America*. Reprint, Washington: Smithsonian Institution Press, 2001.

———. *Souper Tomatoes: The Story of America's Favorite Food*. New Brunswick, N.J.: Rutgers University Press, 2000.

Smith, E[liza]. *The Compleat Housewife*. 15th ed. London, 1753. Reprint, London: Literary Services and Production, 1968.

Smith, Prudence. *Modern American Cookery*. New York: J. and J. Harper, 1831.

Snow, Dean R. *The Archaeology of New England*. New York: Academic Press, 1980.

Staveley, John. *The American Indian Meal and Hominy Receipt Book*. Nottingham, Eng.: N.p., 1847.

Stavely, Keith W. F. "Roger Williams and the Enclosed Gardens of New England." In *Puritanism: Transatlantic Perspectives on a Seventeenth-Century Anglo-American Faith*, edited by Francis J. Bremer, 257–74. Boston: Massachusetts Historical Society, 1993.

Stone, Lawrence. *The Causes of the English Revolution*. New York: Harper Torchbooks, 1972.

Stowe, Harriet Beecher. *The Minister's Wooing* (1859). Edited by Susan K. Harris. New York: Penguin, 1999.

———. *Oldtown Folks* (1869). Edited by Dorothy Berkson. New Brunswick, N.J.: Rutgers University Press, 1987.

———. *The Pearl of Orr's Island: A Story of the Coast of Maine* (1862). Edited by Joan D. Hedrick. Boston: Houghton Mifflin, 2001.

———. *Poganuc People* (1878). Introduction by Joseph S. Van Why. Hartford, Conn.: Stowe-Day Foundation, 1977.

Strother, D. H. "A Summer in New England, First Paper." *Harper's New Monthly Magazine*, June 1860, 1–19.

Tannahill, Reay. *Food in History*. New York: Stein and Day, 1973.

Thimble Club. *Choice Recipes from Old New England*. Manchester, N.H.: L. Cummings, 1937.

Thirsk, Joan. "Patterns of Agriculture in Seventeenth-Century England." In *Seventeenth-Century New England*, edited by David D. Hall and David Grayson Allen, 39–54. Boston: Colonial Society of Massachusetts, 1984.

Thoreau, Henry David. "Thomas Carlyle and His Works." In *A Yankee in Canada with Anti-Slavery and Reform Papers*, 211–47. 12th ed. 1892. Reprint, New York: Haskell House, 1969.

———. *Walden and Other Writings* (1865). Edited by Brooks Atkinson. New York: Modern Library, 1950.

———. *A Week on the Concord and Merrimac Rivers*. 1849. Reprint, London: Dent, 1932.

Trigger, Bruce G., ed. *Northeast*. Vol. 15 of *Handbook of North American Indians*. Washington: Smithsonian Institution, 1978.

Turner, Alice M., comp. *The New England Cook Book: The Latest and Best Methods for Economy and Luxury at Home*. Boston: Chas. E. Browne, 1905.

Twain, Mark. *The Adventures of Huckleberry Finn* (1884). Afterword by George P. Elliott. New York: New American Library, 1959.

Ulrich, Laurel Thatcher. *The Age of Homespun: Objects and Stories in the Creation of an American Myth.* New York: Knopf, 2001.

———. "It 'Went Away Shee Knew Not How': Food Theft and Domestic Conflict in Seventeenth-Century Essex County." In *Foodways in the Northeast,* edited by Peter Benes, 94–104. Boston: Boston University, 1984.

———. *A Midwife's Tale: The Life of Martha Ballard, Based on Her Diary, 1785–1812.* New York: Vintage, 1991.

University of Illinois Extension. "Pumpkins and More: Pumpkin History." <http://www.urbanext.uiuc.edu/pumpkins/history.html>. 24 February 2004.

Vaughan, Beatrice. *Yankee Hill-Country Cooking: Heirloom Recipes from Rural Kitchens.* Brattleboro, Vt.: Stephen Greene Press, 1963.

Verrill, A. Hyatt. *Along New England Shores.* New York: Putnam, 1936.

———. *Foods America Gave the World: The Strange, Fascinating and Often Romantic Histories of Many Native American Food Plants, Their Origin, and Other Curious Facts Concerning Them.* Boston: L. C. Page, 1937.

Vickers, Daniel. *Farmers and Fishermen: Two Centuries of Work in Essex County, Massachusetts, 1630–1850.* Chapel Hill: University of North Carolina Press, 1994.

———. "Work and Life on the Fishing Periphery of Essex County, Massachusetts, 1630–1675." In *Seventeenth-Century New England,* edited by David D. Hall and David Grayson Allen, 83–117. Boston: Colonial Society of Massachusetts, 1984.

[Webster, Mrs. A. L.]. *The Improved Housewife.* 9th ed. Hartford, Conn.: Richard H. Hobbs, 1847.

Weeden, William B. *Economic and Social History of New England, 1620–1789.* 2 vols. Boston and New York: Houghton Mifflin, 1891.

Weinstein, Laurie, Delinda Passas, and Anabela Marques. "The Use of Feathers in Native New England." In *Enduring Traditions: The Native Peoples of New England,* edited by Laurie Weinstein, 169–85. Westport, Conn.: Bergin and Garvey, 1994.

Weston, Jennie M., ed. *A Practical Cook Book: Tried and Approved Recipes Compiled by the Nashaway Woman's Club.* Nashua, N.H.: Phaneuf Press, [ca. 1930s].

Whatsoever Circle. *King's Daughters . . . Cook Book.* Newport, N.H.: Barton and Wheeler, 1903.

Whitehill, Jane. *Food, Drink, and Recipes of Early New England.* Sturbridge, Mass.: Old Sturbridge Village, 1963.

Whiteside, Clara Walker. *Touring New England: On the Trail of the Yankee.* Philadelphia: Penn Publishing, 1926.

Whittier, John Greenleaf. *The Complete Poetical Works of John Greenleaf Whittier.* Boston: Houghton, Mifflin, 1892.

Williams, Roger. *The Correspondence of Roger Williams.* Edited by Glenn W. LaFantasie. 2 vols. Hanover, N.H.: University Press of New England, 1988.

———. *A Key into the Language of America.* 1643. New York: Russell and Russell, 1973.

Wilkie, Richard W., and Jack Tager, eds. *Historical Atlas of Massachusetts*. Amherst: University of Massachusetts Press, 1991.

Wilson, C. Anne. *Food and Drink in Britain: From the Stone Age to the 19th Century*. Chicago: Academy Chicago Publishers, 1991.

Winthrop, John. "A Modell of Christian Charity." In *The Puritans*, edited by Perry Miller and Thomas H. Johnson, 1:195–99. New York: Harper Torchbooks, 1963.

———. *Winthrop's Journal "History of New England," 1630–1649*. Edited by James Kendall Hosmer. 2 vols. New York: Scribner's, 1908.

Winthrop Papers. 5 vols. Boston: Massachusetts Historical Society, 1929–1947.

Winthrop, Robert C. *Life and Letters of John Winthrop*. 2 vols. Boston: Little, Brown, 1869.

Wolcott, Imogene. *The New England Yankee Cook Book*. Preface by Wilbur L. Cross. New York: Coward-McCann, 1939.

Wood, Gordon S. "The Enemy Is Us: Democratic Capitalism in the Early Republic." In *Wages of Independence: Capitalism in the Early American Republic*, edited by Paul A. Gilje, 137–53. Madison, Wis.: Madison House, 1997.

Wood, Joseph S., with a contribution by Michael P. Steinitz. *The New England Village*. Baltimore: Johns Hopkins University Press, 1997.

Wood, William. *New Englands Prospect*. London, 1634. Boston[?]: Reprinted for E. M. Boynton, 1898[?].

Woolley, Hannah. *The Gentlewoman's Companion*. London, 1673.

Wright, Helen S. *The New England Cook Book*. New York: Duffield, 1912.

Wrightson, Keith. *English Society, 1580–1680*. New Brunswick, N.J.: Rutgers University Press, 1982.

Index

in Britain, 234–35, 237; growing, 24, 201, 237, 345 (n. 7); in pottage, 345 (n. 7)

Barlow, Joel, 19–22, 34, 41, 43, 293 (n. 95)

Barrows, Anna, 58, 93, 108, 184, 186, 193, 299 (n. 30), 307 (n. 84), 335 (n. 21)

Barter. *See* Trade: local exchange

Bass, 78, 98; attitudes toward, 109, 110; baked, 110; marrow, 109

Beans: attitudes toward, 49–50; in bread, 11, 50, 235, 239, 347 (n. 11); growing, 49, 50; New World, 50; Old World, 49; pea bean, 50; spoilage, 126. *See also* Pottage

Bears, 150, 194; attitudes toward, 170, 171; meat, 172–73

Bede, Venerable, 81

Beecher, Catharine, 251, 320 (n. 56); *American Woman's Home*, 142, 143, 144–45; *Autobiography of Lyman Beecher*, 253, 254, 355 (n. 93), 358 (n. 21); *Miss Beecher's Domestic Receipt Book*, 19, 27, 28, 35, 42, 55–56, 58, 66–67, 69, 85, 91–92, 98, 102, 103, 108, 110–11, 127, 128, 140, 142, 143, 154, 159, 160, 183–84, 185–86, 187, 189, 191, 192, 193, 194, 195, 204, 206, 209–10, 211, 212, 222, 223, 224, 225, 243, 248, 252, 269, 273, 289 (n. 70), 323 (n. 39), 325 (n. 69), 330 (n. 124), 335 (n. 22), 336 (n. 41), 352 (n. 63), 359 (n. 34); *Treatise on Domestic Economy*, 140, 142–43, 145

Beecher, Lyman, 233, 253

Beef: baked, 186; boiled dinner, 42–43, 69, 181–82, 196, 329 (n. 113); brains, 186, 187; in Britain, 178; calf's head, 187; calf's tongue, 220, 222, 223; calves' feet, 211, 222; as commodity, 180; consumption, 173, 177, 181; corned, 181, 196; corning (pickling), 176–77, 328 (n. 95); feet, 174, 186, 192; heart, 187; liver, 187; lungs,

187; pancreas, 187; pot roast, 184, 329 (n. 119); purchasing, 187, 330 (n. 129); roast, 115, 184–86; steak, 186, 193; stewed, 183, 329 (n. 119); suet, 222; tea, 269; tongue, 186, 187; tripe (stomach), 174, 175, 187; udder, 186. *See also* Cattle

Beer, 74, 214; brewing equipment, 125; pumpkin, 67; spruce, 260, 356 (n. 1); as staple beverage, 24, 124, 201, 235, 260. *See also* Flip

Bees, 148, 213

Bentley, William, 163, 166, 189

Berners, Dame Juliana, 81

Berries: abundance, 198; in Britain, 200, 207; Indian cookery, 199–200, 333 (n. 7); Indian horticulture, 198; in Johnny cake, 38–39; in pudding, 13, 15–17

Blackberries: Indian cookery, 199; in Indian pudding, 15; in Johnny cake, 38; pie, 222

Blackfish, 92, 98; cookery, 110

Blaxton, William, 201

Bliss, Mrs. (of Boston), 341 (n. 98), 352 (n. 63), 359 (n. 34)

Blueberries, 198; Indian cookery, 38; pie, 224; preservation, 209

Boiled dinner. *See* Beef

Boiling: and baking, 186, 330 (n. 124); in hearth cookery, 13–14; by Indians, 39, 66

Boorde, Andrew, 80, 236

Borden, Lizzie, 326 (n. 82)

Bowler, Metcalf, 203, 334 (n. 17)

Bowles, Ella Shannon, 29, 290 (n. 79), 311 (n. 130), 342 (n. 103)

Boyle, Robert, 284 (n. 27)

Bradford, William, 4, 5, 45, 77, 166, 170, 303 (n. 22), 328 (n. 104)

Bradstreet, Anne, 166, 325 (n. 60)

Bradstreet, Simon, 166

Bread
—in Britain, 235–38
—corn: anadama, 290 (n. 79); bannock,

328 (n. 104); as dairy source, 148, 178, 181, 187, 188; environmental impact of, 151; and land, 151; as meat source, 148, 178, 183; ownership of, 173, 179. *See also* Beef

Chadwick, (Mrs. J.), 342 (n. 103)

Champlain, Samuel de, 30, 49, 65

Chapman, John (Johnny Appleseed), 202, 334 (n. 15)

Charles II (king of England), 245, 267

Chase, Mary Ellen, 317 (n. 16)

Chaucer, Geoffrey, 10, 200

Cheese, 125, 126, 188, 189–90, 253, 257, 259, 317 (n. 13); cheddar, 188, 190; Cheshire, 189

Cherries, 198; in Britain, 200, 207; Indian cookery, 38; pie, 224, 342 (n. 102)

Chicken, 323 (n. 27), 324 (n. 42); in battalia pie, 219–20; boiled, 159–60; in Britain, 156–57; broiled, 160; chowder, 160; consumption, 159; curried, 160; domestication, 156; as egg producers, 156, 157, 227; feeding, 157, 165; fricasseed, 160, 323 (n. 41); with oysters, 108; pie, 158, 223, 227, 343 (n. 115); possession, 156, 157; purchasing, 159; roast, 158, 159; salad, 103; sale, 157; scalloped, 160–61; soup, 160; and Thanksgiving, 158, 227, 343 (n. 115); theft, 158

Child, Lydia Maria, 251, 319 (n. 56); *American Frugal Housewife,* 17, 19, 26, 34–35, 37, 55, 57, 69, 90–91, 97, 103, 108, 127–28, 133, 134, 136, 138–40, 143, 154, 159, 160, 168, 175–76, 183, 186, 187, 189, 191, 192–93, 196, 204–5, 210, 211, 222, 223, 242, 246, 256–57, 270, 273, 298 (n. 28), 301 (n. 58), 313 (n. 146), 318 (n. 35), 337 (nn. 47, 52), 342 (nn. 102, 103), 349 (n. 30), 357 (n. 16), 359 (nn. 32, 46); "Appleseed John," 334 (n. 15); *Hobomok,* 296 (n. 136), 300 (n. 54); "Over the River and through the Wood," 69, 187

Chocolate (drink), 242; as commodity, 266–67

Chowder, 90, 95–102; attitudes toward, 96–97, 99–100; chicken, 160; clam, 94, 98, 99, 101; crackers in, 98, 101, 310 (n. 114); fish, 97–101, 309 (nn. 100, 104); and leisure, 96–99, 101; lobster, 101, 311 (n. 130); milk in, 98, 101, 310 (nn. 106, 111); origins, 95–96; potatoes in, 97, 99, 101; scallop, 101; tomatoes in, 97, 101

Cider, 74; attitudes toward, 261–62; in Britain, 260, 356 (nn. 2, 3); and charity, 229, 261, 343 (n. 123); consumption, 261–62, 264; and festive occasions, 253; mills, 262, 356 (n. 8); "Royal," 260, 261; as staple beverage, 24, 124, 201, 260–61; and syllabub, 356 (n. 5)

Civil War, 103–4, 116, 144, 167, 230

Clams, 307 (nn. 74, 84); attitudes toward, 76, 77, 79, 88–95, 306 (n. 70), 308 (n. 92); as bait, 91; chowder, 94, 98, 99, 101; clambake, 51, 89, 90; as fodder, 76; Indian cookery, 78; long, 92, 307 (n. 79); middens, 89; pancakes, 92, 307 (n. 79); puree, 94; roasted, 92; size, 88; soup, 92; steamed, 90, 92, 93; stewed, 90–91, 92–93; varieties, 306 (n. 68)

Cobbett, William, 23, 50, 287 (n. 54)

Cod, 60, 96, 97, 102, 109; attitudes toward, 77, 115; *bacalhau,* 116–17; baked, 110; "Cape Cod Turkey," 116; cheeks, 116, 315 (n. 176); as Massachusetts emblem, 117, 315 (n. 177); salt, 110, 111, 115–17, 264; salt, as commodity, 72–73, 117, 179, 266, 302 (n. 9), 309 (n. 105); salt, with cream sauce, 111, 116; salt, with egg sauce, 115, 116; salt, and salt pork, 196; serving, 115; sounds, 116, 315 (n. 176); "Stamp and Go," 117; tongues, 116, 315 (n. 176)

Coffee, 242, 258, 260, 270–77; attitudes

Drake, Samuel Adams, 104, 115–16
Dutch oven. *See* Baking
Dwight, Timothy, 150, 180

Early, Eleanor, 290 (n. 80), 308 (n. 92)
Edwards, Jonathan, 62–63
Eels, 76, 78, 84, 85–86, 305 (n. 48); attitudes toward, 81–82, 87; boiled,
  84–85; collared, 82–83, 85; fishing,
  81, 84; Indian cookery, 81; pie, 83–
  84, 219; potted, 83; purchasing, 86;
  roasted, 83; soup, 83, 304 (n. 43);
  spawning, 80, 87; spitchcocked, 83,
  84, 85, 87, 304–5 (nn. 43, 58); stewed,
  82, 83, 86
Elderberries: Indian cookery, 38
Election cake, 353 (n. 79), 354 (n. 89);
  and election sermon, 255; and festive occasions, 232–34, 253–56; and
  refinement, 254
Election Day, 254, 353 (n. 82), 354 (n. 85)
Eliot, John, 30
Emerson, Ralph Waldo, 28, 225
Emery, Sarah Anna, 91
Emigration: from Britain, 121, 179;
  sociology, 121–22
Enclosure (land), 122, 178
England. *See* Britain
English, Philip, 267
Environment: Anglo-American impact
  on, 46, 151–52, 197; Indian impact on,
  46, 150–51, 199
Eucharist: secularized, 62–64, 233, 236,
  249–50, 255–56

Farmer, Fannie Merritt, 87, 93, 104,
  186, 311 (n. 128)
Farming: attitudes toward, 21–22,
  33, 64–65, 145–47, 152, 278–79; for
  market, 123, 156–57, 180, 188, 189;
  production, 126; self-sufficient, 124–
  29, 152, 157, 180, 189, 227, 229, 252,
  278–79
Fast food, 196, 249, 333 (n. 163), 355
  (n. 100)

Fasting, 80, 94, 219, 299 (n. 39), 304
  (n. 37), 308 (n. 90); dishes, 83; and
  eels, 81; in Elizabethan England, 76,
  304 (n. 37); in France, 299 (n. 39);
  Lent, 12, 60, 77, 86, 203, 242, 304
  (n. 37)
Fish, 78; abundance, 109–10, 151; attitudes toward, 72, 76–80, 87, 305
  (n. 62); cakes, 111, 117; dried, 125;
  fresh, 110, 111; hash, 111; jelly, 211;
  pickled, 125; pie, 219; purchasing,
  110; salt, 110–11, 125; size, 109; in
  succotash, 308 (n. 98). *See also individual species*
Fishing: attitudes toward, 71, 73–74;
  culture, 74, 76; and farming, 76;
  by Indians, 78; industry, 71–74, 76,
  117–18, 123; small-scale, 111, 113, 129
Flip, 67, 158, 253, 263, 264–66; "bellows-
  top," 264–65; calibogus, 357 (n. 18);
  and festive occasions, 265, 358 (n. 21);
  flip-dogs, 264, 265; and sabbath, 266,
  358 (n. 22)
Food supply: annual patterns, 125, 177;
  improvements in, 59, 126, 177–78,
  201–2, 317 (n. 16); theft and, 125,
  177
Fowl: abundance, 151; in Britain, 148;
  generic cookery of, 154; pie, 219. *See
  also* Chicken; Turkey; Wildfowl
France: attitudes toward, 113, 114, 275–
  76, 322 (n. 26), 360 (n. 59)
Franklin, Benjamin, 162, 246
Frogs' legs, 113; cookery, 114; and Indians, 114
Froissart, Sir John, 31
Frugality, 17, 133–34, 137, 140, 279, 318
  (n. 35), 352 (n. 61)
Fruit: fresh, 199–200, 207–8; and
  health, 207–8, 336 (n. 36); Indian
  cookery, 199–200, 207; Indian horticulture, 199; jelly, 211–12; pie, 221;
  processed, 200, 207. *See also individual varieties*
Frying, 36–38, 290 (n. 82)

Galen, 207
Galenic theory (health), 298 (n. 29),
340 (n. 87)
Game: abundance, 151; attitudes
toward, 171–72; baked coon, 172;
baked rabbit, 172; in Britain, 148–
50; caribou, 150; as clothing source,
150; consumption, 171; hare (Britain), 149; hare (North America),
170, 172; and Indians, 150–51; moose,
150, 170; muskrats, 170; muskrat
stew, 172; porcupines, 170; rabbits,
170; raccoons, 170; squirrel pie, 172;
squirrels, 162, 170, 172. *See also* Bear;
Deer; Venison
Gardiner, Anne Gibbons, 68, 83–84,
102–3, 105, 146, 158, 221, 327 (n. 94),
341 (n. 90), 342 (n. 103)
Gingerbread, 34, 242, 244–52, 351
(n. 51); attitudes toward, 246, 249;
breadcrumbs in, 244; in Britain, 244–
46; commercial, 249; and festive
occasions, 246, 351 (n. 59); flour in,
244–45; without ginger, 352 (n. 60);
hard, 248; honey in, 244, 245; leavening, 246, 248; marzipan, 246, 248, 352
(n. 59); milk, 251; molasses in, 245–
46, 248, 250–52; soft, 246, 248; sour
milk, 251; sugar in, 245–46, 248, 250,
251, 252; water, 251
Glasse, Hannah: *Art of Cookery Made
Plain and Easy*, 83, 89, 97, 98, 167,
168, 190, 191, 192–93, 220, 246, 304
(n. 43), 309 (n. 100), 322 (n. 26),
323 (n. 41), 342 (n. 103), 354 (n. 90);
Compleat Confectioner, 218, 340
(n. 80)
Gluten, 12
Goats, 148; as dairy source, 188
Godey's Lady's Book and Magazine, 69,
93, 106, 116, 127, 243–44, 253, 254,
301 (n. 59), 354 (n. 89)
Goodrich, Samuel G., 128, 318 (n. 20)
Gookin, Daniel, 30, 39, 52, 65, 77, 295
(n. 112), 308 (n. 98)

Gooseberries: preservation, 209
Gore, Christopher, 189, 337 (n. 48)
Gosnold, Bartholomew, 71–72, 115
Gould, John, 64–65
Gower, John, 237
Graham, Sylvester, 28, 243
Grapes, 198; in Britain, 200, 207; in In-
dian pudding, 17; and mercantilism,
146
Groundnuts, 46, 88, 296 (n. 132)

Haddock, 96, 97, 98, 101, 102, 109, 309
(n. 105)
Hale, Sarah Josepha, 251; as *Godey's*
editor, 69; *Good Housekeeper*, 17, 26,
28, 58, 69, 137, 154, 181, 223, 224–25,
248, 272, 336 (n. 36), 359 (nn. 32, 34,
41); *Ladies' New Book of Cookery*, 38,
85–86, 112, 133, 137, 191–92, 193–94,
210, 212, 360 (n. 50); "Mary Had a
Little Lamb," 286 (n. 40); *Northwood*, 69–70, 167; and Thanksgiving,
69–70, 167, 230
Halibut, 109; broiled, 110; fried, 110
Hamilton, Alexander (colonial physician), 306 (n. 70)
Hancock, John, 115, 268
Harrison, William, 10–11, 50, 65, 81,
284 (n. 32), 347 (n. 15)
Harrison, William Henry, 90
Hawthorne, Hildegarde, 93, 101, 104
Hawthorne, Nathaniel: *House of the
Seven Gables*, 297 (n. 16), 360 (n. 55);
Scarlet Letter, 328 (n. 109)
Hazard, Thomas Robinson, 15–17, 25–
26, 27, 29, 31–32, 36, 38–39, 41, 69,
153, 164–66, 203, 205, 249–50, 255,
273–76, 286 (n. 46), 287 (n. 52), 288
(n. 59), 289 (n. 70), 292 (nn. 89, 92),
293 (nn. 98, 103), 294 (n. 107), 302
(n. 66), 305 (n. 62), 321 (n. 17), 339
(n. 72), 352 (n. 69)
Hearth, 13, 33, 52–55, 97, 167, 183, 184,
193, 258, 284 (n. 32), 298 (nn. 17, 28),
319 (n. 56)

Herring, 78, 79, 109, 112

Higginson, Francis, 8, 102, 109

Holmes, Oliver Wendell, 225

Holyoke, Edward, 261

Honey: in Britain, 213; in gingerbread, 244, 245; and Indians, 213; in mead, 213; and sugar, 214

Hopkins, Samuel, 276–77; fictionalized, 166, 258, 259, 276–77

Hotels, 101, 186; Central Hotel (Provincetown, Mass.), 101; Parker House (Boston), 39, 107; Revere House (Boston), 105, 312 (n. 136)

House plans, 33, 126, 188, 317 (n. 19)

Howells, William Dean, 329 (n. 113), 334 (n. 18)

Howland, Mrs. E. A., 98, 134, 204

Huckleberries, 198; in boiled bag pudding, 13; in Indian pudding, 15; in Johnny cake, 38–39; whortleberry pie, 342 (n. 102)

Hunt, William, 298 (n. 28), 301 (n. 64)

Hunting, 153, 170; pigeons, 155–56; turkey, 162, 163

Iberian peninsula, 72, 117, 266

Iceland, 77

Immigration. See Emigration

Indentured servitude, 121

Independence (economic), 73; in Britain, 121, 229; and Catharine Beecher, 140, 142–45; and gender, 129; and Harriet Beecher Stowe, 142, 144–45, 277; and Lydia Maria Child, 138–40; in New England, 121–24, 129, 130, 132, 136–38, 227, 229, 230–31, 252

Indian corn. See Corn

Indians: animal husbandry, 150–51, 161; attitudes toward, 4, 8, 11–12, 20, 30, 33, 41, 43–44, 47–48, 51, 52, 66, 68, 99–100, 171, 198–99, 229, 283 (n. 27), 296 (n. 136), 303 (n. 26), 343 (n. 123); clothing, 150, 162, 324 (n. 52); cookery, 20, 23, 29–31, 33, 38, 39–40, 46–47, 52, 65–66, 70, 77–

79, 81, 96, 109, 114, 152–53, 154, 170, 199–200, 213–14, 290 (n. 82), 291 (n. 84), 292 (n. 92), 294 (n. 111) 295 (n. 112), 296 (n. 133), 308 (n. 98), 322 (n. 22), 333 (n. 7); disease, 5, 6, 281 (n. 4); fishing, 78, 151; forest burning, 150–51, 199, 207; horticulture, 4, 7–8, 49, 70, 112, 150, 151, 198, 199, 281 (n. 8), 282 (nn. 9, 13); hunting, 150–51, 152, 162; and metal pots, 214, 290 (n. 82), 338 (n. 62); ornament, 324 (n. 52); population, 281 (n. 2); preservation, 8, 66, 81; trade with Europeans, 214, 338 (n. 62). See also Abenaki; Iroquois; Narragansetts; Wampanoags

Industrial Revolution (American), 54, 87, 118–19, 129, 130, 142, 230, 252, 256, 266

Inns and taverns, 27, 56, 66, 74, 105, 106–7, 156, 261, 263, 264, 265, 268, 358 (n. 22)

Ireland, 40, 189, 287 (n. 54), 304 (n. 43)

Iroquois, 52, 214

Isinglass, 315 (n. 176); jelly, 211, 212

Jackson, Andrew, 167

Jagger wheel. See Dough spur

Jam. See Preserves

Jamaica. See West Indies

James I (king of England), 115

Jefferson, Thomas, 190

Jelly, 125, 337 (n. 54); apple, 213; calves' feet, 211, 212, 337 (n. 53); cranberry, 212; currant, 212; fish, 211; fruit, 211–12; gelatin, 211–12; and health, 212; isinglass, 211, 212; meat, 211, 337 (n. 52); moss, 212, 338 (n. 55); quince, 213; rice, 212; sago, 212; sassafras, 212; sculpting, 211–12; tapioca, 212

Jeremiad, 61

Johnny Appleseed. See Chapman, John

Johnny cake. See Bread

Johnson, Edward, 9, 66, 68, 77, 113, 171, 179, 199, 221

Market economy, 230–31, 344 (n. 127); in Britain, 120–21, 122–23, 134, 136, 156–57, 178–79, 188; and Catharine Beecher, 140, 142–45; and Harriet Beecher Stowe, 144–45, 230–31; and Lydia Maria Child, 136–37, 138–40; and Mary Hooker Cornelius, 137–38; in New England, 122–23, 129–33, 136, 145–47, 151–52, 157, 179–80, 189

Markham, Gervase, 40, 177, 190, 220, 221, 235, 239, 240

Marmalade. *See* Preserves

Marsh, John, 266

Martha Washington's Booke of Cookery, 245, 246

Maslin (wheat and rye mixture). *See* Wheat

Massachusetts, 208, 246. *See also* Plymouth, Massachusetts; Plymouth Plantation

—cities and towns: Andover, 166, 215, 225; Beverly, 53, 56–57, 59, 93, 202, 320 (n. 59); Boston, 15, 18, 39, 51, 60, 83, 96, 105, 107, 115, 117, 118, 145, 157, 161, 165, 166, 171, 174, 179, 180, 186, 188, 189, 201, 216, 221, 241, 246, 252, 261, 263, 267, 270, 300 (n. 49), 312 (n. 136), 318 (n. 29), 352 (n. 69); Cambridge, 114, 161, 355 (n. 100); Cheshire, 190; Concord, 56; Danvers, 194; Deerfield, 157, 171, 173, 189, 216, 263–64, 283 (n. 25), 289 (n. 73), 307 (n. 74); Fall River, 326 (n. 82); Falmouth, 268; Hadley, 112; Holden, 263; Ipswich, 125; Leominster, 201; Lowell, 54; Marblehead, 74; Medford, 118, 125, 264; Nahant, 99; Nantucket, 38, 111, 112, 355 (n. 93); Natick, 107, 174, 296 (n. 136); New Bedford, 301 (n. 62), 305 (n. 58); Newburyport, 91; Northampton, 182; Northfield (Squakeag), 46; Pepperell, 196; Provincetown, 101; Rockport, 290 (n. 79); Salem, 14–15, 72, 74, 102, 118, 145, 146, 154, 161, 163, 167, 189,

205, 209, 215–16, 225, 227, 267, 273, 298 (n. 16), 320 (n. 59), 339 (n. 72), 352 (n. 69); Taunton, 118; Waltham, 189; Watertown, 113; West Springfield, 314 (n. 165); Woods Hole, 100–101

—counties and regions: Berkshire, 190, 318 (n. 29); Cape Cod, 86–87, 114, 115, 308 (n. 92); Connecticut River Valley, 180, 182; Essex, 125, 158, 177, 215–16; Hampshire, 130, 189; Middlesex, 24, 181, 261, 283 (n. 25)

—fictional settings, as model for, 107, 174, 217

—foods and foodways: apples, 200–201; bakers, 241; cheesemaking, 189–90; cider consumption, 261; cod as emblem, 117; fishing, 72; hunting, 170; livestock ownership and trade, 173, 174, 181; lobster canning, 311 (n. 127); meat consumption, 181

—schools and colleges: Harvard, 261; Phillips Academy, 27, 225

—institutions and customs: colonial elections, 353 (n. 82); General Court, 74; House of Representatives, 117

—rivers and harbors: Boston Harbor, 97, 98, 199; Merrimack River, 113

—settlement, 199; early difficulties, 77

—wildlife: deer, 170; turkeys, 161, 163; turtles, 114

Massasoit, 6, 166, 170

Mather, Cotton, 61, 88, 115, 324 (n. 50)

Mather, Increase, 263

Mead, 213, 260

Meat, 9; butchers, 180; consumption, 180–81, 182; entrails, 174, 175; jelly, 211; pie, 219; preservation, 173–78, 226; salt, 125; salt, as commodity, 118, 123, 179–80, 197, 266; salting, 174; smoked, 125. *See also* Beef; Pork

Melville, Herman, 118

Misson, F. M., 181

Molasses, 17, 351 (n. 54); attitudes toward, 245, 250, 339 (n. 72); as

commodity, 118, 123, 215, 266; consumption, 216, 217; cookies, 251, 252; in gingerbread, 245–46, 248, 250–52; and health, 245; in meat preservation, 176, 327 (n. 94); in rum, 245, 250, 262; substitute, 353 (n. 70); in sugar processing, 215; and Thanksgiving, 226. *See also* Sugar; Sweetener
Morton, Thomas, 162
Mourt's Relation, 6, 281 (n. 3)
Mutton, 326 (n. 82); chops, 193; consumption, 173; purchase, 180

Narragansetts, 6, 22, 30, 199, 281 (n. 8)
New Hampshire, 243, 251; bear hunting, 172; Bristol, 87; fish cookery, 114; Hampton, 154; Isles of Shoals, 225; livestock slaughter, 173–74; Manchester, 87; maple sugaring, 214; Merrimack River, 113; Newport, 108; Portsmouth, 173–74, 189, 198, 216; pot roast, 184; and pottage, 295 (n. 117); squirrel pie, 172; Strawberry Bank (Portsmouth), 198, 199; turkey farming, 161; turtles, 114; Weare, 59; White Mountains, 243–44
Newfoundland, 72, 118
New York: Brooklyn, 105; cheesemaking, 189; Iroquois, 52; Long Island, 43, 52, 130; Narrows Ferry, 306 (n. 70)
Nostalgia, 52–55, 64–65, 92, 93–94, 100–101, 108, 147, 230, 255–56, 286 (n. 46), 318 (n. 20)

Oats: attitudes toward, 11, 19, 24, 30, 346 (n. 9); in Britain, 235, 237; growing, 24, 237; in pottage, 39, 235. *See also* Bread
Oranges: in Britain, 207
Oysters, 307 (n. 74); abundance, 105, 106; attitudes toward, 80, 104–7; in battalia pie, 220; in Britain, 104–5; broiled, 106, 108; cellar, 106–7; depletion, 108–9, 312 (n. 140); as

export, 105; as fertilizer, 105; with fowl, 106, 108, 167–68; fricasseed, 108; fried, 105, 106, 108; fritters, 108; Indian cookery, 78; ketchup, 106; with macaroni, 106; mock, 108, 313 (n. 146); omelet, 106; pancakes, 106; parties, 107, 312 (n. 142); patties, 106–7; peddlers, 105–7; pickled, 105, 107, 108; pie, 105–8; powdered, 106; ragout, 105; roasted, 106; saloons, 105–6; as sauce, 106, 110, 116, 167, 183, 185, 227; scalloped, 106, 108; size, 105, 107, 303 (n. 30); soup, 106, 108; stewed, 105, 106, 108

Parkman, Ebenezer, 96–97, 308 (n. 99), 354 (n. 85)
Parsnips, 127
Patten, Mrs. Francis Jarvis, 252
Peaches: pie, 222; preservation, 209
Pearlash. *See* Leavening: chemical
Pears, 9, 66, 207; attitudes toward, 200; in Britain, 200, 207; marmalade, 210; perry, 260; storage, 208; tart, 221
Peas: in bread, 11, 235, 239; growing, 24, 49
Pellagra, 7
Pickles, 317 (n. 18). *See also* Preservation
Pie
—attitudes toward, 219, 224–26
—in Britain, 219–21
—crust, 84, 204, 206, 218–19, 220, 221–22, 224–25, 340 (nn. 81, 87), 341 (nn. 98, 99), 342 (n. 102); puff paste, 222
—cultural role and customs: for breakfast, 225–26; and harvest, 226; and Thanksgiving, 226–29, 343 (n. 115)
—fish and shellfish: eel, 83, 219; lobster, 103, 311 (n. 121); oyster, 105–8
—fowl, game, and meat: battalia, 219–20, 222; chicken, 158, 222, 223, 227, 343 (n. 115); mince, 175, 220–21, 222, 223, 224, 225, 341 (n. 90); pigeon, 341 (n. 100); squirrel, 172; umble, 219, 341 (n. 90); venison, 172

—fruit and vegetable: apple, 68,
206, 221, 222, 223–24, 225, 226, 341
(n. 93), 342 (n. 103); blackberry,
222; blueberry, 224; cherry, 224, 342
(n. 102); cranberry, 225, 342 (n. 103);
currant, 222, 223; flower petal, 221;
peach, 222; plum, 222, 224; pumpkin, 55, 67–70, 90, 206, 221, 225, 226,
301 (nn. 59, 62, 64); quince, 220, 221;
raspberry, 222, 224; spinach, 221;
sweet potato, 220; whortleberry, 342
(n. 102); young pea, 221
—ingredients: salt pork, 342 (n. 103);
sugar, 220–21, 222, 223–24, 342
(n. 103)
—origins, 218–19
—and preservation, 220, 226–28, 341
(n. 91)
Pigeons: abundance, 154–55; in battalia pie, 219–20; domesticated, in
Britain, 148, 152; extinction, 156; foraging, 155; hunted, 155–56; in Indian
diet, 152, 154; oil source, 154; pie, 341
(n. 100); popularity as food, 153, 156;
potted, 153; stewed, 156
Pigs, 76, 155; in Britain, 148, 178; as
commodity, 178, 179, 180; environmental impact, 151; as meat source,
148, 178; ownership, 173, 178, 194;
reproduction, 178, 194; ringed, 194,
332 (n. 158); slaughtering, 194, 195,
227. *See also* Pork
Pilgrims. *See* Plymouth Plantation
Plagiarism, 17, 134, 252, 285 (nn. 37, 40),
287 (n. 49), 301 (n. 58), 309 (n. 100),
322 (n. 21), 323 (n. 41), 325 (n. 69),
326 (n. 80), 330 (n. 122), 342 (n. 103),
354 (n. 89), 359 (n. 46)
Plums, 198; in Britain, 200, 207; jam,
212; marmalade, 210; pie, 222, 224;
preservation, 209
Plymouth, Massachusetts: Bicentennial, 90; Centennial, 61, 89; dairy,
188; Forefathers' Day, 41, 42, 60–61,
89, 90, 182, 295 (n. 115); Old Colony

Club, 61, 89; Plymouth Rock, 61, 295
(n. 115)
Plymouth Plantation: agriculture, 5–6,
24; apples, 200; chickens, 157; dairy,
188; early difficulties, 5–6, 77, 155;
environmental conditions, 4, 5–6;
fishing, 72, 81, 102, 303 (n. 22); hunting, 153, 170; livestock ownership and
trade, 328 (n. 104); site selection, 5, 6,
79; and Thanksgiving, 166, 170, 226
Pomegranates: in Britain, 207
Pork, 45; attitudes toward, 58, 193–96,
332 (n. 161); bacon, 176; baked, 191,
193; in baked beans, 57, 58, 192; barrel, 196, 327 (n. 89); boiled dinner,
42–43, 69, 181–82, 196; brains, 190,
192; brawn, 190; cheeks, 190, 192;
chops, 193; collared, 175, 192; as commodity, 180; consumption, 173, 177,
181; ears, 190, 191, 193, 211; entrails,
190; eyes, 191, 192–93; feet, 190, 191,
192, 211; fricasseed, 191; ham, 176,
192, 327 (n. 94), 332 (n. 150); head,
190, 191–92, 193, 337 (n. 52); head
cheese, 191–92; heart, 192; liver, 192;
lungs, 192; pickling, 175, 176, 327
(nn. 94, 95); purchasing, 180, 193–
94; and refinement, 194–96; roasted
(cuts), 191; roasted (whole pig), 190–
91, 192–93; salting, 175, 176, 178, 181,
327 (n. 94); sausage, 168, 177, 182,
194, 328 (n. 96); snout, 190, 192, 211;
souse, 174, 175, 176, 190, 191; tongue,
191. *See also* Pigs; Salt pork
Porridge. *See* Pottage
Potatoes, 127, 317 (n. 16); in boiled dinner, 181; in pie crust, 222, 223; in
Thanksgiving, 167–68
Pottage, 22; apple, 204; baked beans,
50, 51–52, 55–65, 298 (nn. 28, 29),
300 (n. 49), 329 (n. 113); barley, 345
(n. 7); Boston Baked Beans, 50–51,
58, 300 (n. 49); and breadcrumbs,
244; in Britain, 39–40, 50, 235, 242,
244; entrails in, 219; in New En-

gland, 40–41, 59, 181–82, 295 (n. 117), 299 (n. 34), 329 (n. 113); spoon-meat, 295 (n. 114); succotash, 39–43, 47, 51, 65, 77, 96, 182, 294 (n. 111), 295 (nn. 112, 117), 308 (n. 98)

Poultry. *See* Chicken; Turkey

Prescott, J. H., 106, 108

Preservation, 59, 67, 124–29, 136–37, 139
—advice, 126–28, 176–77
—in Britain, 124–25, 173–76
—dairy, 125, 126, 128; annual pattern, 317 (n. 13); cheese, 188; equipment, 125; gender roles in, 188–89; milk room, 188, 317 (n. 19)
—fish, 125; cod, 110–11
—fruit, 125, 126, 127–28; apple butter, 206–7; applesauce, 208–9; canning and bottling, 209; cider, 124, 126, 128; drying, 336 (n. 41), 341 (n. 91), 208–9; fruit cheese, 206–7; storage, 208, 341 (n. 91); syrups, 209
—grains and legumes, 124, 126, 127, 316 (n. 9); beer, 124
—house design: in-house environments, 128; milk room, 188, 317 (n. 19); root cellar, 126
—by Indians, 8, 66, 81
—meat, 126, 128, 139, 173–78, 226, 327 (n. 94), 328 (n. 95); sausage, 177
—and pie, 220, 226–28, 341 (n. 91)
—preservatives: molasses, 176, 327 (n. 94); saltpeter, 176, 191, 327 (n. 94); sugar, 125, 176, 209–10, 213, 316 (n. 9), 336 (n. 41)
—processes: brining, 174–77, 328 (n. 95); collaring, 82–83, 192; drying, 125, 127–28, 208, 301 (n. 58); dry salting, 125, 174, 175, 327 (n. 94); pickling, 125, 128, 139, 175, 176–77, 191, 327 (n. 94), 328 (n. 95); potting, 82, 102–3; smoking, 125, 175, 176, 327 (n. 94); sorting, 126
—and Thanksgiving, 227–28
—vegetables, 125, 126, 127, 128, 139, 318 (n. 20)

Preserves, 125, 139, 210–11, 212, 337 (n. 47); jam, 210–11, 212, 337 (n. 46); marmalade, 210–11; pumpkin, 66–67, 300 (n. 55)

Pring, Martin, 72

Prunes: marmalade, 210

Pudding: apple, 205–6, 335 (nn. 27, 28); Bird's Nest, 204, 335 (n. 22); blood, 12; boiled bag, 12–14, 204–5, 293 (n. 95); containers, 12–13, 14, 15, 284 (n. 30), 285 (n. 34); grits, 22; hasty, 19–22, 287 (nn. 49, 51, 52); hominy, 22–23; Indian, 15, 17–19, 205, 286 (nn. 41, 44), 293 (n. 95); Indian cookery, 199; and Lent, 12; mush, 19, 21; plum, 227; polenta, 21; rice and apple, 204, 205; samp, 22; serving, 14–15, 285 (n. 36)

Pumpkin: in beer, 67; boiled, 66; in bread, 34, 35, 67; in Britain, 65; drying, 66, 67, 127–28, 301 (n. 58); in flip, 264; growing, 49, 65; non-food uses, 67; pie, 55, 67–70, 90, 206, 221, 225, 226, 301 (nn. 59, 62, 64); preserves, 66–67; sauce, 66; spoilage, 126; as sweetener, 67, 264; whole, 66, 300 (n. 54)

Quinces, 68; jam, 212; jelly, 213; marmalade, 210–11, 214; pie, 220, 221; preservation, 209, 211

Quincy, Josiah, 27, 264

Rabbits, 324 (n. 42); in Britain, 148

Raffald, Elizabeth, 83

Raspberries, 198; Indian cookery, 38; jam, 210, 212; pie, 222, 224

Recipes: apple pie, 223; apple pudding, 205–6; baked beans, 57; bass, 110; beef à la mode, 183–84; calf's head, 187; chowder, 97–98, 309 (n. 100); doughnuts, 256–57; eels, 82, 85; election cake, 254, 256; Indian pudding, 15; Johnny cake, 32, 36; molasses gingerbread, 248; pumpkin pie, 68;

Ryaninjun bread, 26; soft gingerbread, 246; succotash, 42
Redfield, John Howard, 255–56
Redwood, Abraham, 315 (n. 182)
Refinement (social), 136, 319 (n. 56);
and Catharine Beecher, 319 (n. 56);
and farming, 145; and hearth
cookery, 319 (n. 56); and Lydia Maria
Child, 134, 136, 319 (n. 56); and
mercantilism, 145–46, 320 (n. 59);
and N. K. M. Lee, 146, 319 (n. 56);
and pork, 194–96; and Sarah Josepha
Hale, 137
Revere, Paul, 83
Rhode Island, 153, 205, 305 (n. 62),
321 (n. 17); Bristol, 182, 350 (n. 48);
clambake, 90; Cumberland, 201;
dairy, 188; as model for fictional settings, 157, 166, 213, 258; granite, 286
(n. 46); Jamestown, 19; meat preservation, 176; Narragansett, 15, 38–39,
274; Narragansett Bay, 312 (n. 140);
Newport, 118, 145, 157, 161, 166, 203,
213, 258, 276–77, 315 (n. 182); Newport County, 37, 293 (n. 103); Paw-
tucket, 18, 182; pigeon hunting, 156;
Portsmouth, 29, 170; South County,
37, 165, 293 (n. 103), 339 (n. 72);
South Kingstown, 339 (n. 72); turkey
variety, 153, 164–65; turkeys in, 161;
Washington County, 293 (n. 103)
Rice: and apples, 204, 205
Riedesel, Friedrich von, Baron, 264
Riley, James Whitcomb, 302 (n. 66)
Roasting, 13, 184–85, 330 (n. 122); and
baking, 185–86, 191, 193
Roberts, Robert, 337 (n. 48)
Rollins, Ellen Chapman, 128
Rowlandson, Mrs. Mary, 45–47
Royal Society, 81, 109, 284 (n. 27), 324
(n. 50)
Rum, 215, 260, 262–64, 266, 357 (n. 16);
attitudes toward, 263–64; black-
strap, 264; in bounce, 358 (n. 20);
as commodity, 118, 123, 266; con-

sumption, 263–64, 357 (nn. 12, 14);
distilleries, 262–63, 356 (n. 11); domestic, 263, 357 (n. 12); and health,
264, 357 (n. 16); molasses in, 245,
250, 262; price, 263, 357 (n. 12); and
slavery, 266; West Indian, 263, 265,
357 (n. 12). See also Flip
Rundell, Maria, 354 (n. 90)
Rye: attitudes toward, 9, 10, 24, 235,
237–38; in Britain, 235, 237; growing,
6, 24, 237, 345 (n. 7), 346 (n. 10); in
local exchange, 215–16; in pie crust,
220, 221; spoilage, 127. See also Bread

Sabbath observance, 56, 59–60, 61–62,
115–16
Saleratus, 27, 222, 350 (n. 41). See also
Leavening: chemical
Salmon, 76, 102, 109, 113; attitudes
toward, 103; baked, 110; Indian
cookery, 78; salted, with cream sauce,
111
Salsify. See Oysters: mock
Salt pork: attitudes toward, 196, 333
(n. 162); baked, 196; in baked beans,
58; in boiled dinner, 42–43, 196; in
cake, 243; in chowder, 97, 99, 101; as
currency, 196; with fish, 110, 113, 116;
fried, 196; in pandowdy, 206; in pie,
223, 342 (n. 103); roast, 196; and salt
cod, 196; stew, 196; in succotash, 42;
with turkey, 168, 325 (n. 71)
Scallops, 78, 101, 313 (n. 149)
Scotland. See Britain
Sedgwick, Catharine Maria, 288 (n. 61),
296 (nn. 133, 136)
Sewall, Samuel, 146, 171, 216, 246
Shad: abundance, 112, 113; attitudes
toward, 78, 112; baked, 110, 113;
broiled, 112–13; depletion, 112, 314
(n. 161); as emblem, 113; as fertilizer, 112; festivals, 113; as fodder, 112;
Indian cookery, 78; as prefix, 112;
salted, 110; spawning, 112
Shakespeare, William, 200

Shaw, George Bernard, 245
Shay's Rebellion, 196
Sheep, 148; as dairy source, 188; lamb,
173; ownership, 173. *See also* Mutton
Shellfish: attitudes toward, 84, 88–89,
92, 303 (n. 22); gathering, 77, 78, 79,
88; and Indians, 78. *See also* Clams;
Lobster; Oysters; Scallops
Shipbuilding, 118
Sigourney, Lydia, 208
Simmons, Amelia, 15–16, 32–33, 37,
50, 57, 68, 84, 90, 97, 110, 114, 133,
154, 159, 167–68, 172, 176, 183, 185,
189, 201–2, 204, 205, 209, 210, 221–
22, 241, 242, 246, 289 (n. 65), 317
(n. 16), 327 (n. 94), 335 (n. 27), 349
(n. 30), 352 (nn. 60, 61), 354 (n. 89);
authorship, 285 (n. 37), 297 (n. 6)
Slavery, 230; manumission, 258, 277;
slave trade, 118, 266, 276–77, 315
(n. 182); in sugar industry, 73, 123,
214–15, 266, 338 (n. 69)
Smith, Captain John, 72, 121, 137
Smith, E[liza], 82–83, 183, 191, 245, 351
(n. 59), 356 (n. 2)
Smith, Prudence, 97–98
Smith, Sydney, 235
Spider (fry pan), 34, 35, 38, 108, 113, 294
(n. 105)
Squanto, 6, 81
Stearns, Samuel, 271, 357 (n. 16)
Stevens, Joseph, 201
Stiles, Ezra, 188
Story, Emelyn, 99–100
Stove. *See* Cookstove
Stowe, Harriet Beecher: *American
Woman's Home*, 142, 143, 144–45;
Minister's Wooing, 17–18, 62–63, 157–
59, 166, 213, 243, 257, 258–59, 265,
270, 276–77, 360 (n. 60); *Oldtown
Folks*, 27–28, 41–42, 48, 107–8, 113,
128, 145, 158, 172, 174–75, 181–82, 188,
204, 217, 221, 225, 226–32, 248, 253,
254–55, 257, 261, 265, 351 (n. 59), 353
(n. 79); *Pearl of Orr's Island*, 99, 158–

59, 188, 212, 257–58, 260, 261, 268,
269–70; *Poganuc People*, 208
Strawberries: abundance, 198; in Britain, 207; Indian cookery, 30, 38, 199;
Indian horticulture, 198; marmalade,
210; preservation, 209–10; size, 198;
and sugar, 218
Sturgeon, 78, 109, 110
Succotash. *See* Pottage
Sugar, 9, 197, 213–18, 340 (n. 80). *See
also* Molasses; Sweetener
—attitudes toward, 213, 216–18, 340
(n. 79)
—in cookery: cake, 241, 245–46, 248,
250, 251, 252; jelly, 212; pie, 220–21,
222, 223, 224, 342 (n. 103)
—in preservation: fruit, 125, 209–10,
213; meat, 176
—pre-seventeenth century: in Britain,
213; and Christopher Columbus, 214;
and honey, 213; as medicine, 213, 340
(n. 77); origins, 213; sculpted, 340
(n. 77)
—seventeenth century and after: in
beverages, 262; in Britain, 214, 216–
17; as commodity, 123, 216, 262,
266–67; consumption, 215, 216–17,
339 (n. 72); and dessert, 218; and
honey, 214; industry, 72, 214–18, 250,
262, 266; in local exchange, 215–16;
price, 215, 216, 217; processing, 214–
15; refineries, 217; and slavery, 73, 123,
214–15, 266, 338 (n. 69)
—theft, 215
Sweetener: in baked beans, 57–58; in
brown bread, 28–29. *See also* Honey;
Molasses; Sugar
Swift, Jonathan, 193
Swine. *See* Pigs

Table manners, 21
Tarts. *See* Pie
Taverns. *See* Inns and taverns
Tea, 242, 260, 267–70, 358 (n. 27); in
Britain, 267; as commodity, 123,

266–67; consumption, 267–68; and health, 268–69, 359 (nn. 32, 34); non-tea steeped drinks, 269, 359 (n. 34); origin, 267; smuggling, 267, 268; and socializing, 267, 269–70, 359 (n. 36); sugar in, 217; varieties, 267, 269, 359 (n. 32)

Thackeray, William, 107

Thanksgiving, 53, 54, 145, 226–31, 343 (n. 111); apple pie in, 226; cake in, 227, 343 (n. 114); and charity, 229, 230; chicken pie in, 158, 227–28, 343 (n. 115); and harvest home, 166, 226; mince pie in, 226; pie in, 69–70, 226–29, 343 (n. 115); pumpkin pie in, 69–70, 226; turkey in, 158, 166–67, 227, 230; venison in, 326 (n. 78); and westward migration, 344 (n. 127)

Thimble Club (Manchester, N.H.), 101

Thoreau, Henry David: *Cape Cod*, 86–87; "Thomas Carlyle and His Works," 349 (n. 27); *Week on the Concord and Merrimac Rivers*, 112, 305 (n. 48), 314 (n. 161)

Tin kitchen, 53, 66, 167, 185

Towle, Dorothy S., 29, 290 (n. 79), 311 (n. 130), 342 (n. 103)

Tracy, Nathaniel, 114

Trade: China, 118; with Indians, 214, 338 (n. 62); local exchange, 124, 175, 189, 265, 339 (n. 72); maritime, 118–19, 123, 124, 179, 189, 197, 265, 266–67, 315 (n. 182), 316 (n. 6), 339 (n. 72), 356 (n. 11)

Tradition, invention of, 61, 69, 93–94, 278–80; baked beans, 51, 64; boiled dinner, 182, 196; chowder, 94, 96, 101; clambake, 51, 89; clams, 91; diet, 94; family farms, 145–47, 278–79; fish fry, 113; gingerbread, 250–52; lobster, 91; oyster stew, 94; plainness, 92, 95, 146, 251, 279; pot roast, 184; seashells, 89–90; Thanksgiving, 166; tourism and, 93

Treacle. *See* Molasses

Trout, 78, 110, 305 (n. 62); broiled, 111–12

Trumbull, John, 265

Turbot, 102, 109

Turkey, 153, 194, 324 (n. 50); abundance, 151, 161–62; banquet fare, 165–66; Bell's seasoning, 325 (n. 71); boiled, 168, 227, 325 (n. 69); in Britain, 161, 164; carving, 168; and Christmas, 161; as commodity, 161, 163; domestication, 161, 163; in Europe, 161, 164; feeding, 164–65; gravy, 167, 168; hunted, 162, 163, 167; and Indians, 162, 324 (n. 52); name, 163–64; national bird consideration, 163; non-food uses, 162, 324 (n. 52); with oysters, 167–68, 227; roast, 165–66, 167–68; size, 158; slaughtering, 165, 227, 230; stuffing, 167–68, 325 (n. 71); and Thanksgiving, 158, 166–67, 227, 230; theft of, 166; wild, roasted, 162–63

Turkey (nation), 164

Turkey merchants, 164

Turtle: size, 114–15; soup, 114–15

Tusser, Thomas, 175

Twain, Mark, 225, 276, 360 (n. 59)

Vaughan, Beatrice, 342 (n. 103)

Veal: consumption, 173; roast, 185

Venison, 170; attitudes toward, 148, 170–71; banquet fare, 147, 171–72; collops, 172; hash, 172; pie, 172; roast, 172; and Thanksgiving, 326 (n. 78). *See also* Deer

Verjuice, 125, 316 (n. 8)

Vermont, 225, 226, 250; cheesemaking, 189; Chelsea, 29, 290 (n. 80); fish cookery, 111, 114

Verrill, A. Hyatt, 100–101

Wage labor: in Britain, 121; in New England, 129, 130–32, 138, 231

Wales. *See* Britain

Wampanoags, 6, 45

Wampum, 306 (n. 68)

Warner, Charles Dudley, 225

Washington, D.C., 190

Water, 260

Watson, Elkanah, 318 (n. 29)

Webster, Daniel, 61, 90, 309 (n. 104)

Webster, Mrs. A. L., 17, 36, 84–85, 92, 98, 103, 110, 113, 224, 307 (n. 79), 311 (n. 125), 343 (n. 115)

Westward migration, 129, 144, 201, 230, 344 (n. 127)

West Indies, 72–73, 116–18, 123, 179, 214–15, 250, 262–63, 266, 339 (n. 72)

Whaling, 118

Wheat: attitudes toward, 9, 10–11, 27, 233–34, 236–39, 289 (n. 73), 345 (n. 6), 346 (n. 9), 347 (nn. 14, 15), 348 (n. 20); bolting, 10, 348 (n. 19); in Britain, 234, 235–37; colonial importation, 24, 289 (n. 73); Erie Canal and, 23–24, 55, 221, 293 (n. 98), 348 (n. 24); growing, 6, 11, 23–24, 234, 235, 236–38, 289 (n. 69), 345 (n. 7), 346 (n. 10), 348 (n. 17); maslin, 235, 346 (n. 10); in pie crust, 220, 221; transactions, 283 (n. 25). *See also* Bread

White, John, 72

White, Peregrine, 200

Whittier, John Greenleaf, 334 (n. 20)

Whortleberries. *See* Huckleberries

Wildfowl, 321 (n. 17); abundance, 151, 153; as banquet fare, 152; in Britain, 149, 152; bustard, 152, 153, 166; canvasback duck, 153, 154; "Coot Stew," 321 (n. 18); crane, 152, 153; heron, 152, 153, 166; partridge, 149, 152, 153, 154, 162; peacock, 152, 166; pheasant, 149, 152, 153, 154; plover, 149, 152, 153, 154; potting, 153; quail,

149, 152, 154; reed bird, 154; roasting, 152, 153; snipe, 153, 154; stewing, 152; swan, 152, 153, 166; teal, 149, 153, 154; widgeon, 154; woodcock, 149, 153, 154. *See also* Pigeons; Turkey

Williams, Roger: *Correspondence*, 261–62; *Key into the Language of America*, 22, 30, 31, 65, 77–78, 109, 151, 162, 198, 199

Winslow, Edward, 5, 79, 81, 102, 112

Winthrop, John, 72, 137; Boston Harbor island, 199; *Journal History of New England*, 77, 117, 155; "Modell of Christian Charitie," 145, 256; "Reasons . . . iustifieinge . . . the intended Plantation," 11–12, 122–23, 134, 198–99

Winthrop, John, Jr., 9, 22, 23, 24–25, 161, 261–62, 281 (n. 8), 284 (n. 27), 291 (nn. 83, 84), 294 (n. 111), 310 (n. 114), 316 (n. 9)

Witchcraft, 249–50

Wolcott, Imogene, 87, 94, 101, 108, 191, 205, 206, 252, 290 (nn. 79, 80), 308 (n. 92), 342 (n. 103), 354 (n. 89)

Wolves, 151, 170, 194

Women: and dairying, 188–89; and household production, 129–30, 174, 188–89; and idleness, 131, 318 (n. 29); and outwork, 130–31, 318 (n. 28); and Thanksgiving, 228–29; and unpaid household labor, 131–32, 133, 139

Wood, William, 29–31, 39–40, 65, 76, 78–79, 109, 153, 154–55, 161–62, 170, 171, 198, 199, 303 (nn. 26, 30), 338 (n. 62)

Woolley, Hannah, 301 (n. 59)

Wright, Helen S., 87, 93–94, 104, 108, 286 (n. 44), 300 (n. 55)